law for
social workers

KU-657-054

law for
social workers

9th edition

Hugh Brayne

Helen Carr

OXFORD
UNIVERSITY PRESS

OXFORD

UNIVERSITY PRESS

Great Clarendon Street, Oxford OX2 6DP

Oxford University Press is a department of the University of Oxford.
It furthers the University's objective of excellence in research, scholarship,
and education by publishing worldwide in

Oxford New York

Auckland Cape Town Dar es Salaam Hong Kong Karachi
Kuala Lumpur Madrid Melbourne Mexico City Nairobi
New Delhi Shanghai Taipei Toronto

With offices in

Argentina Austria Brazil Chile Czech Republic France Greece
Guatemala Hungary Italy Japan Poland Portugal Singapore
South Korea Switzerland Thailand Turkey Ukraine Vietnam

Oxford is a registered trade mark of Oxford University Press
in the UK and in certain other countries

Published in the United States
by Oxford University Press Inc., New York

First edition © Hugh Brayne and Gerry Martin 1990
Seventh edition © Hugh Brayne, Gerry Martin, and Helen Carr 2001
Eighth edition © Hugh Brayne and Helen Carr 2003
Ninth edition © Hugh Brayne and Helen Carr 2005

The moral rights of the authors have been asserted

Database right Oxford University Press (maker)

All rights reserved. No part of this publication may be reproduced,
stored in a retrieval system, or transmitted, in any form or by any means,
without the prior permission in writing of Oxford University Press,
or as expressly permitted by law, or under terms agreed with the appropriate
reprographics rights organizations. Enquiries concerning reproduction
outside the scope of the above should be sent to the Rights Department,
Oxford University Press, at the address above

You must not circulate this book in any other binding or cover
and you must impose this same condition on any acquirer

British Library Cataloguing in Publication Data

Data available

Typeset in Stone Serif, Meta, and DIN Mittelschrift
by RefineCatch Limited, Bungay, Suffolk
Printed in Great Britain on acid-free paper by
Ashford Colour Press Limited, Gosport, Hampshire

ISBN 0–19–927551–3   978–0–19–927551–9

10 9 8 7 6 5 4 3 2

Normally our practice is to write a preface explaining our major concerns about changes in the law and changes in the structure of the book. We use the preface to provide the reader with some insight into our thought processes as we update and re-organize the book. For this edition we have a different focus. Allan Levy QC, who died in September 2004, has written the foreword to the book since its third edition. This preface is a record of our thanks for this and our appreciation of his work as a lawyer.

Allan Levy worked for and spoke up for children's rights throughout his career at the Bar. His work led directly to developments in law and procedures, and, therefore, to the contents of this book. He had extraordinary respect for social workers and the work they do in difficult circumstances. But he believed that legal rights and the adversarial system which challenges social work decisions and forces social workers to account for their actions are a vital protection for vulnerable children. He also believed that social workers need to have knowledge of the legal framework in which they work and encouraged us to explain the law as coherently and clearly as we could in order to make the law accessible. His views were not always welcome to social workers. As Andrew Cozens, President of the Association of Directors of Social Services put it in a press release dated 29 September 2004 following the announcement of Allan Levy's death, 'Not all social care directors will always have agreed with some of his analyses or prescriptions. But none will have doubted the goodwill and good intentions with which they were offered, nor the contribution they have made over the years to the steady understanding of the child as the centre of our services, and to the improvement of those services themselves.'

One of his most well known contributions to the practice of social work was his co-chairmanship of the 'Pindown' Inquiry with Barbara Kahan in 1990. This, the first inquiry into residential care, investigated the solitary confinement of 'looked after' children in Staffordshire. The inquiry was extremely critical of local social work practices.

Allan Levy explained in a 2003 article, 'The role of inquiries: a personal view' (**http://www.edgehill.ac.uk/cscsj/pdf/allantalk.pdf**), that 'We ultimately found the practice of isolation and humiliation of children to be decisively outside anything that could properly be considered as good childcare practice. It was, in our view, unethical, unprofessional and unacceptable. In the round it was unlawful. The Inquiry was set the task of making recommendations in order to allay public concern and maintain confidence in the social services department and its protection of the interests of children and the public. Accordingly we made a number of recommendations, all of which were accepted as was the contents of the Report by the local authority and the Department of Health.'

The recommendations alerted the government to the need to take a lead in setting standards for looked after children and led indirectly to the *Quality Protects* initiative, launched by the Department of Health in 1998, to improve a range of childcare services.

Most unusually for a lawyer, his work for the Inquiry achieved improvements in the professional practice of social work. In legal circles Allan Levy was best known for his willingness to challenge the status quo on behalf of individual clients. He acted in a number of high profile and controversial cases, such as that in which he was instructed by the Official Solicitor in a case concerning the compulsory sterilization of a 17 year old Downs syndrome girl, and he also represented (unsuccessfully) an Oxford student who wanted to prevent his girlfriend from having an abortion. Perhaps most significantly, he challenged the public policy bar on compensation claims by children and parents for damages caused by local authorities failing in their childcare duties. In *X v Bedfordshire* [1995] 3 All ER 353 he represented five children who suffered horrific parental abuse, yet despite this were not taken into care. The case went to the House of Lords, which decided that public policy barred legal action against local councils for breaches of their childcare duties. However, he successfully took the case to the European Court of Human Rights where it was reported as *Z and others v UK* [2001] 2 FLR 612.

This made clear the significance of the Human Rights Act 1998, which directly incorporated the European Convention into English law. Allan Levy saw its potential to dismantle the public policy bar which English common law placed in the way of people seeking damages for breach of the duty of care owed to them by those local authorities in whose care they were placed as children. In *Barret v Enfield* BC [1999] 3 All ER 193 he represented the applicant who had been taken into care when he was 10 months old and remained in care until he was 17. During that time he had numerous placements and very little care. He left local authority care with no family or friends, and suffering from a psychiatric illness leading to alcohol problems and a propensity to harm himself. The case established that local authorities could be sued for negligence because of their failures towards children in their care.

He had a continuing concern with the inadequacies of some local authority care of children. He persuaded the Court of Appeal that the Human Rights Act 1998 enabled the courts to take a supervisory role over incomplete care plans when he represented the mother in *In re W and B (Children: Care Plan); In re W (Children: Care Plan)* [2000] EWCA Civ 757. The House of Lords then rejected the approach as deviating too far from the statutory framework of the Children Act 1989. This decision is reported at [2002] 2 AC 291. However, Parliament responded by enacting legislative changes to the Children Act 1989 and by implementing a system of independent review of plans for children in local authority care. Yet again he achieved a rare outcome for lawyers, an important change to social work practice.

Allan Levy continued to challenge the limits of the law. He represented the appellant children and parents in *D v East Berkshire Community Health NHS Trust* [2003] EWCA Civ 1151 [2004] 2 WLR 58 in the Court of Appeal in a case concerning unfounded accusations of child abuse made against parents which led to investigations and the removal of children into care. The children and the parents sued for psychiatric damage. The Court of Appeal held that the Trust had a duty of care to the children but not to the parents. He had intended to represent the parents in their appeal to the House of Lords before he became terminally ill.

His opposition to the lawfulness of the smacking of children provides a further example of his commitment to children's rights. He represented 'A' in the case of *A v UK* (1998) 2 FLR 959 before the European Court of Human Rights. 'A' 's stepfather used the defence of lawful punishment in relation to a charge of 'actual bodily harm', having admitted beating his stepson with a garden cane causing bruising. The Court judgment found the punishment of the child in this way breached Article 3 of the ECHR and that the UK was responsible because its law, which at the time provided parents and guardians with a defence of 'reasonable chastisement' to criminal charges, failed to provide adequate protection or effective deterrence to the beating of children.

He could not understand Parliament's failure to provide what he believed to be effective deterrence to smacking in the Children Act 2004. He gave evidence to the Joint Committee on Human Rights on behalf of the 'Children are unbeatable' alliance that any provision of law which permits smacking fails to meet the UK's human rights commitments and is likely to cause confusion. He wrote in the Observer on 4 July 2004 that, 'Adults cannot pick and choose among the human rights they bestow on children. The right to respect for one's human dignity and physical integrity is fundamental for all of us. Does Parliament still view children as the property of their parents and worthy of less protection than adults, or as holders of human rights including the right to equal protection from assault?' Allan Levy did what lawyers do—that is to defend individual rights against the state—extremely well. Moreover, he acted on behalf of children, who are particularly vulnerable to abuse and whose rights are only recently being recognized by English law. For social workers this can feel like constant criticism. High profile cases appear to highlight only bad social work practice. The adversarialism of the legal system glosses over the difficulties and complexities of social work decision making. The idea of victories over social services in the courts smacks of triumphalism. In celebrating Allan Levy's work we are not condoning these unsavoury aspects of the law for which he certainly had no personal responsibility. Rather, we are celebrating the work of someone who placed the rights of children at the heart of the child care system, who was innovative and energetic in ensuring the accountability of social services to the vulnerable children who rely on dedicated and professional social work and who believed that clear and effective law works for the benefit of both children and social workers. These are characteristics we can all celebrate and which will be sadly missed.

Student resources

The web site for this book can be found at **www.oup.com/uk/booksites/law**. The web site offers the following features, which we hope will enhance your ability to understand the various topics and improve your overall ability to work with legal issues as a social worker.

- Worked examples of exercises—each chapter ends with one or more case studies which contain a legal problem; in chapter 1 instead of a case study there is an issue for you to think about. When you have studied each chapter, perhaps received the classes on this topic and looked up any additional materials (such as the actual statutes, guidance, or case reports), you may find it useful to attempt to write out an answer to these exercises. Once you have given it your best efforts, you can turn to the web site for guidance on how we would approach answering the problem. We do not think you will find all the material you need to answer the questions in the chapter. On some issues you are going to need to refer to a range of chapters, because people's problems cannot be compartmentalized that easily. You are also going to need to get in the habit of looking at legal materials beyond what is in the textbook—not all questions can be fully answered without identifying the actual part of the statute, regulation, guidance, case, etc. You will find our companion text, *Legal Materials for Social Workers* (edited by Hugh Brayne and Graeme Broadbent, published by Oxford University Press, 2002) helpful for this purpose.

- Web links—where we have mentioned a web resource in the chapter, you can find a direct link on the web site to that resource without having to type in the address. At the end of each chapter is a list of useful web sites which will all be linked in this way. We will update these links, for example if new materials become available or known to us, or if web addresses change.

- Glossary—the law contains a lot of jargon. It is easy to forget a word or phrase, even after it has been explained. The web site contains an alphabetical list of glossary terms with short explanations.

- Updates—we will regularly provide updates on what has changed in an area of law since May 2005 (publication date of the 9th edition). To check this click on the relevant chapter number.

■ Lecturer resources

The web site also offers the following material for lecturers using this book in their teaching.

- Test bank of multiple choice questions—the test bank is a fully customizable resource containing 200 multiple choice questions with answers and feedback. The test bank is downloadable into Questionmark Perception, Blackboard, WebCT, and most other virtual learning environments. Also available in print format.

- Lecture outlines in PowerPoint—using the lecturer password provided on request by Oxford University Press, you can access a set of PowerPoint slides for each chapter of the book. These can be downloaded and then adapted for your own use. (To obtain a password, simply go to the front page of the companion web site and, under Lecturer Resources, click on the 'Registration Form' link. Once you have filled in and submitted the form, a password will be e-mailed to you.)

- Lecture notes—we accompany each set of slides with a short discussion on issues which you might like to take into account in teaching this area of law.

ACKNOWLEDGEMENTS

Writing and updating *Law for Social Workers* is a team effort and we are grateful for the input and support we have received in our task over the last six months. Our editorial team at Oxford University Press have been cheerful, reasonable, and resilient when perhaps we have not been. Our copy editor Mick Belson has been the most patient and good-humoured editor we have yet encountered. Their efforts on our behalf have produced what we believe to be a very attractive and user friendly text book. Our colleagues have also been generous in their comments and help. We would like to mention Tim Baldwin and wish him luck in his pupillage at 2 Garden Court and Jeanie Fraser who has ploughed through several draft chapters with enthusiasm.

We have particularly benefited from the thoughtful criticisms provided by anonymous reviewers and we are grateful for their time and effort. We have tried to respond appropriately and we believe the book has benefited. Readers too have very helpfully pointed out some mistakes and omissions. We hope they will continue to do so!

We acknowledge with gratitude permission given by Oxford University Press to reproduce the diagram of the legal system from Professor Martin Partington's Introduction to the *English Legal System*. We also acknowledge permission to use diagrams from the Adoption and Children Act 2003 Explanatory Notes and from the Protocol for Judicial Case Management in Public Law Children Act Cases.

We are grateful that our families continue to be tolerant of the demands of writing to deadlines. In Helen's case, Richard remains cheerfully resigned and Rowan is only mildly irritated when required to forgo time on the computer. Meanwhile Harriet has escaped any stress by backpacking round Australia but diverts her mother with numerous amusing e-mails. Hugh's family has adjusted with humour and tolerance to his new freelance career, even though as a result this book has encroached even more into family time. Both our families note—as do we—that it seems no time since we were preparing the eighth edition.

As usual we cast around for people to blame for mistakes in the text. The government, in its apparently relentless task of improving and modernizing public services, is an obvious scapegoat. In the end though we do, with reluctance, accept responsibility and apologize in advance to our readers for any resultant confusion or exasperation. We do hope that, despite any mistakes, you find useful and even enjoy this edition of *Law for Social Workers*.

CONTENTS

DETAILED CONTENTS

ABBREVIATIONS

AA	Attendance allowance
ABC	Approved behaviour contract
ACPC	Area Child Protection Committee
ASBO	Anti-social behaviour order
AST	Assured shorthold tenancy
ASW	Approved social worker
BAAF	British Agencies for Adoption and Fostering
BASW	British Association of Social Workers
CAB	Citizen's Advice Bureau(x)
CAFCASS	Children and Family Court Advisory and Support Service
CCDPA	Community Care Direct Payments Act
CCETSW	Central Council for Education and Training in Social Work
CDA	Crime and Disorder Act 1998
CDCA	Carers and Disabled Children Act 2000
CDS	Criminal Defence Service
CFR	Children and Families Reporter
CPAG	Child Poverty Action Group
CPO	Child protection order
CPS	Crown Prosecution Service
CRE	Commission for Racial Equality
CRSA	Carers Recognition and Service Act 1995
CSA	Care Standards Act 2000
CSAP	Correctional Services Accreditation Panel
CSDPA	Chronically Sick and Disabled Persons Act 1970
CSO	Child safety order
CYPA	Children and Young Persons Act
CYPP	Children and Young People's Plans
DHSS	Department of Health and Social Security
DIAL	Disability Information Advice Line
DLA	Disability living allowance
DoH	Department of Health
DPEA	Disabled Persons (Employment) Act 1958
DPSCRA	Disabled Persons (Services, Consultation and Representation) Act 1986
DTQ	Detention, treatment, and questioning
DWP	Department for Work and Pensions
EAT	Employment Appeal Tribunals
ECHR	European Convention on Human Rights
ECJ	European Court of Justice
ECtHR	European Court of Human Rights
EOC	Equal Opportunities Commission

EPO	Emergency protection order
EU	European Union
FAO	Family assistance order
GSCC	General Social Care Council
HA	Health Act 1999
HASSASSA	Health and Social Services and Social Security Adjudications Act 1983
HHSRS	Housing Health and Safety Rating System
HRA	Human Rights Act
HSCA	Health and Social Care Act 2001
HSPHA	Health Services and Public Health Act 1968
LAC	Local Authority Circular
LASSA	Local Authority (Social Services) Act 1970
LSC	Legal Services Commission
MAPPA	Multi-Agency Public Protection Arrangements
MAPPs	Multi-Agency Public Protection Panels
MHA	Mental Health Act 1983
MHA 1959	Mental Health Act 1959
MHRT	Mental Health Review Tribunal
NAA	National Assistance Act 1948
NACRO	National Association of Care and Resettlement of Offenders
MASS	National Asylum Support Services
NHS	National Health Service
NHSA	National Health Service Act 1977
NHSCCA	National Health Service and Community Care Act 1990
NOS	National Occupational Standards
NOSP	Notice of seeking possession
NSPCC	National Society for the Prevention of Cruelty to Children
ODPM	Office of the Deputy Prime Minister
PACE	Police and Criminal Evidence Act 1984
PCCSA	Powers of Criminal Courts (Sentencing) Act 2000
RO	Reporting officer
RRA	Race Relations Act 1976
SDA	Sex Discrimination Act 1975
SSCBA	Social Security Contribution and Benefits Act 1992
SSI	Social Services Inspectorate
YOI	Young Offenders Institution
YOT	Youth Offending Teams

GUIDANCE

PART I

The legal framework

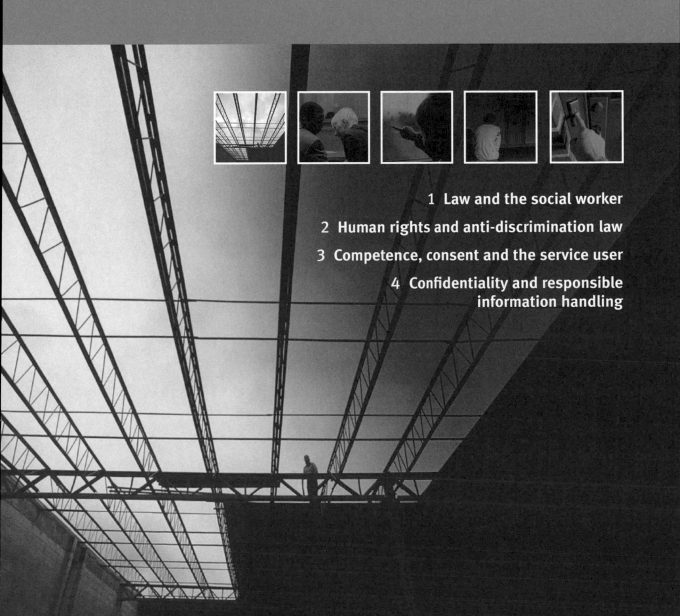

PART I The Legal Framework

The motivation for working to assist vulnerable or socially excluded members of society comes from altruism and idealism. Social workers want to do their best for the people who use their services. It is easy to see law as an irrelevance or even an obstacle to achieving these ideals: by requiring you to practise your profession within a legalistic straitjacket of externally imposed requirements or restrictions law may rob you of the excitement and motivation which underpins your commitment. You may even think it stops you from doing what is best for the service user.

But you must not underestimate the importance of the law. The law may be imperfect, but it is the product of a democratic legislature and an accountable judiciary; it reflects the wishes of the society it serves; it defines, approximately and with manifest imperfections, what society thinks is best for the service user. Laws establish agencies and set out procedures for helping the most vulnerable. Laws set standards for when it is appropriate, and when it is necessary, for action to be taken. Laws provide a framework for holding you to account. The laws relating to the profession of social work in fact give you a lot of discretion to do what you think is best and they cannot work without the exercise of skill, compassion, and wisdom.

The law often needs improving, but, for the social worker and others, it cannot be ignored. It is law, and not ideals, which sets out, sometimes with clarity but sometimes with confusion, what social workers are required to do, who they are accountable to, who they have responsibilities towards, and to some extent the overarching principles which govern public services. This is not to say that law is separate from ethics; best practice is both legally and ethically informed, but the imperative for the social worker in deciding how to respond to complex ethical dilemmas is to ensure that their chosen course of action is lawful.

The first part of the book is designed to introduce you to the key legal principles which inform your practice as a social worker. We start, in **chapter 1,** by considering what it means to be a social worker and the requirements on social workers to act lawfully, competently, responsibly, and ethically. We explain your multiple identities as a professional, as a statutory creation, as a state agent and as an employee. We also introduce you to your responsibilities to the service user.

The legal and ethical basis of those responsibilities is expanded upon in the remaining chapters of this part of the book. In **chapter 2** we outline the human rights framework and the anti-discrimination framework. These underpin both your relationship with your service user and all of the law outlined in the rest of the book. In essence, and imperfectly, these laws dictate that each individual person you work with is treated by the state and by society with integrity and respect. This is closely related to the ethical basis of social work practice.

In **chapter 3** we introduce you to the concepts of autonomy and consent and capacity. These are issues both of ethical and legal importance. The ethical issues arise because service users are entitled to privacy and respect for their wishes, but social work may require the state to override their objections. You need to know when the law permits action without consent, and who is able to provide a valid consent.

In **chapter 4** we look at your potentially conflicting duties to respect the privacy and confidentiality of your service user and to share information where it is necessary to safeguard the service user. The important ethical dilemma you will be required to solve is when is it lawful and ethical to divulge confidential information and override your obligation to respect the autonomy of your service user or other people with whom you have a professional relationship.

1 | Law and the social worker

CASE STUDY

A and another v Essex County Council [2003] EWCA Civ 1848 [2004] 1 WLR 1881

Facts

Mr A and Mrs B were married in 1985. Both had been married before and A had two children from his first marriage. They had no children together and, in 1990, applied to be approved as prospective adoptive parents. Their local authority, Essex, was the relevant adoption agency as defined under the Adoption Act 1976. A and B were interviewed by a social worker and adoption adviser, employed by Essex, who recommended that they were suitable adoptive parents. In June 1991, A and B were approved by the adoption panel.

In June 1994 the adoption panel recommended two young children, a brother and sister, for adoption. The boy was born in 1990 and his sister in 1993. The children had had a very difficult start in life, witnessing and being at risk of physical and emotional abuse. By 1994 they were in the care of Essex. In October 1995 the adoption panel recommended linking A and B with the children. In February 1996 the children were formally placed with A and B, and finally on 1 May 1997, the court made adoption orders.

Following the adoption the boy proved impossible to control, to such an extent that he had damaged A and B's home, health, and family life. The judge referred to evidence of the boy's behaviour as follows: 'B described his behaviour as "spiralling out of control". She has suffered black eyes, split lips, and bruises on various occasions and ended up in hospital as a result of being attacked by him while pregnant. He smashed their greenhouse with a spade, damaged their conservatory, poured gloss paint on the walls and carpets of the hall and their bedroom, and generally behaved violently including attacking other children. On one occasion at a party for the girls he attacked A's father and bit him, he attempted to attack the girls (his sisters), took a carving knife and threatened to kill A, and attempted to electrocute himself with bare wires from his bedside lamp which he had destroyed.' In October 1997 he was diagnosed as suffering from Attention Deficit Hyperactivity Disorder and is medicated with Ritalin. Since 1999 he has been in care appropriate to his special needs.

A and B sought damages from Essex. They alleged that Essex were negligent in particular in failing to inform A and B of the extent of the boy's difficulties of which it knew; had A and B been properly informed they would not have agreed to the placement. The particular points that would have caused them to reject the children had they been aware of them were said to be: the fact that the boy's behaviour may well have had a psychiatric origin or connection and that it could even be permanent in the sense of requiring ongoing specialist support; the reference in the papers to past violence, that respite care would be needed; a recommended reference to child guidance, and 24 hour supervision. Essex denied negligence, in the sense of carelessness, but also denied that it owed A and B a duty of care; it also denied it had caused the problem. Its argument was that a fair and sufficient amount of information was conveyed and it did not accept that A and B would have rejected the children in any event. The question before the court was whether Essex owed a common law duty of care to A and B when acting pursuant to a statutory framework.

The High Court decision

The judge in the High Court found that Essex had been negligent for failing to provide A and B with all the relevant information about the two children whom they were to adopt. This decision represented a considerable extension of the previous law on responsibility for decisions. However he also found that Essex was only liable for injury, loss, and damage sustained between the time when the children were placed with A and B as prospective adopters and the date of the adoption orders. Both Essex and A and B appealed against the decision.

The Court of Appeal decision

The Court of Appeal, whilst still finding that Essex had some responsibility for the inadequate information that A and B received, came to a narrower view of Essex's responsibility. It asked a number of questions. One question was whether individual social workers and others can be held to account in their implementation of the adoption agency's policy and practice on disclosure of information? Other questions also arose. First, is there a duty of care in relation to the contents of the forms and reports which are made? Secondly, is there a duty of care in relation to the communication of the information which the agency has decided that the prospective adopters should have?

It answered the second question first. It saw no difficulty in a duty of care to communicate to the prospective adopters that information which the agency has decided that they should have. The first of the intermediate questions proved more difficult. Clearly the primary duty of social workers, doctors, and others who complete forms on behalf of an agency is to that agency. The reports are required by the agency so that it can fulfill its statutory obligations. Can the compilers of reports simultaneously owe duties toward the people who are the subject matter of those reports and towards the people who may read and rely upon them? For a number of reasons the Court was reluctant to impose such a duty. The first reason it gave was that there was a statutory framework for adoption which was closely regulated 'with a view to ensuring best contemporary practice in this difficult and sensitive exercise in social engineering'. The second reason was that the agency owed its first duty to the child who is the most likely to suffer lasting damage if things go wrong, who rarely has much choice in the matter and is least likely to be able to protect his own interests, which may well conflict with the adults involved. It raised two further considerations. First, prospective adopters are proposing to be parents and like all parents have to be prepared for downs as well as ups. Second, prospective adopters have a trial period within which to get to know the child and decide that they can cope with the upheaval of adoption. For these reasons the Court decided that it is not fair, just and reasonable to impose upon professionals involved in compiling reports for adoption agencies a duty of care towards prospective adopters. It did not rule out a duty of care toward the child, but that was not the question before the court. The Court further held that even if there were a duty of care, that as long as the professional judgement made in the report was one which would be acceptable to a responsible body of opinion within that profession at that time then there would be no breach of duty. In this particular case it decided that the social worker was not in breach of her duty in compiling the form.

Another question the Court answered was whether the agency had a duty of care in respect of the decision about what information should be passed on. The agency has to have a policy about this, but the Court understood that it may be appropriate to depart from that policy in individual cases either in withholding information which would otherwise be given, or in divulging information over and above that contained in the various forms and reports disclosed. It therefore decided that there was in general no duty of care owed by an adoption agency or the staff whom it employs in deciding what information is to be conveyed to prospective adopters. Only if they take a decision which no reasonable agency could take could there be liability. However, once the agency has decided what information should be given, then there is a duty to take reasonable care to ensure that that information is both given and received.

The Court of Appeal therefore decided that the duty of care to the prospective adopters was more restricted than the judge in the High Court had held. A and B did not need to have all the relevant information; they should receive the information which a reasonable and competent agency would provide. However, once the agency decides on that information it has a duty of care in the provision of that information. The Court was clear that Essex had breached that duty of care. Essex had not provided A and B with the information that it had decided they should be provided with. As a result they were liable for all of the harm that resulted from that failure, but only to the point of the adoption order. 'The adoption order changes everything for ever. From that point on the adopters became as much like birth parents as it is possible for them to be.' The Court concluded with a thought-provoking statement of the limits of the law.

> Adoption is not a commercial transaction. It cannot be likened to the sale of goods or even the supply of services. Writing reports about a child is not like writing financial references and reports. The whole process is about doing the best one can for children who have not had the start in life which most of us take for granted. At times during the argument in this case it was easy to forget that (the children) are real people, every bit as real as the adults in the case. . . . The long term calculation of gains and losses involved in this delicate piece of social engineering cannot be done on the cold computer programme of the law.

OVERVIEW AND OBJECTIVES

In each chapter we start with a true case study, designed to flag up live issues which that chapter will touch on.

The case study for this chapter received extensive media coverage. In a story headlined 'Couple sue over adopted "wild child" ', the *Guardian* reported on 17 October 2002 that 'in the first claim for "wrongful adoption" a couple are suing Essex county council for negligence in failing to disclose reports indicating that the boy was "uncontrollable and vicious" and that his appalling behaviour would be "beyond the wildest imagination" of inexperienced adopters.' The case is of great significance for social workers. Do not be distracted by its notoriety or the technicalities of the law on adoption and the law of tort. You will become more familiar with these technicalities as you study later chapters. The case can be appreciated on a more straightforward level than that. It stresses social workers' professional responsibilities to the people who are affected by the decisions they make. It makes it clear that 'doing your best in difficult circumstances' is not always good enough. As you read through the case ask yourself why the social workers did not tell the whole truth to A and B? Can you understand the pressures on them? Put yourself in the position of the prospective adopters—what pressures were upon them? Think about the children involved in this case—how have their lives been damaged by this? Do you agree with the barrister representing Essex who argued that the law must be careful not to impose burdens on social workers which get in the way of the interests of children and their statutory responsibilities? Or do you agree with the High Court judge when he said that the possibility of an award of damages should lead to an improvement in the practice of social work? What do you think the Court of Appeal meant when it did not rule out a duty of care to a child in these circumstances? What are the implications of the decision for your practice of social work? Does the case tell you anything about the extent of your professional responsibilities?

This case highlights a number of important issues which we will be discussing in this chapter which relate to the professional identity of social workers. It focuses on the competence required of professional social workers and the nature and extent of the redress that the law provides to those who are damaged in some way by their actions. This chapter explores the circumstances when your employer can be sued for the mistakes you make. It will also discuss the responsibilities that your employer has to you to ensure you can do your job. The case also highlights some of the problems which social workers face: a hugely demanding role where there is pressure to achieve particular outcomes and where time to complete paperwork properly and consider the full implications of the course of action that you have embarked upon is in short supply. So in this chapter we consider the multiple roles that social workers have, and the legal relationship that they have with those to whom they have responsibilities. (The case study also raises important issues of confidentiality, to which chapter 4 is devoted.)

Using *Law for Social Workers*

The relationship between law and social work is complex. It derives from two inescapable facts. First, social workers are the creation of government; government is therefore accountable to the public for their work and obliged to regulate their activities. Second, social workers as caring professionals are themselves accountable to their users and to the public at large. Social workers are required to account for their actions and inactions to the government and the public within a framework of law which lays down their tasks, the scope of their work, their discretions, and their powers. This book is designed to describe and explain that framework of law.

The goals of *Law for Social Workers* are relatively straightforward:

- to explain the legal system and how it works in practice, so that you can work within it effectively, and use it both to achieve what you think is right and to fulfil your statutory duties;
- to identify the statutory duties of the social worker (or department) in relation to children and adults;
- to identify what you *must* do to fulfil those duties;
- to identify what you *may* do to fulfil those duties;

- to identify and discuss further areas of law where that law impacts most directly on your ability to fulfil your statutory duties.

The result is a long book. The core of the book is Part 3, where we explain statutory duties in relation to children, and Part 4, duties in relation to adults. To exercise your duties and powers you need to know about a range of other areas of law: how the courts work and how you work within them; confidentiality of information; what happens when young people are in trouble; how the law of housing and family law affects children and vulnerable adults, or those they live with; and so on.

We aim to provide a book which covers a range of things you are likely, in practice, to need to know; not everything, and not every last detail. Perhaps the most important starting point, however, is that you cannot and need not know it all. If you know enough, you will know when it is time to call in the lawyer. In fact a key issue in the Climbié inquiry, which is discussed again, particularly in chapter 7, is that social workers should not work alone. Lawyers, along with line managers, should be there to help. Their job is to support you in your goals by providing you with the legal expertise and tools relating to the particular area of law concerned, and to ensure that social work powers are used in a way which is consistent with due process (see chapter 6), human rights and in a non-discriminatory way (see chapter 2). By understanding law we are not suggesting you become equipped with the lawyer's toolkit, but you can be more effective in harnessing the lawyer and the lawyer' toolkit to achieve better outcomes for the service user.

The relevance of law to good social work practice

It is our task to emphasize the relevance and importance of law to social work practice. But we ourselves are lawyers, and we should not presume to talk about what is good social work practice. Law alone is not enough for good social work practice. But failure to practise according to the requirements of the law leaves you open to criticism. In 1998, the Social Service Inspectors at the Department of Health published a report called *Someone Else's Children* (DoH, 1998). This set out the results of a large-scale inspection of local authorities in England and Wales. It gave a dreadful picture of how the law is actually put into practice. It describes 'a catalogue of concerns about how important decisions are made and the arrangements to ensure that children are safe' (Paragraph 1.3). Failure to understand and act within the legal framework let these children down. The law may say that the interests of the child are important, or, where a court is concerned, 'paramount' (Children Act 1989, s. 1). It is the practitioner who carries this into effect. Whether or not the aims of the law—which by and large will coincide with the aspirations of the motivated social worker working within an ethical framework— are achieved is a matter of adherence to law as well as your conceptions of best social work practice.

Criticism of the law is valid and useful; but working outside the law is unacceptable. The rule of law requires the state—which you as a social worker represent—to use its formidable powers according to the law and in an accountable way. Illegal imprisonment of children in care in Staffordshire—'pindown'—was the result of using the authority of the social services department to oppress individuals who should have been entitled to the protection of the law (Allan Levy and Barbara Kahan, *The Pindown Experience and the Protection of Children* (Staffordshire County Council, 1991)). We consider it an illusion to think you can protect the interests of vulnerable people better outside the legal framework than within it. At the very least it will destroy your credibility in court and your chance of obtaining appropriate court orders; at its worst, there may be a disaster, and you will be the first in line for any criticism. 'Professionals involved in child welfare and protection are not moral crusaders. They are empowered in law to act in certain prescribed situations in certain prescribed ways, no more, no less' (D. Platt and D. Shernings, *Making Enquiries into Alleged Child Abuse and Neglect: Partnership with Families* (Pennant, 1996)).

A few technicalities about the book and its web site

The book is accompanied by a dedicated web site, which is not password protected. The address is site at **www.oup.com/uk/booksites/law**.

If a phrase is going to be used a lot, we will abbreviate it after the first time: so '*Legal Materials for Social Workers*, Hugh Brayne and Graeme Broadbent, Oxford University Press 2002' can become just 'Brayne and Broadbent'. The abbreviation will be found in brackets after the full version. The same goes for acronyms—referring to something just by its initials. When we first introduce a new term (for example the European Court of Justice), or if we reintroduce it after a gap, we will give the full title followed by the initials (in this case, ECJ). There is also a table of abbreviations at page xxv.

We try to explain new phrases when they first appear. If you come across a phrase and you do not know what it means, there are two ways to check. First, you can look in the index and see when that phrase was first mentioned, and then refer to that page. We also have a full glossary on our companion web site.

We aim, in this book, and in keeping with the various anti-discrimination laws and ethical codes to which social workers adhere, to avoid language that makes sexist assumptions. We will not write 'he' or 'she' unless we actually mean a male or female person. Sometimes we will alternate 'he' and 'she' where it would be clumsy to always repeat 'he or she' or 'the child' or to use 'they', and sometimes we will make gender assumptions—but we will explain these to you. Of course we do not control all the relevant language. Statutory language is a product of tradition and uses 'he' as a shorthand for 'he or she'—in fact the 1978 Interpretation Act tells us that 'he' means 'she' as well. When we quote a statute or other official document, we give you the actual wording. Judges also sometimes use 'he' as a shorthand for 'he or she'. If we are quoting directly from a case we will use the judge's actual words.

We will try to avoid insensitive labelling; but words like 'the disabled' are statutory terms, so in referring to the law we reproduce those terms for accuracy.

Finally, we are shortly going to be introducing you to cases and statutes. These are the main sources of law—if a law cannot be traced back to a case or a statute, it is of doubtful authenticity, so a law text book is bound to be full of them. Cases are decisions of courts, and are referred to by the names of the people involved—for example *Gillick v West*

Norfolk and Wisbech Area Health Authority (1986). For most purposes reading our summary of the case, and knowing the name and date, is enough; but sometimes you need to find where the case is reported in order to read the full report. We explain how to do this in chapter 5. You can find a full reference, which means details of where it is reported and can be found in a law library, or law database, by looking at the table of cases right at the start of the book. Statutes (Acts) are referred to by the subject matter—for example the Children Act 1989—and statutes (or Acts) are divided into sections and Parts (for example Part 4 of the Act deals with child protection issues, and s. 31 sets out details relating to care orders). We also explain statutes in chapter 5, and you can find an alphabetical list of the statutes referred to in the book in the table of statutes at the beginning.

What is a social worker?

Our answer to this question takes up the rest of this chapter. We identify a range of social work roles and responsibilities which we set out in Box 1.1. We then discuss these further within the chapter. Of course, the identity of a social worker is complex and contested and you may not agree with our conclusions. We think the answer is, ultimately, a matter of values, but those values cannot be translated into effective practice unless they are located within, and based on, legal requirements.

BOX 1.1 Social workers and their identities

The social worker as	This includes	Legal meaning
Professional	• Ethical codes • Values • Competence • Responsibilities	Professional identity implies particular legal responsibilities and carries with it particular powers. Professionals are accountable to society in a number of ways
Statutory creation	The definition and infrastructure of social work	The law both creates and controls the practice of social work
State agent carrying out statutory functions	Particular responsibilities for caring for the vulnerable on behalf of society	The law which governs these tasks is the subject matter of Part 3 & 4 of the book
Employee	The contractual relationship with your employer	Your contractual responsibilities determine your day-to-day responsibilities. Your employer also has responsibilities to you

■ The professional social worker

Professionals have a particular type of relationship with the people who use their services because of the level of expertise and authority that being a professional implies. The law recognizes the particular nature of the relationship and imposes responsibilities to act with care and also intervenes to ensure that the professional has the appropriate qualifications. In this section of the chapter we will look at both of these aspects of your professional identity but we will start with the most fundamental aspect of professional identity, integrity.

Value-driven practice

Professionals are bound by ethical codes and their actions are underpinned by agreed values. These values do not, of course, identify who is a social worker—but they frame the professional ethos that members of your profession hold in common.

The code of ethics for social work was drawn up by the British Association of Social Workers, your professional association, after widespread consultation from a number of sources. The latest code was launched in April 2002 (see **www.basw.co.uk/pages/info/ethics**).

The summary of the values underpinning social work is expressed in the Code as follows:

> Social work practice should both promote respect for human dignity and pursue social justice, through service to humanity, integrity and competence.

We will refer to the *BASW Code of Ethics* again in this chapter.

The state also imposes ethical values upon you. The General Social Care Council (GSCC) was set up by the government to regulate the conduct and training of social care workers including social workers. Box 1.2 sets out the GSCC Code of Practice, which sets out the regulator's view of the values which should underpin social work. The code is available at **www.gscc.org.uk/codes_practice.htm**. We try to make a connection between these core values and the legal issues explored in this book.

Part of our purpose in *Law for Social Workers* is to demonstrate the link between value driven, ethical practice, and legally informed practice. One particular area of practice—cultural awareness—is worth examining in more detail at this stage.

Diversity and social work—the ethical position

The *BASW Code of Ethics* is clear that cultural awareness is a necessity for ethical practice. Paragraph 4.1.6 states that social workers will:

a. acknowledge the significance of culture in their practice, will recognise the diversity within and among cultures and will recognise the impact of their own ethnic and cultural identity
b. obtain a working knowledge and understanding of service users' ethnic and cultural affiliations and identities and of the values, beliefs and customs normally associated with them, recognising that the service user's own values and beliefs may differ;

BOX 1.2 Core values for social work (from GSCC Code of Practice)

Social care workers must:	Reflected in legal obligations
Protect the rights and promote the interests of service users and carers	Respect for human rights and anti-discrimination legislation (chapter 2); awareness of statutory entitlement to services (parts 3 and 4); awareness of areas of law beyond statutory duties (e.g. Family law chapter 13, Housing law chapter 18 and Homelessness law chapter 19
Strive to establish and maintain the trust and confidence of service users and carers	Respect for confidential information and limits to confidentiality (chapter 4)
Respect the rights of service users whilst seeking to ensure that their behaviour does not harm themselves or other people	Awareness and acknowledgement of statutory powers of social workers and others to intervene (Parts 3 and 4); awareness of law on violence and harassment (chapter 17)
Uphold public trust and confidence in social care services	Knowledge of accountability (chapter 3) and legal powers and duties (this chapter, chapter 4 and parts 2 and 3)
Be accountable for the quality of their work and take responsibility for maintaining and improving their knowledge and skills	Includes knowledge of legal processes, inter-agency working, courts (Part 1 and Part 2)

   c. communicate with users, other than in exceptional circumstances, in a language and by means which they understand, using an independent, qualified interpreter where appropriate.

Working Together (DoH, 1999) a document which we refer to extensively in Part 3 of the book, reflects the ethical position. In paragraph 7.24, Race Ethnicity and Culture it states:

> Working in a multi-racial and multi-cultural society requires professionals and organisations to be committed to equality in meeting the needs of all children and families and to understand the effects of racial harassment, racial discrimination and institutional racism, as well as cultural misunderstanding or misinterpretation.

However, paragraph 7.26 makes your professional responsibilities to the service user explicit:

> 'professionals should guard against myths and stereotypes—both positive and negative—of black and minority ethnic families. Anxiety about being accused of racist practice should

not prevent the necessary action being taken to safeguard a child. Careful assessment—based on evidence—of a child's needs, and a family's strengths and weakness, understood in the context of the wider social environment, will help to avoid any distorting effect of these influences on professional judgements.'

Chapter 16 of the Laming Report into the death of Victoria Climbié focuses on the role of race and diversity in the failure of social services and others to respond to Victoria's needs. As Laming points out, in paragraph 16.1 of the Report:

> Victoria was a black child who was murdered by her two black carers. Many of the professionals with whom she came into contact during her life in this country were also black. Therefore, it is tempting to conclude that racism can have had no part to play in her case. But such a conclusion fails to recognise that racism finds expression in many ways other than in the direct application of prejudice.

The report emphasizes that children from every background are entitled to the protection of the law. Paragraph 16.10 states:

> The basic requirement that children are kept safe is universal and cuts across cultural boundaries. Every child living in this country is entitled to be given the protection of the law, regardless of his or her background. Cultural heritage is important to many people, but it cannot take precedence over standards of childcare embodied in law. Every organisation concerned with the welfare and protection of children should have mechanisms in place to ensure equal access to services of the same quality, and that each child, irrespective of colour or background, should be treated as an individual requiring appropriate care.

What we learn is that culturally aware ethical practice is not simple. The law also impacts upon your practice here.

We discuss the race relations legislation, including the duties it imposes on local authorities, as part of the legal framework for combating unlawful discrimination, in chapter 2.

The competent social worker

The second aspect of professional identity we must consider is competence. Professional competence is a key legal and ethical requirement. The BASW ethical code identifies it as an essential value of social work practice. In paragraph 3.5.2 it states that social workers have a duty to:

(a) Identify, develop, use and disseminate knowledge, theory and skill for social work practice;

(b) Maintain and expand their competence in order to provide quality service and accountable practice, appraising new approaches and methodologies in order to extend their expertise;

(c) Use available supervision or consultation and engage in continuous professional development, taking active steps where necessary to secure appropriate supervision.

The state translates this ethical requirement to a legal one by insisting on a rigorous qualification system. Under the Care Standards Act 2000 (CSA) a social worker falls within the general category of 'social care worker' (a category which includes a wide range of people engaged in social care, whether qualified as social workers or not—see below). The CSA, s. 55, defines a social worker as someone who engages in social work (s. 55(2)(a))—the definition does not really help to define what is social work, but there is no doubt that if you act as, or call yourself, a social worker, you must be qualified and registered. In fact it is a criminal offence for anyone else to use the title 'social worker' (s. 61).

You must be registered under s. 56 with the General Social Care Council (GSCC: **www.gscc.ord.uk**) (in Wales the National Assembly). Not only social workers but, under s. 55, any of the following must register with the GSCC/Assembly:

(a) anyone who engages in 'relevant social work' (meaning social work connected with any health, education, or personal services—perhaps a little unhelpful as a definition, but it will have to cover anyone undertaking the duties set out in Local Authority Social Services Act 1970 (LASSA) discussed below);

(b) a person employed in or managing a children's home, care home, or residential family centre, or for the purposes of a domiciliary care agency, a fostering agency, or a voluntary adoption agency;

(c) a person supplied by a domiciliary care agency to provide personal care in their own homes to persons who by reason of illness, infirmity, or disability are unable to provide it for themselves without assistance.

How does a social worker qualify?

The Secretary of State for Health is responsible for determining educational requirements, using powers contained in s. 67(1) CSA. The Secretary of State published the requirements currently in force in 2002—see **www.doh.gov.uk/swqualification/ newrequirements.htm**. But this document is not self-contained. It cross-refers to two further documents, and the actual detail of the competence, knowledge, and skill you will have to acquire are set out in:

1 the National Occupational Standards for Social Work published by the Training Organisation for Professional Social Work at **www.topss.org.uk/pdf/ SW_may2002.pdf.**; and

2 The Quality Assurance Agency for Higher Education benchmark standards for social work degrees at **www.qaa.ac.uk/crntwork/benchmark/social%20policy_text only.html#11.**

In Box 1.3 below we summarize those parts of these requirements which relate to knowledge and understanding of law. There is no minimum law curriculum; a matter of some regret in our opinion.

Under the CSA it is the statutory responsibility of the GSCC (or Welsh Assembly) to approve training courses on behalf of the Secretary of State, to recognize where appropriate foreign qualifications, and to specify post-qualification training requirements.

BOX 1.3 Social work training standards relating to law

National Occupational Standards (NOS)

For each of the areas of competence set out in the bullet points below a student must 'understand, critically analyse, evaluate, and apply . . . knowledge' of:

1 'The legal, social, economic and ecological context of social work practice . . . [English and Welsh], UK, EU legislation, statutory codes, standards, frameworks and guidance relevant to social work practice and related fields, including multi-disciplinary and multi-organizational practice, data protection and confidentiality of information' and

2 'The context of social work practice' including 'international law and social policy'

- 'Prepare for, and work with individuals, families, carers, groups and communities to assess their needs and circumstances

- Work with individuals, families, carers, groups and communities to help them make informed decisions

- Assess needs and options to recommend a course of action

- Plan, carry out, review and evaluate social work practice, with individuals, families, carers, groups, communities and other professionals. Respond to crisis situations

- Interact with individuals, families, carers, groups and communities to achieve change and development and to improve life opportunities

- Interact with individuals, families, carers, groups and communities to achieve change and development and to improve life opportunities

- Prepare, produce, implement and evaluate plans with individuals, families, carers, groups, communities and professional colleagues

- Support the development of networks to meet assessed needs and planned outcomes

- Prepare for, and participate in, decision making forums

- Assess and manage risks to individuals, families, carers, groups and communities

- Assess, minimise and manage risk to self and colleagues

- Manage and be accountable, with supervision and support, for your own social work practice within your organisation'

Quality Assurance Agency benchmarks

Subject specific knowledge should include:

The significance of legislative and legal frameworks and service delivery standards (including the nature of legal authority, the application of legislation in practice, statutory accountability and tensions between statute, policy and practice). The current range and appropriateness of statutory, voluntary and private agencies providing community-based, day-care, residential and other services and the organisational systems inherent within these. The significance of interrelationships with other social services, especially education, housing, health, income maintenance and criminal justice.

The complex relationships between justice, care and control in social welfare and the practical and ethical implications of these, including roles as statutory agents and in upholding the law in respect of discrimination.

CSA s. 62 also gives the GSCC/Assembly the duty to draw up codes of practice for social care workers. These can be accessed on the GSCC web site: **www.gscc.org.uk/**. The core values we quoted in Box 1.1 above were promulgated under these statutory powers by the CSCC. So when it stated the core values of the social work professional and articulated the training required to achieve competence, it did so using explicit statutory powers. Your starting point as a professional is a set of values and, we will show next, powers which derive explicitly from statute.

The responsible social worker

The third characteristic of professional identity we consider is the nature and extent of your professional responsibilities. We consider this in two sections. First, we consider your responsibilities to the service user. Secondly, we look at the duty of care you have to your service users and consider how the law is increasingly holding social workers accountable for their failures.

The service user

The first problem is to identify the social worker's service user. The LASSA duties, which we examine in more detail below as a matter of law, define for you who you owe duties to. The service user is the person to whom you owe a statutory duty.

In any case involving children, each individual child on your case-load is the service user, the person to whom you have statutory responsibilities. You need to build up an individual relationship with each child over and above that you may have with the child's parents or guardians. The Report of the Inquiry into Victoria Climbié—the Laming Report (see chapter 7) is the latest in a long series of reports which make it clear what happens when social workers lose sight of the core statutory responsibility to the child.

This point about service users is not just applicable to children. For example, if you are responsible for the well-being of an older person it is easy to overlook that that person is your service user and that his or her needs are the starting point for assessing what should be done. The pressures of the family can lead you to concentrate on what the family may want, which often may not be what the older person wants or what your statutory duty requires.

Other responsibilities

As the case study at the beginning of this chapter demonstrates, you do, of course, have responsibilities to others, such as prospective adopters, foster parents, and carers. You have duties to society at large, for instance in your responsibility to diminish offending by young people (see chapter 15). These responsibilities may arise from your common law duty of care or from other statutory responsibilities, for instance those arising under the Carers (Recognition and Services) Act 1995(C(RS)A)—see chapter 16. There will be legal consequences if you fail in your professional responsibilities to such people.

Nonetheless, it is critical that your prime focus is the person to whom you have statutory responsibilities.

What is the nature of the responsibility to the service user?

There is a conflict at the heart of the social work role. You have two clear relationships with the service user:

(a) an adviser/friend to the service user, or to those involved with the service user, such as their carers or parents. Such a role is often talked of as 'being an agent of social change'. That is to say that you will be seeking to make life better for the service user. This is often the motivation behind the decision to become a social worker; and

(b) a statutory relationship in relation to the service user. This is more commonly referred to as being 'an agent of statutory control'. This is where you are sometimes required to use statutory powers to protect the service user.

This second function may well involve you in investigations of the conduct of a service user or of those who are close to that service user. The conflict is clear. A friend does not investigate you, or police your behaviour. You may be required to make risk assessments of the future behaviour of the service user. A friend does not work out the likelihood of you behaving badly in the future. The tensions are even more apparent with the increased emphasis on partnership working with other agencies, such as the police—see chapter 7. Friends do not collude with others against our interests.

Acting in the best interests of the service user

Perhaps this gives us an insight into what went wrong in the case study at the beginning of this chapter. The children's social worker very much wanted the children to have this opportunity of a family life. She forgot that her statutory responsibilities were to act in the best interests of the children. Their best interests would have been served by full disclosure of the information about the difficulties of the boy to the prospective adopters. The social worker's wishes for the children overrode her professional judgement.

It is clear that your prime role has to be within the statutory framework that has created social workers. A social worker who fails to bear this in mind will ultimately fail him- or herself and his or her service users. This does not mean that your role as friend and adviser is or should be diminished. Nevertheless you need to build up your relationship with the service user with your statutory role as your first consideration. This is to be honest with that person, which is the best basis for a relationship. The idea of honesty raises questions, however, about the extent to which information is for sharing. The issues are so complex that they require a full chapter to analyse—see chapter 4.

Ethical practice

The *BASW Code of Ethics* gives some guidance on what this means in practice. Paragraph 4.1.1 of the code states that social workers will:

(a) Give priority to maintaining the best interests of service users with due regard to the interests of others;

(b) In exceptional circumstances where the priority of the service user's interest is outweighed by the need to protect others or by legal requirements, make service users aware that their interests may be overridden;

(c) Seek to safeguard and promote the rights and interests of service users whenever possible;

(d) Endeavour to ensure service users' maximum participation in decisions about their lives when impairment or ill-health requires the social worker or another person to act on their behalf;

(e) Not reject service users or lose concern for their suffering, even when obliged to protect themselves or others against them or to acknowledge their inability to help them.

These are not statutory guidelines, but they are drawn up in the light of the law and official guidance and must be respected.

Autonomy and the service user

The ethical principle that every person has a right to self-determination and is entitled to their autonomy is set out clearly in the *BASW Code of Ethics*. In paragraph 4.13 of the code, headed 'self-determination by service users', the code sets out the following:

> Social workers will help service users to reach informed decisions about their lives and promote their autonomy, provided that this does not conflict with their safety or with the rights of others. They will endeavour to minimise the use of legal or other compulsion. Any action which diminishes service users' civil or legal rights must be ethically, professionally and legally justifiable.

These principles are also enshrined in law, through the notion of consent and the duty of confidentiality. Actions taken without consent are unlawful, and in some circumstances criminal. We examine this difficult area of legal and ethical practice in chapter 3.

Legal accountability

The second part of our discussion about the responsibilities of social workers focuses on legal accountability. It is worth noting that the courts are increasingly holding local authorities to account for the mistakes of their employees. Traditionally, local authorities have been protected by the courts from such action for policy reasons—local authorities should be able to carry out the difficult task of child protection without the risk of being sued. For these reasons the House of Lords, in *X (Minors) v Bedfordshire County Council* (1995), dismissed claims by children trying to sue for failures by local authorities. Recently, however, there has been a shift away from this absolute legal immunity. Local authorities can be sued for negligence as long as the three criteria for the imposition of a duty of care are present. The three criteria were explained by the House of Lords in *Caparo Industries plc v Dickman* (1990) as foreseeability of damage (to what extent was the loss or damage predictable), proximity of relationship (how close was the relationship between the person causing the damage and the victim), and the reasonableness or otherwise of imposing a duty. For social workers the relationship with the service user is clearly sufficiently proximate, and the damage to the victim is generally predictable. The stumbling block in the past has been whether it was reasonable to impose a duty.

There has been a range of cases demonstrating that negligence by local authorities is now actionable. Among these are *S v Gloucestershire County Council* (2000), where the child was sexually abused by foster parents and *Barret v Enfield London Borough Council* (1999), where a social worker was careless in implementing decisions made about a child in care. In *W and Others v Essex County Council* (2000), the foster parents successfully sued where they had not been told by the social worker that the foster child had come into care for abusing his sister—a case similar to our case study in this chapter. These cases were distinguished from *X v Bedfordshire* on the basis that the facts in that case concerned the failure of the local authority to take children into care, which was a statutory responsibility which could not be ignored, and not the failure to carry out responsibilities once those responsibilities had been recognized.

The House of Lords considered the extent of the duty of care of local authorities and the professionals it employs to carry out its statutory responsibilities in *Phelps v London Borough of Hillingdon* (2000). This case was the legal authority for the judge's decision in the case study at the beginning of this chapter. In *Phelps*, their Lordships make it clear that local authorities are liable for professional misjudgements by their staff; and where a duty of care arises between a professional and a particular child the professional can be sued if there is a breach of that duty.

Claims against social workers or agencies under the European Convention

We will be devoting half ot the next chapter to human rights questions, including the role of the European Court of Human Rights (ECtHR). For now all you need to know is that individuals have the right to complain against the UK government at the ECtHR if they claim that their rights have been overridden within the UK. The judgment of the ECtHR in *Z and others v The United Kingdom* (2001) (the name under which the *X v Bedfordshire County Council* case was taken to Europe) was that the English law on negligence was valid. However, the children's human rights had been breached and the law of negligence had not provided them with a way of getting a judgment in court; on that basis the Court awarded the children substantial damages against the local authority. The authority's failure to remove the children from the home over a period of four and a half years, during which the children suffered emotional and physical abuse, meant that the authority had breached Article 3 of the Convention— 'No one shall be subjected to torture or to inhuman or degrading treatment or punishment.' The failure of English law to allow the children to sue for breach of Article 3 was a breach of Article 13—'Everyone whose rights and freedoms as set forth in this Convention are violated shall have an effective remedy before a national authority notwithstanding that the violation has been committed by persons acting in an official capacity.'

What this means is that children can sue for breach of their Convention rights in the UK courts where there has been a failure to take appropriate preventive action, and can sue in negligence where local authorities have failed to act properly once the child is in care. However there will be cases where the damage to children arose prior to the Human Rights Act and where *X v Bedfordshire* means that there is no recourse to the common law of negligence. In such cases the only legal action available is to take the case direct to Strasbourg. *DP and JC v UK* (2003) and *E v UK* (2003) are examples of people claiming for breaches of their human rights inflicted on them decades previously.

This does not mean that social workers owe a duty of care to everyone who may be affected by their actions. The duty is only owed where, on the basis of the particular facts of a case, it is fair, just and reasonable that such a duty should exist. This was made clear in *D v East Berkshire Community NHS Trust* (2003). In this case the parents had sued health professionals for psychiatric harm caused by false allegations of child abuse committed by the parents against the children. Their complaint was non-actionable (they had no right to compensation). The court believed there were cogent public policy reasons for concluding that no common law duty of care should be owed to the parents, since the child's interests were paramount and in potential conflict with those of the parents. It would be inappropriate to have the important work of child protection hamstrung by the fear of litigation.

Substantial damages may be available against social services departments for breach of human rights. In *C v Flintshire County Council* (2001), a case concerning a child seriously bullied whilst in care, damages of £35,000 were awarded for pain and suffering, £25,000 for loss of earnings, and over £10,000 for the cost of future psychotherapy.

The social worker as statutory creation

Having considered at some length what it means to be a professional social worker we now turn to the second identity of the social worker which we recognized at the beginning of the chapter, the social worker as a statutory creation.

Local Authority (Social Services) Act 1970

The principal Act imposing the social services function on local authorities (metropolitan boroughs and county authorities) is the Local Authority (Social Services) Act 1970 (LASSA). Social workers employed in local government, as we know them today, were effectively created by this Act. It is not an easy Act to understand. What it does is to establish the framework for local authority social work, and then refer you to all the other statutes that set out social work responsibilities (statutes dated both before and after 1970, since it is amended continuously, most recently in the Children Act 2004). The modern social work professional role did not exist before this statute, and it is to this statute that you look to signpost you to your statutory powers and duties. Although there is plenty of room for good intentions, these do not define your role; the statute does. The statutes tell you who you have responsibilities towards, and to some extent define how those responsibilities shall be exercised.

Section 2 of LASSA requires local authorities to establish a Social Services Committee to administer the social services functions of the local authority. The section is set out in Box 1.4.

 BOX 1.4 Local Authority (Social Services) Act 1970–s.2

'Every local authority shall establish a social services committee, and . . . there shall stand referred to that committee all matters relating to the discharge by the authority of—

(a) their functions under the enactments specified in the first column of Schedule 1 to this Act . . .'

You can refer to the list of relevant enactments (Acts of Parliament) up to 2002 in Brayne and Broadbent. We also consider them in a little more detail below. Whatever the social services department does is watched over by the Secretary of State for Health. This is because s. 7 of LASSA provides:

Local authorities shall, in the exercise of their social services functions, . . . act under the general guidance of the Secretary of State.

Section 7 also provides two other mechanisms to ensure that social services committees are accountable to their users and to the government. s. 7C provides for the Secretary of State to set up inquiries into performance of functions and s. 7D provides for the Secretary of State to take over the running of the authority's functions.

Note that s. 7B which provided for complaints procedures was repealed in England only by the Health and Social Care (Community Health and Standards) Act 2003. s. 7B remains in force for Wales. We shall discuss both the complexities of the devolution settlement and complaints procedures and inquiries together with other mechanisms for dispute resolution and accountability in chapter 5.

While the Local Authority (Social Services) Act 1970 sets out the framework for the provision by the local authority of social services, it is not very specific about the particular way this is to be organized. For instance, it may or may not be of comfort to you to know that the only people within the social services department who actually warrant a specific mention in the Act are the directors of adult social services and directors of children's social services.

LASSA establishes the overall framework. Detailed specific duties, responsibilities, and powers are to be found in other relevant Acts such as the Children Act 1989, the Children Act 2004, or the Mental Health Act 1983. By and large duties are placed by the legislation not on individual social workers but on the employing local authority social services committee. Children's guardians (formerly guardians *ad litem*) in child-care work and approved social workers in mental health work, however, also have duties imposed on them as individuals.

Further powers of the Secretary of State

Some of the specific legislative provisions which emanate from the Local Authority (Social Services) Act 1970 include the power for the Secretary of State to direct the local authority to take certain steps in relation to its social services function.

For example, under the Children Act 1989 there is a provision in s. 44(5) which deals with the exercising of parental responsibility once an emergency protection order has been granted. Paragraph (c) requires that the exercise of these powers 'shall comply with the requirements of any regulations made by the Secretary of State for the purposes of this subsection'. This subsection requires the Secretary of State to act by way of regulations, but in some cases the Secretary of State can act directly. For example, under s. 22, the general duty of the local authority to children can be overridden for the purposes of protecting members of the public from serious injury. By virtue of s. 22(7), in that situation the Secretary of State can tell the local authority what to do. This may be applicable in the case of a child suspected of murder where the matter might become a case for public concern. The Secretary of State would have the politically useful power of being able to say 'I have directed the local authority to place the child in secure accommodation.'

The statutory functions of a social worker

Now let us consider the third characteristic of the social worker which we have identified: the statutory functions of a social worker. In many ways this is the easiest identity to grasp. You are a social worker because of what you do. What you can do is set out in the 1970 statute we mentioned above: LASSA. Schedule 1 to the Act sets out every statutory duty which a social services department must carry out. Although it does not specify that individual social workers carry out these duties, or even mention the social work profession, any department of necessity carries out these duties by employing social workers. These duties are therefore, as a result of your employment as a social worker, your duties. The 1970 legislation suffers from two major defects. First, it does not systematically organize and define social service department duties using any coherent framework or philosophy, or, in fact, any framework at all. It merely lists all the bits of all the existing statutes about what local authorities do for children or for adults and states: this is what the social service departments must do. (See for more detail Brayne and Broadbent chapter 1.) Second, as this list has been added to or amended over three and a half decades, the collection of duties has become less and less coherent. The actual list covers enactments dating from 1933, which specify certain duties to assist children facing criminal proceedings. It sets out the most important sources of social service department duties to adults which date back to 1948 and the beginnings of the welfare state. The 1989 legislation on children is, by comparison, recent. The list is constantly being tweaked, with duties frequently amended and occasionally added. They are cited in full (as of 2002) in Brayne and Broadbent, and are referred to in the relevant parts of this book.

Box 1.5 opposite gives a quick summary of some key LASSA duties.

However, whilst these statutory functions are important, there is, as you are already becoming aware, far more law with which you have to be familiar. None of us can solely be defined by what we do. We have already touched, for example, on the CSA, which specifies statutory duties for social services departments as shown in Box 1.5, but also regulates the standards and training of social workers. (It also provides for inspection of community care and health services.)

But beyond legislation setting out statutory duties to particular service users through schedule 1 to LASSA there is a large, almost limitless, range of other legislation which affects your work: vulnerable adults and children in need may have problems relating to housing, immigration, family, domestic violence, welfare benefits, education, crime, and more. Sometimes the services provided by social workers in carrying out their statutory duties require you to be familiar with these areas of law. Because the work of the police and the criminal courts is so much a part of the work in protecting and assisting children in need, we deal with that area of the law in the section of the book which deals with children, Part 3. Part 5 of the book addresses a small number of other areas of law which we consider to be crucial: housing, family, protection from violence, and immigration. They have an effect on social exclusion in common. People suffering from social exclusion can often meet the statutory criteria for intervention by social services departments. Welfare benefits law affects all vulnerable groups, and is therefore touched on in the chapters below on the client relationship, on children, and on adult community care, as well as within the chapters on family law, housing law, and immigration law.

The rights and responsibilities of social workers as employees

The final identity of the social worker which we consider in this chapter is your identity as an employee of an agency. You have obligations arising from employment law to do the best you can for your employer. This may produce conflicts arising from the handling of individual cases. You may find that you are required by your team leader or area manager to take certain steps, such as seeking a court order, that you may not think is the 'best' course of action. As an employee you are legally required to follow the instructions of your employer. But your professional duty may put you in conflict with your employer. We hope this occurs rarely, but it remains a real possibility. (For the particular case of an approved social worker under the Mental Health Act (MHA)—where

BOX 1.5 Key statutory duties of the social worker

The Acts	Nature of the duties of local authority social services committees
Children and Young Persons Act 1933 and 1963	Support for children involved in criminal prosecution
Children Act 1989	Requirement to provide support for children in need and to protect children at risk of significant harm
Adoption and Children Act 2002	Providing adoption services
National Assistance Act 1948	Providing care services in the community or residential care for those who cannot cope without such services
Health Services and Public Health Act 1968	Additional care services for old people
National Health Service Act 1977	Additional care services for mothers and under-fives
Mental Health Act 1983	Provision of after-care. Provision of specialist approved social workers. Guardianship, involvement in assessment for compulsory admission to hospital
National Health Service and Community Care Act 1990	Requirement to plan community care services, assess individual needs, and make appropriate provision
Carers (Recognition and Services) Act 1995	Assessment of the ability of the carer to provide appropriate community care
Community Care (Direct Payments) Act 1996	Payments to the service user who can then buy community care
Health Act 1999	Framework for co-operation and payments between social services and health authorities
Carers and Disabled Children Act 2000 (*CDCA*)	Extends right of carer to assessment and creates direct right to services for carer
Care Standards Act 2000 (*CSA*)	Establishes framework for quality assurance of care and residential services
Health and Social Care Act 2001 (*HSCA*)	Delineates boundaries between social care and medical care; extends scope for direct payments to service users

Community Care (Delayed Discharges) Act 2003 (CCDDA)	Penalizes local authorities which cannot provide for discharged hospital patient
Children Act 2004 (CA2004) (when in force)	Establishes a children's commissioner; reorganizes aspects of child protection work

the employer cannot give the social worker instructions and the responsibility is individual—please see chapter 16.)

The *BASW Code of Ethics* explains the ethical position with regard to your employer. Paragraph 4.3 a–d states that social workers will:

a. Strive to carry out the stated aims of their employing organization, provided that they are consistent with this Code of Ethics;

b. Aim for the best possible standards of service provision and be accountable for their practice;

c. Use the organization's resources honestly and only for their intended purpose;

d. Appropriately challenge, and work to improve, policies, procedures practices and service provisions which:
    - Are not in the best interests of service users;
    - Are inequitable or unfairly discriminatory; or
    - Are oppressive, disempowering, or culturally inappropriate.

Accountability to your employer

Many social workers are concerned that they may be personally liable if they make mistakes. There is no doubt that if things go wrong you will have to explain your decisions. If you have taken reasonable care, kept your written records properly, and acted within an acceptable level of professional competence then you will be able to do this. If you do make a professional misjudgement there may be several consequences. First, the case may become the subject of an inquiry and you may be blamed in the report. Many feel that such an emphasis on individual social workers is unfair. The Laming report on the death of Victoria Climbié made this point:

> It is not to the handful of hapless, if sometimes inexperienced, front-line staff that I direct most criticism for the events leading up to Victoria's death. Whilst the standard of work done by those with direct contact with her was generally of very poor quality, the greatest failure rests with the managers and senior members of the authorities whose task it was to ensure that services for children like Victoria were properly financed staffed, and able to deliver good quality support to children and families. [paragraph 1.23]

Secondly, you are subject to the risk that you will be disciplined, and even dismissed, as a result of your mistake. The incompetent social worker will always take this risk. As Laming points out, the risk to you is almost always greater than the risk to senior managers.

Finally, the person who suffers may be able to sue for compensation for the effects of your mistake. He or she is far more likely to sue the local authority than you, and even if you are sued you will be indemnified by the local authority. We have discussed earlier the responsibility of the local authority for breach of duty of care or breach of the Human Rights Act by social workers.

Confidentiality as an employee

We discuss in chapter 4 the duty of confidentiality you have to service users and others. Social workers will also have duties of confidentiality which arise from their employment. If you breach a term of your contract, then you may well be disciplined, or even dismissed. Your trade union, professional association, or a lawyer experienced in employment law will have to advise you on procedure.

There may, however, be occasions when you would feel justified in breaching the requirement of confidentiality between you and your employer. For instance a social worker may wish to disclose that the social services department is chronically understaffed or that a colleague is professionally incompetent. The *BASW Code of Ethics* may be of some assistance here. Paragraph 4.3 j states that social workers will:

> Familiarise themselves with the complaints and whistle blowing procedures of their workplace, with the relevant provisions of the Public Interest Disclosure Act and with BASW procedures for complaints against members, addressing suspected or confirmed professional misconduct, incompetence, unethical behaviour or negligence by a colleague through the appropriate organisational, professional or legal channels.

The responsibility is on the social worker to know the internal complaints procedures. Where these do not produce satisfactory results social workers should consult their trade union or professional association for advice. In the last resort the Public Interest Disclosure Act 1999 may provide some assistance.

Public Interest Disclosure Act 1999

The Act is designed to encourage people to raise genuine concerns about malpractice in the workplace by providing legal protection against dismissal or victimization. If a social worker makes a disclosure in good faith to a manager or an employer, he or she will be protected as a whistleblower if he or she has a reasonable suspicion that the malpractice has occurred, is occurring, or is likely to occur. The Act also protects disclosures made in good faith to prescribed regulatory bodies where the whistleblower reasonably believes that the information and any allegation in it are substantially true. Wider disclosures (for instance to the police, the media, MPs, and non-prescribed regulators) are protected if, in addition to the test for regulatory discloser, they are reasonable in all the circumstances and:

- they are not made for personal gain,
- the whilstleblower must have reasonably believed he would be victimized if he or she raised the matter internally or with a prescribed regulator, and
- reasonably believed a cover-up was likely and there was not a prescribed regulator; or had already raised the matter internally or with a prescribed regulator.

If the concern is exceptionally serious, a disclosure will be protected if it meets the test for regulatory disclosures and is not made for personal gain. The disclosure must also be reasonable, having particular regard to the identity of the person it was made to.

Where the whistleblower is victimized in breach of the Act, he or she can bring a claim to an employment tribunal for compensation.

Your employer's responsibilities to you

Local authorities have responsibilities and duties towards you as their employee. The nature and volume of your work, with its associated risks of violence and abuse, place you under a great deal of stress. You have to balance individuals' needs with limited resources, and you are responsible for decisions which have significant implications for people's lives. In *Walker v Northumberland County Council* (1995), where a social worker suffered a nervous breakdown as a result of stress, the court made it clear that all employers have a duty of care and a duty in contract to ensure that the employee is kept safe from psychiatric as well as physical harm. Local authorities who breach this duty may be liable to pay substantial compensation to social workers. In September 2001 headline news was made by a former social worker who received £140,000 damages in settlement of her claim against Worcestershire County Council for a stress-related ill-ness developed through work. In *Gogey v Hertfordshire CC* (2001), a worker in a care home was suspended when concerns were raised about allegations of abuse made by a vulnerable child. The facts on which those concerns were raised were not clear. The Court found that the local authority could suspend the worker only if it was 'reasonable and proper' to do so. So the law should protect you from excessive work pressure and being treated in an arbitrary manner.

▒ What are lawyers?

Having spent all this time considering what a social worker is, it seems only fair to spend a little time considering what a lawyer is. Lawyers share with social workers a pro-fessional identity. They belong to a professional body, the Law Society or the Bar Coun-cil dependent upon whether they are solicitors or barristers, and are bound by a code of conduct. The code of conduct for solicitors however focuses on less complex dilemmas, not acting for people where you have a conflict of interest, and holding money that belongs to clients in a separate account from your own money. This is because lawyers have a much more straightforward relationship with their clients than you have with your service user. If the lawyer and the client disagree on what is the best course of action then the client can sack the lawyer. The child or vulnerable adult who is your service user does not have that freedom. Lawyers are originally not creations of statute; they are creatures of the market, though you will be perhaps reassured to know that the law regulates them closely. From the beginning of state power and the creation of laws to regulate behaviour there has been a demand for lawyers to interpret the law and to argue for the interpretation which best suits their client. This is not to say that the individual lawyer does not have ideals; the prime motivation for working in social welfare law is an idealistic one. However, being a lawyer does not inevitably imply an idealistic vocation, in contrast with the social worker. Lawyers also have different skills from social workers. Their skills lie in the interpretation of complex statutes and cases and in defending the interests of their clients through negotiation and advocacy.

However, it is probably at the quite different level of their view of the world that the essential difference between the social worker and the lawyer is seen most clearly. Social workers want what is best for their service user; lawyers are interested in achieving for the client what he or she wants, and the question of whether it should be what they want is irrelevant. This is best illustrated by an incident involving one of our colleagues, a lawyer. When she was working at a Law Centre she was approached by a 16-year-old woman clutching the hand of a 35-year-old man. The young woman explained that she was in care and she wanted to marry her boyfriend. Our colleague explained the legal process of getting permission from the magistrates. Our colleague was then telephoned by the young woman's social worker, who was outraged at the advice. Marrying the boyfriend was not in the best interests of the young woman in the opinion of the social worker and therefore it was inappropriate to advise her how to go about it. Our colleague was perplexed at the criticism; she considered she was only doing her job. The social worker was perplexed at the lawyer's lack of understanding of the social worker's wider responsibilities to the young woman. Our opinion is that both of these roles are important. We see one of the functions of the book as explaining these different world views and integrating them where appropriate.

EXERCISES

Consider the following three perspectives on social work:

1 The Department of Health gives the following guidance about the nature of social work on its careers web site: **www.socialworkcareers.co.uk/socialwork/socialwork.htm**

Social work is all about people.

Social Workers form partnerships with people: helping them to assess and interpret the problems they face, and supporting them in finding solutions. As advisor, advocate, counsellor or simply as listener, a Social Worker will try to help people to live more successfully within their local communities. Social Work involves engaging creatively with people, their families, friends and other important influences in their lives.

2 On the other hand the Quality Assurance Agency, which specifies the standards which apply for social work degrees, acknowledges at paragraph 2.2.2 that

There are competing views in society at large on the nature of social work and on its place and purpose. Social work practice and education inevitably reflect these differing perspectives on the role of social work in relation to social justice, social care and social order.

www.qaa.ac.uk/crntwork/benchmark/social%20policy_textonly.html#11

3 The British Association of Social Workers contains the following statement in its code of practice (para 4.1.1)

Priority of service users' interest

Social workers will:
Give priority to maintaining the best interests of service users, with due regard to the interests of others;

In exceptional circumstances where the priority of the service users' interest is outweighed by the need to protect others or by legal requirements, make service users aware that their interests may be overridden;

Seek to safeguard and promote the rights and interests of service users whenever possible;

Endeavour to ensure service users' maximum participation in decisions about their lives when impairment or ill-health require the social worker or another person to act on their behalf;

Not reject service users or lose concern for their suffering, even when obliged to protect themselves or others against them or to acknowledge their inability to help them.

In light of the duties set out in LASSA, which include intervention in people's lives, do you think your role is about justice, care or social order? See our web site for our thoughts on this from two lawyers' perspectives.

COMPANION WEB SITE

 For guidance on how to answer these exercises, visit the companion web site at: www.oup.com/uk/booksites/law

WHERE DO WE GO FROM HERE?

This chapter provides the foundation of the book. We have endeavoured to introduce you to our methods, language and priorities. We have considered the relationship between the social worker and the law by identifying the multiple roles of the social worker and by demonstrating how the law, alongside ethics, determines each of those roles. We hope that this has provided an interesting introduction to your studies.

We may have given an impression that Law and ideals are opposites. It is true that we have suggested that you should—indeed must—be guided by the powers and duties as laid down by law. If this might blunt your enthusiasm, we hope that the next chapter will show that law can be a vehicle for social change and the realization of ideals. We will be examining the Human Rights Act 1998 and follow this with legislation protecting people from inappropriate discrimination. These laws have changed, and are changing, the nature of our society. They require you, as a person working in a public authority, to respect individual rights including the right not to be discriminated against unlawfully.

ANNOTATED FURTHER READING

Hugh Brayne and Graeme Broadbent, *Legal Materials for Social Workers* (Oxford University Press, 2002). Chapter 1 provides excerpts from debates and the Seebohm Report leading up to the present day organization of the profession and writing on the nature of social work law.

Quality Assurance Agency, *Social work subject benchmark statement* (Quality Assurance Agency) **www.qaa.ac.uk/crntwork/benchmark/social%20policy_textonly.html#11**—a full analysis of the standards to be achieved in social work education.

Code of Ethics of the British Association of Social Workers **www.basw.co.uk/**—a comprehensive analysis of the standards of professional social work practice, including respect for human rights of service users, obligations to society, and issues concerning use of compulsory powers. It is also referred to extensively in chapter 4 below.

Stephen Nathanson, *What Lawyers Do—A Problem Solving Approach to Legal Practice* (Sweet and Maxwell, 1997)—if you want to look at the world through a lawyer's spectacles, this is readable and informative.

Jonathan Dickens, *Risks and Responsibilities – The role of the Local Authority Lawyer in Child Care Cases* [2004] CFLQ. This article discusses key sticking points in the relationship between local authority lawyers and social workers. It suggests awareness of each others multiple and competing responsibility will improve inter-professional relationships.

We recommend getting into the habit of looking at—and acquiring—the texts of the major pieces of legislation relevant to your area. All legislation likely to affect social workers is collected together in the looseleaf *Encyclopedia of Social Services and Child Care Law* (published by Sweet & Maxwell and updated regularly), together with rules, regulations, circulars, and text. We use it a lot and recommend it to you too.

The legal liability of local authorities for negligence

R. Bailey Harris and M. Harris, 'Local Authorities and Child Protection—The Mosaic of Accountability', [2002] CFLQ 117.

This article is particularly helpful in unravelling a difficult area of law.

2 Human rights and anti-discrimination law

CASE STUDY

Re L (Care: Assessment: Fair Trial) [2002] 2 FLR 730

This was an adoption case. The mother's first child had probably died of abuse aged four months. Not surprisingly the next child was subject to care proceedings, where the threshold conditions for making a care order (risk of significant harm—see chapter 12) were established. The question now for social services and then the court was whether rehabilitation was worth trying. The local authority's psychiatric expert at first recommended a long-term residential assessment; but as a result of discussions with the local authority and the children's guardian he changed his mind and recommended no assessment and therefore no chance of rehabilitation. The main reason was that the mother had refused to accept any responsibility for the death of her first child. Effectively he recommended, as a result, the end of the mother's chances of keeping her child.

Unfortunately the mother had been excluded from this discussion. She complained that her right to a proper determination of her rights had been abused. The judge upheld this complaint, though he did not in fact revoke the care order. He noted that there is a right to a fair trial and there is a right to the same fairness in all forums where rights and responsibilities are decided. This includes making information available to all parties and allowing them to be involved.

The case is of interest because of the way the judge, Munby J, highlighted the draconian powers held by social service departments and those whose opinions they use. Note in particular paragraph 150: 'The fairness which Arts 6 and 8 [of the European Convention on Human Rights] guarantee to every parent—and also, of course, to every child—in public law proceedings imposes . . . a heavy burden on local authorities. But it must never be forgotten that, with the state's abandonment of the right to impose capital sentences, orders of the kind which judges of this Division are typically invited to make in public law proceedings are amongst the most drastic that any judge in any jurisdiction is ever empowered to make. It is a terrible thing to say to any parent—particularly, perhaps, to a mother—that he or she is to lose their child for ever.'

OVERVIEW AND OBJECTIVES

Our case study concerns an abuse of human rights by social services. If at first reading you did not realize, the judge was comparing social workers' powers to seek the permanent separation of a child from her mother to the former power of a court to sentence to death. It is hard to imagine a more draconian intervention by the state in a person's life and family. There is an important human rights dimension to be considered.

Few readers will be unaware that since the Human Rights Act 1998 the European Convention on Human Rights 1950 is now part of the law applied in the courts of England and Wales. Or is it? Few will be unaware that the Act brings about a significant shift in the way our courts make decisions. Or does it? Most will know that legislation now has to be compatible with the fundamental rights set out in the Convention. Or must it? Many people assume that the law requires that all people should be treated the same, regardless of race, gender, disability, sexual orientation, gender reassignment, or age. Laws protect minority and vulnerable groups against such discrimination. Should they? Do they?

We hope to provide you with some tools to answer these questions, so far as they relate to social work practice. You should gain a working knowledge of the basic principles of the Human Rights Act 1998, the Race Relations Act 1976, the Sex Discrimination Act 1975, the Disability Discrimination Act 1995, and emerging laws relating to discrimination based on sexual orientation, gender reassignment, religion, or age.

Of course respect for human rights and the equal rights of all persons starts not from law but from personal and professional values. This respect is articulated in your educational and professional standards (see chapter 1). You would not have got as far as reading this book if these values were alien. But it is not enough to do your best to treat all people with respect and all people equally. Your own conduct and professional integrity, to put it simply, are not sufficient. You need to know the law—from the principles which underpin it through to the duties which it imposes on you and others. You will be judged against the standards laid down, for some rights are not just benchmarks but are enforceable through courts and tribunals.

The Human Rights Act (HRA) and the gradually increasing anti-discrimination laws have created a framework which to some extent pervades all other considerations of law. This is why the chapter comes early in the book—but you may need to return to it. The first part of the chapter outlines how the new approach to law created by the HRA works, and indicates where it can impact on the work of a social worker. The second part of the chapter examines the right not to suffer certain forms of discrimination. We examine the law designed to prevent discrimination in particular circumstances (employment and provision of services in particular) where the discrimination is based on grounds of racial origin, gender, and disability. It is a little artificial to separate out human rights in general from anti-discrimination in particular. But that reflects the way the legislation is currently framed in England and Wales and offers us the easiest way to explain it.

Human rights law

First, we will explain the way the Human Rights Act 1998 (HRA) works; we will then examine briefly the particular articles from the European Convention on Human Rights (the Convention) which set out each particular right.

We do not expect you to become expert human rights lawyers. It is enough that you gain an appreciation for an approach to practice that asks at every turn 'what are the human rights implications of this?' and that you know the approximate extent and limits to the power of the law to enforce human rights and prevent abuse.

Human rights as a concept

'We hold these truths to be self-evident, that all men are created equal, that they are endowed by their Creator with certain unalienable Rights, that among these are Life, Liberty and the pursuit of Happiness . . .' declared the writers of the American Declaration of Independence. However women, native Americans and slaves were not contemplated as beneficiaries until more recently. We think human rights are the product of history, human intelligence and compassion, and that they are not self-evident.

Social work under the Poor Law was concerned with helping the needy and less fortunate and was a form of top down paternalism. Understandings have, in the early twenty-first century, moved forward, and social work practice without an articulated respect for individual rights would now make little sense. In attempting to create a world where each individual has equal value and equal rights—including the right to litigate if those rights are curtailed—Parliament has imposed limits on the powers of those in authority. Those in authority includes the social worker. Rights empower individuals in relation to other individuals and in relation to the state.

New rights?

The UK was the prime force in drafting the 1950 European Convention on Human Rights and Fundamental Freedoms Convention. It did this because it believed that the rights and freedoms enjoyed in the UK should be enjoyed in all Council of Europe countries as a part of the post-war settlement. The Government signed up to the treaty which established the Convention in 1951. But in international law, signing a treaty commits the country's Government but not its courts to obeying its terms. The only enforcement mechanism was criticism from the Council of Europe monitoring procedures set up by the treaty, and from public pressure.

This changed in 1965, when the UK agreed to the citizen's right of direct petition to the European Court of Human Rights in Strasbourg (ECtHR). Since that date, anyone alleging a breach by the UK Government (which includes its public authorities) of their Convention rights has been able to have the dispute adjudicated by this international court.

Before 2000 the UK lost more cases in the ECtHR than any other country. Why? Is it because our Government and laws fail to protect human rights? The principal reason is that all allegations of breach had to go to Strasbourg for adjudication, as the Convention rights were irrelevant in UK courts. A good example illustrating this is the 'gays in the forces' case, *R v Ministry of Defence, ex parte Smith* (1996). Having been dismissed from the armed forces because of their homosexuality, and not for reasons of conduct, four officers tried to get the dismissal reviewed by a court. The case went to the Court of Appeal, where the judges said it was essential to distinguish between a bizarre, irrational decision which no reasonable Government department could possibly come to, and a bad decision which breached human rights. English law only entitled them to strike down an irrational decision, and the court had no power to declare this decision wrong, since its only fault was that it was probably in breach of the officers' human rights.

So they lost their case, and the officers had to take their complaint to Strasbourg. Predictably, the ECtHR upheld the complaint (*Smith v UK* (1999)), and only then was the Government forced to change its policy and admit homosexuals into the forces (or, more accurately, allow those already in the forces to 'come out of the closet'). But this was how things were before the Human Rights Act 1998, before English and Welsh courts could use Convention rights as a basis for decision making.

A comprehensive set of rights?

The Convention is a child of its time—the post-war years when the states of western Europe tried to set their faces both against the devastation of the recent past and against any new form of totalitarianism. So the Convention says many important things about due process, personal integrity and free speech and ideas; but nothing directly about the most elementary of all human needs, a right to enough food and shelter to keep body and soul together. (Lord Justice Sedley, Legal Action Dec 2003 page 19.)

The nearest the Convention rights get to economic rights comes in relation to the avoidance of inhuman or degrading treatment, which has resulted in asylum seekers denied support because they failed to claim asylum soon enough being able to obtain basic support from the government, despite rules designed to prevent this. 'It is thanks to the safety net which [the HRA] required . . . that these people are not starving in the streets' (Sedley LJ in the same article at page 23).

Human rights are not 'embedded' into the UK constitution, as such provisions are in the case of, say, Canada or the US. Human rights protections can be amended or withdrawn by legislation, and indeed the Conservative party has implemented a review of the HRA with a remit including total repeal (LS Gazette 2 Sep 2004 p.4); and the government has 'derogated' (exercised a right not to abide by) certain of the Convention rights (see below).

■ Enforcing human rights

The principal effect of the 1998 Act is to allow allegations of a breach of Convention rights to be raised in front of English courts. The mechanisms by which this is achieved are explained in Box 2.1.

How does this work in practice?

First, where legislation clearly clashes with Convention rights, legislation wins. Parliament has not given away its right to legislate as it sees fit, though it took a House of Lords decision to make this completely clear. They did this in the case of *Re S (Care Order: Implementation of Care Plan)* (2003). The Children Act 1989, as you will see later, gives a local authority broad powers to make decisions, once a child has been made subject to a care order. It is, under clear statutory powers, for the local authority to decide how to exercise the parental responsibilities it acquires under this order. There is no power of

BOX 2.1 Overview of the Human Rights Act 1998

How HRA impacts on:	Obligations created by HRA	Comment
Interpretation of statutes by courts	The words of statutes should be given a meaning compatible with the Convention rights (s. 2)	If statute conflicts with Convention rights statute prevails (s. 3(2)(b)) but a court may declare statute incompatible (s. 4)
Interpretation of case law and delegated legislation by courts	Convention rights prevail over Common Law (ie case law) and delegated legislation (rules made by government departments or public authorities authority)	All existing common law principles and all secondary legislation open to challenge as not human rights compliant (s. 6)
Obligations of public authorities	Public authorities (including social service departments) must act at all times in ways which comply with the Convention rights (s. 6)	A public authority can be taken to court by victim who alleges its actions are not compatible with Convention rights (s. 7)
Decisions of European Court of Human Rights	Human rights law in England and Wales requires ECtHR case law to be treated as part of our law s. 2	Principles derived from cases involving human rights complaints in other countries are equally relevant to challenges against UK

the court to supervise what the local authority does. But what if the authority infringes human rights in the exercise of these powers? Article 6, after all, provides a right to a fair trial when rights and responsibilities are decided, which conflicts with a social services department power to make decisions about the child on a day to day basis. And while Article 8 provides a right to respect for family life, social services have this statutory power to make decisions on, for example, placing the child with foster parents which interfere with the parent–child relationship. In working out the relationship between the Human Rights Act and the Children Act in this case, the Court of Appeal thought the answer was that human rights must override or add to what the Children Act said, and it decided that a court could have a power to keep under review the legality of the actions taken by the local authority under the Act. The Court of Appeal sought to achieve this through laying down milestones which the local authority's care plan must take into account. The local authority would have to report to the court if it departed from these.

The House of Lords robustly rejected this approach. It declared that the way to resolve a clash between what the Children Act said and the principles set out in the Human

Rights Act was not to rewrite the legislation. The Children Act, in its view, unambiguously gave the discretion to the local authority and was deliberately drafted to keep the courts from interfering. It was not the job of the courts to rewrite legislation, even where it failed to comply with the principles of the Convention.

So it appears that courts cannot rewrite clearly drafted legislation to make it HRA compatible. Indeed in the case of *R (on the application of Anderson) v Secretary of State for the Home Department* (2002), the House of Lords said any such attempt would amount to 'judicial vandalism'.

But more recently the House of Lords appears to have indulged in its own rewriting of the statutes, in *Ghaidan v Godin-Mendoza* (2004). The case involved the interpretation of the Rent Act 1977, which permits a spouse, or a couple living together as if they were man and wife, to inherit a tenancy. This case involved a long term relationship between the tenant and his same-sex partner, who was resisting the landlord's claim to possession of the flat now the tenant had died. Could the partner be, in law, a spouse? The European Convention requires human rights laws to be applied without unjustifiable discrimination, and Lady Hale was quite right to declare sexual orientation to be a 'suspect ground'. All the Lords agreed there was no justification for the discrimination against same sex couples on policy grounds. So could they rewrite the statutory wording to achieve a non-discriminatory result? The answer was yes, they should not be bound by the actual wording of the legislation and they could depart from the presumed intention of Parliament; indeed they could effectively modify the statutory words, so long as they did not end up effectively rewriting a whole statute. However, the House of Lords was aware that legislation was already planned to achieve this result, and informal reports indicate they would not have taken this bold step otherwise.

What a court can do if the legislation seems to breach the Convention rights is to declare it 'incompatible'; the Government then has a power to fast-track legislation through Parliament to correct the problem. However, this declaration of incompatibility is of no practical value to the litigant in the case, whose only choice is to give up on the rights he or she has under the European Convention, or take the UK to the ECtHR—where success is probable, given that the legislation has already been declared not compliant with the Convention.

An example of legislation declared incompatible is s. 26 of the Mental Health Act 1983. This—as we will see in chapter 17—gives powers to the 'nearest relative' to take decisions in relation to the detention or guardianship of a person for mental health reasons. In the case of *R (on the application of M) v Secretary of State for Health* (2003) a woman objected under Article 8 (respect for private life) to her adoptive father, as automatic nearest relative, gaining access to her records and being involved in decision-making, when there was no trust or relationship between them. The European Court of Human Rights had in 1998 already ruled that this section had to be changed and the Government had done nothing for five years, so the High Court had no difficulty declaring that it was incompatible with the Convention. Another example of incompatibility was *Bellinger v Bellinger* (2003), where the House of Lords refused to declare a marriage valid where the wife had previously been a man. The European Court of Human Rights had already declared English law, which failed to recognize gender reassignment, to be in breach of the Convention, but the Lords could not change the law, merely declare it incompatible. (Legislation has since changed this law—see below.)

There is also a requirement for draft legislation to be declared compatible with the Convention rights before it is introduced to Parliament. Such a declaration does not, of course, guarantee that it is. For example Article 6 of the Convention declares that a person charged in a criminal court has the right to challenge the witnesses against him or her. Yet the Criminal Justice Act 2003 permits the court to rely on hearsay, which means the witness cannot be challenged by cross-examination in court. (See chapter 6.) Before the Act was passed, the Bill was considered by Parliament's Joint Committee on Human Rights (*Report on the Criminal Justice Bill* (2003)), who stated that any conviction on such hearsay evidence would breach Article 6 of the Convention. The Committee was ignored and the Bill became an Act. Similarly the Committee (Nationality Asylum and Immigration Bill) reported that new powers to refuse asylum support or to deport an asylum seeker to an EU country, both without right of appeal, and to refuse to consider asylum claims from EU countries would breach human rights. But that Bill is now law.

Claims that legislation is incompatible rarely succeed. One example of success was *R (on the application of H) v Mental Health Review Tribunal* (2001). Section 73 of the Mental Health Act was declared to be incompatible with the right to liberty (Article 5), because it required the detained patient to prove she or he should be released, rather than putting the burden of proof on the state to show that there were continuing grounds for detention. (See chapter 17.)

So clearly drafted acts of parliament cannot be overridden by the judges, however badly they breach human rights. But courts can strike down old case law and can strike down statutory instruments (explained in chapter 5) if they are incompatible with the Convention rights.

Has there been any noticeable change in the law?

The United Nations Human Rights Committee monitors countries' human rights records, and in 2001 praised the UK for bringing human rights legislation into its domestic law. But the Act has not eliminated this Committee's criticism of the UK's human rights record: for example, there are not enough women in public positions; there are not enough ethnic minority members of the judiciary; the UK incarcerates children (see chapter 15). Some of these criticisms go into areas of policy and culture, which the Human Rights Act cannot address.

But still the answer is 'yes', there has been a change. Every action of every public authority must be checked for its compliance with the principles of the Convention. For example, the government has decided that tribunals (these are explained in chapter 5) require wholesale reform, because the way they are run is not compatible with Article 6, the right to a fair trial. Pressure comes from cases such as *R (on the application of Bewry) v Norwich City Council* (2001) or *Husein v Asylum Support Adjudicator* (2001). In the former the court said that a local authority cannot administer housing benefit and also hear appeals against its refusal; in *Husein* the immigration adjudicator was appointed by the Home Office, the same Home Office which had made the immigration decision. Therefore, the court ruled, the adjudicator lacked independence.

The balancing of rights and other factors

Convention rights are not absolute. For most individual rights—the right not to suffer torture is a clear exception—there will be an explicit corresponding provision balancing that right with the needs of the state, other individuals, or society. Article 8 (right to respect for private and family life) is an example. Paragraph 1 baldly describes the right:

> Everyone has the right to respect for his private and family life, his home and his correspondence.

But paragraph 2 quickly shows that it has limits:

> There shall be no interference by a public authority with the exercise of this right except such as is in accordance with the law and is necessary in a democratic society in the interests of national security, public safety or the economic well-being of the country, for the prevention of disorder or crime, for the protection of health or morals or for the protection of the rights and freedoms of others.

This leaves considerable discretion to the judges. They must exercise the discretion in light of previous decisions of the Strasbourg Court, and, in due course, the body of human rights case law built up in this country.

A particular principle when carrying out the balancing exercise is that any reduction in individual rights must be lawful proportionate and necessary. We will explain these three concepts in relation to the case example which follows. Let us take the case of *R (on the application of S) v Plymouth City Council* (2002). S wanted to see social services records in order to be able to participate in the decisions that had to be made about her son, who was subject to a guardianship order under the 1983 Mental Health Act (see chapter 16). The local authority thought the son should be moved from his mother's care to a residential environment. This required them to take over the mother's powers of discharge as the nearest relative. The mother had a right under Article 6 to a fair determination of her rights and responsibilities as nearest relative. The local authority championed the son's rights to respect to his own private life (Article 8). The court decided that Article 6, in this case, outweighed Article 8, particularly as there was no evidence that the son objected or that it would damage his interests for his mother to see the file. The displacement of the mother as nearest relative was lawful, in that the Mental Health Act provided powers for a court to order it; it was proportionate, in that the court balanced the rights of the mother against the needs of the son; and it was necessary, in that it could not be avoided if the son was to get what he needed, the independent living which the mother wished to block but the court considered he should have.

In addition to the fact that the rights are balanced against the interests of other people or society at large, be aware that a breach of a right will not automatically lead to a remedy. For example in *R v Robinson* (2002), the Court of Appeal condemned the police for planting an informant in a solicitors' office where fraud against the legal aid fund was suspected. This would interfere with the duty of solicitors to their clients, particularly the duty of confidentiality. But as far as the convicted solicitor was concerned, his conviction for fraud was upheld and the only consequence of the police abuse was the court's condemnation.

Box 2.2 summarizes a few recent cases involving human rights challenges. You will find further examples in every chapter of this book, as human rights questions now pervade all judicial decision making.

 BOX 2.2 Examples of recent human rights challenges

Djali v Immigration Appeal Tribunal (2003)—this case shows the difficult balancing act which courts have to carry out in reconciling the legitimate interests of the state with the personal rights set out under the Human Rights Act. The appellant's wife was suffering post traumatic stress disorder because of her experience in Kosovo. Although the appeal against refusal of asylum was brought by the husband, his wife's right to remain depended on its success. At stake in the appeal were her Article 8 rights to respect for family and private life and Article 3 rights not to suffer inhuman or degrading treatment. The Immigration Tribunal upheld the deportation order against the husband, on the ground that the state has a legitimate aim of maintaining effective immigration policy. The Court of Appeal upheld the decision to refuse asylum, holding that the wife could obtain medical treatment in Kosovo; it is accepted that inhuman or degrading treatment could counterbalance the need to maintain proper immigration control, but this was not proved here.

N v Secretary of State for the Home Department (2003) shows up the difference between protection of rights and provision of other services. To deport N to Uganda could result in her imminent death, as there were no facilities comparable to those in the UK to treat her AIDS. Her asylum claim was nevertheless dismissed and her claim that deportation would be a breach of her Article 3 right was also dismissed. Her treaty rights did not require the UK to protect her from a lack of resources in Uganda.

Evans v Amicus Healthcare Ltd (2003) was a well-publicized case in which the male former partner of the applicant was refusing his consent to her use of fertilized embryos. Although both had consented to the treatment leading to the production of fertile embryos, the relationship between them had now broken up. The relevant legislation permitted the man at any time to withdraw his consent for the storage and use of the eggs. The legislation was clear, and even though refusal meant the loss of the possibility of a pregnancy, the right to family life could not override the very clear provisions of the legislation.

Hooper v Secretary of State for Work and Pensions (2003). The 1992 Social Security Contributions and Benefits Act explicitly gave benefits to widows which are not available to widowers (in fact the legislation has subsequently been amended to provide equality). A group of widowers appealed all the way to the House of Lords, but unsuccessfully. The Lords agreed that the discrimination was manifest, but first it had occurred before the human rights act came into effect in 2000, and secondly, the legislation was unambiguous and it was not the function of the court to overturn the words of the legislation. If these widowers appeal to the European Court of Human Rights they are likely to succeed under Article 14, which did outlaw such discrimination at the relevant time. The English and Welsh courts cannot override clear UK legislation, but that is not the case with the ECtHR.

Connors v UK (2004) is an example of this continuing role of the European court of Human Rights, notwithstanding the Human Rights Act 1998. Mr Connors, a gypsy, was evicted by the local authority for alleged nuisance. He sought judicial review in the High Court on the ground that the facts leading to the decision to evict had not been properly investigated by the local authority, and failed. However when the case was eventually heard in the ECtHR he was successful. The court confirmed, under Article 8—right to respect for family life—that the government must facilitate not hinder the gypsy way of life, and that clear and weighty reasons were required before action which interfered with it. It was a balancing act in every case. See Legal Action August 04, page 13.

A v Secretary of State for the Home Department (2005). After 9/11 the government rushed through powers (Anti-terrorism, Crime and Security Act 2001) to detain foreign terror suspects indefinitely, without charge or trial. The government accepted that this breaches Article 5 (liberty), but used its power under the HRA and the Convention in time of national emergency. Nine detainees successfully challenged their detention, the House of Lords accepting that—as foreigners—this was discrimination under the Convention and that the powers were a disproportionate (and ineffective) response to the terrorist threat.

Summary of the Convention rights

The full text of the Convention rights, which are included within the Human Rights Act, can be accessed directly via **www.hmso.gov.uk/acts/acts1998/19980042.htm**, and also in Brayne and Broadbent. We also give you the full text where it is important within later chapters. The key rights are summarized below.

Article 2 establishes a right to life. This could be relevant to a social services department sued, for example, for failure to protect the right of a child not to be killed by an abusive parent, or failure to properly investigate any such death.

Article 3 is the right not to be subjected to inhuman or degrading treatment, and could be relevant to social workers' duties to protect children and perhaps vulnerable adults from abuse or, in extreme cases, failure of the state to provide economic support.

Article 5 provides a right to liberty and security. This means that a person can be detained only following a proper, lawful procedure. That means that anyone claiming illegal detention—such as, for example, a child locked up without following the procedures under the Children Act set out in chapter 9—already has a remedy and cannot invoke the Human Rights Act. It may be arguable that the detention of immigrants pending the processing of their applications could be in breach, and we have referred above to the incompatibility with Article 5 of the Mental Health Act, s. 73, which requires a detainee to prove that conditions for detention no longer apply.

Article 6, right to a fair trial (see case study above), refers to the requirement for civil rights to be fairly determined, and criminal trials to contain full safeguards. The way you conduct case conferences and make decisions about use of your statutory powers, particularly in relation to children, can also be challenged under this Article.

Article 8 provides a right to respect for family life and private life; any interference with this right must be both lawful and necessary. Much of social work with children comprises use of compulsory powers, or the possibility of their use if other support fails. If the interference is carried out within the legal framework the first test for interference—lawfulness—is satisfied. It is unlikely that you will fall foul of the second test—the interference was necessary—because the Children Act, which is where most of your powers reside, requires a court to be satisfied that the interference was in the interests of a child. But there are some actions taken within other legal frameworks which also interfere with privacy or family life—for example placing a child on an 'at-risk' register. These actions are lawful, but because they are not sanctioned by a court your department and those who participate in the decision-making must be satisfied that, on balance, the action was necessary and the procedure for making the decision fair under Article 6.

Article 14 prohibits discrimination in the enjoyment of Convention rights. An imaginary example of the operation of Article 14 would be a case where social services were shown to have failed to protect a child from inhuman or degrading treatment (Article 3) if the reason was that they were not prepared to get involved because the child is, say, from a Muslim family. Such grounds for discriminating when a Convention right is involved would be unlawful under Article 14, even if the discrimination is not covered under English and Welsh law on discrimination. Similarly removing a child into care (breach of Article 8) could be in breach of the Article if the substantive ground was that the parent was, say, homosexual. (Note that Article 14 does not itself prohibit all forms of discrimination. There is, for example, no right to economic or social provision in the Convention, so denying a person employment or health care on grounds, say, of disability or gender is not on its own a breach of Article 14, which is why the statutes on race, sex, and disability discrimination have to be considered as well.)

Article 13 requires there to be a remedy for any breach of the Convention Articles. Parliament deliberately omitted Article 13 from the HRA, however, because it wanted English and Welsh legislation to be paramount. We noted the example of *Re S* above, where the House of Lords held that local authorities may use their statutory powers under a care order even if the use of those powers breaches Article 8 rights to respect for family life. The only redress is to use the European Court of Human Rights, where the UK is in fact bound by Article 13 and could be held to be in breach.

Department of Health Guidance for Social Workers on Human Rights

Circular LAC 2000 (17) states:

> Social Service Departments should actively develop good practice in a manner suited to the new human rights culture, linking as appropriate the equality and race relations agenda.

This is, perhaps unavoidably, a rather bland statement. Such guidance will work only if human rights issues are taken into account in all aspects of social work. We will raise issues of human rights as they occur throughout the chapters which follow, so that this culture can acquire some meaning for you. The DoH web site is a very good source of further guidance: find it at **www.doh.humanrights/index.htm**. It includes discussion of the relationship between existing human rights cases, the Articles referred to above, and social work situations.

Are we already retreating from human rights?

As the seventh edition went to press in October 2001, we noted that the terrorist attacks on New York and Washington had led to the then Home Secretary declaring that, if necessary, human rights legislation could have to be restricted. We feared then that the optimistic belief that human rights provides a new foundation for all legal thinking could be snuffed out in new legislation or executive action, or by judges simply preferring to support state rights against individual liberty when using their wide discretion. There is now little visible enthusiasm in government pronouncements about the benefits of embedding fundamental rights for all into our laws, and the destitution of asylum seekers who fail to claim asylum immediately on arrival is an early result (see chapter 21). We have seen (page 41 above) the government derogate (which means withdraw) from a part of the UK's treaty obligations in respect of the European Convention. In order to detain foreign suspected terrorists it brought in the Human Rights Act 1998 (Designated Derogation) Order 2001. We saw above that the House of Lords declared this order unlawful.

In fact the courts, often to the dismay of Government, seem to have embraced the human rights opportunities handed to them by the HRA. The Lord Chief Justice, in particular, has expressed his opinion on the duty of the senior judges to uphold human rights if necessary against the wishes of the government. The BBC web site for example on 16 October 2002 quotes the following:

> the courts must be ready to stop the government taking away people's human rights in the name of tackling terrorism, the most senior judge in England and Wales has warned. Lord Woolf said it was 'almost inevitable' that ministers would fail to protect the rights of minorities as they confronted what they said could be an even greater threat than Hitler. Judges would not be popular for stepping in against the government, said the lord chief justice, but that was a price worth paying for guarding democracy.

In a more prosaic way, the following case shows that human rights are so embedded that perhaps it is becoming unnecessary to refer to them. *Re V (a Child) (Care Proceedings: Human Rights Claims)* (2004) involved care proceedings in respect of a baby. The father raised human rights issues: interference with respect for family life under Article 8; right to a fair trial under Article 6. He claimed that to safeguard his Article 8 rights the authority should have funded therapeutic treatment for the family, so that they could have stayed together. The county court judge, in light of these issues, transferred the case to the High Court so that it could consider the human rights issues. The Court of Appeal was critical of the county court decision, and their judgment shows in effect how ingrained the HRA has now become. The following is from the judgment of Wall LJ (our emphasis):

2. ... Articles 6 and 8 of the European Convention for the Protection of Human Rights and Fundamental Freedoms are to a lesser or greater extent engaged *in each and every application issued by a local authority* under Pt IV of the 1989 Act. In every case where the threshold criteria under s. 31 of the 1989 Act are established, the court, in deciding what (if any) order to make, is required to apply the welfare checklist under s. 1(3) of the 1989 Act; to balance the competing art 8 rights to respect for family life of the parties and the child; and to achieve a result which is both proportionate and in the best interests of the child.

3. Every court hearing proceedings under Pt IV of the 1989 Act, (that is the family proceedings court (FPC), the county court and the High Court) has a duty under s 3(1) of the 1998 Act to give effect to the provisions of the 1989 Act in a way which is compatible with convention rights.

4. Any allegation made in care proceedings pursuant to s. 6(1) of the 1998 Act that a local authority has acted in a way which is incompatible with a convention right, including any allegation which involves a breach of a party's rights under either arts 6 or 8 of the convention, can and should be dealt with in the care proceedings by the court hearing those proceedings under s. 7(1)(b) of the 1998 Act. It is neither necessary nor desirable to transfer proceedings to a superior level of court merely because a breach of convention rights is alleged.

Human rights and discrimination

The right not to be unfairly discriminated against is one of the most important human rights. The right has existed, on paper, since the United Nations adopted the Universal Declaration of Human Rights shortly after the Second World War, and is supplemented by UK adoption of additional treaties: see Box 2.3.

The Articles in Box 2.3 are statements intended to bind the UK Government to good practice. In some countries international treaty obligations create rights enforceable by citizens in the courts. This is not the case in England and Wales, except in the case of those rights introduced by way of the Human Rights Act (see above). So all of the international treaty obligations in respect of addressing discrimination are not enforceable, if breached, in the domestic courts, though in fairness to the judges, many make explicit reference to such treaties when trying to arrive at a just solution to a particular case (for example, the *Bulger* case used as the case study in chapter 15).

Article 14 of the ECHR

By contrast with the above UN treaty obligations, the UK has accepted that rights under the European Convention on Human Rights can be enforced in court. We looked at these above. The article that particularly relates to discrimination is Article 14:

The enjoyment of the rights and freedoms set forth in this Convention shall be secured without discrimination on any ground such as sex, race, colour, language, religion, political or other opinion, national or social origin, association with a national minority, property, birth or other status.

BOX 2.3 Extracts from UN treaties

Universal Declaration of Human Rights

Article 2

Everyone is entitled to all the rights and freedoms set forth in this Declaration, without distinction of any kind, such as race, colour sex, language, religion, political or other opinion, national or social origin, property, birth or other status. . . .

Article 23

1. Everyone has the right to work, to free choice of employment, to just and favourable conditions of work and to protection against unemployment.
2. Everyone, without any discrimination, has the right to equal pay for equal work.

Convention on the Elimination of All Forms of Discrimination against Women 1981

Article 1 defines discrimination against women as

any distinction, exclusion or restriction made on the basis of sex which has the effect or purpose of impairing or nullifying the recognition, enjoyment or exercise by women, irrespective of their marital status, on a basis of equality of men and women, of human rights and fundamental freedoms in the political, economic, social, cultural, civil or any other field.

Article 3 requires governments to take

all appropriate measures, including legislation, to ensure the full development and advancement of women, for the purpose of guaranteeing them the exercise and enjoyment of human rights and fundamental freedoms on a basis of equality with men.

Article 4 permits temporary positive discrimination to tackle inequalities.

Article 5 requires government to take measures towards

'the elimination of prejudices and customary and all other practices which are based on the idea of the inferiority or the superiority of either of the sexes or on stereotyped roles for men and women' and 'to ensure that family education includes a proper understanding of maternity as a social function and the recognition of the common responsibility of men and women in the upbringing and development of their children'.

Article 11 deals with employment including

(a) The right to work as an inalienable right of all human beings;

(b) The right to the same employment opportunities, including the application of the same criteria for selection in matters of employment;

(c) The right to free choice of profession and employment, the right to promotion, job security and all benefits and conditions of service and the right to receive vocational training and retraining, including apprenticeships, advanced vocational training and recurrent training;

(d) The right to equal remuneration, including benefits, and to equal treatment in respect of work of equal value, as well as equality of treatment in the evaluation of the quality of work;

(e) The right to social security, particularly in cases of retirement, unemployment, sickness, invalidity and old age and other incapacity to work, as well as the right to paid leave;

(f) The right to protection of health and to safety in working conditions, including the safeguarding of the function of reproduction.

UN Declaration on the Elimination of All Forms of Racial Discrimination 1963

1. Discrimination between human beings on the ground of race, colour or ethnic origin is an offence to human dignity and shall be condemned as a denial of the principles of the Charter of the United Nations, as a violation of the human rights and fundamental freedoms proclaimed in the Universal Declaration of Human Rights, as an obstacle to friendly and peaceful relations among nations and as a fact capable of disturbing peace and security among peoples.

2.1. No State, institution, group or individual shall make any discrimination whatsoever in matters of human rights and fundamental freedoms in the treatment of persons, groups of persons or institutions on the ground of race, colour or ethnic origin.

2.2. No State shall encourage, advocate or lend its support, through police action or otherwise, to any discrimination based on race, colour or ethnic origin by any group, institution or individual.

3. Special concrete measures shall be taken in appropriate circumstances in order to secure adequate development or protection of individuals belonging to certain racial groups with the object of ensuring the full enjoyment by such individuals of human rights and fundamental freedoms. These measures shall in no circumstances have as a consequence the maintenance of unequal or separate rights for different racial groups.

4.1. Particular efforts shall be made to prevent discrimination based on race, colour or ethnic origin, especially in the fields of civil rights, access to citizenship, education, religion, employment, occupation and housing.

4.2. Everyone shall have equal access to any place or facility intended for use by the general public, without distinction as to race, colour or ethnic origin.

The Convention also requires governments to legislate against discrimination, to campaign against prejudice, take positive steps to promote full citizenship rights and benefits, and 'condemn persons claiming superiority of one group against another and to criminalise incitements to violence and organisations which promote violence.'

UN Declaration on the Rights of Disabled Persons 1974

1. The term 'disabled person' means any person unable to ensure by himself or herself, wholly or partly, the necessities of a normal individual and/or social life, as a result of a deficiency, either congenital or not, in his physical or mental capacities.

2. Disabled persons shall enjoy all the rights set forth in this declaration. These rights shall be granted to all disabled persons without any exception whatever.

These we have summarized as rights to:

Dignity, a decent and normal full life, social and political rights, all possible measures to be taken to facilitate self-reliance, treatment and retraining towards rehabilitation, economic and social security, proper employment opportunities, family life as near to normal as possible, legal aid for the protection of rights, protection from exploitation, and the right to be informed of these rights.

UN Convention on the Rights of Mentally Retarded Persons 1971
These rights we have summarised as the rights to:

proper care; education; rehabilitation; guidance; economic security; work to the fullest extent possible; family life as far as possible, with support if necessary; guardianship; protection from exploitation and abuse; and proper procedures to be adopted before any deprivation of normal rights.

The Article 14 protections against unreasonable discrimination seem at first to extend a long way beyond the more limited statutory rights which exist in England and Wales, set out below. However, closer reading shows that Article 14 does not create a free-standing right not to be discriminated against. What it does is to ensure that treaty rights—things like a right to respect for private life and a right to a fair determination of civil or criminal rights—are equally available to all without discrimination. Since, in contrast to the UN treaty rights, the Convention offers no rights to economic, social, or cultural facilities, its Article 14 cannot on its own protect from discrimination in relation to these. For that we still rely on English and, to some extent, European Community laws.

An example of how Article 14 protects from discrimination in the enjoyment of a European Convention right—in this case on grounds of sex—can be seen in the ECtHR decision of *Abdulaziz, Cabales and Balkandali v UK* (1982). A new Conservative Government wished to restrict immigration at a time of mass unemployment. Male workers were the target as they would add to the job seekers.

Rules were introduced which prevented a woman lawfully settled in the UK bringing her husband into this country, unless she was a UK citizen by birth or descent. The rules said nothing about men in the same situation bringing their wives to live with them. The allegation brought against the UK in the European Court of Human Rights was that this breached the wife's right to family life and her right to found a family (Article 8). But the UK government could argue that, under Article 8, this was necessary 'for the economic well-being of the country'. (We have referred earlier to the fact that Convention rights almost always are balanced by such factors.) The ECtHR judges were willing to accept that this restriction on the Article 8 right to family life was justified, and that anyway such a woman could go to the man's home country and start a family there (this was 1983!). But the UK defence still failed, and this was because there was no equivalent rule preventing men from bringing in their wives.

Taking account of Article 14, the UK's approach had resulted in a woman being discriminated against compared with a man. The UK would breach its Convention obligations if it protected its labour market against immigrant men but not immigrant women. (Incidentally despite the rule having the practical result of favouring whites over other racial groups, the Court held that there had been no racial discrimination.)

The scope for using Article 14 rights within the courts of England and Wales will depend on the creativity of lawyers and judges. It is, at least, arguable that old cases relating to the allocation of public sector housing would have to be decided differently. An example is *Tower Hamlets v Ferdous Begum* (1993). In that case, the Court upheld the right of the landlord to refuse housing to prospective tenants who lacked the mental capacity to sign the tenancy. Lack of capacity is unlikely to qualify under the DDA as a disability, but Article 14 could now be used to argue that discrimination on grounds of capacity is a form of unlawful discrimination.

Can law defeat discrimination?

It may help to try to distinguish between two types of discrimination—that which is based on sensible and fair grounds, and that which is based on prejudice and irrationality. As simple examples of acceptable discrimination, it is sensible and fair to discriminate in favour of women by offering obstetric facilities in hospitals, or in favour of visually impaired people by permitting guide dogs in places where dogs are otherwise not allowed. The law's target is to stop decisions being made, either by the state or by individuals, where the reason for favouring one person or group or discriminating against another is unfair and irrational and based on prejudice. The law has since 1970 progressively attempted to define which grounds will be treated as unlawful as grounds for discriminating—so far the main ones are gender, race, or disability. Sometimes even discrimination on these grounds is lawful and desirable (though views differ). The law can accept, or require, discrimination in favour of certain sectors: for example, additional facilities to enable workers with disabilities to carry out employment tasks; preferential access to training for disadvantaged groups.

Discrimination and lawyers

The legal profession is not always in the best position to preach anti-discrimination practice to social workers. We noted earlier that a UN report on human rights progress in the UK in 2001 noted poor progress in getting ethnic minorities into judicial roles. Box 2.4 illustrates a few other problems:

 BOX 2.4 Diversity in the legal professions

From the Lord Chancellor's Department web site Sept. 2004
- The House of Lords now has one woman member, who at 59 is the youngest Law Lord; in the Court of Appeal two out of 36 are women; in the High Court women occupy nine of the 106 positions.
- One judge (since Sept. 2004) in the High Court comes from an ethnic minority background.
- One judge in the High Court is under 50.

From the *Law Society Gazette*
- "Almost a third of female solicitors have experienced sexual discrimination at work, and one in five have experienced harassment." (13 Sept. 2001)
- "A female solicitor who was told by her employers that women who have babies go 'jelly-headed' and are not capable of working to their previous standard has won her unfair dismissal claim." (9 Sept. 2002)
- "It is extremely difficult even now for disabled people to gain employment as solicitors." (4 June 2004)
- "The *Gazette* recently received a press release from a law firm proudly announcing the appointment of the first female partner in its history." (5 Aug. 2004)
- "Black lawyers have had to call for a quota system as the only way to break into the prestigious city firms." (2 Sept. 2004)
- "Some law firms display an 'utterly shocking' lack of knowledge about the law relating to pregnancy." (2 Sept. 2004)

Local authority equal opportunities policy

A local authority should have a written policy on sexual, racial, and disability discrimination (an equal opportunities policy). This policy will go beyond the minimum legal requirements, and will attempt to promote both equality of opportunity and sensitivity to relevant difference for all people affected by the work of the authority. Since April 2001, all public bodies—for example, police, immigration authorities, and, of course, local authorities—have a general duty to work towards the elimination of unlawful discrimination and to promote equality of opportunity and good relations between different racial groups (Race Relations Act 2000, s. 1).

We first focus on sex and race discrimination, where each of the Acts was drafted on similar lines in the 1970s. After this we look at more recent legislation in relation to disability, before finishing with a look at initiatives by both courts and government to address other forms of discrimination.

The legal framework governing discrimination

What follows is not necessarily easy to follow. Discrimination law was not designed as a coherent whole; it has grown in response to public awareness, to European Community requirements, and to human rights law. The result is a hotchpotch. 'The complexity of the existing legislation is unnecessarily difficult for employers, in particular small businesses, to comply with. . . . It hinders victims in their access to justice. Compliance is too dependent on the willingness of individuals to take a case to a court or tribunal with the result that entrenched patterns of systematic discrimination remain. Eliminating institutional barriers requires greater emphasis on changing organisational cultures from within' (*The Need for Reform*, published by the Odysseus Trust at **www.odysseustrust.org** in support of proposals for a single statutory equality framework. This Equality Bill was rejected by Parliament.)

Sex Discrimination Act 1975 (SDA) and Race Relations Act 1976 (RRA)

Definitions can be difficult. For sex discrimination, English law recognizes only two sexes, men and women, which until recently meant the sex which went on to your birth certificate but now includes gender acquired following reassignment treatment. Sex discrimination does not cover discrimination on grounds of sexual orientation, though we will discuss this, as there has been much case law.

For race discrimination, the RRA, s. 1, defines race in terms of colour, nationality, or ethnic or national origins. Race does not cover religion, unless religion overlaps with ethnicity, such as with Sikhs, who were recognized as a distinct ethnic group in the case of *Mandla v Dowell Lee* (1983). Likewise Jews are an ethnic group (*Seide v Gillette Industries Ltd* (1980)). Gypsies are a racial group (*Commission for Racial Equality v Dutton* (1989)), although travellers are not, since traveling is a mode of life not a question of race. By contrast, Rastafarians have not been recognized in law a racial group—so it was lawful to refuse a Rastafarian man a job unless he cut his hair (*Dawkins v Crown Suppliers* (1993)).

Decisions about who is entitled to protection on racial grounds are not always easy or consistent. In Scotland, where legislation is identical, the English were recognized as a national group entitled to protection from discrimination on nationality grounds (*BBC Scotland v Souster* (2001)). But in England the Scots seem to have no separate national identity (*Boyce v British Airways* (1997)).

To comply with a European Community directive, discrimination on grounds of religion was made unlawful in employment in December 2003—see below. Otherwise there is currently nothing to stop discrimination on grounds of religion. In 1997 the Government pledged to introduce legislation to fill this gap; after 11 September it again tried, but failed to produce drafts which satisfied all sides. One problem is that legitimate debate about religious doctrine and practice might be inhibited or even criminalized by any such legislation. But the gap means that the British National Party can attempt to stir up hatred against Muslims without contravening the Public Order Act 1985, because Muslims are not a racial group (*Guardian*, 28 Oct. 1998).

Discrimination on grounds of age is lawful, unless it can be shown that the discrimination affects more women than men (excluding older candidates from jobs can exclude more eligible women candidates than men, because of time taken out to raise a family: that is sex discrimination). But age discrimination in employment will become unlawful by 2006, to comply with an EU directive. We believe age discrimination in the provision of health or social care is effectively unlawful, and we will explain this below.

What is sex/race discrimination?

The simple principle in the legislation is that, in defined circumstances, unless a statutory exception applies, it is unlawful to discriminate against a person on grounds of his or her sex or race. The defined circumstances include in particular employment, provision of goods and services, education, and letting premises.

Direct discrimination

Discrimination can be direct discrimination. This means treating a person less favourably on grounds of sex or race. It covers the now illegal job or property advertisements which used to state, for example, 'no coloureds or Irish need apply'. Sexual or racial harassment is direct discrimination. Employers cannot plead ignorance if harassment occurs—they must stop their employees harassing others. See, for example, *Enterprise Gears Co. Ltd v Miles* (below).

Indirect discrimination

Indirect discrimination imposes requirements that a person of a particular sex or race would have greater difficulty in complying with than other people: for example, a minimum height requirement would exclude many women; a requirement to wear headgear may exclude a Sikh. This indirect discrimination is not unlawful if the requirement can be justified on its merits rather than on gender or race grounds—for example, to seek workers with experience of senior management may well indirectly discriminate against women, or members of some racial groups, who for a variety of reasons are less likely to have such experience, but it will not be unlawful if that experience is genuinely necessary for that job. But a requirement which cannot be justified on such grounds and which indirectly discriminates, such as an upper age limit for job applicants, is unlawful (*Price v Civil Service Commission* (1977)).

Discrimination can occur where a person has objected to unlawful discrimination and is then him- or herself discriminated against. In the case of *Weathersfield v Sargent* (1999) a white employee who quit his job successfully claimed race discrimination against his employers because he had been instructed not to rent vehicles to black or Asian customers. This is victimization, which is discussed again later.

Both men and women are entitled not to be discriminated against on grounds of sex. Additionally the Sex Discrimination Act makes it unlawful to discriminate on grounds of marital status, whatever a person's sex. In fact marital status rarely turns out to be the real issue. For example, it was unlawful to refuse to train a woman as a social worker. Her employer claimed that the investment would be a waste of money on the grounds that she was bound to follow her husband to another part of the country. The tribunal declared that the unlawfulness was not, at root, because she was married, but because she was a married woman: the employer would not have dreamed of treating a married man in that way (*Horsey v Dyfed County Council* (1982)).

European Community law and sex discrimination cases

Back in 1975, the trigger for English legislation on sex discrimination was the Treaty of Rome, which required Member States to remove discrimination on pay and treatment (Article 119 (now 141) and subsequent directives). Though we do not have space for detailed examination of European Community law, you should be aware that it has direct effect: this means that even where the UK Parliament has not passed laws to implement Community directives, they are still applicable in our courts. Using European Community law, as opposed to English law, it has, for example, been possible to get pension and retirement ages equalized (though the process will not be completed until 2020, a delay which the European Court of Human Rights considered to be lawful in the case of *Walker v UK* (2004)). So it is worth asking in any case of sex discrimination that English law cannot deal with: can this be challenged as unlawful under European law? The European Court of Justice (ECJ) deals with difficult Community legal issues, and these decisions are directly applicable in English courts, even where they are incompatible with UK legislation. So lawyers have to read these case reports.

Our first example of an ECJ case is this Danish one: *Tele Danmark AS v Handels- og Kontorfunktionaerernes Forbund i Danmark HG* (2001). The employee had not told her new employers that she was pregnant. She had only been taken on for a six-month contract, and she was now going to be unavailable for most of it. Her employers dismissed her when they found out. The ECJ ruled that she did not have to reveal her pregnancy, even though it virtually wrecked the contract. The dismissal was unlawful because it was pregnancy-related and, therefore, sex discrimination. The decision now binds the English courts. The second example is *Wiebke Busch v Klnikum Neustadt GmBH* (2003), a case originating in Germany. In this case the ECJ ruled that a woman is not required to reveal, at selection, that she is pregnant, even if the job to which she is appointed cannot be done while pregnant and even if she will have to take immediate leave.

It therefore seems to have been the ECJ, not English courts, who have provided the real protection in relation to pregnancy. The best the House of Lords could do on the subject, in fact, was to rule that pregnancy was for a woman in the same category as, say, absence from work for a hip replacement for a man, so an employer could legitimately dismiss one or the other if the pregnancy/hip operation kept them off work (*Webb v Emo Air Cargo* (1993)). The ECJ put the Lords right on how to approach discrimination on grounds of pregnancy in this case, in *Webb v Emo Air Cargo (UK) (No. 2) Ltd* (1995). In fact, under Articles 2 and 5 of the Equal Treatment Directive any dismissal for illness related to pregnancy is automatically unlawful (see, e.g. *Brown v Rentokil* (1998)).

The ECJ has recently been asked to rule on the legality of tight time limits for making claims. In the late 1990s the ECJ had ruled that part-time workers had been wrongly excluded from joining occupational pension schemes, and had been ever since the UK joined what was then the European Economic Community. This was because far more women than men worked part time, and the discrimination was indirect sex discrimination. The government, in a mean response, said they would provide compensation to such workers so long as they had claimed within two years of being excluded from the pension scheme. In reality none of them knew they could bring a claim until the ECJ ruling, so it was effectively a denial of a remedy. In *Preston v Wolverhampton NHS Trust* (2001) the House of Lords, having sought guidance from the ECJ, held that the government's response had effectively barred these part time workers from enjoying the equality that European law dictated, and ordered the government to admit all excluded workers (mostly, of course, women) to the occupational pension schemes.

Examples of unlawful racial and sexual discrimination in employment

Employment discrimination may not be the prime concern of social workers. However, it is by far the area where the law has been most extensively tested. For that reason the case examples should help you to understand how courts and tribunals will interpret the legislation in other areas, in particular provision of services.

Discrimination on grounds of race or sex in the field of employment is unlawful. (There is some doubt about whether employment includes volunteer work: in *Murray v Newham Citizens Advice Bureau* (2001) it did, but in *South East Sheffield Citizens Advice Bureau v Grayson* (2004) it did not). This means not just refusal of a job, but discrimination within all work, including provision of facilities, promotion prospects, training, or selection for dismissal. Moreover, the employer carries a responsibility for what goes on in the work situation. The employer must actively prevent employees behaving in a discriminatory way towards each other, and is liable for employees' actions, unless the employer can show that he or she was unaware of the acts of the employee, and also that he or she had taken reasonable steps to prevent it (in particular through training or supervision of the workforce). An example of how this works is *Enterprise Glass Co. Ltd v Miles* (1990). A male worker made suggestive remarks to a female colleague—direct discrimination on grounds of sex. The employers ignored her complaint, and even promoted the perpetrator. The Employment Appeal Tribunal (EAT) made the employer pay the victim compensation.

Employers must not discriminate in rates of pay. There is a separate process for deal-ing with equal pay claims for women, under the Equal Pay Act 1970, which involves complex rules for making comparisons between the value of different kinds of work. Is canteen work, for example (typically work done by women), worth as much as shipyard work (more often done by men)? The answer was 'yes' in the leading case of *Hayward v Cammell Laird* (1988). To bring this kind of case an expert in job evaluation is necessary.

Not all discrimination in relation to employment is unlawful. We will look now at the most significant exceptions.

If a person of a particular sex or racial group is required for a job for 'genuine occu-pational reasons', it is lawful to discriminate in favour of that kind of person. It is, for example, permissible to insist on a black male actor to play a black male character; it is lawful to seek a person of Bengali origin for welfare work within a Bengali community, if cultural understanding is vital to the work; a women's refuge can insist that its employees are female; an Indian can be sought to provide authenticity as a waiter for an Indian restaurant (but probably not as a cook, since out of sight of the customers it is the ability to cook Indian food not racial appearance that provides the authenticity). Each exception, if challenged, has to be justified as genuine.

It is, perhaps regrettably, lawful to discriminate in selecting someone to work in the employer's own home, for example as nanny or cleaner. And firms with up to four employees may discriminate on sex grounds.

We looked earlier at the protection which European law has provided in relation to discrimination on grounds of pregnancy. What about child care? The Employment Appeal Tribunal turned a blind eye to the real gender differences in child-care responsi-bilities. *British Telecommunications plc v Roberts* (1996) held that a woman returning from maternity leave and seeking a job share was no different from a man suddenly deciding that he wanted to change his hours of work. A better decision was *London Underground v Edwards* (1995), where a woman train driver had to resign when the shift rotas were changed with the result that she could not look after her son. It was held that this shift pattern discriminated against women (who were more likely to be single parents than men). *Visa International Service Association v Paul* (2004) also shows the courts making progress in protecting women's employment rights during maternity. A woman on maternity leave was not informed of an internal promotion opportunity which she might have been interested in. Looking at her qualifications the tribunal found it unlikely she would have been shortlisted had she applied, but it was discrimination against her not to inform her during her maternity leave.

Discrimination permitted by statute

It is lawful to discriminate, in employment and other cases, if statute makes that lawful. Otherwise many decisions and rules in relation to immigration and residence require-ments for state benefits which favour British citizens would be unlawful indirect discrimination. The government has in fact amended the RRA to permit such direct discrimination on race grounds, though in the case of *European Roma Rights Centre and others v Immigration Officer at Prague Airport* (2004), where it might have provided a lawful defence, it denied actually using this power. It said it was not discriminating at all. The applicants had shown that far more Roma than non-Roma were detained for long interviews at Prague airport and refused entry in a Home Office pre-flight screening programme. The House of Lords rejected the Government's argument and declared it to be unlawful racial discrimination.

But UK statutes must bow before European law, and the statutory exception which made men work five years longer than women before drawing a pension was declared illegal by the European Court of Justice (*Marshall v Southampton and South West Hampshire-Area Health Authority (Teaching) (No. 1)* (1986)).

The ECtHR has also upheld challenges to the effect of UK statute. An example is *Willis v United Kingdom* (2002). At the relevant time a widow could claim widow's allowance. ECtHR stated that there could be no justification for such discrimination, and in fact Parliament has legislated to produce a gender neutral widowed parent's allowance as a result.

Positive discrimination

Where a particular racial group, or one sex, is under-represented in a field of employment (throughout the UK), training organizations may offer special training and facilities to attempt to equalize the position. Employers can also offer special training if during the past twelve months a racial group or a sex has been under-represented in their organization. Positive discrimination is also permitted to allow training to be offered to people who have had family or domestic responsibilities. This can help women come back into the workforce but, apart from this exception, it would constitute unlawful discrimination against men.

The ECJ—whose decisions bind English courts—has ruled that positive discrimination must remain within boundaries. Giving preference to women just because they were women was not acceptable (*Kalanke v Freie Hansestadt Bremen* (1995)).

Sex and race discrimination not involving employment

Discrimination in membership of trades unions and in provision of goods and services is unlawful, as it is in partnership agreements where there are at least six partners. A private club with fewer than twenty-five members is exempt from the Race Relations Act 1975 (RRA), so long as it does not discriminate on grounds of colour. So a small Irish-only club would be lawful, but the exclusion of a black Irish person would not.

Discrimination in the provision of rented property is unlawful, with the regrettable exception that a landlord who lives on the premises can indulge her or his prejudice and discriminate on race or sex grounds when choosing tenants. Where premises are used as a hospital or prison, or for caring for certain groups, such as children or people with special needs, single-sex establishments are permitted.

Race or sex discrimination in schooling is not permitted, except that single-sex educational establishments are allowed. For example, Birmingham City Council was found to have breached the SDA by giving fewer grant-aided places to girls than boys (*Birmingham City Council v EOC* (1988)).

Harassment and victimization

Both of these are forms of direct discrimination. For example, a woman who rejected her employer's advances and who was, in retaliation, subject to unjustified criticism, was awarded £12,000 for injury to feelings (*Hay v Bellhaven Brewery Co. Ltd* (1996)). Allegations of harassment require the employer to investigate. Failure to do so can on its own amount to discrimination, since it is a detriment (*Reed v Steadman* (1999)).

In a victimization case *Lisk-Carew v Birmingham City Council and another* (2004) an employee had been dismissed. An employment tribunal, having heard the evidence, rejected his allegation that this was on racial grounds, so the dismissal was in itself fair. However the employer had used as part of the justification for the dismissal the fact that 'You have made repeated unsubstantiated allegations'. The employee was therefore entitled to damages in respect of victimization, even though there was found to be no substance to the actual complaints.

■ Enforcement in race and sex discrimination cases

The Equal Opportunities Commission (EOC) and the Commission for Racial Equality (CRE) both have powers to hold investigations, to require persons or bodies to answer questions about their practices, and if necessary to appear before the Commission. They can issue non-discrimination notices requiring a person or organization to desist from specified discriminatory practices, which can be enforced by injunction in the High Court. The Commissions can also assist individuals in bringing cases against a person or body that has discriminated against them. Both of these bodies, together with the Disability Rights Commission which is mentioned later will in due course be merged into a new Equality and Human Rights Commission.

The victim of discrimination has two direct avenues of complaint, apart from enlisting the help of the CRE or EOC. If discrimination is alleged at work, he or she can bring a case in an employment tribunal—but he or she must not delay, as the time limit for starting the case is normally three months from the date of the last discriminatory act. For example, where a black nurse claimed she had been regraded at a lower level than equivalent white nurses, her application to the tribunal failed because it was started more than three months after the regrading, even though she could clearly show the discrimination continued after then in her relatively lower pay packet (*Sougrin v Haringey Health Authority* (1992)).

A tribunal can declare the rights of the individual, can order compensation to be paid (which can include a sum for distress to feelings, even if there is no other financial loss), and can order the employer to take specified steps to prevent further discrimination against this employee, failure to do so leading to a possible further award of compensation.

Public funding for legal representation is not available in tribunal cases, though legal help (advice) subject to a means test is available in employment cases in many solicitors' firms and advice agencies.

If the discrimination takes place outside the employment field (e.g. refusal to serve someone in a restaurant or to consider them for a partnership) the case is brought in the county court. Proceedings have to be started within six months of the last act complained of, or eight months in the case of discrimination in education. The court can order damages to be paid, including compensation for distress to feelings, and an injunction requiring the discriminator to do or stop doing certain acts (e.g. ordering a landlord to cease harassing a tenant).

Race and crime

A racial element can be part of the definition of a crime. An important example is incitement to racial hatred under the Public Order Act 1986, s. 23, or racially aggravated assault under the Crime and Disorder Act 1998, s. 29. A racial element can also increase the seriousness of an offence when the court decides on sentence (Crime and Disorder Act 1998, s. 63).

Race and sex discrimination and the social worker

We take for granted that a social worker should not discriminate unlawfully in carrying out his or her duties. Your duty, however, if you are a local government employee, goes further than that. Under the RRA, s. 71, all local authorities must have due regard to the need:

(a) to eliminate unlawful racial discrimination; and

(b) to promote equality of opportunity and good relations between persons of different racial groups.

How do you go about this? All services for children and provided as part of community care, whether by the local authority or purchased, should be compliant with the legislation. If you suspect unlawful discrimination in employment practice or provision of services we suggest consultation within your team and with your legal department. You may need to refer cases of racial abuse to the police, as this is likely to involve an offence under the Public Order Act 1986. An employer should take available steps to protect an employee against discrimination or abuse by others, e.g. to protect a teacher from racist abuse by pupils (*Bennett v Essex CC* (2000)). This would apply equally where a council takes no interest in protecting its social workers from racial or sexual abuse.

Positive discrimination is permitted in the provision of education, training, or welfare to meet the special needs of persons of a particular racial group—for example, language assistance for Asian women. A circular from the DHSS (11/77) states that this exemption 'will, for example, enable consideration to be given to special housing or social service arrangements where for example particular Asian or West Indian groups have special needs. These may include residential home provision for children and the elderly'.

Local authority services count as services under the RRA and, by analogy, under the SDA. This was decided in *Conwell v Newham London Borough Council* (1999), where a social worker had complained about the authority's refusal to allow a black child in its care to go on a holiday with a white family. He alleged he was victimised for making this complaint (and, you may have noted above, victimization counts as discrimination if it follows a complaint about race discrimination). His complaint would only succeed if looking after a child in care amounted to a 'service' under the RRA, and the Employment Appeal Tribunal held that it did. The Tribunal confined its judgment to the ruling that the Act applies to such services, and did not comment expressly on the social worker's complaint that the refusal of the holiday with the white family was unjustifiable race discrimination. A reading of the facts of the case suggests to us that it would not have been hard to show that the decision—which was not made by anyone who knew the child or his circumstances, but was purely based on a policy—could only have been based on race grounds rather than the proper weighing up of what was best for the child.

You are permitted under the RRA, in choosing foster parents or making boarding out arrangements for children, elderly persons, or persons requiring special care, to take race into account. Indeed in making arrangements for day care for children, and selecting foster parents for children, your duty goes the other way: the local authority is obliged by the Children Act 1989, Sch. 2, para. 11 to 'have regard' to racial groups. But in making each individual placement decision you still have to choose—depending on whether this is considered best for the child—to place them with someone from their own racial or national background, or not. A blanket policy based on race, such as in *Conwell v Newham*, is open to challenge.

The Disability Discrimination Act 1995

Disabled persons are the largest minority in the world encompassing more than 500 million persons, of which 2/3 live in developing countries. For a very long time disabled persons have been confronted with different kinds of disregard and mistreatment. Together with women and children, legal systems have excluded disabled persons as non-persons. Eugenic population policies were carried out with the aim of eliminating those deemed disabled through sterilization and killing programmes. . . . Modern disability policies [are] much more benign but [are] also based on the assumption of disabled persons not being real citizens (Theresia Degener, 'Disabled Persons and Human Rights: The Legal Framework', in Theresia Degener and Yolan Koster-Dreese, *Human Rights and Disabled Persons* (Martinus Nijhoff Publishers, 1995)).

Anyone invoking the Disability Discrimination Act must have a disability, which is defined as 'a physical or mental impairment which has a substantial and long-term adverse effect on ability to carry out normal day-to-day activities'. Long-term means twelve months (or less if an illness is terminal). Disability can include severe disfigurement and mental impairment. It can also include learning disorders. Paranoid schizophrenia was ruled to be a clear instance of a disability in *Goodwin v Patent Office* (1999), since it impaired the applicant's ability to carry out normal day-to-day activities. Reactive depression can amount to a disability (*Kapadia v Lambeth LBC* (2001)). Day-to-day activities can cover something that may be inessential or confined to a part of the population, such as putting on make-up: *Ekpe v Commissioner of Police for the Metropolis* (2001).

Disability does not yet cover people who have a condition (such as HIV) which causes other people to stop them from doing day-to-day activities which they are otherwise perfectly capable of doing. Planned new legislation will change this, however, in relation to HIV.

It is unlawful to discriminate on grounds of disability in employment, in services (such as shops and restaurants); since October 2004 in public transport (infrastructure, such as new bus design, not yet the service itself); and in selling/letting property. A victim can bring a case before an employment tribunal or a county court.

There are many exceptions to the right not to suffer discrimination on grounds of disability, including:

(a) unsuitability for the job;

(b) a candidate without disability is genuinely more suitable;

(c) the buildings which cause the discrimination complied with building regulations relating to disabled access;

(d) provisions for disabled service-users (e.g. shops, cinemas) would cause real and unavoidable safety problems, or would be too expensive;

(e) lettings where the landlord lives in the premises.

But these exceptions must be proved to apply, and there is an automatic presumption that discrimination is not justified.

Disability discrimination and employment

As with race and sex discrimination, most case law relates to employment. This is inevitable, as the Act has been brought into force in stages, starting with employment. But there are two important differences between this legislation and that relating to sex and race discrimination. First, there is the defence of justification, which cannot be argued in sex and race cases. Second, the Act does not distinguish between direct and indirect discrimination.

An employer must not discriminate against a disabled person in terms of selection procedures or in terms of employment (s. 4), unless such discrimination is justified (s. 5). Discrimination cannot be justified, however, unless the reason is 'material to the circumstances of the particular case and substantial'. This requirement would rule out the defence of 'well, we'd be happy to take you on, but the rest of the workforce wouldn't like it'. Discrimination is not justified if the employer could have made reasonable adjustments to accommodate the needs or abilities of the employee or applicant. Adjustments (s. 6) can include physical changes to premises, changes to work arrangements, training, supervision, or the provision of a helper to the disabled person (e.g. a signer for a deaf person). (The Code of Practice issued by the Department for Education and Employment in 1996 provides extensive guidance and examples. The conclusion we draw from this is that an employer or tribunal will have to show real attempts to meet the needs of an otherwise suitable employee.)

Case law in the employment field is mainly encouraging. In *British Sugar plc v Kirke* (1998), one of the earliest cases, compensation of over £100,000 was paid to a 40-year-old worker selected for redundancy on grounds of his disability (partial blindness). In *Kenny v Hampshire Constabulary* (1999), the applicant had cerebral palsy. He was offered a job, but his needs included help getting to the lavatory. The employers could not find any volunteers, made an application to the Access to Work scheme for help, but gave up waiting and withdrew the offer. The EAT held that the employer's duty to make reasonable adjustments for disabled employees had not been discharged. It was wrong to give up before learning whether the grant had been awarded.

Archibald v Fife Council (2004), though a Scottish case in origin, is important in indicating just how far an employer should go in making reasonable adjustments where a person is disabled, if that would enable the person to continue in employment. The employee was a road sweeper who now could not walk and therefore could not do his current job. The Council could not find her any office work on the same or a lower grade, and refused to consider her for higher grade work without a competitive interview. The House of Lords ruled that it would be discriminatory to dismiss her and she should be given the higher grade post 'provided the taking of this step is a reasonable thing for the employer to do in all the circumstances' (Lord Hope). Note also the helpful clarification on disability discrimination law given by Lady Hale:

> The Act . . . does not regard the differences between disabled people and others as irrelevant. It does not expect each to be treated in the same way. It expects reasonable adjustments to be made to cater for the special needs of disabled people. It necessarily entails an element of more favourable treatment.

But the case law has not been altogether encouraging. It has been held that an employer would not have to make reasonable adjustments, or avoid discriminating, if he or she could not have been expected to know the person was disabled. In *O'Neill v Symm* [1998] IRLR 233, the applicant had been dismissed because of recurrent sickness absences. She had chronic fatigue syndrome, which the appeal tribunal accepted as a disability. The employer had not been told the reason for the absences, and had not enquired whether there might be a disability. It was therefore held that the discrimination was lawful, an encouragement to turn a blind eye. Fortunately, a conflicting decision in 2000 will help to force employers to take more care to find out. In *Hammersmith and Fulham LBC v Farnsworth* (2000), the applicant was dismissed when her history of mental illness was discovered. She had not disclosed this at interview, but the mental illness was not affecting this employment (and had not affected her previous employment). The Employment Appeal Tribunal held that the council could not use its own lack of knowledge of the applicant's illness as a defence, especially as, once the council discovered it, it discriminated against her by sacking her.

The legislation does not prevent justified discrimination. For example, when a person with chronic fatigue syndrome is incapable of returning to work after a prolonged absence, any dismissal is not automatically unfair. But it will be if the employer fails to consider adjustments such as lighter duties (*H.J. Heinz Co. Ltd v Kenrick* (2000) 144).

Disability discrimination in education, goods, and services

The part of the Act making disability discrimination unlawful in housing and educational establishments is already in force. And for goods and services the law came
fully into force in October 2004. This means that the requirement to make reasonable
adjustments under s. 21 DDA has been extended to a much wider range of public
services under the *Disability Discrimination (Providers of Services) (Adjustment of Premises)
(Amendment) Regulations* 2004 This is the reaction of the DRC:

> 1st October 2004 is a landmark for disabled people. From that date service providers will have
> to consider making changes to physical features that make it difficult for disabled people to
> use their services. Pubs, clubs, gym and swimming pools, hospitals, restaurants, shops and all
> service providers will have to make "reasonable adjustments" to their premises or the way that
> they provide their services so that they are not unreasonably difficult for disabled people to
> use. **www.drc-gb.org/open4all/about/why.asp**.

Few challenges in areas other than employment have yet reached the case reports. We
cite three.

In *Manchester City Council v Romano* (2004), the appeal concerned two separate tenancies, but the common issue was the mental illness of the tenants. One had depression and one had borderline personality disorder. Both had, on the evidence, behaved
in such a way as to cause real stress to neighbours. The landlord claimed possession,
saying their behaviour breached the tenancy agreement. Section 22 DDA makes discrimination in housing provision, including an eviction, unlawful if it is on grounds
of disability. A mental disorder can interfere substantially with ability to carry out day
to day activities, and this tenant's problems were considered to fall within the Act.
However, as in all DDA cases, there is a defence of reasonableness, in this case under
s. 24. Could the landlord demonstrate a reasonable belief that the eviction was
necessary to protect others from harm to their physical or mental health? If so the
landlord would also not fall foul of Article 8 of the European Human Rights Convention, respect for private life. If the eviction could protect that person from harm to their
'complete well-being' it could be lawful, notwithstanding the discrimination under
s. 22.

In the earlier case of *North Devon Homes Ltd v Brazier* (2003) the High Court had
come to the opposite conclusion on the facts. Here the tenant was disabled within the
meaning of DDA 1995 as a result of a psychotic illness. Her illness meant that she caused
considerable nuisance to her neighbours as a result of her abusive and aggressive
behaviour. Her landlord sought to evict her using the discretionary nuisance ground of
the Housing Act 1988. The landlord's argument was that any tenant behaving in the
way this particular tenant behaved would have received similar treatment. However,
the High Court made it clear that this approach was not appropriate. The landlord's
decision to evict arose because of the disabled person's behaviour, which was caused by
her disability. The decision to evict a disabled person was only reasonable, as required
by the discretionary grounds of HA 1988, when the landlord (the discriminator) showed
that it was justified under DDA s. 24. In this instance there has been no evidence that
the tenant was a danger 'to the health or safety of any person'.

The other case is particularly interesting for social workers and anyone who talks to people, though it is only a county court case which means that other courts do not have to follow it: *Appleby v Department for Work and Pensions* (2003). The applicant for benefits was deaf and refused to be interviewed by an officer who was behind a glass screen. The officer's frustration that the claimant could not hear her questions became obvious to the claimant, who was distressed. The county court awarded her damages for this discriminatory behaviour. She should have been interviewed in a way which enabled her to communicate effectively, and should not have been subject to the officer's emotional response to her disability.

A Code of Practice, *Rights of Access, Goods, Facilities, Services and Premises*, may be obtained free from the Disability Rights Commission (below).

Enforcement in disability discrimination cases

The Act may have started to alter the culture, but it is not going to abolish discrimination against disabled persons. One expert has described it as 'riddled with vague, slippery and elusive exceptions making it so full of holes that it is more like a colander than a binding code' (Lord Lester, HL Debates (1994)).

The 1995 Act did not originally create the equivalent of the CRE or EOC. However, a Disability Rights Commission was created under the Disability Rights Commission Act 1999, with a statutory duty to promote 'equalization of opportunities for disabled persons' and to 'work towards the elimination of discrimination against disabled persons'. It has powers to investigate, to assist individuals, to issue non-discrimination notices, and to negotiate with employers to ensure compliance with best practice. See **www.drc-gb.org**. It will in due course be absorbed into the new single equality commission.

Other forms of discrimination

New regulations

Under the 1997 *Treaty of Amsterdam* EU states undertook to provide minimum protection against discrimination, so that minimum standards would apply across the EU. In many respects the legislation we have considered above means that the UK already has more advanced standards of protection than is required. However, to comply with the Treaty, the following regulations were brought into force in December 2003.

- The *Employment Equality (Religion or Belief) Regulations* 2003
- The *Employment Equality (Sexual Orientation) Regulations* 2003

These regulations only apply to protect employees, or would-be employees, and not to other victims or potential victims of discrimination. Discrimination, under these regulations, is not identical to the definition of discrimination under the RRA or SDA, and is defined as treating a person less favourably, or applying a provision, criterion or practice which puts persons at a particular disadvantage compared with other persons because of their religion or belief or sexual orientation. Discrimination can include victimizing a person, for example because they have made a complaint or brought proceedings because of alleged discrimination, or harassment which violates a person's dignity or is intimidating, hostile, degrading, humiliating, or offensive. Any less favourable treatment has to be justified by the employer, who has to show that the treatment is 'a proportionate means of achieving a legitimate aim'. An example of a defence might be a small company which can show objectively that it cannot afford to release a Jewish employee on a Friday.

Similar provisions to protect people from discrimination on grounds of age will be required by the Treaty of Amsterdam, but not before 2006.

There is a further interesting by-product of the Treaty of Amsterdam. This treaty requires member states to legislate to prevent discrimination on grounds of race or national origins in the fields of employment, social security, healthcare, and education. On the one hand, the existing legislation for England and Wales goes wider than this, since it looks at colour and nationality as well. But on the other hand our own legislation is narrower in the way that the discrimination is proved. The changes required under the treaty are now reflected in s. 1(A) of the Race Relations Act.

We think it would now make sense to unify EU and national anti-discrimination legislation, particularly on race issues. But that is not planned. So at present, as a result of the new rules, where discrimination arises in employment and is alleged on grounds of sexual orientation, religion or belief, race or national origins, the principles which apply are broader than those which apply if the discrimination is based on gender, colour, or disability or (with the exception of race or national origins) arises in relation to services. You may need to re-read the last two paragraphs, but if you understand, let us look at the new principles. They are:

• Discrimination arises even if it results from false assumptions, e.g. not employing a practising Christian, thinking that such a person will refuse to work Sundays

• Anyone accused of indirect discrimination must show that the action he or she took or failed to take was a proportionate means of achieving a legitimate aim.

• Discriminatory practices can be informal practices which tend to produce a disadvantage, as well as 'requirements' (the word used for indirect discrimination in the sex and race legislation).

• Discrimination by way of harassment is wider than under existing case law and includes conduct which, it is reasonably (in the eyes of who, though?) considered, violates dignity or creates an offensive environment.

The provisions in relation to victimisation are similar to existing legislation on sex and race, as is the defence of discriminating because of a genuine occupational requirement. But where a faith- or belief-based organization tries to exclude non-believers it must show that the adherence to the belief or faith is genuinely necessary for the fulfilment of that function. Preference for working with those who share belief is not acceptable on its own.

Whether this will cause practical difficulties remains to be seen, but it is unnecessarily confusing to have two different tests for discrimination on grounds of race, ethnic or national origin on the one hand, and colour and nationality on the other, and some provisions dealing only with employment, and others covering services.

Sexual orientation and gender reassignment issues

In *Goodwin v United Kingdom* (2002) the appellant was a woman, but she was required to pay her national insurance up to age 65, on the ground that she had been a man before undergoing gender reassignment treatment. Had she been recognized as a woman the requirement would have ended at 60. The European Court of Human Rights upheld the appeal and said she should be treated in all respects as a woman. As a result Parliament passed the the Gender Recognition Act 2004, which creates a mechanism for formal recognition of gender change or confirmation of gender of transsexuals. Applicants apply to a panel for a gender recognition certificate which entitles the person to marry, work, obtain state benefits etc. in their new gender. This will consign previous case law to history, for example the case of *A v Chief Constable of West Yorkshire* (2004). Here a male to female transsexual was refused a job with the police on the ground that she would be unable to carry out intimate searches in her acquired gender because she was not the same sex as the person searched under s. 54 of Police and Criminal Evidence Act 1984 (PACE). The House of Lords said that it cannot be an occupational requirement to be a man, or a woman, to become a police officer, so the appellant was successful in her claim. But the Lords upheld the interpretation of PACE made by the Chief Constable, that A would not, despite now being a woman, be able to lawfully conduct intimate searches of other women because the law did not recognize her as being a woman. Under the 2004 Act she is a woman for all purposes.

Discrimination on grounds of gender reassignment in relation to goods, services, and employment is also expressly made unlawful under SDA s. 2, which has been amended to comply with a decision, not of the ECtHR this time, but of the ECJ: *P v S and Cornwall CC* (1996). The ECJ ruled that dismissal of a person on the ground that she changed sex from male to female was sex discrimination against her as a woman in breach of Article 119 (now 141) of the Treaty of Rome.

We wonder whether the following case is good law. We ask whether a woman suffering from, say, post-natal depression, or a disabled person suffering depression, would have been treated as was the police officer in *Ashton v Chief Constable of Mercia* (2001). Here the officer was suffering depression caused by the gender reassignment treatment, and her work was suffering. The Employment Appeal Tribunal held that her dismissal was on grounds of her performance and not of her gender reassignment, so it was not discrimination.

With sexual orientation the law has made some progress in relation to combating discrimination. The European directive, as we saw, provides remedies for work place discrimination. Adoption legislation no longer requires a couple to be heterosexual (see chapter 13), and the House of Lords has recognized a homosexual couple as having the same rights as any other couple to inherit a tenancy (*Mendoza v Ghaidan*, discussed earlier). A case against the Department of Health has been reported which resulted in a homosexual partner having the same rights as a heterosexual partner to be declared the nearest relative (see chapter 17) when a person became mentally disordered (*Law Society Gazette*, 14 Nov. 2002—we have not located a case report). And the Civil Partnership Act 2004, discussed in chapter 14, will permit same sex partners to obtain rights in respect of property, inheritance and being treated as next of kin very similar to those of married couples.

But otherwise discrimination against homosexuals can be lawful, even when based on prejudice alone, unless they can show that sex discrimination was also involved. For example, a spouse cannot be compelled to testify against a spouse (Police and Criminal Evidence Act 1984, s. 80). But it is not a breach of the Human Rights Act (Article 8 right to respect for family life) to compel a cohabitee to testify (even though a same-sex cohabitee cannot marry and take advantage of s. 80): *R v Pearce* (2001).

Age issues

People can be discriminated against on grounds of age (whether too young or too old), unless this can be proved to lead to indirect race or sex discrimination. We have seen examples of this amounting to sex discrimination above. The Government has introduced a voluntary Code of Practice for employers, available at **www.agepositive.gov.uk/codeOfPractice.cfm?sectionid=90**.

But age discrimination in the provision of health or social care is effectively unlawful. We arrive at this conclusion through a different route—it is not contained in anti-discrimination legislation but in official guidance from the Department of Health. The *National Service Framework for Older People* is a form of guidance published under the authority of the Local Authority Social Services Act 1970, s. 7(1). We will explain the legal impact of guidance issued under the Act more fully in the next chapter. We will, in particular, explain how it is in fact more than guidance—it must be followed. The Framework is accompanied by a Circular which gives it this legal effect, and the Circular (HSC 2001/007: LAC (2001)12 entitled *National Service Framework for Older People)* states:

> NHS services will be provided, regardless of age, on the basis of clinical need alone. Social care services will not use age in their eligibility criteria or policies, to restrict access to available services.

Within the NHS, as a result of the circular, age cannot be used as a factor to deny medical treatment for conditions such as hernia, joint replacement, cancer, or heart problems, unless age is relevant to the clinical assessment of the appropriateness of the treatment (e.g. an older person may face particular complications from surgery).

Similarly avoidance of discrimination on grounds of mental health is a duty of health and social service authorities by virtue of the *National Service Framework for Mental Health*, issued under HSC1999/223 LAC (99)34:

> Health and social services should . . . combat discrimination against individuals and groups with mental health problems, and promote their social inclusion (Standard 1).

■ Future developments in anti-discrimination and human rights

A major development will be the merging of the existing equality commissions dealing with race, sex, and disability, into a new body. The White Paper *Fairness for all: A new commission for equality and human rights* was published in 2004 (available at **www.dti.gov.uk/access/equalitywhitepaper.pdf**) and proposes the following core functions for this body:

- Encouraging awareness and good practice on equality and diversity;
- Promoting awareness and understanding of human rights;
- Promoting equality of opportunity between people in the different groups protected by discrimination law;
- Working towards the elimination of unlawful discrimination and harassment;
- Promoting good relations among different communities, and between these communities and wider society (para. 3.4).

It will carry out these functions in relation to discrimination relating to (para. 3.18):

- men and women;
- people of different racial groups;
- people of different sexual orientations;
- people of different religions or beliefs (including those who do not have a religion or belief);
- people of different ages;
- people who intend to undergo, are undergoing, or have undergone gender reassignment;

as well as;

- to promote the equalization of opportunities for disabled people (para. 3.19).

Clearly it is intended to be an anti-discrimination body more than a human rights body, for its role in relation to human rights is described as an 'additional' role:

- Acting as a centre of expertise on equality and human rights (para. 3.5).

We noted earlier that the Human Rights Act 1998, by incorporating Article 14 of the European Convention, prohibits discrimination only where this prevents enjoyment of Convention rights. The Twelfth Protocol to the Convention is designed to require contracting states not to permit discrimination on any matter by any public authority on grounds such as 'sex, race, colour, language, religion, political or other opinion, national or social origin, association with a national minority, property, birth or other status'. Unfortunately the UK, unlike several European nations, has not ratified the treaty, even though it signed it back in 2000. This means as yet it does not consider it is able to comply. But even when in force as a treaty, it will not change the law in England and Wales without an amendment to the Human Rights Act 1998.

Extension of disability discrimination

The Government has produced a draft Disability Bill which would result in the following (quoted from the DRC web site **www.drc-gb.org/newsroom/newsdetails.asp?id= 602&section=4**):

- The definition of disability will be extended to clearly include more people with HIV, cancer, and multiple sclerosis from the point of diagnosis (at present coverage of these conditions is not guaranteed).

- Extension of the DDA to cover discrimination in relation to transport (at present only the transport infrastructure is covered).

- A duty to promote disability equality will be placed on the public sector (which is already required by the Race Relations Amendment Act). According to the Government, 'A substantial move forward in terms of disability rights will not occur as long as the only mechanism for enforcement is reliant on individual disabled people taking cases.'

- The DDA will cover more functions of public authorities. There is presently a lack of clarity, for example, relating to disabled prisoners and access to pavements and highways.

- The DDA's duties on landlords and managers of premises will be extended to include a duty to make reasonable adjustments to policies, practices, and procedures and provide auxiliary aids and services, where reasonable, to enable a disabled person to rent a property and facilitate a disabled tenant's enjoyment of the premises.

- Any club with 25 or more members will be covered by the Act. This is likely to impact upon political parties.

EXERCISES

What effect does the law have in each of the situations set out in the bullet points?

1 The Jones family comprises Mr Jones, who is Welsh; Mrs Jones who is English, but of African racial background. They have adopted Gemma, who was born in China. They have two children, Matthew, age 12, who has attention deficit hyperactivity disorder, and Christine, age 6, who is confined to a wheelchair. Mr Jones has HIV. Mrs Jones has a severe facial disfigurement following a road accident.

- Mrs Jones, who has a science doctorate and a high-profile research and publication record, is refused several posts for which she meets all of the essential criteria. The University of Anytown told her they might have trouble with the Home Office getting her a work permit. Science Labs plc told her that with her family problems she was unlikely to be committed to the work. Newtown College said the students would find her disfigurement difficult to handle.

- Gemma needs special English language tuition but the school says it is not allowed to spend more money on her than on other children.

- Mr Jones is continuously taunted at work with offensive comments about his multi-racial family. The employer treats this as a joke, and up to now Mr Jones has tried to pretend he does not mind.

- Mr Jones wants a clerical job. He is 45, and he has been told by the local authority that he is too old. He spent much of his twenties and thirties at home bringing up his first family, from whom he is separated, and his new family. He is told by Admin R Us that they do not want anyone around with HIV as it will put off the other staff.

- Mrs Jones takes Christine to the Gateside Cinema, which is situated in an old building recently modernised. They are refused admission because Christine's wheelchair 'will create a safety hazard for other customers'.

- Social Housing Ltd, the family's landlord, has written to say that Matthew's loud behaviour is anti-social and the family will have to leave.

2 You are a social worker for Careborough MBC. Your statutory client is Maggie, a 14-year-old who has been sleeping rough and, you believe, taking drugs. You have been accommodating Maggie with her mother Jane's agreement. Because of Maggie's frequent absconding you are considering secure accommodation. Jane has formed a relationship with John and wants Maggie to come home and the family to make a fresh start. Maggie's father Will wants Maggie to remain in local authority accommodation. You are about to set up a case conference. Maggie's headteacher does not want to participate if Will or Jane are present. Will wants to see copies of a psychologist's report which recommends that it would be disastrous for Maggie to return home or have contact with Will. John's former wife has phoned you to say she thinks John has sexually abused her daughter. Jane is deaf and can only communicate if a signer is present.

- What are the human rights law considerations you should be aware of before the case conference takes place?

COMPANION WEB SITE

For guidance on how to answer these exercises, visit the companion web site at:
www.oup.com/uk/booksites/law

WHERE DO WE GO FROM HERE?

The duty to respect the rights of all people you work with, including those service users or their families in whose lives you are required to intervene, will become a fundamental aspect of your work. It must therefore underpin your understanding of the legal powers you will be using. We will make reference to human rights law throughout the remaining chapters. The requirement to avoid inappropriate discrimination is similarly a pervasive requirement in your work, whether with children or adults.

The next chapter will continue with setting the framework. A care element of the human rights culture is respect for the individual, which includes the right of the individual to make his or her own decisions. We explore the limits to that right and the power of others to override personal autonomy. It is an area which social workers cannot avoid.

ANNOTATED FURTHER READING

Human rights

H. Brayne and G. Broadbent, *Legal Materials for Social Workers* (Oxford University Press, 2002) contains relevant legislation and case law, plus human rights documents from the UN—see chapters 2 and 3.

Liberty is the leading organization monitoring the effectiveness of the Human Rights Act and bringing test cases. It has a range of useful information at **www.liberty-human-rights.org.uk/**.

The Department of Health maintains a web site at **www.doh.gov.uk/humanrights/index.htm** which includes, in particular, useful case studies with reference to actual court decisions on the impact of the Human Rights Act on areas of work which will be relevant to social workers and health professionals.

The Lord Chancellor's Department operates a more general human rights web site at **www.humanrights.gov.uk/**—particularly useful for its links to other sites.

The United Nations has all of the international charters on human rights and discrimination issues at: **www.unhchr.ch/html/intlinst.htm#cov**.

J. Wadham and H. Mountfield, *Blackstones' Guide to the Human Rights Act 1988* (3rd edn., OUP, 2004) provides a very accessible overview of the working of the Act.

C. Gearty and A. Tomkins (eds.), *Understanding Human Rights* (Continuum International Publishing Group, 1997). If you are interested in human rights this series of intelligent and readable essays is very thought-provoking.

D. Kretzmer and E. Klein (eds.), *The Concept of Human Dignity in Human Rights Discourse* (Kluwer Law International, 2002). This volume gets into the fundamental issues of 'why rights' but is also relevant for an exploration of principles underpinning anti-discrimination law.

Discrimination law

North Lambeth Law Centre has set up a do-it-yourself guide to the race discrimination law: **www.rdu.org.uk**.

S. Fredman, *Discrimination Law* (Oxford University Press, 2002) looks at discrimination law and policy, including the human rights perspective.

M. Stacey, C. Palmer, T. Gill, K. Monaghan, and G. Moon, *Discrimination Law Handbook* (4th edn., The Legal Action Group, 2002). A practical guide, written by lawyers specializing in this area of litigation.

R. Townshend-Smith, *Discrimination Law* (2nd edn., Cavendish Publishing Ltd, 2003). Comprehensive guide and up to date.

The Commission for Racial Equality: **www.cre.gov.uk/**—this statutory body has been referred to above. Its web site contains extensive and useful guidance. It can take up suitable cases.

The Equal Opportunities Commission: **www.eoc.org.uk/**—also referred to above and equally useful. It can take up suitable cases.

Disability Rights Commission: **www.drc-gb.org/**—also referred to above and equally useful. It can take up suitable cases.

3 Competence, consent, and the service user

CASE STUDY

Gillick v West Norfolk and Wisbech Area Health Authority and another [1986] 1 AC 112, [1985] 3 All ER 402

Like most parents, Mrs Gillick wanted to raise her teenage daughters in accordance with her own deeply held personal values. But in 1980 her local health authority issued guidance, which had been drafted by the Department of Health and Social Security, to GPs on contraceptive advice for under 16's. She challenged this guidance, a part of which is quoted below, as unlawful:

> Section G The Young.
> There is widespread concern about counselling and treatment for children under 16. Special care is needed not to undermine parental responsibility and family stability. The department would therefore hope that in any case where a doctor or other professional worker is approached by a person under the age of 16 for advice in these matters, the doctor, or other professional, will always seek to persuade the child to involve the parent or guardian (or other person *in loco parentis*) at the earliest stage of consultation, and will proceed from the assumption that it would be most unusual to provide advice about contraception without parental consent. It is, however, widely accepted that consultations between doctors and patients are confidential; and the department recognises the importance which doctors and patients attach to this principle. It is a principle which applies also to the other professions concerned. To abandon this principle for children under 16 might cause some not to seek professional advice at all. They could then be exposed to the immediate risks of pregnancy and of sexually-transmitted diseases, as well as other long-term physical, psychological and emotional consequences which are equally a threat to stable family life. This would apply particularly to young people whose parents are, for example, unconcerned, entirely unresponsive, or grossly disturbed. Some of these young people are away from their parents and in the care of local authorities or voluntary organisations standing *in loco parentis*.
>
> The department realizes that in such exceptional cases the nature of any counselling must be a matter for the doctor or other professional worker concerned and that the decision whether or not to prescribe contraception must be for the clinical judgment of a doctor.

Section 8 of the Family Law Act 1969 (still valid) stated:

> (1) The consent of a minor who has attained the age of 16 years to any surgical, medical or dental treatment which, in the absence of consent, would constitute a trespass to his person, shall be as effective as it would be if he were of full age; and where a minor has by virtue of this section given an effective consent to any treatment it shall not be necessary to obtain any consent for it from his parent or guardian.

She drew an analogy with s. 131 of the Mental Health Act:

> In the case of a minor who has attained the age of 16 years and is capable of expressing his own wishes, any such arrangements as are mentioned in subsection (1) above [for informal admission] may be made, carried out and determined notwithstanding any right of custody or control vested by law in his parent or guardian.

Mrs Gillick argued that both these provisions imply that if 16 is the age for consent always to be valid, surely below the age of 16 parental consent must be required. Was she right, or can children below the age of 16 consent to treatment?

Lord Templeman's judgment, at its core, was that the issue is not just about contraception, which is just one example of medical treatment or advice:

> It seems to me verging on the absurd to suggest that a girl or a boy aged 15 could not effectively consent, for example, to have a medical examination of some trivial injury to his body or even to have a broken arm set. Of course the consent of the parents should normally be asked, but they may not be immediately available. Provided the patient, whether a boy or a girl, is capable of understanding what is proposed, and of expressing his or her own wishes, I see no good reason for holding that he or she lacks the capacity to express them validly and effectively and to authorise the medical man to make the examination or give the treatment which he advises. After all, a minor under the age of 16 can, within certain limits, enter into a contract. He or she can also sue and be sued, and can give evidence on oath. Moreover, a girl under 16 can give sufficiently effective consent to sexual intercourse to lead to the legal result that the man involved does not commit the crime of rape—see *Reg. v. Howard [1966] 1 W.L.R. 13*, 15 when Lord Parker C.J. said: 'in the case of a girl under 16, the prosecution, in order to prove rape, must prove either that she physically resisted, or if she did not, that her understanding and knowledge were such that she was not in a position to decide whether to consent or resist. . . . there are many girls under 16 who know full well what it is all about and can properly consent.' Accordingly, I am not disposed to hold now, for the first time, that a girl aged less than 16 lacks the power to give valid consent to contraceptive advice or treatment, merely on account of her age.

His judgment goes on to make plain that the test of competence—what has become known as *Gillick competence*—is flexible:

> It is, in my view, contrary to the ordinary experience of mankind, at least in Western Europe in the present century, to say that a child or a young person remains in fact under the complete control of his parents until he attains the definite age of majority, now 18 in the United Kingdom, and that on attaining that age he suddenly acquires independence. In practice most wise parents relax their control gradually as the child develops and encourage him or her to become increasingly independent. Moreover, the degree of parental control actually exercised over a particular child does in practice vary considerably according to his understanding and intelligence and it would, in my opinion, be unrealistic for the courts not to recognise these facts. Social customs change, and the law ought to, and does in fact, have regard to such changes when they are of major importance. . . .
>
> In times gone by the father had almost absolute authority over his children until they attained majority. A rather remarkable example of such authority being upheld by the court was *In re Agar-Ellis* (1883) 24 Ch.D. 317 which was much relied on by the Court of Appeal [where Mrs Gillick's case had succeeded]. The father in that case restricted the communication which his daughter aged 17 was allowed to have with her mother, against whose moral character nothing was alleged, to an extent that would be universally condemned today as quite unreasonable.

The case has been much criticised in recent years and, in my opinion, with good reason. . . . The common law can, and should, keep pace with the times. It should declare, in conformity with the recent Report of the Committee on the Age of Majority [Cmnd. 3342, 1967], that the legal right of a parent to the custody of a child ends at the 18th birthday: and even up till then, it is a dwindling right which the courts will hesitate to enforce against the wishes of the child, and the more so the older he is. It starts with a right of control and ends with little more than advice. . . .

Once the rule of the parents' absolute authority over minor children is abandoned, the solution to the problem in this appeal can no longer be found by referring to rigid parental rights at any particular age. The solution depends upon a judgment of what is best for the welfare of the particular child. Nobody doubts, certainly I do not doubt, that in the overwhelming majority of cases the best judges of a child's welfare are his or her parents. Nor do I doubt that any important medical treatment of a child under 16 would normally only be carried out with the parents' approval. That is why it would and should be 'most unusual' for a doctor to advise a child without the knowledge and consent of the parents on contraceptive matters.

OBJECTIVES AND OVERVIEW

Involvement of health and social work professionals in the lives of individuals and families arises because a service user is perceived to need help. But do they want it, and have they consented to receive it? In many, perhaps most, instances, the benefits to be derived from the intervention are so clear that issues of competence, consent and autonomy do not cross anyone's mind. But where there could be a clash of fundamental values, such as in the *Gillick* case, which involved the proper role of the state in providing services to children, the decisions as to who provides the necessary authority or consent for the state's involvement are very difficult. The *Gillick* case involved, ultimately, permitting a doctor not a parent to decide to provide contraceptive advice and treatment to any girl old enough to understand and consent to receiving it.

These are hot topics in the media, which provides a constant supply of difficult issues. There are no easy answers to questions such as whether a baby should be kept alive, whether a boy of 16 can consent to homosexual activity, or whether the consent of a girl of 13 to sexual intercourse can provide a defence to a criminal charge of rape. It is hard to imagine the feelings involved where a hospital wants to let a child die because of the seriousness of the condition and the perceived hopelessness of treatment. No-one can be sure to be right, even in respect of clinical judgement: in a recent high-profile case a parent herself revived her child in the hospital, against the wishes of the doctors, who had given morphine to ease his death: *Glass and another v United Kingdom* (2004). And there is a constant and nagging, but poorly researched, worry about the scale of elder abuse involving allegations of inappropriate treatment against the wishes or interests of the older person by families and care staff.

This is an area where the law struggles to define appropriate procedures and standards. The common law assumes people are rational and informed about their own best interests, and evolved at a time of fierce regard for property interests and individual freedoms, combined with an accepted high level of paternalism in regard to fathers taking responsibility for children and, until the late nineteenth century, their wives. A welfare orientated state cannot rely on these blanket and sweeping assumptions, and needs a different framework for the provision of social and health services, one in which rights to autonomy are respected but where interventions can be made even where they diminish autonomy. It is not easy, but it is important. This chapter gives, we hope, a framework so that when balancing the need to intervene with the need to respect autonomy you are doing so in a way which will be recognized as lawful.

The *Gillick* case we just looked at was decided in 1986, but it remains so important that even today Mrs Gillick's name is used by lawyers and judges as shorthand for capacity to consent to or refuse interventions by health and social work professionals. It raised such important issues that the 1989 Children Act has several implicit references to *Gillick* competence (e.g. in the requirement of courts under s. 1(3) to have regard to 'the ascertainable wishes and feelings of the child concerned (considered in the light of his age and understanding)'). A 'Gillick competent' child can make decisions, and receive or refuse treatment independently of the wishes of those who have parental responsibility for the child.

The key difference between adults and children is that with adults the starting point is always an assumption of competence. With children, there is an assumption—not always a strong assumption, and almost defunct at age 16—that the starting point for capacity and consent is those with parental responsibility. The sources of law for children and adults are separate, so after considering some basic issues, we address them separately.

Without an appropriate consent, implicit or explicitly given by someone with the capacity to do so, interference with another person's physical integrity, property or affairs will be unlawful. It can lead to criminal prosecution or to civil liability. Without consent such interference would require explicit legal authority such as:

- A court order, for example a care or specific issue order under the Children Act 1989, a compulsory detention order under the Mental Health Act 1983, removal to residential accommodation under s. 47 of the National Assistance Act 1947, or a common law declaration of the lawfulness of carrying out medical treatment.

- An explicit police power, for example of arrest under the Police and Criminal Evidence Act 1984, a power to remove to a place of safety under the Mental Health Act 1983 or the Children Act 1989.

- The explicit protection of the current Mental Capacity Bill 2004, which we expect to be enacted shortly after this book is published and which we discuss later.

- Power under the Children Act 1989 s. 3(5) which provides that 'A person who (a) does not have parental responsibility for a particular child; but (b) has care of the child, may (subject to the provisions of this Act) do what is reasonable in all the circumstances of the case for the purpose of safeguarding or promoting the child's welfare.'

- The power of the Department of Work and Pensions under social security legislation to appoint someone to a apply for and receive benefits on another person's behalf, where this is in the interests of the claimant.

Or it would require implicit authority under previous court rulings, or explicit court authorization, for example

- Intervening as a matter of necessity to save life or prevent serious harm (permissible for medical treatment under the common law).

- Other medical interventions including cessation of treatment and pain relief, for example if it is in the best interests of a terminally ill patient.

But given that the starting point is that you can do nothing for or to a service user without an appropriate consent, we need to ask:

- Who is capable of giving that consent?
- When an adult lacks capacity, when is it lawful to intervene?

Our objective for the chapter is to provide you with sufficient understanding that you can answer that question in an individual case. If you need to use compulsory powers, these are dealt with in Parts 3 for children and 4 for adults. Useful additional guidance is available from the Department of Health's *Making Decisions: Helping people who have difficulty deciding for themselves*; *Planning ahead—a guide for people who wish to prepare for possible future incapacity*, May 2003 **www.dca.gov.uk/family/mi/mibooklets/guide5.htm**.

Social work ethics and consent

Cases involving social workers, as compared to health workers, rarely get to court. So the main examples illustrating the principles are in cases, often involving life and death, which social workers probably were not directly involved with. But the principles informing decision making are the same, which is why we have used them. These principles are the same, essentially, as those which underpin your own ethical codes.

The ethical principle that every person has a right to self-determination and is entitled to their autonomy is set out clearly in the *BASW Code of Ethics*. In paragraph 4.13 of the code, headed 'self-determination by service users', the code sets out the following:

> Social workers will help service users to reach informed decisions about their lives and promote their autonomy, provided that this does not conflict with their safety or with the rights of others. They will endeavour to minimise the use of legal or other compulsion. Any action which diminishes service users' civil or legal rights must be ethically, professionally and legally justifiable.

The principle is also enshrined in law, through the notion of consent. Actions taken without consent are unlawful, and in some circumstances criminal. They also breach the right to respect for private life under Article 8 of the Convention on Human Rights (see previous chapter).

We provide here a very brief outline of this difficult area of law. The chapter is full of case illustrations, which are necessary because each situation is different, and ultimately, while broad principles are discernible, judgement is often the key factor, and judgement is exercised by professionals, or in really difficult cases, by courts. Most of the case law relates to health professionals, but the principles will be relevant to decisions which have to be made by social workers in relation to provision of services to children and adults.

Forms of consent

Consent may be express or implied. It is express when someone explicitly agrees to the action being taken. When a person signs a consent form in connection with the Data

Protection Act they are consenting to the holding and using of personal information. Implied consent is a more difficult consent. The law may in certain circumstances deduce from a person's conduct their state of mind, that they agreed to the course of action undertaken. An example is that when you participate in team sports you implicitly consent to the bodily contact that will almost inevitably arise. However, reliance on implicit consent, particularly to the sort of interventions in personal autonomy which arise in the course of social care, is probably not a wise course of action. Interestingly, following the cases involving retention of children's organs for many years for research purposes without explicit consent of the bereaved parents, guidance has just been issued for hospitals, which must now obtain clear and detailed consent from families for post-mortem examinations of their relatives. There have also been successful claims for psychiatric distress caused—see, for example, *AB and others v Leeds Teaching Hospital NHS Trust and another* (2004).

The nature of consent

Lawful consent has three qualities. First, the person must have the capacity or competence to consent; second, they must have sufficient information to enable them to give informed consent, and third, it must have been given voluntarily. Our discussion is concerned with the question of capacity. Your social work expertise will be required to ensure the second and third quality.

Capacity or competence to make decisions—the functional approach

English law in general takes a functional approach to capacity: see *Re C (adult; refusal of medical treatment)* (1994) which we discuss below. This was explained and endorsed by the Law Commission in its report on *Mental Incapacity* (1995).

> In this approach, the assessor asks whether an individual is able, at the time when a particular decision has to be made, to understand its nature and effects. Importantly, both partial and fluctuating capacity can be recognised. Most people, unless in a coma, are able to make at least some decisions for themselves, and many have levels of capacity which vary from week to week or even from hour to hour.

What must be understood?

Clearly if the law requires a total understanding of all of the implications of the decision then few people are going to have legal capacity. The Law Commission suggests that it must be the nature and effect of the decision that are understood. This is consistent with the common law, and was the basis for the Mental Capacity Bill 2004 which we look at the end of the chapter. In *Re C (adult; refusal of medical treatment)* (1994) the patient was required to understand 'the nature, purpose and effect' of the procedure. This is a limited meaning of understanding, but one which means that more people are able to make decisions for themselves. For example, before consenting to surgery a patient will not need to be provided with the research papers where risk is analysed, and would not be capable of forming a useful judgement if these were provided; but the patient is entitled to be informed of the nature and broad extent of risk of a particular type of complication, rather than being told merely not to worry. If the patient cannot under-stand at that general level, informed consent is not possible. The level of understanding can vary: a woman about to lose her child through refusing a clearly indicated caesarian where her own and the child's life is at great risk has been held not really able to understand the decision she is making, and therefore her refusal of consent was not informed and was overruled by a court: *Bolton Hospitals NHS Trust v O* (2002).

Actual understanding or ability to understand?

This is another difficult question which the law provides no clear answer to. It would be logical to require actual understanding, but then if the social worker or the doctor failed to provide sufficient information the person would be deprived of their capacity to consent. In *Gillick* the judges stated that what was important was that someone was capable of understanding the decision, and the gravity of the situation should be taken into account. In *Re L (medical treatment: Gillick competency)* (1998) the court required actual understanding because of the consequences of a refusal of consent. Here the life of a 14-year-old girl was in danger as a result of serious and extensive burns. She was a practising Jehovah's Witness and refused to consent to the medical treatment as it might have required a blood transfusion. The court decided that what was required was actually understanding of the decision. The doctor had not explained to her the nature of the death she would endure if she did not undergo medical treatment. Because of that the court was able to decide that she did not have actual understanding of the decision and was therefore not competent to refuse the treatment. Her consent to receive the treatment, by contrast, would not have had such grave consequences and would probably have been sufficient, even against her parent's objections (though not had she been say aged 10, where a court order would have been necessary, if there was time to obtain it).

But, in the case of an adult, to override clear wishes is unusual. It can happen, for example in the case of the woman in childbirth above, where the problem was tem-porary, urgent and, in the opinion of the court, the woman could not at the time understand the consequences of what she was deciding. In *Macette v Shulman* (1991) a woman refused a blood transfusion and the court accepted this, and it inevitably led to her death. Interestingly this same woman's refusal to consent when she was under 18 had been overruled and she had been treated under the court's consent, not her own.

◼ Establishing competence to provide consent

We stated earlier that you need to start with the assumption that adults are competent. Legal authority for this comes, for example, from *Re T (adult: refusal of treatment)* (1992). Section 8 of the Family Law Reform Act 1969 additionally provides that children aged between 16 and 18 are presumed competent. However, for both adults and 16–18 year olds the presumption of competence is rebuttable. And we have seen in the *Gillick* case that the 1969 Act does not exclude under 16 year olds from providing consent to their own treatment or, in principle, from refusing consent to treatment.

◼ Competence to refuse treatment

There are a number of extremely clear statements that a competent person has freedom of choice, 'whether the reasons for which making that choice are rational, irrational, unknown or even non-existent' per Lord Donaldson in *Re T*, cited above. The principle was revisited recently by Dame Elizabeth Butler-Sloss in the well-known case of *Ms B v An NHS Hospital Trust* (2002). Ms B, who had become completely paralysed following serious illness, sought declarations from the High Court that her continued artificial ventilation against her wishes was unlawful. The judge was satisfied that Ms B was competent to make all relevant decisions and granted the declarations. It should not be assumed that refusal is only possible where a person has no mental health problems. Each situation must be weighed up. In *Re C* (1993) a mental patient had gangrene, but refused treatment. The court decided, on the evidence, that he knew enough about the issues to refuse treatment. As it happens his leg recovered.

However there are many situations with adults and children where competence to refuse treatment is found to be lacking. Competent children cannot, in general, withhold consent. In *Re R* (1991), the Court of Appeal held that although an anorexic 16-year-old girl could be said to be '*Gillick* competent', that fact did not prevent the court ordering that she be given drugs against her will. The Court, in a much-criticized decision, drew the distinction between the ability of the girl to give consent and her right to refuse consent. It said that while she could give valid consent, if she refused this did not mean that others such as parents or the court could not still impose consent on her behalf.

The Court said:

> The failure or refusal of the 'Gillick competent' child is a very important factor in the doctor's decision whether or not to treat, but it does not prevent the necessary consent being obtained from another competent source.

Similarly, in *Re W (A Minor) (Consent to Medical Treatment)* (1993), the Court of Appeal again overrode the refusal of an anorexic to accept treatment. The notion of a competent child involves limited competence. The courts consider that the welfare of the child is not something to be decided solely by the child. The welfare of the child can be decided by others, particularly the court.

Refusal of consent also raises problems for adults—for example, the refusal to undergo a caesarian, which the court overruled (see above). *The NHS Trust v T (adult patient: refusal of medical treatment)* (2004) provides another example, of particular interest because the patient had given a clear advance directive at a time when her mental competence was reasonably clear. She self-harmed to such an extent when in a state of temporary psychosis that she required frequent blood transfusions. Her advance directive stated that she knew the consequences of refusal, and she nevertheless did not consent to future transfusions. She believed her blood to be evil, though she acknowledged in her advance directive that this was a manifestation of her illness. She claimed in the directive that she had sufficient understanding of her situation and her illness at the time of making it to be able to refuse consent. Knowing the situation would arise again, the hospital which treated her applied in advance for court guidance. The judge used guidelines from an earlier case (*Re MB (Medical Treatment)* (1997)) which are helpful to repeat here:

(1) Every person is presumed to have the capacity to consent to or to refuse medical treatment unless and until that presumption is rebutted.

(2) A competent woman who has the capacity to decide may, for religious reasons, other reasons, for rational or irrational reasons or for no reason at all, choose not to have medical intervention, even though the consequence may be the death or serious handicap of the child she bears, or her own death. In that event the courts do not have the jurisdiction to declare medical intervention lawful and the question of her own best interests objectively considered, does not arise.

(3) Irrationality is here used to connote a decision which is so outrageous in its defiance of logic or of accepted moral standards that no sensible person who had applied his mind to the question to be decided it could have arrived at it . . . it might be otherwise if a decision is based on a misperception of reality (e.g. the blood is poisoned because it is red). Such a misperception will be more readily accepted to be a disorder of the mind. Although it might be thought that irrationality sits uneasily with competence to decide, panic, indecisiveness and irrationality in themselves do not as such amount to incompetence, but they may be symptoms or evidence of incompetence. The graver the consequences of the decision, the commensurately greater the level of competence is required to take the decision: *Re T* (above), *Sidaway* (a) [1985] AC 871, at 904 and *Gillick v West Norfolk and Wisbech Area Health Authority and another* [1986] AC 112, 169 and 186, [1986] 1 FLR 224, 234 and 251.

(4) A person lacks capacity if some impairment or disturbance of mental functioning renders the person unable to make a decision whether to consent to or to refuse treatment. That inability to make a decision will occur when:
  (a) the patient is unable to comprehend and retain the information which is material to the decision, especially as to the likely consequences of having or not having the treatment in question;
  (b) the patient is unable to use the information and weigh it in the balance as part of the process of arriving at the decision. If, as Thorpe J observed in *Re C* (above), a compulsive disorder or phobia from which the patient suffers stifles belief in the information presented to her, then the decision may not be a true one. As Lord Cockburn CJ put it in *Banks v Goodfellow* (1870) LR 5 QB 549, 569: '. . . one object may be so forced upon the attention of the invalid as to shut out all others that might require consideration'.

(5) The 'temporary factors' mentioned by Lord Donaldson MR in Re T (above) (confusion, shock, fatigue, pain or drugs) may completely erode capacity but those concerned must be satisfied that such factors are operating to such a degree that the ability to decide is absent.

(6) Another such influence may be panic induced by fear. Again, careful scrutiny of the evidence is necessary because fear of an operation may be a rational reason for refusal to undergo it. Fear may also, however, paralyse the will and thus destroy the capacity to make a decision.

Balancing individual autonomy with welfare

When acting for children the position is clear. Section 1(1) of the Children Act provides that:

When a court determines any question with respect to—
  (a) the upbringing of a child; or
  (b) the administration of a child's property or the application of any income arising from it, the child's welfare shall be the court's paramount consideration.

'Upbringing' under the Act will include decisions about social or health care where for any reason parents cannot make this decision themselves. These are dealt with under s. 8 and are further discussed in chapter 14.

In cases involving children, autonomy involves not only that of the child, but also that of the parent. The tension between autonomy and welfare can be seen, taking a case involving children, in *South Glamorgan County Council v W and B* (1993). Here Douglas Browne J was faced with the problem of a young person who clearly was beyond parental control. She was aged 15. She had refused to do anything she was told. She had, in fact, barricaded herself in the front room of her father's house for eleven months. The local authority wanted an interim care order to have the child assessed. The difficulty was the provisions in s. 38(6) of the Children Act 1989 which deal with the court's powers to make orders for assessments to be carried out when making interim care orders (see chapter 11). This particular subsection has provision for informed consent by the young person, stating 'but if the child is of sufficient under-standing to make an informed decision he may refuse to submit to the examination or other assessment'. The local authority and those acting for the girl put the view to the court that if she refused to submit to the assessment then there was little that anyone could do. The judge would not accept this and gave directions under the inherent power of the court (s. 100) for the authority to remove the child. In effect, he bypassed the provisions of the Act relating to informed consent. He did this without making the girl a ward of court. He said:

In my judgment the court can in an appropriate case—and they will be rare cases—but in an appropriate case, when other remedies within the Children Act have been used and exhausted and found not to bring about the desired result, can resort to other remedies, and the particu-lar remedy here is the remedy of providing authority, if it is needed, for the local authority to take all necessary steps to bring the child to the doctors so that she can be assessed and treated.

Re B (Wardship: Abortion) (1991) illustrates the range of issues which can arise when balancing autonomy with welfare. A 12-year-old girl was pregnant. She herself consented to abortion and was supported by her grandparents. Her mother refused. The local authority and several medical witnesses thought aborting the child would be in the girl's best interests, physically and emotionally. The mother's experts thought the opposite. The court had to decide, and decided in favour of a termination. The welfare rather than consent issues were uppermost, though what the child herself wanted influenced the assessment of what would also be in her best interests.

Legal representation of children

There have been a number of cases concerning the ability of children or young people to appoint guardians or solicitors to act on their behalf. In *Re S (A Minor)* (1993), the Court of Appeal held that a child of 11 could not remove the Official Solicitor as guardian. The Court said:

> The 1989 [Children] Act enabled and required a judicious balance to be struck between two considerations. First was the principle, to be honoured and respected, that children were human beings in their own right with individual minds and wills, views and emotions, which should command attention. Second was the fact that a child was, after all, a child.

In *Re H (A Minor) (Care Proceedings: Child's Wishes)* (1993), the court said a 15 year old did not have the right to address the court on his own behalf.

In *Re N (contact: Minor seeking leave to defend and removal of guardian)*, an 11-year-old child was refused leave to defend s. 8 contact proceedings himself because he did not have sufficient understanding to participate in the proceedings and to give instructions that would be fully considered as to their implications. The judge could perceive no advantages in dispensing with a guardian and bringing an application on his own behalf, and many disadvantages.

These cases point to a view of the courts that, despite the apparent philosophy of legislation, the court retains the right to make such difficult decisions for itself, and, if it feels able, to substitute its view for that of the child or young person. They appear to be particularly reluctant to allow a child to decide to participate in adversarial litigation. The *Gillick* competent child is only a competent person in a very limited sense.

Representation of adults

Family members may claim to speak for the adult, but there may be a conflict of interest. In straightforward litigation where there is no conflict, such as a personal injuries claim following an accident, appointment of a litigation friend on behalf of an adult lacking capacity to conduct the proceedings is relatively straightforward. But where complex decisions have to be made about what is in the adult's own interests and whether he or she has capacity, a court will generally appoint the Official Solicitor to represent the adult's interests in the case.

Proxies

If people are not competent then decisions have to be made for them and others must act as proxies for them. For children those people are generally parents. Each parent or other person with parental responsibility is able to exercise the right to consent individually. However, there may be a duty to consult the other parent in relation to major decisions (see *Re G (a minor) (parental responsibility: education)* (1994)). Also in the absence of agreement between parents, the courts may impose a limitation on the power of one parent to consent, for example, to the changing of a child's surname and require the approval of the court—see chapter 13). In *Re J (child's religious upbringing and circumcision)* (1999) it was held that ritual circumcision did not fall within the power of one parent to consent to, where there was disagreement between the parents. As you will see (in chapter 11) local authorities may acquire parental responsibility under Part 4 of the Children Act. This enables them to consent to treatment etc. on behalf of the children. Parents retain parental responsibility, and therefore the power to consent, although that power may be specifically restricted by the local authority—see chapter 11. The Children Act also provides for a further possible proxy. Section 3(5) provides:

> A person who—
>   (a) does not have parental responsibility for a particular child; but
>   (b) has the care of the child
> may (subject to the provisions of this Act) do what is reasonable in all the circumstances of the case for the purpose of safeguarding or promoting the child's welfare.

Teachers or grandparents are able to make necessary decisions with the authority of this provision.

The court is also a decision maker on behalf of children. The High Court has jurisdiction as part of its inherent jurisdiction, and family proceedings courts in respect of s. 8 orders. We consider the power of the courts to make 'specific issues' orders and 'prohibited steps' orders in chapter 13.

All proxies must make decisions consistent with the welfare, or best interests, of the child.

▪ Filling in the gaps

Re F (adult: court's jurisdiction) (2001).

(Although the case name is *F*, the Court of Appeal judges refer to the patient in this case as *T*.) This is how Butler-Sloss P described the family background of T, an 18 year old with a behavioural age of around five:

> The father was 75 at the date of his death in 1999. The mother is 49 or 50. They married in 1984. The case for the local authority disclosed a picture of chronic neglect, a lack of minimum standards of hygiene and cleanliness in the home, a serious lack of adequate parenting and worrying exposure to those engaged in sexual exploitation and possible sexual abuse of one or more of the children including T. The eight children were said to be suffering significant harm and at risk of so doing, based upon these numerous allegations.

T had been looked after by the local authority with the parents' consent. When T was 17 years old the parents withdrew their consent, and the local authority tried to obtain mental health guardianship. To do this it had to get an order from the court that the mother should be replaced by it as the 'nearest relative' (only a nearest relative can apply for guardianship). But that application failed, for the 1983 Mental Health Act provides for guardianship in the case of a mental impairment only where that is associated with seriously irresponsible behaviour. Wanting to live with her family might be against F's interests, but it did not meet that test. So it was held in the Court of Appeal that there were no grounds for guardianship. That decision was reported as *Re F (Mental Health Act guardianship)* (2000). The Court of Appeal advised wardship, but by that time there were six weeks until T turned 18, when neither wardship nor Children Act powers would be available.

The local authority still could not use the Mental Health Act and applied to the court for a declaration that it would be legal for it to direct the living arrangements of T, thereby preventing her living at home and coming to harm. Complex legal arguments around ancient legal doctrines giving the Crown parental powers over its subjects and the doctrine of necessity took place in the absence of clear statutory powers to intervene in F's living arrangements. The Official Solicitor was brought in to join in the arguments on T's behalf, since T was unable because of her mental impairment to instruct a solicitor.

So here, in the words of her ladyship, was the problem:

> There is an obvious gap in the framework of care for mentally incapacitated adults. If the court cannot act and the local authority case is correct, this vulnerable young woman would be left at serious risk with no recourse to protection, other than the future possibility of the criminal law.

As stated by Sedley J:

> T is so unable to judge what is in her own best interests that no humane society could leave her adrift and at risk simply because she has reached the age of 18.

According to Butler-Sloss P.:

> The assumption of jurisdiction by the High Court on a case-by-case basis does not, however, detract from the obvious need expressed by the Law Commission and by the Government for a well-structured and clearly defined framework of protection of vulnerable, mentally incapacitated adults, particularly since the whole essence of declarations under the inherent jurisdiction is to meet a recognised individual problem and not to provide general guidance for mentally incapacitated adults. Until Parliament puts in place that defined framework, the High Court will still be required to help out where there is no other practicable alternative.

The local authority therefore got the declaration it sought in the Court of Appeal, enabling it to accommodate this young adult away from her family. Sedley J said that no human rights were infringed:

> The purpose [of Article 8, respect for private life and family life], in my view, is to assure within proper limits the entitlement of individuals to the benefit of what is benign and

positive in family life. It is not to allow other individuals, however closely related and well-intentioned, to create or perpetuate situations which jeopardise their welfare.

Practical advice on consent and competence

The Lord Chancellor's Department has produced a helpful leaflet targeted at social care professions. It is called '*Helping People who have difficulty making decisions for themselves—a guide for social care professionals*'. It can be found on the web at **www.dca.gov.uk/family/mi/mibooklets/guide5.htm**. The leaflet starts by affirming the right to autonomy and suggesting methods by which individuals can be helped to make their own decision.

> The basis of the law is that every adult has the right to make their own decisions and is assumed to have capacity to do so unless it is proved otherwise. Some people may need help or support to be able to understand the decision they are being asked to make, to know how to make a choice or to be able to communicate, but the need for help and support does not remove their right to make their own decisions.
>
> The principle applies equally to decisions affecting the personal care and welfare of people who need support. For example, people with learning difficulties have the same rights as other citizens and should be given the help and support they need to maximise their independence and control their own lives. Everyone has a right to determine what happens to their own bodies and valid consent must be obtained from an elderly or disabled person if they are able to give it before providing personal care such as bathing and dressing.
>
> Social care professionals have a key role to play in finding ways of help people who need support to understand what decisions need to be made and why, what the effects might be and whether there are any alternatives. Through their work, they will be in a good position to know the most effective way to communicate with the people they care for and how to explain things in a way they can understand. They may also know of other sources of help and advice which will enable individual to reach a decision and express a choice.

We recommend that you read the leaflet in full. It will help put the complexities of the law into a meaningful practical framework.

The Mental Capacity Bill 2000

This Bill was presented to Parliament in the 2003–2004 session, but at the time of publication has not yet completed its passage through Parliament. If it fails it will almost certainly be reintroduced. It will provide a new and comprehensive framework for assessing whether a person of 16 and over has capacity to make decisions, and the lawfulness of taking action to benefit the person who does not have capacity. The principles are very clearly stated in clause 1:

(2) A person must be assumed to have capacity unless it is established that he lacks capacity.

(3) A person is not to be treated as unable to make a decision unless all practicable steps to help him to do so have been taken without success.

(4) A person is not to be treated as unable to make a decision merely because he makes an unwise decision.

(5) An act done, or decision made, under this Act for or on behalf of a person who lacks capacity must be done, or made, in his best interests.

(6) Before the act is done, or the decision is made, regard must be had to whether the purpose for which it is needed can be as effectively achieved in a way that is less restrictive of the person's rights and freedom of action.

The definitions will, of course, need to be tested by challenges in the courts, but the Bill's definitions seem to us to provide a clear frame or reference. A 'person *lacks capacity* in relation to a matter if at the material time he is unable to make a decision for himself in relation to the matter because of an impairment of, or a disturbance in the functioning of, the mind or brain'. The problem can be temporary—the decision has to be made according to the issue that has arisen at a particular time.

The Bill talks in terms of hypothetical figures D (the person intervening) and P (the person whose capacity is being considered). For our discussion, we limit it to social worker and service user, though please do not conclude that the Bill is limited to this context. Anyone—benign relative, passerby, doctor, etc.—is protected if they act on behalf of another person without consent under the terms of this Bill.

The social worker who decides a service user lacks *capacity to make a decision* is protected if, at the time, and on the balance of probability (a concept we discuss in more detail in chapter 5) the service user is 'unable to understand the information relevant to the decision, [or] to retain that information, [or] to use or weigh that information as part of the process of making the decision, or to communicate his decision (whether by talking, using sign language or any other means)'.

Actions taken must always be in the *best interests* of the service user. This is based on all the circumstances, but in particular 'whether it is likely that the person will at some time have capacity in relation to the matter in question, and if it appears likely that he will, when that is likely to be'. This means there is no point acting now if there is a good chance the service user will have capacity him or herself take the necessary action later. Even though lacking capacity the service user must, as far as possible, 'participate, or to improve his ability to participate, as fully as possible in any act done for him and any decision affecting him [in light of] the person's past and present wishes and feelings [and] the beliefs and values that would be likely to influence his decision if he had capacity', and must consult if appropriate 'anyone named by the person as someone to be consulted on the matter . . . anyone engaged in caring for the person or interested in his welfare . . . any donee of a lasting power of attorney granted by the person' (we discuss these in chapter 15).

The result of going through this checklist is that if the social worker 'reasonably believes that what he does or decides is in the best interests of the person concerned' he or she is acting lawfully, so long as the actions which follow are neither negligent or criminal, and are compliant with the terms of any advance directive (see below). The powers to act include physical restraint and payment out of the service user's available funds for goods and services. We strongly suggest taking legal advice in advance of taking such steps, unless physical restraint is needed in an emergency.

The Bill creates a new *Lasting Power of Attorney*, which we deal with in chapter 15. Controversially, the Act in sections 24–26 gives official recognition to *advance decisions* as to provision or withdrawal of medical treatment. The patient must have set out her or his instructions at a time when they were capable of making decisions of this sort; then, if later lacking capacity in relation to issues the advance decisions covered, the advance decision is activated. This would cover the situation of, say, the woman who clearly refused a caesarian—under the old law, her capacity to consent was judged not when she had the chance to think and decide, but in the middle of a traumatic labour (*Bolton Hospitals NHS Trust v O* (2002) above). Critics worry that old people may be persuaded to sign these in order not to be a nuisance to family and that it opens the door to a form of passive euthanasia.

EXERCISE

A neighbour reports the Lee family to social services because of fears for the welfare of the children. You are admitted to the home by Jasmine Lee and discover the following:

(a) Her daughter Susan Lee, aged 13, appears anorexic and seriously underweight. She also has an unrelated skin disorder. Her mother does not want her to receive treatment for either condition. Susan would like treatment for the skin disorder but does not accept that she suffers from anorexia.

(b) Mrs Lee's mother-in-law, Selina Lee, is aged 75 and speaks no English. Jasmine Lee indicates that her mother-in-law is suffering from serious mental health problems and asks you to take her to a specialist unit for assessment. Mr Lee says he does not want you to take his mother anywhere and he is quite capable of deciding what is best for her.

What are the principles involved in relation to issues of consent to treatment or assessment?

COMPANION WEB SITE

 For guidance on how to answer these exercises, visit the companion web site at: www.oup.com/uk/booksites/law

WHERE DO WE GO FROM HERE?

The next chapter will continue with setting the framework. All social work is based on intelligence—gaining and using accurate information in order to carry out statutory duties to protect and assist service users. There is a human rights element—how much information should the state obtain and hold on individuals and families, how much should it share, and where does the right to privacy and confidentiality prevail. The law is complex, but in our opinion now so important that we have in this edition devoted a full chapter to it.

ANNOTATED FURTHER READING

There are surprisingly few textbooks dealing with this issue. For a good detailed overview, though it relates to health not social care issues, look at A. Grubb, *Principles of Medical Law* (Oxford University Press, 2004).

The web site referred to in the text also provides valuable guidance, from a government perspective:

Department of Health, *Making Decisions: Helping people who have difficulty deciding for themselves; Planning ahead—a guide for people who wish to prepare for possible future incapacity* (May 2003) **www.dca.gov.uk/family/mi/mibooklets/guide5.htm**.

You may find the following case commentary useful: *Re C (Welfare of Child: Immunisation) Room to refuse? Immunisation, Welfare and the role of parental decision making*, K. O'Donnell, CFLQ (2004).

4 Confidentiality and responsible information handling

CASE STUDY

R on the application of S v Plymouth CC and C (an interested Party) [2002] EWCA Civ 388 5 CCLR June 2002 251

Facts

C suffers from a mental disorder and general mental impairment. The local authority had success-fully applied for C to be made subject to a guardianship order under the Mental Health Act 1983 (see chapter 16). His mother wanted to care for C at home with appropriate support from health and social services. The local authority considered that C was better cared for separate from his mother's home. She is his 'nearest relative' as defined by s. 26 of the Mental Health Act 1983. The nearest relative can discharge a patient from guardianship. The mother had attended various care planning meetings and objected to the renewal of C's guardianship. She had not been shown any of the documentation upon which either the guardianship or its renewal was based. She asked to see the material, but was told that she could not see it. The local authority said it was prohibited from disclosing confidential information about C. It was also contended that C lacks capacity to consent to disclosure. His mother sought judicial review of the refusal to disclose the material upon which the guardianship order was based. The judge in the High Court dismissed the application for judicial review. At that stage the mother's solicitors instructed experts who wished to see C's mental health records, assessments, reports, and minutes of case conferences. The local authority's position by the time of the appeal was that it would disclose this material to the mother's experts, but not to the mother or to her solicitors.

The decision of the Court of Appeal

The Court of Appeal allowed the appeal and ordered disclosure to the mother's solicitors and also to the mother. Lady Justice Hale explained that decisions about disclosure were a balancing exercise.

> The simple answer to this case is that, both at common law and under the Human Rights Act, a balance must be struck between the public and private interests in maintaining the confidentiality of the information and the public and private interests in permitting, indeed requiring, its disclosure for certain purposes. There is no evidence from the correspondence leading up to the first instance hearing that the local authority had made any attempt to strike that balance. They began from the proposition that they had no power to disclose this information at all. They then modified this to 'no power without a very good reason'. But in seeking for a reason they looked at the nature of the underlying disagreement between the authority and the mother about where C was to live and not at the legal interests which might support the disclosure of the information.

Lady Justice Hale examined the common law of confidentiality and the Human Rights Act 1998 and set out the legal principles deriving from both which underpin the balancing exercise.

> Hence both the common law and the Convention require that a balance be struck between the various interests involved. These are: the confidentiality of the information sought; the proper administration of justice; the mother's right of access to legal advice to enable her to decide whether or not to exercise a right which is likely to lead to legal proceedings against her if she does so; the rights of both C and his other to respect for their family life and adequate involvement in decision-making processes about it; C's right to respect for his private life; and the protection of C's health and welfare. In some cases there might also be an interest in the protection of other people, but that has not been seriously suggested here.

She also made it clear that the context of disclosure was extremely important.

> But we are not concerned here with the publication of information to the whole wide world. There is a distinction between disclosure to the media with a view to publication to all and sundry and disclosure in confidence to those with a proper interest in having the information in question. We are concerned here only with the latter. The issue is only whether the circle should be widened from those professionals with whom this information has already been shared (possibly without much conscious thought being given to the balance of interest involved) to include the person who is probably closest to him in fact as well as in law and who has a statutory role in his future and to those professionally advising her.

Lady Justice Hale made it clear that C's own perspective must be considered.

> C's interest in protecting the confidentiality of person information about himself must not be under-estimated. It is all too easy for professionals and parents to regard children and incapacitated adults as handing no independent interests of their own: as objects rather than subjects.

Later she analysed C's interest in the question of disclosure.

> C also has an interest in having his own wishes and feelings respected. It would be different in this case if he had the capacity to give or withhold consent to the disclosure: any objection from him would have to be weighed in the balance against the other interests, although as *W v Edgell* shows, it would not be decisive. C also has an interest in being protected from a risk of harm to this health or welfare which would stem from disclosure; but it is important not to confuse a possible risk of harm to his health or welfare from being discharged from guardianship with a possible risk of harm from disclosing the information sought. As *Re D* shows, he also has an interest in decisions about his future being properly informed.

It is on that basis that she reached her conclusion on the balance of interests in the case.

> That balance would not lead in every case to the disclosure of all the information a relative might possibly want, still less to a fishing exercise amongst the local authority's files. But in most cases, it would lead to the disclosure of the basic statutory guardianship documentation. In this case it must also lead to the particular disclosure sought. There is no suggestion that C has any objection to his mother and her advisers being properly informed about his health and welfare. There is no suggestion of any risk to his heath and welfare arising from this. The mother and her advisers have sought access to the information which her own psychiatric and social work experts need in order properly to advise her. That limits both the context and the content of disclosure in a way which strikes a proper balance between the competing interests.

The problem that the local authority faced here was whether to disclose confidential informa-tion they held about a young man, who did not have the necessary mental capacity to consent to disclosure, to someone who disagreed with them about what was in the best interests of that young man. The case provides a typical example of the sort of dilemma faced by social workers in deciding what confidential information to disclose and in what circumstances. It also provides an example of the failure of the local authority to properly address the issues they are required to address in reaching their decision. The decision they reached appears overly cautious and defensive. Why do you think the local authority behaved in this way? To what extent were they influenced by the incapacity of the service user? Or by the fact that they perceived the mother's challenges as inappropriate?

Lady Justice Hale, as she then was (now the first woman appointed to the House of Lords as Baroness Hale of Richmond) provides an excellent explanation of the decision making process which the authority should have followed. She makes it clear that the local authority must balance the various interests of the parties in a manner which is both Human Rights Act com-pliant and which addresses the requirements of the common law on confidentiality. She also stresses that the fact that the authority has information about a person who is incapacitated does not fundamentally change the decision making process. The purpose of this chapter is to help you understand the law which underpins this important aspect of your work.

Information is essential for the protection of vulnerable people. There is a danger that social workers and others interpret the common law and statutory framework in a way which pre-vents them from using information effectively. It is fair to say that social workers' caution could be the result of unduly cautious legal advice. The potential legal barriers to information sharing recently received careful scrutiny within the Laming Report, published in January 2003, into the death of Victoria Climbié which we discuss further in chapter 8. Paragraph 17.115 states:

> The evidence put to the Inquiry was that unless a child is deemed to be in need of protection, information cannot be shared between agencies without staff running the risk that their actions are unlawful. This either deters information sharing, or artificially elevates concern about the need for protection—each of which is not compatible with serving well the needs of children and families.

The Report recommends (recommendation 17) that the Government should issue guidance on the Data Protection Act 1998, the Human Rights Act 1998, and common law rules on confidentiality. You can read the Report at **www.victoria-climbie-inquiry.org.uk**. Guidance was subsequently published by the Department of Constitutional Affairs which is very helpful. You can find this at **www.dca.gov.uk/foi/sharing/toolkit/lawguide.htm**. In addition the govern-ment has made provision within the Children Act 2004 which will require local authorities to establish databases of information about children in order to facilitate contact between pro-fessionals who are supporting individual children or who have concerns about their develop-ment or well being with the aim of securing early and coherent intervention. These provisions will be discussed in more detail in chapter 8.

Further evidence of the potential tragic consequences of failing to share crucial information was considered in the Bichard inquiry. This inquiry was established on 17 December 2003 by the Home Secretary following the conviction of Ian Huntley for the murder of Holly Wells and Jessica Chapman. The inquiry reported on 22 of June 2004. Certain conclusions that Sir

Michael Bichard reached are relevant to this chapter. First, he was extremely concerned at the failure of Social Services to inform the police that Huntley had sexual relationships with girls under 16. Secondly, he noted that the police and others lacked confidence in their ability to share information because of their perceptions of the Data Protection Act 1998.

> It is evident that police officers were nervous about breaching the legislation, partly at least because too little was done to educate and reassure them about its impact. But I do not believe that the current Data Protection Act needs to be revised as a result of these events. It is, as a member of the judiciary said recently, an 'inelegant and cumbersome' piece of legislation, but the legislation was not the problem. I suggest, however, that better guidance is needed on the collection, retention, deletion, use and sharing of information, so that police officers, social workers and other professionals can feel more confident in using information properly.

You can find the full inquiry report on the web at http://www.bichardinquiry.org.uk.

On the other hand we must not forget that social workers may be using information given in confidence, and that individuals are entitled to have their privacy respected. Moreover, the state in its various guises holds a great deal of information about us all. If there is no check on its use there is great potential for oppression. Government too has an interest in ensuring that the information it holds is only used for legitimate and proportionate purposes. It would be all too easy for individuals to lose their trust in the state if it is believed to have abused its powers. The law is complex because of the complexity of the decisions which have to be made. As Lord Falconer puts it in the introduction to the DCA guidance:

> The law, rightly, puts in place safeguards for the use of individuals' data and there are organizational costs involved in meeting those conditions. In a democratic society, it is important that those safeguards exist and are properly applied. This does not mean, however, that further and better use of information should not be made in order to serve the best interests of the individuals, of groups and of society more widely. An appropriate balance must be struck in the specific circumstances that surround each service or policy.

The chapter is at times technical but we hope it gives you an indication of the legal framework. In this area, as in many others within the book, if you have a specific problem you will have to seek specialist legal advice. However an understanding of the basic principles should inform your day to day practice.

In the chapter we set out the relevant provisions of the Human Rights Act 1998 and then explain the basics of the common law of confidentiality. These provide you with your basic tools for lawful practice in this area. We go on to consider the balancing act that the courts undertake when they make difficult decisions about disclosure. If you like, the cases indicate how you should use the legal tools that you have. Next we consider the framework of information legislation, looking at the Data Protection Act 1998 and the Freedom of Information Act 2000. These provide an additional statutory overlay and are designed to ensure that information is handled appropriately by the authorities and that individuals can have access to the information the state has about them. Finally we look at the interaction of the various legal frameworks and explain the decision making process which underpins lawful information sharing. We start, however, by setting out your ethical responsibilities and considering why confidentiality is so important.

◼ The Code of Ethics

The BASW Code of Ethics is a key tool in helping you with the difficult conflicts which can arise in the relationships between professionals and their service users. Paragraph 4.1.7 of the code sets out the ethical position on confidentiality and disclosure. We have set this out for you in Box 4.1.

You will see as you go through this chapter that the ethical principles are reflected in both the common law and the statutory framework. Confidentiality is the starting point, both legally and ethically. This is because social work, like many of the caring professions, is based upon the concept of respecting individual autonomy. Social workers obtain private information about individuals as a result of their privileged position in society. Unwarranted disclosure of that information is a breach of an individual's personal integrity. Moreover, the interests of the community or of the public are generally served by the relationship between a service user and the social worker being confidential. It promotes confidence in public service and trust in social

---

 BOX 4.1 Paragraph 4.17 of the BASW Code of Ethics

Social workers will:

(a) Respect service users' rights to a relationship of trust, to privacy, reliability, and confidentiality and to the responsible use of information obtained from or about them;

(b) Observe the principle that information given for one purpose may not be used for a different purpose without the permission of the informant;

(c) Consult service users about their preferences in respect of the use of information relating to them;

(d) Divulge confidential information only with the consent of the service user or informant, except where there is clear evidence of serious risk to the service user, worker, other persons, or the community, or in other circumstances judged exceptional on the basis of professional consideration and consultation, limiting any such breach of confidence to the needs of the situation at the time;

(e) Offer counselling as appropriate through the process of a service user's access to records;

(f) Ensure, so far as it is in their power, that records, whether manual or electronic, are stored securely, are protected from unauthorized access, and are not transferred, manually or electronically, to locations where access may not be satisfactorily controlled;

(g) Record information impartially and accurately, recording only relevant matters and specifying the source of information;

(h) The sharing of records across agencies and professions and within a multi-purpose agency is subject to ethical requirements in respect of privacy and confidentiality. Service users have a right of access to all information recorded about them, subject only to the preservation of others persons' rights to privacy and confidentiality.

workers and allows people to discuss their problems in the assurance that the information will not be disclosed. Without this assurance people may be unwilling to seek help.

Of course there are circumstances when a social worker owes a greater duty to the community than to the individual who has disclosed information. The social worker may be obliged, or may have the discretion, to breach any obligation of confidence they owe to an individual. The difficulty is recognizing when those circumstances arise. Behaving ethically and legally in problematic circumstances and ensuring that an individual service user is appropriately protected involves difficult dilemmas. The cases indicate how the courts think that these dilemmas should be solved but the lessons from the cases are not straightforward. We know that each case must be decided on its own merits. We also know that effective interdisciplinary working is essential for the protection of vulnerable people. The Human Rights Act 1998 provides you with some assistance in balancing the right to confidentiality with the need of the state to intervene.

The Human Rights Act 1998

We have already described the significance and the impact of the Human Rights Act 1998 for your social work practice. Every decision you make must comply with the Human Rights Act. We set out the European Convention Articles which are of particular relevance to decisions about confidentiality in Box 4.2. We have emphasized the important words in bold.

Human Rights and privacy

It is important at this stage to consider the distinction between privacy and confidentiality. There is no right to privacy recognized in English law, as distinct from the legal protections given to confidential information. However the European Court of Human Rights is increasingly stressing the legal significance of privacy as the two cases set out in Box 4.3 indicate.

The common law duty of confidentiality

The common law provides individuals with a cause of action for damages if there is a breach of the legal duty of confidentiality. We discuss what we mean by common law in chapter 5. For the time being all you need to know is that the branch of common law that we are concerned with here is tort. The courts recognize that certain people, particularly professionals such as social workers and lawyers, owe duties to those who rely upon them. If they breach those duties without justification then the court can interfere, either by making an award of damages or by making an order, known as an injunction, prohibiting the disclosure of the relevant information. Note that the duty of confidentiality extends to children, the dead, and incompetent adults.

BOX 4.2 Extracts from key Articles

Article 6—Right to a fair trial

(1) In the determination of his civil rights and obligations or of any criminal charge against him, everyone is entitled to a **fair and public hearing** within a reasonable time by an independent and impartial tribunal established by law. **Judgment shall be pronounced publicly but the press and public may be excluded** from all or part of the trial in the interests of morals, public order or national security in a democratic society, **where the interests of juveniles or the protection of the private life of the parties so require,** or to the extent strictly necessary in the opinion of the court in special circumstances where publicity would prejudice the interests of justice.

(3) Everyone charged with a criminal offence has the following minimum rights:

   (a) **to be informed** promptly, in a language which he understands and in detail, of the nature and cause **of the accusation** against him;

   . . .

   (d) **to examine or have examined witnesses against him** and to obtain the attendance and examination of witnesses on his behalf under the same conditions as witnesses against him;

   . . .

Article 8—Right to respect for private and family life

Everyone has the right to respect for his private and family life, his home and his correspondence.

There shall be **no interference by a public authority with the exercise of this right except such as is in accordance with the law and is necessary in a democratic society** in the interests of national security, public safety or the economic well-being of the country, for the prevention of disorder or crime, for the protection of health or morals, or for the protection of the rights and freedoms of others.

Article 10—Freedom of expression

Everyone has the right to freedom of expression. This right shall include freedom to hold opinions and to receive and impart information and ideas without interference by public authority and regardless of frontiers. This article shall not prevent States from requiring the licensing of broadcasting, television or cinema enterprises.

The **exercise of these freedoms,** since it carries with it duties and responsibilities, **may be subject to** such formalities, conditions, **restrictions** or penalties as are prescribed by law and are necessary in a democratic society, in the interests of national security, territorial integrity or public safety, for the prevention of disorder or crime, for the protection of health or morals, **for the protection of the reputation or rights of others, for preventing the disclosure of information received in confidence,** or for maintaining the authority and impartiality of the judiciary.

BOX 4.3 The increasing importance of privacy

Peck v United Kindom (2003)

On the evening of 20 August 1995, at a time when he was suffering from depression, Mr Peck walked alone down Brentwood High Street, with a kitchen knife in his hand, and attempted suicide by cutting his wrists. He was unaware that he had been filmed by a closed-circuit television (CCTV) camera installed by Brentwood Borough Council.

The CCTV footage did not show the applicant cutting his wrists; the operator was solely alerted to an individual in possession of a knife. The police were notified and arrived at the scene, where they took the knife, gave the applicant medical assistance and brought him to the police station, where he was detained under the Mental Health Act 1983. He was examined and treated by a doctor, after which he was released without charge and taken home by police officers.

The council sought to publicize the value of CCTV and used the incident to demonstrate how CCTV had ensured that prompt action was taken to protect Mr Peck's life. Footage of the incident was used in the local paper and in a national television programme. Mr Peck was identifiable from this footage.

The Court observed that, following the disclosure of the CCTV footage, the applicant's actions were seen to an extent which far exceeded any exposure to a passer-by or to security observation and to a degree surpassing that which the applicant could possibly have foreseen. The disclosure by the Council of the relevant footage therefore constituted a serious interference with the applicant's right to respect for his private life.

Perry v United Kingdom (2003)

Mr Perry was arrested in connection with a series of armed robberies and released pending an identity parade. When he refused to take part in an identity parade, he was covertly video taped by the police in a police station and later identified by two witnesses. Mr Perry was subsequently convicted.

The European Court of Human Rights has ruled that Mr Perry's right to respect for private life under Article 8 of the ECHR was breached by the police as their covert video taping had gone beyond the normal use of their station camera and was not in accordance with the law. The police had not followed procedures laid out in the applicable code of practice, had not informed Mr Perry or his solicitor that the tape was being made or obtained his consent and had not informed him of his rights in that respect.

These developments are very much in line with your ethical responsibilities set out in the *BASW Code of Ethics* and you should be aware that there is likely to be an increasing emphasis on privacy in the courts. However, this chapter is primarily concerned with confidentiality, and the responsibilities that the law imposes on you in handling personal and confidential information.

Breach of confidence is a tort which protects the collection, use, and disclosure of personal information. Not all information is protected. There are three basic requirements. First, the information must be confidential. The courts will generally not protect information which is in the public domain or readily available from another source. However they may act to limit further disclosure even if the information is already in the public domain. Moreover, the cases that we discussed earlier about the increasing importance of privacy indicate that the public/private divide is not clear-cut. Mr Peck's suicide attempt was in a public place, but he did not anticipate that it would be televised to 9 million viewers, and he had the right to be protected from that dissemination of information. In addition the information should have a degree of sensitivity and value which gives it the quality of confidentiality.

Second, the information was communicated in circumstances giving rise to an obligation of confidence. If you guaranteed that you would not disclose the information that would give rise to the obligation. However the obligation can also be implied from the relationship between the person who communicated the information and the recipient. If there is a professional relationship such as exists between a lawyer and their client or a social worker and service user then information divulged is likely to give rise to the obligation of confidence. The obligation will extend to information you learn indirectly, for instance from a relative of a service user, because the information was received in your professional capacity.

Third, there must have been an unauthorized use of the information. If a service user gives you permission to divulge particular information then the tort cannot arise. However, the service user could give you permission to disclose information only in certain circumstances or to certain people. Communication of the information in breach of those requirements would give rise to the tort. Moreover, the service user must have capacity to consent to the disclosure.

However, confidentiality is not an absolute right. Just cause or excuse and acting in the public interest are defences to an action of breach of confidence. You can breach a duty of confidentiality to prevent serious crime. Government departments and local authorities owe duties of confidentiality when the relevant circumstances arise in the same way that individuals do. As there may be uncertainty about when it will be in the public interest to disclose information legislation is sometimes used to provide clarity. Sometimes the legislation prevents the disclosure of information by imposing specific obligations of confidence, for instance in the Abortion Act 1967. Sometimes legislation requires that local authorities, for instance, disclose information. For example, the Child Support (Information, Evidence and Disclosure) Regulations 1992 impose an obligation to disclose information. Other legislation provides for a power to make disclosures in certain circumstances. For instance s. 115 of the Crime and Disorder Act 1998 gives the power to certain public authorities to disclose information where the disclosure is necessary or expedient for the purposes of that Act. The legislation does not *require* disclosure to be made in such circumstances. Rather there would need to be a balancing act between the obligation to maintain confidentiality and the need for disclosure. In many ways then the common law reflects the requirement of proportionality and justification imposed by the Human Rights Act 1998. The provisions in the Children Act 2004 are another example of legislative provision designed to create clarity on the principles underpinning lawful information sharing. These provisions will be discussed in more detail in chapter 8.

▦ The balancing act . . .

What you have learned so far from consideration of your ethical responsibilities, the Human Rights Act 1998 and the common law duty of confidentiality is that whilst the starting point is that information is confidential, there may be a range of circumstances which justify disclosure. Your role is to balance the competing interests. In Box 4.3 and Box 4.4 we set out in summary the balancing exercise which you must undertake.

▦ Themes from the cases

This section of the chapter discusses the balancing exercise set out in Box 4.4 and Box 4.5 in greater detail. We suggest that nine themes to the balancing exercise emerge from the cases and we examine these themes next. Our first four themes illustrate reasons for maintaining a duty of confidentiality. The five remaining themes are more

---

BOX 4.4 The basic duty to protect confidences

Confidences should be kept because	But, bear in mind . . .
Privacy is protected both legally and ethically—Article 8 of the ECHR, the common law, statute such as the Data Protection Act, etc., and the social work code of ethics	This is only a starting point and in exceptional cases both legally and ethically disclosure will be necessary. Note that Human Rights jurisprudence requires that disclosure must be necessary and proportionate.
Litigation privilege protects communications with lawyers	The cases show that it is strong but not immutable and the privilege is limited to the litigants.
Children require privacy	Not in serious criminal cases, or in cases of anti-social behaviour.
Public interest immunity	It is in the public interest that certain facts, such as the identity of police informers is kept confidential. Note, however, that Human Rights jurisprudence limits the extent of public interest immunity.

BOX 4.5 Reasons to disclose information

Disclosure is required because	But, bear in mind . . .
Child protection and partnership working requires information to be shared	There is no presumption of disclosure; each case must be considered on its own merits.
Allegation should be spelled out—Article 6 of the ECHR	Article 6 has great weight, but must be weighed against the public interest. There may be Human Rights issues against disclosure too . . .
Secrecy damages trust	Personal information should be kept private, and disclosed only as far as necessary.
Open media—Article 10 of the ECHR	Sources will have to be protected disclosed if it is in the overriding public interest.
s. 12 of the Human Rights Act reinforces that article	
Other reasons—particularly relating to the abuse of children by professionals and others	But only where there is evidence of a pressing need and disclosure must be limited.

concerned with the justification for the disclosure. Each decision requires a balancing of personal and public interests, and where decisions require an interpretation of the ECHR, consideration must be given to whether the interference with a right under Article 6, 8, or 10 is both necessary and proportionate, has a legitimate aim and is authorized by the law.

Bear in mind that the decision to disclose information requires more rigorous analysis than the maintenance of confidentiality. Public interest, the general justification for disclosure, is a slippery concept. This is particularly so for social workers whose role ranges from caring for the individual through broader statutory responsibilities to protect the vulnerable right through to the investigation of harmful, often criminal activities. Social workers are also required to work in partnership with a number of state agencies including the police. The courts demonstrate an increasingly sophisticated understanding of the professional role of the social worker and provide some case specific examples of appropriate and responsible information handling.

◼ Four themes keeping information confidential

Theme 1: confidences should be kept

Government guidance sets the tone:

> 'Normally, personal information should only be disclosed to third parties (including other agencies) with the consent of the subject of that information', *Working Together under the Children Act* (DH 1999 revision).

Do not forget that even with consent there is a limit on the extent of disclosure. Information should be disseminated no further than is necessary to achieve the aim of disclosure.

Confidentiality is a starting point

This provides a starting point, but it does not override other competing themes. There are some circumstances where confidentiality can be almost guaranteed. Lawyers' communications with and on behalf of their clients are the nearest we can get to a concept of an absolute privilege. But even here professional codes of conduct require breach where intention to commit a crime leading to serious personal injury is revealed, or where breach of confidence is dictated by a need for child protection. Lawyers also have 'litigation privilege': the right to talk to witnesses and obtain reports for the purpose of preparing actual or probable court cases and not to disclose the material if it is unhelpful. Later in this chapter we examine this in more detail in particular the case of *Re L (Police Investigation: Privilege)* (1996), which became, at the European Court of Human Rights, *L v UK (disclosure of expert evidence)* (2000). That case reveals that there may be circumstances where even this privilege can be breached, if there is an overriding need to protect children.

Litigation privilege

Litigation privilege is explained in the case of *S County Council v B* (2000), where the Family Division, notwithstanding the House of Lords decision in *Re L*, maintained that litigation privilege is absolute. The father of triplets had obtained the court's leave in care proceedings to obtain a medical report on serious injuries to one of them. The report was disclosed to the court in these proceedings. But the father was also involved in criminal proceedings and for those proceedings had instructed a different expert, hoping the new expert would support his defence. He refused to disclose the report in the care proceedings, or even to reveal the identity of the expert, presumably because it was unhelpful to his version of events. The children's guardian, suspecting the information would be helpful to a decision on what was the best outcome for all three children, sought an order to compel him to disclose it. The Family Division held that, while the paramount duty to the welfare of the child dictated what happened within the care proceedings, it did not in fact override the privilege of a party to communicate in absolute confidence with her or his adviser and witnesses if that privilege had arisen in the course of other proceedings. The father could not be compelled to breach his litigation privilege. This litigation privilege is restricted to the litigant in the case, so, for example, expert witnesses have no privilege and cannot guarantee confidentiality.

Exceptional disclosure to the police

Many agencies hold their records under 'an express or implied undertaking to hold it in confidence'. Police investigating crime can obtain warrants to search the records of agencies such as social services, and, subject to judicial discretion, which we consider below, will be able to use the material in criminal prosecutions notwithstanding the confidential nature of the contents. But while powers exist to force disclosure under a court order, those holding it must still start from an assumption of confidentiality, as paragraph 28 of the circular *Personal social services: confidentiality of personal information*, DoH Circular LAC(88)17 indicates (emphasis added):

> The disclosure of personal information [to the police] may exceptionally be justified if it can help to prevent, detect or prosecute a serious crime . . . Before such a disclosure is made at least the following conditions must be satisfied:
>
> > the crime must be sufficiently serious for the public interest to prevail. A record should be kept of when information is disclosed for this purpose;
> >
> > it must be established that, without the disclosure, the task of preventing or detecting the crime would be seriously prejudiced or delayed;
> >
> > satisfactory undertakings must be obtained that the personal information disclosed will not be used for any other purpose and will be destroyed if the person is not prosecuted, or is discharged or acquitted;
> >
> > request from a police officer of suitably senior rank, e.g. superintendent or above.

Paragraph 30 continues:

> In addition, evidence may come to the attention of staff which may justify disclosure on their own initiative to the police so as to protect another individual. The most common example of this is in cases of child abuse.

A number of reported cases reinforce the view that confidentiality is the starting point for personal information. We have summarised these in Box 4.6.

Theme 2: personal information deserves protection

Privacy is the starting point in many statutes concerned with storing personal data, whether manually or electronically. Data no longer required for the purposes for which they were obtained should be destroyed: see for example *Guardian ad litem and reporting officer service: retention and destruction of records*, LAC (95)18. The impact of these statutes on the work of social workers will be considered later in the chapter.

Additionally the common law—influenced but not radically altered by the Human Rights Act—has long respected confidentiality of personal data. But such respect is not absolute. When the mistress of a professional footballer wanted to tell the story of her adulterous affair to the press, the Court of Appeal saw no overriding public interest in refusing her this opportunity. See *B and C v A* (2002), *Independent*, 19 March 2002.

BOX 4.6 Some case examples emphasizing the starting presumption of confidentiality

R v Birmingham City Council, ex parte O (1982): social service committee records (in the actual case concerning the background of adoptive parents) cannot be divulged to other members of the same local authority (in this case a member of the authority's housing committee).

Re M (Care Proceedings: Disclosure: Human Rights) (2001): the mother had admitted to a social worker involved in care proceedings that the injuries to the child had been caused by her shaking him. The social worker reported this to a case conference, without the court's permission. The police therefore heard of the existence of this statement and wanted to see it for the purposes of criminal proceedings. The Family Division restated the general principle: 'it is on the person seeking disclosure to make out a positive case to justify breaching that code of confidentiality.' In deciding whether to exercise the discretion to order release of the information the judge held that the child's interests would be better served by the mother receiving therapy and avoiding criminal proceedings. She denied the police the access to the statement which they needed for a prosecution.

S v S (Chief Constable of West Yorkshire Police Intervening) (1999): the mother had fled with the child to a women's refuge. The father sought under Children Act 1989, s. 8, a residence order and an order to prohibit the mother from taking the child out of the jurisdiction; he asked the court under the Family Law Act 1986 to order the police to divulge to the court the address of the refuge. The police successfully resisted the application, as they were able to satisfy the court of the child's present safety without the court knowing the address.

In each case there is a balancing act between privacy rights and the interests of those (including media—see below) wishing to disclose personal information. There can be instances when the balance tips strongly in the direction of privacy: in *Venables and another v News Group Newspapers Ltd and others* (2001), the lives of the two boys who, in a case which shocked the nation, had killed a 2-year-old boy continued to be at risk from vigilantes long after their adulthood and release. A life-long ban on identification of the new names and whereabouts of the released killers was justified.

Theme 3: children in particular require protection against intrusion

The *Gillick* case, which we discuss in chapter 3, considers the nature of the legal and ethical responsibilities to protect the confidential information disclosed by children. Whilst in many circumstances the need to protect children will mean that your duties extend to the whole family, there will be occasions where the information which a child discloses to you must remain secret from their parents. The controversial case reported in numerous newspapers in May 2004 of a 14-year-old girl whose school arranged for her to have an abortion without the knowledge of her parents highlights the dilemmas. Following the controversy the Department of Health published new guidelines emphasizing that doctors and other health professionals have a duty of care and confidentiality regardless of the patient's age. A doctor or health professional is able to provide contraception, sexual and reproductive health advice and treatment, without parental knowledge or consent, to a young person under 16 years of age, provided that:

- she/he understands the advice provided and its implications;
- her/his physical or mental health would otherwise be likely to suffer and so provision of advice or treatment is in their best interest.

The *Daily Telegraph* (31 July 2004 see **http://www.telegraph.co.uk/new**) reported that the 'document infuriated pro-life campaigners who said it made a mockery of the concept of parental responsibility'.

Ann Widdecombe, the Tory MP, said: 'What worries me is the blanket description "under-16s". What about 10-year-olds? Surely the parents of 10-year-olds need to know if their children are sexually active, let alone having an abortion.'

Paul Tully, of the Society for the Protection of Unborn Children, said: 'In the vast majority of cases, the support that a teenage girl needs in these situations is the support of her parents.'

All of these comments would be valid if those responsible for deciding whether to maintain confidentiality in this situation made their decisions without careful reference to the principles we are discussing in this chapter. But the child's and the parents' interests in being informed may not always—as a matter of judgement and, if necessary, of law—be identical.

Children in court

Tensions are not only visible within families. The legal system also attempts to reconcile its public role with the need to protect children.

All courts and tribunals are, in principle, open to the public and to press reporting. See, for example, Magistrates Courts Act 1980, s. 121(4); *Scott v Scott* (1913), and of course ECHR Article 6(1). This principle is further explored below. However, there has long been a consensus that there is little public interest in disseminating the private affairs of children, including their wrongdoing. The idea is internationally accepted. For example the United Nations adopted the Beijing Rules in November 1989, which state in relation to criminal proceedings involving children:

8.1 The juvenile's privacy shall be respected at all stages in order to avoid harm being caused to her or him by undue publicity or by the process of labelling.

8.2 In principle, no information that may lead to the identification of a juvenile offender shall be published . . .

Thus we find in English law a range of statutory protections for keeping cases involving children private in both criminal and civil cases. For criminal cases the Children and Young Persons Act 1933 applies:

S. 47(2): . . . No person shall be present at any sitting of a youth court except—
(a) members and officers of the court;
(b) parties to the case before the court, their solicitors and counsel, and witnesses and other persons directly concerned in that case;
(c) bona fide representatives of newspapers or news agencies.

S. 49(1): The following prohibitions apply . . . In relation to any proceedings to which this section applies, that is to say—
(a) no report shall be published which reveals the name, address or school of any child or young person concerned in the proceedings or includes any particulars likely to lead to the identification of any child or young person concerned in the proceedings; and

(b) no picture shall be published or included in a programme service as being or including a picture of any child or young person concerned in the proceedings.

Additionally, under s. 37(1) judges or magistrates are empowered to clear the court (but not to evict the press) where a witness is aged under 18.

Adoption proceedings under the old law, and we expect under any new rules under the new adoption law (see chapter 13) must be in private. In all other civil proceedings courts are empowered to hold their proceedings in private. The power derives from a number of sources: for example the Civil Procedure Rules 1998, rule 37; Family Proceedings Courts (Children Act 1989) Rules 1991, SI 1395; this general power has been confirmed by the Court of Appeal in *Clibbery v Allan* (2002) (see below).

For Children Act 1989 cases this becomes the presumption:

> Unless the court otherwise directs, a hearing of, or directions appointment in, [Children Act] proceedings . . . shall be in chambers. (Family Proceedings Rules 1991, SI 1247, r. 4.16(7))

The Children Act moreover requires under section 97(2) that:

> No person shall publish any material which is intended, or likely, to identify—
>   (a) any child as being involved in any proceedings before the High Court, a county court or a magistrates' court in which any power under this Act may be exercised by the court with respect to that or any other child; or
>   (b) an address or school as being that of a child involved in any such proceedings.
> (4) The court or the Lord Chancellor may, if satisfied that the welfare of the child requires it, by order dispense with the requirements of subsection (2) to such extent as may be specified in the order.

The rules are backed by enforcement powers. Under s. 12 of the 1960 Administration of Justice Act it is a contempt of court to publish certain information given in private proceedings.

> (1) The publication of information relating to proceedings before any court sitting in private shall not of itself be a contempt of court except in the following cases, that is to say . . . where the proceedings—(i) relate to the exercise of the inherent jurisdiction of the High Court with respect to minors; (ii) are brought under the Children Act 1989; or (iii) otherwise relate wholly or mainly to the maintenance or upbringing of a minor, . . .

Orders banning publicity

While these provisions appear at first sight to be comprehensive, there are some proceedings where the affairs of a child may be involved and which are not protected. For example, domestic violence proceedings under Family Law Act 1996, Part IV, are not protected and press reports are not restricted, unless an order is made (the grounds for which are narrow). In deciding whether to make an order, the interests of the children are not paramount, although they are a factor. So in what circumstances will the court ban publicity? We have provided some case examples in Box 4.7.

Criminal proceedings

However there have been some moves away from this approach within criminal proceedings, where there is an evolving rhetoric of toughness on youth crime. The results of

BOX 4.7 Some case examples of protecting children from publicity

In *A v M (Family proceedings: publicity)* (2000) the mother's allegations of violence by the father had been rejected by the court, so she repeated them to the newspapers. The father sought an injunction on the basis that this public airing of her grievances was damaging for the children. The injunction was granted, even though interests of the children under the legislation were only one factor.

In *Re G (Celebrities: Publicity)* (1999), the parties were celebrities. The judge had banned all publicity of any sort; the parents themselves were happy with this, but the press wanted to maintain a right to publish details of the divorce and existing photographs. The Court of Appeal held that a total ban on all mention of the case and all use of photographs went too wide. The court would allow existing photographs to be printed. Publicity about the proceedings should, however, be restricted to a statement issued by the court.

In *A Local Authority v A Health Authority* (2004) the local authority had carried out a report into a care home, which looked after children and vulnerable young adults. The report contained some lurid matters. The correct approach to publication was to assume that there was a right to publish until the Court was satisfied for good reasons that publication would be so disadvantageous to the children concerned that the Court was driven to restrain publication so far as it related to children.

It seems from the above that children, if not adults, are protected, if not from all publicity, at least from unrestricted publicity.

this shift in philosophy are apparent in amendments to the Children and Young Persons Act 1933, s. 49, to allow a naming and shaming approach for very serious crimes:

(4A) If a court is satisfied that it is in the public interest to do so, it may, in relation to a child or young person who has been convicted of an offence, by order dispense to any specified extent with the requirements of this section restrictions imposed by subsection (1) above in relation to any proceedings . . .

Anti-social behaviour orders

The anti-social behaviour order (ASBO), which we discuss in chapter 18, was brought in by the Crime and Disorder Act 1998, s. 1. This order works partly through publicity. Proceedings against individuals for anti-social behaviour are generally widely reported to demonstrate that people can do something to stop aberrant behaviour. Under the Crime and Disorder Act 1998, applications for ASBOs against juveniles are generally heard as civil matters in the magistrates' courts where there are no automatic reporting restrictions, although the court has the power to impose restrictions to protect the identity of a person under 18.

The predictable problem this throws up can be seen in *Medway Council v BBC* (2002) 1 FLR 104. The local authority obtained anti-social behaviour orders on eight children from the magistrates' court. The authority's motivation, the court noted in the case, had been in part to make an example of these problem children. But these problem children were also troubled children; indeed they soon came to be recognized as children in need under s. 17 of the Children Act and children at risk of significant harm under s. 47 (see chapters 9 and 11). The same council now had to view the children from its Children Act perspective. It applied for a care order for one of the children. Given its responsibilities to the child's welfare it now needed to restrict, not encourage, publicity. Any information revealed in the care proceedings themselves was protected (Children Act 1989, s. 97(2), above), but the council additionally sought an injunction to prevent an interview with the child's mother about the anti-social behaviour order being broadcast. The Family Division refused an injunction: the publicity related to proceedings over which it had no control, and (to paraphrase) it was too late to lock the stable door.

The Anti-social Behaviour Act 2003 provided the Government with an opportunity to deal with the inconsistencies between the two approaches. Instead it dealt deal with a different anomaly, the fact that when youth courts made ASBOs following convictions for other offences, automatic reporting restrictions used to apply. Following the implementation of the Anti-Social Behaviour Act 2003 automatic reporting restrictions are no longer imposed when the youth court makes an ASBO. However, the court retains discretion to apply reporting restrictions where it considers it to be appropriate, and the court is also required to consider the welfare of the child under the Children and Young Persons Act 1933. Automatic reporting restrictions will continue to apply to the conviction that precedes the ASBO. This lifting of the automatic reporting restrictions for ASBOs attracted a great deal of hostile parliamentary comment. For instance one member of the House of Lords pointed out the damaging consequences of *The Sun* newspaper's 'Stop a Yob' campaign:

> This is the antithesis of responsible, local community involvement; it is vigilantism of the press. It is very difficult and dangerous to use publicity in this way because people interpret and react to information in an extremely unpredictable way. When difficult, dysfunctional and often disturbed youngsters are concerned, whose behavior is indeed unpleasant and intimidating, the risks are magnified. Such children are rarely shamed or humiliated into positive social behaviour. They are not only demonised by the process in the eyes of some, they could equally become anti-heroes in the eyes of others. (Hansard, Aoure of Cords, 3 Nov. 2003, col. 546.)

Theme 4: public interest immunity

Public interest immunity is the shorthand for the legal rule which allows public bodies to withhold information on the grounds of public interest. The simple fact that the document or information in question is confidential is not sufficient reason for the withholding of the information. The rule applies only where disclosure would cause real harm to the public interest. So, for instance, in *D v NSPCC* (1978), suppliers of information of the type which could help in child protection work, even if the informants was acting maliciously and providing demonstrably false information, are entitled not to be identified, as this would inhibit informers. In deciding whether or not information should be disclosed the courts have to balance the interests of the person seeking disclosure against the public interest. It was made clear by Lord Hailsham in *D v NSPCC* that 'The categories of public interest are not closed, and must alter from time to time whether by restriction or extension as social conditions and social legislation develop'.

The changing culture in which the rule operates is illustrated by the case of *Gaskin v*

Liverpool CC (1980). Gaskin was a former foster child in the care of a local authority who was refused access to his social services records. He applied to court for disclosure. The Court of Appeal refused, saying that there was a public interest in upholding the proper functioning of the child-care system. The European Court of Human Rights, to which he then appealed, upheld his claim (reported as *Gaskin v United Kingdom* (1990). The confidentiality of public records was important, but Gaskin's right to have crucial information about his early life overrode this public interest, and was protected by Article 8 of the Convention. Note that the case was decided prior to the Access to Personal Files Act 1987 (now part of the Data Protection Act 1998).

◼ And five themes justifying sharing information

Theme 5: child protection work and decisions require information

This particular theme goes to the heart of the social worker's role. It is therefore appropriate that we consider it in detail.

The necessity of sharing information

It is difficult to protect children from abuse if information is not available to the full range of professionals concerned with their welfare. Information should be shared for the benefit of vulnerable individuals and society as a whole. Further, decisions need to be based not on half truths and prejudice but on full and accurate information. *Working Together* (DoH, 1999) comments at para. 7.27, 'Often, it is only when information from a number of sources has been shared and is then put together that it becomes clear that a child is at risk or suffering harm.'

The courts and disclosure

In *Re G (a minor)* (1996), the court made it clear that information recorded as part of the investigation but not filed at court could be disclosed to the police without the permission of the court. To decide otherwise would destroy interdisciplinary arrangements for investigating child abuse, and might even put the child's welfare at risk. Information which has been filed at court requires the permission of the court to be disclosed to anyone not a party. *Re G* also suggested that the guardian *ad litem's* (now the children's guardian's) role was not independent of the court. However, in a recent case, *Re M (A Child) (Disclosure: Children and Family Reporter)* (2002), the Court of Appeal stressed that the relationship between the Children and Family Reporter (CFR) and the judge is a collaborative one. Each has distinct functions and responsibilities in the discharge of which each exercises independently both judgement and discretion. In urgent cases the CFR must be free to report concerns direct to social services and then inform the judge. This indicates growing judicial recognition of the skills and autonomy of child welfare professionals.

Limits to litigation privilege where child welfare is concerned

Where there is an overriding need to protect children then even the well established litigation privilege discussed in theme 1 can be breached. *Re L (Police Investigation:*

Privilege) (1996), which became at the European Court of Human Rights *L v UK (disclosure of expert evidence)* (2000), concerned two children of heroin-addicted parents. One child was admitted to hospital having consumed a quantity of methadone. Both children were made the subject of interim care orders. In the course of the proceedings the parents sought leave from the court to disclose the court papers to a consultant chemical pathologist. They were seeking support for their argument that the consumption of the drug was accidental. The court gave them leave and also directed that the report be filed in the court and made available to all the other parties. The pathologist's report to the mother's solicitor indicated that the mother's version of events was not at all probable. During a child protection conference the police became aware of the contents of this report. They applied on notice to be joined as a party to the care proceedings to seek disclosure of the pathologist's report for the criminal investigation. The House of Lords held that the report should be disclosed. As child protection proceedings are not adversarial the litigation privilege did not apply. This case is indicative of an increasing trend towards disclosure where it is necessary to allow the investigation of possible criminal activity relating to children. Social workers clearly cannot give assurances of confidentiality.

However, in a recent case, *Re AB (Care Proceedings: Disclosure of Medical Evidence to Police)* (2002), the judge, Wall J, pointed out that there is not as a matter of law a presumption in favour of disclosure. Each case must be decided on its own merits. Nonetheless, he pointed out the advantages of disclosure as a matter of good practice in modern interdisciplinary child protection.

Duties and powers to disclose to the police

Social workers may, in the course of their duties, gain information about activities that may interest the police. Legislation provides for some very specific circumstances when information must be disclosed to the police, for instance under the Prevention of Terrorism Act 1989, the Misuse of Drugs Act 1971 and the Police and Criminal Evidence Act 1984. If the particular provisions under these statutes apply then social workers have no choice but to disclose confidential information. We do not have space to detail these provisions, and advise you to take legal advice as soon as a request or requirement to provide information is received. However the more challenging scenario is where legislation gives only a power to disclose information. There has recently been an expansion of disclosure powers. Section 115 (1) of the Crime and Disorder Act 1998 provides:

> Any person who, apart from this subsection, would not have power to disclose information—
>   (a) to a relevant authority; or
>   (b) to a person acting on behalf of such an authority,
> shall have power to do so in any case where the disclosure is necessary or expedient for the purposes of any provision of this Act.

This is a broad provision which impacts upon social services as members of Crime and Disorder Partnerships (discussed in chapter 15—see the reference to the Youth Offending Service) alongside the police and other local authority departments. This provision is not unique. For instance s. 17 of the Anti-terrorism, Crime and Security Act 2001 extends the existing disclosure powers of public authorities contained in sixty-six

Acts where disclosure would assist (amongst other things) criminal investigations, criminal proceedings, the initiation or bringing to an end of any such investigation or proceedings or facilitating a determination of whether any such investigation or proceedings should be initiated or brought to an end.

Decisions to disclose

When should social services choose to use these extensive powers to disclose information? Disclosure is allowed only if it conforms with the public interest exception to the common law duty and the proportionality and necessity requirements of the Human Rights Act 1998. We remind you of the guidance offered by the local authority circular, *Personal social services: confidentiality of personal information*, DoH Circular LAC(88) 17, which we discussed earlier. Disclosure may exceptionally be justified if 'it can help to prevent, detect or prosecute a serious crime'. However, the nature of the relationship between local authorities and the police has changed dramatically since 1988. Emerging partnerships mean that social services are likely to feel greater responsibilities to work with the police. Society has also become more risk averse. What in the past may have been exceptional may become more routine to eliminate risks to children through criminal or anti-social activities.

The Regulation of Investigatory Powers Act 2000

Social workers do much more than provide support for families. They also investigate abuse. It may be that social services acquire information other than through direct information gathering. Local authorities, as public authorities, are able to engage in covert surveillance such as entry to or interference with property, following suspects, and use of informers. There are legal controls on these activities. Covert information gathering is governed by the Regulation of Investigatory Powers Act 2000. The Act claims to ensure that the use of powers to investigate individuals through surveillance or to intercept telecommunication complies with the Human Rights Act, in particular Article 8. (It also implements Article 5 of EU Directive 97/66/EC, which to some extent provides a European framework for handling such information and surveillance.) Public authorities have only the surveillance powers conferred by the Act, and if they exceed these powers they will be acting unlawfully. Surveillance operations to obtain evidence require prior authorization from a designated person. Local authorities can designate Assistant Chief Officers and Officers responsible for the management of investigations. A written record must be kept and include the reasons for granting the authorization and its terms. Necessity and proportionality are the bases for granting authorization. Proportionality is tested against the object to be achieved by carrying out the surveillance in question. The Act establishes a Surveillance Tribunal which will provide judicial oversight of the Act and consider allegations that public authorities have infringed human rights by surveillance activities.

If a local authority fails to get activities authorized then the evidence produced will be tainted if used in any court proceedings, as it will have been obtained in breach of s. 6 of the Human Rights Act. Any prosecution using the evidence will be vulnerable to arguments that evidence acquired in breach of Convention rights should be excluded under s. 78(1) of the Police and Criminal Evidence Act 1984 (see chapter 5).

Decisions to use these powers are likely to be taken at the highest level, but any social worker exceptionally involved in any covert activity should be fully briefed on what is and is not permissible.

Responsible disclosure

Social workers must be effective in their work, and this means an increasing pressure to disclose information to a range of other agencies. The judiciary support this pressure. Nonetheless, information must be disclosed in a responsible way. How it is obtained must conform with statutory procedures. Social service departments should follow the advice of *Working Together* (discussed in chapter 11), anticipate difficulties, and have in place carefully worked out information sharing protocols.

Theme 6: allegations must be spelled out

The last principle went to the core of the role of the social worker and others with legal responsibilities to protect children. This next principle is at the heart of the procedural protections of the Human Rights Act. Article 6—the right to a fair trial—means that anyone subject to an allegation should have full details of that allegation and be able to challenge it. The interaction of Article 6 with other Convention rights and the public interest are illustrated in *The Chief Constable of the Greater Manchester Police v McNally* (2002). The claimant had sought damages from the Chief Constable of Greater Manchester Police for wrongful arrest, false imprisonment, and malicious prosecution. In the course of the trial the judge ordered the Chief Constable to disclose whether a person called 'X' in the proceedings was at any material time a police informer. Counsel for the Chief Constable resisted the application on the basis of our theme 4—public interest immunity based upon the importance to keeping the identity of informants secret. The Court of Appeal set out the human rights issues as follows: 'on the police side the protection of informers, Article 2 the right to life, and Article 8, the right to respect for private and family life; and on the claimant's side, Article 5.5 which provides an enforceable right to compensation to everyone who has been a victim of unlawful arrest or detention and Article 6 (1) the right to a fair trial.' The court dismissed the Chief Constable's appeal. The public interest in this case was in disclosure because of the serious risk of a miscarriage of justice without disclosure of the information requested, the need for redress for wrongful deprivation of liberty over a period of ten months, and the overwhelming public interest in the exposure of serious misconduct by the police. What the court did was to balance the relevant Articles very carefully in response to the specific facts of the case and to give Article 6 in particular great weight.

The context of the case

Whilst Article 6 is absolute and unqualified what it means for there to be a fair trial will depend upon the context of the particular case. Any departures from the normal requirements of an adversarial trial must be proportionate and can happen only if the reason for doing so is legitimate. However, protecting the interests of vulnerable children will often be a legitimate reason. So for instance in *B v UK* (2002) it was decided there was no breach of Article 6 to hear child residence proceedings and pronounce judgment in chambers with the applicant parents being prohibited from revealing any details. The Article 6 requirement to hold public hearings is subject to exception and Article 6(1) contains an express exception for the interest of juveniles; it is also important in child residence cases that the parties are able to speak frankly without the possibility of adverse comment.

Protecting the interests of the service user

These cases illustrate the application of the right to a fair trial when individual interests may have to be compromised in the interests of society. Often what need to be balanced are the rights of one vulnerable individual against another. However the courts are cautious in denying information to parties to litigation.

In *Re X (children) (adoption; confidentiality)* (2002) there was a conflict between vulnerable individuals. Here prospective adopters, concerned about the children being at risk from the wider birth family if confidentiality were breached, insisted that the adoption be anonymous. The solicitor to the birth parents became aware of the identity of the prospective adopters during a review meeting and sought permission to disclose this to her clients who, she believed, had a right to the information. The guardian supported disclosure, whereas the local authority supported anonymity. The judge refused permission to disclose the identity of the prospective adopters, on the basis that there was a real possibility of significant harm to the children. This possibility arose first from the risk of intervention of the parents in the life of the adoptive family in an unplanned and unauthorized way, and secondly, from the increased anxiety of the adopters. He weighed that possibility against the problems of testing the evidence properly, the difficulties in taking instructions from the parents, and all the forensic disadvantage and apparent unfairness to the parent in trying to deal with the issues in the case without knowing what the true position was. He had no doubt that the interest of the children lay in favour of anonymity. The Court of Appeal dismissed the solicitor's appeal. The court agreed that its starting point was disclosure of all the information relevant to the court's decision. But when contemplating non-disclosure the issue came down to striking a fair balance between the various interests involved: the interests of all parties, but particularly the birth parents and the children themselves, in a fair trial of all the issues in the case in which the evidence on each side could be properly tested. The court was not able to say in this case that the judge's exercise of his discretion had been plainly wrong. The interest of the children in maintaining a secure and happy home was so great that it outweighed the formidable but not insurmountable problems facing the parents' legal team in not having all the information.

The case we discussed at the beginning of this chapter, *R on the Application of 'S' v Plymouth City Council* (2002) is a good illustration of the debate about protecting the vulnerable service users through non-disclosure, and demonstrates when the Court of Appeal will overturn too cautious an approach by the local authority supported by the High Court. The case emphasizes that the presumption is weighted in favour of spelling out allegations. However, the exercise of professional judgement will be respected by the courts and will have a profound impact upon the outcome.

Theme 7: secrecy damages trust

Trust is important when people and institutions are involved in long-term relationships where respect for professional expertise is critical and needs to be maintained. The Government recognizes this in its commitment to open government and indeed in the Freedom of Information Act 1999 which we discuss below.

Disclosure can be uncomfortable for social workers

Problems can be caused by social workers who are unwilling to confront individuals with the evidence that they intend to use to make serious decisions, for instance about the future of their parenting. In *Re X (children) (adoption; confidentiality)* (2002), discussed above, a comment was made by the judge that indicates the importance of openness. The court case could have been avoided if the local authority had applied in 2000 for permission to refuse contact between the children and their parents. It could also have applied to free the children for adoption. It chose instead to deny the parents the opportunity of challenging those decisions and then to practise a deception upon them.

Adoption

The difficulties and fragilities of adoption seem to pose particular challenges. We have seen this already in the case study at the beginning of chapter 1. Two Ombudsman decisions indicate the dilemmas which can face social services. In Report 97/A/3857, Mrs W complained about the way a council placed two children with her and her husband with a view to adoption. One aspect of the complaint was the lack of information about the children's behavioural problems. The Ombudsman accepted that social workers had to make difficult decisions about what they could disclose without improperly breaching confidentiality. Some of the information Mrs W asked for could not be disclosed, but the Ombudsman said that the council did not tell her and her husband things which would not have entailed an improper breach of confidence and which they reasonably needed to know, such as information about the children's health and history of abuse. The Ombudsman concluded that as it became clear to the prospective adopters that they had not been told enough about the children, they became increasingly anxious about what they did not know. That prolonged anxiety was an important element of the injustice caused by the way the council acted.

Inappropriate disclosure

The second case demonstrates that openness must be appropriate. Report 97/C/3985 concerned the termination of the induction process between the complainant and child she hoped to adopt without good reason, without proper notice, and without adequate explanation. One particular aspect of the complaint was that the council had allowed the child's foster parents full access to the complainant's adoption form. The Ombudsman commented:

> Whilst it may be perfectly proper for a foster carer, who has an in-depth knowledge and understanding of a child, to play some part in the selection process of a suitable adoptive parent, I can see no justification nor statutory basis for extending this to providing the foster carer with detailed personal and confidential information about the prospective adoptive

parent. It appears to me to be totally inappropriate and unprofessional for such confidential information to be made available to anyone other than the most essential personnel.

The council's action exposed the complainant to unnecessary and unwarranted intrusion into her private affairs.

Theme 8: a free press is desirable

Goodwin v United Kingdom (1996) provides a clear statement of the significance of Article 10 of the Convention. The case concerned the protection of journalists' sources. The ECtHR made it clear that freedom of expression constitutes one of the essential foundations of a democratic society and that the safeguards afforded to the press are of particular importance. Without protection journalists' sources may be deterred from assisting the press in informing the public on matters of public interest. As a result the vital public watchdog role of the press may be undermined and the ability to provide accurate and reliable information may be adversely affected. Orders to disclose sources must be justified by an overriding requirement in the public interest.

An earlier case, *BBC v United Kingdom* (1996), indicates that disclosure can be ordered in the course of criminal proceedings. In social care there may also be an overriding requirement to disclose sources in the public interest. The House of Lords decision, *Ashworth Security Hospital v MGN Limited* (2002), indicates the approach to this issue. The case concerned the right of a newspaper to refuse to reveal its sources. The *Daily Mirror* published an article which included verbatim extracts of the medical records of Ian Brady (one of the Moors murderers), a patient at Ashworth Security Hospital. The hospital had decided to force-feed Brady after he had been on hunger strike for thirty days. Brady had taken judicial review proceedings in relation to the decision, which had been found in those proceedings to be lawful since it was reasonably administered as part of the medical treatment given for the mental disorder from which Ian Brady was suffering. The hearing had been held in private, although the judgment was delivered in open court. Ian Brady's medical records, upon which the decision was based, were then, somehow, disclosed to the *Daily Mirror*. An employee of the hospital was most likely to be responsible, as the data were from the hospital database. The hospital applied for an order to discover the source of the leak. Brady had consented to the leak, but the courts recognized an independent public interest in the hospital maintaining confidentiality and preventing journalistic access. The House of Lords acknowledged the importance of Article 10, and made it clear that any restriction on the right to freedom of expression must meet two further requirements. Any curtailment of the right should meet a pressing social need, and the restriction should be proportionate to a legitimate aim which is being pursued. In this situation that need was the critical importance of trust in the relationship between therapists and patients. Further, it was important to identify the employee to prevent further disclosure and remove the cloud of suspicion hanging over the authority's employees. In addition Article 8 requires that personal data are protected. In this exceptional case disclosure of the source of the leak was ordered. The care of patients at Ashworth is particularly fraught with difficulty and danger which is increased by breaches of confidentiality.

The House of Lords has again paid attention to the tensions between Article 8 and Article 10 of the ECHR in *Campbell v MGN* (2004). In this well-known case it was decided that details relating to a person's attendance at Narcotics Anonymous were confidential because disclosure would be likely to be distressing and offensive to the reasonable person in that situation and disruptive of treatment. The right of privacy in Article 8 had to be balanced against the right of the media to impart information in Article 10. Neither Article had hierarchical priority. The test was whether publication pursued a legitimate aim and whether the benefits of publication were proportion to the harm that might be caused. The restrictions on Article 10 had to be rational, fair and not arbitrary and must not impair the right any more than is necessary. In this case there were no political or democratic values at stake nor was any pressing social need identified. Publication had the potential to cause harm. Accordingly there had been a breach of Campbell's Article 8 right to privacy.

Theme 9: other people may need to know about a person's past

Professionals who abuse

The cases indicate that the courts take the need to protect children very seriously and accept that the interest of any adult concerned may have to be placed second if there is real evidence of a high risk. Professionals who abuse their own children are unlikely to be able to protect themselves from the disclosure of the information to their professional bodies. In *A County Council v W (Disclosure)* (1997) disclosure of the care proceedings to the General Medical Council where the father involved was a doctor was allowed on the basis that disciplinary proceedings would possibly protect other children. In *Re L (Care Proceedings: Disclosure to third party)* (2000) the mother, a paediatric nurse suffering mental and emotional problems, had caused her child significant emotional harm which resulted in an interim care order. The court gave leave to disclose the judgment and the medical reports to the UK Central Council for Nursing. The rights of the mother and child had to be balanced against the public interest in demanding protection from nurses who were or who were potentially unfit to practise.

Other perpetrators of abuse

Even where perpetrators do not have professional responsibilities disclosure may be ordered. In *R v Chief Constable of North Wales, ex p AB* (1997) a married couple released from prison after serving long sentences for serious sexual offences against a number of children rented a caravan on a caravan site as their home. The police informed the site owner of the convictions, and as a result the site owner required the couple to leave. They then sought a judicial review of the police decision to disclose the convictions. The Court of Appeal confirmed the Divisional Court's dismissal of the application. It was compatible with Article 8 because there was a pressing need for the police to disclose material already in the public domain to a caravan site owner, when the material related to paedophiles on the site who were a considerable risk to children and vulnerable adults who might come onto the site during the holidays.

What was critical here was the real evidence of a pressing need for disclosure. Without such evidence the authorities are much more vulnerable, as the following case demonstrates. In *R v Local Authority in the Midlands, ex p LM* (2000) the applicant, who owned a bus company, had his contract to transport school children terminated. This was because of social services and police concerns arising from an allegation against him of indecent assault on his daughter seven years previously, along with a further allegation against him of sexual abuse three years before that. He wished to take up a new contract for school bus services and therefore asked for assurances from the police and social services that such allegations would not be further disclosed. The authorities refused to give those assurances and he sought judicial review of the refusals. The court held that it was not compatible with Article 8 for the police to disclose stale and unproven allegations of sexual abuse to a county council which employed the applicant to provide school transport because there was no 'pressing need' for disclosure.

The way in which the reliability of any information has to be weighed up using evidential principles before the decision is made to pass it on is further considered in chapter 5.

The prerequisites for disclosure

The need for evidence of a pressing need, for limits to be placed on disclosure, and for the responsibilities involved in disclosure to be taken very seriously was restated in *Re C (Disclosure: Sexual Abuse Findings)* (2002). This case concerned an order for disclosure made during care proceedings. The judge in the care case had found that C had sexually abused children and that he was a paedophile who posed a considerable risk to any child. The judge gave the local authority leave to disclose a copy of his judgment to the Department of Health and to any social services department or police force within whose area C might be residing. Following this the police and social services applied for permission to disclose the judge's findings to C's present landlord, a housing association, and to any future landlord. The judge ordered disclosure to the current landlord but refused an order for disclosure to future landlords. The wider disclosure would be difficult to control and the balance of need and harm fell against it. He also ordered that the information be disclosed to the housing association by a police officer of the highest practicable rank, and that disclosure should be to named individuals. This, he stated, 'would assist in bringing home the very sensitive nature of the information concerned and the serious trust being reposed in the relevant individuals'. In the context of the Human Rights Act, it is interesting to note that the judge did not regard the Convention as adding anything of significance to the approach applicable to this application under domestic law.

■ Information legislation

In addition to the themes we have extracted, there are clear legislative requirements governing data held in official records. Social workers must be aware that any information they hold is subject to the statutory framework which controls information handling by public authorities and others, and allows for disclosure in particular circumstances. Those statutory duties are limited by the common law on confidentiality which we have discussed above.

The Data Protection Act 1998

Information held by social services departments is governed by the requirements of the Data Protection Act 1998 which came into force on 1 March 2000. The Act, which incorporates the provisions of the Access to Personal Files Act 1987, requires data controllers who process personal information to comply with a range of data protection principles.

Data controllers are people, including organizations, who decide how and why personal data are processed. 'Personal data' refers to information relating to an identified or identifiable living individual which is processed automatically (including information processed on a computer) or recorded manually as part of a filing system or part of an accessible record. This will include records such as social services files. Processing covers anything done in relation to such data, including collecting them, holding them, disclosing them and destroying them. The eight data protection principles are key to understanding the Act. We have set them out in Box 4.8. You will notice how similar they are to the ethical principles we set out at the beginning of this chapter:

> the detection or prevention of crime, or the protection of members of the public against dishonesty malpractice or incompetence or enabling confidential counselling, or enabling research.

Conditions for processing data

Data Protection Principle One goes on to state that personal data shall not be processed (which includes disclosure) unless: '(a) at least one of the conditions in Schedule 2 is met, and (b) in the case of sensitive personal data, at least one of the conditions in Schedule 3 is also met.' Sensitive personal data are concerned with ethnic origin, political or religious beliefs, trade union membership, physical or mental health, sexual life, and criminal offences. Conditions of most relevance to social services departments within both Schedule 2 and Schedule 3 are the need to protect the vital interests of the subject and for the exercise of a government department or functions of a public nature exercised in the public interest by any person. Schedule 3 includes an additional relevant condition—where there is a substantial public interest in:

Principle One also requires that data subjects—individuals—must be told the identity of the data controllers and the purposes for which their data are to be processed. Individuals should also be made aware of any additional purposes for which their data may be used.

Therefore disclosure can be made for many purposes without obtaining consent and still comply with the Act so long as the information in question was obtained fairly and no breach of the common law was involved.

Access to personal information

The Data Protection Act 1998 provides a right of access to personal information held by *public authorities* and *private bodies*, regardless of the form in which it is held. One important practical implication is that social workers must be aware that individuals are entitled to request a copy of information held about them and that the local authority has an obligation to ensure that information relating to individuals is structured in such

BOX 4.8 The data protection principles

Data protection principles	Comment
Fairly and lawfully processed	Lawfully refers to the requirements found in the common law of confidentiality, administrative law (the processing must not be '*ultra vires*', i.e., outside the authority of the organisation or contrary to statutory provisions) and with the provision of Article 8 of the European Convention on Human Rights.
Processed for limited purposes	Information is held for a purpose. You should be clear what that purpose is and the information should only be used for that purpose.
Adequate, relevant, and not excessive	Only necessary information should be held.
Accurate	You have a responsibility to ensure that the information is accurate and you should have systems in place for checking the accuracy, for instance confirming details with your service user.
Not kept longer than necessary	Once the reason for holding the information is past then the information should be destroyed. There should be a system in place for checking regularly the continuing relevance of information held.
Processed in accordance with the data subject's rights	These are set out in Schedules 2 & 3 of the Act, discussed below.
Secure	Non-authorised people should not be able to get access to the information. You should be clear who has authority to access information and who does not.
Not transferred to countries without adequate protection	Information should not automatically be sent to other countries when the service user moves abroad. The new country may not have similar standards of protection of information.

a way that specific information relating to an individual is readily accessible. Not all information need be disclosed; the right is subject to exemptions. Box 4.9 summarizes the position.

To obtain access the individual must write to the data controller, stating that are applying under section 7 of the Data Protection Act 1998 for access to any personal data

BOX 4.9 Access to information

An individual can see information held about them:

- by anyone on computers (or in other forms where data can be processed automatically).
- in health, social work, housing and school records held on paper. This applies to all information, not just that in 'structured' files.
- in all structured files held by any organization, including government departments, local authorities, the police, employers and private companies. The right applies regardless of when the files or filing system was created.
- when the Freedom of Information Act is fully in force, 'unstructured' information held by any public authority will become accessible under the DPA.

All these rights are subject to a variety of exemptions, which allow certain information to be withheld.

'Structured' files are collections of files or papers organized in a way that makes it easy to find information about a particular individual.

about themselves. The data must be disclosed unless it is exempt information, which we summarize in Box 4.10 below. Note that there is an important additional exemption which relates to social work records which we discuss below.

Access to social work records

A service user is entitled under the Data Protection Act 1998 to see all information held by a local authority social services department, including 'unstructured' information. However there is an important additional safeguard preventing disclosure of certain information. Information can be withheld if disclosure would be likely to cause serious harm to the service user or to any other person's physical or mental health. This includes the physical or mental health of a health or social care professional.

An individual is only entitled to see their own records. A parent would not normally be entitled to see a child's records without the child's consent. If the child is too young to consent, the parent can apply on the child's behalf. Any information which a child has provided in the expectation that it would not be shown to the parents is exempt.

The result of these exemptions mean that a parent who is accused of child abuse is unlikely to be given access to the child's records, or to information provided by the child but recorded on the parent's file. However, the parent should still be able to see other information recorded about him or herself such as the notes of an interview or home visit, so long as disclosure would not expose the child to risk or prejudice law enforcement; if the evidence is to be used in court the right to full disclosure would prevail (as discussed above).

A family member caring for a mentally handicapped adult who cannot give an informed consent to their application has no explicit right of access to that person's file,

BOX 4.10 Exempt Information under the Data Protection Act 1998

Personal information about someone else. This will not normally be released without that person's consent. However, the DPA does allow such information to be disclosed *without consent* if this is reasonable in all the circumstances. If the information can be disclosed in a way that does not identify the individual—for example by deleting the name or other identifying features—then the individual is are entitled to it.

Information that would identify someone who has *supplied* **information**. Only identifiable *individuals*, not organizations, are protected. The exemption does not protect the identity of a health professional, social worker or teacher who has provided information which is recorded on the health, social work, or educational record.

Law enforcement—personal data held for the purpose of preventing or detecting crime, apprehending or prosecuting offenders, or assessing and collecting any tax or duty are exempt if disclosure would prejudice one of those purposes.

National security—information can be withheld on national security grounds.

References are generally exempt. There is no right to obtain a confidential reference from the person or body *which gave it*. But you would be entitled to see a reference *held by the person to whom it was supplied*, except where this would identify the *individual* who gave it.

Information about the course of negotiations between the data controller and the individual are exempt, if disclosure would prejudice those negotiations. General opinions and intentions are not exempt.

Examination marks and examiners' comments are exempt for a short period. An individual is entitled to see these 40 days after the examination results have been announced or five months after the request has been received, whichever is shorter.

Adoption records and reports are exempt.

unless they are acting under a power of attorney or an order of the Court of Protection.

Remember that information about someone else which is recorded on a service user's file, and anything which would identify an individual who has provided information about a service user, will normally be exempt, unless disclosure is reasonable in the circumstances.

The Department of Health has issued guidance on access to social records. This is available on the web at **www.dh.gov.uk/PublicationsAndStatistics/Legislation/ActsAndBills**.

We will consider the workings of the Data Protection Act 1998 in the context of information sharing in the final section of this chapter.

The Freedom of Information Act 2000

The Data Protection Act 1998 gives individuals the right to access information about themselves. The Freedom of Information Act 2000 extends this right to include non-personal information.

The Freedom of Information Act 2000 provides statutory rights for those requesting information. Under the Act any member of the public will be able to apply for access to information held by a wide range of public authorities, including local authorities. The exemptions from the Act are, first, those which apply to a whole category of information, for example, information relating to investigations and proceedings conducted by public authorities, court records, and trade secrets. Information covered by these category-based exemptions is always exempt. Second, are those exemptions which are subject to a prejudice test, for example, where disclosure would or would be likely to prejudice the interests of the UK abroad or the prevention or detection of crime. Information becomes exempt only if disclosing it would or would be likely to prejudice the activity or interest described in the exemption. However, even where an exemption covers the information, the public authority will, in the majority of cases, have to consider whether the information must be released anyway in the public interest. To answer this the public authority will have to consider the circumstances of each particular case and the exemption which covers the information.

Schemes for the publication of information

The Act imposes a duty on public authorities to adopt schemes for the publication of information which must be approved by the Information Commissioner. Whilst the Act does not come fully into force until November 2005 local authorities should already be planning their publication schemes.

The Information Commissioner

The Information Commissioner and an Information Tribunal oversee and enforce both the Freedom of Information Act 2000 and the Data Protection Act 1998. Each statute is concerned with responsible handling of personal information and therefore having one office overseeing the implementation of the legislation should ensure the coherent development of the law.

The web site of the Information Commissioner, **www.informationcommissioner. gov.uk**, contains a range of user friendly and useful explanations of information legislation.

Information governance

The law relating to confidential information illustrates the difficult and conflicting demands upon professionals striving to carry out their responsibilities. In the context of health services the Caldicott review of personally identifiable information in 1997 recommended that 'guardians' of personal information be created to safeguard and govern the uses made of confidential information within NHS organizations. The review advocated a managerial approach, based upon a framework of quality standards for the management of confidentiality and access to personal information.

The Caldicott approach has been extended by the Government to councils with social services responsibilities who were required to appoint a Caldicott guardian by 1 April 2002. Full details are set out in LAC (2002)2. It is anticipated that this new framework will bring together all the requirements, limits, and best practice that apply to the processing of confidential personally identifiable information. Caldicott guardians have been set tasks of auditing exiting systems, procedures, and organisational capabilities relating to confidentiality and security. The eighteen audit areas require consideration of a range of prerequisites for responsible information handling, for example examining the level of information provided to service users about the proposed uses of information, the extent of confidentiality requirements in staff contracts, the extent of information-sharing protocols, and the extent of confidentiality and security training. The results of audits should inform subsequent performance reviews of social services departments. Whilst there is a great deal of value in the approach, it reflects its origins in the context of health care as it does not indicate how the greater policing responsibilities of social services should be incorporated into the framework.

Data sharing—a summary

Both the Laming Inquiry and the Bichard Inquiry made clear the importance of information sharing for the protection of vulnerable individuals. They also made clear that the potential for misunderstandings about the law can stand in the way of effective yet lawful use of information. You are very likely to be involved in data sharing; perhaps you will receive a request for confidential data you hold, or perhaps you will be involved in a data sharing partnership. This section of the chapter attempts to bring together in summary form the complex and overlapping legal issues to indicate what questions need to be answered before data can be shared. We have relied on the guidance from the Department of Constitutional Affairs in drawing up this summary.

Legal Authority

The first question to be considered is whether the body which holds the data has the legal power to do so. If it has, then what are the constraints on that legal power? Does the enabling statute contain a provision preventing the sharing of information in particular circumstances? You may need to ask your lawyers for clarity on these issues.

Human Rights Act issues

Is Article 8 of the ECHR engaged? You must ask whether the proposed data collection and sharing will interfere with the right to respect for private and family life and the home. If the data collection and sharing exercise is carried out with the consent of the people who provide the data then Article 8 is not engaged.

If Article 8 is engaged, then is the interference:

- In accordance with the law?

- In pursuit of a legitimate aim?
- Necessary in a democratic society?

Common law of confidentiality

There are two critical questions here. Is the information confidential? In answering this you have to consider whether its nature, whether there is an obligation of confidence and whether there has been an unauthorized use of the material. If it is confidential then is there an overriding public interest that justifies its disclosure. Here the law overlaps with Article 8.

Data Protection Act issues

First you have to consider whether the Data Protection Act applies. Is the information personal data held on computer or as part of a 'relevant filing system'?

Second, can the information be used in compliance with Data Protection Principle One which required 'fairness'? Third, is the additional use that the local authority wishes to make of the information in compliance with the Second Data Protection Principle? That will depend upon the specified use of the data when they were obtained. If the use of the data by the other department is not compatible with that purpose or purposes then they cannot be transferred. Fourth can one of the conditions in Schedule 2 be satisfied? Additionally if the data are sensitive personal data can one of the conditions in Schedule 3 also be satisfied. Finally do any of the exemptions that are set out in the Data Protection Act apply?

EXERCISES

A. Why is confidentiality important? When do you think confidentiality should be breached? Does your thinking accord with the legal position? The ethical postion? Are there ever circumstances when your ethical obligation is to breach a confidence?

B. In the following circumstances what issues are raised about human rights, your professional responsibilities, and confidentiality? How would you suggest they should be resolved? Do not forget to consider the Human Rights Act 1998 and the Data Protection Act 1998 in preparing your response.

1 The Housing Department of a local authority asks the Social Services Department for any information it has about anti-social behaviour by a particular family.

2 An anonymous caller rings social services because she has seen evidence of physical abuse of a child. The local authority asks the family's health visitor for information.

3 You, a child-care professional, tell the head teacher of a secondary school about your concerns for a particular child. The head teacher tells the child's form teacher.

4 You suspect Mr X of sexual abuse of his grandchildren. Mr X has found himself accommodation with a housing association which is housing him in a block of flats which also accommodates families. You want to tell the housing association of your concerns.

5 When you were visiting a family you overheard a telephone conversation which indicated that one of the adult children of the family was involved in criminal activities. You want to tell the police but your team leader says that the issue is not serious enough.

C. You have serious concerns about Fred who you suspect of having physically and emotionally abused his two sons aged 12 and 14. You have recorded these concerns on both of the children's files. Fred has asked to see his file. He has signed consents from his sons. What are his rights to do so? What information will he be allowed to see?

COMPANION WEB SITE

For guidance on how to answer these exercises, visit the companion web site at: www.oup.com/uk/booksites/law

WHERE DO WE GO FROM HERE?

Our overview of the common law duty of confidentiality and its interface with the Human Rights Act and information legislation illustrates the complexity of the area. Clearly a balance needs to be reached between the necessity to protect children and other vulnerable people and the right to privacy. In our view the law is moving towards greater sharing of information, provided the decision to share is one that is proportionate and necessary. On the other hand, we also see that public opinion is strongly in favour of privacy and resists state intrusion. It is this tension which causes legal uncertainty. We can understand and sympathize with the confusion and bewilderment the law creates for many social care professionals who are at the coal face of this dilemma. The law does not necessarily make your decision making any easier—but it should help clarify the issues you must consider. This chapter is the final chapter in Part 1 of the book. Part 2 moves on to discuss a critical aspect of your professional life—working with the courts.

ANNOTATED FURTHER READING

Confidentiality

H. Brayne and H. Carr, 'Confidentiality, Secrecy and Children's Rights Part 1', (2002) 15(3) *Representing Children* 152.

H. Brayne and H. Carr, 'Confidentiality, Secrecy and Children's Rights Part 2', (2002) 15(4) *Representing Children* 241.

'Privacy and data-sharing: The way forward for public services', published by the Performance and Innovation Unit. The report looks at the issues of privacy and data-sharing in delivering public services, and charts the way forward. **http://www.number-10.gov.uk/su/privacy/annex-a.htm**.

Information sharing

C. Cobley '"*Working Together?*" – *Admissions of Abuse in Child Protection Proceedings and Criminal Prosecutions*' 2004 CFLQ.

This article considers the way in which information is exchanged between the child protection and criminal justice systems. It suggests that tensions between the two systems increase as cases progress.

PART II

Using the legal system

5 **Law and the practice of social work**

6 **Evidence and reports**

7 **Evidence from children**

PART II Using the legal system

Part I laid out the framework of law that determines your responsibilities as a social worker, and the pervasive principles which affect your practice. In Part II, we want to equip you with practical tools for making use of the law, particularly making use of the legal system and court powers.

Chapter 5 explains the legal system and the legal tools that you need in order to navigate the cases, the statutes and the courts. It goes beyond the more traditional account of the legal system as it introduces you to administrative and regulatory mechanisms that exist to control the quality of decision making by the state.

Both agency and court decisions require relevant and reliable information to be kept and presented. To do this you have to understand the rules of evidence, the requirements of writing reports, and the general principles of managing information. **Chapter 6** looks at presenting evidence to the court. How does a court decide what evidence should be taken into account? How do you prepare and present a case so that your evidence will be accepted and persuasive? What do terms like hearsay mean? As well as addressing these questions, the chapter goes on to discuss documentary records and formal reports.

Chapter 7 focuses on the vulnerable witness. How can the evidence of a vulnerable witness—in particular a child victim in a criminal abuse allegation—be preserved and presented in court in a way which does not traumatize them?

Law and the practice of social work

F v Lambeth LBC Also known as F (children: Care Planning), Re (Fam Div) [2002] 1 FLR 217

Facts

J was born in 1984 and his brother K was born in 1988. J's name was put on the child protection register in 1986. In 1989 wardship proceedings were commenced on both brothers. Interim care orders were made in respect of both boys in 1991. The boys were then placed in a children's home. This was an emergency placement, but in the event the boys remained there for four years. Care orders were made in 1992 with leave to implement a rehabilitation of the boys to their parents. In 1993 Lambeth decided not to proceed with the rehabilitation. In 1994 the parents applied to discharge the care orders, but in a report of the child psychiatrist involved in the case since 1991 reported that the boys needed the security of permanent care by substitute parents. Following that report unsupervised contact with the parents was reduced to four times per year. This was later changed to supervised contact at the children's home. From 1995 onwards Lambeth took no further steps to find the boys a family home or implement changes to safeguard or promote their development. In 1996 the boys were removed to another children's home where they have remained. In 1999 the parents applied for unsupervised contact away from the home.

The boys suffer from a variety of difficulties. Both boys are statemented (i.e. entitled to special needs education). J will require life long support. K may or may not be able to function in adult life without support. The consultant psychiatrist who gave evidence on behalf of the Official Solicitor who acted for the boys described them both in her oral evidence as being extremely anxious boys with no secure attachment or emotional commitment to anyone. The parents have problems of their own and there is no prospect of them being able to care for the boys whilst they remain in care, and each of the boys will remain in care until he is 18.

The application before the court was for unsupervised contact. The parents contended that Lambeth had breached its obligations under the Children Act 1989, s. 22(3)(a), and its duty as a public authority under the Human Rights Act 1998 and Article 8 of the European Convention not to act in a manner which is incompatible with the family's right to a family life.

The decision

The parents' application was allowed. Interim contact was ordered five times per year including activities to take place outside the children's home. The judge also held that L had not done anything for the children and the children had drifted in care. The state had failed the parents and the children, gravely and repeatedly, and had itself caused significant harm to children who had been taken into care against the wishes of the parents. Lambeth was in breach of its duties under ss. 22 (3) and 34 of the 1989 Act in a way that meant it had failed to carry out its duties under Article 8. Similarly it had breached the Local Authority Social Services Act 1970, s. 7(1), by its failure to follow the relevant guidance. On the facts there had been no effective planning by Lambeth and it would be required to lodge a care plan with the court detailing the children's future treatment.

The courts also stated that ultimately the only safeguard and guarantee for the proper performance of their functions by public authorities was public awareness and the force of informed public opinion and an informed electorate. The public needed to be told what had been done to this family.

Discussion

This case illustrates the problems which arise when the legal responsibilities that a social services department has to children it takes into its care are not discharged. We will discuss the importance of appropriate case planning later in the book, in chapter 11. Here we are using the case to alert you to the importance of the law to the practice of social work. The judge refers to breaches of duties under the Children Act 1989 and failure to follow guidance under the Local Authority Social Services Act 1970. We will talk about the meaning of duties and guidance later in this chapter. The end result is that the local authority's duties to individuals under Article 8 of the European Convention have been breached. This case is not just about poor social work, it is about social work practice which fails to achieve the minimum standard set by the law. The judge also talks about the necessity of public accountability. It is important that the courts make public decisions about social work practice. This provides a safeguard for individuals and a guarantee of basic standards.

OVERVIEW AND OBJECTIVES

What this chapter is about is decision making within the law. As a practising social worker you are working within the legal framework. To work successfully within that framework you will need to know the rules that govern it and the institutions that police it. You need to be familiar with the tools of the law, statutes, secondary legislation, and cases. You need to know enough about the law to ensure that your decisions are lawful. When decisions are particularly complex you need to know that you should consult lawyers to help you make those decisions. The case also provides an excellent illustration of the fact that failing to take action is every bit as dangerous as taking incorrect action. By the end of the chapter you should also have some understanding of how the law provides public accountability for decisions, whether through court cases, inquiries, or complaints.

This chapter is important although it is largely descriptive and a bit fragmented. It will be a chapter that you will refer to as you are reading later chapters that deal with the detail of the law relating to social work practice. When you are reading this chapter think about what you need to do to feel comfortable with using the law. This book is designed to make the law familiar to you. We use extracts from statutes and case studies to illustrate our points. You must go beyond this and read statutes and cases, visit courts and talk to lawyers about the operation of the law. If you do this your social work skills together with your knowledge of the law will enable you to make legally robust decisions. This chapter should also give you sufficient information about finding the relevant cases and statutes and how to approach them with confidence. Box 5.1 explains the structure of the chapter and highlights the elements of lawful decision making.

BOX 5.1 The legal framework for decision making

Aspects of decision making	Legal tools
Overarching principles of lawful decisions	The rule of law
Making choices and exercising discretion	Administrative law
Amplification of the meaning of statutes	Secondary legislation and guidance
Illustrations of the statutes and areas not covered by statutes	Reported cases
Dispute resolution and formal recognition of decisions	Courts and other judicial hearings
Other methods of accountability for decision making	Inquiries including complaints, maladministration inspection

Some overarching principles

The rule of law

The rule of law means that no matter how much any individual may dislike a law, whilst he or she remains a member of this particular society, they are required to obey the law. The rule of law in a democracy means that we are ruled by politicians in Parliament who can pass whatever laws they see fit, and the citizens have to obey those laws. If a director of children's services (a post created by statute: see below) wishes to provide particular services for children in need then he or she refers to the Children Act 1989—a statute. In that Act he or she finds the rules on which any recommendation can be made to the Social Services Committee (another statutory creation). Suppose that those in political control of the local authority say that they are opposed to providing additional services for children in need—can the director ignore the criteria set out in the statute? Not according to the concept of the rule of law.

The rule of law also means that the courts' function is to interpret the will of Parliament expressed in statute and not to make it up for themselves, unless there is a 'gap' in the statute.

European influences

Parliament has to a certain extent constrained its actions via the Human Rights Act 1998. It has even more fundamentally constrained itself under the European Communities Act 1972 although this has less significance for your practice as a social worker.

In passing the 1998 Act, Parliament has decided that in general it will be bound by the terms of the European Convention on Human Rights. However, it retains discretion whether or not each statute that it enacts will be compatible with the Convention. From 2 October 2000, each statute must contain a statement of compatibility or non-compatibility. Clearly, if the Government states that it does not intend a statute to be compatible, it must explain why and receive Parliament's consent. The 1998 Act also contains a new rule of statutory interpretation which we explain below.

The distinction between private and public law

There is an important distinction to be drawn between public and private law. Public law cases are cases brought by public authorities, such as the social services departments of local authorities. Private law cases are cases brought by private individuals.

For example, care proceedings are an area of public law. Public law proceedings, because they involve public authorities interfering with the way individuals live their lives, are required to conform to certain standards. Those standards are achieved through the operation of the law. The particular area of the law which performs this function is administrative law which we will discuss below.

In contrast, an example of private law would be a dispute between a car owner and a garage over the quality of a repair to the car. If the owner refuses to pay the bill because of dissatisfaction with the quality of the repair, the garage may sue the car owner in the county court. How the dispute is to be resolved by the court is set out in the law of contract and the rules of court. The outcome of the case, though, is not of interest to society as a whole, only to the parties to the dispute.

Sometimes both public law and private law proceedings will arise from a particular situation which has reached the courts. For example divorce proceedings are private law. As you will find out in chapter 15, under the provisions of the Children Act 1989 there are powers during divorce proceedings to require the local authority to carry out an investigation, if the court is concerned about the welfare of the children. One outcome of this investigation can be the local authority commencing care proceedings, which as stated above, are public law.

Administrative law

The state is very powerful and well resourced in comparison with an individual. Administrative law attempts to ensure that justice is done between the state and the individual by embracing particular principles which operate to restrain arbitrary or wrong decision making by the state. These principles are openness (often described as transparency by lawyers and public administrators), fairness, rationality (including giving reasons for decisions), impartiality (which means that decision takers should be independent), accountability, the control of discretion, consistency, participation, efficiency, equity, and equal treatment. These principles can be collectively described as the requirements necessary for fairness, and are often referred to as the requirements of 'natural justice'. Sometimes these principles conflict, and then the decision maker must weigh up the various principles and make the best decision he or she can in the circumstances. Your understanding of professional ethics may help you at this point.

'Natural justice'

Natural justice means that whatever the law is, citizens are entitled to have the law applied fairly, in accordance with common law, and the courts will uphold that right. The mechanism available for people who believe that they have not been treated fairly by the state is to apply for judicial review. Judicial review is the process by which the courts oversee decisions made by public officials and ensure that they have been made fairly. You will come across several cases of judicial review in the case studies we use at the beginning of each chapter.

In general judges will not substitute their decision for the public official's decision. What they will consider is the process of decision-making. We can see what this means in practice by going back to our example of the director of children's services: if he or she were personally to take a dislike to the parents of the child who was seeking services, then he or she might decide merely to recommend to the Social Services Committee that the child should not receive services. In those circumstances the child could seek a judicial review of the decision by stating that natural justice had been infringed since the law was not fairly applied. Facts which were relevant to the decision had not been considered. Facts which were not relevant were considered. The court could make such a ruling, even though according to the Children Act 1989 the Social Services Committee has a discretion and may refuse to provide a particular service to a child in need. For the doctrine of natural justice means that the decision must be arrived at through the correct procedures. The courts would then have the power to overturn the 'decision' of the Social Services Committee or to tell the Social Services Committee to make a fresh decision, this time properly.

The 'Wednesbury principles'

The principles of natural justice are often described by lawyers as the *Wednesbury* principles since they were clearly stated by the judges sitting in a case called *Associated Provincial Picture Houses v Wednesbury Corporation* (1947). By way of information, the actual case concerned the question whether or not cinemas should be allowed to open on Sundays in the town of Wednesbury. The cinema lost. You may also hear lawyers describe decisions as *Wednesbury* reasonable. This is referring to the same principles from the same case.

Proportionality

Decisions made by public authorities are, as you know following the discussion in chapter 2, constrained by the Human Rights Act. One particular requirement imposed by the Act is the need for decisions to be proportionate to the outcome which is sought. So, for instance, in *Re C and B (Children) (Care Order: Future Harm)* (2000), the Court of Appeal allowed a mother's appeal against the making of a care order in respect of two of her three children with a view to placement for adoption. The Court accepted that there were reasons for concern, and that there was evidence on which the judge was entitled to conclude that there was a real possibility of future harm. However, there was no evidence of actual harm to the younger children, or that they were at immediate risk. Intervention, which inevitably impacts on the right to respect for family life, had to be proportionate to the degree of risk, and a care order was not justified.

What does this mean for a social worker making a decision?

These principles are not remote from you, the social worker. When you make a decision about a family or a vulnerable person, if your decision is to be lawful then it must follow these overarching principles. Therefore, you will pay heed to the Human Rights Act 1998 and ensure that where your decision impacts upon a European Convention right (as many of your decisions will) that you have acted in a proportionate way. You will ensure that you have followed the requirements of natural justice, you will have found out all the information that is relevant, you will have considered the relevant information carefully, and excluded from your considerations irrelevant matters. You will ensure that evidence which goes against the interests of, for example, the parents of the child about whom you are making a decision, has been put to the parents, and they have had an opportunity to consider it and respond. You will carefully document your decision-making process, so that if there is a dispute in the future you can demonstrate that your decision making was within the bounds of the law.

Do not be misled about decisions always being about action and intervention. If you do nothing about a case, that is also a decision and should be made as carefully and as thoughtfully as a decision to act. The case study at the beginning of this chapter demonstrates the problems which arise when social workers do not understand that principle.

If you think that this all sounds extremely intimidating, you are right. It is. You have enormous responsibilities when you, a representative of the state, intervene in people's lives. However, the law provides you with a range of tools to enable you to fulfil your responsibilities. Understanding the principles of administrative law and human rights is a very good place to start. Also you will be considerably helped in your task if you allow your decisions to be informed by legislation, guidance and case law. We have set out the bases of lawful decision making in Box 5.2.

■ Statute law

The difference between the common law and statute law

Social workers have 'statutory powers'—what does this mean? It means that their powers and their authority derive from statute. There is a distinct difference between statutory law and common law. Common law can be regarded for our purposes as established, traditional law as defined by the courts and developed from precedents. Statute law is that law that has been passed by Parliament. This is not to say that the

BOX 5.2 Lawful decision making by social workers

Bases of lawful decision making	Why?
Full factual information which has been disclosed and discussed with the parties to the case	In accordance with the principles of natural justice and Article 6.
Full legal information	You are bound by the rule of law. You can only do what the law permits you to do. We discuss this fully below.
Proportionate	Required by the Human Rights Act.
Reasonable and fair	In accordance with the principles of natural justice and the Human Rights Act.
Fully documented	You are accountable for your decisions and you must be able to explain how you reached them.
Decisions must be made without undue delay	Failure to reach timely decisions is prejudicial to those whose interests you should be protecting—and can itself be a breach of the Human Rights Act.

courts do not have a role in statute law. Courts, as you will see later, have a vital role in interpreting the meaning of statutes in particular factual situations and in managing the practice of litigation.

As society becomes more complicated the role of common law diminishes, since more and more statutes are passed dealing with more and more areas of behaviour within society. But common law is not wholly extinct: murder is not a statutory offence, it is a common law offence. This means that you cannot look in an Act of Parliament for a definition of murder, rather you have to look at decisions of courts in the past as to what defines murder. However, the penalty that must be imposed for murder is set out in a statute. There are many other examples where common law provides the legal framework. The law on confidentiality is one we have already discussed.

Procedural law

Court rules and Practice Directions are judge-made law which govern the day-to-day practice of litigation. These rules which are drafted by the Rules Committee are essential to the implementation of legislation. The Rules Committee is a committee of judges with legislative authority.

Statutes

Statutes—Acts of Parliament—start life as Bills. These may be bills sponsored by Government ministers, or private members' bills. Private members' bills are, as the name suggests, bills sponsored by ordinary backbench Members of Parliament. Most bills are Government bills, but within the field of social care there have been some very significant Acts which started life as private members' bills, for instance the Homeless Persons Act 1977 and the Disabled Persons (Services, Consultation and Representation) Act 1986.

Often the subject matter of a bill is discussed extensively before it gets to Parliament. Sometimes the government may publish a Green Paper which will set out a number of proposals to change the law and ask for comments. Green Papers got their name because in the past they were published with green covers. Following this consultation process the government may set out its revised policy objectives in a White Paper. White Papers were originally published with white covers. A relatively recent innovation is the draft bill procedure whereby the government publishes a bill in draft form, before it is introduced in Parliament as a formal bill. This enables consultation and pre-legislative scrutiny before it is issued formally. The Mental Capacity Bill 2005 is an example of a piece of legislation which was originally published as a draft bill and was extensively debated prior to its introduction to parliament.

The formal parliamentary process starts when a bill is presented to Parliament, generally by the minister responsible for it. There are a series of readings, scrutiny, and debates on the bill. Eventually the bill reaches its final form—the Act of Parliament. Even when the Act receives the Royal Assent there is often a long delay before particular sections are brought into effect. If you would like to learn more about the legislative process the parliament web site on **www.parliament.uk** contains a great deal of useful and user friendly information.

Delegated legislation

One of the growth areas of modern life is that of legislation. No matter how long Parliament sits, it still will not be able to pass sufficient legislation in the detail that the running of a sophisticated democracy requires.

Therefore, in most Acts of Parliament there will be found a power for delegated legislation. Delegated legislation, as its name implies, gives the power to some person or body to pass legislation that has the same effect as if it had been passed by Parliament through its normal process of legislation. For the delegated legislation to come into force, normally it must be 'laid before Parliament'. This requires a copy of the proposed delegated legislation to be placed (or laid) in the House of Commons and the House of Lords for a specified number of days. After that the legislation comes into force. It may require a vote without a debate, or the alternative form is where it comes into effect by 'negative resolution'. This means that it will come into force unless sufficient members of Parliament put their names down so as to require a vote to be taken.

Delegated legislation is also known as secondary legislation, or statutory instruments. Statutory instruments come in two forms: Regulations and Orders. It is not important to distinguish between these.

Devolution

This book attempts to cover the law in England and Wales. Doing so has become more complex since the establishment of the National Assembly for Wales. The National Assembly for Wales was set up in May 1999 with powers and functions determined by the Government of Wales Act 1998. This Act gives the Assembly the power to make delegated legislation relating to Wales, to make decisions concerning the budget in Wales, implement European law in Wales, and make recommendations to the UK Parliament in Westminster about primary legislation that affects Wales.

The Assembly can make delegated legislation only on areas devolved to it. There are several areas of importance to social work practice which have been devolved. These include

- Education and training;
- Health and health services;
- Housing;
- Local government; and
- Social services.

The Assembly can make delegated legislation in these particular areas when powers have been given to it by an Act of Parliament. Further details of the powers given to the Assembly by various Acts of Parliament can be found on the Wales legislation online web site.

Inevitably the National Assembly for Wales will have different priorities from the UK Parliament and be interested in different solutions to problems. There will be interesting opportunities to see how different projects proceed and to develop best practice. A useful web site for further information about the impact of devolution on children's services is that run by 4 Nations Child Policy Network. The web site provides up-to-date information on policy issues relating to children and young people in each of the four nations of the United Kingdom (England, Scotland, Northern Ireland, and Wales). It can be found at **www.childpolicy.org.uk**. Box 5.3 provides a summary of the sources of law.

Statutes and secondary legislation as social work tools

Finding statutes

If you are going to know the legal basis upon which your decisions must be based you need to read the appropriate statutory provisions. Statutes are in law libraries and on the Internet. However, it is important that you read the fully amended up-to-date version of the statute. This is not easy without the resources of a full law library or access to a commercially provided database. Our best advice is for you to talk to your legal department to find out what resources it has available for you to use. If you can get access to

BOX 5.3 Summary and commentary on the sources of law

Law	Sources	Comment
Common law	The courts	The advantage of flexibility and expertise but uncertain and lacks the democratic authority of Parliament.
Procedural law	The Rule Committee (the judiciary) and in statute for instance the Supreme Courts Act 1981.	Often overlooked, but critical to the effective implementation of the law.
Statutes	UK Parliament	Democratic authority but slow to enact and the Government may be reluctant to legislate on controversial matters. The Courts have a role in interpreting statutes.
Secondary legislation	UK Parliament and National Assembly for Wales where powers have been given by an Act of Parliament.	Contains the critical detail of legislation. Can be changed relatively easily, but is not extensively scrutinized by Parliament.
Guidance	Parliament	Not binding, but authoritative.

the *Current Law Statute Citator* published by Sweet & Maxwell you will be able to find out which sections of a particular statute are in force. Note that Acts on the HMSO web site are not updated as they are amended.

Reading statutes

Once you find the statute then you must read it. We think it is very important that you feel confident enough to read some statutory materials for yourself and not rely on lawyers to do that for you. This book aims to provide you with a great deal of support in doing just that. If you find a particular word or phrase difficult, then ask your lawyer what he or she thinks it means. The chances are that it is genuinely a difficult word which could be interpreted in several different ways. Your opinion may be correct, or the lawyer's opinion. However, we do not know what a contested word means in law until it has been interpreted by the courts. The courts use a variety of techniques to enable them to interpret statutes in a rational, objective manner. These are the rules of statutory interpretation. Before we go on to discuss these, it may be useful to you to have some general guidance on reading a statute.

The Adoption and Children Act 2002

Let us consider the recent Adoption and Children Act 2002. The date 2002 is the year that the Act received royal assent. It is not necessarily the year when the statute comes into force. Many statutes contain complex provisions which need to be prepared for. The delegated legislation is published after the Act. The Rules Committee needs to consider what the practice requirements of the legislation are. So the commencement date is likely to be later. In the case of a complex piece of legislation like the Adoption and Children Act different parts of the Act will have different commencement dates. At the time of writing we do not know the commencement dates for this Act. Later in this chapter we will tell you how to check the commencement date of a particular statutory provision.

The front cover of the statute has the Royal Coat of Arms, the name of the statute and the words Chapter 38. What this refers to is that it is the 38th statute of this parliamentary session. You can ignore the chapter number in reality. There is also a note to say that explanatory notes have been produced to assist in the understanding of this Act and are available separately. This is a recent innovation. If an Act is one which you will frequently use, the explanatory notes provide a really useful source of information about its provisions. You will see that we refer to the explanatory notes extensively in our chapter on adoption.

The contents of the statute

Turning the page you will see the contents of the statute. You will see that this particular Act is divided into three Parts and then each Part has a number of chapters. Part 1, adoption, is the largest part. It has seven chapters. Each chapter is subdivided. Chapter 2 is subdivided into sections on the adoption service, regulations, and supplemental provisions. In each of the subdivisions there are numbers. These relate to the section numbers of the Act. The contents page therefore provides you with a very useful navigation tool for the whole of the statute. If you are looking to find out how adoption orders are to be made under the new legislation you can very quickly find out which are the relevant sections. A subdivision of Chapter 3 of Part 1 is headed 'the making of adoption orders', and we can see that the relevant section numbers are ss. 46–51.

Sections and subsections

If we look at one of those sections, say s. 49, we can see the typical layout for a section of an Act. The section has a heading, in this case 'Applications for adoption'. It is then divided into subsections which are numbered in brackets. If you want to refer to a particular subsection then you would say s. 49 subsection (1). If you are referring to this subsection in writing you would write s. 49(1).

Schedules

Not everything is contained in the body of the statute. Most Acts have schedules attached which contain further material, usually of a more detailed kind. The Adoption and Children Act 2002 has six schedules. They are listed beneath the contents of the Act. Schedules are set out slightly differently from the main body of the Act. If you turn to Schedule 1 you will see its title, 'Registration of Adoptions'. In small script to the right of the title there is a section number, s. 77(6). This is the section in the Act which gives effect to the Schedule. The Schedule is then set out in paragraphs and subparagraphs. If you wish to refer to a paragraph within a Schedule then you refer to it as paragraph 1(2) of Schedule 1 to the Act. We say 'to' the Act rather than 'of' the Act because the Schedule is attached to the Act.

Amendments

Frequently statutes contain provisions which amend the provisions of earlier statutes. The Adoption and Children Act 2002 is no exception. So for instance s. 113 of the Act provides:

> In section 9 of the 1989 Act (restrictions on making section 8 orders)—
>   (a) in subsection (3)(c), for 'three years' there is substituted 'one year', and
>   (b) subsection (4) is omitted.

What this means is that from the commencement date of this provision of the 2002 Act, that particular section of the Children Act 1989 has to be read in the new way.

Acts can do more than amend particular sections. They can introduce whole new sections into other Acts. In the Adoption and Children Act 2002 new provisions are introduced to the Children Act 1989 to provide for special guardianship. The new sections are introduced by s. 115 of the Adoption and Children Act but they will become ss. 14A–14G of the Children Act 1989. You will always recognize sections of legislation which have been introduced by subsequent legislation because of the use of the capital letter.

Reading statutes—statutory interpretation

Having been through all the procedures and amplification outlined above, you would have thought that the law would be perfectly clear. However, it is not as straightforward as that. There will always be disputes as to what is the particular meaning of a statute, or indeed what is the meaning of a particular word within a statute. It is the function of courts to interpret statutes. This process is called statutory interpretation.

Statutory interpretation has evolved over centuries. When courts have had to decide what a statute says, there has developed a series of so-called 'rules' that guide the courts. Their effect is to set out the approach that should be adopted by the courts. There are three main 'rules': first, the 'literal rule', which says that the words in a statute are taken to have their literal meaning unless such an interpretation produces a nonsensical result. In that case the 'golden rule' applies, which says that if the literal meaning produces an absurd result then you look at it in the overall context of the statute. If these two 'rules' do not help then the 'mischief rule' is applied. This rule states that you interpret the meaning of the word in the light of what the problem or mischief was that the statute was passed to deal with.

An example of the application of statutory interpretation will be in relation to the meaning of the word 'significant' in the Children Act 1989, s. 31. As you will see in chapter 12, the word occurs in the definition of the grounds on which a court may make a care order in respect of a child. No definition of the word is given in the Act and views differ on the word's meaning within the section. We said in earlier editions that soon after the section came into effect we had no doubt that there would be an appeal case that would seek a definition of the word. This proved to be true. If you look at chapter 12, you will see there has been a number of cases on this very point. In trying to define 'significant' the courts have applied the rules of statutory interpretation. Having done that, the lower courts will now be bound to follow the High Court's and Appeal Court's interpretation in all future cases. The meaning of the statute is considered in the light of the unique facts of each case, and the court will always have the chance of saying 'but this case is different'.

The Human Rights Act 1998 has an impact on statutory interpretation, in that it provides that courts must strive to interpret legislation in a way which is compatible with Convention rights and the intention of Parliament (see chapter 2). Where it is not possible to interpret the legislation in this way, the courts may strike down delegated legislation but not primary legislation (although they may make a declaration of incompatibility, which should prompt Government action).

Reading statutes—powers and duties

Something else that you must notice when you read statutes is whether the statute provides you with a duty to act or a power to act. The distinction is relatively straightforward. Where a statute imposes a duty on a person or a body then they have to carry out that duty. There is no choice, however hard the carrying out of the duty may be. Lack of finance, for instance, is not an acceptable reason for not carrying out the duty. Where a statute gives a person or a body a power to do some act, the person or the body may exercise that power but they are not obliged to do so.

The distinction is important for a number of reasons. First, it sets your priorities as a social worker. If Parliament has considered that carrying out a particular action is so significant that it should be a duty upon a social services department then it is a course of action which must be given priority. Second, it is significant when a person is disgruntled by the behaviour of a statutory person or body. If there is a duty then in general the disgruntled person will be able to take court action to enforce that duty. If there is only a power, then it is unlikely that there will be any legal redress—although, if the person can show that the way in which the power was exercised was unreasonable, that could be challenged by a judicial review.

However, it is important to read the scope of the duty in the statute carefully. The law has distinguished between general or target duties which are expressed in broad terms, leaving the public authority with a wide measure of latitude over the steps to be taken to perform the duty owed to the relevant section of the public and personal or particular duties which are specific and precise and which are owed to each individual member of a relevant section of the public. Target duties must be performed, notwithstanding their general nature, they must be discharged in accordance with the principles of public law and they can be enforced like powers through judicial review. However, the public authority has discretion in how it delivers services under the duty and individuals have no personal right of action. One particular general duty we will discuss in chapter 8 is s.17 of the Children Act 1989—the duty to children in need. Personal duties provide no discretion to the public authority and are actionable by the individual who can sue for breach of statutory duty.

Whatever you are doing as a social worker, you should be clear in your own mind whether you are acting under a personal duty, a general duty or a power, and regulate your actions accordingly.

Cases

When we want to know what the law is, we first read the statute. As we explained above, though, this is not always the whole solution. Often it is necessary for the courts to interpret what the words of the statute mean. If there is no statute we fall back on the common law. Whether we are concerned with statutory interpretation or the common law, to find out what the courts have decided we need to look at the law reports. As a good social worker you should spend some time reading law reports, even if only the summaries that accompany decisions.

Reading cases

Lawyers spend much of their academic training learning to read cases. We certainly do not want to condense the expertise that comes with practice into a couple of paragraphs. However we can give you some information which should make the task of reading cases less intimidating. Cases, like statutes, follow a standard format. We have tabulated the standard features of civil cases for you in Box 5.4.

Cases are referred to by their name and a reference to a law report. You may have noticed that when we have told you about a case we then provide with the name of the case and a reference. For instance our case study at the beginning of the chapter is *F v Lambeth LBC*, also known as *F (Children: Care Planning), Re (Fam Div)* (2002). If you want to find that case yourself you will need to follow these directions.

How to find a law report in the library

Step one	Find the meaning of the abbreviation for the law report.
Step two	Find the series of law reports on the library shelves.
Step three	Find the year, and the volume number within that year.
Step four	Find the page number on which the case begins.

[1996]	1	All ER	129
year	volume number	abbreviation	page number

BOX 5.4 The standard features of cases

Feature	Comment
The name of the case, e.g., *F v Lambeth LBC*	The name of the person bringing the case, whether claimant or appellant comes first, followed by the name of the defendant or respondent. The 'v' means versus i.e. against and is usually spoken as 'and'. In children's cases names are not disclosed to preserve anonymity, so cases are named with letters.
The court in which it was heard	The more senior the court the more influential the decision is likely to be.
The name of the judge or judges	Notice who the judges are; as you get more experienced in reading case law you will begin to notice that you agree with some judges' decisions more than you do with others. You will also notice that senior judges make the decisions on the more difficult and controversial areas.
The hearing date(s)	
The headnote	This provides a summary of the case. It sets out the material facts, it indicates the key legal questions to be considered by the court and it summarizes the court's decision.
A list of cases referred to	
Details of the appeal	This gives the legal history of the case setting out the previous hearings and the previous findings of the courts.
The name of counsel appearing in the case	
The judgment(s)	This is the most important aspect of the case. Each judge sitting is entitled to give his or her own opinion, although often the judges simply concur—agree—with each other. The most senior judge gives his or her opinion first and then the others give either supporting speeches or dissenting speeches. There is no set format to the judgment although it tends to be traditional and courteous in style. Nowadays each paragraph is numbered.

The law reports

Frequently used series of general law reports are:

> The Law Reports, currently issued in four series:
> > Appeal Cases (AC)
> > Chancery Division (Ch)
> > Queen's Bench (QB)
> > Family Division (Fam)
> The Weekly Law Reports (WLR)
> The All England Law Reports (abbreviated to All ER)
> Family Law Reports (FLR)

Summaries of recent cases can be found in *The Times* and the *Financial Times*, and in professional journals such as the *Solicitors Journal*, the *New Law Journal, Family Law*, and the *Law Society's Gazette*.

Note that some citations use round brackets instead of square brackets around the date of the report. Round brackets indicate that it is the volume number, and not the date of the report, which is essential if you are to locate it on the shelves. The use of round and square brackets can be summarized as:

> [xxxx] Date is essential. The volumes are arranged on the shelves by year, and the volume number is used only to distinguish between different volumes published in the same year, e.g. [1999] 1 FLR 40.

> (xxxx) Date is not essential, but volume number is essential, i.e. the arrangement on the shelves is by volume number, not by date, e.g. (1980) 70 Cr App R 193.

More and more cases are now being published on the World Wide Web. A citation system which is more suitable for publication on the web has been introduced for all Court of Appeal and High Court (Administrative Division) judgments decided since 11 January 2001 and all High Court decisions since 14 January 2002. The citation should appear in front of the familiar citations set out above. The citation is media neutral, as page numbers are irrelevant on the Web.

The three new forms of citation are as follows:

Court of Appeal (Civil Division)	[2001] EWCA Civ 1, 2, 3, etc.
Court of Appeal (Criminal Division)	[2001] EWCA Crim 1, 2, 3, etc.
Administrative Court	[2001] EWHC Admin 1, 2, 3, etc.

This system fits in with international practice and makes it easier to find cases electronically. Here is an example: *Re O (Supervision Order)* [2001] 1 FLR 923 is a Court of Appeal decision published in the Family Law Reports. It should now be cited as: *Re O (Supervision Order)* [2001] EWCA Civ 16; [2001] 1 FLR 923. The '16' means that it was the sixteenth case heard in the Court of Appeal Civil Division in 2001. 'EW' stands for England and Wales.

Legal electronic databases

Cases are available from legal electronic databases. Lawyers subscribe to services such as Lexis and Westlaw and can search for and find cases which are relevant to the area of law they are researching extremely quickly.

The Internet

Reports of decisions of the House of Lords are available on the Parliament web site (**www.publications.parliament.uk/pa/Id199697/Idjudgmt/idjudgmt.htm**) and the Court of Appeal and the High Court are now published by the court service web site (**www.courtservice.gov.uk/judgments.do**). Decisions are made available extremely quickly. They can be accessed free, the only cost to the end user is the cost of printing the decision.

◼ Dispute resolution

This part of the chapter describes the court system and tribunal system. It then goes on to discuss other mechanisms of dispute resolution and accountability.

The court system

When a dispute cannot be resolved by the people involved, the solution of our legal system is usually for the dispute to be decided by a judicial hearing. Sometimes there is a need to attend a judicial hearing even if there is total agreement between the persons involved; for example, if a couple agree to get divorced, then no matter how much they settle things by agreement they will never get a decree of divorce without a judicial hearing. At some time, every social worker is going to have to attend some form of judicial hearing.

We use the term 'judicial hearing' since it is somewhat wider than just 'court'. For example, apart from courts there are Mental Health Review Tribunals and others which a social worker may be required to attend. From now on, where we use the term 'court', it is intended to include these other forms of judicial hearings. This chapter considers only the particular structure of courts in England and Wales. (Those in Scotland and Northern Ireland have a different legal system.) So what we mean by the term 'court' in this particular chapter is 'courts and other judicial hearings in England and Wales'.

Criminal and civil courts

There are two main divisions of the courts:

(a) criminal; and

(b) civil.

Criminal courts are where the state prosecutes offences and courts impose penalties on those convicted. (In certain circumstances private individuals can take criminal proceedings themselves.) People can be convicted only where the evidence points to guilt 'beyond reasonable doubt'. The parties to proceedings are the prosecution and the defence.

Civil courts are where people can gain remedies for injustices 'proved on the balance of probabilities'. The remedies are normally financial, in the form of damages which compensate someone for loss, or restitutional, putting right the wrong complained of. The courts have a full range of orders available to them, including orders that someone should do or not do a particular act. The parties to proceedings are described in most cases as the claimant, the person or organization asking for a court order, and the defendant, the person who is resisting the order. Social workers are more likely to come across cases where the parties are described as applicant and respondent. There are three main categories of civil cases: family cases, administrative justice cases, and civil and commercial cases.

Frequently the same facts can give rise to both a criminal and a civil 'offence'. If a person driving hits another car then the person may have committed a criminal offence and also be liable to be sued in civil law for damages. The civil case (known as the 'claim') for damages would be totally separate, unconnected with the careless driving charge. A person may be successfully sued for damages arising out of a road accident, without there being any proceedings for driving offences, or vice versa. Because of the different burdens of proof it is also possible for a case to be unsuccessful in the criminal courts but give rise to successful proceedings in the civil courts.

The court structure

The diagram on page 147 gives an overall picture of the court system. Courts are arranged in a hierarchical structure. This means that a lower court must follow decisions of any court higher than itself in the judicial 'ladder' and that there is also a system of appeals against the decision of one court from one level to another. Cases begun in the lower courts can, normally, work their way up to the highest court, by way of appeal. We will return to the question of appeals at a later stage.

The criminal courts

This section looks at the two main criminal courts, namely:

(a) the magistrates' court; and

(b) the Crown Court.

(The youth court is part of the magistrates court and is dealt with in chapter 16.)

Social workers, in their official capacity, will appear in these courts only when presenting pre-sentence reports to assist the court in deciding upon appropriate punishment (unless the social worker is called as a witness to an alleged crime arising from their work, for example if he or she has been assaulted by a client or the client's carer, or is able to give evidence in prosecution for abuse of a child). Social workers may also accompany children to provide support in criminal trials: see chapter 16.

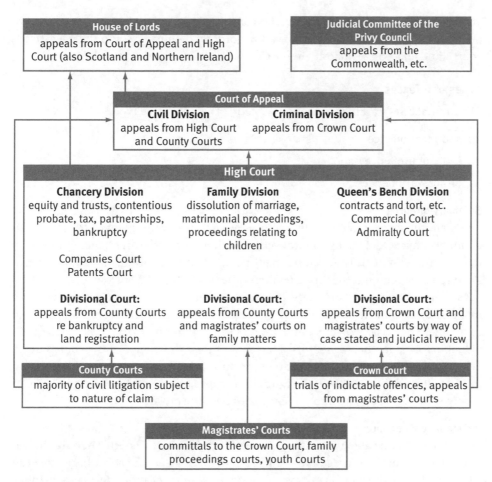

An outline of the court structure in England and Wales

Criminal proceedings in the magistrates' court

All criminal cases begin in the magistrates' court. The vast majority (95 per cent) start there and stay there. They stay there because either there are no powers for the cases to be transferred anywhere else or the person involved (the defendant) agrees to the case being dealt with by the magistrates. They are the backbone of the criminal system. Specially selected magistrates deal with juvenile crime in the youth courts. For all this, magistrates are not professionals; they rejoice in the fact that they are amateur, albeit with some training. Their function is to decide the facts of the cases on the evidence that is put before them. (You should see chapter 6 for fuller details on evidence.)

Magistrates also apply the relevant law to the case. They are not expected to know all the law. The person on whom this burden falls is the only professional lawyer employed by the magistrates' court, namely the court clerk. The clerk will advise the magistrates (collectively known as the 'bench') on points of law that arise during the course of any trial and again when the magistrates consider the appropriate form of sentence or penalty. We say 'any trial', since the vast majority of criminal cases in the magistrates' court—and, indeed the majority in the Crown Court—proceed on a guilty plea.

Types of offences

All criminal cases start in the magistrates' court. There are three types:

(a) summary offences;

(b) indictable offences; and

(c) either way offences.

Summary offences

These are the most common offence. Examples include common assault, less serious criminal damage, and taking a motor vehicle without consent (this offence is known by the acronym 'TWOC'). They can normally be dealt with only in the magistrates' court. Therefore, the court has the limited powers of sentence described below.

As you would expect, summary offences constitute the vast majority of criminal offences dealt with in our courts. They are generally regarded as commonplace and mundane. The social worker should always bear in mind that for the particular individual involved in 'their' case, this is the total of their experience of the court system. Whether it be the first and only time that person goes to court, or whether it is the latest in a long line of appearances, it is of great importance to them. It is too easy for all of us involved in the court system to become blase about the process.

Indictable only offences

These are cases that are 'just passing through' the magistrates' court. They are the serious offences, such as murder, rape, and arson that, for an adult (over 18), can be dealt with only by the Crown Court. A person accused of murder cannot decide to go to the local magistrates' court and get the case dealt with there.

Cases do not go straight to the Crown Court for historical and practical reasons. The practical reason is that where, for instance, a person is accused of murder, it requires a great deal of time for both the prosecution and the defence lawyers to prepare their cases before the trial can take place in the Crown Court. Meanwhile, the question of what is going to happen to the accused person has to be dealt with. The magistrates will decide whether the accused person should be remanded into custody or be granted bail (which would be rare in cases such as murder).

Usually, an indictable only offence is dealt with in the youth court if the accused is under 18—see chapter 16.

Either way offences

These are hybrid offences which, as the name implies, can be dealt with either by the magistrates' court or by the Crown Court before a judge and jury. An example of such an offence is theft. What may appear to be the theft of a small amount may be regarded by many as trivial, but for the defendant the consequences of being convicted of such an offence may be extremely serious. Therefore Parliament has decided, for the present, that the person accused of such an offence can insist on the case being tried before a judge and jury in the Crown Court.

However, if the magistrates consider the case to be not too serious, they can offer the defendant a 'summary' trial. This has the advantage of being dealt with more quickly and sometimes, if the person pleads guilty, on the spot.

If the magistrates or the defendant insist on Crown Court trial, the defence can require the magistrates consider the prosecution evidence to see whether there is a case to answer, before committing the case for trial at Crown Court.

Functions of magistrates' courts

The magistrates' court is divided into different parts. There is the division into the criminal and civil, but there is also the distinction in criminal proceedings between the adult and youth courts, which deal with juveniles under the age of 18. The criminal functions of the magistrates' court are exercised by both the adult and the youth court benches. For fuller details see chapter 16. The magistrates also have important family (civil) functions, which we will consider after looking at the Crown Court.

Magistrates' courts' powers of sentence

Magistrates have restricted powers in relation to the sentences that they can impose. We tend to associate the word 'sentence' with the idea of 'locking someone up'. Many of the offences dealt with by the magistrates' court carry no power of imprisonment, and the heaviest penalty then can only be a fine or perhaps a community rehabilitation order. Where the magistrates have the power to imprison a person the maximum length of the sentence will be governed by the statute. Even where an offence might carry a maximum penalty of several years' imprisonment if it were dealt with by the Crown Court, the magistrates are limited in the length of sentence they can impose. For any one offence committed by an adult they can impose a maximum of only six months' imprisonment, assuming the offence merits such a sentence. In addition, if a person has committed more than one offence, each of which is an either way offence and each of which could have a six-month sentence imposed for it, then the total maximum sentence the magistrates could impose is twelve months' imprisonment (i.e. two six-month sentences to run consecutively). If the magistrates think that their powers, in relation to either way offences only, are inadequate, then after conviction they can commit the person to the Crown Court for sentence. (The youth court does not have this power, although its maximum sentencing powers can be two years. If it thinks an offence particularly serious, i.e. murder or one that can carry a fourteen-year prison sentence for an adult, such as causing death by dangerous driving, or an indecent assault on a woman, the youth court may send the case to the Crown Court for trial—see chapter 16.)

■ Crown Court

The Crown Court is where serious criminal cases are heard before a judge and jury. Whereas the magistrates, in their court, are the deciders of both fact and law (after being advised on the law by their clerk), in the Crown Court there is a separation of these functions. The judge, being a professional lawyer (usually a barrister, but occasionally a solicitor), is the authority on the law. The jury, composed of randomly selected lay people, is the body which decides what the facts are, based on the evidence which they hear.

When sentencing an adult, the powers of sentence of the Crown Court are limited only by the lengths of sentence that are set out either in the statute governing the crime or by common law. The Court's powers on sentencing a person under 18 are more limited—see chapter 16. The Crown Court can impose a maximum penalty of life imprisonment and almost unlimited financial penalties for some offences. The Crown Court hears some criminal appeals from the magistrates' court.

The civil courts

This section will look at the following courts:

(a) magistrates' court;

(b) county court;

(c) High Court.

Civil functions cover such areas as:

(a) matrimonial cases;

(b) contact with children cases;

(c) child-care cases;

(d) contract cases;

(e) personal injuries cases;

(f) administrative law cases;

(g) licensing cases.

You are most likely as a social worker to appear in these courts in family matters as:

(i) an applicant and/or witness in applications for an order under the Children Act 1989. (Details of the relevant law are dealt with in chapters 9–12.)

(ii) a 'welfare officer' presenting a report to the court to assist it in deciding what, if any, type of order should be made. (Reports are dealt with in chapter 6.)

The Hearing in the Family Proceedings Court

The Family Proceedings Court is the name for magistrates courts when they deal with family matters. The magistrates who sit in the family proceedings court receive specialized training in family matters and form the family panel. Family Proceedings

Courts deal with both public and private law matters relating to children. All public law cases start in the Family Proceedings Court.

We shall look in detail at a hearing of an application by a local authority for a statutory order under the Children Act in the magistrates' court. This is to enable you to get an overall picture of the typical format of a case which is probably the hearing that social workers most frequently attend. In most courts there is a similar approach to hearings. Details of the applicable law should be obtained from chapter 12.

It is worth making clear, however, that much of the local authority social worker's time will not be spent with dealing with applications for care orders, since work with children does not inevitably end in an application to the court. It is the philosophy of the Children Act 1989 to try to avoid the need for formal court orders.

Rules of court

The procedures of the court are governed by the rules of court. Those issued under the Children Act 1989 will be the ones the social worker will come across most often. There are two sets of rules: one for the magistrates' court and one for the county court and High Court. In most cases they have identical numbering, except that the county court/High Court rules are prefixed with '4'. For example, rule 18 of the magistrates' court rules deals with the admission of expert evidence: the admission of expert evidence in the county court/High Court is dealt with under rule 4.18. In this book we have omitted the '4', and treat the rules as identical. Where there is a difference in numbering we state it.

The procedure

Rule 25 sets out the procedure in a case where the local authority applies for an order. (More information on evidence and courtroom procedure can be found in chapter 6.) The steps in the procedure are as follows:

(a) The applicant (i.e. local authority or NSPCC) will make an opening statement, through its lawyer, outlining the basis of the case.

(b) The applicant will call witnesses (who will certainly include social workers) to support its case. It is necessary to submit a written statement of evidence before the hearing in the magistrates' court. This may either shorten or lengthen the hearings. This is because a written statement can allow agreed evidence to be quickly introduced but also allows more detailed evidence to be produced which gives the 'other side' plenty of scope for cross-examination. Following *Practice Direction* (1995), in the county court and High Court the written statement is the evidence. The trend in the Family Proceedings Court is to place greater reliance on the written statement. Opening oral evidence will tend to be confined to confirming the written statement.

(c) The other parties (or more usually their lawyers) to the proceedings (which includes the child through his or her guardian, the parents, and grandparents) can cross-examine the applicant's witnesses.

(d) The applicant can re-examine its witnesses.

(e) The other parties may make an opening statement.

(f) The other parties may call witnesses to rebut the applicant's case.

(g) The applicant may cross-examine the other parties' witnesses.

(h) The applicant can make a closing statement.

(i) The other parties to the proceedings can make a closing statement.

(j) The magistrates decide whether the grounds for the order are satisfied.

(k) If there are grounds for making an order, then the applicant and the other parties, in that order, make representations as to the kind of order that should be made. These representations can be supported by evidence given under oath.

(l) The children's guardian, if appointed (see chapter 12), will present his or her report and can give evidence if required. (See also chapter 6 and 7 on evidence and reports.)

(m) The magistrates decide what order they are going to make. The court may decide not to make any order at all (s. 1(5) of the Children Act 1989).

The making or refusing of the order ends the proceedings, unless there is an appeal.

In other family proceedings, such as matrimonial proceedings (other than divorce which is not dealt with in the family proceedings court), the order of proceedings will be similar. That is to say, the person making the application to the court will open the proceedings with the other parties giving evidence in turn. If the social worker is involved at all it will normally only be at the report stage.

Interim hearings

The proceedings that have been described above are called full hearings since, subject to any appeal, once the order is made the legal case is completed. (Lawyers, unlike social workers close their case files once they get a court order.)

Often when a case comes before a court, for a variety of reasons, the court cannot make a final order. There will therefore be a need to adjourn the hearing to another date and, in the meantime, sometimes to make an interim order. This will state what the parties should do during the time the case is adjourned. For instance, if the local authority were making an application for a care order, and an adjournment was needed to enable a report to be obtained from a child psychiatrist, then it would need to be decided where the child was to stay in the meantime. Such directions will be contained in an interim order.

Interim orders can be made in any court proceedings. What the social worker has to appreciate is that they are very common and that you should not be misled by the term. It is easy to fall into the belief that because the applicant is only asking for an interim order it will automatically be a short hearing. Evidence or representations are required, unless the interim arrangements are agreed.

Directions hearings

An important part of preparing a case for hearing is the directions hearing. This is designed to enable the court and the lawyers to decide what procedural matters need to be dealt with. It is very important in the process of managing the case to ensure that the final hearing takes place as quickly as possible, is as short as possible, and deals with those points that are actually in dispute.

Hearings in county court and High Court

The majority of the social worker's dealings with the county court and the High Court will be in connection with children. We shall look mainly at such cases in this section. Such appearances will be:

(a) the result of your authority applying for a care or supervision order;

(b) at the request of the court, where it appears during family proceedings that it may be appropriate for a care or supervision application to be made by the local authority (Children Act 1989, s. 37); or

(c) the most frequent, where the court requires a welfare report to assist it to decide what order should be made in family proceedings (Children Act 1989, s. 7).

Transfer of cases

Under the Children Act 1989 there is the generic concept of family hearings. All public law cases have to be started in the magistrates' court. For the more complex cases there are procedures whereby the cases can be transferred to the county court and then to the High Court. These are dealt with in the Children (Allocation of Proceedings) Order 1991. Essentially, the grounds for transfer are whether the proceedings are exceptionally grave, important, or complex, or because there are already proceedings in the other court or the case can be dealt with more quickly by the other court.

Before the Act came into force, the Government indicated that it both expected and wanted the majority of cases to stay in the magistrates' court. The reasons for this seem to be largely questions of costs, since, as the magistrates are unpaid lay people, costs per hour in the magistrates' court are far less than in the higher courts with professional judges. (This argument ignores the cost, including financial costs, of bad decisions.)

When the Act first came into force there appeared to be a number of magistrates' courts which were reluctant to transfer cases up. The High Court has made a number of comments in different cases about the need to transfer cases up to the higher courts. See, for instance, *C v Solihull Metropolitan Borough Council* (1993) 1 or *Re H (A Minor)* (1993). In this case the court said that magistrates should not hear a case expected to last in excess of two, or at the most three, days. Cases involving serious disputed sexual or other abuse, or cases where children or young people are seeking to make representations which are different from those of the children's guardian, should not be heard in the magistrates' court.

If the magistrates refuse to transfer a case to the county court, this decision can be appealed. It is a matter for your legal advisers to deal with. It is important that you try to ensure that the case is heard in the right court. (See Case Planning in chapter 11 for more discussion of this.) Most people within the child-care system still feel that the full-time professional judges in the county court or the High Court will ensure a more satisfactory hearing. That is not to criticize the magistrates but to accept that there is more expertise in the higher courts.

County court

The divorce court

The county court is the court where most divorces are processed, and it follows that it is the court in which s. 8 Orders under the Children Act 1989 (see chapter 14) will be made ancillary to those divorce proceedings. Ancillary relief refers to the powers of the court to make orders related to divorce or other matrimonial proceedings. Section 7 of the Children Act gives the the court the power to ask either the local authority or the probation service to prepare a report in the course of divorce proceedings. For the requirements of such a welfare report see chapter 6. When presenting your report you will find that the hearing in the county court follows a similar outline to that described for the magistrates' court. The report will be presented at what is stage (k).

Chambers hearings

The county court family hearing takes place in 'chambers', which means that the hearing will be in private. (But rarely in the judge's private chambers from which the term derives; most chambers do not have the room to take all the people who will be involved in the hearing.) There are no press present and some of the formalities, such as the wearing of wigs, are not observed.

Written statements

There is no longer a hearing of the applicant's initial oral evidence. The county court is familiar with the idea of using written statements as the means of setting out both the competing claims of the opposing parties and the evidence that goes to support those claims. The judge, having had the opportunity to read those before the hearing date, will already be in a position to see the areas of dispute. This does not mean that the side opposing the application will not spend a great deal of time cross-examining the applicant's witnesses, and in turn the applicant may spend an even greater length of time re-examining its witnesses!

As the judges are professional lawyers, you will hear them assist the lawyers who are appearing before them, by indicating when the lawyer has to pursue a particular point and when this is not needed. You will hear such statements as: 'I am with you on that point; you have no need to pursue that point; what is your submission on this point?' This may appear confusing to the outsider but is designed both to speed the hearing and to ensure that the lawyers and the judge address the correct questions.

High Court

The High Court has the power to hear all cases relating to children. In practice it hears the more complex cases under the Children Act 1989.

Wardship

The historical role of the High Court in children's cases was that of wardship where the High Court steps in and takes over in place of the child's parent. (The child then becomes referred to as a ward of court.) The authority of the High Court to do this derives from what is described as its inherent jurisdiction.

Prior to the passing of the Children Act, most of the local authority social worker's experience of the High Court would have been in wardship proceedings. Under s. 100 of the Children Act, local authorities no longer have the right to apply in wardship proceedings for a statutory order (i.e. they cannot get a care or supervision order this way). It was thought by many that this would mean an end to wardship hearings. However, wardship is still used by local authorities in particular to get the High Court to make specific orders in difficult cases. In *Re S (A Minor) (Medical Treatment)* (1993), the authority sought an order in wardship to allow a blood transfusion to be given to a child of Jehovah's Witnesses whose parents were refusing to allow this. The court readily granted the order. The interesting aspect of the case was the lack of comment by the court as to why wardship was being used rather than any other order under the Act. (The authority could have applied for an emergency protection order, which we discuss in chapter 12.) There seems to be a continuing role that will be used for wardship in such cases, and the High Court does not appear to be raising difficulties.

Additionally, people other than local authorities can, in certain limited situations, apply to the High Court for a child to be made a ward, and in those circumstances the local authority may well be joined as a party in the proceedings because of immediate interest in the welfare of the child. Social workers will still be involved in such cases.

Supervisory function

In addition the High Court has a very important function of supervising the workings of the Children Act 1989, as it is the court which hears appeals against the decisions of magistrates and the county courts. In this way, gradually, a uniformity of practice in these courts can be brought about. In addition, the more important decisions of the High Court will be reported and influence the development of the law relating to children.

The hearing in the High Court

The hearing in the High Court is very much a copy of the county court hearing. In principle you should expect a 'better class' of hearing in the High Court, since the judges are expected to be of the highest calibre. Practical experience will allow you to draw your own conclusions as to whether or not this is so.

The hearings are again in chambers. The courtrooms used may well be the same rooms as are used for the county court. Indeed you may find yourself appearing before a judge who also conducts hearings as a county court judge. This is because there are provisions for county court judges to be appointed as 'deputy' High Court judges, because of the continuing lack of available High Court judges to meet all the demands for hearings before them.

Civil hearings other than family hearings

All the courts discussed above exercise a civil jurisdiction other than in family matters. These cover such matters as contract disputes, licensing, claims for compensation arising from accidents, etc. The High Court hears applications for judicial review. Normally a social worker will not deal with these cases in the course of their work. Perhaps the main distinction between these hearings and family hearings is that 'normal' civil hearings will take place in open court and will be public. The form of the hearing will be similar to that of a family hearing, although obviously in a contract dispute there will be no place for a welfare officer!

Appeal hearings

The courts of England and Wales are part of an appellate structure. Accordingly, there are normally provisions for a party unhappy with a decision of a lower court to appeal to a higher court.

This section looks at the question of appeals in family matters, since that is the main concern of social workers. The general principles are applicable to other cases.

A dissatisfied party may want to appeal for the following reasons:

(a) They think the court got the facts of the case wrong.

(b) They think that the court got the law applying to the case wrong.

(c) They think that the court in exercising its discretion in the case came to the wrong decision.

Most appeal hearings do not involve hearing the case all over again with the same witnesses. An exception is an appeal to the Crown Court from conviction in the magistrates' court. Normally, however, the appeal court will look at what reasons the lower court gave for arriving at its decision. In some courts the reasons (the judgment) are available in writing. Having heard representations from the parties and having looked at the judgment, the appeal court will give *its* judgment.

Accordingly it will be difficult to succeed in an appeal on ground (a)—only in exceptional circumstances would a lower court be held to have got the facts wrong, since that court at least has heard the evidence directly.

Most decisions are on ground (b): that the lower court misstated or misunderstood the law. The clarification of the law is a prime function of the appeal system.

In the field of family matters it is ground (c) that presents the greatest difficulty. It will be appreciated when dealing with such family proceedings that there can rarely be only one correct decision. The question whether or not to grant a contact order or a residence order will always be a question of balancing a variety of possibly conflicting demands. In any of these types of cases there will always be a certain amount of discretion whether or not an order should be made. The appeal courts, generally, will not interfere in such a case provided that the exercise of that discretion was not unreasonable. Thus an appeal court may say that it would have arrived at a different decision, but if the original decision was within the area of the lower court's discretion then it will not interfere.

So although there is a system of appeals it does not mean that any decision can be overturned. Just because a decision goes against you, do not think that you will have grounds for an appeal.

If you look at the diagram of the court structure you will see that the two highest courts of appeal are the Court of Appeal (which has separate branches—criminal and civil) and the House of Lords. The House of Lords is the court of final appeal. It is bound by the European Court of Justice and the European Court of Human Rights in some cases. To give some understanding of the actual workings of the appeal system: the Court of Appeal will hear about 1,000 cases a year and the House of Lords hears about fifty cases a year. So it will be a rare occasion when you have a case going to either of these courts.

The actual practicalities of appeals are beyond the scope of this book. If you do find yourself in a situation which you think should be the subject of an appeal, you should consult your lawyer immediately.

The Constitutional Reform Act 2004 abolishes the House of Lords and replaces it with a Supreme Court. Full details of the reforms and their implementation will be available on our web site.

Tribunals

The range of tribunals

A great deal of dispute resolution within the English legal system is carried out by tribunals. They hear a large number and a great variety of cases, generally between the citizen and the state, such as in Appeals Service Tribunals which general hear social security appeals; but they also hear citizen against citizen disputes, as in Employment Tribunals. Tribunals are created by statute and are administered by the relevant government department. Tribunals generally consist of three people, with only the chair being legally qualified. Their numbers have dramatically increased over the last fifty years. Currently there are about eighty types. Their purpose is to provide a quicker and less formal forum than the courts and to allow cases to be adjudicated on by people with an expertise in the particular jurisdiction, so for instance psychiatrists sit on Mental Health Review Tribunals and surveyors on Lands Tribunals. Tribunals tend to be of particular importance to social work clients as their lives are likely to be more dependent on decisions made by state bodies. The Council on Tribunals has supervisory jurisdiction over most (but not all) tribunals.

New tribunals

New tribunals are created relatively frequently, partly in response to the increasing complexity of society and also stimulated by Article 6 of the European Convention on Human Rights which requires the existence of courts or tribunals to determine a person's civil rights. One example relevant to social work practice is the Care Standards Tribunal. The Care Standards Tribunal is the operational name given to the tribunal that handles appeals provided for under the Care Standards Act 2000 (CSA). However, in law it is the tribunal that was set up under the Protection of Children Act 1999 (PCA). The 1999 Act provides for a tribunal to hear appeals against decisions of the Secretary of State for Health to include the names of individuals on the list of those considered unsuitable to work with children. The 1999 Act also provides for the Tribunal to hear appeals in respect of decision of the Secretary of State for Education and Skills to restrict or bar a person's employment in schools. The Care Standards Act confers additional functions on the Tribunal, including appeals in respect of the registration of care home and children's homes. It also hears appeals against decisions of the Secretary of State for Health in respect of decisions to include the names of individuals on the list of those considered suitable to work with vulnerable adults and appeals against decisions of the General Social Care Council in England and the Care Council for Wales in respect of the registration of social workers and social care workers. For further information on the work of the Care Standards Tribunal see its web page at **www.carestandstribunal.gov.uk**.

Criticisms of the tribunal system

The tribunal system is criticized on a range of issues. Tribunals are not clearly independent of the government body whose decision is being challenged. Procedures and the quality of decision-making vary enormously. Informality and simplicity of procedure is difficult to achieve in many of the complex social welfare fields in which tribunals operate, so that unrepresented parties feel themselves to be at a disadvantage, yet in the vast majority of tribunals there is no publicly funded legal help available (exceptions being the Mental Health Review Tribunal and the Immigration Appeal Tribunal) to pay for lawyers. As the Legal Action Group points out, those who are unrepresented encounter pitfalls, such as being unaware that an application is without merit, misunderstanding tribunal procedures, preparing inadequately for the hearing, or putting forward irrelevant facts and arguments. The best advice you can give to a client taking a case to a tribunal is to go to their local advice centre as soon as possible for specialist assistance.

Modernizing the tribunal system

The Government set up a comprehensive review of the tribunal system in June 2000 (the Leggatt Review). The report was published in August 2001, entitled *Tribunals for Users: One System, One Service*. It addresses many concerns about the tribunal service—the need for an enhanced role for the Council on Tribunals, a greater standardization of tribunal procedures, better judicial training, and clearer separation from government departments. The report can be found on the Department of Constitutional Affairs web site: **www.dca.gov.uk**.

The Government intends to create an 'increasingly unified tribunal system' with most tribunals brought together under the umbrella of the Department of Constitutional Affairs. It published a White Paper *Transforming Public Services: Complaints, Redress and Tribunals* in July 2004. This goes beyond the Leggatt Review suggesting that a much more radical approach to the reform of dispute resolution is needed, one which concentrates on the needs of the users of the system and on proportionate dispute resolution. It is difficult to assess the practical implications of this until more formal proposals are published. We will endeavour to keep you up-to-date on our web site.

Inquiries

Here we are using the term 'inquiries' to refer to a whole range of investigations/ hearings which take place outside the court system. Local authorities may initiate, participate in, or contribute to many types of inquiries. Some are more formal than others. They are a useful mechanism for dealing with complaints or investigating failure and may prove more helpful in finding out facts than the adversarial system used in the courts. We set out here some of those you may come across.

Inquiries ordered by a minister

These are the type of inquiry with which you are probably most familiar. They arise when a minister, acting under powers conferred upon him or her by statute, orders the local authority to conduct an inquiry. The *Victoria Climbié* Inquiry, which was set up by the Secretary of State for Health and the Secretary of State for the Home Department under the chairmanship of Lord Laming, is a typical example. Inquiries established by statute normally have power to order witness attendance and compel disclosure to the inquiry. The reports of ministerial inquiries are essential learning documents. We will refer to several of them throughout this book.

The Ombudsman

The scope of the ombudsman system

Public ombudsman schemes originated in Scandinavia and were imported into Britain in the 1960s. Ombudsmen are designed to provide a possible source of redress where private individuals have suffered through the poor administration of a public body, such as a local authority. We say 'poor administration' which is also termed 'maladministration', because the ombudsman is concerned only with this area. What the ombudsman looks at is not the failure of the public body to obey the law but its failure to implement the law in a competent way. Ombudsmen are not able to investigate complaints where legal proceedings are possible.

The Parliamentary Ombudsman

The first ombudsman created was the Parliamentary Commissioner for Administration who deals with the administrative failings of government departments. The public does not have direct access to the ombudsman. Complaints must go first of all to Members of Parliament. MPs are not obliged to refer the complaints they receive to the Parliamentary ombudsman if they consider that they can deal with the matter themselves. This filter was introduced to preserve the primary responsibility of Parliament to call the administration to account.

The Local Government Ombudsman

The Local Government Ombudsman (technically called the Parliamentary Commissioner for Local Government) is the officer you are most likely to have dealings with. Typically, in any year there are 15,000 complaints to the local authority ombudsman, 6 per cent of which relate to social services (37 per cent, in contrast, relate to housing departments—mainly the administration of housing benefit). The objective of the local government ombudsman is to provide, where appropriate, satisfactory redress for complainants and assist in the improvement of administration by local government. The local government ombudsman has the power to issue general advice on good local administration. The local government ombudsman is not able to investigate personnel complaints or complaints about the internal running of schools.

The procedure

To apply, it is necessary to have satisfied the ombudsman that all other procedures of internal complaint to the local authority have been tried and exhausted, without giving the complainant redress. (While many complaints will be covered by the local authority complaints procedures, the ombudsman can investigate delays in hearing complaints or allegations that councils are trying to exclude people from using the complaints process.) The complainant has to approach the ombudsman through a local councillor. This is designed to act as a filter, since the requirement to use a councillor should mean that the councillor will have considered all other forms of redress and will have used their influence to solve the difficulty. If the complainant can find no councillor willing to make the application, the complainant can approach the ombudsman direct. The ombudsman then has wide powers of investigation and the ability to look at files and compel people to give information.

An officer of the ombudsman sends a copy of the complaint to the chief executive of the local authority asking for comments. When the investigations are complete the ombudsman prepares a report. This report is made publicly available, with the expectation that if there is a finding of maladministration then the local authority will remedy the fault and, in the appropriate case, pay compensation. The local authority must respond to the report. If the local authority fails to carry out the recommendations of the ombudsman then a further report will be published. This, however, is the only sanction that the ombudsman has. There are no powers of compulsion available to the ombudsman to require the local authority to carry out any of the recommendations contained in the report.

More information is available on the Local Government Ombudsman's web site **www.lgo.org.uk**. The site also contains reports of the Local Government Ombudsman's decisions and details on how to make a complaint.

Other ombudsmen

There are several other examples of ombudsmen which may provide useful redress for your clients. The Health Service Ombudsman investigates complaints about the failures of National Health Service hospitals or community health services and other National Health Service provision. Any member of the public may refer a complaint direct, though normally only if a full investigation within the National Health Service complaints system has been carried out first. More recently a range of specialist ombudsman has been created. For instance the Housing Ombudsman Service deals with complaints against housing associations, and the Legal Services Ombudsman handles complaints about services provided by lawyers. More information about these services can be found on their respective web sites, **www.ombudsman.org.uk/hse**, **www.ihos.org.uk**, and **www.olso.org**.

Inquiries established by the local authority

These can cover a variety of different procedures depending upon the reason for the inquiry, and their remit will vary according to the time and expense constraints, and whether criminal proceedings are pending. For instance they can be chaired by an independent chair or by a member of the local authority, for instance the chief executive. They can be public or private, although due to the sensitive nature of many of these inquiries, they tend to be private. Clwyd Council carried out a series of inquiries into allegations of child abuse in its children's homes prior to the Waterhouse Inquiry being ordered by Parliament. Local authorities, like social services departments, can only carry out functions which they have statutory authority to carry out. Local authorities are empowered to carry out inquiries by the Local Government Act 2000.

Inter-agency inquiries

These can be undertaken by one or more statutory bodies. They may involve local authorities, health authorities, police, or other interested parties. They may be *ad hoc* in nature or subject to standing procedures. The type of inter-agency inquiry which you are most likely to come across is the care review coordinated by the Area Child Protection Committee (ACPC). Guidelines are laid down by the Department of Health, Home Office, Department for Education and Employment. These require each agency which was involved in the issue to review its own conduct. These reviews are then compiled by the Area Child Protection Committee into one report. Note that Area Child Protection Committees are to be replaced by Local Safeguarding Children Boards once the provisions of the Children Act 2004 are implemented. Local Safeguarding Children Boards are fully discussed in chapter 8.

Complaints

Complaints are an important driver for improvement in services. Complaints may be generally defined as expressions of dissatisfaction or disquiet that require a response. It is important not to define complaints too narrowly since this may prevent service users from having a legitimate outlet for their concerns.

Social Services complaints procedure for adults

The complaints procedure for adult service users is currently being reformed. The previous provisions set out in section 7B of the Local Authority Social Services Act 1970 were repealed by the Health and Social Care (Community Health and Standards) Act 2003 which also enabled the Secretary of State to introduce a new regulatory frame-work. At the time of writing the regulations are being consulted upon and the new procedures are due to be implemented from 5 April 2005. The final guidance will be issued as s. 7 guidance under the Local Authority Social Services Act 1970. The complaints procedure will have two stages, the handling and consideration of complaints by the local authority whose actions are complained about, followed, if necessary by independent review by the Commission of Social Care Inspection (see below). Box 5.5 sets out the new procedure.

The Children Act 1989 procedure

The second procedure is that required by s. 26(3) of the Children Act 1989. This requires every local authority to establish a procedure for considering representations about the exercise of its functions under Part 3 of the Act, made by or on behalf of any children looked after or in need—we explain these phrases fully in chapter 9. The requirements are set out in the Representations Procedure (Children) Regulations 1991. The key features of the Children Act procedure are that a designated officer is appointed in the local authority to coordinate the consideration of complaints and that an independent person is appointed to consider the complaint. A response should be given to the complainant within twenty-eight days and a review panel containing an independent person should consider complaints not resolved within twenty-eight days of being notified. From April 2004 a new s. 26A of the Children Act 1989 imposes on local authorities a duty to make arrangements for the provision of advocacy services for children and young people making or intending to make a complaint under s. 24D and 26 of the Children Act. Full details of the requirement are set out in *The Advocacy Services and Representations Procedure (Children)(Amendment) Regulations* (2004) and the accompanying guidance *Providing Effective Advocacy Services for Children and Young People Making a Complaint under the Children Act 1989: Get it Sorted* available on the Department for Education and Skills web site **www.dfes.gov.uk/childrensadvocacy/docs**.

The Children's Commissioner for Wales

The Children's Commissioner for Wales is an independent body which has the role of ensuring that the rights of children and young people are upheld. It was set up following a recommendation in *Lost in Care*, the report of the Waterhouse Tribunal which looked into the abuse of children in care in the former county council areas of Gwynedd and Clwyd. The office of the Children's Commissioner for Wales was established under the Care Standards Act 2000. The Commissioner's functions under this Act include reviewing and monitoring the arrangements for complaints made by service providers, whistleblowing, advocacy, the provision of advice and information, the power to examine particular cases, providing other assistance, and making reports. In 2001 the Children's Commissioner for Wales Act extended the Commissioner's role to all children. It also gave him the power to review proposed legislation and policy from the National Assembly for Wales considering the potential effect that it might have on children, and to make representations to the National Assembly for Wales about any matter that affects children. Peter Clarke is the Children's Commissioner for Wales. The web site is at **www.childcom.org.uk**.

BOX5.5 The new procedure for social services complaints

Stage One – Handling and Consideration by Local Authorities

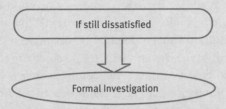

Local Resolution

Complaint brought to the attention of the person or organization providing social services locally

If still dissatisfied

Formal Investigation

Investigation of the complaint by the local authority and production of a report with findings, conclusions and recommendations. The authority subsequently makes an adjudication (decision) concerning the outcome of the complaint

If still dissatisfied

Stage Two – Independent Review

CSCI to assess the eligibility of the complaint for review and where appropriate will take one of the following actions to consider the complaint further:

Independent Complaints Panel
Commission Investigation
Referral to the Local Government Ombudsman
Decision of No Further Action reuired (NFA)

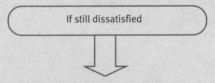

If still dissatisfied

Complaint about the local authority actions and decisions referred to
The Local Government Ombudsman

Complaint about the CSCI Complaints Review Service referred to
The Parliamentary Ombudsman

The Children's Commissioner for England

The Children Act 2004 establishes the office of Children's Commissioner for England with the function of promoting and safeguarding the rights and interests of children in England. In deciding what constitutes the rights and interests of children the Commissioner is required to have regard to the United Nations Convention on the Rights of the Child. The role is similar to the Children's Commissioner for Wales but does not include the power to review all proposed legislation to assess its impact upon children. Most significantly, the Government has resisted any emphasis on individual children's rights. The Minister for Children, Margaret Hodge, said that the Government wanted the Commissioner to consider the wider interests of children rather than getting 'bogged down' in 'policing children's individual rights' like the Children's Commissioner for Wales. In addition some influential bodies believe that the role will not be sufficiently independent of the Government, for instance the NSPCC is concerned that ministers will have the power to direct the Commissioner to carry out inquiries and would also like the Commissioner to have the power to require the Government and relevant bodies such as local authorities, children's charities or youth organizations to respond to his/her recommendations. For full information and commentary on Children's Commissioners see the *Guardian* web site **www.society.guardian.co.uk/ children**. England's Children's Commissioner is Professor Al Aynsley-Green, and the web site is **www.childrenscommissioner.org**.

■ Inspection and audit

The Government is committed to improving the performance of public services. One particular mechanism by which it does this is via inspection and audit.

The Commission for Social Care Inspection

The Commission for Social Care Inspection brings together the work previously undertaken by the Social Services Inspectorate, the SSI/Audit Commission joint review team, and the social care functions of the National Care Standards Commission. Its primary function is to promote improvements in social care by ensuring that there are consistent levels of service and protection for vulnerable people using care services.

The inspectorate:

- Carries out local inspections of all social care organizations;
- Registers services that meet national minimum standards;
- Carries out inspections of local social service authorities;
- Publishes an annual report to Parliament on national progress on social care and an analysis of where resources have been spent;
- Validates all published performance assessment statistics on social care;
- Publishes the star ratings for social services authorities.

For full information on the work of the inspectorate look at its web site **www.csci.org.uk**.

The Commission for Healthcare Audit and Inspection

The Commission for Healthcare Audit and Inspection, known as the Healthcare Commission was launched on April 1 2004. It took over the private and voluntary health-care functions of the National Care Standards Commission and the functions of the Audit Commission in respect to national studies of efficiency, effectiveness and economy of healthcare. It is anticipated that the Healthcare Commission will take over the functions of the Mental Health Act Commission, subject to the passing of further legislation.

Its role is to:

- Encourage improvement in the quality and effectiveness of care, and in the economy and efficiency of its provision;
- Inspect the management, provision, and quality of health-care services and tracking where, and how well, public resources are being used;
- Carry out investigations into serious service failures;
- Report serious concerns about the quality of public services to the Secretary of State;
- Publish annual performance ratings for all NHS organizations and produce annual reports to Parliament on the state of health care;
- Collaborate with other relevant organizations including the Commission for Social Care Inspection;
- Carry out an independent review function for NHS complaints.

For full information on the work of the Commission see its web site **www.chai.org.uk**.

There has been continuous change in the organization of the regulation of social and health care inspection. Further upheaval is likely. The Chancellor announced plans for the merger of the Commission for Social Care Inspection and the Health Care Commission on 16th March 2005.

Children's services

The Children Act 2004 provides for a new joint system of inspection of local children's services. The joint area reviews are designed to 'evaluate the extent to which, taken together, the children's services being reviewed improve the well-being of children and relevant young persons (s.16(4) Children Act 2004). Box 5.6 sets out the persons and bodies to which the section applies.

The purpose of the inspection regime for children's services is to ensure that the services work together to safeguard children—see the discussion of the Children Act 2004 in chapter 8.

Achieving public accountability

It is clear there is a multitude of mechanisms to achieve the essential public accountability referred to in the case study at the beginning of this chapter. In Box 5.7 we list them and provide a summary of the advantages and disadvantages they bring.

BOX 5.6 Joint area reviews—relevant persons and bodies—s.16(5) Children Act 2004

The relevant persons and bodies are:
- The Chief Inspector of Schools.
- The Adult Learning Inspectorate.
- The Commission for Social Care Inspection.
- The Commission for Healthcare Audit and Inspection.
- The Audit Commission for Local Authorities and the National health Service in England and Wales.
- The Chief Inspector of Constabulary.
- Chief Inspector of the National Probation Service for England and Wales.
- The Chief Inspector of Court Administration.
- The Chief Inspector of Prisons.

BOX 5.7 A summary of the different forums for public accountability

Forum	Advantages	Disadvantages	Comment
The courts	Prestigious Extensive expertise and specialist knowledge	Expensive and time consuming. Can be very alienating to people unfamiliar with its operations.	Very few cases that you are involved in will get reported in the law reports. Decisions which are reported tend to arise from very complex factual circumstances which you may feel have little relevance to your day to day practice.
Tribunals	Less formal hearings, with greater accessibility and speed	Different tribunals run on different procedural rules. Sometimes the informality can work to the disadvantage of the vulnerable person. Generally no funded legal help available.	You are likely to become increasingly familiar with tribunals because of the influence of the Human Rights Act.

Inquiries	Public inquiries are very influential on subsequent practice.	Public inquiries are expensive and time consuming. Other inquiries may be held in private and provide very little public accountability.	
Complaints	These provide a speedy informal system of addressing issues of concern to ordinary people.	Children and vulnerable people may find it very difficult to complain.	
Local Government Ombudsman		Limited compensation.	
Children's Commissioner for Wales	Provides a service which children need since they find it difficult to complain or influence policy and the law. It will also provide a useful coordinating role.	England's Commissioner has limited role.	It will be interesting to see the extent of the added value the Children's Commissioner provides.
Social Services Inspectorate	Can concentrate on standards of management and day to day procedures which makes them more relevant to social work practice.	Does not deal with individual complaints, although should take service users views into account. May be seen as insufficiently independent of national government.	
National Care Standards Commission	As above. The Commission also has flexibility to respond to service needs, for instance through the establishment of the Children's Rights Director.	As above. Continued legal and procedural developments mean it is difficult to keep track of the functions.	

Reading statutes

Find the Care Standards Act 2000—on the Web or find a paper copy. Now answer the following questions:

1 How many parts are there to the Act?

2 What is the title of Part IX and how many chapters does it have?

3 How many Schedules are there to the Act?

4 Find s. 11 of the Act. Does this impose criminal or civil liability on the person who fails to register?

5 Find s. 16 of the Act. What is the legal status of regulations made under this section?

6 Look at s. 23. What powers does the minister have? What statutory duties are imposed upon him?

7 What section of the Act deals with the title 'social worker'? Write, in your own words, what it provides.

8 How does the Act define 'vulnerable adults'?

9 Has s. 81 of the Act come into force?

10 Is your version of the Act up to date? How do you know?

Reading cases

Find *Gillick v West Norfolk and Wisbech Area Health Authority* (1986) and answer the following questions:

1 In which court was the case heard?

2 Name the judges.

3 When was the case heard? On what date was the judgement handed down?

4 Who were the parties to the case?

5 Set out briefly the legal history of the case.

6 Is the case one of statutory interpretation, or is it about the common law?

7 Was the decision of the court unanimous?

8 Who were the barristers in the case? Who were the solicitors?

9 Find Lord Scarman's judgment and copy it. If you have time, read it. It is a good decision to read as it has been extremely influential, as you will find out in the next chapter.

Accountability

A service user is dissatisfied with a decision you have made. Outline the various options open to her and indicate in which circumstances which option is likely to be most appropriate.

The Ombudsman

Find the Local Government Ombudsman's site on the Web. Find the decisions on complaints about Social Services. What types of complaint are most common?

COMPANION WEB SITE

 For guidance on how to answer these exercises, visit the companion web site at: www.oup.com/uk/booksites/law.

WHERE DO WE GO FROM HERE?

This chapter makes it clear that you are operating in a legal arena. Statute and common law define your role and responsibilities. Secondary legislation and guidance provide detailed information. This chapter has also aimed to describe that legal arena to you and to provide you with some tools so that you can navigate it to the best of your ability. Whilst it is a complex and extensive arena it will become more familiar with practice. Disputes are inevitable, and we have described the most familiar forum for dispute resolution, the courts. The courts, as the case study at the beginning of the chapter made clear, do not only resolve disputes. They also provide public accountability. We have described other mechanisms available to both your service user and to the public to ensure that social work decisions are of the highest standard.

The most important message to conclude this chapter is that the law determines what you do. Social workers must be able to account for their decisions. In addition, any correct answer that a social worker can give, when asked why he or she took a particular course of action, must include the statement 'I took the step because that was what appropriate social work practice demanded within the framework of the law'. Without the ability to say that, the professional social worker will have failed themselves and, more important, their service user. The next chapter looks more closely at the courts and in particular the evidence upon which courts make their decisions.

ANNOTATED FURTHER READING

The legal system

If you would like to read more about the English and Welsh legal system there are a number of books available. We enjoyed Martin Partington's *Introduction to the English Legal System* (3rd edn., Oxford University Press, 2003). It is written in a very accessible style and covers all the institutions we have discussed in this chapter.

Reading law

For more information on finding and reading cases and statutes we recommend J. Holland and J. Webb, *Learning Legal Rules* (5th edn., Oxford University Press, 2003). Again this is a very user-friendly text which provides a great deal of support to anyone new to reading law.

Evidence and reports

Re D (Sexual Abuse Allegations: Evidence of Adult Victim) [2002] 1 FLR 723

A long time ago—sixteen years in fact—a man had fostered a girl. His own granddaughter now needed a good home, and the family proceedings court had to decide in the course of care proceedings if, once again, he was a suitable person to look after a child. The assessments of his capabilities, both now and then, were good. But there was a problem. In 1985 the foster child had made an allegation that he had touched her inappropriately. The girl had not made a statement, and had not been interviewed by the police or any child protection group. The local authority had not followed it up because it thought her account was unreliable.

Now, after sixteen years, 'for some reason [social workers] questioned her about these unresolved allegations of 16 years ago. They did not take a statement from her. They did not hold a formal interview with her; it was informal and sympathetic. They did not have it audio-taped; they did not have it video-taped; they did not keep an accurate record of the interview. I understand there were some relatively scrappy notes, but nothing was available to the magistrates.' In the family proceedings court 'the social worker gave . . . an astonishingly vague and generalised picture of what this young woman was saying happened 16 years ago.' (The quotations are from the words of Lady Justice Butler-Sloss in the Court of Appeal.)

Despite this the family proceedings court believed the evidence. In its own words: 'The account she gives now is coherent. The windows of opportunity for the abuse have been confirmed by the grandfather in evidence. The account is of an abuse of affection and an escalation of abuse. In our view, the most probable explanation for why she is telling the story now is because it is true and it happened as she now describes it.'

In a tone verging on anger the Court of Appeal ruled that the magistrates had had no right to accept this flimsy evidence and make a finding based on it without obtaining the evidence of the alleged victim and weighing it against that of the grandfather. Consider this rebuke:

No court in the land should accept a social worker's account of an interview without a careful transcript of how the interview took place. It is extraordinary that if the magistrates were going to rely upon what this alleged victim said, that the child protection arrangements were not put in force and that the police were not involved. The police have no hesitation in charging, and the Crown Prosecution Service in prosecuting, those who have abused children on the allegations being made after the children have grown up. We know that there are cases in which people are prosecuted for offences which took place 20 or 30 years earlier. If the local authority wish to rely on this sort of evidence in any case, the court would expect them to be in touch with the police and there should be a formal, joint interview of the person making the allegations. To do it in this sloppy half-hearted way in a sympathetic interview, without any sort of rigour of questioning, and to have that accepted by the court as evidence that brands a man as a sexual abuser, is entirely unacceptable.

OVERVIEW AND OBJECTIVES

The case study shows what happens when best intentions are substituted for decision-making according to rules, systematic analysis of evidence, and due process. To be fair, the issue is not just about social workers and misplaced good intentions: in August 2004 a consultant pediatrician was reprimanded by the General Medical Council for his overzealous and unprofessional insistence to police investigating a cot death that a father must have killed his child. The consultant, apart from watching a television programme, had no knowledge of the facts of the case, but was sure that his expertise offered the correct understanding (see **www.http://news.bbc.co.uk/1/hi/health/3542880.stm**).

We hope to help you develop an understanding of the reasons why rules of evidence matter, and a reasonable understanding of what those rules are. We also want you to develop a respect for the fair, properly conducted trial. If we are successful you will retain a critical approach—some rules of evidence may well interfere with the proper tasks of the social worker; some may achieve the wrong balance between the duty of the state to protect and the rights of the person who you think they need protecting from. Experience may well teach you that some courts do not achieve, and some judges or magistrates may not seem to aspire to, the balanced fairness required. In any event you will, we hope, recognise that there has to be a balance between various interests. This balance is maintained in large part by rules of evidence.

Here, then, are our aims for the chapter. To:

- explain basic concepts
- look at the relationship between evidence, fairness and truth
- demistify technical rules, including questions of relevance, admissibility, hearsay, and standard of proof
- address any worries you may have about giving evidence yourself in court
- identify requirements for keeping records and preparing reports.

■ What is evidence? Why does it matter? Isn't it just for lawyers?

When are you likely to need to go to court? Let us take an example. You believe the department should take a child into care; child abuse is alleged. You have a statutory power to start care proceedings, but your department cannot get care without a court order. The court will not make an order until it decides what are the facts, which means it has heard evidence. You are involved in preparing and presenting at least some of that evidence. And if the alleged abuser is prosecuted you may be called as a witness in a separate court case. As well as deciding what are the facts—in this case whether and what abuse occurred—the civil and the criminal court also needs expert information to decide whether a care order is justified, or in deciding on a sentence.

The lawyers can prepare the ground and can argue the case; but they do not have first hand knowledge of the facts, and they are not experts in social work. They advise, and they act on the instructions their clients (in this case your department) give them in light of that advice. They can help you prepare evidence, but they cannot testify or present expert opinion—that is for you.

Evidence is technical but not impossible

Rules of evidence are complex. History is largely to blame. The issues in a case used to be decided by illiterate juries, so rules of evidence were made up by the judges on a piece-meal basis, mainly to stop the jury hearing things that they were thought ill-equipped to weigh up. Many of these old rules have now been simplified through legislation, but sometimes traces or memories of a rule remain which is not needed or has been abolished. Fortunately, in cases involving families and children, legislation has led to the courts relaxing the grip of the evidential rules.

It is worth trying to remember that rules are designed—even the old and complex ones—to help achieve fairness. They are not intended to make things difficult, even if that is sometimes the result. Courts, by and large, want to achieve a fair result according to law, and a starting point is to assume that courts and lawyers will treat you fairly as a witness, and will give all parties a fair hearing. This includes helping you with technical difficulties so that your evidence can be used.

Why evidence is important—a due process model

There are a number of ways in which decisions can be made by judges. We shall indulge in a caricature of three of them, and then look at the model we think applies in the courts of England and Wales.

An arbitrary model

A distinguished judge seemed to have spoiled a fine career with a bad decision. He was summoned before the Lord Chancellor to explain how he went about trying cases. He described how he would roll dice for each party; whoever got the best score would get the desired decision. When asked why the present decision was so bad, he said that he was getting old; he must have misread the dice! So this model (taken from fiction) gives a random outcome, unless you believe in divine intervention. There is no need for witnesses and evidence. It is no more likely to arrive at the truth than the medieval test for witches—guilty if she swims, innocent if she drowns.

If you think this model has, in fact, been applied in a case you have been involved in, consider an appeal.

A compassionate model

Here the court sets some kind of test/ordeal in order to form a judgment over which party merits its compassion. Solomon, for example, in his famous judgment, had to decide between two women who both claimed to be the mother of the child. His solution (would he have actually carried it through?) was to split the child down the middle and give half each. Fortunately one of them, in horror, said she would give up her claim in order to save the child. Solomon believed he had revealed the true mother, and he awarded her custody. The role of a compassionate assessment of the competing interests of the parties is not excluded from our system; however, the difference between our system and Solomon's is that the court cannot invent tests; it must exercise compassion using criteria recognized by law and taking into account recommendations from people like social workers, and on the basis of the admissible and relevant evidence before it.

Social workers—or other experts, such as the cot death expert referred to above—imposing best intentions onto the 'facts' are falling into the 'compassionate model' trap.

A legalistic model

In Shakespeare's *Merchant of Venice*, Shylock has lent a fortune to Antonio. Antonio must in due course either repay the loan or a pound of his own flesh. When Antonio's ships are wrecked and he cannot find the money, Shylock initially insists on his legal entitlement, the pound of flesh. Antonio's 'lawyer' persuades the judge that Shylock must indeed have what the contract says: one pound, no more and no less, and no drop of blood. Using this model the exact words of a contract or rule are enforced. There is no exercise of judgement, compassion, no room for deviation or relaxation from rules. Justice is not considered.

There are of course other models. For example, anthropologists describe traditional Inuit society as resolving some conflicts by a singing duel. But we hope this light-hearted overview prepares you for the model which applies in advanced democratic societies.

An evidence model

In this model a court cannot make decisions on the basis of whim, or pure compassion; its decisions must be rational and the process must be fair. The court itself must remain aloof from the contest, and hear what all parties wish to say about the issue causing the dispute. Decisions must be predictable in the sense that they are based on the law, which is known and published in advance. It must not take into account anything that the parties say, therefore, apart from what the law deems to be relevant to this particular type of dispute. Unlike the compassionate model, it cannot set tests (or traps) for the parties. Unlike the pound of flesh model it cannot apply rules in a purely mechanistic way, and must balance adherence to rules with outcomes which are just. In England and Wales since 2000 the model must operate within an explicit human rights framework (see Box 6.1 below). We will not examine the other components of a fair trial, but the way in which evidence is handled is the cornerstone.

BOX 6.1 Article 6 of the European Convention on Human Rights—Right to a fair trial

1 In the determination of his civil rights and obligations or of any criminal charge against him, everyone is entitled to a fair and public hearing within a reasonable time by an independent and impartial tribunal established by law. Judgment shall be pronounced publicly but the press and public may be excluded from all or part of the trial in the interests of morals, public order or national security in a democratic society, where the interests of juveniles or the protection of the private life of the parties so require, or to the extent strictly necessary in the opinion of the court in special circumstances where publicity would prejudice the interests of justice.

2 Everyone charged with a criminal offence shall be presumed innocent until proved guilty according to law.

3 Everyone charged with a criminal offence has the following minimum rights:

(a) to be informed promptly, in a language which he understands and in detail, of the nature and cause of the accusation against him;

(b) to have adequate time and facilities for the preparation of his defence;

(c) to defend himself in person or through legal assistance of his own choosing or, if he has not sufficient means to pay for legal assistance, to be given it free when the interests of justice so require;

(d) to examine or have examined witnesses against him and to obtain the attendance and examination of witnesses on his behalf under the same conditions as witnesses against him;

(e) to have the free assistance of an interpreter if he cannot understand or speak the language used in court.

In this model evidence is required so that the factfinder—judge, magistrate, jury, tribunal—can decide what are the facts and then use them to make a decision on what the outcome of the case will be. Lord Diplock, giving a judgment in the House of Lords, explained the evidential model for fact finding in this way (the emphasis has been added):

> The requirement that a person exercising . . . judicial functions must base his decisions on evidence means no more *than it must be based upon material which tends logically to show the existence or non-existence of facts relevant to the issue to be determined*, or *to show the likelihood or unlikelihood of the occurrence of some future event the occurrence of which would be relevant.* It means that he must not spin a coin or consult an astrologer, but may take into account any material which as a matter of reason has some probative value . . . (*R v Deputy Industrial Commissioner, ex parte Moore* (1965)).

The evidence model applies beyond courts to any formal decision making process or enquiry. In Box 6.2 you can see where things can go wrong if you depart from its basic principles.

BOX 6.2 Judicial observations relating to the evidence based approach Lillie and another v Newcastle City Council and others

In 1990 in Newcastle two nursery workers were suspended for allegedly abusing children in their care. At their criminal trial the judge withdrew the case from the jury because the evidence was flawed. The local authority then set up a panel to investigate the allegations, chaired by an eminent professor of social work. This panel determined that the two workers were guilty of systematic abuse. The nursery workers then sued the members of the enquiry panel, and the City Council which appointed them, for libel. To win their case they had to prove not just that the findings were wrong but that they had been reached through malice. They succeeded, and were each awarded the maximum sum available: £200,000.

The enquiry had been led by an eminent, and caring expert in social work and had held an exhaustive two months hearing into the truth of the allegations. Yet the libel judge, Eady J, found it had completely failed in its duty to investigate objectively and in accordance with principles of justice.

One of the recurring features of this case has been the willingness of psychologists, professional or amateur, to impose pre-conceived stereotypes or theories upon the facts of the case. I have had to remind myself that evidence must always come first and theory kept in its proper place. [para. 97]

[I]t is obvious with the benefit of hindsight (and indeed should have been obvious at the time) that they were simply not equipped for the task. In any event, none of them apparently had any expertise in conducting such an enquiry or in legal principles or processes (as to which, it emerges from their Report in several places that they were, in any event, quite disdainful). [para. 133]

Two facts emerged with clarity. Professor [B] and his colleagues believed that the Claimants were guilty of child abuse on a very extensive scale, as summarised in their Report, at the time it was published. I am equally satisfied that, despite their protestations, some of them had formed that view at the outset of their inquiry and never wavered. [para. 1333]

It emerged early on in Professor [B]'s testimony that he has a fundamentally different attitude towards the weighing and analysis of evidence from that of a lawyer. At several points, it became apparent that he is rather dismissive of what he called 'a forensic approach'. He resorted from time to time to impressionistic mode, referring to his 'professional judgment' and to discussions in academic and other published work. His colleagues were similarly minded. Indeed, Ms [J] [a member of the enquiry panel] voluntarily espoused the word 'impressionistic'. Yet the issue of whether any given individual has raped or assaulted a small child, or for that matter upwards of 60 small children, is not a matter of impression, theory, opinion or speculation. It should be a question of fact. [para. 1136]

The Professor is entitled to be disparaging about the criminal justice system, or 'forensic analysis', or the testing of evidence in cross-examination. Many people are. Such criticism from the sidelines may or may not be made on an informed basis. But surely when such a critic steps forward to take on the responsibility of condemning a fellow citizen as being guilty of such wicked behaviour, a little humility may be thought appropriate. One would certainly expect a willingness to address the strength or weakness of the factual evidence relevant to the individual concerned. [para. 1137]

Do the courts ever depart from the evidence model for decision making? Of course. Such decisions may then be open to criticism. Here is an example which we think, in fact, is wrong: *R (on the application of X) v Chief Constable of the West Midlands* (2004). A social worker was accused of rape. At the ID parade the victim picked out someone else and the charge was dropped. That should perhaps have been the end of the matter. On the evidence he was not a rapist. But by this stage he had not only lost his job, but the police passed the information, via a criminal record certificate, to prospective employers. It was not, in fact, a criminal record, but an abandoned criminal allegation. The police, challenged via judicial review, claimed they had no choice under the Police Act 1997 s. 115. The High Court disagreed, holding that inclusion of information of this sort was not automatic; natural justice required manifestly doubtful information to be weighed up and the person concerned to have the opportunity to present his case. Section 115 states that 'The Secretary of State shall also request the chief officer of every relevant police force to provide any information which, in the chief officer's opinion . . . might be relevant for the purpose described in the statement under subsection. The Court of Appeal said that the interests of children and the 'clear' language of s. 115 required information to be included in the certificate regardless of its quality. We think this is unjust and wrong. In our opinion the Chief Constable had a power and a duty to use his discretion using the evidential model.

■ Evidence or truth?

The review of the criminal justice system which led, in part, to the Criminal Justice Act 2003 characterizes the criminal process as 'a search for truth in accordance with the twin principles that the prosecution must prove its case and that defendants are not obliged to incriminate themselves' *Justice for All*, Cm 5563, 2002). We are not convinced that this accurately sums up the trial process. Truth may be obscured—sometimes quite rightly—by the rules of evidence. One of the shortcomings of the evidential model is that truth may be a casualty to a rule-based process, as is reflected by the apocryphal story in Box 6.3.

 BOX 6.3 Evidence or truth

It was a hot summer's day in the county court. Everbody was feeling testy. The old judge was listening to a particular witness, who was talking about the contents of a document that the witness had written and had sent to a person involved in the case. Mr Darby, the barrister, had a copy of the document in his hands and was slowly drawing out its contents from the witness. 'Mr Darby,' said the judge 'do you have a copy of this document?' 'Yes your Honour I do.' 'Am I to see it then?' 'No your Honour.' 'Am I not to know the truth of this wretched document. Am I not to hear the truth then, Mr Darby?' 'No, your Honour, that is not your function.' 'What, then, pray, Mr Darby, is my function?' 'Why, your Honour, your function is to hear the evidence, not the truth. And as your Honour will be aware those are not the same thing!'

A Deputy Director of Social Services, echoing the judge in Box 6.2, said on radio some time back that courts should concern themselves with truth, not evidence. He was clearly frustrated by the severe difficulties in getting the evidence of young children against their alleged abusers into court. (There has been progress on this issue since then—see chapter 7.) But courts have to be pragmatic. Truth can never be finally agreed, since a court's findings on the facts have to be based on evidence which—by definition in the case of a dispute—is inconsistent. Judicial fact-finding is not a scientific search for a truth which, with enough effort, will be uncovered. Courts decide, in the light of statutory guidance and cumulative experience, how much information they are able to consider and then they make a quick decision. The appeal process is there if they make irrational decisions or clearly ignore important evidence.

As well as having to erect pragmatic boundaries around the amount of evidence they can cope with, there are laws which stop courts hearing certain types of evidence, even if it may be highly significant. Privilege is an example. An eminent judge who died in 2004 went, according to the obituary, to his grave without revealing the name of a former client from his days as a barrister who had admitted to him that he had committed a murder for which an innocent man was serving life imprisonment. The rules of his profession, which any court would have recognized, prevented him ever divulging this evidence, even though it was highly probably true, even though it would enable an injustice to be corrected. It was privileged information, privileged because the law supports as a very high priority the ability of people to talk in complete confidence with their lawyers. (We discussed this kind of information in chapter 4 above.)

Other limits to truth seeking may be dictated by policy considerations. Consider the dilemma, for example, in ordering a blood test that might reveal that the man a child has called 'Daddy' for many years is not his or her biological father. See *Re H and A (Children) (Paternity: blood tests)* (2002): the husband knew nothing about his wife's affair until her ex-lover brought paternity proceedings in respect of the twins. When the husband accidentally discovered this he said he would leave if it turned out the twins were not his. Blood tests could destroy the family, according to the judge who refused the husband's request for a test which would reveal the truth In fact on appeal the court said illegitimacy was no stigma and the truth should be found, but the case illustrates the power of the courts to ignore evidence for policy reasons.

Technical rules

Evidence must be relevant—but what is relevant?

The law requires that evidence be 'relevant' or it will be excluded. Relevance has a commonsense meaning. If you are dealing with care proceedings, for example, your personal knowledge of the family circumstances, your professional judgement, and your experience may have led you to a feeling, which you have articulated persuasively in child protection meetings, that this child should be removed from home. But the court has to make the decision, not you. You have to present it with the evidence which it will treat as relevant, which may not be identical to your view. How will it decide what evidence is relevant?

The answer is that a court can treat as relevant only matters which law—statute or case law—has said are relevant. By law we mean the law which covers the particular issue in dispute. In the present example you will have to look at the Children Act 1989, s. 31. (For more detail on this see chapter 12.) This tells you that the court can make a care order if—in fact only if—it is satisfied that the child:

- has suffered significant harm, or
- is likely to suffer such harm, and
- that this harm is attributable to the standard of care of the parents or to the child's being beyond parental control,
- the proposed order is in the best interests of the child (s. 1).

Any facts which are going to help the court to decide one or more of these questions is called a *fact in issue*. What is a fact in issue will vary according to the law relating to the particular case. And they are not strictly 'facts' until they have been proved, but the lawyers call them facts in issue even while they are still allegations. For a s. 31 application, if your evidence cannot help the court with its decision on these criteria, it is not—and cannot be—legally relevant. It does not matter if you think it is relevant. If you start to talk about something else, the court will tell you to stick to the point. This happens at some point to every lawyer and to every social worker. Even if you think the court has made a mistake as to what is relevant, you must tailor your evidence to what it tells you is relevant, because the court's job is to interpret the law, including the law which determines what is relevant.

The rule on relevance can be stated as follows: evidence is relevant if it logically helps to prove, or disprove, a fact in issue. For this purpose put aside any thoughts as to whether the evidence is believable or not. You must assume in deciding if it is relevant that the evidence could be believed. Whether it is in fact believed is a matter for assessment by the judge, magistrate, jury or tribunal after the evidence has been received. (Of course, there is no point anyone tendering relevant evidence which is not likely to be believed.)

We will try now to identify actual facts in issue, using the 'significant harm' test under the Children Act 1989, s. 31. The issues that the court has to determine are whether such harm has occurred, or is likely to occur, and whether such harm can be attributed to a lack of parental care. Facts that will help the court to decide these issues are relevant facts, and if there is disagreement on them they are in issue. Let us assume a child has a bruise. No one disputes the existence of the bruise at the particular time, so that is not a fact in issue, even though it is relevant. A fact in issue might be how a bruise was caused. The parents say it was accidental. The social worker gives evidence from which it can be concluded that it was not. Relevant evidence on this particular fact in issue will be evidence that—if believed—would help to prove or disprove that it was caused non-accidentally. Medical evidence, facts observed by neighbours, the child's account, the parents' accounts, your own observations, your opinions on the family's behaviour, previous findings of non-accidental injury—these can all be relevant to this one fact in issue.

Several facts are usually in issue in any case. A court must consider all the relevant evidence and, on each of the facts in issue, decide whether the fact is established or not.

To seek to prove significant harm to a court, a series of incidents may be alleged; evidence may be given as to the harm that a child has suffered, that the child has turned to criminal behaviour, or is not attending school, or has disturbed behaviour, and so on. Evidence on any such allegations will then be admissible as relevant, if the court agrees it will help it to form a conclusion on the s. 31 issues of significant harm and lack of care.

The courts have to decide, in such a case, what has happened in the past. They consider relevant evidence and decide if the child has suffered significant harm and whether it is attributable to the lack of parental care, etc.

The court then goes back to what are the legal requirements for making a care order and finds that before it can make a care order it must also make decisions under the Children Act, s. 1 on what order is best for the child, if any, and all the other factors listed. Any fact relevant to this decision now becomes a further fact in issue—for example the court will need evidence on what the result of an order is likely to be, who is going to provide what to safeguard the child's interests, why an order will advance the child's interests more effectively than not making an order etc. Why? Because s. 31 requires a court to make these decisions, and it cannot do so without evidence and advice to guide it.

Rules under the Children Act 1989 help the courts and the parties to pinpoint what are facts in issue in a children case. Applications for any order must include a form setting out what are alleged to be the grounds for the desired order and what are the applicant's future plans for the child. Other parties have to reply by stating what aspects of the applicant's case they agree or disagree with and what allegations of fact they wish to put forward. In all cases in court—civil and criminal—procedural rules state what the parties must commit to paper before the trial. In a criminal case this will be found in the charge sheet and prosecution witness statements; in a civil case in an exchange of documents called pleadings backed up by witness statements on both sides. So the areas of factual dispute become narrowed by the time that evidence is presented to the court. Evidence is then required, and is relevant, only on the issues where there is a dispute.

Previous decisions of the courts also help to determine what factual evidence will be relevant. Again, taking 'significant harm' as an example, the courts have given some guidance on what might amount to significant harm. Truancy from school has been recognized as constituting 'significant harm' (*Re O* (1992): see chapter 12), and so evidence of truancy becomes relevant. Disagreements about whether, when, or how the truancy took place become facts in issue. Another example of case law clarifying what has to be proved comes again from the 'significant harm' test. Section 31 provides that it must be proved (among other things, as a ground for a care order) that the child '*is* suffering'. Does '*is*' mean *now*—in court, today? In *Re M R (Minor) (Care Order: Significant Harm)* (1994) (see chapter 12), it was held that the time to look at the evidence of the harm is the date that when the local authority instituted proceedings to protect the child.

■ Evidence or representations

By and large, when making a finding on the relevant facts, the courts can take into account only 'evidence'. Evidence, as we see later in this chapter, means the testimony of witnesses, the contents of documents, and the production of objects in court.

But there is another category of information which a court can take into account in making certain decisions; this information is not treated as 'evidence' and is not always subject to the same rules.

Let us consider an example. Having heard the relevant evidence and having ascertained the necessary facts in a care case, that a child has suffered harm due to lack of parental care, or in a criminal case that a person has committed an offence, the court can now hear representations from people who are not testifying as witnesses of fact, for example the lawyers. These representations are not subject to technically complex rules as to what is admissible, and are, of necessity, based largely on second-hand information and full of opinion (both of which are problems for witnesses giving evidence, as we see below). For example, in a mitigation speech after a conviction, the lawyer may say 'I have heard from the defendant's employer that a job awaits him if he is not sent to prison, and in my opinion it will be more likely to reduce the risk of further offending if he remains in the community.'

It will also be the role of the social worker to make representations. For example, assume that the court is satisfied that significant harm has occurred under s. 31, and that this relates to the standard of parenting. You may be asked to give a welfare report to the court and be available for questioning on it, for the purpose of representing, or giving your professional opinion, to the court what particular order should be made and why. Or the question of the appropriate sentence could be part of the advice you give in a pre-sentence report to a youth court.

In a child protection case you will normally provide your evidence (on the facts in issue) and your representations (on your opinion as to how the court should decide in the light of the evidence) in one written statement. When you are cross-examined it will be on both aspects—the evidence and the representations. But there will also be occasions when you will be delivering a report not on behalf of your agency, but as a servant of the court (see the last part of this chapter for when you take on these different roles); the same principles apply, your report and any questioning in court you may face on its contents do not consist, technically, of evidence but of representations, and the rules of evidence are relaxed.

Whether you are giving evidence or making representations, what you say must be justifiable and can be challenged both in cross examination and by evidence or representations which contradict it.

When you make a representation it will contain a mixture of factual information—i.e. what you believe to be facts—and opinion. If what you say in the course of a representation is challenged as factually inaccurate, the court must either ignore it, and any conclusions that derive from disputed facts, or require you to prove the point on evidence. For example, in a welfare report in care proceedings you say that the family live in squalor and do not provide a good home for the children. The latter point is your opinion, and you do not have to prove it. The court will weigh it up in the light of your overall credibility, expertise, any other opinion and information available, and the facts you rely on. But the point about the squalor will either go unchallenged, or the parents can challenge you to prove it. The alleged squalor then becomes a fact in issue. No conclusions can be based on it unless it is proved to the court by relevant evidence. It may not be important as an underpinning to your representation, in which case you can concede it; it may be vital to the decision on what order to make, and through your lawyer you will have to call evidence to prove the point.

Another example could be in a pre-sentence report on a juvenile, where you say that he or she has an alcohol problem, or missed several appointments with you without excuse. If the young offender challenges these allegations, the court has to ignore them unless you can prove them by producing evidence. It hardly needs saying that it is not a good idea to make allegations unless they need to be made to underpin your recommendations and you can, if necessary, demonstrate that they are true.

◼ Who has to prove what? What is the standard of proof?

This issue is not an abstract question just for legal scholars, as the recent high profile successful appeals of Sally Clark, Trupti Patel, and Angela Canning have shown. They were convicted in separate cases of murdering their babies, the main evidence being that of medical experts who said there was no other credible explanation than murder. The Appeal Court's acquittals of Clark and Canning, and the Crown Court's acquittal of Patel, was headline news, and the resulting case reports indicate a need for extreme care with expert evidence: see *R v Cannings (Angela)* (2004). Although these cases dealt with the criminal offences, there has followed a flood of appeals against care orders based on allegedly similar flawed expert evidence. The question of who has to prove what, and to what level of proof, suddenly became of interest to the public at large. An interesting case study which summarizes some of the issues is that of *Re U (A Child) (Serious Injury: Standard of Proof)* (2004) see Box 6.4.

To explain the balance of probability in a civil (i.e. family) case, let us again assume that the issue is whether there has been significant harm caused to the child because of a lack of parental care. The court has heard medical evidence, on one side showing that the bruise is not consistent with an accident; evidence that the father has been known to beat another child in the family; that there was a three-day delay before bringing the child to the doctor: yet on the other side there is medical evidence that suggests a plausible accident consistent with what the parents are saying; there is evidence from a relative of domestic harmony.

How does the court decide what actually happened and whether it is attributable to quality of parenting? It must do so, in a civil case, on the balance of probabilities. This means, for each fact which it has to decide, it metaphorically puts all the relevant and admissible evidence for each side into a pair of imaginary scales; the more convinced the judge or magistrates are by a particular bit of evidence, the more it weighs in the

BOX 6.4 Court of Appeal guidance on standards of proof in abuse cases

Two mothers wished to overturn findings in care proceedings that they had abused their children. One involved a finding of airways obstruction, and the other a series of eleven non-accidental injuries. We quote from the judgment of Butler-Sloss LJ, giving guidance on how a court in family proceedings should approach this kind of evidence:

[23] .... (i) The cause of an injury or an episode that cannot be explained scientifically remains equivocal.

(ii)   Recurrence is not in itself probative.

(iii) Particular caution is necessary in any case where the medical experts disagree, one opinion declining to exclude a reasonable possibility of natural cause.

(iv) The court must always be on guard against the over-dogmatic expert, the expert whose reputation or *amour propre* is at stake, or the expert who has developed a scientific prejudice.

(v)   The judge in care proceedings must never forget that today's medical certainty may be discarded by the next generation of experts or that scientific research will throw light into corners that are at present dark.

. . .

[25] Contrast the role of the judge conducting the trial of a preliminary issue in care proceedings. The trial is necessary not to establish adult guilt, nor to provide an adult with the opportunity to clear his name. The trial of a preliminary issue is the first, but essential, stage in a complex process of child protection through the medium of judicial proceedings. The state, in the form of the local authority, in order to establish a foundation for intervention in the life of the family, must satisfy the court—

(a) that the child concerned is suffering, or is likely to suffer, significant harm; and (b) that the harm, or likelihood of harm, is attributable to-(i) the care given to the child or likely to be given to him if the order were not made, not being what it would be reasonable to expect a parent to give to him . . . (See s. 31(2) of the Children Act 1989.)

[26] It is for the purpose of satisfying that threshold that the local authority seeks to prove specific facts against the parent or parents. Only if it succeeds in that task can its application for a care or supervision order proceed. Thus the preliminary issue of fact constitutes the gateway to a judicial discretion as to what steps should be taken to protect the child and to promote his welfare. In those circumstances we must robustly reject [the] submission that the local authority should refrain from proceedings or discontinue proceedings in any case where there is a substantial disagreement amongst the medical experts. For the judge invariably surveys a wide canvas, including a detailed history of the parents' lives, their relationship and their interaction with professionals. There will be many contributions to this context, family members, neighbours, health records, as well as the observation of professionals such as social workers, health visitors and children's guardian.

[27] In the end the judge must make clear findings on the issues of fact before the court, resting on the evidence led by the parties and such additional evidence as the judge may have required in the exercise of his quasi-inquisitorial function. All this is the prelude to a further and fuller investigation of a range of choices in search of the protection and welfare of the children. A positive finding against a parent or both parents does not in itself preclude the possibility of rehabilitation. All depends on the facts and circumstances of the individual case. In that context the consequences of a false positive finding in care proceedings may not be as dire as the consequence of the conviction of an innocent in criminal proceedings.

[28] So it by no means follows that an acquittal on a criminal charge or a successful appeal would lead to the absolution of the parent or carer in family or civil proceedings.

In one of the two appeals permission to appeal was refused, as the judge had been entitled to rely on the medical evidence in coming to her conclusions. In the other, permission to appeal was granted as the medical evidence, taken alone, was not sufficiently cogent to be relied on to pass the balance of probabilities test. However, the appeal was then dismissed as the weight and credibility of the non-medical evidence supported the conclusion that the mother had been responsible for the injuries sustained by the child.

scales; it then looks to see which way the scales tip. If they tip at all, that fact is accepted or rejected. That may not be the end of the case, as there has to be a further balancing exercise for each fact in issue; for example, after finding, on the balance of probabilities, that the child has suffered significant harm, the evidence on the question 'Was it caused by a lack of parental care?' must be weighed in the same way.

What happens, however, if the scales do not move at all and there is perfect balance? In other words, if the court is unable to decide who to believe and whose evidence is more convincing on the particular fact in issue. The solution to what might be an impasse is that whoever is alleging a fact has the burden of proving that fact. In care proceedings, it will be the social service agency that alleges the significant harm, and that it is due to lack of parental care. It therefore has the burden of proof on each of these facts in issue, and it must discharge that burden by producing relevant evidence on each which the court accepts as more cogent than the evidence put to rebut that allegation. If they are not proved on the balance of probabilities and the scales refuse to tip, the order cannot be made.

This may produce a result that you are uncomfortable with. Take the case of *Re O and N (Children) (Non-accidental injury: burden of proof)* (2002). The father admitted causing some injuries, but other injuries could have been caused by either him or the mother. It was important to know whether the mother was to blame, because s. 31 of the Children Act required a decision to be made on whether the child was at risk of significant harm from her. The trial court thought that unless she could explain the injuries assumptions should be made that she was to blame; but the Court of Appeal said that if the scales did not tip she had no need to explain anything. But such a result is rare. For example in a case where experts disagreed, but the majority thought the child's death at the parents' home, and symptoms of retinal haemmorhage, indicated non-accidental injury: this was sufficient to tip the scales, even though some experts only thought it more probable than not, and therefore not certain, and even though other experts disagreed (*Re A (A child) (Non-accidental injury: medical evidence)* (2002). If the scales do tip on the harm issue, s. 1 of the Act still requires that the agency must put into the metaphorical scales evidence which convinces the court on the balance of probabilities that the order it seeks is the best outcome for the child.

The burden of proof in a criminal case requires more than just tipping these imaginary scales. In fact, despite the blindfolded statue of justice at the Old Bailey holding a pair of scales, the use of scales does not apply. The defence do not have to prove their story, and the prosecution must prove theirs beyond reasonable doubt. This was reaffirmed by the High Court in *Evans v DPP* (2001), which affirmed that the right to have the prosecution prove the case is a human right under Article 6 of the European Convention. And it was restated very clearly following the *Cannings* case (see above), from which the Court of Appeal in *Re U* (above) drew the following clear principle to illustrate the burden of proof in a criminal case:

> In a criminal trial for murder or manslaughter arising out of a series of sudden infant deaths a jury is not entitled to convict and a guilty verdict cannot be deemed safe unless a natural cause of death, whether explained or unexplained, can be excluded as a reasonable (and not fanciful) possibility.

The same set of facts can be in issue in both a criminal and a civil case, for example when a child has allegedly been sexually abused. The alleged perpetrator may be acquitted in the criminal proceedings because there is reasonable doubt about his or her guilt. On the same evidence in the civil court, a care order can be made because the court is satisfied that, among other things, a person committed those acts and the child has suffered significant harm—the court is satisfied on the balance of probabilities.

■ A higher standard of proof in serious abuse cases?

Does the civil standard of tipping the scales on the balance of probability apply equally in all civil cases? In theory the answer is 'yes', but the courts have ruled that some facts should be harder to prove than others. An example of this occurs where, in care proceedings, it is alleged and becomes a fact in issue that a named person has abused a child. The case of *In re G (a minor)* (1987) suggests that where allegations of criminal conduct are made in care proceedings against a named individual, before accepting those allegations as true, a higher standard of proof is required than merely the balance of probabilities, but proof beyond reasonable would be too strict. And in *Re W (Minors)* (1990), Butler-Sloss LJ said:

> Grave allegations of sexual abuse made in a statement by a child . . . would, unsupported, rarely be sufficiently cogent and reliable for a court to be satisfied on the balance of probabilities that the person named was indeed the perpetrator.

(Contrast this cautious approach to the child's evidence with the decision of the Court of Appeal to convict a man for rape on the evidence of a 6 year old (*R v Norbury* (1992)). See Questions of Credibility in chapter 7.)

It may be that the court does not need to determine the identity of the abuser to make a finding of the necessary facts for a care order under s. 31 Children Act. In *Re W* the court was able make an order to protect the child, deciding that on the balance of probability significant harm had occurred or was likely, and the s. 31 requirements were satisfied without deciding who had caused it. Again, in *Lancashire County Council v B (A Child) (Care Orders: Significant Harm)* (2000), where the court could not decide whether it was the childminder or the parents who had injured the child, the significant harm was still made out. But if it was important to know if a particular individual had committed the abuse, the standard of proof would be higher.

The standard of proof can also arise as an issue in a civil case where allegations supporting, say, an application for a care order are made against someone who is not a party to the case? This happened in *Re S (Minors)* (1997). The local authority wished to bolster its case by referring to allegations that the stepfather had assaulted his niece (now an adult). The stepfather did not want this issue decided in his absence, and he was allowed to intervene in the case to defend himself against these specific allegations, which then had to be decided according to the standard set out above in *Re G* and *Re W*.

Sometimes the burden of proof is defined in statute or regulations. An example of this is the Sex Discrimination (Indirect Discrimination and Burden of Proof) Regulations 2001, brought in to comply with a European Union directive. Under this someone alleging sex discrimination must establish sufficient facts for the tribunal to presume that direct or indirect discrimination could have occurred. The respondent then has the burden of proof of showing that it did not. You may recall from reading chapter 2 that the new rules on discrimination on grounds of sexual orientation, race or national origins, also place the burden of proof not on the alleged victim but on the alleged discriminator, who has to demonstrate that their actions either did not discriminate or, if they did, did so in a legitimate and proportionate manner.

It may be worth digressing for a moment to consider the burden of proof required for certain decisions your department has to make, where your department is acting in a quasi-judicial capacity. When a local authority investigates allegations of child abuse, the very decision to investigate is made after weighing up evidence. That decision must be arrived at in a way which replicates what the courts do, and in particular must be based on evidence properly weighed up. In *R(S) v Swindon Borough Council and Another* (2001), a man had been acquitted of indecent assault on the child of the woman he was living with. The local authority was still worried, and decided it had a duty to investigate under s. 47 Children Act (see chapter 11). The man tried to get a court order compelling the authority to stop on the grounds that it did not have sufficient evidence. In fact he was unsuccessful in this case because the amount of evidence required to investigate is by definition less than that required to make a court order or to bring a criminal charge. But the point here is that some evidence must exist to trigger the investigation, and an improper investigation which is not based on sufficient evidence properly evaluated can indeed be halted by court order (*L and P v Reading Borough Council and Chief Constable of Thames Valley Police* (2001)).

You will note there are, in the statute, lower burdens of proof when a local authority seeks an Emergency Protection Order (chapter 12) compared to when it seeks a care order.

Interestingly a higher standard of proof seems to be required for more serious abuse allegations, a view we have difficulty accepting. It is not an approach confined to child abuse, and perhaps the view that serious allegations require more robust proof is sensible in other areas of social policy. But we find it strange that the greater the risk to the child, the harder it is to prove the harm actually occurred, which would trigger the power to protect the child. *Re H and R (Child Sexual Abuse: Standard of Proof)* (1996), was a decision on this difficult point, and was reached by the House of Lords by a majority of 3:2. Their ruling was that serious abuse is less likely to occur than minor abuse; therefore serious allegations require more cogent evidence than other allegations. The court did not have any expert evidence on probabilities—it was essentially armchair science. Research might reveal the opposite. What makes this decision—to refuse a care order under the Children Act 1989, s. 31—bizarre is that all the courts which had heard the original evidence and the appeals thought on the *actual* evidence the child's allegations were more credible than the man's denials. Nevertheless, the child's siblings were denied the protection of the 1989 Act on the basis of being at risk of serious harm because the allegations against the man were so serious! The principle has been repeatedly upheld, most recently in *Re ET (Serious Injuries: Standard of Proof)* (2003).

◼ Inferences and presumptions

We have said that the party raising allegations and therefore putting a fact in issue must prove each and every one of them. But proof can be achieved by inference, and occasionally by presumption, as well as by evidence. Imagine that a person is identified running away from a jeweller's shop carrying a bag marked 'swag', and evidence is given that items found in the bag are identical to items missing from the shop. An inference can be made in relation to proving the facts in issue for a theft charge, which include that this person took them, dishonestly intending to keep them. Most findings of fact require inferences to be drawn from the direct evidence given.

Let us give two examples. It is 1.20 a.m. The accused is sitting in his stationary car on a road; the keys are in the ignition. It turns out his blood alcohol level is over the limit. He denies that he was driving and there is no direct evidence to contradict his assertion. Do the circumstances lead to an inference that he was driving? And if so is it a safe inference? The answer was 'yes', and his appeal against conviction was refused: *Whelehan v DPP* (1995). In *Secretary of State for Work and Pensions v Jones* (2003) a man was refusing the DNA test which would determine whether or not he was the father of the child. The court had evidence that he had lived with the mother at the time of conception, but the mother had named the husband as the father on the birth certificate. The court inferred that refusal to take the test was enough, in these circumstances, to prove the man to be the father for child support purposes.

Inferences are sometimes not easy. A parent delayed seeking medical help for a child's injury. Can a court infer from this that the parent inflicted the injury? On its own the inference is unsafe, but it may be combined with other evidence, such as the nature of the injury or the doubtful explanation given for it. The court may or may not draw the inference depending on the other evidence presented, the credibility of all the evidence, and of course the judge's or the magistrates' own experience (or prejudice). A social worker is alleged to have committed sexual assaults and then fails to attend the tribunal which has to decide whether he should remain on the Consultancy Service Index or be listed as unsuitable to work with children. The tribunal was entitled to draw an adverse inference from his unaccounted absence: *Secretary of State for Health v C* (2003).

Some inferences can be made as a matter of law. For example, under the Criminal Procedure and Investigations Act 1996, a defendant on a criminal charge must supply details of the nature of his or her defence before trial. If they do not, and there is no recognized reason for the failure, the court is entitled draw adverse inferences from this and to see the inference as strengthening any other evidence against the accused. In chapter 15 we will discuss the power of the court to draw inferences from a suspect's silence when being questioned about an alleged crime by the police.

Often a court should be warned against a 'common sense' inference. In child-abuse cases it takes experience to realize that a child may conceal the abuse because of threats made and/or misplaced guilt. A jury might infer from silence that the alleged abuse did not take place, and it might require expert evidence to explain the psychological processes which can lead a child to denial and delay.

Inferences may, but need not be, drawn from the particular facts, Presumptions go further—the law says that they should be drawn unless the evidence proves otherwise. The Court of Appeal has explicitly stated that it can be presumed that a 1-month-old baby should be with the mother, so the father who claims residence has to prove the baby's welfare requires baby and mother to live apart (*Re W* (1992), *Re D* (1999)). In *T-R and W (Children)(Adoption: Expert Evidence)* (2001), the Court of Appeal rejected expert medical opinion that a 9-month-old child should reside with her family in Tanzania rather than the mother, even with evidence of the mother's alcohol abuse, and presumed the child and mother should be together Another example of a presumption in family law is that a child benefits from contact with the father: (*Re R* (1993)). (Contact issues are considered in relation to children in care in chapter 12 and in family disputes in chapter 14.)

▣ Judicial notice—using common knowledge to replace evidence

Monday follows Sunday; cars in the UK are driven on the left. Some facts do not have to be proved. The judge (magistrate or other factfinder) takes 'judicial notice' of such a fact. But if something apparently well known is in dispute the court will prefer to hear the evidence. In the days when adultery allegations in divorce had to be proven in a full trial, a husband tried to rely on the well known fact that pregnancy does not last 12 months, and since he had been away for 12 months he could not be the father of the child. The case went to the House of Lords, where the majority refused to assume without specialist evidence that this was completely impossible. (The husband did get his decree, however, as a GP had given his opinion at trial that such a gap between intercourse and birth had never been known, and this could be the required expert evidence: *Preston-Jones v Preston-Jones* (1951).)

◼ Questions of credibility: who will the court believe?

When all parties have had a chance to present their evidence the court must decide on the issues. It must not sit on the fence and wait, like a patient scientist, for more data. To decide the case it must in many cases decide whether one witness is to be believed (or, euphemistically, relied on) rather than another on a particular fact in issue.

In a criminal case, the magistrates or the jury decide whether they believe one story or another. In a civil case, it is the magistrates or the judge. It is up to these factfinders to decide what is credible and what is not. There is normally no right of appeal on the basis of 'well I wouldn't have believed that evidence', unless no reasonable factfinder hearing that evidence could possibly have believed it. (The only exception to this is the automatic right of a complete rehearing by way of appeal to the Crown Court from a conviction in a magistrates court.)

The decision on the evidence will always be that of the judge, magistrates or jury. The following is an example of that principle. A judge rejected the unanimous opinion of social workers, guardian *ad litem* (now children's guardian) and consultant paediatrician, who all advised that the mother posed a risk of significant harm and who all advised adoption. The judge decided the non-accidental injuries were not the mother's fault and, so long as the decision was explained by the judge and not perverse, the Court of Appeal would not overturn it: *Re B (Care: Expert Witnesses)* (1996).

As we have indicated, a decision on the fact in issue cannot be avoided. So in *Re X (Non-accidental Injury: Expert Opinion)* (2001) we find the parent's experts explaining a child's bone fractures by saying the child had brittle bone disease. However, the local authority experts testified that in their opinion there is no such thing. Here was a straight conflict of expert opinion. The court had to make a decision; it could not wait for scientific certainty; it accepted the evidence of the local authority witnesses, so significant harm under Children Act, s. 31, was proved on the balance of probability.

The next chapter will cover the issue of credibility of the child witness.

◼ Is evidence always required?

In most civil proceedings, the parties can agree to settle all or part of a case, so some key facts are not in issue. However, in cases where social workers are concerned, this is rare. In care proceedings, even if the parent admits the facts and accepts the recommenda-

tions, the court can make the order only if the grounds are made out to its satisfaction—
that is what the statute requires. And there may be other reasons for wanting a full
hearing of the evidence. *Re M (Threshold Criteria: Parental Concessions)* (1999) is an interesting example. Three adopted children each alleged sexual abuse against the adoptive
father. In criminal proceedings he was acquitted, but (as we saw above) this means
only that the evidence did not satisfy the jury beyond reasonable doubt, and it was not
conclusive proof that he did not do the deed. But the adoptive father did not want to
continue as an adoptive parent. He effectively conceded the criteria for a care order by
admitting his bad parenting and his subsequent rejection of the children. However, the
Court of Appeal decided that the children needed to be listened to, and a judicial finding was needed on the issue of abuse in case the adoptive father ever applied for contact.
Therefore, the court must hear and make a finding of fact on the abuse allegations.

Sometimes, of course, evidence can be dispensed with. For example, a defendant in a
criminal case pleads guilty; or a court makes an interim care order without hearing the
full argument or evidence, because the parties agree (see further chapter 11). And, of
course, sometimes a judicial decision is not needed: under the Children Act, for
example, the authority working in partnership with the parents can meet the needs of a
child, for example by taking the child into accommodation, without seeking additional
powers under a court order.

◼ Testimony, documents, and direct observation—types of evidence

Our courts, as we observed above, are the product of history. The rules evolved when
few people could read or write; it was necessary either to have oral evidence or do
without. Nowadays, there can be a choice, but despite some erosions of the rule, the
norm is still that evidence should be presented orally. There are obvious criticisms of
this bias towards hearing the witness in person—expense and delay, and, as we shall see
in criminal cases, loss of potentially useful evidence—but it has the attraction of giving
parties their day in court, the chance to see clearly what the case for or against them is,
and to challenge the evidence of the other parties directly. This is the process of 'justice
not only being done, but being seen to be done'. Judges, magistrates, and juries are
heavily influenced when asserting credibility by the appearance and manner of a
witness in the witness box.

But as well as the witness speaking in the witness box in response to questions there
are two other categories of evidence: documentary evidence (which includes audio and
video tapes, computer data, and photographs) and real evidence. The court allows
documents as evidence. But there are problems in the form of the hearsay rule if you
actually want to get the court to read what the documents say and to take account of the
contents. Reports and written statements (see below) are, by definition, documentary
evidence.

Real evidence means things which relate to the facts in issue—for players of Cluedo,
the piece of lead piping or the revolver which was the murder weapon; on a more
mundane level, in a road accident case, the brake cylinder which was allegedly defective
and led to the crash. Surprisingly, people are real evidence, including their demeanour

in court, which is relevant to whether they are to be believed. What they actually say in court, of course, is oral evidence.

Evidence on the same fact can come from all three types of evidence: for example, the particular fact in issue is an alleged injury to a child. A witness can give oral evidence that she saw the injury being inflicted, or the resulting injury; a doctor can submit a written report and even an X-ray—these are items of documentary evidence; a scar on the child's body could be looked at by the court as real evidence (although there would have to be compelling reasons to put a child through that when other satisfactory documentary or oral evidence is available, such as a photograph, a medical report, or medical testimony).

Excluded evidence

Some evidence, which at first sight appears to be relevant, is not admissible because it falls within one of the ancient rules excluding it.

Character evidence in criminal trials was until recently one such rule. A person's bad character, including previous crimes, was as a matter of law not relevant as evidence, with a few exceptions such as where the past actions showed a distinctive course of conduct which pointed the finger at guilt on this occasion. Now, under the Criminal Justice Act 2003, this has been relaxed.

Another such rule is evidence the criminal court considers to be intrinsically unfair. This is excluded under s. 78, Police and Criminal Evidence Act. For example a criminal court may—not, however, must—withdraw evidence obtained through a trick or an illegal search if the overall result is unfair to the accused.

Hearsay evidence

The hearsay rule excludes a witness's evidence being given without the witness being available to be questioned on it. This rule of exclusion has long been relaxed in civil proceedings, which means in child protection proceedings in particular, and has also been relaxed under the 2003 Criminal Justice Act. But it has not exactly been abolished. And it helps to understand what is hearsay, even if it is admissible in evidence, because the reasons why it used to be excluded are still valid in considering its weight in a trial.

If A has first-hand knowledge of a fact in issue, the courts want to hear it from A. If B gives A's evidence—'I know the facts because A told me'—the only facts that can be tested in court are whether A really did tell B, whether B's memory of what A said is accurate etc.—but the accuracy of A's memory or firsthand observations of the relevant facts cannot be tested at all. The court calls that hearsay. The exclusionary rule simply stated, with exceptions, that it would be better not to even hear such evidence. But it is worth being aware that even with the relaxation of the exclusionary rule, the second hand evidence can lack the weight of first hand testimony from a witness who has been cross examined on it.

Incidentally, not all reported speech is hearsay. Imagine Jane says the words 'John is a swindler'. Jane denies saying this. John sues for defamation. Bill claims he heard what Jane said, so if he is to help prove that part of his case John has to call Bill as a witness. Is it hearsay for Bill to tell the court what, according to him, Jane said? The purpose of his evidence will not be to prove that John is a swindler. The fact in issue is 'Did Jane *say* that John is a swindler? Or did she not?' It is only hearsay if the court needs to make a decision on the truth of the second-hand statement. Merely making a decision on whether it was said or not is not hearsay, it is just another factual observation by, in this case, Bill.

The hearsay 'rule', once hearsay is identified, looks simple enough: hearsay should not be used. The trouble is, such an approach excludes potentially helpful evidence. Witnesses die, disappear, forget, lie, and get embarrassed, confused, or frightened. What they said at the time, particularly if it is written or officially recorded, may be more reliable than what they may say from the witness box. And in most circumstances now such reasons will be perfectly acceptable to justify admitting hearsay evidence, in criminal as well as civil trials. But the reasons why previously the courts refused to admit it may still be good reason for trying to get the witness to court rather than to bring the witness's evidence to court at second hand. And in criminal cases, ultimately, a court can exclude evidence which is too unfair, which hearsay evidence could be.

Hearsay in child protection proceedings

The most significant hearsay evidence, from your point of view, is probably the evidence of children. If a child tells you that he or she has been hit, or sexually abused, by a parent, that statement is of crucial importance to a care case or a criminal case. There is often no other convincing evidence of the relevant facts, particularly the identification of the perpetrator.

Under s. 96 of the Children Act, in cases involving the upbringing, maintenance, or welfare of children, hearsay evidence is allowed. Out-of-court disclosures by children can be evidence in any case in which matters concerning children are in issue. In fact anything written or said out of court, by any person, not just a child, can be evidence in this type of case. (See the next chapter, however, for discussion on the issue of 'disclosure'.) Under s. 45 the same rule permits hearsay in emergency protection proceedings (see chapter 11).

The overall expectation is that in child protection proceedings, and in private family law disputes about children, the CAFCAS officer is expected to tell the court what the child would wish to say—the child should not have to testify.

So if a court is considering the future of children, it should do so with all the available information before it. It would rather receive the information, weigh it, and reject it, than not hear it at all—even if it is hearsay. Only in that way can all relevant issues be considered, and the child's best interests be protected.

We would remind you of the case study with which this chapter started: *Re D (Sexual Abuse Allegations: Evidence of Adult Victim)* (2002). The Court of Appeal angrily rejected conclusions drawn by magistrates about abuse allegations put before the court by a social worker when the adult witness had neither given the evidence in court herself (but could have) nor made a statement. The evidence was admissible according to the rules, but the court should never have relied on it in that form.

Hearsay in criminal cases

We will see below that in criminal proceedings too the admissibility rules for hearsay have been relaxed: but courts are bound to take a similar approach to that in *Re D* and robustly reject evidence which is flimsy and untested when serious matters (which all criminal charges are) fall to be decided. For Article 6 of the European Convention on Human Rights provides (amongst other things) the fundamental right for the accused:

> to examine or have examined witnesses against him and to obtain the attendance and examination of witnesses on his behalf under the same conditions as witnesses against him.

This is another way of restating the hearsay rule. In criminal cases the court generally expects any witnesses who know something of relevance to the case against the accused to come to court; if they cannot testify from the witness box the court will have to be very careful to weigh up whether it can be used at all, and that will depend on how reliable it is likely to be, and the reasons for not bringing the witness to court. So evidence of what other people said, for example evidence contained in your file notes, records, or recollections of interviews with the child, and reports from neighbours are all likely to breach the principle of a defendant having a proper chance to challenge evidence directly, but the court will have to weigh up the fairness of admitting such evidence. There is no absolute rule to bar it: a court can allow *any* hearsay evidence to be used, under the 2003 Criminal Justice Act. But it will have to weigh up if it is in the interests of justice, and it will wish to see a good reason why it is impossible or inappropriate to insist on the witness attending.

But even with these relaxations of the hearsay rule, criminal courts generally insist on witnesses whose evidence can be tested. Even videos of interviews with children—documentary hearsay—are only admitted if the child has been made available for cross-examination at or before the trial (see next chapter). So you have to understand why the police may be reluctant to refer the case for prosecution when you yourselves have what seems like an open and shut case showing child abuse.

There has always been an important exception to the hearsay rule in criminal proceedings. It is known as confession evidence. We will introduce the concept here, but explain it in more detail in chapter 15. Words that go against the interest of the party speaking them, for example a suspect 'coughing' to the police, can be quoted back in court as evidence of the truth of what was said, so long as the confession was not extracted improperly. A simple example in a careless driving prosecution would be a driver after a road accident who says: 'I'm sorry, I just wasn't paying attention.' These words can be quoted back in court as evidence of carelessness. Such 'I wish I'd never said that' statements are called confessions (or admissions in a civil case). Unless doubt can be cast over the circumstances in which a person has confessed, it is considered to be very reliable evidence. It is a form of hearsay because the person is not giving the confession as a witness in the witness box.

The same rule giving particular credence to admissions applies in a civil case. So if a parent admits to a social worker 'I hit my child', the court will pay considerable attention to the social worker repeating that admission in care proceedings as well as in a criminal prosecution. The parent may of course deny that he or she did say those words. You will have to be able to convince the court of the accuracy of your recollection, backed up by meticulously kept notes. You will also have to be careful to avoid receiving information in confidence from a parent, or anyone else, since you know that it may become key evidence in court proceedings involving children. There is nothing to stop you discussing your allegations with the parents out of court, and repeating to the court what they tell you, but we suggest that, just as the police must caution suspects before they are questioned, you should inform people that what they say to you cannot be guaranteed complete confidence—such an assurance would be wrong, because your duty to protect a child through giving all relevant evidence to the court would override any personal preference for confidentiality. (We discussed this in chapter 4.)

Hearsay and anti-social behaviour orders

You will in two later chapters (15 on criminal justice and 18 on violence, anti-social behaviour, and harassment) encounter a court order which is neither criminal nor civil: the anti-social behaviour order, an order made in the magistrates' court. It has the characteristics of a criminal sentence: a person is found to have behaved in a way society wishes to deter, and a court order is made which can lead to a conviction if it is breached. But the legislation which creates it (Crime and Disorder Act 1998) specifically allows hearsay evidence and specifically makes it a civil hearing, in which the balance of probabilities applies, not proof beyond reasonable doubt. Because of its quasi-criminal nature, the order has been subject to a human rights challenge, on the ground that unrestricted hearsay in a criminal charge breaches the right to test the prosecution's allegations (Article 6 of the Convention—see above). The argument failed in the Divisional Court: *R (on the application of Chingham) v Marylebone Magistrates Court* (2001). Perhaps this decision augurs badly for any human rights challenge to the use of more hearsay made possible under the new Criminal Justice Act.

Hearsay—admissibility and weight

You will now have the impression that a great deal of hearsay, (i.e. second-hand evidence) can, after all, be admitted. But we do not wish to give the impression that courts see hearsay as in itself desirable as an alternative to evidence from witnesses in court. Let us consider, for example, the welfare report. (See below for further discussion of reports.) It is based on discussion with various interested parties and, to do a fair job, it must report the essence of the discussions. The welfare officer recommends to the court that, for example, the child should not live with the father. This is based on interviews with the mother, who makes allegations about the father's brutality. To act on the recommendation, the court inevitably places some weight on those hearsay statements. The opinion of the Court of Appeal (*Thompson v Thompson* (1986), confirming what a judge had said in an earlier case) was:

> Some hearsay is unavoidable in such a document, and in respect of comparatively uncontroversial matters is likely to be unobjectionable; but I think it is important that a reporting officer should report his own observations and assessments, and that where he is constrained

to pass on second-hand information or opinions he should endeavour to make this explicit and should indicate the source and his own reasons, if he has any, for agreeing with any such opinions. Where a judge has to arrive at a crucial finding of fact he should found them upon sworn evidence rather than on an unsworn report.

This opinion was supported by Butler-Sloss LJ in *Re W (Minors)* (1990):

I agree that the liberty to tender hearsay evidence could be abused. I cannot imagine that any judge would allow a grave allegation against a parent to be proved solely by hearsay, at any rate in a case in which direct evidence could be produced.

This means that hearsay will not be excluded, but a case where the relevant facts are entirely based on such evidence will not usually be easy to prove.

We would like to finish this section on hearsay with some words of common sense, which should be applied in the preparation of any evidence, not just material containing hearsay. They were written by Roger Maunday in the *Law Society's Gazette* (1986) 29 Oct, 3221: '[E]vidence is appraised on its merits by a judicious application of common nous, a balance being struck between direct and indirect evidence, between reliable, confirmed or reasoned reports of facts on the one hand and fickle gossip on the other.' Our advice therefore is to go for the best evidence you can get, which means witnesses who can tell the court the facts from their own personal experience, but not to be afraid of bringing relevant, second-hand evidence, so long as you are prepared to be cross-examined on the sources and reliability of such evidence.

Hearsay and representations to the court

When we discussed representations earlier (attempts to advise the court in reaching its decision, rather than evidence of facts in issue) you may recall that these are not evidence; the rules of evidence do not apply, and hearsay is not excluded. The Children Act clarifies the position as to representations made in a report to the court; under s. 7, any matter referred to in the report, whether hearsay or opinion, is admissible so long as it is relevant. Nevertheless, we would remind you that if representations to the court include statements of fact which are in dispute (for example in deciding whether to make a care order after the significant harm test has been satisfied a statement that 'F is not capable of looking after this child'; a statement after a conviction on what the sentence should be such as 'D has no prospects of getting a job and has few ties in the community') the court cannot rely on them, and if the fact is important to the decision it may have to be proved by evidence.

Expert and opinion evidence

Courts have traditionally had an abhorrence of witnesses offering opinions: 'Give us the facts. We will form our own opinions.'

Like the rule which excludes hearsay, the rule excluding opinion evidence is easy to state but hard to apply with certainty. What appears to be a simple fact, such as 'The car was going fast', or 'She was drunk' or even 'The person I saw was John' is, on reflection, nothing other than the observer's opinion as to drunkenness, speed, or a person's features. But the court allows a witness to give their opinion of facts that could not easily be conveyed in any other way, so the examples above cause no problem. The opinion can be stated: whether it is believed is another matter. Coming closer to the borderline, statements such as 'She looked frightened' or 'He was trying to avoid me'—statements which are giving an opinion as to someone else's state of mind—will usually be admissible as the only way of saying what was observed. But from a layperson, a statement such as 'This injury was not an accident', or 'I think she was behaving negligently' will be refused.

Sometimes courts cannot make up their minds about the evidence without the help of an expert. In areas such as mental health and child care, opinion evidence is allowed and is usually crucial. The Civil Evidence Act 1972 expressly permits experts to give their opinion to the court, if they are experts in that subject (*Re M and R* (1996)). The courts presume that as a qualified social worker you are an expert on issues of general child care (see *F v Suffolk County Council* (1981)). Judges should accept expert evidence, or make clear why they have not accepted it, according to the Court of Appeal. In *Re M (Child: Residence)* (2002) the judge had rather liked the impression the father gave from the witness box and thought him capable of caring for the child. Three expert witnesses had all agreed that he had a severely damaged personality. The Court of Appeal stated that the judge was wrong to be guided by his inexpert impression in these circumstances and should have either accepted their evidence or given clear reasons for coming to the opposite conclusion.

Expert opinion and research findings

Aside from disagreements between children's guardians and social workers, expert opinion (including in a report which you have submitted) may be attacked by, for instance, the parent's lawyer because the social work principles are wrong or weak. In difficult, complicated cases there may well be grounds for assisting the court by referring to particular 'learned' writings, either in the report or in oral evidence on a particular topic.

Let us take an example to illustrate. You are dealing with a case of a child who, you say, has been physically abused. To counter the obvious contention by the parents' lawyer that the injuries were accidental, you may well wish to draw the court's attention to research findings about the characteristics of families that are liable to batter their children. To do this you may, for example, refer to the conclusions contained in articles such as Kempe, C. H. (1978) *Recent developments in the field of child abuse*. Child Abuse and Neglect, 2(4): 261–7) or Ghate, D., Hazel, N., Creighton, S. J., Finch, S., and Field, J. (2003) 'The National Study of Parents, Children and Discipline in Great Britain, Key Findings' **www.nspcc.org.uk/inform/Research/Summaries/ParentsChildrenAndDisciplineSummary.pdf,** or refer to the findings of the various enquiries into the death of children such as the Laming Report into the *Climbié* case. Referral to Kempe would show, for example, that such assaults are prevalent amongst families where the parents are under 21 years old, where neither works, where the child subject to the abuse is the father's stepchild, and that such battering is likely to recur unless the family dynamics are altered. With that information the court may agree there is sufficient evidence of the risk of significant harm and agree with your recommendation as to the type of order that they make.

As an expert in social work, you are entitled to state your professional opinions and you must explain where you derive these from. But if you are going to refer to such published work then you have to be careful to ensure that it is within your competence so to do. This means that you have to have an expertise in the area, which may be because it is within the general body of social work knowledge (usually taught as part of general training) or you have a particular expertise. This may be because you have obtained a certain qualification or because you have had long experience in a given area. That being the case there is no reason why you should not include reference to such work in your report. You should discuss with your agency lawyer whether you will need to disclose in advance the opinion and the support for it to the other parties to the proceedings and, if appropriate, supply copies of the extracts from the relevant publications to which you may refer.

The danger in including research findings in your report is that the other side may have the opportunity to test you in cross-examination on your knowledge, and if it is shown to be lacking then you may end up weakening, rather than strengthening, your case. This danger is greater where you seek to rely on a controversial or 'new' theory. If you are in any doubt discuss it with your agency lawyer. If there is any doubt then your lawyer may well advise that either a 'proper' (i.e. a more eminent) expert witness should be brought in or there should be no allusion to the point during the hearing.

Against that there is the other trap, that you ignore your expertise and your professional standing. The courts accept that you, by virtue of being a social worker, are already an expert on questions of general child development (*F v Suffolk County Council* (1981)). Therefore do not be afraid to say, if it is true, 'In my professional opinion and in the light of the evidence I think . . .'. This indeed is the essence of the service that you should render to the court, viewing the facts before the court through your professional eyes and giving the court the benefit of that expertise.

Excluding evidence in a criminal trial because of unfairness

Rules of evidence have evolved according to what the judges and Parliament, at any given time, think is a fair process and a fair balance between competing interests. Since the incorporation of the European Convention on Human Rights (see chapter 2) the idea of what is fair can be benchmarked against the standard of Article 6. There are many aspects of this right to a fair hearing, most of which were already entrenched in English law before the Human Rights Act brought Article 6 into our courts. For example, the processes of justice should not take place in secret; judges should not have a personal involvement in a case; any forum, whether a court or a case conference, where important decisions are made should include opportunity for those who are affected to put their case. The Police and Criminal Evidence Act 1984, s. 78, encapsulates one aspect of this approach: any evidence in a criminal case which in fairness should not be put before the court will be excluded. For example evidence may be relevant but likely to have an effect that prejudices the court rather than helps to determine the issues. A court should remove this from its mind or from the jury.

But notwithstanding the Human Rights Act and s. 78, some evidential material which arguably should not be heard and which arguably leads to an unfair hearing fails to be screened out. An example is *Attorney General's Reference (No 3 of 1999)* (2001) (a reference means the Attorney General wants a ruling on a legal issue from the House of Lords or Court of Appeal on a particular aspect of the case, even though the verdict or sentence in the actual case will still stand). In this case DNA evidence should have been destroyed because the accused had been acquitted: Police and Criminal Evidence Act 1984. The police retained it, without legal authority to do so. It was then used to link the same accused to a rape, and to obtain his conviction. The accused's complaint about this had been under Article 8 of the ECHR, an interference with respect for private life. The House of Lords held that, even though any interference with his private life must be 'in accordance with law', the conviction could stand. The curious reasoning was that under s. 78 the court had weighed up the fairness of using this illegal evidence and decided to go ahead. Therefore it was illegally held but legally used in court!

A fair trial has long been assumed to include the right not to be tried in a criminal case on the basis of past history. Convictions and character used to be seen as irrelevant to the issues being tried. We saw above that this rule has been relaxed, which means the prosecution case may be strengthened in any case where the accused has had convictions or charges against him or her.

You should be aware that the requirement for a fair hearing requires the prosecution to disclose to the defence in a criminal case any information that may undermine the prosecution case, as well as the materials they intend to rely on at trial. For example, in *R v M* (2000) social services had investigated at the time (fifteen years previously) worrying signs of injury and abuse. The records showed the social workers at the time thought there was no abuse, and each aspect of the allegations was documented with details of their enquiries. But when the man was prosecuted many years later, he was not told about these records, and was advised somewhat negligently that he should plead guilty. The Court of Appeal decided these records were crucial and that the conviction was based on a plea which should not have been entered. The same principles would apply in a civil case if the allegations were of a similar nature—parties subject to accusations or investigation should have access to the information required for them to present their case. (Any *hearsay* element of producing the file is then dealt with either by the relevant witnesses being called, or the files being used in evidence, which is permitted in the civil case and, particularly if the witnesses are untraceable, dead, abroad, or unlikely to remember, also in a criminal case.)

▮ Evidence and you—being a witness

Traditionally, the Law of England and Wales has favoured oral evidence. Witness evidence can be tested by cross-examination, and the credibility of the evidence can be judged from the demeanour of the witness. Courts have more recently moved towards allowing much more written evidence in trials. In all civil proceedings which you encounter as a social worker (Children Act cases being the most important) any evidence from a witness must first be put before the court as a written statement. You will go into the witness box only after the judge (or magistrates) and the other party have read your statement.

In criminal cases, however, the oral tradition remains paramount. In child protection work you are working with the police and Crown Prosecution Service, whose duties include charging suspects; the best way to protect a child's interests may be for an abuser to be prosecuted. Therefore, you also need to understand matters of criminal evidence and procedure. In what follows, we are assuming that you are preparing to appear as a witness in a civil case brought by social services. Where the procedure differs in criminal cases, we point this out.

Your agency lawyer should prepare, or assist you in the preparation of, documentary and real evidence. But no one can be a witness for you. In this part of the chapter, we will describe the procedures for oral testimony, and as we go along try to answer some common questions which cause anxiety.

Must I give evidence?

Anyone can be compelled to attend court as a witness in child protection proceedings and to testify, including reluctant parents *Re Y (A Child) (Split Hearing: Evidence)*, (2003).

But, as an agency social worker, this question will rarely arise; you have the relevant personal knowledge of the facts, and you are a party to the case. You are not going to need to compel your own attendance. It is possible, however, that another party will want to force you to attend, for example to testify in a case where you are no longer the key worker, perhaps on behalf of a parent. And if anything goes wrong, you can be compelled to attend by any statutory inquiry: the social worker who refused to attend the *Climbié* Inquiry notwithstanding being summonsed was convicted of a criminal offence (see chapter 8 for more details of this important inquiry).

If you are likely to require a witness from outside your agency, for example a health visitor, then frequently you will find that a witness order is required, as they may be instructed by their employer not to attend court unless one has been served. You, and your lawyer, must be aware of which agencies have adopted this policy.

If your evidence is important you must give it in court, even if you are frightened. The case of *Re W (Children) (Family Proceedings: Evidence)* (2002) makes this clear. The particular fact in issue here was the social worker's evidence that she had seen the father with the children, despite the mother's promise that this man would not be involved. Was it in the children's interests for her to continue to care for them? The social worker who had seen the man with the children wanted to be screeened from view and to remain anonymous, but the same approach would apply if she had applied to be excused from appearing and to have her statement read out.

Here is why the social worker was scared to be seen to testify, from the judgment of Thorpe LJ:

the father is an agricultural worker who has been brought up from his earliest boyhood to regard rough shooting as the prime recreation in life. He has always had, until police removal, a series of shotguns. Much of the professional concern hinges around his access to guns, his experience in using them and his repeated wild threats to do away with family members, himself, professional people (particularly social workers), the guardian and the experts should he lose his children at the end of the case. This dimension of violence and of threats to kill has led to repeated changes in the social work responsibility.

But here is the decision of Thorpe LJ:

As a generalisation, I think it must be recognised that social workers up and down the country, day in day out, are on the receiving end of threats of violence and sometimes of actual violence from adults who are engaged in bitterly contested public law cases at the end of which the parents face permanent separation from their children, at least during their child-hood and adolescence. Social workers generally must regard this as a professional hazard. I have not myself ever had experience of a local authority seeking anonymity for a professional worker in these circumstances. I am unaware of any previous ruling to this effect. Obviously the court must exercise a discretion, and it is quite impossible to set any useful bounds on the exercise of that discretion. Perhaps it is enough to say that cases in which the court will afford anonymity to a professional social work witness will be highly exceptional.

What order do things proceed in?

Whoever has to prove the case will usually be required to call their witnesses first. In a criminal case, therefore, prosecution witnesses testify before defence witnesses. In care proceedings, the applicant (your department or the NSPCC) goes first. When it is your turn the usher leads you to the witness box and gives you a choice of card. One contains the oath, the other the non-religious affirmation. The wording of the oath differs for different religions, and, if you do not affirm, the book you hold in your hand should be appropriate to your religion. There are three stages in giving evidence as a witness: examination, cross-examination, and re-examination. In the examination and re-examination you are being questioned on behalf of your own 'side'—usually, of course, the lawyer for your employing authority. On cross-examination you are being questioned on behalf of all the other parties in turn.

Examination

This stage is bypassed in civil proceedings, including Children Act cases, because every witness must submit to the court and copy to the other parties a statement of what it is they will be saying as a witness. That statement is read in advance of the hearing, and witnesses go straight into the ordeal of being cross-examined. In the family proceedings court, occasionally a bench will ask the witness to go over the evidence before there is a cross-examination, even though there is a witness statement. In that case what we say below about examination in criminal proceedings will apply.

Examination in criminal proceedings

In a criminal case, 'special measures' are applied to permit a vulnerable witness to pre-record his or her evidence on video tape. The examination stage is then bypassed. This is discussed in the next chapter. What follows is directed at the non-vulnerable witness, such as the social worker. If you are involved in a criminal case, your evidence will first be taken orally. (The statement you will have made to the police does not go before the court unless you are to be cross-examined about it.) The process is called 'examination in chief'. You will be asked questions by the prosecution lawyer. These questions must not be put in such a way as to suggest the answer—that would be a leading question. For example, you cannot be asked 'Did you see him hit the child?' but instead 'Did you see anything?'; 'Yes'; 'What did you see?'. Leading questions are permitted where the answer is not in dispute, such as when you are asked at the beginning of your examination 'Are you Joan Wilson, of 10 Burdon Terrace, Cliffside, and are you employed by Northshire Social Services Department in Area 3?'.

So, under examination you cannot be told what to say. You have to produce the 'right' answers of your own accord. One of the worst fears of a lawyer is of the witness who does not come 'up to proof', because the lawyer is prevented from saying 'Wait a minute, that's not what you told me before'. A lawyer cannot normally cross-examine his or her own witness, and is stuck with the answers given.

Therefore you need to know exactly what it is that you are going to say in evidence. Preparation comes in here. The term 'up to proof' in fact derives from a document called a proof of evidence. When legal proceedings are likely, the lawyer who plans to call you will take a statement (or proof of evidence) from you, have it word-processed, and get you to check it and sign it. In a criminal case, the statement is usually taken by a police officer, and the statement will usually be disclosed to the defence before trial.

In civil cases the witness statements are filed at court and revealed to the other parties in advance. If any statement needs amending, the court's permission is needed. So a statement has to be drafted with attention to accuracy. In the witness box in a criminal case you will not have the proof in front of you. It is permissible and sensible to re-read your statement shortly before going into the witness box, and even at this late stage it is better to tell the prosecution lawyer before giving your evidence that parts are inaccurate than to have inconsistencies exposed in the witness box.

Cross-examination

This stage applies in both civil and criminal cases. You gave your evidence by written statement. Alternatively, the examination finishes, and you are asked to 'wait there'. All other parties' lawyers now have the opportunity to cross-examine you in turn. The most important part of the English trial is the cross-examination. This is where the testing takes place. Cross-examination allows the advocate to put to you leading questions, i.e., questions which do suggest the answer. 'I think you've got it wrong; it wasn't half-past five when you called, it was well after six, wasn't it?' 'How can you be so sure?' 'So you were wearing a watch; how is it that you do not have one on today? Do you usually take your watch off before coming to court?' and so on. Something to avoid is finding yourself being cross-examined on aspects of the statement that are put in the lawyer's words, not your own. Courts will be angry if you express doubts about what is in your statement (*Alex Lawrie Factors Ltd v Morgan* (2000)). Before you sign it, read your statement and ask yourself if you are ready to be cross-examined on it. (Technically what is in your statement is a form of hearsay known as a self-serving statement, but any witness can be cross-examined on inconsistencies.)

Cross-examination can be an unpleasant experience. You will perhaps take a dislike to the person subjecting you to this. But understanding the purpose of cross-examination may assist in remaining objective about it.

If a witness makes any factual allegation, the other parties are assumed to accept it as correct unless they challenge it in cross-examination. So even when it is quite obvious that you are not going to change your story, you will have to answer questions such as 'That's not what happened, is it?' or even 'I suggest to you that what you have said is pure fabrication'. The lawyer does not expect, or even hope, that you will buckle under the weight of this skilful cross-examination and suddenly admit that you have made it all up. But he or she has a duty to put the question to you, and the benefit for that lawyer may be that it flusters and confuses you. It is going to happen to you. Do not take it personally just because someone is insinuating that you are wrong in your recollection or judgement.

More worrying is the apparently friendly question which softens you up for the sharp follow-up question. You may wonder what the questioner is getting at. If you are unsure, then the best advice is to answer the question in as matter of fact a way as you can, and let him or her reveal the strategy. Long, complex answers, given under pressure, may well contain things that you are not confident about, or even that contradict your earlier evidence. Short replies—but not monosyllabic—create fewer hostages to fortune. (If in doubt, remember KISS—Keep It Simple, Stupid!)

But giving evidence is an art, and giving short answers may itself allow a false picture of your position to emerge. Consider the following exchange:

Q: You were concerned about June?
A: Yes.
Q: Very concerned?
A: Yes.
Q: Did you discuss this with your management?
A: Oh yes, we had many meetings and case conferences.
Q: There was considerable concern throughout the department?
A: Yes.
Q: June was a constant preoccupation?
A: Yes.
Q: Then why did you visit only twice before you applied for a protection order?

How should the witness have answered these questions? Perhaps he or she was too eager to give the apparently 'correct' answer. There is no correct answer except what you consider to be the truth. The witness has acquiesced with an exaggeration of the truth, falling into the same trap as the witness who does not know when to stop.

Occasionally a skilled cross-examiner will trip you up. You will say something which you think on reflection is wrong. The immediate temptation is to cover your tracks, to pretend it is consistent with the other evidence you have given. But you risk digging yourself into a deeper hole, and a good cross-examining lawyer will allow you to dig deep before pointing out the inconsistencies in what you have just said. We suggest: 'I think I have just said something which gives the wrong impression', or even 'I made a mistake when I said that; what I meant to say was . . .'.

Tips for answering questions

There is a convention which you can use to your advantage. It can be used in examination and cross-examination. Although the lawyer asks you the questions, your answers must be addressed to the bench. This means, to do it properly, turning your head to face the bench after the lawyer has finished framing the question. Doing this slowly, particularly after a difficult question in cross-examination, gives you thinking time, and shows you to be in control of the situation. Sometimes you will be told to 'Watch the pen!' To the uninitiated this makes no sense at all. Apart from the High Court, where there will be a stenographer or a tape recorder, you will find that the clerk of the court or the judge is taking a longhand note of everything that is said. Watching the pen means pausing frequently as you speak, resuming only when the pen is still. If you comply with this requirement, not only will the court be impressed by your obvious control of the situation and your court experience, but you will also gain valuable time to think about what it is you wish to say next. If you feel nervous, this is natural. So, in fact, do the lawyers and the other witnesses. Perhaps the judge is nervous. Speak slowly and deliberately, pause for breath, and remember that how you feel is probably worse than how you look.

Re-examination

This is the mopping-up operation. It is too late to introduce new evidence, but your own lawyer will get you to clarify points that have been raised in cross-examination, to explain inconsistencies. If you have taken a straightforward approach to the cross-examination, this will be mercifully brief. It may not even happen at all.

We will now consider some more questions which commonly concern witnesses.

Can anyone help me with my evidence?

The simple answer is 'No'. Once in the witness box, you are on your own. Preparation of your evidence gives some assistance, as long as it is still your own evidence and truthful. There is nothing to prevent you discussing what you will say (so long as no one coaches you or suggests lying) and re-reading your notes and witness statement before you go into the witness box.

Can I refuse to answer questions?

No, unless the answer would incriminate you—i.e. leave you vulnerable to criminal charges. This is an unlikely risk to you personally. In fact, since the Children Act, s. 98, you are unlikely to see a witness being allowed to refuse to answer a question on this ground, for it no longer applies in a case involving children. The result is that in care proceedings a person alleged to have abused a child must answer questions about the allegations, even if the answers could lead to a criminal prosecution. The Act puts the need to protect children above other civil liberties.

Transcripts of civil proceedings can be disclosed to the police for use in criminal cases, if the judge gives permission. This makes the right not to answer questions a little meaningless, since the witness can then be cross-examined in a criminal trial as to why he or she refused to answer questions (*Re L* (1999)).

Can I refer to notes?

In all cases the court will also allow a witness to refer to notes that were made by that witness, or verified by that witness, 'substantially contemporaneously' with the events that are recorded in them. This means as soon as possible in the circumstances. You may therefore refresh your memory from the case notes, if, in accordance with good practice, you made these notes when the incidents were fresh in your mind, and not days or weeks or months later. You will not be able to refer to anyone else's notes to help you remember the facts—the maker of the notes would have to be called personally or, in a children's case, those notes could themselves be evidence. Before being allowed to refresh your memory, you will be asked a few questions about when you made the note.

You may be asked to explain why you took, or failed to take, a particular course of action, and in that case you may refer to case notes made by you, or anyone else. This is, technically, different from refreshing your own memory.

Your notes will be kept in a case file. If you have it with you, you will be able to flick back and forward to refresh your memory according to the questions asked. There is one problem. When it comes to cross-examination, the opposing lawyer will ask to take a look at the notes. If the notes are contained in a file, you have to hand over the whole file. There will be a dramatic pause while the lawyer peruses the notes, and suddenly you may get a totally unexpected question: 'But it says here that . . .'. How will you cope with the realistic need to refresh your memory without the problems caused by handing your whole file to the opposition? The simple answer would be to extract only those notes which are relevant, although under cross-examination about incidents you had thought irrelevant the absence of your notes will now be painful. And the court may object to your selection only of parts of what, in essence, is one continuous document, and refuse to allow you to rely on the extract.

There are two safe options. One is to rely on memory only. This is advisable only if your memory is clear, for it will be fully tested under cross-examination.

The other (recommended) option is to use the whole file. You should, as a matter of course, have prepared every entry in the knowledge that it may be the subject matter of skilled cross-examination. Every opinion must then be justifiable, every fact accurately recorded, with the name of the person making the note (and the time and place) also recorded. Your legal department should already, as a matter of course, have informed any other parties of material within the files which are helpful to them (see *R v M* above).

In a children case, the decision whether to rely on your notes to refresh your memory should be discussed with your lawyer and your line manager.

Can I withhold information from my file?

Even if you do not choose to bring your file to court, as you will see in chapter 12, a person called a children's guardian can inspect your file, take copies, and produce the contents in court whether you like it or not. There is, as we discussed in chapter 4, no concept of privilege for what social workers put in their files, and if potentially relevant, a court will not allow it to be withheld.

Can I give the court my opinion?

Sometimes you will be giving evidence as an expert witness (see above), and sometimes (perhaps within the same case) not. In conveying opinions about one sample of handwriting matching another, or interpretations of medical symptoms, you are not an expert, and not entitled to offer opinions to the court. But in areas such as child behaviour, or causes of stress in families, if it is relevant, the court will allow you to voice those opinions, because you are in a better position than a court to judge these matters. In fact, frequently, a large part of what you have to say will consist of your opinion; but you must confine your opinions to areas where you have expertise. (Courts do not consider that social workers generally have expertise in diagnosing sexual abuse: *Re N* (1996). You will therefore need to tell the court what you have directly observed, not what you think it means. Nor are you expert in matters of credibility of child witnesses.)

You will of course be required to defend your opinion. You will have to state what experience or research or reading you based that opinion on, and in what circumstances you might modify it. You must be prepared to hear it contradicted by another witness, and to have it dismissed in favour of another interpretation of the facts. It is therefore worth anticipating very hard questions on your opinions in cross-examination; and if you cannot justify them before you get to court, perhaps they are unjustifiable, or perhaps you are the wrong person to call as the witness on this point.

What if my opinion is different from that of my employer?

Imagine that your opinion was not accepted at a case conference, and it was decided to apply for a care order, even though you think that this is not in the child's best interests or that the relevant admissible evidence is weak.

As an employee of your agency, you must abide by directions given to you by your seniors. If you are told to instruct your lawyers to commence care proceedings, you do so. Of course, as a professional, you make plain that in your view this is not the best course. If at all possible, you should avoid going into the witness box. It may be that your lawyer decides there is sufficient evidence from other witnesses to make out the grounds. But the other parties may notice and comment on your absence, and may even serve you with a witness order, in which case you will have to attend. Alternatively, your lawyer may decide that without your evidence of the facts of which you have firsthand knowledge, the case will not be made out.

So you find yourself in the witness box and the cross-examination begins. You are asked directly whether you think these parents are incapable of caring for the child. What is the answer?

You are now a professional social worker under oath, sworn to tell the truth. Your duty is to the court first, to your employer second. You state as accurately as you can what your observations and opinions are. Any alternative would be perjury. There is nothing unprofessional about giving evidence which damages your agency's case. What would be unprofessional would be if you had not made the difference in viewpoint known to your agency before giving the evidence. If you fear that this situation may arise, you should inform your lawyer and your senior at the earliest opportunity.

One example of this dilemma is *Re C (Interim Care Order: Residential Assessment)* (1997). A psychologist and the social workers gave evidence in care proceedings that they considered that a residential assessment of the child and parents would help to determine whether the parents should have the child returned to them. The Assistant Director of Social Services refused to pay the estimated costs of £24,000, and gave evidence contradicting that of her team, who had said that an assessment was needed. The House of Lords considered, on balance, that an assessment should be ordered. What matters for the present discussion is that there was no suggestion in the judgment that there was anything wrong with social workers disagreeing with their manager in the witness box.

Am I allowed into court when I am not giving evidence?

This matter was considered in the case of *R v Willesden Justices ex parte London Borough of Brent* (1988). At the commencement of the care proceedings the mother objected to the presence of the social worker in court, as she was later to be called as a witness. The justices excluded her, and the local authority applied to the High Court for judicial review of that decision. The court decided that as a general rule the party to the case has a right to be present throughout. If an agency is the party, it is represented through the social worker who deals with the case and therefore he or she retains the right to be present. But this is subject to the court's overall discretion to allow witnesses and non-parties to be present and also to exclude people, even the social worker who personifies the agency. But as a general rule, even in children and family cases where proceedings are not open to the public, the social worker who gives instructions to the lawyer, and the expert witness waiting to be called, not only may, but should, be present in court.

Can I give evidence from file records that someone else made?

We have referred to how you can refresh your memory as a witness from your notes, which can include looking at your file. But looking at the notes which someone else made is a different type of issue. The notes are important so that the court gets a full picture, not just the parts that you have been involved with. But to tell the court what happened in, say, 2001, when you were not involved until 2005, is hearsay. In presenting any evidence, whether in the witness box or in a written statement, you must make it clear to the court where it applies that you are testifying from your own knowledge. Where on the other hand you are repeating information supplied by others, you must give a full explanation of the source, and the date and circumstances in which any file record was created or other information supplied. The more careful the record keeping—and the evidence of careful record keeping—the more likely the hearsay content is to be useful as evidence.

If something is recorded on the file which is of great importance to your case, and the person who originally made the note is available, then calling the witness, if necessary using a summons, should be considered.

Writing reports

This part of the chapter is concerned with the essential paperwork needed for effective social work practice. The case study in Box 6.5 demonstrates the need for effective file keeping. It is not just a question of accumulating evidence—in *Re E* the social work files stood four feet high—the information needs to be managed. You need comprehensible information to manage cases on a day-to-day basis, to enable you to know when court applications are necessary, and to provide reports to the court to support your applications.

 BOX 6.5 Case study *Re E (Care Proceedings: Social Work Practice)* **(2000)**

The five children of a family were subject to constant emotional, physical, and sexual abuse. The matter first came to the attention of social workers in 1979 when the eldest child, then aged 4, was placed on the child protection register. The children exhibited characteristics of serious sexualized behaviour, emotional disturbance, anti-social conduct, suicidal tendencies, and parental rejection. The pattern was repeated over a twenty-year period, during which time, according to the evidence in the law report, the social workers took no effective action and repeated referrals were ignored. After hearing an application brought by the local authority in respect of the three younger children, the judge, Bracewell J, found that the threshold criteria (significant harm—see chapter 12) were established. She was deeply disturbed by the inadequate social work response to the abusive parenting of all of the children. One of the problems was the state of the evidence kept by the social services authority. She set out the following principles:

1 Every social work file should have as the top document a running chronology of significant events kept up to date as events unfold.

2 Lack of cooperation by parents is never a reason to close a file or remove a child from a protection register.

3 Referrals by professionals such as health visitors and teachers should be investigated and given great weight.

4 Those with power of decision making should never make a judgement without having full knowledge of the files and consulting those professionals who know the family.

5 Children who are part of a sibling group should not be considered in isolation, but in the context of the family history.

6 Cases should be time-limited and an effective timetable laid down within which changes need to be achieved.

The judge commented as follows:

> Had these matters been looked at and followed in the current case, effective intervention would have occurred many years ago to protect these children from the years of dysfunctional parenting which has left them so damaged and vulnerable. I hope that the lessons to be learnt from this case will assist local authorities up and down the country in dealing with other similar cases.

Your reports will inform internal decision making and, if a case goes to court, will for better or for worse, ensure that the department is accountable for its actions.

Files

The basis of all written information and evidence-based decision-making is a well-kept file. Files have many purposes including to record:

- who is who—the persons involved, addresses, dates of birth, who is related to whom;
- what has happened—when, where and who (including who provided what information);
- assessments and reasons;
- decisions, reasons, targets, review arrangements and responsibilities.

As we saw above, your file can be inspected by a children's guardian if court proceedings are underway. And we saw that your file may be inspected during the proceedings. It may, of course, also be inspected within the local authority as part of an internal auditing process. You will be vulnerable to criticism if it is not well organized. As the Laming Report into the *Climbié* case makes clear, you and colleagues must be able to rely on accessible, accurate and relevant information for decision-making purposes.

All authorities have their own file-keeping protocols, but the essential purpose is the same. A file should put you in control. A good file will accurately, fully and clearly record at least the following:

- a chronology of significant events;
- a family tree;
- a regularly updated summary;
- discussions within the team;
- decisions made.

The purpose of a chronology is to provide a comprehensive, concise, and objective overview of the case rather than a précis of every entry on the file. The summary provides an overview for anyone who has to read the file. The importance of these and the record of discussions and decisions is indicated in the following extract from *Someone Else's Children*, which was a report of the Social Services Inspectorate (Department of Health 1998, also **www.doh.gov.uk/pdfs/sechildren**). It stated:

> The majority of [Social Services Departments] had policies on file formats and these were usually complied with. The actual filing within the modules was somewhat erratic. It was often difficult for us to find materials and key documents such as birth certificates, care orders and agreements to accommodate; these were frequently not on current files. (10.1)
>
> . . . most files we saw were useful working tools. They contained copious, full and up-to-date recording. However, this was frequently poorly structured and often had little obvious focus. Except in court cases, most case records lacked social histories and chronologies, and regular summaries were also rare. We saw little evidence of files being properly audited by line managers. (1.43)

[Case notes] were usually up-to-date and for the most part readable. However, they rarely contained an outline of the purpose of the interview, such as the issues to be pursued or the social worker's evaluation of the interview. They appeared to reflect unstructured information gathering exercises rather than focused pieces of work. (10.3)

Social histories and chronologies were rare except where cases were involved with court proceedings and although transfer summaries were relatively common, regular three-monthly case summaries were very rare even when it was clear policy and procedure to provide them. (10.5)

We saw no proper evidence of supervision discussions on any of the case files we examined. Although we were told that formal supervision records were kept, children's files did not show the detail. Very few authorities have systems to ensure that all children looked after were discussed during workers' supervision. (5.9)

Recording a decision to take no action

In the *Re E* case study in Box 6.5, the judge was particularly concerned about decisions to take no action. Such decisions should not be taken without full knowledge of the file and consultation with the professionals who knew the family. Lack of cooperation from parents or carers is not a reason for no action. On the contrary this should provide a spur for further investigation. Where children are part of a sibling group, information on all children should be recorded within the context of their family history. If no action is taken the file must indicate review dates and, of course, should document information considered and decisions taken on review. Taking no action is a very important decision and the file must clearly show the care with which that decision was taken and the information on which it was based.

Recording a decision to take action

Once you have decided to take action, the production of good statements and reports, considered in the rest of the chapter, is dependent on the original file source. Not only is good file management good practice, you are unavoidably accountable as a result of its contents and quality. The report of the Social Services Inspectorate we just considered is just one example of how you are accountable for your files, since the Inspectorate may have occasion to inspect yours. If anything goes wrong, your file will be scrutinized in any enquiry. And of course the courts may want to see it in protection proceedings.

Types of reports

There are three main types of report that you will have to produce:

- Internal agency reports, which are used for management purposes, and decision making in particular cases, for child abuse case conferences, for cases reviews, etc.

- Court reports (reports making representations), which may be referred to as 'welfare reports' or 'social enquiry reports' or, in a criminal case, 'pre-sentence reports'. Often the report will be produced by the social worker after the relevant facts have been proved or agreed, but sometimes it is prepared in anticipation of the facts being proved. Or, except in a criminal case, it may be a report which the court can use both in relation to the facts in issue and the decision-making which will follow if those facts are proved. The social worker is acting under a statutory duty to provide information to the court, and the report is intended to assist the court in knowing what type of order then to make. An example of this would be a pre-sentence report required under Criminal Justice Act 2003 ss. 157–8, before sentence in youth court hearings (see chapter 15).

- Statements for your agency lawyer (or evidential statements), which form the basis of the evidence that you are going to give in court. They are internal and are not submitted to the court or provided to other parties. If you are going to give oral evidence, the final version of this internal document will be called your *proof of evidence*. It is drafted by your agency lawyer and sets out all the relevant evidence which you intend to give in court. If, as is normal in a civil case, your evidence is submitted to the court in written form, your lawyer will produce a *witness statement*, which is broadly similar. In both cases, though the lawyer drafts it, it is your evidence and you must check it for accuracy and completeness.

Let us try to clarify the difference between the different categories of report (while pointing out that there can be no rigid division). Assume your agency is seeking a care order. You will first have to produce for your lawyer an evidential statement. This is an internal document. It ensures that the lawyer has a full and accurate account of the evidence which you can give (which can include hearsay evidence—see above). Based on the contents of this statement the lawyer can, if the case is going forward to court, complete the application form; at a later stage the lawyer can prepare from this your witness statement, which has to be filed with the court under the court rules. If the court then decides, on the evidence received, that the grounds for making an order are proved, then the court may wish to see a welfare report making representations that will have been prepared. It may well give a wider picture of the child's family, situation, etc.

The evidential statement—which has to be kept up to date—will form the basis of all of these reports or statements.

Much of the advice below is generic, although there are particular requirements for particular types of report.

Reports in care proceedings

In care proceedings under the Children Act 1989, s. 31, if the court is satisfied that there are grounds for making an order (the threshold criteria of significant harm) it will then consider whether a care order or a supervision order should be made. At this point you switch roles; you are not concerned with proving grounds; you are concerned with assisting the court with deciding the best type of order to make. The court will consider a welfare report that it has asked you for under the Children Act 1989, s. 7. The decision it makes on what is best for the child will be based both on the representations in this report, and also its view of the evidence it has considered when deciding the threshold has been met. Deciding what order to make in light of the earlier evidence and your welfare report is the second part of the two-stage process talked of in *Humberside County Council v B* (1993) (also discussed in chapter 12). This case illustrates the need for clear thinking about the purpose of particular reports. The High Court found that the magistrates had confused findings about the threshold criteria (significant harm had occurred or was likely) with the requirements of the welfare principles which dictate how decisions are then made and are contained in s. 1. The court said that there should be a two-stage decision process. In stage 1 the court asks if he threshold criteria have been met; if they are this gives the court the power to move on to the second stage of looking at the wider issues of the welfare of the child and what sort of order, if any, should be made. Witness statements and reports by the local authority should ensure that the necessary information is available to the court at both stages of the process.

The witness statement filed at the beginning of the proceedings will be largely concerned with proving the case: showing that the threshold criteria are met. The welfare report deals with stage 2.

In addition to the witness statement and the welfare report there is a possibility of you submitting an additional statement with the leave of the court. You can do this before being requested to provide a s. 7 welfare report, and the time for it is immediately prior to the final hearing. It is our view that if the court has not already ordered a separate welfare report to be prepared under s. 7, the additional witness statement filed with the court would contain the following:

(a) A summary of the local authority's case: the facts relating to the child and family; a chronology of events; a summary of the history of the case, and the reasons why the proceedings have been brought.

(b) The results of any assessment that has taken place since the proceedings commenced. (This may refer to a witness statement of an expert who carried out the assessment or part of the assessment.)

(c) Why the court should not apply the no order principle (s. 1(5): see chapter 8).

(d) The views of the local authority in relation to the welfare checklist and how it should be applied in this case (s. 1(3): see chapter 8).

(e) Why the court should make a care or supervision order (as is appropriate).

(f) The local authority's care plan and its proposals for contact if a care order is made (s. 34(11)). (For further discussion of care plans see chapter 10.)

When are reports called for in family proceedings?

Under the Children Act 1989, s. 8, there is a variety of orders that can be made: contact orders, prohibited steps orders, residence orders, and specific issues orders. The court can consider making these in any family proceedings, whether or not they have been applied for. (For more on these s. 8 orders, see chapter 14.)

Having heard evidence from the parents, and before actually making any of these orders, the court can ask either the local authority or CAFCAS (see chapters 5 and 10) to prepare a report to assist it in deciding what type of order should be made, even if there is no intention of the children being made the subject of any care or supervision application (Children Act 1989, s. 7).

Rule 13 of the Family Proceedings Courts (Children Act 1989) Rules 1991 (see chapter 5) requires the welfare local authority or CAFCAS to serve it on the court at least five days before the hearing. It also requires the report writer to attend the court hearing unless excused by the court. When the court has decided a report is necessary, Rule 14 enables it to give specific directions about the preparation of the welfare report, in particular the scope of the report and the timescale for preparing it.

In family proceedings the court can, under s. 16 of the Children Act, make a family assistance order. Before making such an order the court may ask for a welfare report. (For further discussion of this, see chapter 9.)

Under the Children Act 1989, s. 37, the court can require the local authority to investigate the situation of a particular child. If, as a result of the investigation, the local authority decides that an application for a care or supervision order should be made then it should make an application in the usual way. If the local authority does not consider that an application should be made it must report this fact to the court. It must give its reasons for not applying and set out any services or assistance it intends to give to the family. There is no requirement in the rules to do this by way of report, but, unless your lawyer or manager decides otherwise, we would advocate this. (For further discussion of s. 37, see chapter 10.)

When is a pre-sentence report called for?

Under the Criminal Justice Act 2003 ss. 157–8 (not yet in force, but the wording is the same as in the Powers of Criminal Courts (Sentencing) Act 2000) there is a requirement for courts in all cases involving an offender under 18 years of age to consider a pre-sentence report before making a sentencing decision. The report may be written by a probation officer, social worker, or member of the Youth Offending Team (the YOT is explained in chapter 15). The Home Secretary has not used his statutory power to specify what the contents should be. However the report must comment on the factors which a court needs to take into account in using its sentencing powers, which are set out in chapter 15. Note that your report must be given to the parent or guardian of the child as well as to the court and prosecution, unless it would cause significant harm to the child to do so.

Guidance on preparing reports and statements

There are several reasons for taking the utmost professional care. Firstly, lives are affected.

The second reason is that is that you may be sued. Professionals such as surveyors, lawyers and doctors have in law always been liable to pay compensation if they are negligent in preparing reports. Social workers used to be protected from this type of claim, but in *Phelps v Hillingdon LBC* (2000), the House of Lords recognised that a duty of care can arise where a person is employed to carry out professional services as part of the authority's statutory duty to children with special educational needs. This is a clear precedent for social workers, whose statutory duties are, for these purposes, very similar to those of an education authority. We discussed this in chapter 1.

A third reason is the possibility, remote but real, of a failure such as the *Climbié* case, leading to detailed scrutiny.

A shoddy report will not always produce such damage, but you should approach report preparation as a competent, skilled professional.

A suggested pro forma

Much of what is said is applicable to all reports, but internal evidential reports and statements, whilst perhaps containing the same full information, do not have to be laid out in such a formal way.

Several questions must first be asked:

1. What will be the conclusion of this statement or report?

2. To whom am I trying to express this conclusion?

Then there is a third question, particularly in respect of the evidential type statement:

3. Can I defend the contents, to colleagues, managers, other agencies, and, if necessary, under cross-examination?

These may seem to be odd questions to start with, particularly the question about the conclusion. However, by adopting this approach you should avoid the risk of merely repeating the contents of a previous report and then change the conclusion and possibly add a new paragraph to 'bring the report up to date'. Write the report knowing where it is leading. The contents must be written so that, without distorting any facts, they are logically leading to the conclusion you put forward, not the conclusion of any previous report.

In all but the simplest case, if you are preparing a court statement presenting evidence or making representations, you will discuss it with your lawyer. The discussion will be assisted if you have given your lawyer, in advance, a report about the child's family background, the department's views, etc., so that you both have something in writing to refer to. At that discussion you will jointly examine the options that may be available in the court proceedings. The lawyer will be able to advise you as to the likely outcome of the proceedings.

For example, if you feel in a particular case that to protect a child it is necessary to remove the child under a court order (and often you may be told by your team leader or recommended by a child protection conference to adopt that course of action) and the lawyer says that there is insufficient evidence to satisfy a court to enable it to grant the order, then you and your managers will need to reconsider the case. Such reconsideration may be either to collect such evidence or to change tack.

Having agreed your conclusion, you then proceed to the next question: to whom am I trying to express this conclusion? Your report is going to the courts, either the magistrates or a judge. You are addressing a decision maker who requires particular information based upon particular statutory criteria. This is a different audience from the case conference where you will put forward opinions for discussion and do not have to focus on one outcome.

Department of Health guidelines

No social worker should write any report without studying the guidelines issued by the Department of Health. The latest version was published in 1996. It is called: *Reporting to Court under the Children Act: A Handbook for Social Services*. Extracts are set out below. Additionally *A Framework for the Assessment of Children in Need and Their Families* (Department of Health, 2000) is of help in compiling statements or reports. Use of the *Framework* should provide evidence to help, guide, and inform judgements about children's welfare and safety from the first point of contact, through the processes of initial and more detailed case assessments. We refer to the *Framework* in chapter 10. We have taken both these publications into account in the recommendations which follow.

In any statement or report you write for court during the course of family proceedings, as defined in the Children Act 1989, s. 8, you must have regard to the welfare checklist in s. 1. This is reproduced in chapter 8. As the court is required to take account of these matters, and its decisions can be appealed if it does not, it is essential that your witness statement or report deals with all these issues. This is especially true in the conclusion, where you will be directly addressing the type of order that the court should be making. Remember that the court can always choose not to make any order, or the court can substitute a s. 8 order, even where such an order is not applied for. So, in your statement or report you need to explain why the court ought to follow your recommendation instead of making no order or making a s. 8 order.

Content of reports—Children Act proceedings

In this section we look at the form of the welfare report, using the family proceedings court as an example.

The typical layout of a magistrates' court report should be as follows:

(a) Name of magistrates' court and date of court hearing.

(b) Name of person(s) about whom the report is prepared.

(c) Name of person preparing the report and the identity of their agency.

Only these details should appear on the front page of the report, which should otherwise be blank, apart from clearly indicating that the contents are confidential. This is because you owe a duty of confidentiality to the person(s) about whom the report has been prepared. If the front page sets out any other details then there is the danger that the information may be seen by people for whom it is not intended, merely by being left on a courtroom desk, whether by you or others to whom the report has been given. With this suggested layout, if that happens, then with the information that can be obtained from the front page the report can be returned to those in whose possession it should be without the finder being any the wiser as to the actual contents. The next page then continues with:

(d) Sources of information from which the report is compiled.

(e) Family members; names, dates of birth, marital status, address, education/ qualifications/current occupation (if any) and financial details (if relevant).

This should be in diagrammatic form. You may understand that 'Billy' is in fact John Brown, who is Susan's second cousin's husband, but will anybody else? Diagrams make things clearer.

(f) A narrative family history.

(g) A narrative history of the service user.

(h) A narrative history about the reason for the court appearance.

In the evidential statement this will be the part that contains the evidence to satisfy the threshold criteria in s. 31 of the Children Act.

Which way round these appear can be a matter of personal choice. There may be some element of repetition in these sections.

(i) The results of any assessment that has taken place since the proceedings commenced.

(j) Why the court should not simply apply the no order principle.

(k) The views of the local authority in relation to the welfare checklist and how it should be applied in this case.

(l) Why the court should make a care or supervision order (as is appropriate).

(m) The local authority's care plan and its proposals for contact if a care order is made (s. 34(11)).

(n) A conclusion and final recommendation.

The actual recommendation should be for a single order, rather than suggesting a choice, since your function is to advise the court what you, as a professional, think to be appropriate. The function of the court then is to arrive at its decision on the information before it, including your recommendation, and it is entitled to diverge from what you say. However when children's guardians (see chapter 9) present statements or reports, they are acting for the court, and not making representations to obtain an order on behalf of an agency. In these circumstances, it was decided in *Devon County Council v C* (1985), if the court does not follow the recommendation it must give cogent reasons, otherwise there will be good grounds for an appeal. If you presented your recommendations not on behalf of the court but on behalf of your agency, if the court does not make the order you recommended you should still discuss with your lawyer whether there are grounds to appeal.

A good example of what the court expects is to be found in the judgment of the Court of Appeal in *H v H, K v K* (1989):

> In the High Court and county court in child proceedings a welfare officer directed by court order to investigate and report has a duty to give to the court all the information which he considers to be relevant and is not restrained by the hearsay rule from including relevant but

otherwise inadmissible information. He may consider it necessary to and often does provide the judge with a full picture of the family, investigate many sources and interview many people, including grandparents and other relatives, teachers, doctors and the children themselves. What the children have to say may be relevant not only to their state of mind but as to important facts derived from the child which the court should know. Unless [the officer] is entitled to present this information, it would be extremely difficult for [the officer] to comply with the task [the officer] is directed by order to perform. Equally, [the officer's] usefulness to the court would be substantially diminished. The reliance on the report and the weight to be attached to any information contained therein is, of course, a matter for the judge. I would just add for completeness that a social worker directed by an order of the court to provide a report in place of a welfare officer . . . would seem to me to be in the same position for that purpose as a court welfare officer.

At the point at which your report is relevant to the court, the court has already heard the evidence and decided that there are grounds on which it is now empowered to make *some* form of order, or that the young person has committed an offence. In care proceedings it must be borne in mind that the Children Act 1989, s. 1(5), specifically lays a duty on the court not to make an order unless 'it considers that doing so would be better for the child than making no order at all'. Therefore, your report should be designed to help the court decide, first, whether making any order would be better for the child, and then what is the order that should be made in the best interests of the child.

The regulations under the Adoption and Children Act 2002 have not yet been published. When available they will provide additional guidance. We will provide an update on our web site.

Content of pre-sentence reports

For these reports a similar framework should be adopted. We discuss here the particular requirements of such a report.

You will see in chapter 15 that the basis on which the court considers sentencing is what is defined as the seriousness of the offence. It is on this basis that a custodial or community sentence may be given. The report therefore must look at the seriousness of the offence. It must include any information that may be relevant to the length of sentence and look at the question of a sentence in the community where liberty would be restricted by means of supervision requirements, etc.

There is a step-by-step approach to sentencing. This approach dictates the format that needs to be adopted for that part of the pre-sentence report looking at sentencing. For sentencing of young offenders the welfare question is relevant, although not paramount, when the court is considering sentencing.

It should show the details of the court, hearing date, the name of the person for whom the report is prepared, and the name of the person and agency preparing the report. This should be all that is on the front page for the same reasons we discussed above.

Then inside the report will be:

(a) The basic facts of name, address, age and date of birth and the offence charged.

(b) Sources of the report.

(c) A discussion of the current offence(s). This should look at seriousness and questions of aggravation (if relevant).

(d) Relevant information about the offender.

This is where you would bring to the attention of the court any particular factors to be considered. Is this a first offence? If not, does it go against pattern? Are there special circumstances? Have previous sentences worked?, etc.

(e) Conclusion and Proposal.

The report should make a clear recommendation about the type of sentence and the length of sentence. It should justify this by stating what effect the sentence should have. Since the Crime and Disorder Act 1998 states that the principal purpose of the youth justice system is to reduce offending this should be explicitly addressed in your recommendation.

The report's recommendations

The key element of your statement or report is what you recommend. Drawing on the information contained in the rest of the report, applying your professional knowledge, experience, and expertise your recommendation should assist the court in reaching its decision about the correct order to make. That part of the report is very likely to be challenged in cross examination and argument in children cases, though normally unless the defendant is in profound disagreement, not with a pre-sentence report. Grounds for a challenge will be either that your professional judgement is wrong, perhaps based on incorrect principles or reasoning, or it is simply based on incorrect information.

The fact that you are challenged does not mean you are wrong. If you were not challenged, there would probably not have been a court hearing, as your strategy for promoting the child's welfare would not be in dispute. There will always be valid grounds for challenging your judgement, since your opinion is based on expertise and experience, not inescapable logic.

There will be legitimate divergence of opinion; it is common for a guardian to make a different recommendation to that of the agency social worker. But a court will not be pleased if there has been no attempt to resolve them before the hearing. You should also try to identify areas of agreement with the other parties (in particular the parents) so that the court can focus in terms of evidence and representations heard on any areas of disagreement. You will know before the date of the hearing what the guardian's report is going to say. Rule 13 requires that in the absence of a specific direction, a welfare report must be filed five days before the hearing. Any other written statement which is going to be relied on needs to be served before the hearing (rule 17). Normally the discussions between the agencies, the parties and the children's guardian will have taken place much earlier and the reports' recommendations will be known before then.

Agreeing on some or all of the issues

It should be for your lawyer to arrange for a meeting to see whether there can be agreement, if not between all parties then at least between the agency and the guardian. It should go without saying that all parties and their lawyers should be given the opportunity to attend such a meeting. This is not to usurp the function of the courts, or to compromise anybody's professional standing or their duties to their clients. If properly and professionally dealt with it should be in the very best interests of all, since it may avoid a contested hearing, which rarely assists anyone. All parties, including the parents, should be represented, and it will be their decision on legal advice whether or not to accept any compromise proposed.

This meeting may then produce an agreed draft order that can be put before the court. This course of action was approved in *Devon County Council v S* (1992). It is to be appreciated that none of the above can take place if the reports of both the guardian and the agency social worker are not available at an early stage prior to the hearing. If the parties do not have the reports early enough then the case will be adjourned to enable the reports to be properly considered. Therefore it is in everybody's interests to make the reports available as soon as possible, even before the dates set by any court directions.

Disputed factual evidence in reports

As we discussed earlier, facts asserted in representations cannot be relied on if they are challenged, unless they are first proved. When preparing your report you should discuss the factual contents with the parties, and in particular in children's cases with parents. If at this stage there emerges a dispute over the matters of fact contained in your report then you should consider whether the disputed parts are important or can be omitted. If you are unable to remove those parts you should state within the report that there is dispute about the validity of these 'facts'. This does not prevent you including your opinion on those facts but in such a fashion as 'If these are the facts then my professional opinion would be . . .'. It is then up to the other party's lawyers to challenge the facts in dispute and the agency's lawyer to 'prove' the facts by way of evidence.

Jargon

There is a fine line between jargon and professional language. In choosing your words, it helps to remember that your reports are going to be read by non-professionals. It may, however, be impossible to make the report accessible to all interested parties, since some may have poor educational attainment levels, and you will then have to assume that their advisors will explain difficult parts of the report to them. Without talking down, or losing essential meaning, you should be using simple, direct, language where that choice is available. Technical terms where essential should be accompanied by a clear definition, understandable by someone who is not a social scientist, which includes the lawyers, judges and magistrates. One of the worst things that can happen is for your lawyer to be asked from the bench: 'What does your witness mean?'

For example: Which is better? Which is clearer to the lay person?

Tommy has considerable difficulty in adequately relating to his peer group in the educational setting.

Tommy does not have many school friends.

Colleagues can sometimes find clearer ways of saying something in a report that, because you are too close to it, you have been unable to find. Also a fresh mind can spot howlers, which can be innocent but can be dangerous. Imagine the social worker who could not understand why the court would not allow Susan to live with her step-father. The same worker then noticed that in the report, the phrase 'Susan repeatedly insisted that her stepfather liked her' had become a simple typing error 'Susan repeatedly insisted that her stepfather licked her'! To quote from the evidence of the unfortunate, overworked team leader who received the most blame in the report into the death of Kimberley Carlile: 'It is a curious yet repeatedly observed phenomenon of social work that it is much easier to perceive the errors in other people's work than in one's own.'

Redrafting after a 24-hour break also helps.

■ Official guidance

Our advice is not enough. Even more vital is to follow official guidance—see Box 6.6.

 BOX 6.6 Extracts from the Department of Health Guidelines, *Reporting to Court under the Children Act*

The local authority's evidence must demonstrate that the course of action it proposes is in the child's best interests. This must not be achieved by including in its statements only those facts and opinions which support the local authority's position. The courts have clearly established that where the welfare of children is the paramount consideration, there is a duty on all parties to make full and frank disclosure of all matters relevant to welfare whether these are favourable or adverse to their own particular case. This includes the disclosure of information by local authorities to parents which may assist in rebutting allegations against them.

In considering which facts are relevant and any opinion which you wish to add to your evidence, you should distinguish:

- matters to be described factually as a result of your direct observations;
- your opinion or interpretation of behaviour or events which you have observed;
- matters recorded on the file or told to you by others which are relevant to the case but which you cannot personally verify; and
- your opinion of the reasons for the order being sought and the care plan based on your overall professional experience.

Justifying your conclusion

The document should make it clear to the reader how you arrived at your conclusions. Have you demonstrated the factual basis for each part of your conclusion? In assessing the risk to the child, have you explained what would need to change for the child to be safe within the home?

Set out the options available to the court and assess each in turn. Your position on each option should be substantiated by the evidence in the body of the statement. Drawing these together is likely to assist the court in its own analysis and in drafting reasons for its decisions.

The conclusions of other parties should be taken into account and the reasons for differences of opinion should be clearly recorded.

Based on your analysis, present a recommendation where appropriate to do so.

It may not be appropriate to put forward a 'hard and fast' position at an early stage. Giving a provisional opinion in an early statement allows for a later change of position, where justified, and is likely to be seen as more balanced and reasonable.

Always review what you have written. It is helpful if you can get a colleague to look at it as well. As you read, consider whether your statement:

- is well-focused;
- takes account of the guiding principles of the Children Act as appropriate;
- reflects the requirements of the relevant section of the Act;
- is balanced and fair overall, giving credit where it is due to family members;
- includes all relevant facts whether or not they support the local authority's conclusion;
- verifies significant facts and justifies opinions;
- avoids unnecessary repetition of material available in other court documents;
- presents information with sensitivity, in a way which does not make relations between parties worse;
- makes references to race, nationality, colour or country of origin which are relevant to the context;
- avoids applying your own cultural or moral values to other cultures (assumptions may be implicit in your choice of words); and
- takes account of changes that have occurred in the period leading up to the final hearing.

Reports other than court reports

You will still be required to write up your file and from the contents of that prepare reports for your team leader, your district manager, higher management, case discussions and child protection conferences or reviews. So we find in *Working Together (Department of Health)*:

7.47 Good record keeping is an important part of the accountability of professionals to those who use their services. It helps to focus work, and it is essential to working effectively across agency and professional boundaries. Clear and accurate records ensure that there is a documented account of an agency's or professional's involvement with a child and/or family. They help with continuity when individual workers are unavailable or change, and they provide an essential tool for managers to monitor work or for peer review.

In doing these tasks you will still be required to have regard to the law. The information that you put into the case file, and hence the other reports, should, to the best of your knowledge, be truthful and as far as is possible within your direct knowledge. It should be recorded as soon as possible after the events which are described, with the date and authorship clearly marked, so that if you later have forgotten the detail your note carries the credibility of being a record contemporaneous with the events.

The comments on evidence in the earlier part of the chapter have already made it clear that when you are in court you may well be put in a position where the file has to be shown to the court and the other parties' lawyers. Or in the very worst of your nightmares you have to face a public inquiry when all of the files will be taken to pieces. Always bear that in mind when you are writing up your case file. Ask yourself 'If this entry were to be read out in court would I be able to justify it, explain it, clarify it etc?'.

A further point on the question of access to information is that presented by the Children Act 1989, s. 42, which states:

> (1) Where a person has been appointed as a guardian *ad litem* [now children's guardians] under this Act he shall have the right . . . to examine and take copies of
>   (a) any records of, or held by, a local authority and the NSPCC or other authorised person which were compiled in connection with the making, or proposed making, by any person of any application under this Act with respect to the child concerned; or
>   (b) any other records of, or held by, a local authority . . . in its social services function relating . . . to that child.'

The section goes on to say that the guardian can use those records as evidence in the relevant proceedings. Bearing in mind that in most court hearings involving children there will be a children's guardian appointed, then your files are going to be open both to your service users (and their lawyers) and to the courts through the guardian.

EXERCISES

Reminder: some of the tools you need to deal with this question will come from your understanding of other chapters, for example powers to apply for a care order under the Children Act (chapter 12) or questions of confidentiality (chapter 4).

1. You are a social worker for Lamingshire Social Services. You are seeking a care order in relation to a 12-year-old child, Kylie. The local authority's case is based on the following information:
   - Kylie has told you 'in confidence' that her parents beat her every night;
   - The head teacher last year suspended Kylie's brother for stealing money from the staffroom;
   - The file note made by a previous social worker involved in the case states that neighbours have reported hearing a girl shouting 'get off me Dad' coming from the house; this neighbour wishes to remain anonymous;
   - You have reached the conclusion that Kylie's emotional and intellectual development would be aided if she were to live with a foster family pending a decision by the Crown Prosecution Service on whether to prosecute Kylie's father;
   - A doctor who examined Kylie when her parents brought her to casualty has written in her report that the bruising is consistent with a fall down the stairs, a version of events given at the time by the parents and Kylie herself;

- The father has at various times told you that he has a drink problem and that he does not have a drink problem.

What are the evidential issues involved in bringing this evidence to the Family Proceedings Court?

2. You are the key worker in a case where the case protection conference has decided it is appropriate to make an application to court for a care order. The facts of the case are that the father of the child has been convicted of violent assault on the child and is imprisoned. The mother suffers from depression and is unable to provide an acceptable level of care for the child. The child is the subject of an emergency protection order. What reports will it be necessary for you to prepare for the court proceedings?

3. You take over a case from a colleague who is retiring. The case concerns Frank, the youngest child of a family of nine. Frank is now 10 years of age. The case papers date back several years. There has been no action on the file for two years. It appears that three years ago there was some concern expressed about the mother's parenting skills, and the drug addiction and erratic behaviour of the father. You can find no evidence of court applications on the file. There is a note saying that Frank's brother, Tom, was also causing the department concern. The note is dated 1999. Frank's school have now been in touch with the department to express concern about Frank's sexualised behaviour. What documents would you expect to find on the file? Are there any other files you should consider? How would you organise the file?

COMPANION WEB SITE

 For guidance on how to answer these exercises, visit the companion web site at: www.oup.com/uk/booksites/law

WHERE DO WE GO FROM HERE?

This chapter has concentrated on setting out advice on how to use the courts to obtain the best outcomes for service users, by understanding the nature of evidence, how the courts evaluate evidence in order to reach decision, and how to organize information for use in court.

The rules of evidence are a subject of some complexity, and for academic lawyers a study of never-ending interest. We hope that, as a social worker, you move from this chapter with some reassurances: first, that, whatever the complexities, the rules have a purpose, which is to protect and balance the interests of all parties caught up in the vortex of allegations and the exercise of state power over the lives of individuals; secondly, the rules cannot prevent you getting on with the job which you are required by statute to undertake, in particular protecting the interests of children. Thirdly, you should have the tools to prepare and present evidence, including reports, to the court in civil and, if required, in criminal proceedings.

The next chapter takes a look at a very particular part of the law of evidence—the rules governing use of children's testimony in court, particularly in criminal proceedings.

ANNOTATED FURTHER READING

Evidence law

C. Tapper (ed.), *Cross and Tapper on Evidence* (Butterworths, 1999)—for anyone really interested in the law of evidence this is the definitive textbook, well written and authoritative.

Going to court

The following web site called Witness in Court may help you or those you are helping in preparation for a criminal court appearance—**www.homeoffice.gov.uk/cpd/pvu/. witness.pdf**. For a civil court appearance the following is useful, and includes detail like what do I call the judge?: **www.courtservice.gov.uk/forms_and_guidance/guidance/ex341.pdf**.

Reports

Additional information on reports for Children Act cases is provided in *Clarke Hall and Morrison on Children* (Butterworths, Looseleaf, updated regularly).

You should ensure that you read the Government publications referred to in this chapter and available on the Department of Health web site **www.doh.gov.uk**.

Evidence from children

Case Study Re B (sexual abuse: expert's report) [2000] 2 FCR 8, [2000] 1 FLR 871, [2000] 1 FLR 875, [2000] 1 FLR 898

The allegations in this case had involved both criminal proceedings against a father for sexually abusing his daughter (subsequently abandoned by the prosecution) and, the present appeal, a civil dispute between the parents over contact with the child. The mother wished to use the evidence of a consultant psychiatrist in court to help prevent the father having contact. The GP had referred the mother and daughter to her. The extracts from the judgment of Thorpe LJ, who refused to allow the psychiatrist's report, illustrate the clear difference between talking to the child for evidential purposes and for therapeutic purposes.

> 6. Dr Bazeley-White prepared the report in response to that request. It is dated 15 September and it describes in detail the work that Dr Bazeley-White had done, presumably all of it therapeutic in character. It is to be noted that at the first interview with F, the doctor introduced anatomically correct dolls which were then undressed and used as an aid to elicit from the child a description of detailed sexual activity which she said she had experienced with her father. In identifying the adult with whom F had had these experiences, the doctor asked a large number of questions, many of which were in leading form. She ended her report by expressing her opinion that F had plainly been sexually abused by her father and that there should be no unsupervised contact in the future.
>
> 12. I do not criticise Dr Bazeley-White for conducting an interview with F that immediately introduced anatomically correct dolls and then proceeded to a string of leading questions. Obviously, those characteristics are in clear breach of the guidelines that have been available to consultants, at least since the publication of the Report of the Inquiry into Child Abuse in Cleveland 1987 (1988) (Cm 412) (the Cleveland Report). But her function was therapeutic and it may be that in her professional judgment that is what the child's therapy required. Where I criticise Dr Bazeley-White was in ever accepting instructions to prepare a forensic report. She should have had the experience and the judgment to perceive that she was disqualified from making any forensic contribution by the nature of her medical reference and by the nature of the work that she had done in response to that reference.

The chapter looks at the thorny question of the child as a court witness. This means under-standing courts' fears—as articulated in this case study—that witnesses' evidence may become contaminated before it is heard, and the damaging experience of being a witness. We look at powers to compel a child to testify. We will consider questions of credibility and ways of protecting the child from some of the trauma of testifying, which include putting the evidence on tape, and we raise issues of confidentiality of video tapes. The child may, of course, be a victim of an alleged crime. We cannot list all the possible crimes which can be committed against a child, but there is a comprehensive list of sexual offences involving children and vulnerable adults listed in LAC 2004(17) Sexual Offences Act 2003 available at **http://www.dh.gov.uk/assetRoot/04/08/31/06/04083106.PDF**.

The evidence of a child may be critical to the outcome of a case, particularly a criminal case where there may be no other convincing evidence against the accused. It can also be relevant to hear from the child in a civil case, but this is rarely needed in Children Act proceedings since the child's voice can and should be presented through the children and family court reporter (see chapter 6).

Introduction

We have summarized in Box 7.1 the rules which govern whether a child's evidence can be given in court. In brief, children are generally considered competent (i.e. acceptable) as witnesses, though they may not be required (in civil proceedings) or allowed (in criminal proceedings while aged under 14) to take the oath or affirmation.

But competence is not enough—using children's evidence creates a problem for a number of reasons: first, they are (often wrongly) considered less likely to give good evidence than adults; secondly, the experience of being a witness is even more unpleasant and potentially damaging for them than it already is for a mature adult. Nevertheless, what they have experienced can be of integral importance in a court case, and their voice must somehow be heard by the court.

 BOX 7.1 When can a person give evidence in court?

Criminal trials

All witnesses: must be capable of understanding the questions and giving answers which can be understood (Youth Justice and Criminal Evidence Act 1999 s. 53). Need not swear an oath/affirmation

Under 14: must not take the oath/affirmation if giving evidence

14 and above: may give sworn evidence if witness understands particular solemnity of the occasion and need to tell the truth

Civil trials

All witnesses: should testify on oath/affirmation if capable of understanding the meaning of the oath/affirmation

Under 18: May give unsworn evidence if witness has sufficient understanding of duty to tell truth (Children Act 1989 s. 96)

There are special rules protecting vulnerable witnesses who give evidence in court. But the interests of protecting the child witness have to be balanced, particularly in a criminal case, with the right to a fair trial. Even those most worried about the damaging effect on children of testifying will recognize the claim of a person charged with an offence (or accused in a civil case of child abuse) to a fair opportunity to challenge the allegations.

A third problem arises where the child is the alleged victim of criminal behaviour, such as sexual abuse. The needs of the courts for evidence and the needs of the victim for therapy come into conflict. Let us take these issues in turn, starting with the testimony versus therapy problem.

▪ Witness contamination fears

Courts do not want evidence to be rehearsed or contaminated. Cases have been thrown out because social workers or therapists have talked to the child about his or her story. Such a result does not protect the child. If a case is thrown out because of contaminated evidence, the child may then feel that he or she was not believed. Yet if no one can talk to the child until after the court proceedings, he or she will be denied the help and support that it is the social worker's duty to provide whenever '. . . his health or development is likely to be significantly impaired . . . without the provision for him of . . . services [from the local authority]': Children Act 1989, s. 17(10)(b). The Court of Appeal has advised social workers that an interview carried out for therapeutic purposes would very rarely be acceptable for use as evidence in a criminal court: *Re D (Minors) (Child Abuse: Interviews)* (1998). You have to decide in advance what the purpose of the interview is. Childline has produced a report on this conflict between the needs of justice and therapeutic support—*Going to Court: Child Witnesses in Their Own Words* (available from Childline, tel. 0208 239 1000).

The case of *Re T (A Minor) (Procedure: Alleged Sexual Abuse) (No. 2)* (1997) provides a warning, as well as a depressing chronicle of bad practice which failed to protect a child who may indeed have been sexually abused. We quote from [or paraphrase] the judgment of Thorpe LJ:

> It is depressing to see how badly this case has been managed by all the professionals who have been involved in what is, after all, a classically simple case of possible child sexual abuse within a single family. . . .
>
> The social services department, quite rightly, referred the case immediately to a skilled physician. [His report was ignored.] It was followed by a joint investigative interview which was very badly handled. The one thing that all accept was that it was conducted so ineptly that it has no residual value but it seems to have convinced the social services that this was a family in which the only child had been sexually abused by the father. . . . Thereafter, the social worker in the case seems to have impressed upon the mother the need to release the child from guilt feelings by repeatedly reassuring him that he was not bad and that all evil was attributable to his father. It seems to me that social services need to await the outcome of the family justice proceedings before initiating a management policy that creates a belief system

in the child. The issue of whether or not a child has been sexually abused in our society is for decision by the court and it seems to be essential that other agencies await that decision before introducing management counselling or therapy that pre-judged the issue.

(The opportunity to obtain an opinion from a psychologist had also been inexplicably ignored.)

> The next mistake to bedevil the case came . . . when the court welfare officer embarked on a 90 minute play interview with the child. . . . He started out with a complete misunderstanding as to what is the appropriate approach [having stated in his evidence that children cannot fabricate such evidence and that he was prepared to flout the recommendations of the Cleveland Report on interviewing children!].

The criticisms of accepting and reinforcing one view as to what happened continue for several more pages. As a social worker you may disagree with the idea that you are not entitled to decide on the truth of allegations of abuse. As a social worker within the legal system you are going to need to suspend such views if you want to bring credible evidence before the courts. Credible evidence will be enhanced if you follow the guidelines. Moreover, as pointed out by Thorpe LJ, if you are totally committed to one view of what happened and ally yourself closely with that view in your case management (in this case the view that the mother was right and the father had played with the son's penis), how will you work with the family if the court does not come to the same conclusion? And how will the mother feel about the court's decision? Is it appropriate for you then to tell the mother that the court got it wrong?

◼ The damaging experience of being a witness

Victims of crime sometimes say that the experience of giving evidence in court is as bad as the original crime. If true, which it undoubtedly is for many, it must be deeply distressing for many child witnesses. Article 6 of the European Convention on Human Rights explicitly requires an accused to have the right to challenge the evidence. We cannot imagine a fair system—however heinous the allegation, from paedophilia to terrorism—which abrogates this right. However bad the crime, there is no point punishing a person whose guilt has not been proved in a fair trial; and there is a serious risk of punishing the wrong person while the guilty person remains unpunished if the evidence is not robustly tested. Many miscarriages of justices have been corrected, belatedly, because the trial was unfair. Therefore any procedure which requires the evidence of the child to be put before the court must balance the interests of the child and the interests of the accused.

All witnesses should be protected from humiliating and aggressive cross-examination. Judges have a duty to ensure that questioning is relevant and dignified; barristers and solicitors are required to adhere to codes of conduct which permit them rigorously to promote their client's cause but not to distress and humiliate the witness. For this reason the accused is prevented from questioning the alleged victim in person in a trial involving sex offences, and any child under 14 where the alleged offence is kidnapping, child neglect, or involves violence (Youth Justice and Criminal Justice Act 1999, ss. 34 and 35). But in all cases, including those where the accused cannot cross-examine the witness him- or herself, she or he needs to challenge what the witness is saying. The same applies in a civil case, if a person is alleged to have behaved in a particular way. If that behaviour is a fact in issue in the case, that person must have a right to test the evidence before a finding is reached by the court. (See above for the process of cross-examination.) Their barrister or solicitor must interrogate the witness forcefully, trying to produce from the witness an account which supports her or his client's version of the facts in issue.

Cross-examination can even include putting to the witness questions about past sexual conduct, which is excluded if the purpose is merely to show a propensity to a particular sexual behaviour (Youth Justice and Criminal Evidence Act 1999, s. 41), but is allowed if it is actually relevant as a fact in issue. For example in *R v T (Complainant's Sexual History)* (2001) the questioning was held to be relevant because the defendant's case was that the alleged victim, his niece, had previously made false allegations of the same type against other members of his family. Similarly in *R v A (Complainant's Sexual History)* (2001) the House of Lords permitted questioning of the alleged victim about past sexual history in relation to the specific defence of consent. (Although such a line of questioning could not be relevant in a child sex abuse case, where consent is impossible, it shows that there is a risk of even a child being questioned on sexual behaviour if it can be shown to be of relevance to rebutting an aspect of the prosecution case.)

The experience is an ordeal for anyone. For a child it will be particularly difficult. The rest of the chapter focuses mainly on measures to protect a child witness from aspects of the ordeal of giving evidence in court. But the other aspect, the fear that a child is somehow not such a credible witness as an adult, will be explored next.

▮ Will a child be believed?

Children's evidence used to be treated as inherently unreliable. Because children were thought incapable of taking the (religious) oath because of the intellectual feats required to understand perjury and damnation, this was another bar. Now, in both criminal and civil cases, to appear as a witness, a child does not have to give sworn evidence. Children's evidence no longer requires independent supporting evidence (known as corroboration); this used to be required in criminal proceedings, but it was dropped in response to a growing recognition that even quite young children tend to be truthful, and because sometimes, particularly in child abuse cases, there is no evidence independent of the child's which points to the involvement of the accused. It was felt by Parliament that the resulting inability to obtain convictions was unjust to the victims of abuse. So now a court can base its decision, if it wishes, entirely on what a child has told it. But common sense says that, child or adult, a single witness is not always persuasive without some other evidence to support the story told.

To decide whether to accept the evidence of a child there does not have to be a special hearing within a trial on this point, nor does the judge or magistrate have to hear evidence on the child's capability from a psychologist or other expert, though in a criminal case the Youth Justice and Criminal Evidence Act explicitly allows the court to use an expert to advise (s. 54). Assuming the child does give evidence, it is then for the jury or magistrates to decide what weight to give it (*Gibson v DPP* (1997)).

In *R v B* (1990), the Court of Appeal upheld a conviction where the principal prosecution witness was the 6-year-old victim giving evidence by video link. And in *R v Norbury* (1992) the Court of Appeal upheld a conviction for rape and indecent assault based on the uncorroborated evidence of a 6 year old. The judge had stated that he was helped in deciding on her competence by seeing her video interview and hearing from the social workers and police officers who were present when the video was made.

There is nothing inherently wrong with using the evidence of a child as young as 4 in a criminal case (normally by means of a video link and a pre-recorded video). The judge will first assess whether the child is capable of giving intelligible testimony, before the evidence goes to the jury (*DPP v M* (1997)).

By comparison there is also no bar to receiving and believing the evidence of an octogenarian with Alzheimer's given via a video recording (see below for evidence given by vulnerable witnesses under special measures) using the same test as for children under the Youth Justice and Criminal Evidence Act, that she could understand the questions and her answers could be understood. The defendant of course could call medical evidence to challenge her mental competence and could point out to the jury that the witness was not available in court for cross-examination: the issue is that the Court of Appeal said it was possible to receive and rely on this evidence: *R v D* (2002).

There have been many cases where the courts have come up with different answers to an interesting question: can one witness (a psychologist) give evidence about whether another witness (a child) is telling the truth? Generally, courts are unwilling to be told who is credible and who is not, and prefer to reserve such decisions to themselves (or to a jury in the Crown Court). We hope that the debate is now over, following the Court of Appeal case of *Re M and R* (1996). The Court said that the Civil Evidence Act 1972 puts beyond doubt the admissibility of such expert evidence. But the opinion can be given only by someone qualified to give it: as a social worker you would not be seen as qualified to go beyond your observations of fact into opinions on credibility. (As we have seen in *Gibson v DPP* above, the fact that this evidence is admissible does not mean the court needs it, or even wants it, in order to decide what weight to give a child's evidence.)

■ Can a child be compelled to testify?

The answer to this question is mixed. In principle, a child can be summonsed to attend, like any other witness. But under s. 44 of the Children and Young Persons Act 1933, a criminal court should have regard to the welfare of any child involved in proceedings, and may exceptionally decide that the child should be spared from giving evidence. The court may make this decision either after the child has been summonsed (*R v Highbury Magistrates' Court ex parte Deering* (1996)), or even before issuing the summons (*Re P* (1997)). The welfare of the child is important but not paramount, as this is not a Children Act matter. If dispensing with the child's evidence means a prosecution will collapse, the judge must take this into account. It could be damaging for the child for an alleged abuser not to be tried.

■ Protecting the vulnerable witness from trauma: evidence by video and other special measures

The measures we are about to consider are explicitly designed for criminal trials. In civil trials (which include care proceedings) hearsay evidence is admissible, and so there is rarely a need to hear directly from a child witness. The judge or magistrates have the task of deciding the case on the balance of probabilities, not of testing it to the point where no reasonable doubt remains. So they can be told at second hand what a child said, or they can choose whether to see, for example, a video of an interview with the child. This may be enough for the court to make a finding of fact or to help the court determine what order to make. However, what follows in the discussion about ensuring that the evidence is not contaminated, particularly in recording a video interview, applies equally in a civil case if the court is to rely on what the child is recorded as saying.

In criminal proceedings there has been a possibility since 1991 of protecting the child witness through using pre-recorded videos of the child's statement, or through cross-examining the child through a CCTV. The Youth Justice and Criminal Evidence Act 1999 now contains and extends this legislation and provides for 'special measures' to apply where the evidence in criminal trials will come from 'vulnerable and intimidated witnesses'. Facilities must be available for the special measures in the relevant court. For a list of possible measures see Box 5.5. Measures in the current Criminal Justice Bill will extend the power to take a witness's evidence via CCTV to any witness where the facilities are available and the court thinks it desirable.

Under s. 16 of the 1999 Act, a child aged under 17 (when the decision on special measures is taken) is automatically eligible for special measures. Any other witness is eligible if the court decides that the quality of her or his evidence is likely to be diminished by reason of mental disorder, intellectual or social impairment, or physical disability. In addition, any witness may become eligible for special measures if the court decides that:

• the evidence will be diminished in quality as a result of fear or distress;

• the witness lacks full capacity because of mental disorder, social or intellectual impairment, or physical disability;

• the witness is a complainant in a sexual abuse case.

BOX 7.2 Special measures for vulnerable witnesses

(a) *Screening (s. 23—not yet in force in the magistrates court)*: This is to prevent the witness from seeing the accused (but it does not provide reassurance that the accused cannot see the witness).

(b) *Evidence by live link (s. 24)*: A court is permitted to move to a different venue to avail itself of facilities for this.

(c) *Evidence in private (s. 25—not yet in force in the magistrates court)*: The accused or his or her lawyers cannot be removed, and the press can be removed only if a sexual offence is alleged, or there are allegations of witness intimidation.

(d) *Removal of wigs and gowns (s. 26)*.

(e) *Video recorded evidence in chief (s. 27)*: The evidence in chief—that is the evidence the witness gives first, before cross-examination—can be pre-recorded. The court has to be satisfied that this is in the interests of justice, weighing the prejudice to the accused against the desirability of seeing the evidence. The main issue with child witnesses is the risk, or allegation, that in preparing the video recording the child has been in some way coached. Details of the circumstances in which the video was made must be provided to the other side. The court will usually not admit the recording if the witness cannot be cross-examined on it.

(f) *Video recorded cross-examination and re-examination (s. 28)*: This is an entirely new departure and addresses the criticism of the old law which did not provide any safeguards for the child witness against the terrors of cross-examination. Cases collapsed because it could be too traumatic for a child to be cross-examined at trial by a barrister whose job it was to undermine his or her credibility. A special measures direction can now provide for the cross-examination (and re-examination) of the witness on pre-recorded video. It is a small step only, of course, because the cross-examination is still carried out by a lawyer whose job it is to discredit parts of the evidence. The video must be made in the presence (which can be electronic presence) of the other party's lawyer and of the judge. The witness is usually then spared from participation in the trial, but exceptionally the judge can have the witness recalled.

(g) *Restriction on who can cross examine (s. 35)*: A child or a vulnerable witness in a sexual offence trial cannot be cross-examined by the accused in person.

(h) *Examination of witness through intermediary (s. 29)*: A court may approve an intermediary who puts the questions to the witness. An interpreter has always been allowed to do this, but this could now include a social worker or other person who can assist the witness. This can be carried out with live video links and in conjunction with pre-recorded video cross-examination. This is being piloted as the intermediaries are recruited and trained. It raises human rights issues—will the accused get a fair trial if he or she cannot hear the evidence of the witness directly?

The court will exercise its discretion to decide what special measures, singly or in combination, are appropriate. But where the witness is a child (under 17 for these purposes, which includes someone who becomes 17 after the video of the evidence is made), s. 21 provides that, where the relevant equipment is available:

(a) evidence in chief *must* be by way of pre-recorded video;

(b) any live evidence *must* be given by way of CCTV link.

Does the absence of the witness from the courtroom—particularly in a situation where it is automatic—violate the defendant's right to a fair trial (the opportunity to mount a full challenge to evidence against her or him under Article 6)? For though a court can override these requirements it is unlikely to do so if the witness has been promised this facility, and in any event there is no discretion for the court if the child witness is the alleged victim in a sexual offence trial. In *R (on the application of D) v Camberwell Green Youth Court* (2003)), the court said this would not interfere with the defendant's rights, and anyway the vulnerable witness has rights which require a balancing act.

The social worker may have involvement in preparing a pre-recorded video. Although the Act came into force in 2000, in preparing you for the task, a number of cases and guidance documents relating to the earlier legislation remain relevant.

The pre-recorded interview can be with a social worker or other non-lawyer. It is attractive for two reasons. First, the interview is more relaxed for the child than an appearance in the witness box; second, the evidence may be of higher quality, as the video can be made long before the trial, before detail is forgotten. There is, however, a serious problem in the procedure if sparing the child an ordeal is an important factor. The person accused of the violence or abuse has the right to challenge the child's evidence by cross-examination, so the child still has to give live evidence, though, as we have seen, this can be organized before the trial. But the task of the cross-examining defence lawyer is still to destroy the credibility of the child's evidence and to get an acquittal, not to protect the child from pain.

The Criminal Justice Act 2003, s. 116, allows evidence in the witness's absence (i.e. hearsay evidence) if the witness is too afraid to come, but the court has to be convinced that this would be fair to the accused. This is unlikely. Courts like to see prosecution evidence tested.

Under the Youth Justice and Criminal Evidence Act 1999, s. 27, the judge can require the pre-recorded material to be edited before it is shown to the jury to remove inadmissible or unfair evidence (such as an inadmissible reference to a person's previous record, or irrelevant prejudicial material). And the court may require those who made the video to give evidence about how it was made (Court of Appeal, *Practice Direction* (1992)).

It is not good practice to conduct an interview with a child without recording the interview. Butler-Sloss LJ in *Re W* (1993) quotes with approval what Latey J said in an earlier case:

> [C]ases have shown . . . that the precise questions, the oral answers (if there are any), the gestures and body movements, the vocal inflection and intonation, may all play an important part in interpretation.

Also experts can watch the video, without further interviews with the child. So, unless you are reporting spontaneous statements by the child, courts will want to see the tape, not to hear your recollection of what happened in the interview.

Guidance on conducting evidential video interviews

The use of pre-recorded video material raises the whole question of 'disclosure' work with children. The first concern of a social worker or doctor will be to work with a child to try to overcome the damage caused by abuse. In this kind of therapeutic contact with the child, it may be necessary to encourage the child to bring up past events which the child is suppressing. But the evidential interview is not, and cannot be, conducted on the same lines, and is rendered worthless as evidence for a trial if there is a suggestion that the interviewer has put words in the child's mouth.

You must be specially trained for this kind of interview. You must be familiar with the Cleveland Guidelines and *Working Together* (see chapter 8), and with the case law and guidance that have grown around the use of video material. The Home Office published guidance in 1992 (the *'Memorandum of Good Practice on Video Recorded Interviews with Child Witnesses in Criminal Proceedings'* (HMSO, 1992)), which has now been replaced with *Achieving Best Evidence in Criminal Proceedings: Guidance for Vulnerable or Intimidated Witnesses including Children* **www.homeoffice.gov.uk/docs/bestevidence vol1_text.pdf**. This guidance states:

> [I]t is recommended that this Guidance be used, in conjunction with other relevant guidance, as a key resource in the training of police and social workers involved in the investigative interviewing of children and vulnerable or intimidated adult witnesses. It should also be used as a resource by those concerned with providing pre-trial support and preparation and those involved in the trial process. (para 3).

We have selected a small number of quotes from the guidance, which are set out in Box 7.3.

 BOX 7.3 Extracts from *Obtaining Best Evidence*

Para 2: Thorough planning is essential to a successful investigation and interview. Even if concerns about the child's safety necessitate an early interview, an appropriate planning session is required which identifies key issues and objectives. Time spent covering and anticipating issues early in the criminal investigation will be rewarded by an improved interview later on. It is important that, as far as possible, the case is thoroughly reviewed before an interview is embarked upon to ensure that all issues are covered and key questions asked, since the opportunity to do this will in most cases be lost once the interview(s) have been concluded.

Para 2.3 Referral information may give clues to likely charges, but should not be used to drive the interview solely towards confirming earlier suspicions or allegations. The interviewer should keep an open mind as to what may or may not have happened to the child, and should not seek only to elicit details which will prove a hypothesis about the child's experience(s) constructed on the basis of the initial information. In abuse investigations, the possibility of gathering additional evidence from a medical examination of the child or from the scene of the alleged abuse should also be discussed.

This guidance is essential reading for any person interviewing children with a view to their evidence being potentially available to a court. The courts will expect that the person who interviews the child on behalf of the multi-disciplinary team investigating allegations of abuse will be a trained specialist. You must, if that person is going to be you, read the guidance in full, for if the guidance is ignored, the evidence may be thrown out. That does not help the child.

The old concept of children having something to disclose is out. 'It must be remembered that non-disclosure of abuse is an acceptable outcome of an interview, either because the child has not experienced nor witnessed any maltreatment, or because the child is not ready, able or willing to tell now' (para. 2.31). That implies prejudgement of what the child may tell you. Your opinion that the child is withholding what he or she knows is potentially relevant, because in court you are an expert witness interpreting for the court what the child's behaviour means. But if, because you 'know' what happened, you prompt the child in preparing or recording a video interview, you have destroyed the child's evidence. (In fact you do not 'know' unless you witnessed the abuse; you have an opinion about what happened, and the court does not want that opinion to influence what other witnesses say.)

Judges have long been critical of poor questioning technique. You can see examples of the courts' attitude to bad questioning technique in civil cases in a series of reports starting at [1987] *Fam Law* 269. The judges rejected suggestive questioning, particularly in combination with the use of the anatomically correct dolls, and they rejected the allegations of sexual abuse apparently made by children on tape. They did so notwithstanding expert evidence from psychologists interpreting the answers to the questions as being evidence of sexual abuse. If you are involved in 'disclosure' work, these cases (although old) must be read; they show clearly that the courts reject the idea of the interviewer going in with the preconceived idea that there is something there to disclose. The consistent theme of the judgments is that putting suggestive questions to a child leads to unreliable disclosure. So yes, the evidence is admissible, but no, it is probably not persuasive unless the questioning has been very open. Jenny McEwan put it well, writing in the *Journal of Child Law*, vol. 2, No. 1, p. 24:

> Judicial dislike of cross-examination technique in disclosure interviews is well known. The courts frown upon hypothetical and leading questions, 'pressure', reminding the child of what she allegedly said elsewhere and disregard of the answers actually given.

Guidance was also given on evidential interviewing in *R v H and others* (1992). Hollings J insisted in particular that one person should co-ordinate the investigation on behalf of a multi-disciplinary team, and this includes preparation of video evidence.

If pre-recorded evidence is used in a criminal case, the prosecution has to supply details to the defence of when it was made, who was there, and who conducted the interview. The recording will not be used if of poor quality, since the jury need to be able to assess the credibility of the witness, which means being able to see him or her and hear clearly. A side view from a distance led to valuable child evidence against a teacher accused of indecent assault being thrown out in *R v P* (1998).

A parent should not be present: *Re N* (1996).

The availability of pre-recorded video evidence probably encourages guilty pleas, once the accused knows it is available and has seen it. Research at Leicester University has shown that this type of evidence is easier for lawyers, judges, and juries to understand, and makes it more likely that children will testify ((1992) *LS Gaz*, 22 Jan., 10).

Everything said about good practice for interviewing in relation to criminal allegations is applicable where the court is deciding a civil law issue. In *Re M (Sexual Abuse Allegations: Interviewing Techniques)* (1999), the father wanted contact, seven years after his children (then aged 2 and 5) had given an eight-hour taped interview containing allegations of abuse. Leading questions had been put and the mother had been present. The mother now wished to rely on this evidence to prevent resumption of contact. It was held that the evidence was badly flawed and breached the Cleveland Guidelines (but, given the children's hostility to seeing their father, contact was limited to postcards to the children, and photographs and school reports to the father).

Another possible way to keep the child witness out of court

The Children and Young Persons Act 1933 has always permitted hearsay evidence to be put into evidence in criminal cases, if attending as a witness would harm a child (including emotionally). A Government Circular (LAC 88(10) Annex C) encourages social workers and others to use this power. But the evidence has to be taken by

BOX 7.4 Further samples from *Achieving Best Evidence*

Although it is important to guard against undue influence of the child by another adult, it may be helpful to the child (and to the process of securing an account) if someone is present to offer support, especially if the child is very young or upset. [para. 2.42]

Interview supporters should never offer the child inducements, such as a toy or trip in return for general cooperation or answering particular questions. Persons involved as a witness in the case in any capacity (i.e. not just someone who has seen the incident in question) cannot take on the role of witness supporter. This would include a parent to whom the child first disclosed abuse . . . [para. 2.43]

Interviewers should have clear objectives for assessment(s)prior to interview, and should apply this guidance on talking with children during such assessment. For example, they should avoid discussing substantive issues (in any detail) and must not lead the child on substantive matters. Interviewers should never stop a child who is freely recalling significant events. Instead . . . the interviewers must make a full written record of the discussion, making a note of the timing and personnel present, as well as what was said and in what order. The interviewers should begin by explaining the objectives of the interview to the child . . . [para. 2.52]

A child witness may be judged by the investigating team, and/or by those professionals responsible for the welfare of the child, to require therapeutic help prior to giving evidence in criminal proceedings. It is vital that professionals undertaking therapy with prospective child witnesses prior to a criminal trial adhere to the official guidance: *Provision of Therapy for Child Witnesses Prior to a Criminal Trial: Practice Guidance*. [para. 2.90] questioning the child in front of a magistrate, and medical evidence is required of the likely harm. The child is spared some, but by no means the whole, of the ordeal and some delay is averted. The reason this procedure is hardly ever used is presumably that prosecutors do not believe that the child's evidence will be as strong as it would be if given at the trial.

Avoiding delay where children are witnesses

Children should be spared the normal months of delay before a criminal case gets to trial. Under the Criminal Justice Act 1991, cases of violence or sexual abuse involving child witnesses should be given priority in the court's timetable.

Confidentiality of video tapes

This is a problem with several dimensions. A child may be prepared to talk only if assured, for example, 'Daddy will never be told'. This is a promise you cannot make, since the tape may be needed in evidence. The other significant problem is that the accused must have a fair chance to know exactly what evidence is going to be given against him (or occasionally her). Fairness, looked at from this angle, dictates that he sees the tape and has a chance to prepare his defence. But to have tapes of this sort circulating as currency in prison, as happens with some written statements, is recognized as unacceptable, and tapes will be passed to the lawyer only on strict undertakings not to release them to the accused or copy them.

Further support for the child

Giving evidence, even with the benefit of a screen or by video link or pre-recorded interview, is bound to be distressing for a child. We quote some helpful advice from *Childright*, January/February 1990, No. 63, at p. 12:

> Not all child witnesses and their carers receive emotional support from an outside source, and even if they do it is not inevitable that a support worker will accompany them to court. After a not guilty verdict, family anger can be very intense. It is important for someone to be available to pick up the pieces and access to a private room is very helpful.
>
> The verdict must be explained to the child. He or she may need to talk, even if the parent/carer wishes to see the trial as a closed chapter. If the result seems unfair to the child, or even if it is what the child wanted, the court experience and its aftermath can churn up emotions of regret and guilt. In the event of an acquittal, children's feelings about not being believed can be devastating. Whatever the verdict, the explanation should.

Childline and the NSPCC have produced a video for anyone helping a child prepare for attending court. The details are available on **www.nspcc.org.uk/html/home/ informationresources/newvideoforyoungwitnesses.htm**.

EXERCISE

Reminder: some of the tools you need to deal with this question will come from your understanding of other chapters, for example powers to apply for a care order under the Children Act (chapter 12) or questions of confidentiality (chapter 4). The case study builds on that used in the previous chapter.

You are a social worker for Lamingshire Social Services. In the previous chapter you were seeking a care order in relation to 12-year-old child, Kylie. You may recall that the local authority's case is based on information which included the following:

- Kylie has told you 'in confidence' that her parents beat her every night;
- A doctor who examined Kylie when her parents brought her to casualty has written in her report that the bruising is consistent with a fall down the stairs, a version of events given at the time by the parents and Kylie herself.

The Crown Prosecution Service intend to prosecute Kylie's father. Your department agrees that this is in Kylie's interest, and that it cannot proceed without Kylie's testimonhy. What are the legal issues involved in her being a witness?

COMPANION WEB SITE

 For guidance on how to answer these exercises, visit the companion web site at: **www.oup.com/uk/booksites/law**

WHERE DO WE GO FROM HERE?

This chapter has had a narrow but important focus—how to prepare and support a child or other vulnerable witness whose evidence is important in a criminal case. We put it into the part of the book which deals with understanding evidence, but the practical use you will put this information to is in relation to child protection, and the next part of the book introduces you to your statutory duties towards children, and the legal principles which will help you to be effective.

The next part of the book is about your statutory responsibilities to protect and promote the welfare of children. When it goes well you won't go near a court—but everything you do must be within a framework of law, knowing that your work may end up under scrutiny from a court of law.

ANNOTATED FURTHER READING

Home Office, *Achieving Best Evidence in Criminal Proceedings: Guidance for Vulnerable or Intimidated Witnesses including Children* **www.homeoffice.gov.uk/docs/.bestevidencevol1_text.pdf**—essential reading as it is the official guidance for all involved and is taken into account by courts.

Home Office, *Provision of Therapy for Child Witnesses Prior to a Criminal Trial Practice Guidance* **www.homeoffice.gov.uk/docs/therapybook.pdf**. From the introduction: 'The guidance makes it clear that the best interests of the child are paramount when deciding whether, and in what form, therapeutic help is given. We hope that it will be helpful for all practitioners, especially those in the criminal justice system, NHS, social services departments and voluntary child care organisations.'

Royal College of Psychiatry, *The Evidence of Children* (Royal College of Psychiatry, 1996), available at **www.rcpsych.ac.uk/publications/cr/cr44.htm**—makes proposals to improve the way in which evidence is obtained from child witnesses.

J. Spencer and R. Flin, *The Evidence of Children* (2nd edn., Blackstone Press, 1993)—it is a pity this book has not run to further editions, as it usefully combines a social scientific and a legal analysis of the issues, in readable language.

K. Müller, *An Inquisitorial Approach to the Evidence of Children* (Port Vale University, South Africa) **www.crisa.org.za/downloads/ia.pdf**—analyses the responses of children to questioning under different circumstances.

Law Commission of New Zealand, *The Evidence of Children and other Vulnerable Witnesses* (Paper 26, 1997). **www.lawcom.govt.nz/documents/publications/PP26.pdf**—a good overall analysis of the range of issues involved.

H. Westcott and J. Jones (eds.), *Perspectives on the Memorandum. Policy, Practice and Research in Investigative Interviewing* (Arena, 1997)—provides a range of different views on the Memorandum of Good Practice and issues relating to interviewing children. Although the Memorandum has been replaced with *Achieving Best Evidence*, the book is primarily about interviewing children and its relevance is not diminished.

S. Hollins with V. Sinason and J. Boniface, *Going to Court*, illustrated by B. Webb (Royal College of Psychiatrists, 1994). This is a picture book without words which can be used with a young person who is preparing to go to court. Now out of date in relation to the video evidence.

Home Office, *Provision of Therapy for Child Witnesses before a Criminal Trial* **www.homeoffice.gov.uk/docs/provision.html**.

PART III

Responsibilities towards children

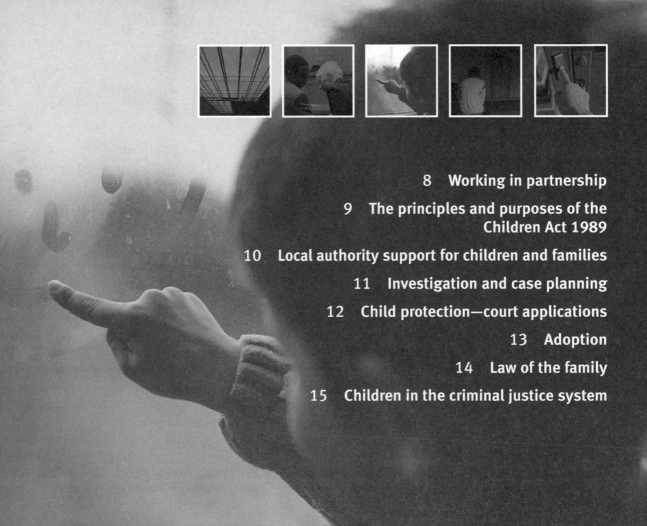

PART III Responsibilities towards children

This part of the book considers the range of statutory duties the social worker has towards children. The Children Act 1989 provides the legal framework for these responsibilities.

Chapter 8 sets out how social services departments should work with other agencies which have a role in safeguarding children. Those agencies can be statutory, such as the police and health authorities, or voluntary. Working with these agencies ensures that the most effective outcomes for children are achieved. Chapter 8 starts with an extract from the Laming Report of the Inquiry into Victoria Climbié. This is an important inquiry, which is shaping the future of social services and which emphasizes the importance of agencies working together to safeguard children. It then explains the government's legislative response in the Children Act 2004 before going on to consider interagency working.

Chapter 9 considers Part 1 of the Children Act 1989 which sets out the overarching principles of the law relating to children. We explain the critical importance of the welfare principle and the other principles which are set out in the legislation.

Chapter 10 explains the responsibilities that local authorities have towards children in need, and 'looked after' children. It is important to note that local authority responsibilities do not depend on a court order, if children are in need or are accommodated by the local authority, then the local authority has a range of responsibilities towards those children which it must fulfill. We draw particular attention to the needs of children who are in care to be prepared for adult life. Long-term plans need to be formulated as soon as possible, so as to avoid children 'drifting' in care, with local authorities failing to address their specific needs.

Chapter 11 describes the local authority responsibilities to investigate cases where there are concerns about the welfare of children and to assess the needs of children. Investigations may be required by the court, or as a result of an agency or a member of the public expressing concerns about a child. It is vital for social workers to respond appropriately. However, responsibilities do not end with investigation—there is some overlap here with the concerns of chapter 10—because social workers need to plan for court proceedings or other long-term formal solutions. In this chapter we consider the protocol for judicial case management in public law Children Act cases which integrates the planning process for children with the court process.

Chapter 12 sets out the law relating to applications for court orders. There is a range of court orders available to the local authority, ranging from orders which provide for the long-term care of the child, to short-terms orders which enable the local authority to respond to emergency situations. Different considerations apply in each of these orders, reflecting the extent to which they interfere with the integrity of the family, the duration of the order, and the nature of the circumstances in which the application is made.

Chapter 13 describes the provisions of the Adoption and Children Act 2002. This important piece of new legislation was enacted because of government concern to modernize and increase the use of adoption. The Act also includes a new type of provision—special guardianship orders—which enables children to have long-term security in circumstances where there are good reasons for not permanently severing their links with their birth family.

Chapter 14 explains family law—the private law that you need to understand as it forms the basis of the law which governs family life. You also need to be familiar with family law in order to understand the options which are available in cases of family breakdown and so that you know when the intervention of public law proceedings may be appropriate.

Chapter 15 goes in a different direction. It explains the criminal justice system relating to children. What is interesting is that the philosophy of the criminal justice system is quite different from that of the Children Act, despite the fact that in each arena we are concerned with the needs of children.

8 Working in partnership

CASE STUDY

The following is an extract from the Victoria Climbié Inquiry Report of an Inquiry by Lord Laming Cm 5730:

1 Introduction

'Victoria had the most beautiful smile that lit up the room.'

1.1 This Report begins and ends with Victoria Climbié. It is right that it should do so. The purpose of the Inquiry has been to find out why this once happy, smiling enthusiastic little girl—brought to this country by a relative for a 'better life'—ended her days the victim of almost unimaginable cruelty. The horror of what happened to her during her last months was captured by Counsel to the Inquiry, Neil Garnham QC, who told the Inquiry:

> The food would be cold and would be given to her on a piece of plastic while she was tied up in the bath. She would eat it like a dog, pushing her face to the plate. Except, of course that a dog is not usually tied up in a plastic bag full of its excrement. To say that Kouao and Manning treated Victoria like a dog would be wholly unfair; she was treated worse than a dog.

1.2 On 12 January 2001, Victoria's great-aunt, Marie Therese Kouao, and Carl John Manning were convicted of her murder.

Abuse and neglect

1.3 At his trial, Manning said that Kouao would strike Victoria on a daily basis with a shoe, a coat hanger and a wooden cooking spoon and would strike her on her toes with a hammer. Victoria's blood was found on Manning's football boots. Manning admitted that at times he would hit Victoria with a bicycle chain. Chillingly, he said, 'You could beat her and she wouldn't cry . . . She could take the beatings and the pain like anything.'

1.4 Victoria spent much of her last days, in the winter of 1999–2000, living and sleeping in a bath in an unheated bathroom, bound hand and foot inside a bin bag, lying in her own urine and faeces. It is not surprising then that towards the end of her short life, Victoria was stooped like an old lady and could walk only with great difficulty.

1.5 When Victoria was admitted to the North Middlesex Hospital on the evening of 24 February 2000, she was desperately ill. She was bruised, deformed and malnourished. Her temperature was so low it could not be recorded on the hospital's standard thermometer. Dr Lesley Alsford, the consultant responsible for Victoria's care on that occasion, said, 'I had never seen a case like it before. It is the worst case of child abuse and neglect that I have ever seen.'

1.6   Despite the valiant efforts of Dr Alsford and her team, Victoria's condition continued to deteriorate. In a desperate attempt to save her life, Victoria was transferred to the paediatric intensive care unit at St Mary's Hospital Paddington. It was there that, tragically, she died a few hours later, on the afternoon of 25 February 2000.

1.7   Seven months earlier, Victoria had been a patient in the North Middlesex Hospital. Nurse Sue Jennings recalled:

> Victoria did not have any possessions—she only had the clothes that she arrived in. Some of the staff had brought in dresses and presents for Victoria. One of the nurses had given her a white dress and Victoria found some pink Wellingtons which she used to wear with it. I remember Victoria dressed like this, twirling up and down the ward. She was a very friendly and happy child.

Victoria's injuries

1.8   At the end, Victoria's lungs, heart and kidneys all failed. Dr Nathaniel Carey, a Home Office pathologist with many years' experience, carried out the post-mortem examination. What stood out from Dr Carey's evidence was the extent of Victoria's injuries and the deliberate way they were inflicted on her. He said:

> All non-accidental injures to children are awful and difficult for everybody to deal with, but in terms of the nature and extent of the injury, and almost systematic nature of the inflicted injury, I certainly regard this as the worst I have ever dealt with, and it is just about the worst I have ever heard of.

1.9   At the post-mortem examination, Dr Carey recorded evidence of no fewer than 128 separate injures to Victoria's body, saying, 'There really is not anywhere that is spared—there is scarring all over the body.'

1.10   Therefore, in the space of just a few months, Victoria had been transformed from a healthy, lively, and happy little girl, into a wretched and broken wreck of a human being.

Abandoned, unheard, and unnoticed

1.11   Perhaps the most painful of all the distressing events of Victoria's short life in this country is that even toward the end, she might have been saved. In the last few weeks before she died, a social worker called at her home several times. She got no reply when she knocked at the door and assumed that Victoria and Kouao had moved away. It is possible that at the time, Victoria was in fact lying just a few yards away, in the prison of the bath, desperately hoping someone might find her and come to her rescue before her life ebbed away.

1.12   At no time during the weeks and months of this gruelling Inquiry did familiarity with the suffering experienced by Victoria diminish the anguish of hearing it, or make it easier to endure. It was clear from the evidence heard by the Inquiry that Victoria's intelligence and the warmth of her engaging smile shone through despite the ghastly facts of what she experienced during the 11 months she lived in England. The more my colleagues and I heard about Victoria, the more we came to know her as a lovable child and our hearts went out to her. However, neither Victoria's intelligence nor her lovable nature could save her. In the end she died a slow lonely death—abandoned, unheard, and unnoticed.

1.13   [not reproduced—the paragraph is a tribute to Victoria's parents]

What went wrong?

1.14 I recognize that those who take on the work of protecting children at risk of deliberate harm face a tough and challenging task. Staff doing this work need a combination of professional skills and personal qualities, not least of which are persistence and courage. Adults who deliberately exploit the vulnerability of children can behave in devious and menacing ways. They will often go to great lengths to hide their activities from those concerned for the well-being of a child. Staff often have to cope with the unpredictable behaviour of people in the parental role. A child can appear safe one minute and be injured the next. A peaceful scene can be transformed in seconds because of a sudden outburst of uncontrollable anger.

1.15 Whenever a child is deliberately injured or killed, there is inevitably great concern in case some important tell-tale sign has been missed. Those who sit in judgement often do so with the great benefit of hindsight. So I readily acknowledge that staff who undertake the work of protecting children and supporting families on behalf of us all deserve both our understanding and our support. It is a job which carries risks, because in every judgement they make, those staff have to balance the rights of a parent with that of the protection of the child.

A lack of good practice

1.16 But Victoria's case was altogether different. Victoria was not hidden away. It is deeply disturbing that during the days and months following her initial contacts with Ealing Housing Department's Homeless Persons' Unit, Victoria was known to no less that two further housing authorities, four social services departments, two child protection teams of the Metropolitan Police Service (MPS), a specialist centre managed by the NSPCC, and she was admitted to two different hospitals because of suspected deliberate harm. The dreadful reality was that these services knew little or nothing more about Victoria at the end of the process than they did when she was first referred to Ealing Social Services by the Homeless Persons' Unit in April 1999. The final irony was that Haringey Social Services formally closed Victoria's case on the very day she died. The extent of the failure to protect Victoria was lamentable. Tragically, it required nothing more than basic good practice being put into operation. This never happened.

1.17 In his opening statement ot the Inquiry, Neil Garnham QC listed no fewer than 12 key occasions when the relevant services had the opportunity to successfully intervene in the life of Victoria. As evidence to the Inquiry unfolded, several other opportunities emerged. Not one of these required great skill or would have made heavy demands on time to take some form of action. Sometimes it needs nothing more than a manager doing their job by asking pertinent questions or taking the trouble to look in a case file. There can be no excuse for such sloppy and unprofessional performance.

A gross failure of the system

1.18 Not one of the agencies empowered by Parliament to protect children in positions similar to Victoria's—funded from the public purse—emerge from this Inquiry with much credit. The suffering and death of Victoria was a gross failure of the system and was inexcusable. It is clear to me that the agencies with responsibility for Victoria gave a low priority to the task of protecting children. They were underfunded, inadequately staffed and poorly led. Even so, there was plenty of evidence to show that scarce resources were not being put to good use. Bad practice can be expensive. For example, had there been a proper response to the needs of Victoria when she was first referred to Ealing Social Services, it may well be that the danger to her would have been recognized and action taken which may have avoided the need for the later involvement of other agencies.

OVERVIEW AND OBJECTIVES

The Inquiry into the death of Victoria Climbié was established after Victoria's death after months of neglect and mistreatment by her carers. The Inquiry, chaired by Lord Laming, was unique in that it was established under three separate statutes and looked at the roles of three key services: the police, social services, and the health services.

The first eighteen paragraphs of the Laming Report are powerful reading. It is particularly moving that Laming puts Victoria Climbié at the heart of the report as the paragraphs set out above illustrate. We recommend that you read the whole report, although it is a very long and stressful read. There is no doubt that it will prove to be a key influence on future social work provision. Throughout the report, Laming identifies poor practice by social workers and the managers of social services, and we will alert you to the relevant recommendations throughout this part of the book. However, a major focus of the report is the need for all agencies working with children to work together effectively so that positive outcomes for children are maximized.

As you read through the eighteen paragraphs ask yourself what went wrong and who has to accept responsibility for Victoria's death? How was it that so many different agencies had contact with Victoria yet there was no official recognition of the extent to which she was at risk? How can a similar tragedy be prevented from happening again?

In this chapter we concentrate on the Government's response to the Laming Report and look at what partnership working means for social workers. We consider in some detail the agencies which share your statutory responsibilities towards children and other vulnerable people and explain their roles. We also briefly consider the range of problems which vulnerable people may face and describe a range of voluntary sector agencies which provide advice and assistance to those families. By the end of the chapter you should have a clearer understanding of how your role complements the roles of other professionals concerned with vulnerable people. The chapter starts with an outline of the Children Act 2004 which provides the legislative framework for improving service provision for children.

In the *Guardian* (Clash of Cultures—19 May 2004) David Brindle writes: 'At the heart of the bill' (as it then was) 'is the concept of integrated working by professional in the best interests of the child, breaking down existing structural and attitudinal demarcations. This is going to prove an awful lot easier to legislate for than to achieve on the ground.' He suggests that the government thinks it will take ten years before the change in culture becomes the norm. As you read through this chapter think about how effective cross-agency working could improve outcomes for children and other vulnerable people, and then consider how practices need to develop in order to achieve this. Also consider whether you think that changes in the law are the best way to ensure that the necessary changes to traditional professional practice happen. How long do you think it will take to achieve, and what responsibility do you have as a new entrant to the profession?

■ The Government response to the Report of the Climbié Inquiry

'Every child matters'

In September 2003 the Government published the Green Paper *Every Child Matters* Cm 5860. This set out its full response to the Laming Inquiry. You can find the Green Paper at **www.dfes.gov.uk/everychildmatters/**.

The Green Paper set out five outcomes for services for children to work towards. These outcomes are:

- Being healthy
- Staying safe
- Enjoying and achieving
- Making a positive contribution
- Economic well-being.

These broad outcomes indicate that the Government is recognising the need for a more holistic approach to children's services. Effective outcomes for children cannot be separated from other initiatives such as *Sure Start*, raising educational achievements and youth justice provision. Other related documents were published on the same date. These included *A Better Education for Children in Care*—a report by the Social Exclusion Unit and *Youth Justice—The Next Step*, which sets out more detailed proposals to build on recent youth justice reforms.

The Government also published on that date, *Keeping Children Safe*—its response to the Laming Report and the Joint Inspection report *Safeguarding Children*. This can be found at **www.dfes.gov.uk/everychildmatters/pdfs/KeepingChildrenSafe.pdf**.

The response identifies particular weaknesses within the child protection system. The following extract from the introduction to the report indicates the gravity of Government concerns.

What is wrong with the system now?

7. The reports show that the legislative framework for safeguarding children set out in the Children Act 1989 is basically sound. However, there are serious weaknesses in the way in which it is interpreted, resourced and implemented.

8. The Victoria Climbié Inquiry Report showed that the system failed comprehensively, because of ill-trained and overworked staff, who were unsupported by their managers or more senior staff in their organizations, and because of senior staff failing to take responsibility for the quality of children's services in the organization. *Safeguarding Children* showed that, although Victoria's was an extreme case, there were issues emerging from it that are also relevant elsewhere.

9. Particular problems include:

- Organizations (and therefore their staff) give different levels of priority to the safeguarding of children, and work to different standards. This makes it difficult for professionals to work together effectively;

- Leading on from this, Area Child Protection Committees are often weak, with no authority and few resources to carry out their functions. In addition, they often suffer from lack of senior representation from organisations other than social services;

- In practice, the system does not always focus on the child's needs. For example, in Victoria's case, the focus was on the needs of the adults responsible for her, rather than the child herself;

- Senior managers, right up to Chief Executives and Chairmen, do not know enough about, and take enough responsibility for, the actions of their staff;

- Social services staff may make decisions about whether or not to assess a child's needs (and if there is no assessment, the child will not receive any services) based on whether the child appears to be 'in need' or a 'child protection' case.

  However, since it is rarely clear without an assessment whether or not a child is in fact being harmed, this causes two main problems: first, children and families do not get services early enough to prevent harm, and secondly, staff in other organizations describe all referrals as 'child protection' in a well-meaning attempt to ensure that the children concerned get support;'

- Many of the organizations working with children and families have difficulties recruiting and retaining skilled and qualified staff;

- Many staff are not adequately trained in safeguarding children. This is a particular problem for staff who come into contact with children and families on a regular basis, but are not considered to be 'child protection specialists';

- There are some fundamental deficiencies in basic professional practice, often made worse by poor managerial practice;

- In many areas, there is too much local guidance, which is often out of date, and does not necessarily provide practitioners with the information they need;

- Many staff do not know when to share information about a child and family, and what information can and should be shared under what circumstances;

- Children in custody are not adequately safeguarded; and

- Multi-Agency Public Protection Arrangements, although in very early stages of development, have already begun to develop very different practice across the country' (paras. 7–9 of the Introduction).

It is within this context then, of serious concerns about fundamental and systemic failings and recognition of the need to improve standards of services and 'joined up' effective partnership working that Parliament passed the Children Act 2004.

The Children Act 2004

The Government in their document, *Every Child Matters: Next Steps*, published on 4 March 2004 simultaneously with the Children's Bill and available on the Web at **www.dfes.gov.uk/everychildmatters** explained that the Act 'is the first step in a long-term programme of change. It creates the legislative spine for developing more effective and accessible services focused around the needs of children, young people and their families (para. 2.2). It describes the principal purposes of the legislation as putting the improvement of children's well-being at the heart of government policies by creating:

- Clear, shared outcomes embedded in legislation
- An independent champion for the views and interests of children
- Robust partnership arrangements
- improved local arrangements for child protection
- Clearer accountability for children's services
- A new integrated inspection framework
- A legislative basis for better sharing of information.

Box 8.1 summarizes the provisions of the Children Act 2004 and indicates where the provisions are more fully explained within this book.

Comment on the Children Act 2004

As you would expect, a wide variety of organizations have commented upon the Act. You may find their perspectives helpful in developing your own understanding of the provisions. For instance head teachers representatives have concerns about the appointment of directors of children's services who are not educationalists, see the web site of the secondary heads association at **www.sha.org.uk/cm** and the NSPCC considers that the provisions are not sufficiently robust in a number of ways—see **www.nspcc.org.uk**. The Children's Society is concerned about the weak protections that the legislation provides for children who are asylum seekers or are in prison—see **http://www.the-childrens-society.org.uk**. For a full discussion of the background to and implications of the Children Act 2004 access the Guardian web site **www.society.guardian.co.uk/children**. Details about the implementation timetable will be published on our web site when it is available.

■ The key provisions of the Children Act 2004

The duty to cooperate to improve well being

The Act is designed to create a holistic approach to children's services. Service providers must cooperate in order to improve children's well-being. Section 10 of the Act, which is set out in Box 8.2 creates the statutory framework for this to happen. It requires local cooperation between local authorities, key partner agencies ('relevant partners') and other relevant bodies ('other bodies or persons'), including the voluntary and community sector, in order to improve the well-being of children in the area. The duty to make the arrangements to improve well-being is placed on the local authority and a duty to cooperate with the local authority is placed on the relevant partners. As well as underpinning wide cooperation arrangements, these duties and powers are also designed to provide the statutory context within which agencies will be encouraged to

BOX 8.1 A summary of the Children Act 2004

Subject matter	Sections	Outline comment	Detailed explanation
Children's Commissioner for England	ss. 1–9 Sch 1	Creates a Children's Commissioner for England. The role is more limited than the Children's Commissioner for Wales but will include the promotion and safeguarding of the rights and interests of children (and certain groups of vulnerable young adults) in England. The Commissioner will also be able to hold inquiries—on direction by the Secretary of State or on his own initiative—into cases of individual children with wider policy relevance in England or, on non-devolved matters, in other parts of the UK.	In chapter 5
Improvement of well-being	ss. 10–11 (Eng) ss. 21–23 (Wales)	Places a duty on local authorities to make arrangements through which key agencies cooperate to improve the well-being of children and young people and widen services' powers to pool budgets in support of this.	Later in this chapter
Safeguarding children	s. 11	To ensure that, within this partnership working, safeguarding children continues to be given priority the Act places a responsibility for key agencies to have regard to the need to safeguard children and promote their welfare in exercising their normal functions.	Later in this chapter
Information databases	s. 12 (Eng), s. 24 (Wales)	The Act provides for the creation of databases holding information on all children and young people to support professionals in sharing information to identify difficulties and provide appropriate support.	Later in this chapter (for further information on the law on privacy see chapter 4)
Local safeguarding boards	ss. 13–16 (Eng) ss. 31–34 (Wales)	These provisions establish statutory Local Safeguarding Children Boards to replace the existing non-statutory Area Child Protection Committees.	Later in this chapter

Children & Young People's Plans	s. 17	A new duty on children's services authorities to plan for the provision of services to children. The plan links with the duty to cooperate.	Later in this chapter
Director of children's services	s. 18 & Sch 2 (Eng)	Local authorities in England will be required to put in place a director of children's services to be accountable for, as a minimum, the local authority's education and social services functions in so far as they relate to children.	See later in this chapter
Lead member for children's services	s. 19 (Eng)	The Act also requires the designation of a lead member for children's services to mirror the director's responsibility at a local political level.	See later in this chapter
Inspections of children's services	ss. 20–24	This provides for the creation of an integrated inspection framework and for inspectorates to carry out joint reviews of all children's services provided in an area.	See chapter 5
CAFCASS functions in Wales	ss. 35–40	This allows for the devolution of CAFCASS services in Wales to the National Assembly.	
Private fostering	ss. 44–47	This strengthens the existing notification arrangements for private fostering, with a reserve power to introduce a registration scheme should these not prove effective.	Not further discussed
Child minding and day care	s. 48 & Sch 4	These provisions clarify and simplify the registration of child minders and providers of day care.	Not further discussed
Education		In support of the integrated approach to inspection this section extends existing intervention powers in relation to education functions of local authorities to children's social services.	Not further discussed
Reasonable punishment	s. 58	This restricts the grounds on which the battery of a child may be justified as reasonable punishment.	Not further discussed but see discussions on NSPCC web site
Child safety orders	s. 60	This removes the power to make a care order at a lower threshold than would be usual under the Children Act as a sanction for not complying with a Child Safety Order.	See chapter 18

BOX 8.2 Section 10 of the Children Act 2004—cooperation to improve well-being

(1) Each children's services authority in England must make arrangements to promote cooperation between—
  (a) the authority;
  (b) each of the authority's relevant partners; and
  (c) such other persons or bodies as the authority consider appropriate, being persons or bodies of any nature who exercise functions or are engaged in activities in relation to children in the authority's area.
(2) The arrangements are to be made with a view to improving the well-being of children in the authority's area so far as relating to
  (a) physical and mental health;
  (b) protection from harm and neglect;
  (c) education, training and recreation;
  (d) the contribution made by them to society;
  (e) emotional, social and economic well-being.
(3) In making arrangements under this section a children's services authority in England must have regard to the importance of parents and other persons caring for children in improving the well-being of children.
(4) For the purposes of this section each of the following is a relevant partner of a children's services authority in England—
  (a) where the authority is a county council for an area for which there is also a district council, the district council;
  (b) the police authority and the chief officer of police for a police area any part of which falls within the area of the children's services authority;
  (c) a local probation board for an area any part of which falls within the area of the authority;
  (d) a youth offending team for an area any part of which falls within the area of the authority;
  (e) a Strategic Health Authority and Primary Care Trust for an area any part of which falls within the area of the authority;
  (f) a person providing services under section 14 of the Learning and Skills Act 2000 in any part of the area of the authority;
  (g) the Learning and Skills Council for England.
(5) The relevant partners of a children's services authority in England must cooperate with the authority in the making of arrangements under this section.

integrate commissioning and delivery of children's services, underpinned by pooled budgeting arrangements, in Children's Trusts (discussed below). As you read the section notice the recognition of the range of bodies which are responsible for children's well-being, the extensive delegation of responsibilities and the role of the local authority as the 'enabler' of effective provision. Notice also the specific mention of the importance of parents within the section.

BOX 8.3 Specified agencies in s. 11 of Children Act 2004

- Children's services authorities.
- District councils which are not children's services authorities.
- Strategic Health Authorities.
- Primary Care Trusts.
- Special Health Authorities.
- NHS trusts and foundation trusts.
- Police authority and chief officer of police.
- Probation boards.
- Youth Offending Teams.
- Governors of prisons.
- Any person providing services under s. 114 of the Learning and Skills Act 2000.

 BOX 8.4 The duty to make arrangements to safeguard and promote welfare—s. 11(2) Children Act 2004

Each person and body to whom this section applies must make arrangements for ensuring that—

(a) their functions are discharged having regard to the need to safeguard and promote the welfare of children; and

(b) any services provided by another person pursuant to arrangements made by the person or body in the discharge of their functions are provided having regard to that need.

Children and Young People's Plans (CYPP)

Children's services authorities are required by s. 17 of the Act to prepare and publish a strategic plan which will explain how they intend to carry out their responsibilities towards children and young people. Regulations will be made which will set out the details to be covered by the plan. In particular the plan must set out how the authority will cooperate with other bodies to improve well-being under s. 10 of the Act. In addition regulations will specify:

- the period to which the plan is to relate
- when and how it must be published
- how it is to be kept under review
- the consultation requirements.

The duty absorbs a number of other local authority planning obligations in relation to children. There will no longer be a need for separate Education Development Plans, Early Years Development and Childcare Plans, School Organization Plans, Behaviour Support Plans, Class Sizes Plans, Children's Services Plans or Local Authority Adoption Services Plans.

The Explanatory notes to the Act expand on the requirement, 'We intend the CYPP to be based on the five outcomes for children and to contain a statement of local vision for children and young people, key outcomes, a strategic analysis, actions (with timescales), references to joint planning with key partners, performance management and review of children's services, and to outline the consultation undertaken in its preparation. The intention is that regulations will provide for the CYPP to relate to successive periods of three years. The authority will have to publish the CYPP and to review it annually.'

Safeguarding children

Section 8 of the Act imposes a duty on specified agencies, set out in Box 8.3, to make arrangements to ensure that their functions are discharged having regard to the need to safeguard and promote the welfare of children.

The aim of the duty (set out in Box 8.4) is to complement the general cooperation duty in the specific area of children's safeguards by:

- ensuring that agencies give appropriate priority to their responsibilities towards the children in their care or with whom they come into contact;
- encouraging agencies to share early concerns about safety and welfare of children and to ensure preventative action before a crisis develops.

This duty requires agencies to actively consider the need to safeguard children and promote their welfare in the course of carrying out their normal functions. The duty will require agencies that come into contact with children to recognize that their needs are different from adults.

The Department of Health has published key documents which provide guidance on inter-agency working to safeguard children—*Working Together to Safeguard Children*, (Department of Health, 1999) and *Safeguarding Children: A Joint Chief Inspector's Report on Arrangements to Safeguard Children* (Department of Health, 2002). These reports, which are vital reading for you, are available on the Department of Health web site at **www.doh.gov.uk/ssi/childrensafguardsjoint.htm** and are also available free from DH Publications, PO Box 777, London SE1 6XH. We will discuss these documents later in the chapter when we consider the different roles of agencies working with children.

Local safeguarding children boards

The Children Act 2004 provides that children's services authorities in England and Wales must establish Local Safeguarding Children Boards to ensure that the necessary local arrangements are in place for co-coordinating the work of the key agencies in safeguarding children. In essence Local Safeguarding Children Boards replace and put on a statutory footing the functions of Area Child Protection Committees as set out in *Working Together to Safeguard Children* (see above). Section 13 of the Act, which we summarize in Box 8.5, sets out membership of the Board.

Section 10 (7) sets out the crucial duty to cooperate. This is set out for you in Box 8.6.

Section 14 sets out the objectives of the Local Safeguarding Boards—see Box 8.7. Regulations and guidance will provide the details of the functions and procedures of Local Safeguarding Boards. We will publish those details as they become available.

BOX 8.5 Representatives on Local Safeguarding Children Boards—s. 13 Children Act 2004

The following bodies/persons must be represented on the Board:

- the children's services authority which establishes the Board;
- if that children's services authority is a county council, then the district council must be represented;
- chief officer of police;
- local probation board;
- youth offending team;
- relevant Strategic Health Authorities and Primary Care Trusts;
- NHS Trust and NHS foundation trusts;
- a person providing services under s.114 of the Learning and skills Act 2000;
- CAFCASS;
- the governor of any secure training centre;
- the governor of any prison;
- other bodies or persons as may be provided for in regulations.

The Board may also include representatives of other relevant persons or bodies as the children's services authority which established it considers appropriate following consultation with the Board.

Information databases

Section 12 of the Children Act 2004 provides for the establishment and operation of databases about all children and other young people to whom ss. 7 and 8 of the Act apply or s. 175 of the Education Act 2002. What this means is that there will be an electronic file on all of England's 11 million children which will include information which would be regarded as confidential under the common law. This has alarmed civil liberties groups such as Liberty (see their web site for comment **www.liberty-human-rights.org.uk**) although the pilot databases being developed by local authorities have only put the most basic information into files and they are making great efforts to obtain parents' consent when it seems appropriate to add anything more.

The purpose of the databases is to facilitate contact between professionals who are involved with individual children or have concerns about their development, well-being or welfare with the aim of securing early, coherent, intervention. It is also intended that the data will enable effective service planning. Thus the function of the databases is related directly to the duties in ss. 10 and 11 of the Children Act 2004. The information to be included in the database(s) is set out in Box 8.8. No other information is to be included.

Certain people and bodies are required by the Act to disclose information for inclusion in the database(s). These are the bodies identified in s. 11(1) of the Act and set out in Box 8.3. In addition educational bodies must disclose necessary information. So governing bodies of schools and further education colleges, the proprietors of

BOX 8.6 Section 13(7)—The duty to cooperate

In the establishment of a Local Safeguarding Children Board under this section—

(a) the authority establishing it must cooperate with each of their Board partners; and

(b) each Board partner must cooperate with the authority.

BOX 8.7 The objective of Local Safeguarding Children Boards—s. 14 Children Act 2004

The objective of a Local Safeguarding Children Board is:

(a) to coordinate what is done by each person or body represented on the Board for the purposes of safeguarding and promoting the welfare of children in the are of the authority by which it is established; and

(b) to ensure the effectiveness of what is done by each such person or body for those purposes.

BOX 8.8 Information to be held about children and young people s. 12(4) Children Act 2004

- Name, address, gender, date of birth.
- An identifying number.
- The name and contact details of person with parental responsibility for the child, or who has care of her or him.
- Details of education provision, including the name and contact details of any educational institution attended.
- Name and contact details of any person providing primary medical services in relation to the child.
- The name and contact details of any person providing services to the child as are specified by the Secretary of State in regulations.
- Information as to the existence of any cause for concern in relation to the child.
- Other information (not including medical records or other personal records) as may be specified by the Secretary of State in regulations.

independent schools and the Learning and Skills Council for England will have to disclose information, alongside other persons or bodies as may be specified in future regulations.

Other people and bodies are permitted to disclose the relevant information. These include registered child minders, people registered to provide day care under the Children Act 1989, voluntary organizations, the Inland Revenue, registered social landlords and other bodies or persons which may be specified in future regulations.

Local authority administration

Local authorities are empowered by s. 18 of the Children Act 2004 to appoint a director of children's services and a director of adult social services and they will at some future date be required to do so. The appointments will remove the current statutory requirement to appoint a chief education officer and a director of social services. The functions of the director of children's services will include (s. 18(2)):

- local authority education functions (other than those relating to adults);
- social services functions for children;
- functions in relation to young people leaving care;
- functions under ss. 10–12 and 17 of the Children Act 2004;
- any function delegated to the authority by an NHS body relating to children;
- any other function prescribed by regulations.

In addition directors of children's services will be expected to steer local cooperation arrangements in relation to children's services. Two or more local authorities will be able if they so wish to appoint a director of children's services jointly.

Section 19 of the Children Act 2004 requires a local authority to designation one of their members as lead member for children's services. This is designed to ensure political leadership of children's services. Further detail on which member should be designated as the lead member and the role and responsibilities of the lead member will be set out in guidance issued by the Secretary of State.

Children's Trusts

Children's Trusts are not provided for within the Children Act 2004. However they are the vehicle which the government has designed to provide a framework for organizations to work together in a local partnership where this assists them to commission and, where relevant, directly provide services for children, in particular those children with a combination of health, educational, and social care needs. Trusts can include other services such as Connexions, Youth Offending Teams, and Sure Start. A range of other local partners—such as the police, voluntary organizations, housing, and leisure services—can also become involved.

The model is essentially flexible, so that Children's Trusts may be based in single local authority areas or may provide services across a wider area. A Children's Trust will have the following core features:

- short and long term objectives covering the five green paper outcome areas;
- a children's services director in overall charge of delivering these outcomes and responsible for services within the Trust and coordination of services outside the organization;
- single planning and commissioning function supported by pooled budgets. This would involve developing an overall picture of children's needs within an area, and developing provision through public, private, voluntary and community providers to respond to those needs.

Children's Trusts are designed to achieve the integration of frontline service provision. Examples of integrated services include:

- co-located services such as Children's Centres and extended schools;

- multi-disciplinary teams and a key worker system;

- common assessment framework across services;

- information-sharing systems across services so that warning signs are aggregated, and children's outcomes are measured across time;

- joint training with some identical modules so that staff have a single message about key policies and procedures such as a child protection and can learn about each other's roles and responsibilities;

- effective arrangements for safeguarding children;

- arrangements for addressing interface issues with other services, such as services to parents with mental health problems.

Most areas are expected to have Children's Trusts by 2006. You can find up to date information on Children's Trusts on the department for education and skills web site at **www.dfes.gov.uk/childrenstrusts**.

Responsibilities on agencies

In this part of the chapter we discuss the ways in which agencies must take joint responsibility for outcomes for children. *Working Together to Safeguard Children*, the details of which we set out earlier, remains a relevant and useful interpretation of what it means for agencies to work together.

Paragraph 1.5 of the report states that safeguarding children means:

- all agencies working with children, young people, and their families take all reasonable measures to ensure that the risks of harm to children's welfare are minimized; and

- where there are concerns about children and young people's welfare, all agencies take all appropriate actions to address those concerns, working to agreed local policies and procedures in full partnership with other local agencies.

The report emphasizes the need to create a culture of safeguarding children which pervades all services and staff. It concludes that there are still some areas where the need is not recognized and the implementation policies are not in place.

Crime and child protection

Safeguarding Children also included within the definition of safeguarding the responsibilities of agencies, particularly the police and probation services in respect of potentially dangerous persons who present a risk of harm to the public, including children. Since the mid-1990s, there has been a range of developments in criminal justice legislation aimed at protecting children and other vulnerable people. They include the legislation set out in Box 8.9.

BOX 8.9 Recent developments in criminal legislation

Legislation	Requirement
Sex Offenders Act 1997	Requires specified sex offenders to register with the police.
Crime and Disorder Act 1998	Introduced Sex Offenders Orders which give the police powers to monitor the activities of people subject to the orders.
Protection of Children Act 1999	Requires the disclosure of criminal backgrounds of those with access to children.
Criminal Justice and Courts Services Act 2000	Requires police and probation services to set up joint arrangements for the assessment and management of offenders at high risk of causing serious harm.
Sexual Offences Act 2003	A major overhaul in the sexual offences framework including the extension of the abuse of position of trust offences set out in the Sexual Offences (Amendment) Act 2000.

Roles and responsibilities

The following discussion of roles and responsibilities draws heavily on *Working Together to Safeguard Children* (Department of Health, 1999) and *Safeguarding Children: A Joint Chief Inspector's Report on Arrangements to Safeguard Children* (Department of Health, 2002). You can replace the old terminology of Local Area Protection Committees and directors of social services with the new terminology of Local Safeguarding Children Boards and directors of children's services where appropriate.

The lead responsibility of social services

Safeguarding Children sets out explicitly the lead role of social services and provides a useful summary of its functions. Paragraph 3.11–3.13 states:

> Local councils with social services responsibilities have the lead role in responding to children in need and ensuring that all agencies work together to protect children from significant harm . . .
>
> Social workers take a lead role in:
> - Responding to children and families in need of support and help;
> - Undertaking enquiries following allegations or suspicion of abuse;
> - Undertaking initial assessments and core assessments as part of the Assessment Framework;
> - Convening strategy meetings and initial and subsequent child protection conferences;
> - Court action to safeguard and protect children;
> - Coordinating the implementation of the child protection plan for children on the child protection register;
> - Looking after and planning for children in the care of the council;
> - Ensuring that children looked after are safeguarded in a foster family, children's home or other placement.

To fulfil these and their other duties, social services staff work in partnership with police officers, teachers, health personnel and all other relevant professionals and agencies.

Specific duties on agencies

The Children Act 1989 places two specific duties on agencies to cooperate in the interests of vulnerable children. The first of these is s. 27 of the Children Act 1989 set out in Box 8.10.

Part 3 of the Children Act 1989, which we discuss in chapter 10, places a duty on local authorities to provide support and services for children in need, including children looked after by the local authority and those in secure accommodation. The authority whose help is requested in these circumstances has a duty to comply with the request, provided it is compatible with its other duties and functions.

The second duty is in s. 47 of the Children Act 1989 set out in Box 8.11.

We discuss s. 47 of the Children Act 1989 fully in chapter 11.

 BOX 8.10 Agencies' responsibilities under s. 27 of the Children Act 1989

Section 27 provides that a local authority may request help from:
- any local authority;
- any local education authority;
- any local housing authority;
- any health authority, Special Health Authority, or National Health Service Trust;

and
- any person authorized by the Secretary of State in exercising the local authority's functions under Part 3 of the Act.

 BOX 8.11 Agencies' duties under s. 47 of the Children Act 1989

Section 47 places a duty on:
- any local authority;
- any local education authority;
- any housing authority;
- any health authority, Special Health Authority or National Health Service Trust;

and
- any person authorized by the Secretary of State to help a local authority with its enquiries in cases where there is reasonable cause to suspect that a child is suffering or is likely to suffer, significant harm.

The responsibilities of other agencies

Chapter 3 of *Working Together* outlines the main roles and responsibilities of statutory agencies, professionals, the voluntary sector, and the wider community in relation to child protection.

Education services

Schools and colleges, whether state or independent, have a critical role in the protection of children. Schools are often the place where abuse is first noticed. Schools do not have a direct investigative responsibility in child protection work, but schools and colleges should assist social services departments by referring concerns and providing information for s. 47 child protection enquiries. Paragraph 3.14 of *Working Together* states as follows:

Throughout the education services:
- All staff should be alert to the signs of abuse and neglect, and know to whom they should report concerns or suspicions;
- All schools and colleges should have a designated member of staff with knowledge and skills in recognizing and acting upon child protection concerns. He or she should act as a source of expertise and advice, and is responsible or coordinating action within the institution and liaising with other agencies;
- All schools and colleges should be aware of the child protection procedures established by the ACPC (Area Child Protection Committees) and where appropriate, the Local Education Authority (LEA);
- All schools and colleges should have procedures for handling suspected cases of abuse, including procedures to be followed if a member of staff is accused of abuse;
- Staff with designated responsibility for child protection should receive appropriate training;
- The school health service has a vital role to play in promoting and maintaining the health of school children and in safeguarding and promoting their welfare;
- School governors should exercise their child protection responsibilities, in particular in response to allegations against head teachers, and in ensuring that there are school child protection policies in place;
- In every LEA a senior office should be responsible for coordinating action on child protection issues across the Authority;
- All schools should have an effective whole school policy against bullying and head teachers should have measures in place to prevent all forms of bullying among pupils;
- Where a state school is concerned that a child may have 'disappeared' or any aspect of a pupil transfer which gives rise to concerns about a child's welfare, it should report its concern to a person specified in ACPC guidance or to the LEA officer with designated responsibility for child protection;
- Teachers at a school are allowed to use reasonable force to control or restrain pupils under certain circumstances. Other people may also do so in the same way as teachers provided they have been authorized by the head teacher to have control or charge of pupils. All schools should have a policy about the use of force to control or restrain pupils.

Local Education Authorities are core members of local Area Child Protection Committees and are responsible for ensuring that maintained schools, staff, and governors are fully integrated in and familiar with local multi-agency child protection procedures.

Health services

Individual health professionals such as general practitioners, midwives, health visitors, and school nurses are extremely well placed to contribute to child protection. Hospital staff, particularly those working in accident and emergency departments, should be fully aware of child protection procedures. Mental health practitioners, particularly those working with child and adolescent mental health services, can provide evidence of child abuse or neglect. Everyone involved should be fully trained in child protection procedures. Strategic leadership should be provided by health authorities and primary care groups and primary care trusts. *Working Together* (para. 3.19) sets out the role of health services as follows:

> The involvement of health professionals is important at all stages of work with children and families:
>
> - Recognising children in need of support and/or safeguarding, and parents who may need extra help in bringing up their children;
> - Contributing to enquiries about a child and family;
> - Assessing the needs of children and the capacity of parents to meet their children's needs;
> - Planning and providing support to vulnerable children and families;
> - Participating in child protection conferences;
> - Planning support for children at risk of significant harm;
> - Providing therapeutic help to abused children and parents under stress (e.g. mental illness);
> - Playing a part, through the child protection plan, in safeguarding children from significant harm; and
> - Contributing to case reviews.

Primary Care Trusts are core members of Area Child Protection Committees and will be represented on Local Safeguarding Children Boards. They will be expected to work in partnership with local authorities in the creation of Children's Trusts. They have the responsibility to appoint 'designated' doctors and nurses for child protection. All National Health Service staff who have contact with children or provide services to children and their families owe a duty of care to safeguard and protect children by recognizing and reporting situations of possible child abuse and, where appropriate, providing assessments and reports within the context of local child protection procedures.

The Laming Report and the health services

Chapters 9 to 12 and Recommendations 64 to 90 of the Laming Report are concerned with the failures of the health care system to protect Victoria Climbié. These range from Recommendation 77:

> All doctors involved in the care of a child about whom there are concerns about possible deliberate harm must provide social services with a written statement of the nature and extent of their concerns. If misunderstandings of medical diagnosis occur, these must be corrected at the earliest opportunity in writing. It is the responsibility of the doctor to ensure that his or her concerns are properly understood.

to Recommendation 89:

All GPs must devise and maintain procedures to ensure that they, and all members of their practice staff, are aware of whom to contact in the local health agencies, social services and the police in the event of child protection concerns in relation to any of their patients.

These recommendations are valuable. We remain convinced, however, that if all the provisions and the spirit of *Working Together* had been followed by the health professionals who had contact with Victoria, she would not have died.

Day care services

Day care services including family centres, early years centres, nurseries, childminders, playgroups, and holiday and out-of-school schemes play an important role in the lives of large numbers of children. As *Working Together* points out (at para. 3.55), 'All those providing day care services should know how to recognise and respond to potential indicators of abuse or neglect, and should know what to do when they have concerns about a child's welfare.'

The police

The Police Service has a commitment under the Children Act 1989 to protect children from abuse. In addition to their duty to investigate criminal offences the police have emergency powers to enter premises and ensure the immediate protection of children believed to be suffering from, or at risk of, significant harm. *Working Together* at para. 3.64 points out that 'such powers should be used only when necessary, the principle being that wherever possible the decision to remove a child from a parent or carer should be made by a court'.

Police responsibilities extend to other policing duties such as protecting the interest of child witnesses, exercising powers in connection with 'care' issues, missing children, and children who offend. They also are involved with pro-active operations against those who exploit children including child sex abusers and curbing child prostitution and child pornography. They work closely with the National Probation Service in delivering the Minimum Requirements for Multi-Agency Public Protection Arrangements (MAPPA) and Panels (MAPPs) (see below).

All police forces have child protection units which take primary responsibility for investigating child abuse allegations within the family, or committed by a carer, where the alleged victim is under 18 years of age.

The police will be a key partner on Local safeguarding Children Boards and where Youth Offending Teams are part of Children's Trusts, the police may also work closely as partner with the Trust. The role of the police is children's issues is reflecting in the national policing plan.

The Laming recommendations on the police

Chapters 13 to 15 of the Climbié Report and Recommendations 91–108 respond to the failure of the police to protect Victoria. The recommendations range from Recommendation 92:

> Chief Constable must ensure that crimes involving a child victim are dealt with promptly and efficiently, and to the same standard as equivalent crimes against adults.

to Recommendation 99:

> The *Working Together* arrangements must be amended to ensure that the police carry out completely, and exclusively, any criminal investigation elements in a case of suspected injury or harm to a child, including the evidential interview with a child victim. This will remove any confusion about which agency takes the 'lead' or is responsible for certain actions.

The National Probation Service

The National Probation Service was created in April 2001 by the Criminal Justice and Court Services Act 2000. It provides a national service delivered through forty-two local probation areas. National strategies and guidance are developed and issued by the National Probation Director. In the context of safeguarding children it undertakes the key tasks of:

- Assessment of offenders, particularly the risk of serious harm to children;
- The provision of reports to courts and the Parole Board;
- Supervision of offenders in the community on orders and licences including their enforcement;
- Provision of accredited programmes including the sex offender treatment programme.

The Criminal Justice and Court Services Act 2000 also placed a duty on the National Probation Service, in collaboration with the police, to make joint arrangements for the assessment and management of the risk posed by sexual, violent, and other offenders who may cause serious harm to the public. These arrangements are referred to as Minimum Requirements for Multi-Agency Public Protection Arrangements (MAPPA) and Panels (MAPPs). Initial guidance on the implementation of the duty was published in March 2001. The guidance includes:

- Establishing strategic management arrangements for reviewing and monitoring the effectiveness of the arrangements made and for revising as necessary or expedient;
- Establishing and agreeing systems and processes for sharing information and for inter-agency working on all relevant offenders;
- Establishing and agreeing systems and processes to ensure that only those critical few that require additional consideration are referred to MAPPs.

The criteria for referral were:

- imminence of serious harm;
- may require unusual resource allocation;
- serious community concerns;
- media implications;
- need to involve other agencies not usually involved;
- establishing and agreeing systems and processes for the MAPPs for the highest risk cases, including young offenders;
- considering resource allocation and multi-agency training;

- establishing community and media communications;
- agreeing the annual report and statistics.

The Prison Service

The Prison Service has a key role in relation to safeguarding children within its establishments that hold young people under the age of 18. Since April 2000 the Youth Justice Board (see below) has been responsible for contracting all secure provision of children either on remand or after sentence. Many 16 and 17 year olds are placed in prison service establishments (see chapter 15). These establishments are required to develop comprehensive child protection procedures covering circumstances where:

- Young people disclose past abuse;
- Young people are at risk form other prisoners;
- Allegations are made against prison officers.

In addition, within the broader remit of the prison service are responsibilities to work with others to protect children from dangerous offenders through:

- An appropriate disclosure of abuse;
- Communication and referral of concerns allegations to social services and police;
- Assessment of the risk offenders might pose to children;
- Monitoring contact of prisoners with children through telephone, letters or visits.

Youth Justice Service

The Crime and Disorder Act 1998 established that the principal aim of the Youth Justice Service was the prevention of offending by children and young people. It required each local authority with social services and education responsibilities to establish Youth Offending Teams as multi-disciplinary teams including probation officers, police officers, social workers and health and education workers. The Youth Justice Board was established to have oversight of these local arrangements. It has developed national standards for youth justice work and sets targets for local services. The work of the Youth Offending Teams is discussed further in chapter 15.

The voluntary and private sectors

There are a range of voluntary sector organizations and private sector organizations which play an important role in the lives of children. *Working Together* categorizes the main activities as follows:

- Helplines: national helplines are now operated on a free 24 hour basis by both Child Line and the National Society for the Prevention of Cruelty to Children. Child Line's service is available for all children in trouble or in danger while the NSPCC's service exists primarily for adults who have concerns about children. In addition, Parentline is developing a national support helpline for parents under stress. All of these services, along with many other smaller helplines, provide important routes into statutory and voluntary services for children in need and for those whose needs include safeguarding from significant harm.

Helpline numbers are as follows:

Child Line 0800 11 11

NSPCC 0808 800 5000

Parentline 0808 800 2222

- Provision of Direct Services: Both voluntary and private sector organisation provide a range of services for children and families. Their work is particularly central in the family support field and as the main providers of day care services. Other services include:
- advocacy projects for looked-after children and for parents and children who are the subject of s. 47 enquiries and child protection conferences—see chapter 11;
- providing independent persons and visitors;
- home visiting and befriending/support programmes;
- support to disabled children and their families including the provision of short-term breaks;
- services for children who are victims or witnesses of crimes;
- specialist services for disabled children and those with health problems (e.g. interpreters for deaf children; information on rare medical conditions or disabilities; the provisions or loan of specialist equipment)
- work in schools and other areas with peer support programmes;
- therapeutic work with children and families particularly in relation to child sexual abuse.

We will provide links to a range of these service providers on our web site.

- Public Education/Campaigning: Voluntary organisations fulfil a key role in providing information and resources to the wider public about the needs of children and resources to help families. A further important role fulfilled by the sector is that of advocacy, both in terms of individual cases and through campaigning on behalf of wider groups on specific issues. This often takes place through involvement in local Area Child Protection Committee activities.

Paragraph 3.76 points out the critical nature of the work carried out in the voluntary sector. 'While the NSPCC alone among voluntary organisations is authorised to initiate proceedings under the terms of the Children Act 1989, voluntary organizations undertake assessments of need and provide therapeutic and other services to children who have been abused.' Voluntary sector and private sector organizations require clear guidance and procedures in place to ensure appropriate referrals and cooperation with Area Child Protection Committees.

Housing authorities

Housing authorities and their staffs have day-to-day contact with a wide range of people and may become aware of concerns about the welfare of particular children. Procedures and guidance should be in place to ensure that housing officers know how to make appropriate referrals. Housing can also make contributions to meeting the health and developmental needs of children, and duties to provide accommodation, or advice to assist in the acquiring of accommodation for families with children, are critical to this. Our chapters on housing advice and homelessness (chapters 19 and 20) should be helpful for you here. Housing authorities also play an important role in the management of the risk posed by dangerous offenders, including those who are assessed as presenting a sexual or other risk to children. As para. 3.81 of *Working Together* points out, 'Appropriate housing can contribute greatly to the ability of the police and others to manage the risk such individuals pose.'

CAFCASS

The Children and Family Court Advisory and Support Service (CAFCASS) was established in April 2001 as a non-departmental government body. It brings together in one organization covering England and Wales support services in family proceedings that had been previously provided separately namely;

- The Family Court Welfare Service, formerly part of the probation service;
- The guardian *ad litem* and reporting officer service, formerly a responsibility of councils;
- The children's division of the Official Solicitor's Department as an Associate Office of the Lord Chancellor's Department.

From the implementation of the relevant provisions of the Children Act 2004 the National Assembly for Wales will take over the functions of CAFCASS for children who are ordinarily resident in Wales.

The principal functions of CAFCASS are set out in the Criminal Justice and Court Services Act 2000. These are in respect of family proceedings in which the welfare of children is or may be in question to:

- Safeguard and promote the welfare of children;
- Give advice to any court about an application made to it in such proceedings;
- Make provision for children to be represented in such proceedings;
- Provide information, advice, and other support for children and families.

CAFCASS is a core member of Area Child Protection Committees and will be represented on Local Safeguarding Children Boards.

The Crown Prosecution Service

The Crown Prosecution Service advises the police on possible prosecutions and takes over prosecutions begun by the police. It is responsible for the preparation of cases for court and for their presentation at court. It works in partnership with the police, the courts, and other agencies throughout the criminal justice system. The role of the Crown Prosecution Service is to prosecute cases firmly, fairly, and effectively when there is sufficient evidence to provide a realistic prospect of conviction and when it is in the public interest to do so. We discuss this more fully in chapter 18 when we consider the role of the Crown Prosecution Service in cases of domestic violence.

There are three principles which underpin the approach of the Crown Prosecution Service to allegations of child abuse, expedition, sensitivity, and fairness. *Safeguarding Children* points out (at para. 3.31) that Crown Prosecution Services should ensure that child abuse cases are given preferential treatment in the review process; that intervals between the key stages of the prosecution process are the minimum consistent with the completion of all relevant tasks; that high standards of timeliness are achieved; and that child abuse cases are dealt with by lawyers and caseworkers of appropriate experience.

Advice and assistance to the service user

The service user is likely to be facing a number of problems. Jacqui Smith pointed this out in her speech to the Association of Directors of Social Services in April 2003 which set out the government's initial reaction to the Laming inquiry.

> . . . child protection is one end of the spectrum that links to a range of other issues and to social exclusion, in its broadest sense. The impact on children of poverty, poor housing, domestic violence, truancy and exclusion from school, crime, drugs and mental health problems are serious and both impact on the children you are responsible for and need the services that you manage in order to address them. The nature of the way that we need to work to tackle these social problems means that social care workers and social services department will increasingly need to work in new ways, in new places, with new partners.

One particular partner which you should not ignore is the voluntary sector. You have a range of statutory duties towards the service user, but he or she may need independent advice on a range of matters which fall outside your expertise, or even where the advice is needed to challenge your department's actions. Box 8.12 sets out a number of agencies which may be able to provide advice and assistance to vulnerable people. A more complete list is available on Liberty's web site at **www.yourrights.org.uk**. Whenever you recommend an advice centre you should ensure that it offers a satisfactory standard of advice. You can do this by using those agencies which have obtained the Legal Services Commission's 'quality mark' in the particular area of legal advice. Quality marked agencies can be identified through quality marked referral agencies (e.g. libraries or social services departments) or by looking at the Community Legal Service Directory via **www.justask.org.uk**.

BOX 8.12 Advice agencies

Name of organization	Brief description of services	Contact
Citizens Advice Bureaux (CAB)	Free impartial advice by both volunteers and professional advisers in local bureaux throughout the country. Details of local citizens advice bureaux are available from the umbrella organization, Citizens Advice. The web site also provides a useful advice guide.	**www.nacab.org.uk**
Law Centres	Law Centres provide free and independent professional legal services to people who live and work within their catchment areas. Law Centres tend to specialize in immigration,	**www.lawcentres.org.uk**

	employment law, social security, mental health, housing, and community care issues. Information on Law Centres is available from their umbrella organization, the Law Centres Federation.	
Shelter	Shelter is a national organization which campaigns for homeless and inadequately housed people. It runs a number of Housing Advice Centres, a telephone advice line, and a web site. You can access these services via the web site.	**www.shelter.org.uk**
DIAL	DIAL is a national organization for a network of 140 local disability information and advice services run by and for disabled people. The web site contains useful resources for disabled people and the carers including how to find a local DIAL, fact sheets, and links to other organizations.	**www.dialuk.org.uk**
Independent Advice Centres	There are a very large number of independent advice centres. Information about these advice centres is available from the Federation of Independent Advice Centres.	**telephone: 020 7489 1800**

High Street lawyers

There are a huge number of solicitors' firms available. You are unlikely to find a solicitor with the expertise the service user requires in every firm. The Law Society runs a panel of specialist child care solicitors. These are solicitors who have undertaken specialist training and have expertise in public child care cases. Their names can be found from the Law Society web site, **www.lawsoc.org.uk**.

The Legal Services Commission awards franchises for solicitors to carry out work in a variety of areas such as crime, civil litigation, family work, and housing. You can find the details of franchised law firms from their web site, **www.justask.org.uk**.

Legal representation in cases involving child protection is automatically available from the Legal Services Commission and there is no means testing. For advice on other problems there is a means test and often a limit on the help that can be provided.

EXERCISES

1 You are investigating an anonymous phone call which expresses concern about a particular family. The caller tells you that there is a young baby and three other children under 10 in the family. Which agencies are likely to have information about the family? What is their role in protecting children? Can you ask for assistance from them?

2 A child has been assaulted by her father. What agencies are likely to become involved as a result of the assault? What duties do they have to help with investigations into the incident?

3 What is your opinion about the national database on information about children? Do you think that it is a major invasion of our privacy that is open to abuse by professionals or is it a reasonable attempt to create an electronic safety net for children?

COMPANION WEB SITE

 For guidance on how to answer these exercises, visit the companion web site at: **www.oup.com/uk/booksites/law**

WHERE DO WE GO FROM HERE?

The purpose of this chapter is to help you understand where social services fits into the organizational framework which exists to support and protect children. It has also suggested that you should be aware of other specialist advice organisations which may help your service user. You should not see your work with service users as separate from the poverty, poor housing, and vulnerability to crime and anti-social behaviour that affect their everyday lives. If you can do something to help, even if it is only pointing them in the right direction, you will have achieved something positive for them. The next chapter concentrates on the principles and purposes of the Children Act 1989 which provides the overarching legal framework for the protection of children.

ANNOTED FURTHER READING

The Laming Report on the Victoria Climbié Inquiry is available on **www.doh.gov.uk**—it is a report which repays careful reading.

You will find responses from various organizations on their respective web sites to the Laming Report and to the Children Act 2004 For instance, BASW on **www.basw.co.uk** and the Local Government Association on **www.lga.gov.uk**.

You should read as many of these responses as you can. You can learn a great deal about the role of organizations, and their relationship with the social worker, as well as understanding their strategic perspective on the protection of children.

The *Guardian* web site **www.society.guardian.co.uk/socialcare**—this web site has a wide selection of articles on social issues and agencies and an archive of reports on Victoria Climbié. It is particularly helpful on the Children Act 2004 and contains a wealth of information including a timeline of child protection initiatives.

You can find an example of a Children and Young Person's Strategic Plan on Bromley Council's web site **www.bromley.gov.uk**. The site also provides copies of the Annual Review of the plan.

Check our web site for information on the publication of regulations and guidance on the Children Act 2004.

9 The principles and purposes of the Children Act 1989

CASE STUDY

R (On the application of the Howard League for Penal Reform) v The Secretary of State for the Home Department, Department of Health) [2002] EWHC 2497

The facts

The application for the Howard League for Penal Reform (the leading non-governmental organization concerned with penal issues and policy in the UK), concerned the extent of the duties owed by the state to the children—young people under the age of 18—whom it detains.

Statistics presented to the court by the Howard League present an appalling picture of the Young Offender Institutions' (YOI) population. Over half of the children in YOIs have been in care. Significant percentages report having suffered or experienced abuse of a violent, sexual, or emotional nature. A very large percentage has run away from home at some time or another. Very significant percentages were not living with either parent prior to coming into custody and were either homeless or living in insecure accommodation. Over half were not attending school, either because they had been permanently excluded or because of long-term non-attendance. Over three-quarters had no educational qualifications. Two-thirds of those who could be employed were in fact unemployed. Many reported problems relating to drug or alcohol use. Many had a history of treatment for mental health problems. Disturbingly high percentages had considered or even attempted suicide.

The Howard League identified four problems in particular affecting children inside YOIs—bullying, on a very large scale; drug use, on a very significant scale; self-harming by a significant minority of inmates; and suicidal thoughts and, in a few cases, suicide attempts.

The law

The judge, Munby J, reviewed the provisions of the Children Act 1989, the Prison Act 1952, and human rights law. The Children Act does not refer to YOIs or to the Prison Service. It does not regulate YOIs; it does not confer or impose powers or duties on either the Prison Service or the Secretary of State for the Home Department. On the other hand, as Munby J pointed out, 'there is nothing in the 1989 Act which expressly excludes, either from the class of children to whom a local authority owes duties under s. 17 or from the class of children to whom it owes duties under s. 47, those of the children "within their area" . . . who are for the time being incarcerated in a YOI.' Munby J, also drew attention to the express provisions in the Act for the promotion of children's welfare. 'S. 1 (1) (a) provides that: When a court determines any question with respect to . . . the upbringing of a child . . . the child's welfare shall be the court's paramount consideration'. However, that principle only binds the court. 'Local authorities are under no common law or equitable duty to promote children's welfare. Nor are they under any general statutory duty to do so.'

Human rights law imposes on the Prison Service enforceable obligations, to have regard to the 'welfare' principle within the UN Convention and the European Charter; and to take effective steps to protect children in YOIs from any ill-treatment, whether at the hands of Prison Service staff or of other inmates, of the type which engages either Article 3 or Article 8 of the European Convention.

Conclusions

The Children Act does not apply to the Prison Service or the Secretary of State for the Home Department. But the duties which a local authority would otherwise owe to a child under either s. 17 or s. 47 of the Act do not cease to be owed merely because the child is currently detained in a YOI. However a local authority's functions under the Act take effect and operate subject to the necessary requirements of imprisonment. The particular way in which the Children Act applies in respect of YOIs was not reviewed by the judge. This could be properly determined only in the context of a particular factual situation. In the current hearing there was no specific case being considered. However, he made four points:

1 Neither the Governor nor the Secretary of State can abdicate responsibility for the management of a YOI and its inmates.

2 Judges are limited in what they can do in relation to a child detained in a YOI because YOIs are in an area which has been entrusted by Parliament to another public authority. Local authorities have similar limitations. A local authority cannot remove a child from a YOI and place it in local authority accommodation. Nor could a constable remove a child from a YOI and take him to a place of safety.

3 Whilst very large numbers of children in YOIs are children in desperate need, it does not follow that they are, in the statutory sense, children whose needs will not be properly met without the provision of local authority social services.

4 In deciding what positive obligations a local authority may have with respect to the provision of services by it, it is entitled to take into account the limitations upon its resources and other claims upon them.

OVERVIEW AND OBJECTIVES

Munby J's decision provides a valuable opportunity to consider the principles of the Children Act 1989 in the challenging context of Young Offenders Institutions. The decision may mean an increased involvement of local authorities in the lives of children in YOIs. The government gave an indication about its response to case in the Children Act Report 2002:

> The Department of Health is working with the Home Office, the Youth Justice Board and the Prison Service to consider the implications of the Munby judgement, together with a recommendation of the Joint Chief Inspectors' report *Safeguarding Children*, that the Home Office and Youth Justice Board should issue revised guidance to the prison service and the ACPC member organisations on the requirements and arrangements to safeguard children in prisons and Young Offender Institutions.

The aim of this chapter is to look at the overall structure and philosophy of the Act and at some common definitions in relation to children and the law. This is to give you a basic understanding of the law in this area, before we look at the more detailed provisions. However, this book is not a book on the Children Act 1989. You must have your own full copy of the Act to function adequately in this area.

In this chapter we shall look at:

(a) the overall structure of the Children Act 1989;
(b) the philosophy behind the Children Act 1989;
(c) some relevant concepts;
(d) principles applicable to court proceedings under the Children Act 1989;
(e) the role of children's guardians and CAFCASS.

The overall structure of the Children Act 1989

The Act has over 100 sections and fifteen schedules. It is a very large piece of legislation. It is divided into 'Parts'. The 'Parts' group together different sections under headings We reproduce, below, in Box 9.1, an outline of the Parts in the Children Act and the main chapters in this book where we consider those Parts. We do not have the space to examine every Part in great depth. We concentrate on those Parts the 'field' social worker will have to be familiar with.

The philosophy of the Act

Guidance and regulation

A comprehensive exposition of much of the philosophy of the Children Act can be found in *The Introduction to the Children Act 1989, The Care of Children, The Principles and Practice in Regulations and Guidance* (Department of Health, 1991) and the ten volumes of *Guidance and Regulations on the 1989 Children Act* published by the Department of Health. Social workers need to be familiar with all these. A word of clarification and warning: these excellent books contain guidance which has to be considered by all local authorities, as they are issued under s. 7 of LASSA 1970. They are not the final statement of the law. They reflect the government view of what it hopes the words of the Act say. Therefore, while you should read them, do not take them to be the final, definitive statement of the law. So, in *Re M (A Minor) (Secure Accommodation Order)* (1995), we find a Court of Appeal judge saying: 'In my judgment section 1 was not designed to be applied to Part III of the Act of 1989. To that extent I would disagree with volumes 1 and 4 of the Department of Health's *Children Act Guidance and Regulations*, although I do agree that the welfare of the child is an important consideration.' It is the courts that finally decide what the law means and, whilst helped by guidance, the social worker has to consult with his or her lawyers for the best interpretation.

BOX 9.1 The Parts of the Children Act 1989

Part Number	Title	Chapter Number and comment
Part I	Introductory	Chapter 9 Outlines key principles underpinning the legislation.
Part II	Orders with respect to Children in Family Proceedings	Chapter 14 This deals with the private law proceedings. Key section is s. 8.
Part III	Local Authority Support for Children and Families	Chapter 10 Children in need. Key section is s. 17. Concerned with public law proceedings.
Part IV	Care and Supervision	Chapter 12 Deals with care orders and supervision orders concerned with public law proceedings.
Part V	Protection of Children	Chapter 11 Sets out the key s. 47 local authority duty to investigate.
		Chapter 12 Provides for Emergency protection orders and other short term measures to protect children concerned with public law proceedings.
Part VI	Community Homes	Essentially regulatory.
Part VII	Voluntary Homes and Voluntary Organizations	These Parts, set below and to the left, whilst important, fall outside of the scope of this textbook.
Part VIII	Registered Children's Homes	
Part IX	Private Arrangements for Fostering Children	
Part X	Child Minding and Day Care for Young Children	
Part XA	Child Minding and Day Care for Children in England and Wales (inserted by the Care Standards Act 2000)	
Part XI	Secretary of State's Supervisory Functions and Responsibilities	
Part XII	Miscellaneous and General	

The underlying philosophy

It may be easier to understand the philosophy of the Children Act 1989 if you have some knowledge of the complex and perhaps contradictory forces which led to its implementation. One major impetus was the need to address a number of child abuse scandals. These ranged from reports of social service failure for instance in *Whose Child?*—Report on the death of Tyra Henry, London Borough of Lambeth 1987 and *A Child In Mind*—Report on the death of Kimberley Carlile, London Borough of Greenwich 1987 to reports of overzealous social work for instance in the *Report of the Inquiry into Child Abuse in Cleveland* 1987. Another impetus was the need to provide a legal statement of the increasing importance of children's rights. These had been articulated in the courts as a result of the *Gillick* judgment (see chapter 3) and in international commitments, such as the United Nations Convention on the Rights of the Child 1989.

Finally the Act provided a reaffirmation of the belief that the best place to bring up children is usually within their family. This is clearly stated in the published guidance.

> [T]he Act's philosophy [is] that the best place for the [child] to be brought up is usually in the [child's] own family and the [child] in need can be helped most effectively if the local authority, working in partnership with the parents, provides a range and level of services appropriate to the [child's] needs. To this end the parents and [the child] (. . . where [the child] is of sufficient understanding) need to be given the opportunity to make their wishes and feelings known and to participate in decision-making. (*Guidance and Regulations on the 1989 Children Act*, vol. 2.)

Thus the philosophy is that the child should be brought up with the child's family, and the local authority should be providing support to that end. This needs to be both understood and, more importantly, accepted by all those who carry out statutory work under the Children Act 1989. To do otherwise is rather like saying, when asked for directions to get somewhere, 'well, I wouldn't start from here'.

In addition to this concept is the belief that the state, in the shape of the local authority, should not, normally, take control of a child's life unless some strict statutory criteria are met. These criteria—described as the threshold criteria—are the grounds for care and supervision orders contained in s. 31 of the Act—see chapter 12.

Some relevant concepts

The welfare of the child

There are three different welfare duties in the Act. These are set out in Box 9.2.

The Children Act 1989 requires the welfare of the child to be the paramount consideration only when the court is making a decision under its powers under the Act. Even then, if the Act lays down other statutory considerations, the welfare of the child is not paramount.

BOX 9.2 The welfare duties in the Act

- A court making a decision as to the upbringing of a child must have the welfare of the child as the paramount consideration (s. 1(1)). This is unless there are statutory requirements that apply different criteria. (For example, the court can never make a care order if the significant harm test is not satisfied. This is true even if the welfare of the child would be best served by the care order.)
- A local authority must safeguard and promote the welfare of a child, in its area, who is in need (s. 17).
- A person who has the care of a child but not parental responsibility can do what is reasonable in all the circumstances for the purpose of safeguarding or promoting the child's welfare (s. 3(5)).

It is only when a court is dealing with a case that affects a child directly that that child's welfare is paramount. So, when the House of Lords was considering what should happen to a young baby born to a 16-year-old mother in care, it had to put the welfare of the baby as being paramount above that of the baby's mother (even though the mother was under 16 and, as such, a child). This was because the court was dealing with an application concerning the baby—not the mother (*Birmingham City Council v H (No. 3)* (1994)).

The welfare concept would be better expressed if it were stated that the Children Act requires everybody to safeguard and promote the welfare of children as far as is possible, because that is the primary and universal duty.

Human rights and the welfare of the child

Article 8 of the Human Rights Convention specifically relates to respect for family life, which could potentially conflict with the welfare of the child unless the court is satisfied that interference by a public authority is warranted. Local authority and social work decision making will need to justify any interference in family life. Decisions will need to be proportionate. See *Re C and B (Children) (Care Order: Future Harm)* (2000) and in general chapter 2. Overall, however, lawyers' views are that the requirement that the welfare of the child be the court's paramount consideration is consistent with Convention case law and within the margin of appreciation (allowance for local circumstances) permitted to national authorities under Article 8, and is therefore compatible with that Article.

■ Respect for the child

This is a concept that is difficult to define but which pervades all the questions of how the law looks at the child. There are two particular aspects. First, that the child and not the parents, for instance, is the focus of your decision making and, second, you should take account of the wishes and feelings of the child in your decision making.

The child is your primary responsibility

In dealing with children you need to recognize that the law regards the child as your primary responsibility. You cannot escape the comment made on behalf of the British Association of Social Workers to the Jasmine Beckford inquiry, which fully endorsed it:

> [the] clear and unequivocal view that in any child abuse case the primary client for the social worker is the child. The many conflicts are easier to resolve if social workers always bear in mind who is the primary client.

The wishes of the child

Conflict is inevitable between parent and child at some stage of the child's development. Part of the growing process is the assertion of the child's independence. When the state becomes involved in the essentially private area of family life, the real difficulty is for the state to ascertain when that independence should be allowed to become a reality. Clearly a 6-month-old baby cannot be independent, and if the parents fail the child then the state must step in and assume parental responsibility. But what is to be said for a 12-year-old child or a 16-year-old young person? If their parents fail, what consideration has to be given to the wishes of the child or young person?

For a statutory recognition of this concept we need to look at s. 22 of the Children Act 1989 which we set out in Box 9.3.

 BOX 9.3 The wishes of the child—s. 22 of the Children Act

(4) Before making any decisions with respect to the child whom they are looking after, or proposing to look after, a local authority shall, so far as is reasonably practicable, ascertain the wishes and feelings of—
   (a) the child;
   (b) his parents;
   (c) any person who is not a parent of his but who has parental responsibility for him; and
   (d) any other person whose feelings the authority consider to be relevant, regarding the matter to be decided.

(5) In making any such decision a local authority shall give due consideration—
   (a) having regard to his age and understanding, to such wishes and feelings of the child as they have been able to ascertain;
   (b) to such wishes and feelings of any person mentioned in subsection (4)(b) to (d) as they have been able to ascertain; and
   (c) to the child's religious persuasion, racial origin and cultural and linguistic background.

The child is mentioned before the parents or any other person in this section. This suggests that the child's wishes are to be the first consideration. This applies whether or not the child is subject to a court order. It should also be borne in mind that if any matter concerning the child is taken to court, then the court will apply the welfare principle, placing the child's welfare as paramount, i.e. coming before and overriding anyone else's welfare or convenience.

Respect for the child's autonomy

The statutory responsibilities are expanded by the decisions of the courts, notably the *Gillick* case discussed below and more fully in chapter 3. In dealing with any children, you have to ensure that an appropriate level of respect is given to the child as an individual who is entitled to separate consideration in his or her own right. As the Cleveland Report put it, 'the child is a person not an object of concern'. As a result of the respect principle, you will find courts and local authorities are required, throughout the Act, to take into account the wishes and feelings of the child. (This does not necessarily mean carrying out those wishes.)

Respect for the child does not mean the child has absolute rights above all others. This point is well made in the extract from Sir William Utting's report, *People Like Us* (Department of Health, 1997) set out in Box 9.4.

BOX 9.4 People like us

10.1 Mention of children's rights provokes a sour response in some quarters, along the lines that the Children Act destroyed parental authority to control and discipline children. There is indeed a set of difficult issues about control and discipline, but they are of long standing and have little to do with the Children Act. Underlying the Act is a strong sense of the value of children, and one of its main purposes is to safeguard and promote their welfare. In the narrower area of rights, however, it specified circumstances in which they were to be consulted about what was provided for them, and their views were to be taken into account. It is also clear that they have a right not to be physically or sexually abused, and to have factors such as race, culture and religion considered when decisions are made about them.

10.2 These are and remain important. Around them, however, have grown myths of child dominance and omnipotence. A proportion of staff polled for their views by one voluntary body believed that the Children Act 'enabled young people to make decisions that they are ill-equipped to make'. A similar proportion percipiently observed that staff used the Children Act as an excuse for inaction in protecting young people. This view was echoed in a personal submission which deplored 'the growing tendency for the SSD spokesperson to say that the Children Act prevented them from doing their job properly'. The Children Act does not say that children must always have their own way, or that they must always be believed. Such loose attributes are made by adults grasping for excuses for welshing on their responsibilities to children.

◼ Partnership with parents under the Children Act 1989

Whilst partnership with parents is not a legal requirement under the Children Act guidance makes it clear that a local authority is required to work, as far as possible, in partnership with children and their families. For instance:

> ...the Act's philosophy that the best place for the child to be brought up is usually in his own family [The wording chosen here can be criticised. S. 17 makes clear that the first duty is to promote and safeguard the child's welfare and only then to try and keep the child with the family.] and the child in need (who includes the child with disabilities) can be helped most effectively if the local authority, working in partnership with the parents, provides a range and level of services appropriate to the child's needs. To this end the parents and the child (where he is of sufficient understanding) need to be given the opportunity to make their wishes and feelings known and to participate in decision-making. (DoH, *Guidance and Regulations*, vol. 2)

The Department of Health has issued a volume of guidance: *The Challenge of Partnership in Child Protection: Practice Guide* (DoH, 1995).

The principle is reflected in the statute in a number of ways set out in Box 9.5.

There are a number of ways in which the state can and does promote the involvement of parents to participate in Children Act 1989 proceedings. Parents with parental responsibility are automatically parties to the proceedings and parents without parental responsibility have the right to be notified of public law proceedings. Parents are entitled to public funding in most public law proceedings without any means test and in dealing with social services, parents of looked-after children have a right to be consulted, a right to have their views taken into account and a right to participate in case conferences. The courts have also insisted on fair procedures, particularly since the advent of the Human Rights Act 1998 see *Re L (Care Assessment Fair trial)* (2002).

 BOX 9.5 Partnership with parents under the Children Act

(a) accommodation of children looked after should be provided as a consumer-led service (s. 22);

(b) that accommodation should be near the children's parents;

(c) contact with parents is presumed if a child is in care (s. 34), and during emergency protection (s. 44) or police protection (s. 46);

(d) care orders do not remove parental responsibilities (s. 2(6));

(e) abolition of care by stealth, i.e. that the placing of a child or young person into local authority accommodation cannot lead, of itself, to that child or young person becoming subject to any form of statutory control; and

(f) the duty of the local authority to consult parents when they accommodate a child (s. 20) or provide services (s. 17).

Limits on partnership

However, it is important to note that the concept of partnership with parents and families does not remove the overriding duty of the local authority to safeguard and promote the welfare of the child. Allowing partnership to become paramount is both misapplying the law and bad practice. As *Someone Else's Children* (DoH, 1998) stated:

> [Social Service Department's] were overwhelmingly committed to the concept of partnership with children's families. This was sometimes detrimental to the best interests of the child, as successive attempts were made to assess and rehabilitate. This practice was driven by a view often reinforced by local authority legal advisers that it was essential to demonstrate to Guardian *ad litems* and the courts that no stone had been left unturned before resorting to the judicial system. Such defensive practices contributed to case drift. (1.34)

Parental responsibility

The concept of continuing parental responsibility is critical to the Act. Married parents, unmarried mothers and, since 1 December 2003, when the relevant section of the Adoption and Children Act 2002 was implemented, unmarried fathers who are registered on the birth certificate gain parental responsibility automatically; unmarried fathers who are not registered on the birth certificate or whose child was born before December 2003 have to apply to court to acquire parental responsibility. See s. 2 of the Act and further chapter 14. Parental responsibility is defined—as far as it can be defined—in s. 3 of the Act set out in Box 9.6.

The Department of Health, in its Introduction to the Act, explained that s. 3 'emphasizes that the duty to care for the child and to raise him to moral, physical and emotional health is the fundamental task of parenthood and the only jurisdiction for the authority it confers'.

Once acquired parental responsibility continues. The only way in which parental responsibility can be terminated is via an adoption order: see chapter 13. However, the extent of parental responsibility can vary. It is at its most extensive when exercised by parents and guardians. It is less extensive when it is given to non-parents in residence orders (see chapter 14) and when given to local authorities as a result of a care order. It is most limited in scope when the child is the subject of an emergency protection order and parental responsibility is given to the applicant for the order (see chapter 12).

 BOX 9.6 The meaning of parental responsibility s. 3(1)

(1) In this Act 'parental responsibility' means all the rights, duties, powers, responsibilities and authority which by law a parent of a child has in relation to the child and his property.

Informed consent

The principle of 'informed consent' permeates the Act. As a general rule anyone (including a local authority) with parental responsibility can give a valid consent to the treatment of a child. (There are important limitations on the local authority's power when it has parental responsibility by virtue of an emergency protection order—see chapter 12.) However, there are limits on the powers of those with parental responsibility. First, irreversible medical treatment for non-therapeutic purposes (such as sterilization) should take place only with the leave of the court. Second, the age and understanding of the child are significant. The older and more mature a child becomes the less the parent is entitled, as a matter of right, to know about and manage the child's affairs. The child does not have to wait for the age of majority (18) to be able to decide matters in his or her own right; that informed choice can be made at an earlier age. This statement of the law is based upon the decision of the House of Lords in *Gillick v West Norfolk and Wisbech Area Health Authority* (1986). The case concerned the question whether or not a parent was entitled to be informed that a child under the age of 16 was going to be given contraception. The notion of the Gillick competent child is built into the statute. There are several examples of statutory provisions along the lines of 'but if the child is of sufficient understanding to make an informed decision he may refuse to submit to the examination'. We discussed consent and capacity in chapter 3.

Limits on autonomy

Our discussion on the legal competence of children in chapter 3 indicated that there are a number of difficulties in treating the *Gillick* competent child as capable of having informed consent. Court decisions do not completely support the notion of autonomy for children, yet the statutory statements within the Act are clear. The social worker must follow the requirements of the Act. However, in some extreme circumstances there may be the need to seek court approval to override the wishes of children if you consider that their decision is not in their own best interests.

Refusal to consent

One difficulty that is raised by the idea of informed consent is 'what happens if the child refuses to consent?'. Volume 3 (2.32) of the *Guidance and Regulations* makes it clear that in that situation it is a matter for the doctor to decide. This is in accordance with official guidance given on patient consent to treatment or examination.

The position of parents

The court also has powers to override the decisions of parents to refuse medical treatment for their children. In *Re A (Children) (Conjoined Twins: Surgical Separation)* (2000), the Court of Appeal sanctioned the separation of conjoined twins against the wishes of the parents, even though the result would be the death of the weaker twin. The court in these circumstances makes its decision based on the best interests of the child and not on the reasonableness of the parents' refusal of consent.

▇ Diminishment of court proceedings

This applies only in the public law area of the Act. Its provisions are to be found tucked away in Schedule 2, Part I, paragraph 7, which we set out in Box 9.7 below.

This provision imposes a duty on local authorities, and in carrying out your responsibilities you should be looking for ways in which to give effect to it.

▇ Principles applicable to court proceedings under the Children Act

There are three main principles that guide courts under this Act, all of which are found in s. 1 of the Act. They are:

(a) the welfare principle (s. 1(1));

(b) the non-delay principle (s. 1(2)); and

(c) the no order principle (s. 1(5)).

The welfare principle

When a court (but only a court) considers any matter concerning the welfare of the child, the court shall treat the child's welfare as its paramount consideration. This means that although the Act tries to balance the rights of the child and the rights of the parents, finally the court must do what the court sees as being best for the child. (That is the function of the court, to arrive at a hard decision which not all the parties may agree with.)

Not all court decisions

The welfare principle in s. 1 does not apply to all decisions by the court. Within the Act there are sections that have specific statutory requirements for the court to consider. If

BOX 9.7 The diminishment of court proceedings

Every local authority shall take reasonable steps designed—

(a) to reduce the need to bring—
  (i)   proceedings for care or supervision orders with respect to the children within their area;
  (ii) criminal proceedings against such children;
  (iii) any family or other proceedings with respect to such children which might lead to them being placed in the authority's care; or
  (iv) proceedings under the inherent jurisdiction of the High Court with respect to children;

(b) to encourage children within their area not to commit criminal offences;

(c) to avoid the need for children within their area to be placed in secure accommodation.

the Act gives such requirements the court must follow these. It cannot apply only the s. 1 paramount welfare principle. For example, s. 10(9) deals with applying for leave to make an application for an order by a private individual. There are specific grounds for the court to consider (*Re A & W* (1992)). Where an application is made to place a child in secure accommodation under s. 25, again, specific statutory criteria apply (*Re M (A Minor) (Secure Accommodation Order)* (1995)). The court (per Butler Sloss LJ) said in that case:

> This duty cast upon the local authority to safeguard and promote the welfare of the child is not the same duty cast upon the court by section 1 to place welfare as the paramount consideration. Other considerations can and frequently do affect the local authority's approach.

So, even if a court is dealing with a specific case involving children under the Children Act, the welfare principle may not be paramount. It cannot override statutory time limits, such as the length of time an emergency protection order may last. It will not allow the court to go behind established principles of law. In *Re M (A Minor) (Appeal) (No. 2)* (1994), the guardian *ad litem* sought to introduce evidence before the Court of Appeal of the effect on the child of being told that the child would have to return home to the mother. The child became hysterical and distressed. The court would not allow the evidence to be introduced. Yet another example is the case of *Nottinghamshire CC v P* (1993).

The non-delay principle

The court 'shall have regard to the general principle that any delay in determining the question is likely to prejudice the welfare of the child' (s. 1(2)). The 'question' here means the question on upbringing the court is deciding. In addition to the emphasis in the Children Act 1989 decisions of the ECHR in connection with Article 6 emphasize the need for appropriate speed in decision making and the Green Paper 'Every Child Matters' also stresses the importance of timely and effective planning and decision-making for looked after children (see chapter 8). One of the most depressing features of the legal system's response to children is delay. There are myriad reasons for this. All those concerned with children are anxious to avoid delay. The introduction of this particular section does nothing of itself to reduce the causes for those delays.

Avoiding delay

In any proceedings involving children, both in private law and public law, there are sections which provide that the court shall:

(a) draw up a timetable with a view to determining the question without delay; and

(b) give such directions as it considers appropriate for the purpose of ensuring, so far as is reasonably practicable, that that timetable is adhered to.

These provisions are to be found for private law in s. 11 and for public law in s. 32. The rules, under the Children Act, require the holding of a directions hearing (rule 14) for the court to make arrangements for preparing the case and hearing it. The first item to be addressed is the timetable for the proceedings. The non-delay principle will be applied.

In an effort to assist all participants in court proceedings to achieve faster resolution of cases the Department of Constitutional Affairs has produced a protocol—an agreed procedure—for the handling of public law Children Act cases. We will discuss this protocol, which came into effect on 1 November 2003, in chapter 11. Its aim is the completion of all cases within an overall timetable of not more than 40 weeks (save in exceptional or unforeseen circumstances). LAC (2004)1 which provides useful guidance for local authorities on the implementation of the protocol is available on the Web at **www.doh.gov.uk/publications/coinh.html**. The guidance, which stresses the need for early planning of interventions, is issued under s. 7 of LASSA by the Department for Education and Skills.

The 'no order' principle

The court should not make an order unless it considers 'that doing so would be better for the child than making no order at all' (s. 1(5)). It is important to realize that the 'no order' principle is a principle for the court, not for social workers.

The first *Annual Report on the Children Act* (Cm. 2144) showed a considerable drop in the number of court proceedings taken under the Children Act compared with similar provisions under the former law. Whilst the cutting of the number of orders may not, of itself, be a bad thing, it does not appear to be that simple. For instance, the figures show that only 2,300 emergency protection orders were made compared with 5,000 place of safety orders in the previous year. Only 1,600 care orders were made compared with 6,200 care orders under the old law. There is anecdotal evidence that many social workers and local authority legal departments are taking the view that the 'no order principle' means that cases should not be taken to court. This view is, to some extent, supported by the report itself:

> 2.20 A recent [Social Services Inspectorate] study examined these decision-making processes in four local authority areas in an attempt to address this issue. Arising from the study and Departmental discussions with a number of local authorities was a belief that the 'no order' principle requires authorities to demonstrate that working in partnership has broken down or been exhausted before an order will be made.

> 2.21 This was not the intention of the legislation. Where a local authority determines that control of the child's circumstances is necessary to promote his welfare then compulsory intervention, as part of a carefully planned process, will always be the appropriate remedy. Local authorities should not feel inhibited by the working in partnership provisions of the Children Act from seeking appropriate court orders. Equally, the existence of a court order should not of itself impede a local authority from continuing its efforts at working in partnership with families of children in need. The two processes are not mutually exclusive. Each has a role to play, often simultaneously, in the management of a child at risk.

Since that first report was published, there has been an increase in the number of applications for orders to the courts. However, the general point about the misunderstanding of the no order principle remains true. The duty of the social worker is to promote and safeguard the welfare of children who are in need. Therefore, the 'no order' principle should not in any way inhibit the social worker from taking statutory steps, including going to court, to carry out this duty. It is not the function of the social worker to second-guess the court and say, 'well the court may apply the no order principle and therefore I will not take any action'. Only when it is clear that it is a hopeless case should you consider not going to court because of the 'no order' principle.

In addition to these three main principles we find others, as set below.

No compulsory intervention by the state without an application

This is a reflection of the philosophy of the Act and is applicable to both private and public law elements of the statute. Where a court is faced with a child that it perceives to be at risk then the court has no power permanently to commit the child into the hands of the state without there being before it an application by the local authority or authorised person. You will not be able to obtain any court order without having made an application to the court.

A salutary case to read is *Nottinghamshire CC v P* (1993). In this case the local authority applied for an order under s. 8 of the Children Act that a self-confessed child abuser stepfather vacate the household and that the children should have no contact except under supervision. The court held that, since the effect of the order was in fact to make a residence and contact order, it could not make that order. Local authorities are specifically excluded from applying for such orders (s. 9(2)). As the authority wished to ensure that the children were not put at risk by seeing their father unsupervised, they would have been better to apply for a care order. This is the view that the High Court judge and the Court of Appeal took. As the report of the judgment states:

> ... the route chosen by the council was wholly inappropriate. In cases where children were found to be at risk of suffering significant harm within s. 47 a clear duty arose on the part of the local authorities to protect them. . . . The council persistently and obstinately refused to undertake what was the appropriate course of action and thereby deprived the judge of the ability to make a constructive order. . . . The position was one which it was hoped would not recur.

Here the Court of Appeal found itself totally frustrated by being unable to make the order asked for. The local authority was seeking to obtain the effect of a care order by the back door. This is clearly contrary to the concept that the only basis on which statutory control can be obtained is by an application which satisfies the significant harm test.

The welfare checklist

This is found in the Children Act 1989, s. 1(3). It is applicable to all court proceedings in both private and public law, except court proceedings under Part V (the emergency protection of children). It consists of a uniform checklist to which the courts need to have regard when they are faced with a dispute concerning any child. It is applicable whether the dispute is between individuals, or a local authority is applying for an order. Section 1(3) is set out in Box 9.8.

Each point in the checklist is considered separately. There is no priority in the order in which the points appear. If you are seeking an order from the court, you must give careful attention to the checklist in your presentation of evidence and within your report. Also, expect in any disputed case to be cross-examined under each heading.

'Mix and match'

This is a useful expression derived from the Department of Health publication, *An Introduction to the Children Act*, where it states:

> . . . [a] full menu of orders is also available to a court hearing a local authority application for a care or other order in respect of a child. Thus a court might, for example, order that a child live with a suitable relative or friend rather than make a care order in favour of the local authority. Or it may mix and match by, for example, ordering that a child live with a non-abusing parent and making a supervision order at the same time.

The best order in the circumstances

What it means is that the court should always seek to choose the best order for the child, and that choice is not limited to the orders that the parties have applied for. But the court cannot make a care or supervision order unless it has been applied for. How this works in practice can be seen in the case of *C v Solihull Metropolitan Borough Council* (1993). A 12-month-old child had suffered a non-accidental injury. The magistrates' court refused to grant a local authority application for a care order but returned the child subject to a supervision order with no conditions attached. On appeal, the High Court made a residence order which no one had applied for, with conditions attached, and an interim supervision order.

 BOX 9.8 The welfare checklist—s. 1(3)

A court shall have regard in particular to—

(a) the ascertainable wishes and feelings of the child concerned (considered in the light of his age and understanding);

(b) his physical, emotional and educational needs;

(c) the likely effect on him of any change in his circumstances;

(d) his age, sex, background and any characteristics of his which the court considers relevant;

(e) any harm which he has suffered or is at risk of suffering;

(f) how capable each of his parents, and any other person in relation to whom the court considers the question to be relevant, is of meeting his needs;

(g) the range of powers available to the court under the Children Act in the proceedings in question.

Family proceedings

Most proceedings in any area of family law are defined as 'family proceedings'. Inclusion in this category means that, if they have any family proceedings before them, the courts are free—in fact obliged—to apply the 'mix and match' principle, and make the best order for the child, not necessarily the one applied for, and quite possibly where no one has applied for an order under the Act.

The list of family proceedings is given in the Children Act 1989, s. 8(3) and (4) as amended. We have reproduced this in Box 9.9.

Not family proceedings

It is important to remember that proceedings under Part V of the Act (protection of children) are not family proceedings. So there can be no 'mix and match', only an emergency protection order, or a child assessment order, or no order at all.

Family assistance orders

In any family proceedings the court can, under the Children Act 1989, s. 16, make a family assistance order, where the court is satisfied that there are exceptional circumstances and the people named in the order agree. Only the court can make the order; it cannot be applied for by a party. When a family assistance order is made the officer named in the order is to advise, assist, and (where appropriate) befriend the person named in the order.

This order is intended to be a short-term order; it can last for only a maximum of six months. It is to help the family over the difficulties that have led to the court appearance.

In *Re C (Family Assistance Order), Re* (1996), when the local authority said that it did not have the resources to implement the order, the court held that it had no power

---

 BOX 9.9 Family proceedings for the purposes of the Children Act

(a) High Court proceedings relating to children under the residual powers of wardship (see chapter 5)

(b) Matrimonial Causes Act 1973—proceedings for divorce and other related matters (see chapter 14)

(d) Adoption Act 1976 (see chapter 13)

(e) Domestic Proceedings and Magistrates' Court Act 1978—disputes between married parties in the magistrates' court (see chapter 14)

(f) The Family Law Act 1996 (see chapter 14)

(g) Matrimonial and Family Proceedings Act 1984—involving divorce proceedings (see chapter 14)

(h) Children Act 1989, Parts I, II and IV (see the other various chapters relating to children); and

(i) Sections 11 and 12 of the Crime and Disorder Act 1998.

to force the authority to do so. Nor would the court compel a local authority under a family assistance order to accompany a child to visit that child's father in prison (*S v P (Contact Application: Family Assistance Order)* (1997)).

The role of children's guardians

The role of the guardian is one, historically, that has been long known to the court. Out of the context of child care, the guardian—also known as the child's 'next friend'—acted on behalf of children in court actions such as a claim for damages arising from an accident.

Maria Colwell

Guardians were introduced into the statutory framework of child care law following the report of the Maria Colwell Inquiry published in 1974. In that case Maria was killed by her stepfather, having been returned from the care of the local authority following the revocation of the care order with the consent of the local authority. It was felt that the tragedy could have been avoided if Maria had been separately represented in the proceedings. A person acting solely on behalf of Maria could have argued that it was not in Maria's best interest for the care order to be revoked.

The Children Act 1989 contains the duty for courts to appoint guardians *ad litem* 'unless it is satisfied that it is not necessary' to safeguard the child's interests (s. 41(1)). Following the creation of CAFCASS (see below) the term 'children's guardian' is used instead of 'guardian *ad litem*' (Family Proceedings (Amendment) Rules 2001)). The guardian then has to appoint a solicitor for the child (Family Proceedings Rules (1991). The rules permit the older child who is *Gillick* competent and who is in conflict with the recommendations of the children's guardian, to instruct the solicitor for the child directly.

The functions of the guardian

Rules of court set out the functions of the guardian. The way in which the guardian works is by a process of investigation involving interviewing the local authority personnel, the child, the parents, relatives, and any other persons the guardian considers relevant. The guardian then prepares a report stating what the guardian considers to be in the best interest of the child's welfare. This report must be made available to all parties to the proceedings in advance of the final hearing.

Resources

In tandem with the lawyer acting for the child, the system ensures that the child's interests are protected and his or her rights respected and upheld by the court. Since the commencement of the Children Act 1989, you can expect guardians to be involved in proceedings concerning children, even at the stage of the application for an emergency protection order. The practical difficulty is one of resources, there not being sufficient suitably qualified people to act as guardians. In some parts of the country, this shortage is delaying proceedings.

Inspection of records

The guardians have the advantage of s. 42 of the Children Act 1989, which provides that a guardian has the power to inspect any local authority or NSPCC records relating to the child who is the subject of the court proceedings. In addition, in *Re R (Care Proceedings: Disclosure)* (2000), the court held that the guardian had a right to see a report compiled by the Area Child Protection Committee on the child's half sibling who had been killed by the child's father. Having inspected those records the guardian may take copies, and those copies shall be admissible as evidence both in the guardian's report and, if the guardian gives oral evidence, during the proceedings.

Your approach to the handling of any case must be carried out in the full knowledge that an officer of the court, the children's guardian, is possibly going to have the chance both to look at and produce in court all the records that you have made. More important, that person may be able to draw the court's attention to the fact that although you claim to have done a particular thing, there exists no record of this fact in your case notes. Accurately and comprehensively record all your actions and decisions as soon as possible after the events.

The children's guardian will be selected from those employed by the Children and Family Court Advisory and Support Service—CAFCASS.

Children and Family Court Advisory and Support Service

The Children and Family Court Advisory and Support Service (CAFCASS) was created by the Criminal Justice and Court Services Act 2000, ss. 11 to 17 and Schedule 2. It is designed to carry out the functions set out in s. 12 of that Act, i.e. to:

(a) safeguard and promote the welfare of children;

(b) give advice to any court about any application made to it in any family proceedings;

(c) make provision for the children to be represented in such proceedings; and

(d) provide information, advice, and other support for children and their families.

CAFCASS—a non-departmental public body—came into operation on 2 April 2001. It unites the Family Court Welfare Service (FCWO) (which advises the courts in private law cases), the Children's Guardian Service and Reporting Officers Service and the Children's Division of the Official Solicitor's Department. This integration should allow guardians to be freed from the previous potential conflict of interest as they were funded and administered by local authorities. It also releases the FCWO from the control of the Home Office. In addition, there is the potential for a national and child-focused service to assist the courts in making critical decisions about children which allows for a beneficial sharing of expertise.

EXERCISES

1 Read the whole of this chapter carefully and construct a checklist for yourself of the issues you will need to consider before recommending that your department makes a court application in respect of an individual child.

2 Locate and read one of the articles listed below. Summarize the article in 100–150 words.

3 Try to construct a time line of events leading up to the Children Act 1989 and then onwards to the present. Include the UK's international commitments. You will find a helpful start on the Guardian Society web site.

COMPANION WEB SITE

For guidance on how to answer these exercises, visit the companion web site at: **www.oup.com/uk/booksites/law**

WHERE DO WE GO FROM HERE?

In this chapter we have considered a number of aspects of Part 1 of the Children Act, in particular its philosophy, structure, overarching principles, and the principles which guide decision making by the courts. This chapter serves as an introduction to the remaining chapters about your responsibilities to children. However, it is more than an introduction. If you understand the purposes and the principles upon which the Act is based you are going to be in a far better position to understand your role within the Act. The next chapter considers Part 3 of the Act, local authority responsibilities to children in need. Part 3 is the cornerstone of the Act, if you like the chassis of the Children Act Bus.

ANNOTATED FURTHER READING

We strongly recommend owning and reading your own copy of the Children Act 1989. We also recommend further reading of a specialist text on the Children Act, such as R. White, P. Carr, and N. Lowe, *The Children Act in Practice* (3rd edn., Butterworths, 2002).

The welfare principle

J. Eekelaar, 'Beyond the Welfare Principle', 14 C&FLR 237—a stimulating article which argues that the very ease of the welfare test encourages an unwillingness to pay proper attention to all the interests that are at stake in decision making.

E. Jackson (2002) Conception and Irrelevance of the Welfare Principle, Modern Law Review vol. 65 no. 2 p. 176—this article looks at the use of the welfare principle in decisions about fertility treatment.

H. Reece (1986) The Paramounting principle: Consensus or Construct 49 Current Legal Problems 267.

The best interests of the child

M. Woolf, 'Coming of Age?—The Principle of "the Best Interests of the Child" ' [2003] EHRLR 205. This article contrasts the approaches of the ECtHR and the English courts in decisions about the best interests of the child.

Children's rights

There is a host of information available on children's rights. A useful introduction to the issues can be found in C. Booth, 'In Search of Children's Rights', Editorial [2003] JLGL. You can access a variety of web sites giving you access to the text of the UN Convention on the Rights of the Child for instance **www.unicef.org/crc** or the vibrant and punchy web site of the children's rights alliance for England **www.crae.org.uk**.

The Howard League for Penal Reform

You may be interested in the other work on behalf of children in custody undertaken by the Howard League for Penal Reform who took the case against the government which formed the case study featured in this chapter. They have produced reports on girls in prison, the use of Anti-Social Behaviour Orders against children and deaths of children in custody. Their web site **www.howardleague.org/** provides a range of useful information.

10

Local authority support for children and families

R (on the application of G) v Barnet London Borough Council
R (on the application of W) v Lambeth London Borough Council
R (on the application of A) v Lambeth London Borough Council [2003] UKHL 57 [2004] 1All ER 97

Facts

These three cases were heard together by the House of Lords. They concern the lack of residential accommodation suitable for the children if they were to remain within the family unit without the risk of significant harm to their welfare. The children were children in need of adequate housing.

G is a person from abroad who is a Dutch national of Somali origin. Her son was born in 1999. G left the Netherlands because of social ostracism because of her child's illegitimacy and she came to the UK to look for the child's father. She was refused income support and housing because she did not satisfy the habitual residence test. She then sought assistance from Barnet council as the local social services authority. The council assessed the child's needs as best served by the return of both mother and child to Holland where they would be immediately entitled to accommodation and other benefits. G applied for judicial review of the decision. It was common ground she was suitable to look after her son and that was not in his best interests to be removed from her care. It was also common ground that if the mother refused to return to the Netherlands, the council intended to place the child with foster parents and to provide no accommodation for the mother. The judge granted her application, the local authority appealed and the Court of Appeal allowed its appeal.

W, the mother of two children born in 1987 and 1998, was evicted from her home in February 2001. She was found by the local housing authority (Lambeth) to be intentionally homeless because there were substantial arrears of rent. She applied immediately to the local social services authority (also Lambeth) for assistance in securing private sector housing for herself and her two children as a family unit, but that authority declined to help her. She was able to find temporary accommodation with a niece between August 2001 and January 2002. She said that no other member of her family was able to help her to house her family.

At her solicitors' request Lambeth social services carried out assessments of the needs of her children in January 2002. The assessing officer found nothing exceptional and said that the council's social services department did not provide accommodation for the families of children in need. They would place the children with extended family members as a short-term measure whilst W sought alternative accommodation. But if the need arose, the authority would make provision for the children alone. Her application for judicial review of the refusal of the local social services authority to provide assistance with accommodation was dismissed. The Court of Appeal dismissed her appeal.

In A's appeal, two of her three children were in need because they were disabled. Assessments of the needs of A's children under the Children Act 1989 indicated that the family needed to be re-housed. A sought an order compelling the local social services authority to find and provide suitable accommodation which provided for the children's assessed needs. The High Court and the Court of Appeal held that the court had no power to intervene to make such an order.

In all three cases the parents argued that the effect of s. 17 of the Children Act 1989 was that, once there had been an assessment of the needs of an individual child in need, there was a specific duty on the local social services authority to provide services to meet the child's assessed needs, and that it followed that, if the identified need was the provision of residential accommodation, the child had an absolute right to that accommodation. In G's and W's appeal the parents contend that the effect of s. 23 of the 1989 Act, which requires a local social services authority looking after a child to make arrangements to enable him or her to live with a parent or with relatives or friends, was to put the authority under a duty to make arrangements to enable the child to live with his or her parent.

Held

The House of Lords decided (by a majority) that s. 17 of the Children Act 1989 set out duties of a general nature only which were not intended to be enforceable as such by individuals. The 'general duty' was owed to all the children who were in need within the area of the local social services authority and not to each child in need individually. It provided the broad aims which the local social services authority was to bear in mind when it was performing the 'other duties' set out in Part III of the 1989 Act and the 'specific duties' set out in Part 1 of Sch. 2 to the 1989 Act as to which it had a discretion as to how it should meet the needs of each individual child in need. Although the services which the local social services authority provided could include the provision of accommodation, the provision of residential accommodation to rehouse a child in need so that he could live with his family was not the principal or primary purpose of the legislation. Housing was the function of the local housing authority.

Section 23 of the Act did not impose an obligation on a local social services authority to provide accommodation for the parent or other persons. Section 23 was concerned with the way a local social services authority was to discharge its obligation to provide accommodation for a child whom it was looking after. It required the local social services authority to make arrangements to allow the child to live with a parent or other specified person unless that would not be reasonably practicable or consistent with his welfare. The provision assumed the parent of the child already had accommodation which the child could live in with his parent. It was concerned with placement, not housing. Accordingly the appeals were dismissed.

OVERVIEW AND OBJECTIVES

The House of Lords decided that the duty under s. 17 of the Children Act to an individual child is very limited. The duty is

- a general duty and not a targeted, specific duty owed to an individual child
- intended to be for the benefit of all the children in need in the local social services authority's area in general

- discharged by providing a range and level of services appropriate to meet the various needs of children in its area.

Even assessment of a particular child's individual needs does not transform the general duty to a specific duty owed to the child as an individual.

So, although social services departments are able to provide accommodation under s. 17, this is not the principal purpose of the legislation. In other words, whilst a homeless child is very likely to be a child in need and should be accommodated by social services, this does not impose a duty upon the local authority to provide accommodation for the child's family as well. The decision demonstrates the desperate plight of some families who for one reason or another are excluded from welfare provision. It is clear that social services departments are inevitably constrained in the support they can give to children in need because of limited resources.

   As you read this chapter consider the extent of the services that social services departments can offer to children in need and the way in which those services underpin the philosophy of the Children Act 1989. Also consider the limited resources available to authorities, particularly deprived urban authorities. What impact does this have on the successful operation of the Children Act 1989? By the end of the chapter you should know the range of powers and duties available to social services departments to assist children 'in need'.

▉ Introduction

Part 3 of the Children Act contains a range of duties which are imposed upon local authorities. These duties are summarized in Box 10.1.

 BOX 10.1 The duties contained in Part 3 of the Children Act

Section	Description
17	The general preventive duty to 'children in need'
18(1)(3)	Day care for some under fives who are 'children in need'
20	Provision of accommodation for some 'children in need'
22, 23, 24(1)	Duties to children and young persons looked after by the local authority
23A, 23B, 23C, 23D, and 24	Duties to some people who have been in care
26	Duty to establish a complaints and independent review procedure
Schedule 2 part 1	Provision of services in the community

These duties have been amplified by two important pieces of legislation, The Children (Leaving Care) Act 2000 and The Care Standards Act 2000. This chapter will consider these duties, in particular:

- The general duty in s. 17 of the Children Act to safeguard and promote the welfare of children within their area who are in need;
- The range of services which may be provided for children in need;
- Local authority responsibilities to 'looked after' and accommodated children;
- Duties to people who have been in care;
- Complaints/representation and planning/review procedures.

It will also note the provision of secure accommodation by local authorities, the particular problems facing 'looked after' children and the role of the voluntary sector in supporting vulnerable families.

Part 3 is extensive and affects every area of service provision under the Children Act 1989. It ranges from providing for very basic 'one-off' support to ensuring that young people who have left care still have support available to them.

The provision of local authority support

Local authority support, designed to safeguard and promote the welfare of the child in need, and enabling the child to be brought up with his or her family, is a cornerstone of the Children Act 1989. The local authority works in partnership with the child and the child's parents. The aim is to provide positive support to avoid the need, as far as possible, for the local authority to have to seek statutory control.

The promotion of welfare

The welfare principle requires the courts to treat the child's welfare as the paramount consideration. For local authorities the requirement is that they safeguard and promote the welfare of children within their areas who are in need. To discharge this duty the local authority has to carry out a balancing act. There will always be a conflict between what it may want to do for an individual child and what it can do, given its resources and the demands of other children whose welfare it has to safeguard and promote. This was the problem that social services departments faced, in the case study at the beginning of the chapter. The *Guidance to the Children Act* recognizes this and advises, 'The outcome of any service provision under this power should be evaluated to see whether it has met the primary objective, namely to safeguard and promote the child's welfare' (*Guidance and Regulations*, vol. 2, p. 6).

Section 17

Section 17(1) of the Children Act sets out the general preventive duty which local authorities owe to 'children in need' in their area. We reproduce s. 17(1) in Box 10.2.

> **BOX 10.2** Section 17 (1)—the general duty on local authorities
>
> (1) It shall be the general duty of every local authority (in addition to the other duties imposed on them by this Part)—
>
> (a) to safeguard and promote the welfare of children within their area who are in need; and
>
> (b) so far as is consistent with that duty, to promote the upbringing of such children by their families
>
> by providing a range and level of services appropriate to those children's needs.

'Children in need'

The local authority's duty to safeguard and promote the welfare of a child extends only to those children who are 'in need'. Being in need is therefore a necessity if a child is going to benefit from the general duty.

Who are 'children in need'?

The Government carries out a census of children in need in England every two years. The National Assembly carries out the same exercise for Wales. The results of the third national survey in England are based upon a survey of provision in a 'typical' week in February 2003 and are available on the web at **www.dfes.gov.uk**. It estimates that in that week there were 388,200 children and young people known to be in need of social service provision. The figures are remarkably similar to the results of the previous census.

The number of children who received services during the census week who are supported within their family or independently (as opposed to 'looked after'—*see* below) was 164,400. Abuse and neglect are the biggest single reason for services and account for 35 per cent of all children served during the census week. However, this ranges between ethnic groups—with, for instance, abuse and neglect being the reason for 44 per cent of mixed-race children and 26 per cent of black children receiving services. Low income is the reason for 11 per cent of black children receiving services, and 3 per cent of white children receiving services.

12,500 children in need were children seeking asylum. This represents 6 per cent of children in need. Black and ethnic minority children (not including asylum seekers) comprise at least 16 per cent of children in need. They are overrepresented in the statistics by a factor of between 1.2 and 1.7.

The definition of 'children in need'

For a definition of a child in need we have to look at s. 17(10) which we set out in Box 10.3.

The majority of children and young people with whom the local authority is going to come into contact will fall within the definition of 'children in need'. The definition is

BOX 10.3 Children in need—s. 17(10) and (11)

(10) For the purposes of this Part a child shall be taken to be in need if—

(a) he is unlikely to achieve or maintain, or to have the opportunity of achieving or maintaining, a reasonable standard of health or development without the provision for him of services by a local authority under this Part;

(b) his health or development is likely to be significantly impaired, or further impaired, without the provision for him of such services; or

(c) he is disabled, and 'family', in relation to such a child, includes any person who has parental responsibility for the child and any other person with whom he has been living;

(11) For the purposes of this Part, a child is disabled if he is blind, deaf or dumb or suffers from mental disorder of any kind or is substantially and permanently handicapped by illness, injury or congenital deformity or such other disability as may be prescribed; and in this Part—

'development' means physical, intellectual, emotional, social or behavioural development; and 'health' means physical or mental health.

broad to emphasize the preventive element of the local authority's role. There are three different elements of the definition:

(a) reasonable standard of health or development;

(b) significant impairment of health or development;

(c) disability.

These are separate and distinct bases on which 'need' should be considered. As *Guidance and Regulations*, vol. 2 says:

It would not be acceptable for an authority to exclude any of these three—for example, by confining services to children at risk of significant harm.
(Significant harm is an important concept with the Act which we consider in chapter 12)

The local authority must consider the provision of services for those who fall within any of the headings. It is the local authority that makes the decision whether or not a particular child is or is not in need (*Re J (Specific Issue Order: Leave to Apply)* (1995)). The need for a holistic model for assessing children's needs is emphasized in *A Framework for the Assessment of Children in Need and Their Families* (Stationery Office, 2000), jointly published by the Department of Health, the Department of Education and Employment, and the Home Office and available on the Department of Health web site at **www.doh.gov.uk**.

'Looked after'

This term is not actually defined specifically in the Children Act 1989. To become 'looked after', the child, first, has to be in need. In addition, to be looked after the child has either to be the subject of a care order, or be supplied with accommodation by the local

BOX 10.4 The general duty of the local authority in relation to children looked after by it

(1) In this Act, any reference to a child who is looked after by a local authority is a reference to a child who is—

  (a) in their care; or

  (b) provided with accommodation by the authority in the exercise of any functions (particularly those under this Act which stand referred to their social services committee under the Local Authority Social Services Act 1970, apart from functions under ss. 23B and 24B.

(2) In subsection (1) 'accommodation' means accommodation which is provided for a continuous period of more than 24 hours.

(3) It shall be the duty of a local authority looking after any child—

  (a) to safeguard and promote his welfare; and

  (b) to make such use of services available for children care for by their own parents as appears to the authority reasonable in his case.

Note 'care' in subsection (1) means the local authority has a court order for that particular child.

authority. This is explained in s. 22 set out in Box 10.4. The 'looked after' child has access to the range of services the local authority provides for children in need. It is important to note that once a child is looked after the child becomes subject to the Placement of Children Regulations 1991. We discuss this and the responsibilities of local authorities to accommodated children more fully in below. 'Looked after' children are likely to be in more serious need than children in need living with their families.

Outcomes for 'looked after' children

The *Children Act Report 2003* provides some interesting statistical information about the life chances of looked after children.

- the proportion aged 11 and obtaining level 4 in KS2 English and maths was only 49 per cent of the proportion for all children;

- of those who were in year 11, 43 per cent did not sit a GCSE/GNVQ examination;

- 9 per cent of those in year 11 gained 5 GCSE (or equivalent) passes at grade A*–C (compared to 53 per cent of all children).

The Social Exclusion Unit report 'A better education for children in care' published in September 2003 provides further information. 27 per cent of looked after children had statements of special educational needs compared with 3 per cent nationally. Children in care are ten times more likely to be permanently excluded from school and children in care are also more likely to be bullied, with six out of ten respondents consulted by the SEU saying they had been bullied, compared to one in six children responding to a Youth Justice Board survey.

Looked after children are not only educationally deprived. Offending outcomes are also poor. Whilst the vast majority of children looked after for over a year have not offended in the last year the data provided in the Children Act Report 2003 shows that looked after children are three times more likely to have received a final warning or conviction during the course of a year, when compared with their peers.

The Children Act Report 2003 can be obtained from **www.dfes.gov.uk/childrenact report/docs** and the Social Exclusion Unit report from **www.socialexclusion.gov.uk**.

■ Services for a child in need

Having established that the child is in need, the local authority has the power to provide the appropriate services. Section 17(4A) (inserted by the Children Act 2004) requires the local authority to ascertain and take appropriate account of the child's wishes regarding the provision of services.

These services may be supplied direct to the child or to other members of the child's family (s. 17(3)). A wide definition of 'family' is given (in s. 17(10)) so that it encompasses any family grouping you are likely to encounter. It is acceptable to target the services on someone other than the child, provided that this is done with the aim of promoting and safeguarding the welfare of the particular child in need, who is your client.

So if a mother was finding it difficult to cope with a child because she also had the responsibility of looking after an elderly parent, it would be possible to use the budget for the provision of services to children under s. 17 to provide the elderly parent with day care facilities, so as to enable the child's mother better to look after the child.

Cash help

The services can, if necessary, be provided by means of cash assistance, as the Children Act 1989, s. 17(6)–(9) set out in Box 10.5 shows.

These important powers mean that if the need can be met by cash then there is nothing to stop the local authority giving cash. The local authority is entitled to take into account the resources of the child and the family before providing assistance. The majority of people who receive cash are likely to be in receipt of family credit or income support and therefore will not have to repay the money received.

Accommodation

Section 17 powers include the provision of accommodation—this was made explicit by the insertion of a new phrase into subsection (6) of s. 17 which came into effect in November 2002. Guidance on the provision of accommodation is provided by the Department of Health LAC (2003) 13.

Direct payments

Section 17A and 17B of the Act allow local authorities to make direct payments to persons with parental responsibility for a disabled child or provide vouchers instead of services which would otherwise have been provided for them by the local authorities.

BOX 10.5 Assistance in kind or in cash

(6) The services provided by a local authority in the exercise of functions conferred on this by this section may include *providing accommodation and giving* assistance in kind or, in exceptional circumstances, in cash.

(7) Assistance may be unconditional or subject to conditions as to the repayment of the assistance or of its value (in whole or in part).

(8) Before giving any assistance or imposing any conditions, a local authority shall have regard to the means of the child concerned and of each of his parents.

(9) No person shall be liable to make any repayment of assistance or of its value at any time when he is in receipt of income support or family credit under the Social Security Act 1986.

This increases the flexibility, for instance, in making arrangements for a carer's short-term break.

Specific duties

In addition to the general duty in the Children Act 1989, s. 17, Schedule 2 to the Act contains a number of specific duties relevant both to children in general and children who are looked after. Schedule 2 is set out in Box 10.6.

Publicity

Paragraph 1 of the Schedule requires the local authority to give publicity to services that the Act requires it to provide and also to services provided by voluntary groups. The information must to be published and steps taken to ensure that it reaches the people who need it.

Prevention of neglect and abuse

Paragraph 4 focuses on the prevention of abuse and neglect. The appearance of the words 'reasonable steps' diminishes somewhat the duty set out in paragraph 4. The steps that may be taken are to prevent 'ill treatment or neglect'. This is a lower standard than the 'significant harm' test in s. 31 of the Act and therefore enables help to be given at an earlier stage. Neglect is not defined in the Act and therefore has to be given its normal meaning. Ill treatment includes sexual abuse and forms of ill treatment which are not physical: s. 31(9) Children Act 1989.

Accommodation of abusers away from the family home

Paragraph 5 gives a power to the Social Services Department to help a suspected abuser find accommodation and pay for it. The limit in the power is that there can be no compulsion applied to the man. This power is in addition to the power of a court to

BOX 10.6 The Children Act 1989, Schedule 2

1. *Identification of children in need and provision of information*

   (1) Every local authority shall take reasonable steps to identify the extent to which there are children in need within their area.

   (2) Every local authority shall—

   (a) publish information—

   (i) about services provided by them under sections 17, 18, 20 and 24 and

   (ii) where they consider it appropriate, about the provision by others (including, in particular, voluntary organisations) of services which the authority has power to provide under those sections; and

   (b) take such steps as are reasonably practicable to ensure that those who might benefit from the services receive the information relevant to them.

2. *Maintenance of a register of disabled children*

   (1) Every local authority shall open and maintain a register of disabled children within their area.

   (2) The register may be kept by means of a computer.

3. *Assessment of children's needs*

   Where it appears to a local authority that a child within their area is in need, the authority may assess his needs for the purposes of this Act at the same time as any assessment of his needs is made under—

   (a) the Chronically Sick and Disabled Persons Act 1970;

   (b) the Education Act 1981;

   (c) the Disabled Persons (Services, Consultation and Representation) Act 1986; or

   (d) any other enactment.

4. *Prevention of neglect and abuse*

   (1) Every local authority shall take reasonable steps, through the provision of services under Part 3 of this Act, to prevent children within their area suffering ill-treatment or neglect.

   (2) Where a local authority believes that a child who is at any time within their area—

   (a) is likely to suffer harm; but

   (b) lives or proposes to live in the area of another local authority they shall inform that other local authority.

   (3) When informing that other local authority they shall specify—

   (a) the harm that they believe he is likely to suffer; and

   (b) (if they can) where the child lives or proposes to live.

5. *Provision of accommodation [to the suspected abuser] in order to protect child*

   (1) Where—

   (a) it appears to a local authority that a child who is living on particular premises is suffering, or is likely to suffer, ill treatment at the hands of another person who is living on those premises; and

   (b) that other person proposes to move from the premises; the authority may assist that other person to obtain alternative accommodation.

(2) Assistance given under this paragraph may be in cash.

(3)...

6. Provision for 'disabled' children

Every local authority shall provide services designed—

(a) to minimise the effect on disabled children within their area of their disabilities; and

(b) to give such children the opportunity to lead lives which are as normal as possible.

7. Provision to reduce need for care proceedings etc. [This has already been described as the diminishment of court proceedings principle.]

8. Provision for children living with their families

Every local authority shall make such provision as they consider appropriate for the following services to be available with respect to children in need within their area while they are living with their families—

(a) advice, guidance and counselling;

(b) occupational, social, cultural or recreational activities;

(c) home help (which may include laundry facilities);

(d) facilities for, or assistance with, travelling to and from home for the purpose of taking advantage of any other service provided under this Act or of any similar service;

(e) assistance to enable the child concerned and his family to have a holiday.

9. Family centres

(1) Every local authority shall provide such family centres as they consider appropriate in relation to children within their area.

(2) 'Family centre' means a centre at which any of the persons mentioned in subparagraph (3) may—

(a) attend for occupational, social, cultural or recreational activities;

(b) attend for advice, guidance or counselling; or

(c) be provided with accommodation while he is receiving advice, guidance or counselling.

(3) The persons are:

(a) a child;

(b) his parents;

(c) any person who is not a parent of his but who has parental responsibility for him;

(d) any other person who is looking after him.

10. Maintenance of the family home

Every local authority shall take such steps as are reasonably practicable, where any child within their area who is in need and whom they are not looking after is living apart from his family—

(a) to enable him to live with his family; or

(b) to promote contact between him and his family,

if, in their opinion, it is necessary to do so in order to safeguard or promote his welfare.

11. Duty to consider racial groups to which children in need belong

Every local authority shall, in making any arrangements—

(a) for the provision of day care within their area; or

(b) designed to encourage persons to act as local authority foster parents, have regard to the different racial groups to which children within their area who are in need belong.

exclude a suspected abuser when making either an emergency protection order or an interim care order.

Support for children living with their families

Paragraph 8 requires the local authority, in accordance with the philosophy of the Children Act 1989, to support the child who is living with his or her family. The Schedule provides a wide range of provisions that the local authority should consider making.

Family centres

Paragraph 9 clearly states that the assistance of a family centre can be given to someone other than a particular child. This, again, is on the basis that the overall aim must be to safeguard and promote the welfare of a particular child.

Again we see the philosophy spelt out, requiring the local authority to take steps to enable children they are not looking after to live with or to have contact with their families.

Housing

The Social Services Department's responsibility implies the need to ensure that the family is kept together, although clearly it cannot take on an open-ended commitment to pay the rent and arrears. Ultimately, it may be that the Social Services Department might have to seek care orders to house the children. This is because the statutory duty is to the individual children rather than to the family as a whole.

Diversity

This is a requirement for the local authority to take account of race and ethnicity in the provision of day care and recruiting foster parents. Where a local authority is 'looking after' a child, there is a requirement before making any decisions in respect of that child to give due consideration to the child's religious persuasion, racial origin, and cultural and linguistic background (Children Act 1989, s. 22(5)(c)) Box 10.6 sets out the provisions of Schedule 2.

▨ Other sources of support

Voluntary sector organizations

The Act recognizes, in s. 17(5) set out in Box 10.7 below, that the voluntary sector has a critical role in providing services for children in need.

There are hundreds of voluntary sector projects working to support children and their families in a multiplicity of settings. Box 10.8 contains some information on some of the national voluntary sector organisations which help families in need. You should get to know your own local organizations, and what help they can offer.

BOX 10.7 Section 17 (5)—the role of the voluntary sector

Every local authority—

(a) shall facilitate the provision by others (including in particular voluntary organizations) of services which the authority have power to provide by virtue of this section or sections 18, 20, 23, 23B to 223 D 24 A or 24B and

(b) may make such arrangements as they see fit for any person to act on their behalf in the provision of any such service.

BOX 10.8 Some national voluntary sector organizations

Organization	Information	Contact
Barnado's (UK)	Runs nearly 300 projects with children affected by poverty, homelssness, disability, bereavement, and abuse.	www.barnados.com
The Children's Society (UK)	Works to help vulnerable children and young people.	www.the-childrens-society.org.uk
Family Fund Trust	Provides grants and information relate to the care of severely disabled children.	www.familyfundtrust.org.uk
Gingerbread	Enables lone parents to meet others who are bringing up children alone. The web site offers information on welfare benefits.	www.gingerbreadorg.uk
National Children's Bureau	Works with policy makers and professionals of all sectors to share good practice in creating child-centred services.	www.ncb.org.uk
NCH Action for Children (UK)	Runs over 320 projects to help vulnerable children and their families. It tackles issues relating to families in need, social exclusion and special needs.	www.nchafc.org.uk
Young Minds	Aims to promote the mental health of children and young people through a parents' information service, training and consultancy, advocacy, and publications.	www.youngminds.org.uk
Youth Clubs UK	Activities and support for all young people, including voluntary work and educational opportunities for young people.	www.youthclubs.org.uk

Local authority accommodation

Accommodation

The local authority may consider that the only way to safeguard and promote the welfare of a child is through the provision of accommodation. Accommodation is defined in s. 22(2) of the 1989 Act as meaning accommodation which is provided for a continuous period of more than twenty-four hours.

Concerns

Government concerns about the experience of children in care, and in particular the conclusions of *Lost in Care—The Report of the Tribunal of Inquiry into the Abuse of Children in Care in the Former County Council Areas of Gwynnedd and Clwydd since 1974* have informed recent developments of the law, in particular the Care Standards Act 2000 and the Children (Leaving Care) Act 2000. The Social Exclusion Unit Report 'A better education for children in care' published in 2003 and discussed above indicates that there is a long way to go in improving the outcomes for looked after children. It provides some key statistics:

- At any one time, around 60,000 children are in care. In 2001–2, 41 per cent of children in care were aged 10 or under.
- Most children—80 per cent—enter care because of abuse or neglect, or for family reasons. Less than 10 per cent enter care because of their own behaviour.
- Two-thirds live in foster care and one in 10 in children's homes.
- One in four children in care lives outside their 'home' local authority.
- Between one-quarter and one-third of rough sleepers were in care.
- Young people who have been in care are two and a half times more likely to be teenage parents.
- Around a quarter of adults in prison spent some time in care as children.

Below we consider responsibilities to care leavers, the regulatory framework, and the responsibilities of local authorities for maintaining links with families. We start our discussion of accommodation by setting out the nature of the service that local authorities provide.

A consumer-led service

Accommodation is a 'consumer-led service' Official guidance sets out the preferred approach:

> The accommodation of a child by a local authority is now to be viewed as a service providing positive support to the child and [the child's] family. In general, families have the capacity to cope with their own problems, or to identify and draw upon resources in the community for support. Some families however reach the stage where they are not able to resolve their own difficulties, and are therefore providing inadequate care for their child or are afraid of doing so.

They may look to social services for support and assistance. If they do this they should receive a positive response which reduces any fears they may have of stigma or loss of parental responsibility. (Children Act 1989 Guidance and Regulations, Vol. 2, 'Family Support, Day Care and Educational Provision for Young Children'.)

The status of accommodated children

If a local authority is providing accommodation for a child the local authority is 'looking after' the child. 'Looked after' children are defined in s. 22(1) of the Children Act 1989 which is set out in Box 10.9 below. The section makes it clear that 'looking after' covers both children subject to court orders and those who are not. The provision of accommodation does not in itself mean that the child is in 'care', it does not affect the parental responsibilities of any person or give the local authority parental responsibility. It is only if the local authority has a court order that it has any control over the child. A child subject to a care order will automatically be looked after by an authority and provided with accommodation.

The exclusion of accommodation provided under s. 17, s. 23B, and s. 24B from the definition of looked after children removes such children from the obligations placed upon local authorities under the Children Act 1989 and the Children (Leaving Care) Act 2000 (see below).

The local authority duty to looked after children

This duty is provided for in s. 22 (3)–(5) of the Children Act 1989 which we have set out for you in Box 10.10. Notice the responsibilities upon local authorities to take into account the wishes of the child, his or her parents and other people who are important to the child. The authority is also obliged to take into account the child's religious and cultural needs.

The extent of the duty to provide accommodation

Section 20 (1), which we set out in Box 10.11, places a duty on an authority to provide accommodation for a child for whom there is no one with parental responsibility or who has been abandoned, or where the person who has been caring for the child is unable to provide suitable accommodation or care.

 BOX 10.9 Section 22(1) of Children Act 1989—looked after children

In this Act, any reference to a child who is looked after by a local authority is a reference to a child who is

(a) in their care; or

(b) provided with accommodation by the authority in the exercise of any functions (in particular those under this Act) which are social services functions with the meaning of the Local Authority Social Services Act 1970 apart from functions under s. 17, s. 23B, and s. 24B.

BOX 10.10 Section 22(3)–(5) of Children Act 1989—the duty of local authorities to looked after children

(3) It shall be the duty of a local authority looking after any child—

    (a) to safeguard and promote his welfare; and

    (b) to make such use of services available for children cared for by their own parents as appears to the authority reasonable in his case.

(4) Before making any decision with respect to a child whom they are looking after, or proposing to look after, a local authority shall, so far as is reasonably practicable, ascertain the wishes and feelings of—

    (a) the child;

    (b) his parents;

    (c) any person who is not a parent of his but who has parental responsibility for him; and

    (d) any other person whose wishes and feelings the authority consider to be relevant,

    regarding the matter to be decided.

(5) In making any such decision a local authority shall give due consideration—

    (a) having regard to his age and understanding, to such wishes and feelings of the child as they have been able to ascertain;

    (b) to such wishes and feelings of any person mentioned in subsection (4) (b) to (d) as they have been able to ascertain; and

    (c) to the child's religious persuasion, racial origin and cultural and linguistic background.

BOX 10.11 The duty to provide accommodation

Section 20(1) Every local authority shall provide accommodation for any child in need within their area who appears to them to requires accommodation as a result of

(a) there being no person who has parental responsibility for him;

(b) his being lost or having been abandoned;

    or

(c) the person who has been caring or him being prevented (whether or not permanently, and for whatever reason) from providing him with suitable accommodation or care.

The power to provide accommodation

The local authority also has power to provide accommodation for a child even though there is someone who is willing and able to provide accommodation, if the local authority considers that the provision of accommodation would promote the child's welfare (s. 20(4)). This power may well be used to protect a child by removing the child from the unsatisfactory home setting. However the provision of accommodation for a child under the age of 16 under this section is subject to parental consent (s. 20(7)). Without that consent no accommodation can be provided. If a child has been provided with accommodation and parental cooperation is withdrawn then, if you are seeking to protect the child, you should consider applying for an emergency protection order.

A service for families

Section 20 makes it quite clear that the provision of accommodation without a care order or criminal supervision order is only provided on a 'service' basis. This is spelled out in s. 20(7) and (8) set out in Box 10.12.

Removal of a child from accommodation

The 'at any time' in s. 20(8) means that no notice need be given to the authority. This is in contrast to the previous law where, after a six-month period in local authority accommodation, notice of the removal of the child had to be given. If you are supplying accommodation to a particular child and you are notified of the possibility of the child's removal by the child's parents, and you consider this to be against the welfare of the child, then you should consider whether there are grounds for an emergency protection order. The grounds are discussed in chapter 12. If a child is subject to a court order in favour of the local authority, a parent has no right to remove the child from the accommodation without the local authority's consent.

A young person in accommodation

A young person of 16 or over is in control of whether or not he or she receives or stays in accommodation. This is because of s. 20(11):

> (11) Subsections (7) and (8) [power of parents to refuse accommodation and to remove the child] do not apply where a child who has reached the age of sixteen agrees to being provided with accommodation under this section.

 BOX 10.12 Section 20(7) and (8)

(7) A local authority may not provide accommodation under this section for any child if any person who—

   (a) has parental responsibility for him;

   (b) is willing and able to—
      (i)   provide accommodation for him; or
      (ii) arrange for accommodation to be provided for him, objects.

(8) Any person who has parental responsibility for a child may at any time remove the child from accommodation provided by or on behalf of the local authority under this section.

Accordingly, the parents may disagree about the future of the young person but the choice is always that of the young person.

Disputes between parents

If one parent has a residence order in their favour, the other parent cannot remove the child from accommodation without first successfully applying to the court for a residence order in their favour. If neither parent has a residence order and both parents have parental responsibility (see chapter 14), then either parent could remove the child, as stated in s. 20(8). This could mean that one parent places the child into accommodation and the other parent removes the child from that accommodation. This would be a good example of where the parent who wants the child to stay in the accommodation should apply to the court for a prohibited steps order under s. 8 (see chapter 14). Remember that s. 8 orders, other than a residence order, cannot be made where the child is subject to a care order.

No residence orders

Where there is no residence order in favour of a parent, then there can be management difficulties. If during the breakdown of a marriage the mother were to place a child under the age of 16 into local authority provided accommodation, what is to stop the father removing the child? The simple answer is nothing. The Act is quite clear that if a parent objects to the provision of accommodation, or seeks, at any time, to remove the child, then the local authority cannot prevent it.

The only guidance in this situation is to look to the Children Act 1989, s. 3(5), which states that a person without parental responsibility but who has care of the child may, subject to the Act, do what is reasonable in all the circumstances of the case for the purpose of safeguarding or promoting the welfare of the child. The local authority is covered by this section, not having parental responsibility, and it has to do all it can to safeguard and promote the welfare of the child. Unfortunately this does not give clear guidance as to what to do when the drunken father turns up at 2 a.m. It cannot be promoting the welfare of the child to allow the child to go with the father, and yet the statute says you should. What will be required here are negotiating skills. If these fail, then an application for an emergency protection order would have to be made, or a request should be made to the police to take the child into police protection (see chapter 12).

The supply of accommodation

There are provisions in s. 23, set out in Box 10.13, as to how the local authority may supply accommodation. These provisions are subject to regulations. This accommodation can be 'supplied' by placing a child with his or her family or a relative or other suitable person, or by placing the child in a suitable home. Section 23 makes the child's family the first choice when considering where to place the child. Other forms of accommodation can be local authority community homes, voluntary homes, registered children's homes, or other homes provided by the Secretary of State. When accommodated by the local authority, there is a duty to maintain the child.

BOX 10.13 The supply of accommodation s. 23

(1) It shall be the duty of any local authority looking after a child

   (a) when he is in their care, to provide accommodation for him; and

   (b) to maintain him in other respects apart from providing accommodation for him.

(2) A local authority shall provide accommodation and maintenance for any child whom they are looking after by—

   (a) placing him (subject to subsection (5)) and any regulations made by the Secretary of Sate with

     (i) a family;

     (ii) a relative of his; or

     (iii) any other suitable person,

   on such terms as to payment by the authority and otherwise as the authority may determine;

   (aa) maintaining him in an appropriate children's home or

   (f) making such other arrangements as—

     (i) seem appropriate to them; and

     (ii) comply with any regulations made by the Secretary of State.

Foster parents

A child in care or being looked after on a voluntary basis can, under s. 23, be provided with accommodation by being placed with foster parents. Foster parents are suitable people selected by the local authority to provide accommodation and maintenance for a child being looked after. The selection and registration of foster parents are subject to the detailed guidance of the Foster Placement (Children) Regulations 1991. Section 23 allows the local authority to pay any person with whom it has placed a child, but the local authority can recover all or part of the costs from the parents unless the parents are in receipt of particular benefits (s. 29).

Responsibilities to care leavers

The local authority is acting as parent to the children it accommodates. One role of parenting is to prepare children for independence. Another is to provide continuing support after the child has left home. Research into the life chances of young people living in and leaving local authority care indicated that local authorities in general failed in these two roles. The Children (Leaving Care) Act 2000 attempts to address these failings. The explanatory notes to the Act state that its main purpose is to:

> . . . help young people who have been looked after by a local authority move from care into living independently in as stable a fashion as possible.

To understand the amendments and new duties it introduces into the Children Act it is necessary to explain some key definitions We have set these out in Box 10.14.

Duties to care leavers

The Children (Leaving Care) Act introduced a new paragraph 19A into Schedule 2 to the Children Act 1989. Paragraph 19A imposes a duty on local authorities which is set out in Box 10.15 below.

Subparagraph (4) of paragraph 19A requires that a local authority carry out an assessment of the needs of each eligible child for the advice, assistance, and support that would be appropriate for the local authority to provide. They will then prepare a pathway plan, which is defined in s. 23E. The pathway plan should take over from the care plan. The plan is to be reviewed regularly ((5) of 19A).

Relevant and former relevant children

The amended s. 22 of the Act and the new ss. 23A to 23C impose duties on the local authority towards children and young people formerly looked after by them. Section 22 is amended so that local authorities can provide accommodation to a child who has left care, without the fact of their doing so classifying him as still being 'looked after'. Section 23B set out in Box 10.16 contains the duties of the responsible local authority towards relevant children. Section 23C provides for similar duties towards former relevant children.

 BOX 10.14 Definitions used in the Children (Leaving Care) Act 2000

(a) Eligible children—those children in care aged 16 and 17 who have been looked after for 13 weeks or more.

(b) Relevant children—those young people aged 16 and 17 who meet the criteria for eligible children but who leave care. The Regulations exclude certain groups, such as children who return home permanently and children who receive respite care.

(c) Former relevant children—those who before reaching the age of 18 were either eligible or relevant children.

(d) The responsible local authority—the local authority who last looked after an eligible or relevant young person.

 BOX 10.15 Preparation for ceasing to be looked after

19A It is the duty of the local authority looking after a child to advise, assist and befriend him with a view to promoting his welfare when they have ceased to look after him.

BOX 10.16 The duties towards relevant children s. 23B

(1) It is the duty of each local authority to take reasonable steps to keep in touch with a relevant child for whom they are the responsible authority, whether he is within their area or not.

(2) It is the duty of each local authority to appoint a personal adviser for each relevant child (if they have not already done so under paragraph 19C of Schedule 2).

(3) It is the duty of each local authority, in relation to any relevant child who does not already have a pathway plan prepared for the purposes of paragraph 19B of Schedule 2—

    (a) to carry out an assessment of his needs with a view to determining what advice, assistance and support it would be appropriate for them to provide him under this Part; and

    (b) to prepare a pathway plan for him.

BOX 10.17 Qualifying persons

Section 24(1) In this Part 'a person qualifying for advice and assistance' means a person who—

(a) is under twenty one; and

(b) at any time after reaching the age of sixteen but whiles still a child was, but is no longer, looked after, accommodated or fostered.

Section 23D and 23E set out the details of personal advisers and pathway plans. Section 24 defines those qualifying for advice and assistance as set out in Box 10.15. The definition includes care leavers as a whole as well as children and young people leaving accommodation provided by certain other providers.

Section 24(4) establishes a duty on a local authority to keep in touch as it thinks appropriate with any child whom it has looked after. Section 24B(5) obliges authorities to provide, or enable the young person to pay for, suitable vacation accommodation should it be needed, if they are in full-time higher education or further education. These provisions are amplified by The Children (Leaving Care) (England) Regulations 2001.

▧ Regulatory framework

The whole field of 'looking after' is dominated by regulations that have been issued under the Children Act 1989. The most important are:

(a) Arrangements for Placement of Children (General) Regulations 1991;

(b) Foster Placement (Children) Regulations 1991;

(c) Placement of Children with Parents etc. Regulations 1991;

(d) Contact with Children Regulations 1991;

(e) Definition of Independent Visitors (Children) Regulations 1991;

(f) Review of Children's Cases Regulations 1991; and

(g) Representations Procedure (Children) Regulations 1991.

Copies of all these regulations are included in Volume 3 of the Department of Health's *The Children Act 1989 Guidance and Regulations—'Family Placements'*. This book is essential. The regulations set down procedures, specify dates, forms, the types and nature of review, and time limits. They govern who should be consulted about steps to be taken by a local authority concerning a child, and so on. In this chapter, we have the space only to give outline coverage of this large area, and you must read this Department of Health guidance.

The Care Standards Act 2000 strengthened the registration and regulation provisions for children's homes and established the National Care Standards Commission for England with similar provision in Wales. The National Care Standards Commission has published national minimum standards for children's homes which cover a range of issues from effective and comprehensive placement plans to the countering of bullying. The functions of the National Care Standards Commission have now been taken over by the Commission for Social Care Inspection—see chapter 5. Children's homes are also subject to regulation—see The Children's Homes Regulations 2001 No. 3967. There have been a number of other innovations designed to enhance provision for children such as the introduction of Children's Commissioner for Wales and for England. These regulatory mechanisms are discussed in chapter 5.

Promoting family links

One finding of research into children who have been looked after by local authorities in the past was the concept of the child being 'lost in care'. This arose when a child may have been provided with accommodation (placed in voluntary care under the old law) at some time of crisis within the family. The child being out of the family may have relieved that particular crisis, but the reception of the child took place without any forward planning and the child just went on to 'hold' in the accommodation. The parents, relieved of the pressures, were often not encouraged to keep up contact and time passed, so that links were lost. Further crises with other families meant that the original child was not given attention and eventually the child became 'lost' in care.

The Children Act 1989 addresses this problem in a number of ways.

It treats all children regardless of the route by which they came to be looked after by a local authority in the same way. We start with s. 23(6) and (7), which seeks to promote this contact between child and parent. These subsections are set out in Box 10.18 below.

The regulations set out the requirement for a written plan before any placement is made. All the people involved in the plan, including the child (so far as is consistent with age and understanding), should be consulted about it. The plan must include the proposals for contact. Volume 3 of the *Guidance and Regulations* sets out

BOX 10.18 The promotion of contact with the family

(6) Subject to any regulations made by the Secretary of State for the purposes of this sub-section, any local authority looking after a child shall make arrangements to enable him to live with—

(a) a person falling within subsection (4) [that is a parent]; or

(b) a relative, friend or other person connected with him, unless that would not be reasonably practicable or consistent with his welfare.

(7) Where a local authority provide accommodation for a child whom they are looking after, they shall, subject to the provisions of this Part and so far as is reasonably practicable and consistent with his welfare, secure that—

(a) the accommodation is near his home; and

(b) where the authority are also providing accommodation for a sibling of his, they are accommodated together.

at paragraph 2.62 the suggested contents of such a plan. This approach to producing the plan was endorsed in *Manchester City Council v F* (1993). See case planning in chapter 11.

Schedule 2

There are comprehensive powers contained in Schedule 2 (which we discussed above) to assist the maintaining of links with the child's family. By way of an example: one allegation that may be made against a social worker is that having provided a child with accommodation s/he then places the child with a foster parent remote from the child's parents. To visit the child, the parents may have to get two buses and a train, and find this difficult. As a consequence the visits to the child drop off, and this is then used as an argument for saying that the parents do not really care for the child. The parents would say: 'This, of course, was what the authority was trying to prove all along. Indeed this was the very reason why the child was placed with these particular foster parents.' Often the truth is closer to the fact that the harassed placement officer had only those foster parents available on the day the child had to be supplied with accommodation. Using the powers in Schedule 2, paragraph 16 should remove this argument. It provides that if the authority believes that visits could not be made without undue financial hardship, then the authority is permitted to make payments to any parent, or indeed any relative, friend, or person connected with the child. These payments can cover not only the cost of travel but subsistence and other expenses that may be involved. The payments need not be subject to a requirement for repayment, and indeed cannot be subject to that condition if the parents are in receipt of benefits.

■ A child subject to a court order

All that we have said above about the treatment of a child being looked after will be applicable to a child under a care order. We discuss care orders in chapter 12. However, there are some aspects of care orders which are relevant to our current discussion.

Links with families when children are subject to care orders

It is important to note that the statutory duty to consider placing the child with the child's family applies even if the child is subject to a care order. See the comments of the Court of Appeal in *Re T (A Minor) (Care or Supervision Order)* (1994). Put another way, the making of a care order does not require the local authority to remove the child from the child's home. This is often misunderstood, as in *Re A (Supervision Order: Extension)* (1995). This was resisted by the mother and at that time by the local authority in the mistaken belief that they would not be able to leave the child with her mother if a care order was made.

If such a placement is made, it must be done in accordance with the Placement of Children with Parents etc. Regulations 1991.

Placement of the child with parents whilst in care

If it is intended to place a child in care with a parent of the child, s. 23(5) will permit this only if it is done in accordance with the Placement of Children with Parents, etc. Regulations 1991. The purpose of these Regulations is to ensure that when the decision is made to place at home a child who is the subject of a court order without the order being discharged, control and supervision is exercised over that procedure. The Regulations to some extent address the perceived fears that such a placement might go wrong and are designed to avoid such situations as happened with Maria Colwell (see chapter 9).

Before deciding to return the child, the 'respect for the child' principle dictates that the child's wishes be ascertained. The local authority must also obtain the written comments of all those agencies involved in the welfare and protection of this child, including the health authority, the education authority, and the police, and must notify the people it has consulted, in writing, of the decision taken.

The Regulations also provide a framework for the practical social work that will be needed to prepare the child and parent for the child's return. There has to be a written agreement with the parent recording the objective and plan of the placement, the arrangements for supervision, details of health, and educational arrangements. The agreement must record the fact that the child can be removed if the authority considers that the child's welfare is no longer being promoted. Whilst the agreement need not be signed, guidance in Volumes 3 and 4 suggests that signing it may be good practice.

On the return home, the register, which has to be kept of such returned children, must record the fact of the return and further record the regular visits of the social worker to the child that have to be undertaken. The first has to take place within one week and the visits then have to take place at intervals of six weeks at the most.

Having placed a child in care with the parents the authority must not allow the situation to drift. It must review the placement within the first three months and then at six-month intervals. The reviews are to see whether the purpose of the placement is being met. If the placement is successful, the authority should consider whether to seek to discharge the care order. These reviews must be recorded in writing, as must the regular visits.

Contact

Under s. 34, where a child is under a care order there is a presumption that the child will have reasonable contact with his or her parents. Before the making of any care order the authority shall inform the court of the plans it intends to make for contact between individuals and the child (s. 34(11)). The court can then define the extent of the contact that should take place. The presumption also applies whenever the local authority accommodates the child under an emergency protection order or a child assessment order.

At the stage of making a care order the court has power under s. 34 to make what is in effect an interim contact order, with specific provision for a further hearing with a view to making provision for contact at the subsequent hearing (*Re B (A Minor) (Care Order: Review)* (1993)).

Contact decisions

At the same time as a care order is made, or following a later application by either the local authority or the child, or the child's parents or others who had a residence order, the court may decide the amount of contact (s. 34(2), (3)). The court may instead make an order authorizing the local authority to refuse contact between the child and his or her parents (s. 34(4)). Section 34—with the rest of the Children Act—was written to ensure compliance with the European Convention. This judicial scrutiny of contact is necessary to satisfy the Human Rights Act 1998, and means that decisions to terminate parental contact are very likely to comply with Articles 6 and 8 of the Convention.

Local authority restriction of contact

There is also a general power given to the local authority in respect of contact under s. 34(6). If the authority believes that it would not promote the welfare of the child to allow contact, then it may refuse contact, but only as a matter of urgency and then only for a period of up to seven days. During that period it would have to make an application to the court for an order. The use of the word 'urgency' implies that the situation which has arisen must have occurred within the recent past, this power not being available to solve long-standing difficulties.

Variation or discharge

The parent can apply to the court to vary or discharge the order under s. 34(9). The child concerned may also use both s. 34(4) to stop a parent seeing him or her, and s. 34(6) to vary such an order.

Contact with Children Regulations 1991

These Regulations cover contact between a child in care and the child's parents and others. The Regulations are applicable to all children looked after by the local authority.

Importantly, paragraph 3 of these Regulations allows the local authority and the parents to vary a court order under s. 34 by means of an agreement in writing.

Reviewing the local authority plans for a child subject to a care order by contact application

Unless there has been an order to refuse contact under s. 34(4), or an order preventing a person from applying without leave of the court for contact under s. 91(14), then parents may apply to the court to consider the contact arrangements (s. 34(3)). If an application has been made and the application has been refused, then the parents must wait six months before applying again for contact unless they obtain the leave of the court (s. 91(17)).

Challenges to the local authority plans for the child in care can be made during the regular reviews. Importantly, the decision in *Re B (Minors) (Care: Local Authority's Plans)* (1993) has indicated that the Court of Appeal views s. 34 as another possible way of challenge. In this case it was argued that the discretion of the local authority with a care order could not be challenged and the court could not look at the local authority's long-term plans. The court would not accept this and said:

> If, however, a court was not able to intervene, it would make a nonsense of the paramountcy of the welfare of the child, which is the bedrock of the Act, and would subordinate it to the administrative decision of the local authority in a situation where the court is seized of the contact issue. That cannot be right.

This means that whilst the local authority has a wide discretion in caring for the child, this discretion can be reviewed by the courts when looking at the contact issue.

Independent visitor

A step that can be taken when links with the child's family have failed is the appointment of an independent visitor (Sch. 2, para. 17 and Definition of Independent Visitors (Children) Regulations 1991). The function of the visitor is not to encourage links but to act as a form of replacement for the family. If the child has had infrequent contact with his or her parents or has not been visited or lived with them during the preceding twelve months, the authority shall appoint such an independent visitor. Therefore, an independent visitor can be appointed at any stage if there is infrequent contact. An independent visitor must be appointed if there have been no visits to the child during the preceding year. The role of the visitor is to visit, befriend, and advise the child. In doing this the authority must apply the 'respect for the child principle' and the child has the right of informed consent to object to the initial appointment and to the continuation of the appointment (Sch. 2, para. 17(6)).

The visitor is entitled to recover reasonable expenses incurred in the exercise of this function. The appointment of such visitors is subject to the reviews of children being looked after.

It is depressing to read the following:

In our ... inspection, we found that SSDs were not always aware of their duty to provide independent visitors for children who are not in regular contact with their own families

- 9 out of 17 SSDs had no scheme at all.
- 3 authorities were not meeting the need.
- other authorities contracted with voluntary organizations to provide a service.

We saw evidence from the files we looked at that social workers should have been aware of this duty and should have acted upon it. (*Someone Else's Children*, 8.15)

It needs to be emphasized that this is a statutory duty.

Reviews of children being looked after

One extremely important responsibility that local authorities have to looked after children is the requirement to review regularly the position of and plans for each looked after child (s. 26 Children Act 1989). Each authority is required to appoint an independent review officer (s. 26(2)(k)) who must participate in and chair the review, monitor the performance of the local authority and where appropriate refer a case to CAFCASS (s. 26(2A)).

The nature and format of the reviews are set down in Review of Children Regulations 1991 as amended by the Review of Children's Cases (Amendment) (England) Regulations 2004 which came into force on 27 September 2004. The regulations stipulate that the independent review officer must be truly independent of the matter in hand, and be a registered and experienced social worker. Reviews must keep any s. 31A plan (see below) for the child under review and if there is no plan for the future care of the child one must be prepared. Reviews are to be held within four weeks of the initial placement, again not more than three months after that first review, and subsequently every six months. A review must also be carried out before the specified times if the independent reviewing officer so directs. There are stipulations as to who should be consulted before a review, who should attend, and the matters for consideration. Worcestershire County Council have published a useful explanation of reviews targeted at the child or young person who is the subject of the review. It is available on **www.worcestershire.gov.uk/ home/cs-social-childrenandfamilies/**.

If cases are referred to CAFCASS by the IRO it may if appropriate start court proceedings against the local authority seeking an order requiring it to put right its failings in relation to the care plan. The options for court action are judicial review proceedings, a compensation claim or a freestanding Human Rights Act 1998 application. We expect that very few cases will be referred to CAFCASS by the IRO. The mere threat of such action should stimulate appropriate responses from the local authority.

Section 31A plans

Section 31A of the Children Act 1989 provides that 'No care order may be made with respect to a child until the court has considered a section 31A plan.' Therefore every child who is subject to a care order subsequent to the implementation of the section will have the benefit of a care plan which has been scrutinized by the courts. These plans will continue to be scrutinized by IROs.

The requirements of s. 31A care plans are set out in Box 10.20.

We will provide information about the implementation of this section of the Children Act 1989 and the relevant regulations when such information becomes available. In the meantime, the care plan should accord with *The Children Act 1989 Guidance and Regulations 1991* (DoH) as supplemented by the Local Authority Circular (LAC(99)29) *Care Plans and Care Proceedings under the Children Act 1989.*

■ The restriction on the liberty of a child being looked after

It is important for social workers to understand that the only basis on which the liberty of a child or young person accommodated by the local authority may be restricted is in accordance with the Children Act 1989, s. 25 (unless the child is remanded from a criminal court—see chapter 15).

BOX 10.20 Section 31A of the Children Act—care orders: care plans

(1) Where an application is made on which a care order might be made with respect to a child, the appropriate local authority must, within such time as the court may direct, prepare a plan (a 'care plan') for the future care of the child.

(2) While the application is pending, the authority must keep any care plan prepared by them under review and, if they are of the opinion some change is required, revise the plan, or make a new plan, accordingly.

(3) A care plan must give any prescribed information and do so in the prescribed manner.

(4) For the purposes of this section, the appropriate local authority, in relation to a child in respect of whom a care order might be made, is the local authority proposed to be designated in the order.

(5) In section 31(3A) and this section, references to a care order do not include an interim care order.

(6) a plan prepared, or treated as prepared, under this section is referred to in this Act as a 'section 31A plan.'

The restriction of liberty

The restriction of liberty does not only mean locking a door. Anything that goes beyond the bounds of ordinary domestic security will probably be a restriction of liberty. The failure to understand or accept this was the cause of the 'pin-down' affair in Staffordshire. All social workers involved in caring for children and young persons should read the report on this experience (Allan Levy QC and Barbara Kahan, *The Pindown Experience and the Protection of Children* (Staffordshire County Council, 1991)).

Guidance

The Control of Children in Public Care: Interpretation of the Children Act 1989 was issued by the Department of Health in 1997. The Chief Inspector, commenting on the guidelines, said:

> the proper use of physical restraint—which must be reasonable and justified—requires skill and judgment.

The guidelines make it clear that the use of physical restraint to prevent children putting themselves or others at serious risk or to prevent serious damage to property can be justified. Staff in these situations should act as a responsible parent would. The attitude of authorities to the use of secure accommodation seems to be varied, and many social workers would regard the use of secure accommodation in any but the most extreme of cases as a failure. Others may be more sanguine about its use.

What is secure accommodation?

Secure accommodation is accommodation that restricts the liberty of a child (s. 25). Detailed regulations have been issued under this section (written in the light of 'pin-down') in respect of the type of accommodation and who may be placed in it. See *The Children Act 1989 Guidance and Regulations*, Vol. 4, 'Residential Care', and the Children (Secure Accommodation) Regulations 1991.

Section 25 Children Act 1989

Section 25 prescribes that the restriction of liberty and the use of secure accommodation are available in strictly limited circumstances. A child may not be placed in secure accommodation unless:

(a) it appears that the child has a history of absconding; and

(b) is likely to abscond from any other type of accommodation; and

(c) if the child absconds, he or she is likely to suffer significant harm; or

(d) if the child is kept in any other type of accommodation, the child is likely to injure himself or other people.

Under the section a child or young person whom a local authority is looking after may be placed in secure accommodation by a local authority only for a limited period of time; up to seventy-two hours in any period of twenty-one days.

It is not necessary for the child to be the subject of a care order before he or she can be placed in secure accommodation. But if the parent objects and there is no care order, in that situation the child must not be placed in secure accommodation.

Court application

If the authority wishes to keep the child in secure accommodation for a longer period than that prescribed by the Regulations, then it must make an application for an authority from a court. A court can grant such an authority only if it is satisfied that the criteria of a history of absconding, etc., set out above, are fulfilled. In doing this the court does not apply the welfare principle (*Re M (A Minor) (Secure Accommodation Order)* (1995)). Six hundred and forty one secure accommodation orders were made in 2003 compared with 526 in 2002 (source: the Children Act Report 2003).

Legal representation

What is important from the social worker's point of view is the fact that the court cannot grant an authority unless the child is legally represented. Section 99 states that where an application for a secure accommodation order is being made, the child/young person must be granted the necessary funding. Rule 25 requires notice of the proceedings to be served on all relevant parties. A children's guardian should be appointed. Secure accommodation orders involve a serious deprivation of liberty, and therefore procedural safeguards are extremely important.

Cases

In the light of this, the decisions in *A Metropolitan Borough Council v DB* (1997) and *Re C (A Minor) (Medical Treatment: Courts' Jurisdiction)* (1997), are worrying.

In the first case the court said that a maternity ward was secure accommodation and ordered that the 17 year old be detained there. The young woman was a crack-cocaine addict, who lived in squalor and had received no antenatal care until very shortly before the birth of her child. Two days prior to the birth, she was admitted to hospital suffering from pre-eclamptic fits brought on by high blood pressure. She then discharged herself from hospital. The local authority obtained an emergency protection order and sought permission to detain her in the maternity ward. The court granted permission, saying that it was the restriction of liberty that made a particular place into secure accommodation.

In the second case, the local authority was granted authority to detain an anorexic young woman without reference to s. 25 under the court's inherent powers contained in s. 100.

There was a greater respect for the procedural safeguards in the next case. In *LM v Essex CC* (1999), Holman J expressed the view that once the criteria justifying a secure accommodation order ceased to be made out, the local authority should no longer keep the child in such accommodation. He also held that the court had no power to discharge or set aside such an order. If a local authority declined to release a child once it appreciated that the basis for the order was no longer present, a writ of *habeas corpus* would be appropriate. If the local authority failed to conclude that the grounds for the order no longer existed, the appropriate procedure might be judicial review.

The European Convention

The question arises whether secure accommodation orders made under s. 25 comply with Article 5 of the European Convention on Human Rights. Article 5(1) lists a finite set of circumstances in which persons may be deprived of their liberty, one of which is educational supervision. Despite the fact that the Children Act criteria make no reference to such supervision, the Court of Appeal in *Re K (Secure Accommodation Order: Right to Liberty)* (2001), rejected the argument that s. 25 was incompatible with the Convention, as the local authority has a duty to provide education for all those aged under 16. The Court did, however, leave open the question whether the words 'for the purposes of educational supervision' covered the facts of a particular case.

Seeking to place a child into secure accommodation will always cause the social worker the greatest of difficulties, both personally and professionally. It is difficult in such situations to see how to square your duty to the child with your wider duty to society.

Representations from children and others

Someone Else's Children considered complaints procedures and reported that:

> . . . young people we met had little confidence in the complaints process and felt that their concerns were not heard:
>
> 'You never get believed but have to believe everything told to you. They never tell you what people say about you, but what I say has to be written down.'
>
> Young people told us that, when they were better informed about the process, their confidence in it increased. (4.30)

It is one of the core principles of the UN Convention on the Rights of the Child that children's views and wishes should be at the forefront of the decision making process. The Children Act 1989 enacts this principle and *Every Child Matters: Next Steps* (see chapter 8) re-affirmed the governments commitment to it.

Representations

Under the Children Act 1989, s. 26(3)–(8), there are important provisions requiring local authorities to establish a representations procedure in relation to the discharge of any of their functions of providing support for children and their families under Part 3 of the Act. The procedure will extend to functions under Part 4 or 5 of the Act and the discharge of functions under the Adoption and Children Act 2002 when regulations to do so are implemented.

The provisions require the authority to consider representations (including complaints) from those listed in Children Act 1989 s. 26(3) and s. 26(3B). These are as follows:

(a) any child or parent of such a child in need or being looked after by the authority;

(b) a person with parental responsibility for such a child;

(c) any local authority foster parent; and

(d) any other person the authority consider has sufficient interest in the child's welfare;

(e) any person for whose needs provision is made by the Adoption Service;

(f) any other person to whom arrangements for the provision of adoption support services extend;

(g) any other person which the authority consider to have sufficient interest in a child who is or may be adopted.

Provision has been made by the Health and Social Care (Community Health and Standards) Act 2003 to extend the representation procedures to those people affected by special guardianship but these provisions have not yet been implemented.

Section 24D of the Children Act 1989 extends the requirement to consider representations to representations from former accommodated children up to the age of 24.

The expression 'representations' is wider than 'complaint' and will allow for comments about the way in which a particular case is being handled.

Procedure

The Representation Procedure (Children) Regulations 1991 as amended require the local authority to appoint an officer to be responsible for the coordination of complaints. Any representations are to be put in writing by the officer, even if given verbally. There must be at least one person independent of the authority who takes part in the procedure. The consideration of the complaint must take place within twenty-eight days of the complaint being received.

After consideration, all people who may be interested must be notified within twenty-eight days of the result.

Panel

If the complainant is not satisfied, then the local authority must, again within twenty-eight days, appoint a panel to consider the representations. The panel also has to contain at least one independent person. It is possible for the independent person to be the same person who considered the written representations. Alternatively, a separate independent person may be appointed.

This panel can consider both written and oral representations. If the independent person on the panel is different from the one who considered the written representations, then that independent person may make oral representations before the panel.

Importantly, the person making the representations has the right to be accompanied by someone who may speak on that person's behalf. This clearly includes a solicitor or other advocate.

Local authority duties

Where representations are made and have been considered, the authority shall:

(a) have due regard to the findings of those who considered them (i.e. so that the representation procedure is not a toothless public relations exercise);

(b) take steps to notify in writing those who have made the representations of the decisions reached and of action to be taken;

(c) give appropriate publicity to this procedure.

The regulations require the local authority to prepare regular reports of the complaints and their outcomes. These should be supplied to the Social Services Committee and be published in an annual report.

Further review

Section 116 of the Health and Social Care (Community Health and Standards) Act 2003 has inserted a new provision into the Children Act 1989, s. 26ZA, which, once implemented, will require introduce new regulations for further consideration of representations by the Commission for Social Care Inspection.

Advocacy

It is clearly not sufficient for children and young people to have a procedure available to them. They must feel able to access the procedure and make their representations fully. Section 26A of the Children Act 1989 requires that local authorities make provision for advocacy services to support children and young people.

The section is set out in Box 10.19 below.

The duty will be extended to further consideration of representations when that provision is implemented. The Advocacy Services and Representations Procedure (*Children*) (*Amendment*) Regulations 2004 which came into force on 1 April 2004 require local authorities to provide the person or child with information about advocacy services and offer him or her help in obtaining an advocate. the Regulations also say who may not be an advocate, set out what local authorities must do when they receive representations or become aware that a child or young person is intending to make representations and require local authorities to monitor compliance, They also amend the Representations Procedure (Children) Regulations 1991 to ensure that an appointed advocate is involved throughout the process. The regulations and guidance to local authorities have been issued under s. 7 of LASSA 1970 as LAC (2004) 11.

 Box 10.19 Section 26A Children Act 1989—Advocacy Services

Every local authority shall make arrangements for the provision of assistance to—

(a) persons who make or intend to make representations under section 24D; and

(b) children who make or intend to make representations under section 16.

EXERCISES

1 Sheila contacts the social services department because she has concerns about her 14-year-old daughter, Claire. Claire has been refusing to go to school because she believes that her mother needs her to help at home. Sheila, a single mother, has 2-year-old twins and she cares for her elderly mother at home. What help can you offer the family?

2 Fred contacts the social services department. He wants you to assess the needs of his three children, all aged under 10, because he is about to be evicted by his housing association for non-payment of rent and the local housing department has found him intentionally homeless. On a brief consideration of the facts, you believe that Fred's children are not vulnerable. Is there any help your department can offer Fred?

3 Jameel has been living with foster parents for two years, since he was 13. He was placed there following his mother's remarriage to a man who has in the past been violent towards Jameel. Jameel's mother has now left her husband and would like Jameel to return to her care. Jameel does not want to return. What advice can you offer?

4 If Jameel's wishes are ignored and he is returned home, can he make a complaint? If he can, explain the procedure to him and the help that is available to him.

COMPANION WEB SITE

 For guidance on how to answer these exercises, visit the companion web site at: www.oup.com/uk/booksites/law

WHERE DO WE GO FROM HERE?

Part 3 of the Children Act is a wide ranging Part of the Act which contains a range of powers and duties necessary to ensure the welfare of children in need. Many children can be supported in their own families, and the Act contains a range of provisions to ensure that, where appropriate, children can remain with their families. Inevitably some families will fail to support their children. Part 3 of the Act sets out the responsibilities of local authorities to those children that they are required to look after, including preparing children and young people for the time when they leave care. However outcomes for 'looked after' children are very poor and the Government has set itself demanding targets to improve those outcomes. Part 3 straddles the two concerns of the Act, supporting families and caring properly for those children who require protection either through accommodation or through court orders. The next chapter considers how social workers investigate concerns about children, and plan for the appropriate provision of services, and where necessary, for court applications.

ANNOTATED FURTHER READING

More extensive information on Part 3 of the Children Act can be found in specialist texts on the Children Act 1989 such as:

R. White, P. Carr, and N. Lowe, *The Children Act in Practice* (3rd edn.; Butterworths, 2002).

Advice for young people in case is provided by:

Voice for the Child in Care—a national organization offering advice, help and advocacy to young people and care leavers, **www.vcc-uk.org**. Their web site includes a PowerPoint presentation on the milestones towards children's advocacy.

Carelaw—**www.carelaw.org.uk**—This web site was launched to help and advise young people currently in local authority care or preparing to leave care. The site has been created by NCH with the Solicitors Family Law Association.

A useful and interesting article on the scope of Part 3 of the Children Act 1989 is John Murphy 'Children in need: the limits of local authority accountability' [2003] 23 Legal Studies 103.

Participation by young people

The Government's proposals on increasing the participation of young people in service provision are set out in:

Children and Young People Unit, *Listening to learn: core principles for the involvement of children and young people* (Department for Education and Skills, 2001).

The particular needs of disabled children are considered in *Consulting with Disabled Children and Young People*, Findings No. 741 (2001), The Joseph Rowntree Foundation, **www.jrf.org.uk**.

An interesting article on complaints procedures (although now out of date) is C. Williams, 'The Practical Operation of the Children Act Complaints Procedure' [2002], Child and Family Law Quarterly 25.

Children in need & housing

D. Cowan (2004) Child & Family Law Quarterly 16.3 (331). In a case commentary on the House of Lords case *R (G) v Barnet LBC*, discussed at the beginning of the chapter, Cowan considers Lambeth's policy, which survived the House of Lords ruling, of offering accommodation only to children in need, without their family. He argues that these decisions make the general duty in s. 17 (1) irrelevant; also, paradoxically, housing legislation gives greater protection to households with children than the Children Act 1989.

11

Investigation and case planning

CASE STUDY

In Re S (Minors) Care Order: Implementation of Care Plan) In Re W (Minors) (Care Order: Adequacy of Care Plan) [2002] 2 A.C. 291

In the first case the judge made final care orders in respect of two children but the local authority failed to implement the care plan, which included working with the mother with a view to reuniting her with her children. The mother appealed against the making of the care order on the ground that the judge should have made an interim care order. In the second case the judge made final care orders in respect of two boys even though the care plan for their immediate future, including the placement, was far from certain, because he was satisfied that it would be impossible for them to return to live with their parents at that time. The parents appealed on the ground that the judge should have refrained from making a final care order until the uncertainties had been resolved.

The Court of Appeal heard both appeals together, dismissing the appeal in the first case and substituting an interim care order in the second case. The court, however, regarded elements in the way care orders were made and implemented as incompatible with the rights of parents and children under Articles 6 and 8 of the European Convention and, using s. 3 of the Human Rights Act 1998, reinterpreted the Children Act 1989 to make it compatible with the Convention. A new procedure was introduced, by which the essential milestones of a care plan were identified and 'starred'. If a starred milestone was not achieved within a reasonable time after the date set at trial, the local authority was obliged to inform the child's guardian of the position. Either the guardian or the local authority would then have the right to apply to the court for further directions. The court also laid down guidelines to give judges a wider discretion to make an interim care order and defer making final care order.

The local authority in the second case and the Secretary of State for Health appealed against the introduction of the new procedures by the Court of Appeal. The mother in the first case appealed against the making of a final care order in respect of her children and argued that without the starring system the 1989 Act would be incompatible with Articles 6 and 8 of the Convention.

Held

The appeals of the Secretary of State and the local authority were allowed, and the appeal of the mother was dismissed. The House of Lords made a number of important points.

1 The Human Rights Act 1998 reserved the amendment of primary legislation to Parliament and any purported use of s. 3 of the Act which produced a result which departed substantially from a fundamental feature of an Act of Parliament was likely to have crossed the boundary between

interpretation and amendment (we discussed this issue, with reference to this case, in further detail in chapter 2);

2 A cardinal principle of the Children Act 1989 was that the courts were not empowered to intervene in the way local authorities discharged their parental responsibilities under final care orders; that the starring system was inconsistent with that important element in the scheme of the Children Act 1989 and passed well beyond the boundary of interpretation;

3 Sections 7 and 8 of the Human Rights Act 1998 did not provide a legal basis for the introduction of the starring system since it would impose obligations on local authorities in circumstances where there had been no finding that they had acted or were proposing to act unlawfully or breach a Convention right and that accordingly the introduction of the starring system could not be justified;

4 There may be some circumstances where some child care decisions made by local authorities could not be challenged in the courts. That, however, was a lacuna (gap) in the statute and not a question of incompatability;

5 When considering whether a care plan was sufficiently certain to enable a final care order to be made the court should normally have before it a care plan which was sufficiently firm and particularized for all concerned to have a reasonably clear picture of the likely way ahead for the child for the foreseeable future. The degree of firmness of the plan would vary, as would the detail, from case to case. However, in order to be fair to the parents and the child's guardian the care plan had to be appropriately specific;

6 The courts must bear in mind the general principle that any delay in determining issues relating to a child's upbringing was likely to prejudice the child's welfare;

7 The courts should also guard against encroaching into areas which were properly within the administrative discretion of the local authority.

OVERVIEW AND OBJECTIVES

This important case should be read in full. It may help you to understand the case to reread chapter 2 on human rights. The case reflects concerns about the inadequacies of the care system and the role of the courts in helping to improve the system. It focuses on the division of responsibilities between the courts and local authorities. Courts are about the resolution of disputes, making decisions on particular issues at particular times. The courts cannot have day-to-day responsibility for a child. As Lord Nicholls of Birkenhead said in this case, 'The court cannot respond with immediacy and informality to practical problems and changed circumstances as they arise.' Nonetheless, the Court of Appeal, in suggesting a starred milestone approach to care plans, highlighted the need for some constraint on the operations of local authorities. Lord Nicholls indicated that this was not a role for the courts but that the problem was one for Parliament to solve.

Parliament's solution has been twofold:

(i) to introduce s. 31 A into the Children Act 1989 which requires plans—s. 31A plans—to be drawn up containing specific prescribed information when the local authority is applying for a care order, and

(ii) to introduce the role of the Independent Reviewing Officer (IRO).

The Review of Children's Cases (Amendment) (England) Regulations 2004 require all local authorities to have IROs in place to chair the statutory review meetings of all looked after children from September 2004.The IROs are responsible for monitoring the local authority's review of the care plan,with the aim of ensuring that actions required to implement the care plan are carried out and outcomes monitored. The Regulations give IROs a new power to refer a case to CAFCASS to take legal action as a last resort where a child's human rights are considered to be in breach. Both these initiatives are considered more fully in chapter 10.

What this chapter is about is the process of investigation and case planning. As you read this chapter think about the steps involved from the initial expression of concern about a child to effective protection of the child and finally through to a satisfactory long-term outcome. Achieving the latter depends upon a number of stages, investigation, assessment, and planning and using court orders where necessary. You should not think of these as separate stages but overlapping. In particular, planning for the future of the child concerned is a critical stage which should begin as soon as possible.

◼ Introduction

This chapter will look at three critical stages of child protection from which follow an initial expression of concern. In appropriate cases, these stages will be crucial to successful court proceedings by a local authority. We shall consider:

- the investigation of child protection concerns;
- the bureaucratic structures designed to protect children; and
- case planning including the protocol for judicial case management in public law Children Act cases.

Working Together to Safeguard Children (1999) published by the Department of Health, the Home Office and the Department for Education and Employment and *The Framework for the Assessment of Children in Need and their Families* (2000) are essential documents for this chapter. They are available on the Department of Health web site **www.doh.gov.uk/qualityprotects**. The Victoria Climbié Inquiry (see chapter 8) expressed concern that the guidance did not make it clear what was expected of front line staff. The government therefore published '*What To Do If You're Worried A Child Is Being Abused*' which was designed to clarify *Working Together* and *the Framework*. Information on the role of this publication is available in LAC(2003)11.

Subsequently the green paper *Every Child Matters* pointed out that the current system of multiple assessments of children by different people is both alienating and inefficient. It therefore proposed a common assessment framework (CAF) designed to provide earlier intervention and more effective protection for children. This common assessment framework will draw upon *The Framework for the Assessment of Children in Need and their Families* but is likely to have a different focus, in particular it may place less emphasis on the lead role of social services. The Department for Education and Skills is leading the development work on a common assessment framework with a

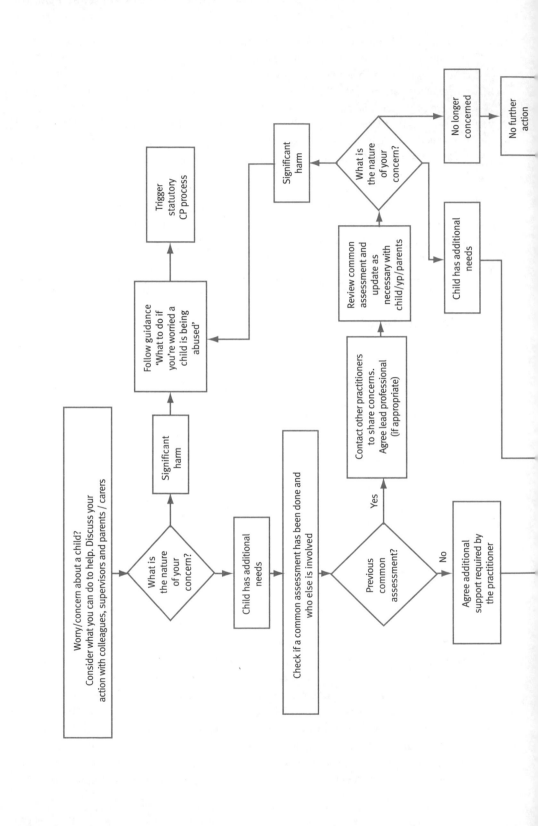

Worry/concern about a child?
Consider what you can do to help. Discuss your
action with colleagues, supervisors and parents / carers

What is the nature of your concern?

Significant harm

Follow guidance 'What to do if you're worried a child is being abused'

Trigger statutory CP process

Child has additional needs

Check if a common assessment has been done and who else is involved

Previous common assessment?

Yes

No

Contact other practitioners to share concerns. Agree lead professional (if appropriate)

Agree additional support required by the practitioner

Review common assessment and update as necessary with child/yp/parents

What is the nature of your concern?

Significant harm

No longer concerned

Child has additional needs

No further action

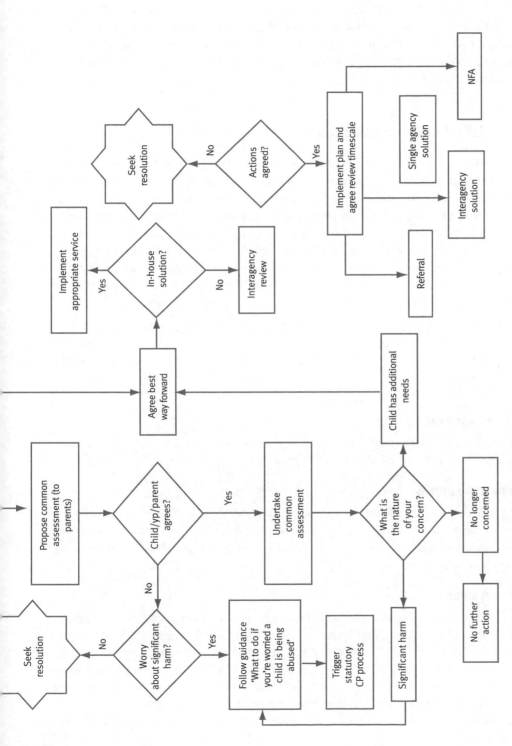

Figure 11.1 An illustration of how the CAF process might work.

consultation period of August–November 2004 with phased implementation planned from April 2005. Some indication of how the common assessment framework may work is set out in Figure 11.1 which is reproduced from the DfES consultation paper. However this chapter describes the current framework of assessment and the diagram certainly indicates that where child protection concerns are involved the procedures will be similar to those operating in 2004. We will endeavour to keep you up to date with developments on our web site.

Initial referral and assessment

The first step in the whole process of child protection is the initial referral. 263,900 assessments of children were completed in 2002–3 (Children Act Report 2003). The protection of children is dependent upon everyone who works with children or is in contact with them being able to recognize indicators that a child's welfare or safety may be at risk. Many cases will not need to go beyond the initial referral. The effectiveness of the child protection system relies on effective partnership with those people who may spot problems and then on the responses of social services to those initial indicators. The Victoria Climbié Inquiry highlights the critical importance of effective procedures from the time of the initial referral. Paragraph 1.17 of the report states:

> In his opening statement to the Inquiry, Neil Garnham QC listed no fewer than 12 key occasions when the relevant services had the opportunity to successfully intervene in the life of Victoria. . . . Sometimes it needed nothing more than a manager doing their job by asking pertinent questions or taking the trouble to look in a case file. There can be no excuse for such sloppy and unprofessional performance.

Initial assessment

Working Together provides clear guidance on how to carry out the initial assessment. Paragraph 5.13 and 5.14 are set out in Box 11.1.

Avoiding the pitfalls

The initial assessment and enquiries are obviously critical to successful child protection. *Working Together* summarizes research which identified ten common pitfalls which may prevent effective initial enquires. The advice is extremely valuable. Box 11.2 below sets out the summary.

The next steps

The result of the initial assessment may be that no further action needs to be taken. It may be that the child is a 'child in need' and the family will benefit from additional support and practical help in promoting the child's health and development. Chapter 10 sets out the responsibilities of the local authority to children in need. It may that there are concerns sufficient to prompt a s. 47 inquiry—we discuss this below. It may be that there is a need for a parallel police investigation. It may be that the child's life is at risk, or there is a likelihood of serious immediate harm. In that case the social services

BOX 11.1 *Working Together*—the initial assessment

5.13 The initial assessment by the social services department of all children in need—whether or not there are child protection concerns—should be completed within a maximum of seven working days of the date of referral. However the initial assessment period may be very brief if the criteria for initiating s. 47 inquiries are met. Using the framework set out in the *Framework for the Assessment of Children in Need and their Families* it should address the questions:

- What are the needs of the child?
- Are the parents able to respond appropriately to the child's needs? Is the child being adequately safeguarded from significant harm, and are the parents able to promote the child's health and development?
- Is action required to safeguard and promote the child's welfare?

5.14 The process of initial assessment should involve: seeing and speaking to the child (according to age and understanding) and family members as appropriate; drawing together and analysing available information from a range of sources (including existing records); and obtaining relevant information from professionals and together in contact with the child and family. All relevant information (including historical information) should be taken into account.

5.15 In the course of this assessment, the social services department should ask:

- Is this a child in need? (s. 17 of the Children Act 1989)
- Is there reasonable cause to suspect that this child is suffering or is likely to suffer significant harm? (s. 47 of the Children Act 1989)

5.16 The focus of the initial assessment should be the welfare of the child. It is important to remember that even if the reason for a referral was a concern about abuse or neglect which is not subsequently substantiated, a family may still benefit from support and practical help to promote a child's health and development.

5.17 Following an initial assessment, the social services department should decide on the next course of action, following discussion with the child and family, unless such a discussion may place a child at risk of significant harm. Where it is clear that there should be a police investigation in parallel with a s. 47 inquiry, the considerations at para. 5.36 should apply. Whatever decisions are taken they should be endorsed at a managerial level agreed within the social services department and recorded in writing with the reasons for them. The family, the original referrer, and other professionals and services involved in the assessment should as far as possible be told what action has been taken, consistent with respecting the confidentiality of the child and family concerned, and not jeopardising further action in respect of child protection concerns (which may include police investigations).

department must act quickly to secure the immediate safety of the child. Legal advice should be obtained as soon as possible. Full details of the emergency protection order and the other available court orders are set out in chapter 12. Details of the power to exclude perpetrators of violence or other abuse from the family home are set out in chapter 18. The s. 47 enquiries should proceed in parallel with seeking protection via the courts. Whatever decision is made, it should be endorsed at managerial level and

BOX 11.2 From *Working Together*, initial assessment and enquiries: ten pitfalls and how to avoid them

1. Not enough weight is given to information from family, friends and neighbours.

Ask yourself: Would I react differently if these reports had come from a different source? How can I check whether or not they have substance? Even if they are not accurate, could they be a sign that the family are in need of some help or support?

2. Not enough attention is paid to what children say, how they look and how they behave.

Ask yourself: Have I been given appropriate access to all the children in the family? If I have not been able to see any child, is there a very good reason, and have I made arrangements to see him/her as soon as possible, or made sure that another relevant professional sees him/her? How should I follow up any uneasiness about the child/ren's health or well-being? If the child is old enough and has the communication skills, what is the child's account of events? If the child uses a language other than English, or alternatively non-verbal communication, have I made every effort to enlist help in understanding him/her? What is the evidence to support or refute the young person's account?

3. Attention is focused on the most visible or pressing problems and other warning signs are not appreciated.

Ask yourself: What is the most striking thing about this situation? If this feature were to be removed, or change, would I still have concerns?

4. Pressures from high status referrers or the press, with fears that a child may die, lead to over-precipitate action.

Ask yourself: Would I see this referral as a child protection matter if it came from another source?

5. Professionals think that when they have explained something as clearly as they can, the other person will have understood it.

Ask yourself: Have I double-checked with the family and the child/ren that they understand what will happen next?

6. Assumptions and pre-judgements about families lead to observations being ignored or misinterpreted.

Ask yourself: What were my assumptions about this family? What, if any, is the hard evidence which support them? What, if any, is the hard evidence which refutes them?

7. Parents' behaviour, whether cooperative or uncooperative, is often misinterpreted.

Ask yourself: What were the reasons for the parents' behaviour? Are there other possibilities besides the most obvious? Could their behaviour have been a reaction to something I did or said rather than to do with the child?

8. When the initial inquiry shows that the child is not at risk of significant harm, families are seldom referred to other services which they need to prevent longer-term problems.

Ask yourself: Is this family's situation satisfactory for meeting the child/ren's needs? Whether or not there is a child protection concern, does the family need support or practical help? How can I make sure they know about services they are entitled to, and can access them if they wish?

9. When faced with an aggressive or frightening family, professionals are reluctant to discuss fears for their own safety and ask for help.

Ask yourself: Did I feel safe in this household? If not, why not? If I or another professional should go back there to ensure the child/ren's safety, what support should I ask for? If necessary, put your concerns and requests in writing to your manager.

10. Information taken at the first inquiry is not adequately recorded, facts are not checked, and reasons for decision are not noted.

Ask yourself: Am I sure the information I have noted is 100 per cent accurate? If I didn't check my notes with the family during the interview, what steps should I take to verify them? Do my notes show clearly the difference between the information the family gave me, my own direct observations, and my interpretation or assessment of the situation? Do my notes record what action I have taken/will take? What action all other relevant people have taken/will take?

recorded in writing with the reasons. The family, the person who originally expressed concern, and other professionals and services involved in the assessment should be told what action has been taken, consistent with respecting the confidentiality of the child and family (see chapter 4).

Referral from the courts

The vast majority of referrals are going to be from social care and health professionals and others who have contact with children. In the course of any family proceedings not involving a local authority, a court may have legitimate reasons to be concerned about the care of children. If that is the case the court has the power under s. 37 of the Children Act 1989 to give directions to a local authority to investigate and consider whether care proceedings should be brought.

The powers of the court under s. 37

Section 37 is set out in Box 11.3 below.

This is a comprehensive section that has wide implications for the local authority. It gives the residual power to the court to require the state, via the local authority, to consider intervention in the affairs of a family. The court can exercise the power in any family proceedings and the use of these powers can lead to a supervision order, or indeed a care order, being made. For instance, if a court was considering an application for a divorce and became concerned about the welfare of the children, it could ask the local authority to undertake a s. 37 investigation. The use of s. 37 is considered again in chapter 14.

The procedure

The procedure is dealt with under r. 27 of the Magistrates' Court Rules and r. 26 of the County Court and High Court Rules. Before making a direction under s. 37, the court

BOX 11.3 Section 37 investigations

(1) Where, in any family proceedings (i.e. other than care proceedings) in which a question arises with respect to the welfare of any child, it appears to the court that it may be appropriate for a care or supervision order to be made with respect to him, the court may direct the appropriate authority to undertake an investigation of the child's circumstances.

(2) Where the court gives a direction under this section the local authority concerned shall, when undertaking the investigation, consider whether they should—

(a) apply for a care order or for a supervision order with respect to the child;

(b) provide services or assistance for the child or his family; or

(c) take any other action with respect to the child.

(3) Where a local authority undertake an investigation under this section, and decide not to apply for a care order or supervision order with respect to the child concerned, they shall inform the court of—

(a) their reasons for so deciding;

(b) any service or assistance which they have provided, or intend to provide, for the child and his family; and

(c) any other action which they have taken or propose to take, with respect to the child.

(4) The information shall be given to the court before the end of the period of eight weeks beginning with the date of the direction, unless the court otherwise directs.

(5) The local authority named in a direction under subsection (1) must be—

(a) the authority in whose area the child is ordinarily resident; or

(b) where the child does not reside in the area of a local authority, the authority within whose area any circumstances arose in consequence of which the direction is being given.

(6) If, on the conclusion of any investigation or review under this section, the authority decide not to apply for a care order or supervision order with respect to the child—

(a) they shall consider whether it would be appropriate to review the case at a later date; and

(b) if they decide that it would be, they shall determine the date on which the review is to begin.

will deal with the main application before it. This would normally be by way of making an interim order pending the s. 37 investigation. It will then adjourn the hearing. A written direction is served on the local authority. If, after investigating, the local authority decides not to apply for an order (i.e. in accordance with s. 37(3) above) then it needs to inform the court in writing.

Explanations of inaction are required

Even if a care or supervision application is not made, the local authority is still required to explain its actions, the reasons for non-action, and its plans for the future. If the court makes a direction under s. 37, the court can appoint a guardian to act on behalf of the child.

The local authority decides

Although it is possible to envisage circumstances in which the local authority and guardian may disagree over the course of action, it remains solely the choice of the local authority whether or not to apply for an order. If in those circumstances the court prefers to pay greater attention to the views of the guardian, which is to be expected, then the court cannot compel the local authority to make an application for a care order.

Interim care or supervision orders pending s. 37 investigations

There are provisions in the Children Act 1989, s. 38, for making interim orders during the s. 37 investigations. Box 11.4 sets out the court's power.

This section, strictly speaking, is an exception to the principle that no care or supervision order may be made without an application being made to the court. Under s. 37 of the 1989 Act, no application need be before the court for it to have the power to make an interim care or supervision order. However, before a full care or supervision order can be made it is necessary for a local authority actually to make an application, so the principle is essentially intact.

If the court has ordered a s. 37 investigation and is thinking of making an interim care or supervision order, it must be certain, first, that the normal test for an interim order is satisfied. Section 38(2) is set out in Box 11.5 below.

 BOX 11.4 Section 38—the power to make interim orders

(1) Where—

    (a) in any proceedings on an application for a care order or supervision order, the proceedings are adjourned; or

    (b) the court gives a direction under section 37(1), the court may make an interim care order or an interim supervision order with respect to the child concerned.

 BOX 11.5 There must be reasonable grounds for an interim order

s. 38(2) A court shall not make an interim care order or interim supervision order under this section unless it is satisfied that there are reasonable grounds for believing that the circumstances with respect to the child are as mentioned in section 31(2) (i.e. the grounds for a care order—the likelihood of significant harm, the child beyond parental control).

The words 'reasonable grounds for believing' mean that the grounds do not have to be 'proved' before an interim order can be made, but merely that there have to be some grounds for believing that a full order may be made. The making of an interim order does not presuppose that a full order will be made. You will find more information about interim care orders in chapter 12.

Section 8 residence orders during or after s. 37 investigation

An alternative course open to the court would be to make a s. 8 residence order. (For further discussion of these, see chapter 14.) It has the power in any family proceedings to make a s. 8 order, even though it has not disposed of the main proceedings (s. 11(3)).

Time limits

One of the practical difficulties is the requirement that the investigation under the Children Act 1989, s. 37, be completed within a period of eight weeks, unless 'the court otherwise directs'. The resource implications for s. 37 are immense, and in the absence of greatly increased resources the court may need to 'otherwise direct' in many cases.

■ The local authority's duty to investigate (s. 47)

Prompting the duty to investigate

If the initial assessment or the result of enquiries following referral from the court indicate that there is reasonable cause to suspect that a child is suffering or is likely to suffer significant harm then the local authority is placed under a statutory duty to investigate. The duty also arises if a child is the subject of an emergency protection order, is in police protection, or has contravened a ban imposed by a curfew notice under the Crime and Disorder Act 1998. The meanings of significant harm, police protection, and emergency protection order are discussed in chapter 12. There has been inserted, in the case of a breach of a child curfew order only, a requirement for the enquiries to be commenced as soon as practicable and, in any event, within forty eight hours of the authority receiving the information.

Section 47 makes it clear that the main responsibility for the protection under the Act falls on local authorities. Section 47(1) is set out in Box 11.6.

Low-level threshold

Note that the local authority has an overall duty to make inquiries as soon as it has 'reasonable cause to suspect' the possibility of significant harm. This is a relatively low-level threshold for triggering action, and is lower than the threshold for justifying interim care or supervision orders, or emergency protection orders. These, by contrast with the s. 47 inquiries, involve a compulsory intervention in the lives of both child and family (see chapter 12) and therefore require a different balance to be drawn between the concerns of the state to protect children and the rights of individuals.

BOX 11.6 The local authority's duty to investigate

47(1) Where a local authority—

    (a) are informed that a child who lives, or is found, in their area—

        (i)   is the subject of an emergency protection order; or

        (ii) is in police protection; or

        (iii) has contravened a ban imposed by a curfew notice within the meaning of Chapter I of Part I of the Crime and Disorder Act 1998;

    or

    (b) have reasonable cause to suspect that a child who lives, or is found, in their area is suffering or is likely to suffer significant harm, the authority shall make, or cause to be made, such enquiries as they consider to be necessary to enable them to decide whether they should take any action to safeguard or protect the child's welfare.

In the case of a child falling within paragraph (a)(iii) above, the enquiries shall be commenced as soon as practicable and, in any event, within forty-eight hours of the authority receiving the information.

The objective of local authority enquiries under s. 47

Working Together, para. 5.33, makes it clear that the objective of local authority enquiries conducted under s. 47 is to determine whether action is needed to promote and safeguard the welfare of the child or children who are the subject of the inquiries. The *Framework for the Assessment of Children in Need and Their Families* provides a structure for helping to collect and analyse information obtained in the course of the s. 47 enquiry. *Working Together* stresses that this 'core assessment' is critical to the s. 47 inquiry process, and that it should be completed by the time of the child protection conference or within forty-two days of the commencement of the assessment.

'Any action'

The 'any action' referred to in s. 47(1)(b) may constitute applying for a court order or providing any form of support under Part 3 of the Children Act—see chapter 10. *Working Together* emphasizes that placing a child's name on the child protection register or initiating care proceedings is not the only way of protecting children. Providing access to a wide range of support services to help children in need is likely to be equally important.

Court applications

Despite this emphasis, s. 47(3) goes on to state that the enquiries should in particular be directed towards establishing whether the local authority should make any application to court.

Statutory requirements

In making its inquiries, the local authority is required actually to see the child unless it is satisfied that it has sufficient information (s. 47(4)).

If in making the inquiries the local authority finds matters concerned with the child's education it is required to consult the relevant education authority (s. 47(5)).

Where the local authority does try to carry out this statutory duty and is refused access to the child or is denied information as to the child's whereabouts, the authority is required to apply for an emergency protection order, a child assessment order, a care order, or a supervision order unless satisfied that the child's welfare can be satisfactorily safeguarded without doing so (s. 47(6)). These court orders are explained in chapter 12. The requirement to make an application to court if access is refused, again, is a statutory duty, albeit that there is a narrow area of discretion.

Next steps

Once the local authority has concluded its inquiries under s. 47, it has to consider what is to be done. Even a decision not to make a court application prompts a positive duty—to consider whether it is appropriate to review the case at a later date. Subsection (8) sets out the overriding statutory duty on the local authority if it concludes that action is necessary. It must take action—'so far as it is both within their power and reasonably practicable for them to do so'. If the local authority concludes as a result of its enquiries that the child needs some form of support, it must supply that support. If it fails to do so then its decision may be liable to judicial review. If the local authority believes that court proceedings are required, the local authority must take proceedings. Box 11.7 sets out s. 47(7) and (8).

Recording of decisions

Whatever the outcome of the s. 47 inquiries, decisions should be recorded, and parents (together with professionals and agencies who have been significantly involved) should receive a copy of the record.

 BOX 11.7 Section 47(7)–(8)—the duty to take action

(7) If, on the conclusion of any enquiries or review made under this section, the authority decide not to apply for an emergency protection order, a child assessment order, a care order or a supervision order they shall—

(a) consider whether it would be appropriate to review the case at a later date; and

(b) if they decide that it would be, determine the date on which that review is to begin.

(8) Where, as a result of complying with this section, a local authority conclude that they should take action to safeguard or promote the child's welfare they shall take that action (so far as it is both within their power and reasonably practicable for them to do so).

BOX 11.8 Section 47—the duty on other agencies

47.(9) Where a local authority are conducting enquiries under this section, it shall be the duty of any person mentioned in subsection (11) to assist them with those enquiries (in particular by providing relevant information and advice) if called upon by the authority to do so.

(10) Subsection (9) does not oblige any person to assist a local authority where doing so would be unreasonable in all the circumstances of the case.

Cooperation from other agencies

The local authority may require assistance from other bodies and authorities. This duty, in s. 47(9), (10), and (11) is set out in Box 11.8. We consider the relationship between other agencies and social services departments in chapter 8.

The nature of the duty

The requirement on the local authority is to do all within its power to safeguard or promote the welfare of a child brought to its attention as being at possible risk, in partnership with other agencies if appropriate. The aim of the legislation has been to avoid the local authority being put in a situation of saying 'we would like to do this but we do not have the legal power'.

This is merely emphasizing the concept of 'diminishment of court proceedings' discussed in Chapter 9 which, in turn, is a reflection of the overall philosophy of the current law relating to children. This is that the local authority shall do all that is within its power to safeguard children and should apply for court orders only as a final and last resort, but always bearing in mind that it should apply for a court order if that is necessary.

The inquiry process

Section 47 inquiries need to be carried out effectively and skilfully. Paragraph 5.36 of *Working Together* sets out some key concerns about interviewing children. We have set out this paragraph in Box 11.9.

The *Framework for the Assessment of Children in Need and Their Families*

Working Together gives guidance on the investigation process. It, in turn, refers to the *Framework for the Assessment of Children in Need and Their Families*. The *Framework* points out that assessment is based on full understanding of what is happening to the child in the context of the family and the wider community. The Department of Health has produced ten family assessment questionnaires, including the Strengths and Difficulties Questionnaire and the Parenting Daily Hassles Scale, but unfortunately this information is not included in the *Framework*. Nonetheless, it is essential that social workers carrying out any investigation should work within the framework supplied by these documents.

BOX 11.9 Obtaining information from children

5.36 Children are a key, and sometimes the only, source of information about what has happened to them, especially in child sexual abuse cases, but also in physical and other forms of abuse. Accurate and complete information is essential for taking action to promote the welfare of the child, as well as for any criminal proceedings which may be instigated concerning an alleged perpetrator of abuse. When children are first approached, the nature and extent of any harm suffered by them may not be clear, nor whether a criminal offence has been committed. It is important that even initial discussions with children are conducted in a way that minimises any distress caused to them, and maximises the likelihood that they will provide accurate and complex information. It is important, wherever possible, to have separate communications with a child. Leading or suggestive communication should always be avoided. Children may need time, and more than one opportunity, in order to develop sufficient trust to communicate any concerns they may have, especially if they have communication difficulties, learning difficulties, are very young, or are experiencing mental health problems.

Additionally, the implications of the use of videotaped interviews as evidence in criminal trials of alleged perpetrators, as allowed under the Youth Justice and Criminal Evidence Act 1999, will need to be borne in mind. There will be the need to work within the official guidance *Obtaining Best Evidence* issued to deal with the running and recording of such interviews (see chapter 7). The practical difficulties of the overlapping nature of the process of such investigations are fully explored in the Department of Health book, *The Challenge of Partnership in Child Protection: Practice Guide* (HMSO, 1995). This should be added to your essential reading.

The structures designed to protect children

Working Together

The child protection structure is not laid down in any one piece of legislation, nor by the decisions of the courts in common law; rather it has evolved through a series of reports, government circulars, and individual decisions by local authorities. The key document is *Working Together to Safeguard Children—a guide to inter-agency working to safeguard and promote the welfare of children* published by the Department of Health, the Home Office, and the Department for Education and Employment in 1999. This provides guidance on the system of cooperation between agencies seeking to protect children. *Working Together* is issued under s. 7 of LASSA 1970. The following discussion is based on *Working Together*.

The mechanisms for child protection in summary

The structure for protection of children consists of:

- The Area Child Protection Committee;
- The Child Protection Register;
  and
- The Child Protection Conference.

Each of these will be discussed in turn.

The Area Child Protection Committee

Note that the Area Child Protection Committee is to be replaced by Local Safeguarding Children Boards once the relevant provisions of the Children Act 2004 are implemented. We describe the statutory nature of Local Safeguarding Children Boards in chapter 8. However their nature and functions will not be very different from the current non-statutory Area Child Protection Committees.

The Area Child Protection Committee is more commonly referred to by its initials, ACPC. It is the framework underpinning the child protection system. An ACPC exists in each local authority area. It is an inter-agency forum for agreeing how the different services and professional groups should cooperate to safeguard children in their area, and for making sure that arrangements work effectively. The responsibilities of the ACPC, described in para. 4.1 of *Working Together*, are set out in Box 11.10.

 BOX 11.10 The responsibilities of the ACPC

(a) To develop and agree local policies and procedures for inter-agency work to protect children, within the national framework provided by *Working Together* (this is done by the issuing of Local Procedural Handbooks, which are issued to hospitals, schools, and other bodies who deal with children, setting out what is to be done in cases of suspected child abuse);

(b) to audit and evaluate how well local services work together to protect children, for example through wider case audits;

(c) to put in place objectives and performance indicators for child protection, within the frameworks and objectives set out in Children's Services Plans;

(d) to encourage and help develop effective working relationships between different services and professional groups, based on trust and mutual understanding;

(e) to ensure that there is a level of agreement and understanding across agencies about operational definitions and thresholds for intervention;

(f) to improve local ways of working in the light of knowledge gained through national and local experience and research, and to make sure that any lessons learned are shared, understood, and acted upon (these issues can arise from local inquiries or national inquiries, for instance the Laming Inquiry into the death of Victoria Climbié);

(g) to undertake case reviews where a child has died or, in certain circumstances, been seriously harmed, and abuse or neglect is confirmed or suspected; to make sure that any lessons from the case are understood and acted upon; to communicate clearly to individual services and professional groups their shared responsibility for protecting children, and to explain how each can contribute (details on the operation of case reviews are set out in Part 8 of *Working Together*);

(h) to help improve the quality of child protection work and of inter-agency working through specifying needs for inter-agency training and development, and ensuring that training is delivered (this emphasises the key importance of training in tackling child abuse); and

(i) to raise awareness within the wider community of the need to safeguard children and promote their welfare, and to explain how the wider community can contribute to these objectives.

ACPCs and Children's Services Planning

The responsibility of social services departments to produce a children's services plan is explicit in *Working Together*. The plans should 'look widely at the needs of local children, and the ways in which local services (including statutory and voluntary services) should work together to meet those needs' (*Working Together*, para. 4.7). The local authority should take a holistic view of how it can better promote the welfare of children; it should consider the roles played by education, housing, youth services, culture, leisure, and other departments as well as social services, and produce a plan to which all local services are committed. ACPCs must contribute to the plan and work within its frame-work. ACPCs should have 'a clear role in identifying those children in need who are at risk of significant harm, or who have suffered significant harm, and in identifying resource gaps (in terms of funding and/or the contribution of different agencies) and better ways of working' (*Working Together*, para. 4.9).

ACPC membership

Working Together states that ACPCs should have members from each of the main agencies responsible for working together to safeguard children. We have considered the contributions that statutory and voluntary agencies make to the safeguarding of children in chapter 10. Membership is to be determined locally but should include minimum representation from those agencies set out in Box 11.11.

 BOX 11.11 Minimum membership of the ACPC (taken from para 4.11 of *Working Together*)

- Local authorities (education and social services);
- Health services;
- The police;
- The probation service;
- The NSPCC (when active in the area);
- The domestic violence forum (when active in the area);
- The armed services (where appropriate, and especially where there is a large service base in the area).

BOX 11.12 Other relevant representation

- Adult mental health services;
- Child and adolescent mental health services;
- The coroner;
- The Crown Prosecution Service;
- Dental health services;
- Drug and alcohol misuse services;
- Education establishments not maintained by the local authority;
- CAFCASS;
- Housing, cultural, and leisure services;
- The judiciary;
- Local authority legal services.

The ACPC should make appropriate arrangements to involve others in its work as needed. Paragraph 4.12 of *Working Together* set out in Box 11.12 makes suggestions as to additional members. The list is not intended to be exhaustive. We explain the roles of these organizations in chapter 8.

ACPC Protocols

Working Together (para. 4.18 set out in Box 11.13) makes it clear that it is a major responsibility of the ACPC to put in place a wide range of local protocols.

As a field social worker you will not normally be involved with the ACPC, unless you

BOX 11.13 The range of required protocols

(a) How s. 47 inquiries and associated police investigations should be conducted and, in particular, in what circumstances joint inquiries are necessary and/or appropriate;

(b) quick and straightforward means of resolving professional differences of view in a specific case, e.g. on whether a child protection conference should be convened;

(c) attendance at child protection conferences, including quora;

(d) involving children and family members in child protection conferences, the role of advocates as well as including criteria for excluding parents in exceptional circumstances;

(e) a decision-making process for registration based upon the views of the agencies present at the child protection conference;

(f) handling complaints from families about the functioning of child protection conferences; and

(g) responding to children involved in prostitution.

have the misfortune to be caught up in a case review arising out of the serious injury or death of a child where child abuse has been suspected, as the ACPC has the responsibility, according to *Working Together*, for carrying out such reviews. More information about the work of ACPCs can be found on the Department of Health web site at **www.doh.gov.uk/acpc**.

Child protection register

The function of the child protection register
The ACPC will monitor the information that comes from the child protection register (known variously as the 'at risk register' or often 'the abuse register'). The function of this register is often misunderstood. It is essentially a management tool that records the fact that a child has been or is suspected of being abused or is believed to be at risk of being abused. It can also be used to record the names of suspected/known abusers. It should serve to 'ring alarm bells' when a professional faced with a new situation of proved or suspected child abuse consults the register on a later occasion. It will give them the details of previous incidents and inform them who are the professionals currently involved so that a full and adequate investigation can be carried out.

It is not a 'legal' document—it has no statutory force and of itself offers no 'real' protection. The mere act of placing a child's name on the protection register does not give any agency the legal grounds to take any action in relation to that child.

Maintaining the register
The maintaining of the register is normally carried out by a designated officer within the social services department, although in some parts of the country this function is carried out by the NSPCC. Access to the register is restricted to those professionals who are offering services direct to the child. There must be careful control over access to the information since there will normally be little or no judicial check on what the register contains.

Entries on the child protection register
Although the register is not a statutory device, the placing of a person's name on the register is capable of being reviewed, in exceptional circumstances, by the courts. In *R v Norfolk County Council ex parte M* (1989), it was suspected that a plumber who had visited a child's house had indecently assaulted her and exposed himself to her. The case conference decided that his name should go on the register and that his employers should be told. He successfully claimed that there had been no adequate investigation and that it was an abuse of process, in those particular circumstances, to place his name on the register as the abuser. (See chapters 2 and 6 for more discussion about the rights issues and the evidential processes by which the decision to make an entry may be affected.)

Interests of the adult are secondary to the interests of the child
Against this should be placed the decision in *R v Harrow London Borough Council ex parte D* (1990), where the mother of children who were placed on the register sought judicial review of that decision. She complained that she had not had the chance to know

the allegation against her even though she had made a written submission to the conference. The Court of Appeal refused to grant a judicial review. It held that in the circumstances of the case the council had to act fairly: 'In balancing the adequate protection for the child and fairness for the adult, the interest of the adult may have to be placed second to the needs of the child'. Whilst approving the *Harrow* decision in the *Norfolk* case, the court pointed out that the main failing there had been the informing of the employer, rather than, necessarily, placing the names on a register. Accordingly, every time, a decision to place a person's name on the register should be taken only after careful consideration.

Well-founded allegations

In *R v Lewisham London Borough* (1991), the court held that where unproved allegations of sexual abuse were made against a foster parent, the authority must not adopt a policy of telling all future foster parents of the children who had been fostered that he was a sexual abuser. The council had to weigh in each case the interests of the children against the harm done to the foster parent. This again points to an approach of carefully checking all facts and making careful decisions about their disclosure. The results would have been different if the allegations were well founded and the social workers acted in good faith (*R v Devon County Council ex parte L* (1991)).

Complaints procedures

In *R v Hampshire CC ex parte H* (1999), the Court of Appeal pointed out that while judicial review could be available in respect of decisions of child protection conferences, it would be rare for it to be the appropriate procedure, complaints procedures being more apt. However, the Court stressed the need for evidence to justify entering a name on the child protection register.

Current information on child protection registers

Statistical information about children on child protection registers is available for England at **www.dfes.gov.uk/rsgateway/DB/VOL/v000444/index.shtml** and for Wales at **www.wales.gov.uk/keypubstatisticsforwalesheadline**. As at March 2004, there were around 26,300 children on child protection registers in England, with slightly more boys than girls. Neglect was the most common reason for both boys and girls to be placed on the register.

Child protection conference

Dual purpose

The child protection conference is the basic instrument of the case-by-case child protection system. It has a dual purpose: (i) to make judgements about the likelihood of a child suffering significant harm in the future; and (ii) to decide whether future action is needed to safeguard the child and promote his or her welfare, how that action will be taken forward, and with what intended consequences. It is at the child protection conference that the investigative process and the planning process for children coincide.

Multi-disciplinary forum

The child protection conference is the forum in which the multi-disciplinary consideration of a child seen to be 'at risk' takes place. It is multi-disciplinary since at the conference there will (or should) be representatives from all the agencies who have dealings with the child or the child's family. Its central role and its relationship with the other structures and legal obligations of the local authority in the protection of children are made clear in diagrammatic form in Appendix 5 of *Working Together*, reproduced at the end of this chapter.

Calling the conference

Calling the conference will be the direct responsibility of the social services department or the NSPCC, both of which have statutory powers. The initial conference should be called only after an investigation under s. 47 of the Children Act 1989. Any other agency involved with the child should have its request for a conference dealt with as soon as possible.

Attendance

Paragraph 5.55 of *Working Together* suggests a list of possible attenders at the initial child protection conference. The list is set out in Box 11.14.

The ACPC protocol

The relevant ACPC protocol should specify a required quorum for attendance and list who should be invited to attend. Accordingly, the child protection conference may well have an average attendance of ten, and on some occasions can have over twenty people present. Those attending should be there because they have a significant contribution to make, either because of professional expertise or from knowledge of the family, or both.

Involving the child, the parents and other family members

Parents used to be systematically barred from child protection conferences and review meetings. The reason often given was that the people present would be inhibited

---

 BOX 11.14 Possible attenders at the initial child protection conference

- Family members (including the wider family);
- Social services staff who have undertaken an assessment of the child and family;
- Foster carers (current or former);
- Professionals involved with the child (e.g. health visitors, midwife, school nurse, children's guardian, paediatrician, education staff, early years staff, the GP);
- Those involved in inquiries (e.g. the police);
- Local authority legal services (child care);
- NSPCC or other involved voluntary organizations;
- A representative of the armed services, in cases where there is a service connection.

from talking frankly. This was challenged, and the decisions of the European Court of Human Rights on the failure of local authorities to involve parents in the decision-making process were partly responsible for the changes in practice and procedure. Best practice is explained in paras. 5.57 and 5.58 of *Working Together* set out in Box 11.15.

Complaints by family members

Parents and others can use the complaints procedure (see chapter 10) if they feel they have not been treated properly by the conference. They may also, in more limited

---

 BOX 11.15 Involving the child and family members—*Working Together*

5.57 Before a conference is held, the purpose of a conference, who will attend, and the way in which it will operate, should always be explained to a child of sufficient age and understanding, and to the parents and involved family members. The parents should normally be invited to attend the conference and helped fully to participate. Social services should give parents information about local advice and advocacy agencies, and explain that they may bring an advocate, friend or supporter. The child, subject to consideration about age and understanding should be given the opportunity to attend if s/he wishes, and to bring an advocate, friend or supporter. Where the child's attendance is neither desired by him/her nor appropriate, the social services professional who is working most closely with the child should ascertain what his/her wishes and feelings are, and make these know to the conference.

5.58 The involvement of family members should be planned carefully. It may not always be possible to involve all family members at all times in the conference, for example, if one parent is the alleged abuser or if there is a high level of conflict between family members. Adults and any children who wish to make representations to the conference may not wish to speak in front of one another. Exceptionally, it may be necessary to exclude one or more family members from a conference, in whole or in part. The conference is primarily about the child, and while the presence of the family is normally welcome, those professionals attending must be able to share information in a safe and non-threatening environment. Professionals may themselves have concerns about violence or intimidation, which should be communicated in advance to the conference chair. ACPC procedures should set out criteria for excluding a parent or carer, including the evidence required. A strong risk of violence or intimidation by a family member at or subsequent to the conference towards a child or anybody else might be one reason for exclusion. The possibility that a parent/carer may be prosecuted for an offence against a child is not in itself a reason for exclusion although in these circumstances the chair should take advice from the police about any implications arising from an alleged perpetrator's attendance. If criminal proceedings have been instigated the view of the Crown Prosecution Service should be taken into account. The decision to exclude a parent or carer from the child protection conference rests with the chair of the conference, acting within ACPC procedures. If the parents are excluded or are unable or unwilling to attend a child protection conference, they should be enabled to communicate their views to the conference by another means.

circumstances, use judicial review procedures or challenges under the Human Rights Act 1998. Clear, fair, and transparent procedures are obviously vital.

In *Scott v UK* (2000), the European Court of Human Rights held that there had been no breach of the mother's rights under Article 8 of the Convention when a local authority decided that, as a result of her continued alcohol problems, it would no longer plan to rehabilitate her with her child, despite her exclusion from the meeting where that decision was made. The court took a broad view of the decision-making process. While the mother had not been present at the actual meeting when the decision against rehabilitation was made, she had been involved in the overall planning process. The more you can involve the parents, the better the general process of decision making is seen to be. In this way an individual procedural error can be remedied and human rights litigation avoided. Of course, parental involvement is important not just for human rights reasons, but also because participation increases the prospects of a successful intervention.

Confidentiality of child protection conference/reviews

All discussions that take place within the child protection conference or review are intended to be confidential. Without total confidentiality the professionals attending will be unable to share frankly all their information and concerns. All professionals involved in child protection, including medical practitioners, have been informed by their appropriate professional bodies that their duty of confidentiality to their client/ patient is overridden by their duty to contribute to the protection of a child at risk. Thus, at a child protection conference or review, there should be no difficulties about a frank exchange. *Working Together* provides useful guidance on sharing information which is set out in Box 11.16.

 BOX 11.16 Sharing information

7.27 Research and experience have shown repeatedly that keeping children safe from harm requires professionals and others to share information; about a child's health and development and exposure to possible harm; about a parent who may need help to, or may not be able to, care for a child adequately and safely; and about those who may pose a risk of harm to a child. Often, it is only when information from a number of sources has been shared and is then put together that it becomes clear that a child is at risk of or is suffering harm.

7.28 Those providing services to adults and children will be concerned about the need to balance their duties to protect children from harm and their general duty towards their patient or service user. Some professionals and staff face the added dimension of being involved in caring for, or supporting, more than one family member—the abused child, siblings, an alleged abuser. Where there are concerns that a child is, or may be at risk of significant harm, however, the needs of that child must come first. In these circumstances *the overriding objective must be to safeguard the child* [emphasis added].

In *Re M (A Minor) (Disclosure of Material)* (1990), the court specifically excluded the records of the child protection conference from a general duty to disclose information to the parties to court proceedings. The court said:

> Case conferences bring together people of different disciplines from the local community to discuss the protection and welfare of a child. . . . For them also the disclosure of the contributions made at a case conference and recorded may have adverse results and the possibility of such disclosure may even inhibit some from attending, an effect which could only be to the detriment of children in the community. Such records ought not to be lightly exposed to general scrutiny and the work for children jeopardised without careful and cogent reasons for their disclosure.

See chapter 4 for a more extensive discussion on confidentiality.

Action and decisions for the conference

If a child is at continuing risk of significant harm the child protection conference must take a number of actions.

First, the child protection conference will look at the child in question and recommend at the initial conference whether the child's name should be placed on the child protection register. The entry of a name can be in various categories, depending on whether or not abuse is known or suspected and whether the abuse is physical, sexual, emotional, or neglect. The classifications are made for management purposes to give an overview of trends, if any.

The registration of a child's name should be accompanied by a child protection plan. The child protection conference agrees the child protection plan in outline.

The outline child protection plan

Working Together sets out the functions of the outline child protection plan in para. 5.69 which is set out in Box 11.17.

Local authority responsibilities

The child protection conference does not decide whether any statutory proceedings should commence in relation to a particular child. The conference can make a

---

 BOX 11.17 The outline child protection plan

5.69 The outline child protection plan should:

- Identify risks of significant harm to the child and ways in which the child can be protected through an inter-agency plan based on assessment findings;
- Establish short-term and longer term aims and objectives that are clearly linked to reducing the risk of harm to the child and promoting the child's welfare;
- Be clear about who will have responsibility for what actions—including actions by family members—within what specified timescales; and
- Outline ways of monitoring and evaluating progress against the plan.

recommendation that proceedings are commenced but the responsibility for the actual decision and the commencing of the proceedings lies squarely with the local authority. It is conceivable for a local authority, having considered the recommendation of the child protection conference, to decide to reject the recommendations and not to commence proceedings. This would have to be when the local authority is satisfied that the child's welfare can be satisfactorily safeguarded without proceedings being commenced, in accordance with the Children Act 1989, s. 47(6). The same is true in relation to the placing of the child's name on the register. It must be stressed that not to follow the recommendation of the case conference would be wholly exceptional.

Police and Crown Prosecution responsibilities

A similar situation exists in relation to a decision to prosecute for a criminal offence arising out of the abuse of a child. The decision to prosecute or not should be taken in consultation with the child protection conference. Nevertheless, the responsibility will still rest with the police and then with the Crown Prosecution Service.

The key worker

The child protection conference, once it has decided that a child's name is placed on the register, will require that a key worker be appointed. The key worker is then required to draw up a plan that will address the concerns that have led to the child's name being placed on the register. The key worker will be either a local authority social worker or an NSPCC social worker. The role of the key worker is set out in paras. 5.75 and 5.76 of *Working Together*, detailed in Box 11.18.

The Core group

Whilst at the early stages the child protection conference may need to be quite large, *Working Together* advises the appointment of a 'core group' once long-term planning has

---

 BOX 11.18 The role of the key worker

5.75 When a conference decides that a child's name should be placed on the child protection register, one of the child care agencies with statutory powers (the social services department or the NSPCC) should carry future child care responsibility for the case and designate a member of its social work staff to be the key worker. Each child placed on the child protection register should have a named key worker.

5.76 The key worker is responsible for making sure that the outline child protection plan is developed into a more detailed inter-agency plan. S/he should complete the core assessment of the child and family, securing contributions from Core Group members and others as necessary. The key worker is also responsible for acting as lead worker for the inter-agency work with the child and family. S/he should coordinate the contribution of family members and other agencies to planning the actions which need to be taken, putting the child protection plan into effect, and reviewing progress against the objectives set out in the plan. It is important that the role of the key worker is fully explained at the initial child protection conference and at the core group.

been formulated. This group includes the key worker and should work to implement and review the plan. Any major changes such as deregistration of the child should be taken back to the child protection conference. The core group can provide a much less intimidating forum for children and parents to work with the authority.

Care plans

Planning for children

The case study at the beginning of this chapter demonstrates the problems caused by inadequate planning or failure to implement agreed plans. Effective planning for children should be a major focus of activity for social work. In the report of the *Victoria Climbié* inquiry, Lord Laming recommended that the focus of the case conference should be on establishing an agreed plan to safeguard and promote the welfare of the particular child—see Recommendation 13. The key worker supported by the core group should work to implement and review the plan for the child which was outlined by the case conference. As we have made clear already in this chapter, *Working Together* puts a great deal of emphasis on the care plan.

All children should be planned for

Good care plans should be prepared for all children looked after by the local authority. There is extensive advice available on good care plans. Chapter 2 in volume 2 of *Regulations and Guidance* provides information about the planning process for children's placements. The guidance identifies four stages: inquiry, consultation, assessment, and decision making. This volume gives excellent suggestions and a checklist of whom to involve in the planning process and how to carry it out. The guidelines set out in the Children Act 1989 *Regulations and Guidance*, Vol. 3, 'Family Placements', at paras. 2.43–2.62, apply to children who are accommodated and to statutory reviews. Paragraph 2.62 sets out the key elements, which we have reproduced in Box 11.19.

Assessment

In every case, the process of assessment of the case should be undertaken on a continuing basis. Assessment is a normal part of good social work practice. The Social Services Inspectorate in its report, *Someone Else's Children*, found that it was often only in cases involving court proceedings that there was evidence of care plans being properly prepared. Some of their comments are reproduced in Box 11.20.

Care plans for court

Local Authority Circular, LAC (99) 29, 'Care Plans and Care Proceedings under the Children Act 1989', sets out guidelines for the preparation of plans for court cases. The guidance is important and can be obtained from the Department of Health (tel. 0541 555 455) and on the DoH web site **www.open.gov.uk/doh.** The guidance advises setting out the contents of care plans in five sections:

• overall aim;

• child's needs, including contact;

• views of others;

BOX 11.19 Key elements of care plans

- the child's identified needs (including needs arising from race, culture, religion or language, special educational or health needs);
- how those needs may be met;
- aim of plan and timescale;
- proposed placement (type and details);
- other services to be provided to the child and/or family either by the local authority or other agencies;
- arrangements for contact and reunification;
- support in the placement;
- likely duration of the placement in accommodation;
- contingency plan, if the placement breaks down;
- arrangements for ending the placement (if made under voluntary arrangement);
- who is to be responsible for implementing the plan (specific tasks and overall plan);

  the extent to which the wishes and views of the child, his parents, and anyone else with a sufficient interest in the child (including representatives of other agencies) have been obtained and acted upon and the reasons supporting this or explanations of why wishes/ views have been discounted;
- arrangements for notifying the responsible authority of disagreements or making representations;
- arrangements for health care (including consent to examination and treatment);
- arrangements for education; and
- date of reviews.

BOX 11.20 Some observations from *Someone Else's Children*

As with previous child care inspection our consistent finding was that assessment practice was more structured and coherent where there had been child protection investigations or court proceedings. (7.4)

Although most children looked after had care plans which they were aware of and felt involved in the production of, the quality of the plans were variable, frequently short term and often rather sketchy. (8.16)

. . . We saw some evidence to suggest that social workers were beginning to see assessment as a separate task to be specially commissioned outside of the normal social worker's normal job. (7.3)

- placement details and timetable; and

- management and support by local authority.

The circular also points out that care plans need to be signed by senior managers to ensure accountability and authority-wide commitment.

In *Re CD and MD (Care Proceedings: Practice)* (1998) Bracewell J recommended that the handbook *Best Practice in Children Act Cases*, issued by the Children Act Advisory Committee in June 1997, should be consulted by all those involved in decision making in care proceedings, in preparing for court. In this case her Ladyship criticized the local authority for reacting to events with the family instead of having clear goals and expectations.

Parents

Local authorities are urged to bear in mind the principles underpinning Article 8 of the European Convention for the Protection of Human Rights, and consultation with parents is emphasized. The guidelines stress the need fully to consider contact (a requirement under s. 34(11) of the Children Act).

Working with your lawyer

The local authority lawyer's role in the preparation of cases for court has been transformed by the protocol for judicial case management of public law Children Act cases which came into force on 1 November 2003. The protocol is designed to improve the outcomes for children by reducing unnecessary delay in public law Children Act cases by achieving the completion of all cases within an overall timetable of not more than 40 weeks (save in exceptional or unforeseen circumstances). LAC (2004) 1 issued under s. 7 of LASSA provides guidance for local authorities on the implementation of the protocol which it points out should be read in conjunction with LAC(99)29.

Paragraph 7 of the guidance states:

> The protocol has been produced to assist all participants in the process (including judges, magistrates, lawyers, guardians, social workers, and other experts) by providing them with a common, timed framework for the case management of every case at every stage and every level. To this end, it sets out the '6 Steps' that every Public Law Children Act Case should go through and includes guidance on the documentation for the conduct of each of the steps. As is apparent, the protocol does not radically change the procedure (no rule changes are required), rather it seeks to distil and streamline the process to its essentials and change the culture within which the proceedings takes place.

The guidance reminds local authorities 'that undertaking core assessments when required by the *Framework for the Assessment of Children in Need and their Families* (Department of Health, et al 2000) and within the required timescales, in order to evidence the care plan presented in the proceedings, is key to reducing delay' (para. 12) and that 'early work around reducing delay and implementing the protocol has identified the key role that pre-planning plays in avoiding delay in care cases. This early planning allows issues to be identified and addressed prior to the application being made to the court and in particular helps to avoid the need for additional assessments to be undertaken later in the process and the associated delay. Successful use of pre-planning relies on effective joint working between local authority legal services and social workers' (para. 15).

The protocol provides extensive information about how cases are to be managed and you will learn a lot from reading it closely. It is available on the Web at **www.courtservice.gov.uk/using_courts/protocol/**. Perhaps what is most important for you to be aware of in detail is the expectation of the court in terms of document preparation at the stage of application for an order. We have copied that part of the protocol for your information at Figure 2. Note in particular the requirement for a social work statement and a social work chronology. The other part of the protocol which you will find particularly useful is appendix F: Social Services Assessment and Care Planning Aide-Memoire which summarises the various requirements for action at every stage from initial referral.

STEP 1: The Application

Objective   Target time: by DAY 3

To provide sufficient information about the Local Authority's (LA) case to enable:

* The parties and the Court to identify the issues
* The Court to make early welfare and case management decisions about the child.

LA Application   on DAY 1

When a decision is made to apply for a care or supervision order the LA shall:

* File with the Court an application in **form C1**
* Set out in **form C13** under 'Reasons' summary of all facts and matters relied upon in particular, those necessary to satisfy the threshold criteria and/or
* Refer in the Reasons to any annexed schedules setting out the facts and matters relied upon
* Not state that the Reasons are those contained in the evidence filed or to be filed.

Directions on issue   on DAY 1

On the day the application is filed (**DAY 1**) the Court shall:

* Issue the application
* Issue a notice in **form C6** to the LA fixing a time and a date for the First Hearing which shall be not later than on **DAY 6**
* Appoint a Guardian (unless satisfied that it is not necessary to do so to safeguard the child's interests)
* Inform CAFCASS of the decision to appoint and the request to allocate a Guardian.

Allocation of the Guardian by CAFCASS   by DAY 3

Within **2 days** of issue (by **DAY 3**) **CAFCASS** shall inform the court of:

- The name of the allocated Guardian or
- The likely date upon which an allocation will be made.

Appointment of the Solicitor for the Child   on DAY 3

When a Guardian is allocated by **Guardian** shall on that day:

- Appoint a solicitor for the child
- Inform the Court of the name of the solicitor appointed
- In the event that the Guardian's allocation is delayed and the Court has already appointed a solicitor, ensure that effective legal representation is maintained.

Where a Guardian is not allocated within **2 days** of issue, the **Court** shall on **DAY 3**:

- Consider when a Guardian will be allocated
- Decide whether to appoint a solicitor for the child.

In any event on the day the appointment is made the Court shall on **DAY 3**:

- Notify all parties on **form C46** of the names of the Guardian and/or the solicitor for the child who have been appointed.

LA documents   by DAY 3

Within **2 days** of issue (by **DAY 3**) the **LA** shall file and serve on all parties, the solicitor for the child and CAFCASS the following documents:

- The **forms C1 and C13** and any supplementary forms and notices issued by the Court
- Any relevant **court orders** relating to the child (together with the relevant Justices Facts and Reasons in **form C22** and any relevant **judgments** that exist)
- The **initial social work statement (appendix B/3)**
- The **social work chronology (appendix B/2)**
- The **core or initial assessment** reports (**appendix F**)
- Any **section 37 report**
- Any other **additional evidence** including specialist assessments or reports which then exist and which are relied upon by the LA.

EXERCISES

Consider the following evolving scenario and then answer the questions arising.

Mary, the 6-year-old child of Tom and Ann, was found at school with a series of dark bruises on her back. She was examined by a paediatrician who said that they were the result of being hit and that there were some additional fingertip bruises on her arm. Mary said her dad had hit her. When questioned, Tom denies hitting Mary. Ann, whilst not saying what happened, talks about Tom's drinking and problems in the marriage. There are financial difficulties and the family want to be rehoused. There is a new baby, Peter, who is 3 months old. Ann appears to be finding coping a strain. Your initial conclusion (which may only be an instinctive feeling) is that the current pressures faced by the family are responsible for the situation in which Tom takes out his frustrations by hitting Mary.

1 What further enquiries would you make?

2 What, if any, statutory duties arise?

You discuss the case with colleagues, there is a child protection case conference.

3 Who would you expect to be present at the case conference?

4 What questions need to be decided at the initial case conference?

The case conference decides to register Mary. You are the key worker.

5 How would you explain that decision to Tom and Ann?

6 Who would you expect to be in your core group?

The social services department decides that you need a court order to protect Mary. You think that Mary and Peter should in the long term remain with Tom and Ann. This view is accepted. At some stage you hope that the department will have to have only minimal involvement.

7 Outline your statutory responsibilities to prepare a plan?

8 What are the key elements of the care plan?

COMPANION WEB SITE

 For guidance on how to answer these exercises, visit the companion web site at: www.oup.com/uk/booksites/law

WHERE DO WE GO FROM HERE?

You have read in this chapter an account of the structures which are designed to protect children. They rely on effective cooperation and clear understanding of roles. You also know something of the process of responding to concerns about particular children, and the need to move from investigation of possible abuse to starting the planning process which is necessary for the future welfare of a child. You have seen how investigations and planning prepare the social worker for a potential court application. Our next chapter sets out the law underpinning the range of court orders available to protect children. Remember, successful outcomes from court applications rely on the work the social worker has already carried out, investigating the case and planning for the child.

Planning

J. Hann and M. Owen, 'The Implementation of Care Plans and its Relationship to Children's Welfare' (2003) 15(1) Child and Family Law Quarterly 71.

An interesting piece of research into what constitutes a good or bad care plan.

Official guidance on planning and reporting

Reporting to the Court under the Children Act, a Handbook for Social Services (HMSO, 1996).

Children Act Advisory Committee, *Handbook of Best Practice in Children Act Cases* (HMSO, 1996).

A critical commentary on the case study at the beginning is provided by N. Mole, a leading human rights lawyer, in *Re W & B, RE W (Care Plans) and Re S (Minors) (Care Order: Implementation of Care Plan) Re W (Minors) (Care Order: Adequacy of Care Plan)*. A note on the judgment from the perspective of the European Convention for Protection of Human Rights and Fundamental Freedoms is in (2002) 14 Child and Family Law Quarterly 447.

Investigating child abuse

R. Smith, 'The Wrong End of the Telescope: Child Protection or Child Safety' (2000) (24)(3) J of SW & FL 247. This article provides a critique of the narrow focus and limited aspirations of *Working Together to Safeguard Children*.

B. Corby 'Towards a new means of inquiry into child abuse cases 2004 vol 25 no. 3 J of SWL 229. This article suggests there should be a more realistic approach to child protection cases.

The protocol for Judicial Case Management in Public Law Children Act cases

P. Cooper, A new Protocol for Care Cases

This article is on the web at **www.city.ac.uk/icsl/dps**

It is a full explanation of the operation of the protocol designed for solicitors and barristers but very useful for social workers.

T. Hale, Public Law Children Act cases: is the protocol for judicial case management working?

Another article on the web at **www.lawzone.thelawyer.com**

Hale, a solicitor in private practice, is sceptical about the effectiveness of the Protocol.

<table>
<tr><td>12</td><td>**Child protection—court applications**</td></tr>
</table>

CASE STUDY

LU (A Child) and LB (A Child) [2004] EWCA Civ 567

Facts

The child LU, born in 2001, suffered a series of breathing problems during 2001 whilst alone with the mother. On each occasion the child was admitted to hospital. Once in hospital checks were done and the child was not found to be suffering from any disease or illness. The mother, who was very young, took an overdose during this time and was assessed by her health visitor as suffering from post-natal depression.

The issue before the judge was whether the evidence established to the satisfaction of the court on the balance of probabilities that the threshold set by s. 31 of the Children Act 1989 had been crossed. He found that the 'combination of medical evidence, the lack of credibility of the mother and the stresses to which she was subject all compel me to a finding that, . . . this mother has on four occasions . . . deliberately obstructed the upper airway of [LU] thereby causing her harm which involved hospital admissions and invasive investigation'.

The child LB was born in October 1999 with certain disabilities. Prior to the birth the mother was suffering from depression for which she received medication. LB was admitted to hospital on several occasions in her first year for failing to thrive. Once in hospital she put on weight. The mother was depressed, suicidal, and described the baby as a devil. However, gradually the mother's mental health improved and social services closed the case file in May 2001. Then, in September 2001 LB was admitted as an in-patient. During six days in hospital she suffered eleven episodes of rigor with potentially life-threatening consequences.

The judge found that the mother had been present or nearby on each of the eleven occasions when the child suffered rigors. She also found the mother to be an 'unimpressive witness who did not tell the truth about many aspects'.

The two cases were heard together by the Court of Appeal. The Court was faced with issues which had been raised in previous Court of Appeal decisions. One of these in particular is likely to be familiar to you—*R v Cannings* (2004) where a mother's conviction for the murder of her child was overturned on appeal because of uncertainties about the medical evidence. The other Court of Appeal decisions related to the higher standard of proof required for the imposition of anti-social behaviour orders and sex offenders order.

The Court of Appeal refused the mother permission to appeal in LU and dismissed the appeal of the mother in LB. It reasserted that the standard of proof in child protection cases remains the balance of probabilities test set out in *Re H (Minors) (Sexual Abuse: Standard of Proof)* (1996) which we discuss below. The Court made it clear that the responsibilities of local authorities under the Children Act 1989 had not been changed by the decision in *Cannings* and it remained their task to protect the child, to assess the issues within their competence and expertise, to rely upon their legal team to advise on the strength and credibility of the medical evidence and to continue to prepare applications for care orders based upon the civil standard of proof.

The Court of Appeal have therefore given a clear steer to the courts about the overwhelming importance of the protection of children when making decisions about the likelihood or not of parents inflicting injuries upon a child. It suggested that the care proceedings were a 'prelude to a further and fuller investigation of a range of choices in search of the protection and welfare of the children. A positive finding against a parent or both parents does not in itself preclude the possibility of rehabilitation. All depends on the facts and circumstances of the individual case. In that context the consequences of a false positive finding in care proceedings may not be as dire as the consequences of the conviction of an innocent in criminal proceedings' (Butler Sloss LJ, at para. 27).

As you work through this chapter notice how the legislation and the case law attempt to strike a balance between the need to protect children and the rights of individuals to a family life. The legislation sets out checks and balances on the responsibilities of the state. The courts supervise the state intervention, ensuring that it provides appropriate protection for children, but preventing intervention which oversteps the boundaries set by Parliament.

OVERVIEW AND OBJECTIVES

This chapter is concerned with Parts 4 and 5 of the Children Act 1989. Part 4 deals with care and supervision. Part 5 is concerned with child protection. These parts of the Act contain the compulsory orders which require in general an application to a court. The exception to this requirement is the power of the police to remove a child to a place of safety under s. 46 of the Act. It is the courts which ensure that local authority action is legitimate. Legitimacy requires that the statutory provisions are observed and that the protections provided by the Human Rights Act are maintained. A key concept which justifies compulsory intervention in family life and which underpins both Part 4 and Part 5 of the Act is *significant harm* which we will discuss at length in this chapter. We will start the chapter by providing a summary of the range of orders available under the Children Act 1989. We will then describe the longer term orders available under Part 4 of the Act—care orders and supervision orders—before turning to the short-term orders contained in Part 5.

Court orders cannot of course be considered separately from the process of protecting children. They need to be considered as part of the investigation, assessment and planning process. They can also not be separated from case management and you need to be aware of the protocol for judicial case management in public law Children Act cases which we discuss in chapter 11. However, in this chapter we are primarily concerned with the legal characteristics of court orders.

As we set out the requirements and effects of each order, compare and contrast these. Which orders are easier to obtain? What impact does the order have on the parent(s)' parental responsibility? What constraints are there on the powers of the local authority? Why is s. 46 an exception to the general requirement of supervision by the courts?

All statutory references in this chapter are to the Children Act 1989, unless otherwise stated. The rules referred to are the Court Rules applicable to either the magistrates' court or county court or High Court, as explained.

The range of court orders and powers

The full range of orders and powers available under Parts 4 and 5 of the Act is set out in summary tabular form in Box 12.1 opposite.

Long-term orders for the protection of children

Care and supervision orders

Care orders and supervision orders are orders which are available to provide for the long-term welfare of the child. Care and supervision orders require exactly the same grounds to have been proved to the court. The difference between the two orders concerns control over the child involved. The court decides, in the case of a care order, that the local authority needs to have effective parental control over the child. This need not necessarily involve the removal of the child from home. A care order gives the local authority the power to protect a child through acquisition of parental responsibility. That may involve removing the child, but equally it can and does permit the child to be left at home. A supervision order puts the child under the supervision of a social worker or probation officer. If the court makes a supervision order the child will not normally be removed from home, although there are powers to direct the child to live at a specified address for a limited period. Supervision orders are less intrusive, and if the balance between a care order and a supervision order is equal, the court should adopt the least interventionist and most proportionate approach.

Intervention must be proportionate

This was made clear by the Court of Appeal in *Re O (Supervision Order)* [2001] EWCA Civ 16, [2001] 1 FLR 923. The Court of Appeal considered the relationship between a care order and a supervision order in the light of the need for intervention to be proportionate to the risk to the child, as required by the Human Rights Act 1998. In the particular case the risk was felt by the Court to be at the low end of the scale, and that provided the parents cooperated and the local authority delivered the necessary range of services to protect the child, a supervision order (rather than the care order requested by the local authority) was appropriate. The Court indicated that previous case law was not necessarily helpful on this distinction, as each case has to be decided on its own facts and the requirements of the Human Rights Act 1998 must be considered.

Therefore, the actual decision as to which type of order the court will make will depend on how serious the court considers the case to be. To this end the social worker can make recommendations to assist the court.

Care orders

7,387 care orders were made in 2003 compared to 6,335 in 2002 (Children Act Report 2003).

To restate a principle from chapter 9 the only way in which a child may be 'in care'

BOX 12.1 The range of orders and powers in Parts 4 & 5

Order/Power	Section	Comment
Care Order	s. 33	A long-term order which commits the child to the care of the local authority. It provides extensive powers to local authorities but requires evidence which demonstrates to the court that a child is suffering, or likely to suffer, significant harm and that the harm or likelihood of harm is attributable to a lack of adequate parental care or control.
Supervision Order	s. 35	An order which places the child under the supervision of a social worker or probation officer. The grounds upon which an order can be made are identical to the care order.
Interim Care/Supervision Order	s. 38	Orders made pending a full hearing of the application for a care order. An initial interim order cannot last longer than 8 weeks. Subsequent interim orders cannot last longer than 4 weeks.
Emergency Protection Order	s. 44	A short-term order which either removes the child on a short-term basis, or allows the child to be kept in a place of safety or requires an alleged abuser to leave the family home. The grounds for the emergency protection order are much easier to prove but successful applicants gain limited powers.
Child Assessment Order	s. 43	A short-term order (maximum 7 days) which provides for the compulsory assessment of the child's state of health and development.
Removal and Accommodation of Children by Police	s. 46	No court order is necessary for the police to implement this power which enables the police to remove a child or to keep a child in a safe place.
Child Recovery Order	s. 49	Enables the return of the child to a 'responsible person'.

under the Children Act 1989 is by an application for a care order being made to the court and the court granting the care order. Without a care order the child is not 'in care'.

Why apply for a care order?

A care order should be applied for only when the principle of the diminishment of the need for court proceedings has been tried or considered and been found to be unsuccessful or inapplicable. This means that the alternatives to care we set out in chapter 10—the support for the family in cash or otherwise or alternative forms of accommodation—have been considered. If no other course of action is suitable there is a duty, under s. 47 of the Children Act, to commence care proceedings if this is the appropriate way to promote and safeguard the welfare of the child. Do not allow confusion over the 'no order' principle, which we discussed in chapter 9 to obscure the need to seek care or supervision orders in appropriate cases.

Applications

Section 31(1) of the 1989 Act determines who may apply for a care order: Box 12.2 sets out the subsection.

You will see that a distinction is made between the application, which can be made by *any* local authority or the NSPCC, and the actual care order which is made to a *designated* authority. The purpose of this is to ensure that the local authority close to the children concerned has the long term responsibility for managing and implementing the care plan. The designated local authority is defined in s. 31(8) of the Children Act 1989 as the local authority where the child is ordinarily resident or where the child does not reside in the area of a local authority, the authority within whose area any circumstances arose in consequence of which the order is made. Periods spent in accommodation provided by or on behalf of a local authority are disregarded in determining 'ordinarily resident' (s.105(6). In *Re H (Care Order: Appropriate Local Authority)* (2003) the Court of Appeal decided that time where the child is accommodated by a family member at the behest of the local authority should count in deciding in which local authority a child is ordinarily resident.

The grounds for a care order

These are contained in s. 31(2) set out in Box 12.3.

These grounds are known as the 'threshold criteria' since they set out the minimum criteria which should exist before there is justification for the court even to contemplate

---

BOX 12.2 Section 31(1) of the Children Act

(1) On the application of any local authority or authorised person [only the NSPCC is authorized], the court may make an order—

    (a) placing the child with respect to whom the application is made in the care of a designated local authority; or

    (b) putting the child under the supervision of a designated local authority or a probation officer.

BOX 12.3 Section 31(2)—the grounds for a care order

(2) A court may only make a care order or supervision order if it is satisfied—

    (a) that the child concerned is suffering, or is likely to suffer, significant harm; and

    (b) that the harm, or likelihood of harm, is attributable to—
        (i) the care given to the child, or likely to be given to him if the order were not made, not being what it would be reasonable to expect a parent to give to him; or
        (ii) the child's being beyond parental control.

compulsory intervention in family life. The court need go on to apply the welfare principles contained in s. 1 only if it is satisfied that the threshold criteria apply.

Significant harm

The key phrase within s. 31(2) is significant harm. What does this mean? What is 'significant' in relation to 'significant harm'. On this the Act is silent. The High Court and the Court of Appeal have decided that the meaning of significant is not a question of law. Whether harm is significant is a matter for the court to decide as a question of fact.

A two-stage process

In *Humberside County Council v B* (1993), Booth J heard a case in which the mother and father were both diagnosed as suffering from schizophrenia. The child involved was six months old at the time of the High Court hearing. Whilst the baby was developing well, there were occasions when she was left unattended. When an aunt was looking after the baby she found her to have bruising on her arms and thighs. A paediatrician had concluded that this was consistent with non-accidental injury. The local authority was granted an interim care order, and thus the magistrates were satisfied that there was a likelihood of significant harm. On appeal the High Court was asked to rule that the harm suffered by the baby was not significant. The judge formulated a two-stage process that the courts have to go through:

> So it can be seen that the definition of harm is a very wide one. [T]he local authority has submitted that the question whether or not a child is suffering or likely to suffer significant harm is a question of factual proof as to which the welfare of the child is not relevant: that submission I accept . . .
>
>   The court, on being satisfied as to the criteria, is then required to have regard to the welfare of the child, and to the matters set out in s. 1 of the Act. In my judgment it is at that stage that the court is determining a question with respect to the upbringing of the child so that the welfare of the child must be the court's paramount consideration. . . . It follows therefore in my judgment that the court has to follow a *two-stage process* in determining whether or not to make a care or supervision order. The *first stage* is to determine whether or not the significant harm test in s. 31(2) is satisfied. If it accepts that as a matter of factual proof, and the criterion is satisfied, then the court must go on to the *second stage* where it must consider whether or not to make an order, and at that stage it must apply the provisions of s. 1 of the 1989 Act. The court is not confined in those circumstances to making a care or supervision order . . . [s.] 1(3)(g) requires the court to consider the range of its powers under the Act . . .

Where the justices fell into error [which was the granting of the interim order] . . . was to confuse the welfare considerations under s. 1 with their findings as to the likelihood of significant harm which . . . is a matter of factual proof. Having been satisfied as to that criterion on the evidence before them, it was then for the justices to consider whether or not to make an order. In relation to that, it was incumbent upon them . . . to consider all the circumstances of the case including the nature of significant harm which they considered would be likely that [the baby] would suffer, in relation to all matters under s. 1 of the Act including the harm which she would be likely to suffer by the continuing separation from the parents [emphasis added].'

To clarify, in considering an application for a care or supervision order, a court must:

(a) be satisfied that the grounds in s. 31 (the threshold criteria) are met; and

(b) decide whether, by applying the grounds in s. 1, to make an order and what order to make (see the diagram at the end of the discussion of supervision orders).

A similar child

In *Re O* (1991) the court examined 'significant harm' and said that the s. 31 criteria were made out when the local authority had done all that they could in relation to truancy. School non-attendance itself was liable to cause harm, and in the long run this could be significant. This perhaps was an unexpected result, particularly when the Children Act introduced the Education Supervision Order (s. 37, which we discuss below). It abolished the previous power to take a child into care for school non-attendance. The decision in this case may have the effect of reintroducing this power. The court made these comments:

In relation to whether the harm is significant, on behalf of the [child] it is said that the comparison which has to be made is with a similar child under s.31(10) and that there is no evidence that she has suffered significant harm compared with a similar child.

In my judgment, in the context of this type of case, 'similar child' means a child of equivalent intellectual and social development, who has gone to school, and not merely an average child who may or may not be at school. In fact, what one has to ask oneself is whether this child suffered significant harm by not going to school. The answer in my judgment, as in the magistrates' judgment, is obvious.

At what stage is significant harm to be assessed by the court?

In *Northampton County Council v S* (1992), the court considered at what time the significance of the harm should be considered. In this case the mother had two children, a girl born in 1986 and a boy born in 1989. The children had different fathers. Following a non-accidental injury the children were taken into voluntary care under the old law. The Children Act then came into force. The local authority applied for a care order. The father of the boy sought a residence order that the boy only was to live with the boy's grandmother. The magistrates granted the care order. The father appealed to the High Court. The High Court had to consider the meaning of 'suffering significant harm'. What is the effect of the present tense? It held that the phrase referred to the period immediately before the action commenced. Ewbank J said:

That means the court has to consider the position immediately before the emergency protection order, if there was one or an interim care order, if that was the initiation of protection, or, as in this case, when the child went into voluntary care. In my judgment, the family proceedings court was quite entitled to consider the position when the children were with the mother prior to going into care and was correct in doing so.

The case of *Newham London Borough Council v AG* (1993) saw some important points made by the Court of Appeal. The case concerned a girl who was aged 2 years 3 months. Her mother was aged 20 and was a schizophrenic. The local authority had concerns about both the mother and the grandmother. The grandmother appeared to be unable to accept that her daughter was ill. In September 1989, the mother was admitted to hospital after swallowing bleach. She discharged herself. Again she was admitted to another hospital. The mother had told a health visitor that she had hit and pinched the baby three or four times when in the previous hospital. She had threatened to give bleach to the baby. To protect the girl the local authority made an application in wardship in February 1990 (that is before the Children Act came into force). Importantly, however, the judge did apply the significant harm threshold test under s. 31 of the Children Act, and this approach was supported by the Court of Appeal. It enabled the Court of Appeal to consider the application of the significant harm test. Stephen Brown, President of the Family Division, gave the leading judgment and said:

> [1] . . . we should not approach the interpretation of s. 31(2) of the Children Act on the basis that the phrase 'likely to suffer' should be equated with 'on the balance of probabilities' . . . (However, this comment should be read in the light of the decision of the House of Lords in *Re H and R, Re (Child Sexual Abuse: Standard of Proof)* (1996), see below.)
>
> [2] . . . It is true that first of all the court has to be satisfied that the child concerned is suffering or is likely to suffer significant harm, but in looking to the future the court has to assess the risk. Is this child likely to suffer significant harm? . . . It is important to bear in mind that the judge had to make an assessment of the future risk in the light of the evidence before him. That is entirely a matter for the judge. It is the duty he has to discharge in the exercise of his discretion. . . .

(We have numbered the paragraphs for clarity.)

The higher courts seem to be saying that the question of significance is one of fact and that the lower courts are in the best position to make decisions about significance on the evidence presented to them.

The meaning of harm

This does not mean that there are no aids to understanding the meaning of 'significant'. To help us understand s. 31(2) we have s. 31(9) and (10) which we have set out in Box 12.4.

The dictionary definition

When lawyers are looking for a meaning of a word that is not statutorily defined they turn to dictionaries. This is in accordance with the rule of statutory interpretation described in chapter 5. What we find is 'significant: having, conveying a meaning; full

BOX 12.4 Section 31(9) and (10)—the meaning of harm

(9) In this section—

'harm' means ill-treatment or the impairment of health or development;

'development' means physical, intellectual, emotional, social or behavioural development;

'health' means physical or mental health; and

'ill-treatment' includes sexual abuse and forms of treatment that are not physical including for example impairment suffered from seeing or hearing the ill-treatment of another.

(10) Where the question of whether harm suffered by a child is significant turns on the child's health or development, his health shall be compared with that which could reasonably be expected of a similar child.

of meaning, highly expressive or suggestive, important, notable' (*Oxford Dictionary*). Fowler's *Modern English Usage* says 'the primary sense of significant is conveying a meaning or suggesting an inference'. This guidance appears to indicate that 'significant' encompasses more than just the question of magnitude of harm. For example, what is the effect of bruising caused by a child being pushed over; is this likely to be seen as insignificant as against a fractured arm caused by a parent hitting the child? The latter must amount to significant harm. Added to this is the question of what an accidental broken arm amounts to. It may not be 'significant' or lead to any conclusion. If we are told the story behind the accident, a child left alone in a house perhaps, then it may be 'significant'. This use of the dictionary definition was indeed endorsed in *Humberside County Council v B* (1993).

Future harm

Looking further at s. 31(2), we see that it is possible to obtain a care order on the basis of *present significant harm* or the *likelihood of future harm*, in contrast to an emergency protection order which can only be granted on the likelihood of future harm. Nevertheless, a care order cannot be based purely on past harm. A decision under the Children and Young Persons Act 1969 continues to be relevant. In *Re D (A Minor)* (1987), the House of Lords decided that a court could infer future harm from past events. In this case the mother's drug addiction during pregnancy provided the grounds for a care order afterwards because the resulting harm continued. This view prevailed in *Northampton County Council v S* (1992), referred to above.

The reasonable parent

The harm or likelihood of harm has to be attributable to the fact that the care given or likely to be given to the child (as appropriate) is not what a parent would reasonably be expected to give to the child. This means the care that should be given to this particular child whose case is before the court by a *'reasonable'* parent. Therefore, you have to look at the child in his or her context (home, surroundings, locale, etc.) and ask what a reasonable parent in that situation would be expected to do. This was the point made in *Re O* (1992), mentioned above.

This gets around the difficulty that if you were to look at most of your clients' situations then often you might be able to say that it would be possible to offer the children a 'better' home. The failing of the parent should be such that it is incapable of being overcome by the range of support services that the local authority is allowed to deploy as we have described in previous chapters.

In *Northampton County Council v S* (1992) (the facts are given above), the point was made that the carer to be considered was the one responsible for the child prior to action being taken. In this case it was suggested that the grandmother could care for the child now, and that with the grandmother the child would not be likely to suffer significant harm. The court ruled that this was not relevant and that it should not look at the hypothetical care that might be given by others who could now be considered as possible carers. The judge said:

> ... the question arises whether the justices ought to consider the care being offered by the grandmother in assessing the threshold condition rather than the care which is actually being provided by the mother. The answer in my judgment is clearly "No". *The threshold test relates to the parent or other carer whose lack of care has caused the harm referred to in section 31(2)(a).* The care which other carers might give to the child only becomes relevant if the threshold test is met. The fact that the threshold test is met does not mean that the family proceedings court does have to make a care order. They have the choice once the threshold conditions are met of making a care order, of making a supervision order, or of making any other order under the Children Act (or, we would add, making no order) [emphasis added].

The decision in this case was endorsed and specifically approved in the case of *Re M (Minor) (Care Order: Significant Harm)* (1994). The House of Lords stated that it would be contrary to the intention of the Act to use any other approach. So, the point at which the court is to consider whether or not the threshold criteria are met is at the 'date at which the local authority initiated the proceedings for protection under the Act' (Lord Mackay 433) following which arrangements were put in place to protect the child.

Some may think that this approach is unfair to parents. Parents may have agreed to a child being accommodated in order to avoid care proceedings. A considerable delay may occur between the initiation of action to protect a child and the final hearing. During that time things could have changed considerably. Should any changes not be taken in account by the court?

The answer is that such changes will be considered by the court, at the second of the stages set out by the decision in *Humberside County Council v B* (above). That will be when the court considers, with the application of the welfare criteria in s. 1, whether or not to make an order.

The meaning of 'likely'

One of the vexed questions of interpretation of s. 31 is the meaning of 'likely' in s. 31(2). This was considered by the House of Lords in *Re H and R (Child Sexual Abuse: Standard of Proof)* (1996). In this case the House also considered the standard of proof that is required in cases where allegations of abuse are made.

The facts

The mother had four children. Two, C and D, aged 16 and 13, were the children of her husband, from whom she was separated. Two, T and M, aged 9 and 2, were the children of the mother's cohabitee. In 1990, C alleged that the cohabitee had sexually abused her. He was charged with rape but was acquitted. The local authority then proceeded with applications for care orders in respect of the three younger children under s. 31 of the Children Act 1989, based only on the alleged sexual abuse of C. The judge found that the mother and her cohabitee were lying and expressed considerable suspicion that the alleged abuse *had* taken place. But he held that, as the case depended solely on C's allegations, he was not satisfied on the balance of probabilities proportionate to the gravity of the offence that the allegations were true. Therefore, he could not proceed to consider whether the children were likely to suffer significant harm in the terms of s. 31(2)(a). He dismissed the applications.

The appeal

The local authority, supported by the guardian *ad litem*, appealed on the ground that even if the judge was not satisfied that abuse had in fact occurred, nevertheless the allegation itself and the judge's suspicion ought to be taken into account so as to fulfil the requirements of s. 31 relating to the interpretation of 'likely to suffer'. The House of Lords, in dismissing the appeal, held that the judge had been right to adopt a two-stage approach, and had fairly weighed up the matter relating to the allegations of sexual abuse. They concluded that the allegations had not been established to the requisite standard of proof, which is the balance of probabilities. The judge had rightly dismissed the applications. It was not open to him on the evidence, since he had rejected the only allegation which gave rise to the applications, to go on to a second stage and consider the likelihood of future harm to the children. The majority of the House adopted what was claimed to be the traditional test.

The standard of proof

The balance of probability standard means that a court is satisfied an event occurred if the court considers that, on the evidence, the occurrence of the event was more likely than not. When assessing the probabilities the court will have in mind as a factor, to whatever extent is appropriate in the particular case, that the more serious the allegation the less likely it is that the event occurred and, hence, the stronger should be the evidence before the court concludes that the allegation is established on the balance of probability. Fraud is usually less likely than negligence. Deliberate physical injury is usually less likely than accidental physical injury. A stepfather is usually less likely to have repeatedly raped and had non-consensual oral sex with his under age step-daughter than on some occasion to have lost his temper and slapped her. Built into the preponderance of probability standard is a generous degree of flexibility in respect of the seriousness of the allegation.

Although the result is much the same, this does not mean that where a serious allegation is in issue the standard of proof required is higher. It means only that the inherent probability or improbability of an event is itself a matter to be taken into account when weighing the probabilities and deciding whether, on balance, the event occurred. The more improbable the event, the stronger must be the evidence that it did occur before, on the balance of probability, its occurrence will be established (per Lord Nichols in majority judgment).

Balancing the various interests

Many commentators have found it difficult to understand this test as being different from the test the House purported to reject. However, the concluding remarks of Lord Nichols seek to justify the position:

> These are among the difficulties and considerations Parliament addressed in the Children Act when deciding how, to use the fashionable terminology, the balance should be struck between the various interests. As I read the Act, Parliament decided that the threshold for a care order should be that the child is suffering significant harm, or there is a real possibility that he will do so. In the latter regard the threshold is comparatively low. Therein lies the protection for children. But, as I read the Act, Parliament also decided that proof of the relevant facts is needed if this threshold is to be surmounted. Before the section 1 welfare test and the welfare 'checklist' can be applied, the threshold has to be crossed. Therein lies the protection for parents. They are not to be at risk of having their child taken from them and removed into the care of the local authority on the basis only of suspicions whether of the judge or of the local authority or anyone else. A conclusion that the child is suffering or it likely to suffer harm must be based on facts not just suspicion.

The effect of this important judgment is to make it harder for the local authority to satisfy the standard of proof required by the courts if the allegations of abuse are based upon improbable events. However, it is a much easier test to satisfy than the criminal standard of proof which requires evidence to be beyond reasonable doubt. Since the decision by the House of Lords there have been a considerable number of decisions by the Court of Appeal which have followed this line of legal authority. The most recent confirmation was in *Re U (A Child) (Serious Injury: Standard of Proof): In re B (A Child)* (2004), the case study at the beginning of this chapter The Court of Appeal found that the balance of probabilities—taking into account that the more improbable an event the stronger must be the evidence that it had occurred—was the correct approach the courts must take to the evidence. Changes to the standard of proof in other areas of civil proceedings were not applicable to child protection cases. They could be distinguished as they were applications under a different statute—the Crime and Disorder Act 1998. Nor were the responsibilities of local authorities changed by the decision in *R v Cannings* (2004).

The courts have said that the test applies not just in public law applications by local authorities, but also in private law applications by individuals for s. 8 orders: see *Re N (Residence: Hopeless Appeals)* (1995).

Uncertainty about the perpetrator of abuse

Another category of cases which cause problems with the standard of proof are those cases where there is no doubt that one or both parents have caused injury to the child but it is unclear from the evidence which parent is responsible. In *Re O and N (Minors); In Re B (A Minor)* (2003) the House of Lords made it clear that where it is uncertain which of a child's parents is responsible for causing the child significant harm, the judge in proceedings by the local authority under s 31(2) of the Children Act 1989 should proceed on the assumption that each was a possible perpetrator. Therefore the threshold condition of attributability could be fulfilled although the identity of the carer who was the perpetrator of the physical harm already done was not known.

Working Together

Working Together to Safeguard Children (DoH 1999) provides some guidance on how to establish significant harm. It emphasizes that there are no absolute criteria on which to rely, but that the whole context of the family and the child's development needs to be considered. We set out a useful paragraph in Box 12.5 below.

Being beyond parental control

'Being beyond parental control' in s. 31(1)(b)(ii) should present few difficulties as this definition is imported from previous legislation and is largely a self-explanatory matter of fact for the court to decide. An example of the use of this concept can be found in *South Glamorgan County Council v W and B* (1993), and also in *M v Birmingham City Council* (1994).

At the end of the discussion of supervision orders there is a flow diagram that shows a summary of the evidential steps to obtaining a care or supervision order. If you are the applicant you should ensure that you have evidence and argument on each point.

◼ The effect of a care order

Section 33 of the Children Act describes the effect of a care order. This is set out in Box 12.6. The essential function of a care order is that it gives the local authority parental responsibility; it makes the local authority the child's parent—with all the implications that are contained in that phrase.

 BOX 12.5 Paragraph 2.18 from *Working Together*

To understand and establish significant harm, it is necessary to consider:

- The family context;
- The child's development within the context of their family and wider social and cultural environment;
- Any special needs, such as a medical condition, communication difficulty, or disability that may affect the child's development and care within the family;
- The nature of harm, in terms of ill-treatment or failure to provide adequate care;
- The impact on the child's health and development; and
- The adequacy of parental care.

It is important always to take account of the child's reactions, and his or her perceptions, according to the child's age and understanding.

BOX 12.6 The effect of a care order

s. 33(1) Where a care order is made with respect to a child it shall be the duty of a local authority designated by the order to receive the child into their care and to keep him in their care while the order remains in force.

(2) Where—

(a) a care order has been made with respect to a child on the application of an authorised person (i.e. NSPCC); but

(b) the local authority designated by the order was not informed that the person proposed to make the application (there is a requirement for the local authority to be informed of applications),

the child may be kept in the care of that person until received into the care of the local authority.

(3) While a care order is in force with respect to a child, the local authority designated by the order shall—

(a) have parental responsibility for the child; and

(b) have the power (subject to the following provisions of this section) to determine the extent to which a parent or guardian of the child may meet his parental responsibility for him.

(4) The authority may not exercise the power in subsection (3)(b) unless they are satisfied that it is necessary to do so in order to safeguard or promote the child's welfare.

(5) Nothing in subsection (3)(b) shall prevent a parent or guardian of the child who has care of him from doing what is reasonable in all the circumstances of the case for the purpose of safeguarding or promoting his welfare.

Parental responsibility under a care order

Sharing parental responsibility

The mere fact of making a care order and giving parental responsibility to the local authority does not remove parental responsibility from the parents (s. 2(5) and (6)). What happens is that the principal responsibility rests with the local authority, with the parents' responsibility remaining an ever-present feature. Indeed, s. 33(3)(b) echoes the philosophy of the Act in that it seeks to encourage the local authority to look at ways in which it can share the care of the child with the child's parent, albeit that this is by way of a power not a duty on the local authority.

The welfare of the child

Section 33(4) then goes on to indicate that although the local authority may share the care of the child with his or her parent, it may not exercise this power unless it is necessary to do so in order to safeguard or promote the child's welfare. This means that a local authority should not adopt the attitude that, in every case where a child has parents, there should be steps to rehabilitate the child with those parents. It is more subtle than that. Local authorities are encouraged to look towards rehabilitating a child, but only in those cases where this will safeguard or promote the child's welfare. What s. 33(5) is saying is that, although the granting of a care order does give the local authority parental responsibility, it does not mean that the parents can wash their hands of their responsibility for the child, especially where the local authority is seeking to share the care of the child with the parents. If, for example, a child subject to a care order was placed back with a parent (which would need to be done in accordance with the Placement of Children Regulations) and the child was neglected by the parent, then it would not be open to the parent to say 'it was the local authority's fault—we were not responsible because the local authority had a care order'.

Limits on the local authority's parental responsibility

Section 33(6), (7), (8), and (9) imposes limitations on the power of the local authority in possession of a care order in respect of the child. We set out a summary of those in Box 12.7 below.

Planning

In making applications to court it has always been necessary for the local authority to present its plans for contact (s. 34(11)) and its proposals for the future care of the child if a care order is made (*Manchester City Council v F* (1993)). This responsibility is made explicit as a result of the insertion of a new subs. (3A) into s. 31. This provides that 'no care order may be made with respect to a child until the court has considered a section 31 A plan'. Section 31A care plans are discussed in chapter 10. Note that this proposal has not yet been implemented.

Once a care order is made the local authority has the task of deciding how to look after the child.

 BOX 12.7 Limiting the local authority's parental responsibility

Whilst a care order is in force the local authority may not:

(a) cause the child to be brought up in a different religious persuasion (this can present problems in the choice of foster parents);

(b) cause the child to be adopted without a court order;

(c) appoint a guardian for the child (that is a testamentary guardian for when the parents die); or

(d) cause the child to be known by a different surname (again this needs to be watched with foster parents); or

(e) allow the child to be removed from the United Kingdom without the leave of the court (except for periods of less than four weeks).

In care—but at home

Do not forget that the making of a care order does not automatically mean that the child must be removed from the home. The local authority's duty once a care order is made is still that contained in s. 17, i.e. to safeguard and promote the child's welfare and, as far as is consistent with that duty, to encourage the child to be with his or her family. A care order adds to this a power, if necessary, to remove the child.

Discharge of care orders

The procedure for the discharge of care orders is identical to that for supervision orders. Section 39 provides the powers for the variation and discharge of both care and supervision orders. Applications can be made by the authority, the child, or the parent. In the case of a supervision order the child may be living with a person who does not have parental responsibility, for example a relative. In that case that person may apply for the supervision order to be discharged.

The welfare principle

There are no particular requirements for a court to consider when deciding an application to have a care or supervision order discharged except to do what is best for the welfare of the child (the welfare principle). The court does have the power, when an application is made to discharge a care order, to substitute a supervision order. In those particular circumstances under s. 39(5) the court does not have to apply the significant harm test in s. 31 which would otherwise apply when considering a supervision order.

Unsuccessful applications

If an application to discharge a care or supervision order, or to have contact with a child in care, has been unsuccessful, then a further application may not be made for a period of six months (s. 91(15)). But there are provisions for the court to grant leave to make an application within the six-month period.

Rehabilitation

In attempting to rehabilitate a child the local authority does not have available any particular court order. The choice is either a care order or a supervision order, or no order at all. The court does not have the power to make an order requiring either the local authority or the parents to undertake a rehabilitation plan. This is a situation in which the absence of the availability of wardship for local authorities is a real loss. The problem is that the court cannot impose restrictions or conditions on a full care order. (See *Kent County Council v C* (1992).)

Discharge of care order by a residence order

There is an alternative way to have a care order discharged and that is by an application for a s. 8 residence order. Under s. 91(1), the making of a residence order discharges any care order. Applications for a residence order are made under s. 10(4) and (5). For the purposes of seeking to discharge a care order by this means the following people could apply:

(a) The mother or father.

(b) Any person with whom the child has lived for a period totalling at least three years out of the last five, ending at the latest three months ago.

(c) Any person who has the consent of the local authority. A foster parent will come within this category unless the child has lived with the foster parent for a period of three years or the foster parent is a relative of the child. Then they can apply without consent. (A relative is defined in s. 105 as a grandparent, brother, sister, uncle, aunt, or step-parent.)

Applications with leave

In addition to these people, the court has power under s. 10(9) to grant leave to any person, except a foster parent, to apply for a s. 8 order. In considering whether to grant leave the court has to have regard to a number of points:

(a) what form of order is sought;

(b) the connection with the child;

(c) the risk that the application would disrupt the child so as to harm the child; and

(d) where the child is looked after by the local authority, what plans the authority has for the child and the wishes and feelings of the child's (actual) parents.

Whilst a hearing for leave ought to be shorter than the full hearing, experience does not always bear this theory out. In an extreme case an authority may be faced with a number of persons seeking leave to apply for a residence order with the consequent pressures on staff dealing with a series of legal proceedings. Of course, the granting of leave does not mean that the residence order itself will be granted. That is decided at a full hearing on the basis of what is in the child's best interest. The decision in *Re B (Minors) (Contact)* (1994) said that a court could refuse leave without a full hearing, if it was clear that leave should be refused. Therefore, if an application had just been refused by the Court of Appeal and the same parent applied in the magistrates' court for leave for a contact order, the court could refuse.

Supervision orders

2,383 supervision orders were made in 2003 compared with 1,538 in 2002 (Children Act Report 2003).

Identical grounds

The grounds for making a supervision order are exactly the same as those for a care order. They are set out in s. 31(2) (i.e. the likelihood of significant harm or the child being beyond parental control). Indeed all the provisions of s. 31 are applicable to the making of a supervision order. Therefore the questions of the meaning of 'significant harm' etc., which we discussed when looking at care orders are just as applicable.

Choosing supervision orders

A supervision order is an alternative to a care order. In the Act there is no guidance on when a supervision order, rather than a care order, should be made. The decision is going to be the decision of the court, although the court will listen to the representations of all the parties, which can include a children's guardian, before coming to that decision. The order is made to either a local authority or a probation officer.

The Act creates three distinct supervision orders—the one made in the course of civil proceedings which we are considering here, the education supervision order which we look at below, and one made in criminal proceedings which we consider in chapter 15.

The value of a supervision order

An interesting case which considered the need for a supervision order is *Re K (Supervision Orders)* (1999). Here the local authority and the mother agreed that the threshold criteria in s. 31 were satisfied. They also agreed that a supervision order would be the appropriate way to safeguard the interests of the children. However, the children's guardian thought that the obligations of the local authority to safeguard the interests of the children under s. 17, as children 'in need', were sufficient to deal with their welfare. The judge found that as a concession had been made by the mother which appropriately reflected the gravity of the case, there was no need for a full investigation by the courts. He made it clear that a guardian should not lightly propose a contentious hearing. While accepting that the least intrusive order possible should be made, the supervision order imposed duties on the mother as well as on the local authority, which would be useful if the mother did not continue to cooperate, and that in practice the result of the supervision order would be to secure the allocation of a social worker and therefore greater protection for the children.

The effect of a supervision order

Section 35 of the Children Act sets out the effect of a supervision order. Its provisions are set out in Box 12.8 below.

There are no definitions of the terms 'advise', 'assist', or 'befriend' to give any guidance. The order need not specify a particular person in respect of a local authority. Note that a probation officer can be a supervisor only with the agreement of the probation authority and where the probation officer is already dealing or has dealt with another member of the child's household (Sch. 3, para. 9). This means that the majority of supervision orders will be made in favour of the local authority. Schedule 3 to the Act gives more detailed guidance on what a supervision order means.

The responsible person

The first paragraph of Schedule 3 introduces the idea of the 'responsible person' who is either a parent or someone with whom the child is living. This 'responsible person' can

BOX 12.8 Section 35—the effect of a supervision order

(1) While a supervision order is in force it shall be the duty of the supervisor—

   (a) to advise, assist and befriend the supervised child;

   (b) to take such steps as are reasonably necessary to give effect to the order; and

   (c) where—

      (i) the order is not wholly complied with; or

      (ii) the supervisor considers that the order may no longer be necessary, to consider whether or not to apply to the court for its variation or discharge.

have duties imposed upon them in addition to any requirements that are imposed on the supervised child. But the responsible person has to consent to playing this role.

Requirements

The court, under a supervision order, can require the supervised person to obey certain directions given by the supervisor. Amongst these are that the supervised child:

(a) be required to live at a specified address for a specified period;

(b) present themselves to a specified person at a specified time and place; and

(c) participate in specified activities.

In addition, the responsible person can be required to:

(a) take all reasonable steps to ensure that the supervised child complies with directions given by the supervisor or contained in the order;

(b) keep the supervisor informed of the supervised child's address; and

(c) attend at a specified place to take part in any specified activities.

The supervision order can require the supervised child to submit to a medical or psychiatric examination, or to submit to such examinations as are required by the supervisor. This requirement is subject to the informed consent of the child, if the child has sufficient understanding. It is also possible for the court to require specified medical or psychiatric treatment, but if psychiatric the court must have first heard the evidence of a Mental Health Act approved doctor. The order can also require the child to keep the supervisor informed of his or her address.

Time limits

There are time limits on the supervision order. Any particular supervision order may not last, initially, for more than a period of one year, but the supervisor can apply to the court to have it extended for up to three years from the date on which the order was first made. The significant harm test need not be satisfied.

Can you replace a supervision order with a care order?

The answer is clearly 'No'. The 'no order without an application' principle means there has to be a fresh application by the local authority. In making any new application the threshold criteria must be satisfied afresh. So in *Re A (Supervision Order: Extension)* (1995), the local authority obtained a twelve-month supervision order in respect of an 11-year-old child. Before the expiry of the twelve-month period the local authority applied for an extension of the order. The guardian *ad litem* recommended that a care order be made in place of a supervision order. The Court of Appeal held that on an application for an extension of a supervision order, the court could make only a further supervision order and could not make a care order.

Discharge of a supervision order

This is dealt with in s. 39. We discuss the procedure, which is identical to that of the discharge of a care order above.

Education supervision orders (s. 36)

If a local education authority (which in most areas is the same authority as the social services department) can satisfy the magistrates' court that a particular child is both of compulsory school age and not being properly educated (s. 36(3)), the court may make an education supervision order. Section 36(4) defines a child as being properly educated only if the child is receiving efficient full-time education suitable to age, ability, and aptitude and any special educational needs that the child may have. An application for an order cannot be made if the child is in the care of the local authority, and the education department must consult with the social services department before the application is made. The order is designed to ensure that children do not go into care merely for school non-attendance.

The effect of an education supervision order

Under Schedule 3, Part III, there are detailed provisions as to the effect of the education supervision order. In essence the supervisor has to advise, assist, and befriend the child and give directions to the child to ensure that the child is properly educated. Chapter 3 of volume 7 of *Guidance and Regulations* considers the order in detail.

The directions might include directions for the child and parents to attend meetings to discuss the child's education or for the child to see an educational psychologist. Under the provisions there is the need to consult with the parents and child before the directions are made. If parents persistently fail to comply with directions that are reasonably given they may be fined, on conviction, in the magistrates' court. There is no penalty for the child.

Time limits

The education supervision order lasts for twelve months or until the child is no longer of compulsory school age (whichever is the shorter). It can be extended for up to three years.

Appeals

Lastly, we will look, briefly, at the particular methods of appealing decisions in relation to care and supervision orders. There is a particular provision for appeals in s. 40.

The aim is to allow the court to decide what will happen to a child where an application for an order is dismissed and there is to be an appeal. This is a safety net provision. No application will be made without an investigation by the local authority or authorized person, and it therefore follows that there should have been reasonable grounds for concern. The safety net that is provided gives the court the power to make an order of the type originally sought, pending the hearing of the appeal.

The requirement that needs to be satisfied is that there must have been an interim order made at an earlier stage in the proceedings. This means that at an earlier stage a court believed that there were reasonable grounds for believing that a final order might be made.

The order made pending appeal is not an interim order since the dismissal of the application is an end to the proceedings as far as the lower court is concerned. The length of time that the order will last is strictly limited to the 'appeal period', which means that the order will last only until the hearing of the appeal. There are provisions for the appeal court to extend the period until it is practicable for it to hear the appeal. In *Re O* (1992), the court held that the magistrates had no power to stay (suspend) such an order pending an appeal.

As we have indicated earlier, if you are involved in a case where your application is dismissed you should immediately seek the advice of your agency lawyer.

A flow chart setting out the key questions for determining the outcomes of an application for a care or supervision order is set out in Box 12.9 opposite.

■ Interim care and supervision orders

Interim care or supervision orders are usually made when for one reason or another the full hearing cannot take place. Section 38(1) of the Children Act, set out in Box 12.10, provides the power for the court to make an interim care or supervision order.

We have already discussed in chapter 11 the provisions relating to interim orders made following the court's direction to a local authority to make an investigation under s. 37. To recap:

(a) the court must have reasonable grounds for believing there are grounds for the full care order;

(b) the making of the interim order does not mean that there will be a full order; and

(c) the court must act judicially in making an order.

Hearings are not always necessary

This does not mean that there will always have to be a hearing with evidence being given. Inevitably after the first interim order is made, within the constraints of the

BOX 12.9 Getting care order/supervision order

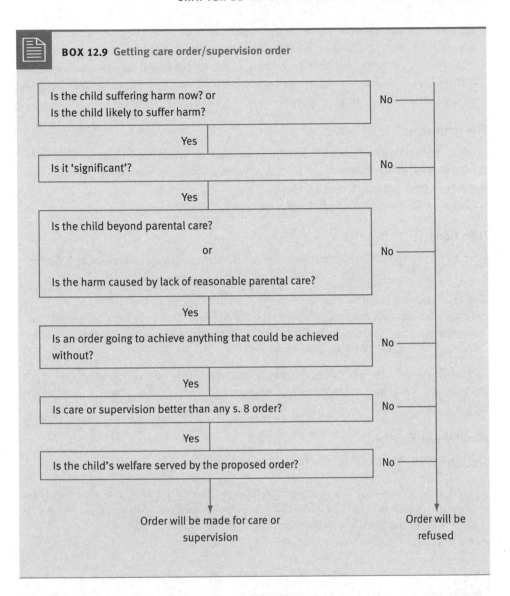

Is the child suffering harm now? or Is the child likely to suffer harm?	No
Yes	
Is it 'significant'?	No
Yes	
Is the child beyond parental care? or Is the harm caused by lack of reasonable parental care?	No
Yes	
Is an order going to achieve anything that could be achieved without?	No
Yes	
Is care or supervision better than any s. 8 order?	No
Yes	
Is the child's welfare served by the proposed order?	No

Order will be made for care or supervision

Order will be refused

 BOX 12.10 Interim care or supervision orders

(1) Where—

   (a) in any proceedings on an application for a care order or supervision order, the proceedings are adjourned; or

   (b) the court gives a direction under section 37(1),

the court may make an interim care order or an interim supervision order with respect to the child concerned.

timetable provisions below, there are occasions on which everybody is agreed that for one reason or another a further interim order will need to be made—the medical report is not available, there is no available court time, etc. In this case the court could make an interim order without hearing evidence but merely hearing representations from the applicant, as happened in *Devon County Council v S* (1992).

The timetable

Section 38(4) sets out a timetable for the granting of interim care or supervision orders. It is not reproduced verbatim here since it is unnecessarily complex and unclear. What it appears to say is set out in Box 12.11.

This approach was approved in *Gateshead MBC v N* (1993).

Directions

When making an interim order, the court has the power to give directions as follows:

> S. 38(6) Where the court makes an interim care order, or interim supervision order, it may give such directions (if any) as it considers appropriate with regard to the medical or psychiatric examination or other assessment of the child; but if the child is of sufficient understanding to make an informed decision he may refuse to submit to the examination or other assessment. (This is another example of *informed consent*.)

Section 38(7) specifies what directions may be given. This subsection is an exact reproduction of s. 44(8) and (9) relating to emergency protection orders which is discussed below.

Medical examinations

The important provisions of rule 18 must be noted:

> (1) No person may, without the leave of the justices' clerk or the court, cause the child to be medically or psychiatrically examined, or otherwise assessed, for the purpose of the preparation of expert evidence for use in the proceedings.

 BOX 12.11 Timetabling interim care and supervision orders

(a) an initial interim order may not last more than eight weeks;

(b) if the initial interim order has been made for a period of less than eight weeks then any subsequent orders may be made for a period or periods that will not exceed that eight-week period starting on the date on which the initial order was made;

(c) if any interim orders are made after that initial eight-week period then those further interim orders may not exceed a four-week period, although they may be made for periods less than four weeks; and

(d) any number of interim orders could be made subject to the non-delay principle.

. . .

(3) Where the leave of the justices' clerk or the court has not been given under (1) no evidence arising out of an examination or assessment to which that paragraph applies may be adduced without the leave of the court.

The message here is quite clear. If you are going to have any medical examination, investigation, or any other type of assessment carried out, then obtain the leave of the court.

Assessments during interim care orders

In *Re C (A Minor) (Interim Care Order: Residential Assessment)* (1996), a 4-month-old child was admitted to hospital suffering from non-accidental injuries. The child's parents, aged 16 and 17, were not able to give a satisfactory explanation of the injuries. An emergency protection order was made, and then an interim care order under s. 38 of the Children Act 1989. The field social workers decided that in-depth assessment of the child and the parents together needed to be undertaken as soon as possible at a residential unit. However, their managers refused to agree to, or pay for, the residential assessment and decided to apply for a care order so that the child could be placed in a permanent alternative placement with a view to adoption.

At first instance, the judge held that she had jurisdiction under s. 38(6) to order a residential assessment. Having weighed the cost (estimated at £18,000 to £24,000) against the recommendations from the professionals involved, she decided to exercise her discretion by ordering the local authority to carry out the residential assessment.

The House of Lords held that s. 38(6) and (7) conferred jurisdiction on the court to order or prohibit any assessment which involved the participation of the child, and was to provide the court with the material to enable it to reach a proper decision at the final hearing. In exercising its discretion the court would have to take into account the cost of the proposed assessment and the fact of local authorities' lack of resources. In this case their Lordships ordered the assessment. The care plan here indicated that the local authority was going to place the child for adoption. To allow the local authority to decide what evidence was to go before the court at the final hearing would allow the local authority by administrative decision to pre-empt the court's judicial decision.

Reducing delay

The final provision relating to interim orders is s. 38(10):

(10) Where a court makes an order under or by virtue of this section [an interim order] it shall, in determining the period for which the order is to be in force, consider whether any party who was, or might have been, opposed to the making of an order was in a position to argue his case against the order in full.

This is designed to cope with a situation where a parent has not had the opportunity to instruct lawyers to act on their behalf at the time of the interim hearing. The court should then consider making an interim order for just sufficient time to enable a lawyer to be properly instructed. This is another reflection of the Act's aim to try and reduce the delays that can be present in such cases.

Power to exclude alleged abuser while the interim order is in force

The Family Law Act 1996 amended the Children Act to include a new s. 38A—a power in interim care orders to require an alleged abuser to leave the house in which the child is living. The court would have to be satisfied of the following:

(a) that there is reasonable cause to believe that if a person is excluded from a dwelling house in which the child lives, the child will cease to suffer or cease to be likely to suffer significant harm; and

(b) another person living in the same house, whether or not a parent, is able and willing to give to the child the care which it would be reasonable to expect a parent to give; and

(c) that person consents to the inclusion of the exclusion requirement.

There are also powers of arrest available, subject to certain requirements. The difficulty with this power is that it does require the consent of the person who is to care for the child. This would normally be the mother. In the absence of her consent it is not possible to compel the alleged abuser to leave. While this power is a welcome addition to the interim order, the requirement of consent may mean that it is not used as much as could be expected. There is an identical power in relation to the emergency protection order which we discuss below.

A fail-safe provision

Section 38(3) requires that the court makes an interim supervision order when making a residence order in certain circumstances. We set out s. 38(3) in Box 12.12 below.

This section covers the situation where the court, instead of making an interim care order, decides to make a s. 8 residence order, say to a grandparent. As a 'fail safe', the court is required to make an interim supervision order. An example of this in practice is *C v Solihull Metropolitan Borough Council* (1993) which we discussed above. It needs to be stressed again that the making of any particular interim order does not mean that type of order will be made as a final order.

 BOX 12.12 Section 38(3)

Where, in any proceedings on an application for a care order or supervision order, a court makes a residence order with respect to the child concerned, it shall also make *an interim supervision order* with respect to him unless satisfied that his welfare will be satisfactorily safeguarded without an interim order being made.

Short-term orders to protect children

We will now discuss the orders and the police power set out in Part 5 of the Act. These provisions are all short term. The most important of these is the emergency protection order. 2,061 emergency protection orders were made in 2003 compared with 1,728 in 2002 (Children Act Report 2003).

The emergency protection order—a summary

An emergency protection order is a short-term order that either:

(a) removes the child on a short-term basis; or

(b) allows the child to be kept in a place of safety (for instance, a hospital); or

(c) requires the alleged abuser to leave the family home (see below).

An emergency protection order is not an end in itself. It is a critical step in the local authority's investigation under s. 47 which will lead to the local authority being satisfied about the child's welfare or will lead it to begin care proceedings.

Emergency protection orders are provided for within s. 44 of the Children Act. Section 44(1) is set out in Box 12.13 below.

 BOX 12.13 Section 44(1)—the emergency protection of children

(1) Where any person ('the applicant') applies to the court for an order to be made under this section with respect to a child, the court may make the order if, but only if it is satisfied that—

    (a) there is reasonable cause to believe that the child is likely to suffer significant harm if

        (i) he is not removed to accommodation provided by or on behalf of the applicant; or

        (ii) he does not remain in the place in which he is then being accommodated;

    (b) in the case of an application made by a local authority—

        (i) enquiries are being made with respect to the child under section 47(1) (b); and

        (ii) those enquires are being frustrated by access to the child being unreasonably refused to a person authorized to seek access and that the applicant has reasonable cause to believe that access to the child is required as a matter of urgency; or

    (c) in the case of an application made by an authorized person—

        (i) the applicant has reasonable cause to suspect that a child is suffering or is likely to suffer, significant harm;

        (ii) the applicant is making enquires with respect to the child's welfare; and

        (iii) those enquires are being frustrated by access to the child being unreasonably refused to a person authorised to seek access and the applicant has reasonable cause to believe that access to the child is required as a matter of urgency.

The key features of an emergency protection order

Duration

The emergency protection order may be granted for a period of up to an initial eight days, extendable, once only, for a period of up to a further seven days—s. 45. These are the maximum periods allowed. It may well be that the court will decide that the order should last for a shorter period.

The different forms of emergency protection order

The emergency protection order is not designed to be granted without careful consideration of the grounds by the court. There are two forms the applications can take:

The 'any person basis' under s. 44(1)(a)

The 'any person' includes a social worker. The court, on the application of any person, may grant an order if a version of the significant harm test is satisfied. Where any person applies for it, the court may grant an emergency protection order only if the court is satisfied that there is reasonable cause to believe that the child is likely to suffer significant harm unless removed to accommodation provided by the applicant or unless allowed to remain in present accommodation.

'Likely to suffer significant harm'

This type of application is designed to cover situations where for instance a social worker is notified of a child with severe injuries and believes that the child should be removed from home for the protection of the child. The ground is that the child is likely to suffer significant harm. The social worker or other applicant has to be able to put evidence before the court that will satisfy the court as to this likelihood. That means that there will have to be evidence that there is a possibility that the harm which has already been inflicted will be repeated—so a 'one-off' incident cannot be a ground for granting an emergency protection order under this subsection.

Alternatively, the 'any person' emergency protection order envisages the situation where a child has been admitted to hospital and the parents are threatening to remove the child, and the court believes the removal would be likely to cause the child significant harm. It would also be possible to make an application where a child is being looked after by a local authority in accommodation and the parents are again threatening to remove the child.

The obstruction of investigation basis under s. 44(1)(b)

Here, if the investigations of a local authority or the NSPCC are obstructed then the court may grant an emergency protection order without being satisfied on the significant harm test—but, like the child assessment order (discussed below), the applicant has to be satisfied there is a risk of significant harm.

The court would need to be satisfied that the access was being unreasonably refused by the parent. The court would have to ask whether this parent was, in all the circumstances, being unreasonable. The local authority would have to show that access was required as a matter of urgency. An application on these grounds may be simpler to obtain than one where you have to satisfy the court that the child is actually suffering significant harm.

Part of continuing investigation

An application under s. 44(1)(b) is to be made by the local authority only as part of a continuing investigation under s. 47 of the Children Act. That is the investigation the authority or NSPCC has to carry out when it has reasonable cause to suspect that a child is suffering or is likely to suffer significant harm. (This again reminds us of the need for social workers to keep careful case notes of their actions, since it would be perfectly reasonable for the court to ask what steps had been taken under s. 47, and in the absence of being satisfied, it will be reluctant to grant an emergency protection order.)

Parents

An order may be granted in the absence of the parents (i.e. without notice of the hearing), but as with the child assessment order there are provisions for the parents to seek to have the order discharged under s. 45(8). At that stage it would be possible for the parents to state that access will be granted and, if the statement is believed by the court, for the basis of the local authority application to be totally undermined.

Common elements between these different forms of emergency protection orders

Even though the court may be satisfied that the grounds for an emergency protection order exist, it still need not grant one, for it has to apply the 'welfare' principle and the 'non-intervention' principle which are contained in s. 1 of the Children Act. This means that it has to be satisfied that the order is in the best interests of the child and necessary for its protection. It does not have to consider the welfare checklist in s. 1. Presumably, the justification for the exclusion of the welfare checklist is that there is not the time to collect the necessary evidence.

Safeguards

The various safeguards in this section all point to the need for the social worker to be adequately prepared before rushing off to seek an emergency protection order. Adequate preparation means that you will need to have answers ready for all the points that the court requires: the grounds (harm or obstruction of your investigation), the welfare of the child, and the need to intervene.

The operation of an emergency protection order

An emergency protection order does not give the applicant an unfettered licence in respect of the child. Box 12.14 sets out the relevant subsections of s. 44.

Not to produce the child is a criminal offence (s. 44(15)). Producing the child means showing the child to you. If you have such an order and ask for the child to be produced and he or she is not produced, you must draw the person's attention to the explanatory notes attached to the order and warn them that failure so to do will render them liable to criminal proceedings.

If the child is produced then you may take him or her to, and/or keep him or her in, accommodation.

BOX 12.14 The operation of emergency protection order

Section 44(4) While an order under this section ('an emergency protection order') is in force it—
- (a) operates as a direction to any person who is in a position to do so to comply with any request to produce the child to the applicant;
- (b) authorizes—
    - (i) the removal of the child at any time to accommodation provided by or on behalf of the applicant and his being kept there; or
    - (ii) the prevention of the child's removal from any hospital or other place in which he was being accommodated immediately before the making of this order; and
- (c) gives the applicant parental responsibility for the child.

- (5) Where an emergency protection order is in force with respect to a child the applicants—
    - (a) shall only exercise the power given by virtue of subsection (4)(b) in order to safeguard the welfare of the child;
    - (b) shall take, and shall only take, such action in meeting his parental responsibility for the child as is reasonably required to safeguard or promise the welfare of the child (having regard in particular to the duration of the order); and
    - (c) shall comply with the requirements of any regulation made by the Secretary of State for the purpose of this subsection.

Power to exclude alleged abuser

The Family Law Act 1996 amended the Children Act to include s. 44A—which provides a power in an emergency protection order to require an alleged abuser to leave the house in which the child is living. There are also powers of arrest available, subject to certain requirements. Box 12.15 sets out what needs to be demonstrated to the court.

Consent

The difficulty with the exclusion power is that it requires the consent of the person who is to care for the child. This is normally the mother. In the absence of her consent it is not possible to compel the alleged abuser to leave. Note that an identical power to exclude an alleged abuser exists in relation to interim care orders (see above).

 BOX 12.15 Factors necessary for an exclusion requirement

- (a) that there is reasonable cause to believe that if a person is excluded from a dwelling house in which the child lives, the child will cease to suffer or cease to be likely to suffer significant harm; and
- (b) another person living in the same house, whether or not a parent, is able and willing to give to the child the care which it would be reasonable to expect a parent to give; and
- (c) that person consents to the inclusion of the exclusion requirement.

Guidance on the exclusion requirement

In *Re W (Exclusion: Statement of Evidence)* (2000), the judge set out guidance on the relevant procedure. While it is not necessary for the local authority to make a specific application, there does need to be a separate statement of evidence supporting the case for an exclusion requirement. The consent can be given orally in court or in writing. If it is in writing, it should clearly state that the person giving consent understands the provision.

(See chapter 18 for a more detailed discussion of legal remedies relating to domestic violence.)

Limited power of removal under an emergency protection order

The power to remove the child is to be used only where it is necessary to safeguard the welfare of the child. This means that if you have obtained an order and then go to the house and find the child is safe, you are not permitted to remove the child.

It is easy to imagine an extreme case where this might be applied: you receive an anonymous telephone call stating that it sounds as if a child is being beaten to death in a certain house. You go to the house, knock on the door, get no answer but hear the sounds of a child sobbing and screaming. You knock next door and are told that there is a child in the house and that 'they are an odd lot'. You go to court and are granted an emergency protection order under s. 44(1)(b) (on the ground that you are investigating and your investigation is being obstructed). You go to the house with the emergency protection order, a surprised parent opens the door holding a cheerful, smiling toddler with no visible signs of injury. The parent readily agrees to you examining the child undressed and there are no signs of injury. When asked about the noise of crying, the parent says that they were listening to a play on the radio, about a child-beating case, which may explain the sounds, and they had the radio up very loud and therefore your knocks were not heard. Clearly s. 44(5)(a) applies and you would have no grounds for the removal of the child, despite holding the emergency protection order.

Assistance of other professionals

Most cases are not so clear-cut and this particular subsection may in practice prove challenging. The only sensible advice is to err on the side of caution and not be afraid to remove the child if in doubt. To assist you in making the decision as to whether removal is necessary, you may want to have the assistance of some other professional person when you go to the house. In these circumstances you may ask the court to make a direction under s. 45(12), which states that the court may direct that the applicant may be accompanied by a doctor, nurse, or health visitor, if the applicant so chooses.

Parental responsibility under an emergency protection order

The local authority, or whoever was the applicant, will also gain parental responsibility, but this does not mean that the parent of the child loses parental responsibility. The exercise of parental responsibility under an emergency protection order in accordance with s. 44(5) means that only steps that are reasonably required during the order (which will be eight, or at the very most fifteen, days) may be taken by the person with temporary parental responsibility. This does not mean that a child may, for instance, have their school permanently changed; only temporary educational provision can be made. It does not mean that a child may be allowed to undergo a cosmetic surgery operation, but it would allow for an emergency operation.

Contact

There is a general presumption that the parent will have reasonable contact with the child whilst an emergency protection order is in force, unless a direction under s. 44(6) is made. We set out the direction power below.

Medical examinations

Medical examinations are allowed only for purposes that promote or safeguard the welfare of the child. This means that any examinations required for the purpose of preparing your case prior to applying for a care order would not be permitted unless you have the additional power contained in s. 44(6).

This subsection sets out the directions that the court can make at the time of granting the order. The court may decline to make any directions under this subsection. The possible range of directions are:

(a) the contact which is, or is not, to be allowed between the child and any named person;

(b) the medical or psychiatric examination or other assessment of the child.

The question of medical examinations is further dealt with in s. 44(7) and (8), which provide:

(a) that a child may give informed consent to any medical examination;

(b) that the court may order that there should be no medical or psychiatric examination, or that such an examination shall take place *only if further permission is obtained from the court.*

The need for directions

If you are seeking an emergency protection order and you or your agency feel that there may be the need for some form of medical examination, then you should, at the time of the application, seek a direction from the court. Some lawyers would argue that despite the absence of directions it would still be possible to have an examination carried out. Our advice, nevertheless, is to seek a direction from the court. If it is not sought at the time of the initial application and it is decided that such an examination ought to be carried out then a direction should be sought under the provisions of s. 44(9).

This point of view is reinforced by rule 18(1) of the relevant court rules, which states:

> No person may, without leave of the court, cause the child to be medically examined or psychiatrically examined or otherwise assessed, for the purposes of the preparation of expert evidence for use in the proceedings.

Religious objections to treatment

The position of children of Jehovah's Witnesses and parents with similar religious objections to treatment needs particular mention. The use of emergency protection orders would not provide the degree of parental responsibility to override the parents objections to treatment. *In Re R (A Minor) (Blood Transfusion)* (1993), Booth J stated that the use of an emergency protection order in such cases was not appropriate. Either the inherent jurisdiction of the High Court should be used, or the local authority should apply under s. 8 to a High Court judge.

Variation

Section 44(9) deals with applications to vary the order whilst it is still in force. If directions have been made about contact with parents or other people, or medical examinations, then an application can be made to vary these.

Limits on the emergency protection order

Returning the child before the emergency protection order expires

Given the drastic effect of an emergency protection order, the Act contains various provisions to mitigate the disruption caused to the child and family. Section 44(10) requires that although an emergency protection order may have been granted, the child should be kept away from 'home' only as long as is required, and if it is safe the child should be returned 'home'. These provisions are set out in Box 12.16.

Once it is safe to return the child, then, you must do so. In the case of a child needing the emergency operation, once the operation has taken place then the child should be 'returned' (albeit that the child may stay in hospital). The duty to return in s. 44(11) is an important example of the necessary checks and balances built into the legislation. The state has a power to intervene in children's lives where it is necessary to protect them, that power must not be excessive. If there is no need to keep the child, the Act says the child should be returned.

Returned to whom?

You can return the child to a different person—not the parent, not the person caring for the child at the time of the emergency protection order—only with the court's permission (s. 48(11)).

BOX 12.16 Section 44(10)

Where an emergency protection order is in force with respect to a child and—

(a) the applicant has exercised the power given by subsection (4)(b)(i) [removed a child] but it appears to him that it is safe for the child to returned; or

(b) the applicant has exercised the power given by subsection (4)(b)(ii) [prevented the child from being removed from accommodation] but it appears to him safe for the child to be allowed to be removed from the place in question,

he shall return the child or (as the case may be) allow him to be removed.

The emergency protection order continues

The return of a child under this subsection does not bring the emergency protection order to an end. Section 44(12) states that if, having returned the child at any time whilst the order is still in force, it appears to the applicant that the child should again be removed, then that can be done. This is without the need for a fresh application. So suppose the parent of the child who had the emergency operation did try to remove the child from the hospital against medical advice, the current emergency protection order would give the power to stop this.

Applications to discharge an emergency protection order

The next 'check' on the emergency protection order is the right of the parent to challenge the order. This right of challenge is not total. The relevant section is s. 45. The right to apply for a discharge is not available for the first seventy-two hours of an emergency protection order. Neither does it apply for a parent who was present at the hearing of the application for the emergency protection order (i.e. was given the chance to put their side of the case to the court). Such a parent has no right to seek to have the order discharged at any time.

Similarly, there is no right to have an order discharged after that order has been extended. This is because rule 4 of the relevant court rules requires that an extension application take place only after notice has been given to all parties. So again, the parents will have had their chance to put their side of the case.

The application to discharge the order can be made by the child (through his or her guardian) or the child's parents.

No appeals

The Act allows for any particular emergency protection order only to be discharged, not to be appealed against.

Section 45(10) provides:

(10) No appeal may be made against the making of, or refusal to make, an emergency protection order or against any direction given by the court in connection with such an order.

This point was clearly made in *Hounslow London Borough Council v A* (1993) and *Re P (Emergency Protection Order)* (1996).

This would not exclude an application for judicial review if the circumstances were appropriate. However, the case study at the beginning of this chapter indicates that the basis for an application for judicial review is very limited. There is a need to ensure that the expertise of the Family Proceedings Court is appropriately applied. If the emergency protection order was made by the High Court, there can be no judicial review of that decision.

Additional powers to protect children

Disclosure of information

Section 48 of the Children Act 1989 gives additional powers which may be relevant. For instance, you may not know exactly where the child is who may be in need of emergency protection. The court may include a provision in the emergency protection order requiring a person who may have information about the child's whereabouts to disclose that information (s. 48(1)). The order may also authorise an applicant to enter premises and search for the child, although this section in any event requires that the parents or whoever is in control of the premises cooperate. If you are prevented from entering premises or gaining access to the child, or it appears to the court that you may be, the court can issue a warrant authorizing the police to assist the entry and search.

Other children

You may believe that there are other children on the premises who also ought to be the subject of an emergency protection order. If so, you may seek an order authorizing a search for them. If the child is found and you are satisfied that the grounds for an emergency protection order exist, the order authorizing the search has effect as if it were an emergency protection order. This is useful when you are not able to identify all the children in the family, or, for instance, where there is evidence of the existence of a paedophile ring but the number and identities of the children involved are unknown.

Recovery orders

Lastly, the Act gives you powers through the mechanism of recovery orders (s. 50) in respect of a child in care, or the subject of an emergency protection order or in police protection, where the child has unlawfully been taken away, has run away, or is staying away from the 'responsible person'. A responsible person is anyone who has the care of the child by virtue of a care order or an emergency protection order. The order operates as a direction to produce the child, or to disclose his or her whereabouts, and authorizes a constable to enter named premises and search for the child, using reasonable force if necessary.

Practical considerations for emergency protection orders

Record keeping

There is a clear need for meticulous record keeping of the social worker involved so that the evidence of the investigation, which is one branch of the grounds for an emergency protection order, can be shown, together with the details of obstruction by the parents that would be required.

Before taking action

Whatever the situation is in which you intend seeking an emergency protection order, always stop to think clearly about why you want an emergency protection order and what you are going to do with it. Always try and consult with a colleague, even if your particular management guidelines allow you to take such steps without consultation.

Refusal of an emergency protection order

If an emergency protection order is refused then, in principle, there does not appear to be any bar to making another application. This is particularly true if further information becomes available concerning the likelihood of potential harm to the child.

Identification

A small practical point is that under s. 44(3) of the Children Act a person seeking access to a child for an investigation must produce some duly authenticated document stating that they are authorized to seek access. All local authority social workers are such authorized persons. Failure by you to produce such proof, if asked for, is just the sort of point that a lawyer acting for a parent would love to have as an opening question in cross-examination. The mere failure to have identification does not on its own prevent you obtaining the order, but it makes you look less professional to the court. Also, the explanatory notes that are part of the statutory form of the emergency protection order have a box telling the parent to ask anyone who tries to carry out the order for evidence of their identity.

Out-of-hours applications

The magistrates' courts' rules allow a single justice (magistrate) to hear an application for an emergency protection order (rule 2(5)). If the hearing is to be made without notice, leave of the clerk to the justices has to be obtained (rule 4(4)). Therefore, in applying out of the normal court time for an order, the applicant needs to contact the justices' clerk first, if the hearing is to take place without the parents.

Time limits

There is a long list of tasks for the social worker to complete in the short period of time that the emergency protection order lasts. Fifteen, let alone eight, days is a very short period of time, especially when lawyers and courts are involved. Given the chance for parties to seek a discharge of the order and to seek contact with the child, the entire time between the granting and expiration of the order could be occupied with court hearings instead of carrying out the intended assessment.

To set this in some context, we reproduce in Box 12.17 a list of possible tasks following an emergency protection order. (This, slightly modified, is taken from J. Bridge, S. Bridge, and S. Luke, *Blackstone's Guide to the Children Act 1989* (Blackstone Press, 1990).)

▉ Summary of the key features of the emergency protection order

In Box 12.18 opposite, we provide a summary of the key features of the emergency protection order.

▉ Child assessment orders

Section 43 of the Children Act allows the local authority to obtain a child assessment order. This provides for the compulsory assessment of the child's state of health and development, if need be by removing the child from the home. It would probably be better called a child investigation order, since it allows only a limited amount of assessment. It was introduced at a very late stage in the Bill's passage through

BOX 12.17 Tasks that may be necessary during the emergency protection order

(a) Arrange for accommodation for the child.

(b) Place the child with foster parents or in an institution, and explain to the child what is happening and give sufficient information to those who will be caring for the child to do so appropriately.

(c) Explain to the parents why their child has been removed from them, and discuss concerns and allegations with them.

(d) Spend further time with the child, to be satisfied that the child's welfare is being met, and also ask the child about any concerns or allegations.

(e) Take the child for medical examination and/or treatment, and obtain the doctor's diagnosis, having obtained leave of the court, if required.

(f) Make decisions about who the child should be allowed to have contact with (from those listed in s. 47(11)).

(g) Arrange for such contact to take place.

(h) Instruct the authority's solicitor in time for extension hearings. Consider making application for directions governing contact or medical examination. Instruct the local authority solicitor to commence appropriate proceedings, and provide sufficient information for the solicitor to do so.

(i) Discuss the case with a children's guardian if one has been appointed.

(j) Convene a child protection conference, ensuring a sufficient number of those involved with the family attend.

(k) Keep under review whether it is safe to return the child home.

(l) Decide, with senior social work staff, whether action needs to be taken to promote or safeguard the child's welfare.

(m) Attend court in respect of an application for an interim care order.

Parliament. The child assessment order can trace its history back to the Kimberley Carlile report. In that case, the social worker was prevented by the stepfather from seeing Kimberley. There were doubts whether or not the legal powers then available were sufficient. The report recommended the institution of an order such as the child assessment order. Prior to its introduction the Government had stated that it was against the idea of such orders. The figures from the *Annual Reports* on the Children Act show that the order has not proved very popular. Box 12.19 sets out the relevant provisions of s. 43.

The necessity of the order

To obtain an order you need to show to the court not that, objectively speaking, the child is at risk, but that you have reasonable cause to believe the child *is* at risk. Then

BOX 12.18 Key features of the emergency protection order

Feature	Provision	Section	Note
Grounds	Child likely to suffer significant harm or cannot be seen where child is at risk of suffering significant harm. Must apply the welfare principle and the non-intervention principle but not the welfare checklist.	s. 44(1)	See the full discussion of significant harm earlier in this chapter.
Duration	8 days—possible extension for additional 7 days.	s. 45(3), (5)	Could be for a shorter period.
Application	Any person can apply.		This includes the police.
Discharge	Certain persons may be able to apply for discharge between 72 hours after commencement of order and 8 days.	s. 45(8), (9)	Cannot apply during extension of EPO.
Parental responsibility	Grants a very limited parental responsibility to the local authority. The parent of the child does not lose parental responsibility.	s. 44(4)	This is a critical check on the scope of the EPO.
Directions	Court has the power to order contact, medical and/or psychiatric reports, assessment, etc.	s. 44(6)	The child's informed consent is required.
Emergency	The EPO may be made by a single justice with the leave of the clerk if the parents are not alerted to the proceedings.	Family Proceedings Court (Children Act 1989) Rules rr. 2(5), 4(6)	The order should be made by a full court if possible. Decisions about whether to inform parents about the application must bear in mind any danger to the child(ren) involved.
Child	Must be named or described as clearly as possible.		

you must show that an assessment of health and development is required actually to find out whether the child is suffering or is likely to suffer significant harm. Having satisfied the court of this you then have to show that you could not make a satisfactory assessment without the order.

BOX 12.19 The child assessment order—s. 43

(1) on the application of a local authority . . . for an order under this section, the court may make the order if, but only if, it is satisfied that—

    (a) the applicant has reasonable cause to suspect that the child is suffering, or is likely to suffer, significant harm;

    (b) an assessment of the state of the child's health or development or of the way in which he has been treated, is required to enable the applicant to determine whether or not the child is suffering, or is likely to suffer, significant harm; and

    (c) it is unlikely that such an assessment will be made, or be satisfactory, in the absence of an order under this section.

(2) . . .

(3) A court may treat an application under this section as an application for an emergency protection order.

(4) No court shall make a child assessment order if it is satisfied—

    (a) that there are grounds for making an emergency protection order with respect to the child; and

    (b) that it ought to make such an order rather than a child assessment order.'

Is an emergency protection order more appropriate?

Whenever there is a child at risk the question whether or not the child would be safe if left in his or her home will be uppermost in most people's minds. That is why this section states that the court shall not make a child assessment order if it thinks that the child should be removed from the home. This would be done by means of an emergency protection order which we discuss above.

If there are no grounds for making an emergency protection order then the court may grant the application for the child assessment order. This 'fail-safe' measure may explain why the courts are reluctant to grant a child assessment order, preferring to grant an emergency protection order. We suspect that such an attitude prevails with senior management within local authorities.

In some circumstances, though, it may well be that there are just no grounds for an emergency protection order until after an assessment order is granted.

Planning for an assessment

Just as the child assessment order is not intended to be dealt with on a 'without notice' basis, neither does the assessment have to begin on the day the order is made. Section 43(5) specifies that the date on which the order may begin can be set by the court. This enables a plan for an assessment to be made, in advance, to begin at some future date.

Speed

The order may last for only seven days. It is difficult to make an adequate form of assessment within that timescale. This is particularly true when you consider that the Framework for the Assessment of Children in Need and Their Families (see chapter 11) talks of the first week being the investigation period and of assessment taking up to twelve weeks. Clearly, all that the assessment in a child assessment order is capable of achieving is to show whether other court orders should or should not be applied for.

If an order is granted then its purpose will be to allow this limited type of assessment to be carried out. To this end the order may include directions for the child to be produced for medical or psychiatric examination. Such examinations are subject to the informed consent of the child (discussed in chapter 3).

Removal for assessment only

The order does allow the child to be compulsorily removed from the home, but only for the purposes of the assessment, and, if that occurs, there are provisions for reasonable contact by the child with parents or other persons. These are contained in s. 43(9) and (10) which is set out in Box 12.20 below.

Therefore, the child may be removed only if the court order says so. This would be where it was necessary for the child to attend for a short residential assessment. The order is not designed to protect the child by removal from the home—that is the function of the emergency protection order.

Parents must know of the application

An application for a child assessment order cannot be made on a 'without notice' basis. It must be made when the parents have been told of the hearing and have the chance to be represented there (rule 4(4)).

 BOX 12.20 Section 43 (9) and (10)—limited removal from home under the child assessment order

(9) The child may only be kept away from home—

   (a) in accordance with directions specified in the order;

   (b) if it is necessary for the purposes of assessment; and

   (c) for such period as may be specified in the order.

(10) Where the child is to be kept away from home, the order shall contain such directions as the court thinks fit with regard to the contact that he must be allowed to have with other persons while away from home.'

Variation and discharge of a child assessment order

It may be that the order having been made, the arrangements for the assessment cannot be carried out on the set date. If a variation becomes necessary, or even if a discharge of the order is required, the court can do this under rule 2(3).

◼ Removal by the police to accommodation

Police powers

The police are very much in the 'front line' when it comes to dealing with social problems. It is therefore to be expected that they will, in the course of their duties, come across children at risk who need protection. The police are given powers under s. 46 of the Children Act to take those children into police protection. The powers apply to children whom the police find and contain no provisions enabling the police to search for a child. They can be used for runaways or for abandoned children, or where the police come across children with drunk parents or living in unhygienic conditions.

A revised Home Office Circular 'The duties and powers of the police under the Children Act 1989' (HO Circular 44/03) was published on 8 September 2003. The purpose of the circular was to give greater clarity to all police officers about when and how they should use police protection powers under the Children Act 1989. It is available at **www.homeoffice.gov.uk/docs2/hoc4403.html**.

No court order necessary

The police are not equipped to deal with children at risk, and therefore the police are required to arrange to place the children in suitable accommodation. They also have the power to ensure that a child remains in suitable accommodation such as a hospital (s. 46(1)(a) and (b)). Neither of these powers (to remove a child or to keep a child in a safe place) requires a court order. The police therefore have powers which a social worker does not.

Duties to notify

As soon as the police have taken a child into their protection they have to notify the relevant local authority, notify the child, if appropriate, of what steps are to be taken, take steps to discover the wishes of the child concerned, move the child to suitable accommodation, and inform the designated officer of the fact that a child has been taken into police protection (s. 46(3)).

The 'designated officer' within the police is clearly the liaison point between the local authority and the police in these cases, and every social worker should be aware of who this person is—every police force is required to appoint one—see chapter 8.

The police also have to inform the child's parent of the fact that the child has been taken into police custody. The police do not obtain parental responsibility for the child by taking the child into police custody but must do what is reasonable to safeguard or promote the child's welfare (s. 46(9)).

The relationship with emergency protection orders

If the police think that an emergency protection order should be sought then they have to apply for it. They can do this whether or not the local authority is aware of the application or, more importantly, whether or not the local authority agrees with the making of such an application (s. 46(7) and (8)). If a child is in police protection that triggers the duty for a local authority to carry out an investigation under s. 47. Of course police protection may be the first step in a long process which may result in a final court order.

Time limits and contact

No child may be kept in police protection for more than seventy-two hours, and during that time the police must allow both the child's parent and anybody having a contact order under s. 8 to have reasonable contact with the child (s. 46(10)).

However, if the child in police protection has been placed in local authority accommodation then it is for the local authority to arrange contact (s. 46(11)). Therefore, for the best of reasons, whenever the police take a child into their protection, they will wish to accommodate the child with the local authority as soon as possible. Either the police or, more probably, the local authority can apply for an emergency protection order if appropriate.

The relationship between the police and social services

The question whether the social worker should use their own powers under the Act or turn to the police will be a decision that will greatly depend on the circumstances of the particular case and the extent and nature of the cooperation and liaison between the local police and the social services department.

In an extreme case, if you believe that a child is in serious physical danger, you can ask a police officer to exercise their powers under the Police and Criminal Evidence Act 1984, s. 17, to enter any premises and to search for and remove the child. No court order is required. The police may also arrest without warrant any person who has committed any offence where the arrest is necessary to protect a child from that person (Police and Criminal Evidence Act 1984, s. 25). The police also have powers under the Crime and Disorder Act 1998 to remove truants either to home, or to a place of safety.

■ Practical points relevant to all applications for orders

Application forms

Applications for all orders under the Act have to be commenced by lengthy application forms that are prescribed in the rules. The forms provide the court with the necessary background detail concerning the child and the child's family and the nature of the order sought. This will enable the court and the other parties to have as full a picture as possible concerning the child, even before any hearing takes place.

Any amendment to the form once it is filed with the court requires the leave of the court. You need to get the form right first time if possible. It is preferable to get your agency lawyer to draft the application form and deal with the directions.

Emergencies

There are provisions under r. 4(4) for the proceedings to be held without notice (i.e. for the application to be made by one party in the absence of the other parties), and in those circumstances for the application to be filed with the court at a later date.

Directions hearings

All new public law applications begin in the magistrates' court. The application forms enable the magistrates' court to decide whether the case will be dealt with in that court, in a higher court, or in a different geographical location. At the same time the court will be able to consider whether at this stage a children's guardian should be appointed. These decisions will be made at a directions hearing. The procedure for these hearings is set out in r. 14. This states that the clerk of the court may make directions concerning the conduct of the proceedings, including the matters set out in Box 12.21 below.

The application will need to be supported by evidence by means of written statements.

These provisions mean that the social worker is going to have done a considerable amount of background work prior to seeing the agency's lawyer. The social worker will supply the lawyer with a full report from which a detailed proof of evidence and draft witness statements can be prepared.

 BOX 12.21 Typical matters considered at a directions hearing

(a) the timetable for the proceedings;

(b) varying the timetable (including the time limits set out in the rules);

(c) whether the attendance of the child is required;

(d) the appointment of a children's guardian;

(e) the timetable and arrangements for the service of documents;

(f) what evidence (including experts' reports) will be submitted;

(g) what welfare reports will be required under s. 7 (see chapter 11);

(h) whether the case should be transferred to another court because of the need for speed, or the complexity and seriousness of the case; and

(i) whether to consolidate the case with other proceedings (such as divorce proceedings).

Guidance on the directions hearing and planning is to be found in *Re D (Minors) (Time Estimates)* (1994) and in the suggested form of directions in the *1993/94 Annual Report* of the Children Act Advisory Committee.

The court will be looking to have the final hearing at the earliest possible stage. Under s. 32 the court is under a duty to draw up a timetable for a hearing for care proceedings.

Written reasons for decisions

The requirement under r. 21 for the magistrates' court to give written reasons for its decisions appears to have caused some difficulties.

In *Hertfordshire County Council v W* (1993), the magistrates thought that when dismissing an application for an interim care order they were not required to give written reasons. The High Court held that they must do so.

In *Hillingdon London Borough Council v H* (1992), the High Court said that the magistrates had to give written reasons at the time of the announcement of their decision. They could not meet later to give full written reasons. This point was emphasized in *Hertfordshire County Council v W* (1993). Here the magistrates failed to give reasons for their decision at the time of announcing the decision. As a result their decision was held to be void.

Guidance

In *Oxfordshire County Council v R* (1992), important guidance was given to magistrates about how to approach the setting out of their reasons for their decisions which we set out in Box 12.22 below.

Agreed draft orders

Where all parties agree a draft order there is no need for a full hearing of all of the evidence. In *Devon County Council v S* (1992), the court was given an agreed order. Nevertheless, the magistrates insisted on hearing evidence before interim and final orders. The High Court said that whilst the court should not merely rubber-stamp such an order, it was not necessary to have a full hearing of evidence. What was needed was sufficient evidence to enable them to make the judicial act of making the order.

 BOX 12.22 Guidance on setting out reasons

(a) There are certain minimum findings and reasons which must be stated, so that the parties and the appellate court can see how the magistrates have approached their task.

(b) A good starting point is the statutory framework within which the magistrates are working (under s. 1). Using the statutory criteria as a checklist, the findings of fact and reasons can be built around them without undue length.

EXERCISES

1 Work through the various court orders in this chapter and produce a grid of their main features, such as duration, directions, discharge, etc.

2 In the following scenarios, consider what order you may be seeking and why.

    (a) Jon has been found wandering in the street by the police. He is bruised and crying. He is about 3 years old.

    (b) Tim is 11 years old. The head teacher of his school has contacted you with the following information. He is underweight and dressed in cast-off clothes. He is the youngest child of a family of seven. He has been absent from school on numerous occasions during the last year. When you consult your records you find that two of the older children in the family have had short periods subject to a care order. There is a note on the file suggesting that Tim's mother finds it difficult to cope. You have talked to Tim, who seems depressed and tells you he is unhappy at home.

    (c) Lizzie has serious drug addiction problems. She has tried to stop her drug abuse but frequently relapses. Her children, who are aged 5 and 9, are neglected. You suspect that in the long term the children would progress better with a foster placement.

3 Sarah is the subject of an emergency protection order. What are your responsibilities to Sarah and her parents during the period of the order?

4 Paula's child, Ian, is subject to a care order and has been placed with a foster family for the last six years. Ian has told Paula that he is unhappy in his placement. Paula would like to apply for the discharge of the care order. How does she go about this?

COMPANION WEB SITE

 For guidance on how to answer these exercises, visit the companion web site at:
www.oup.com/uk/booksites/law

WHERE DO WE GO FROM HERE?

This chapter has explained the range of court orders which your department may apply for to protect children. These orders must not be seen separately from the need to plan appropriately for children which we discussed in chapter 11. One way of planning for children is to consider their needs for permanence. The following chapter on adoption and special guardianship sets out the legal framework for finding children new families on a permanent basis.

ANNOTATED FURTHER READING

Further guidance on the range of orders is provided by specialized texts, such as R. White (ed.), *Clarke Hall and Morrison on Children* (Butterworths, 2000). This loose leaf encylopaedia is authoritative and up to date.

The work of the courts

C. Mullins, 'At work with the Principal Family Judges' [2003] Law Society's Gazette 28.

Threshold criteria

An interesting recent article on the threshold criteria is B. Posner and P. Diaz (2002), 'Everything We Always Wanted to Know About the Threshold Criteria' [2002] Family Law 850.

M. Hayes, Case commentary, Re D and N; Re B. Uncertain Evidence and Risk Taking in Child Protection Cases, C & 7 LQ (2004) 16.1 (63)

Hayes argues that the House of Lords applied different standards of proof at the threshold and welfare stages of care proceedings. She proposes that a 'real possibility' test is applied at all stages of proceedings. This test would strike the correct balance between protecting children from future risk and interfering, perhaps wrongly, in their lives and in the lives of their parents.

T. Booth, W. Booth & D McConnell (2004). Parents with Hearing Difficulties, Care Proceedings & The Family Courts: Threshold decisions and the moral matrix C & 7 LQ (2004) 16.4 409

This paper investigates how social sciences and the courts handle child protection cases involving parents with learning difficulties and explores the factors that are weighed in the balance when decisions are made in the best interests of the children from such families.

Police protection

J. Masson, 'Police Protection—Protecting Whom?' (2002) 24(3) J of SW of 72. An overview and critique of the use of police protection under s. 46 of the Children Act 1989.

Historical overview

J. Masson, 'From Curtis to Waterhouse: State Care and Child Protection in the UK 1945–2000', in S. Katz, J. Eekelaar, and M. Macken (eds.), *Cross-Currents: Family Law and Policy in the United States and England* (Oxford University Press, 2000).

13 Adoption

CASE STUDY

Re G [2002] EWCA Civ 761, 2002 WL 10395

This case arose out of what the Court of Appeal described as 'difficult care proceedings' brought by the local authority in respect of the five children of the family. G, aged 6, was the eldest. There were two sets of twins, N and C, who were 3, and C and T, who were 18 months. All five children had the same mother, but G had a different father. Care orders had previously been made. The adoption case was the local authority application to free these two sets of twins for adoption.

G and two of the twins had suffered serious physical injuries. But in the care proceedings the judge at the county court had been unable to decide which of the parents was responsible for which of the injuries. A care order had been made in respect of all five children. G was at the time of the adoption application settled with her maternal grandmother. The twins were placed with experienced foster parents.

Because of the age of the foster parents, around 50, there were doubts whether the foster parents could act as adoptive parents. However, the foster parents had provided excellent care for the children, who were very attached to them. The twins' father's brother and his wife, who were a childless couple, also wanted to adopt the twins, and the county court judge was impressed with their potential as parents.

The judge had dismissed the local authority freeing application, on the basis that the foster parents would be making their own adoption application. The judge (using Children Act powers—see chapter 12) had also made decisions about contact between the parents and the siblings. He had noted that the preferred view of the local authority and the children's guardian was that contact with both parents should be severed. As far as contact with the mother was concerned the judge had considered that the local authority position was illogical because of the position of G. He had decided that G should keep in contact with her half brothers and sisters and that the mother should continue contact with G. He had also decided that as G would have contact with her siblings it was sensible and beneficial that there should be some contact between the mother and the twins.

The appeal

The appeal was the result of the decision the judge made about the father having contact with the twins. The judge had decided that:

> so far as father is concerned, I regret to say, from his point of view, that I cannot see the same benefit accruing. He is not going to be seeing G. The children are going to be confused by his involvement in the equation and I am afraid that I have come to the view that it is not in the interests of the children to continue contact. I therefore give the local authority permission, under section 34 [Children Act 1989—see chapter 12], to terminate.

The judge had also been asked to consider making a direction about contact between the uncle and aunt and the twins. Whilst he had made no order he had asked that the foster parents be told of his view that contact between them, for instance through birthday cards and telephone calls, and the children would be beneficial.

The father appealed against the order giving the local authority permission to terminate his contact. The Court of Appeal agreed with the father that the reasons for terminating contact with him, whilst allowing it to the mother and to members of the father's family, were not coherent. The Court, reluctantly, allowed the appeal. The judge, Ward LJ, commented:

> [W]hen one is looking at the benefits of contact, in a case like this the benefit is the benefit that comes from the children simply knowing who the natural parental figures are. It is to remove the sense of the ogre, as they reach adolescence and begin to search for their own identity, with the double crisis not only of adolescence itself but of coming to grips with the fact that they are adopted. That is why the current research is in favour of some contact in adoption. It does not seem to me that the judge has analysed why the minimal benefit of keeping the link alive does not operate as much for father as for mother. He does not look into the long term and analyse whether there is some benefit to the children in knowing that this father has kept in touch with them, despite the adoption. . . .
>
> It seems to me that there will be even more confusion for the children if they are to be able to have contact with their paternal uncle but not to have any contact with their father, and I do not see that the judge explains why that distinction can, and should, properly be drawn.

OVERVIEW AND OBJECTIVES

We are not concerned here with the legal technicalities of the case—applications to free for adoption arise under the Adoption Act 1976 and will not be considered in this chapter, which looks at the provisions of the Adoption and Children Act 2002 which is gradually replacing the Adoption Act 1976—but with the nature of adoption and the relationship children have with their birth family. The case raises a number of questions which will continue to be relevant. Why do you think that the local authority was opposed to continuing contact with the birth parents? What do you think would be the right course of action in relation to the uncle and aunt? Can children handle the messy complexities of difficult birth families? Can adoptive parents? Do you agree with the Court of Appeal judge that there should be an analysis of the potential benefit of children knowing that their father has kept in touch with them? As you read this chapter think about the different responsibilities you have, to the child, to the prospective adopters, to the birth family; think about the conflicts that may arise, and consider how the law, if at all, helps you to resolve those conflicts.

By the end of this chapter you should be familiar with the new legal framework, the new emphasis on adoption as a useful solution for children's problems and the range of powers available to social services to support the adoption process which will continue to be available after the making of adoption orders. You will also learn about the alternative to adoption, special guardianship. The most important legal fact to note, however, is that the Adoption and Children Act 2002 requires the welfare of the child throughout its life to be the paramount consideration of the court or adoption agency. Holding onto that fact should help you resolve the dilemmas you will inevitably face.

Introduction

Local authorities should plan for the long-term future of all the children they look after. The Waterhouse report, *Lost in Care—The Report of the Tribunal of Inquiry into the Abuse of Children in Care in the Former County Council Areas of Gwynnedd and Clywdd since 1974* (to be found on the Web at **www.doh.gov.uk/lostincare**) points out the 'lamentable' effects of failing to do so. There is now a legal obligation to consider permanence at the four-month statutory review of looked after children, which has been considered in chapter 10. When you consider permanent resolutions you will inevitably find that there are some children who will never be in a position to return to their parents or any other family member. In those circumstances the authority, to safeguard and promote the child's welfare, must look for an alternative permanent substitute family, unless there are compelling reasons not to do so.

If you have come to the conclusion that a permanent substitute family is the appropriate course of action then you are likely to be considering adoption. Adoption has until recently been governed by the Adoption Act 1976. However, the Adoption and Children Act 2002 received Royal Assent on 7 November 2002 and it will be implemented during the lifetime of this edition. We are therefore going to explain the new provisions for adoption and statutory references in the rest of this chapter will be to the Adoption and Children Act 2002 unless otherwise stated. There may be particular reasons why adoption is not appropriate for children; for instance, older children may be unhappy about severing legal links with their birth families. For this reason the Adoption and Children Act 2002 introduces the new legal status of special guardianship orders which allow for a form of long-term placement with legal safeguards that should be considered.

A note of caution: whilst we give you an overview of the law, for full details you need a specialised text, and if you are involved in the adoption process you must consult specialist social workers and your agency lawyer.

Modernizing the law

Adoption is an extraordinary decision for the state to make about a child's life. It severs the ties with the birth family and creates new legal relationships with the adoptive family. The Adoption Act 1976 is over 25 years old. There have been two major domestic legal landmarks in the relationship between children, families, and the state since 1976: the Children Act 1989 and the Human Rights Act 1998. Additionally, the Government ratified the United Nations Convention on the Rights of the Child in 1991 and ratified the Hague Convention on Protection of Children and Cooperation in respect of Inter-country Adoption in 2003. Each of these provisions puts the adoption decision into new perspective. The Adoption Act 1976 has seemed increasingly out of step legally, particularly since the implementation of the Children Act 1989, because of the different weighting given to the welfare of the child under each piece of legislation.

Under the Adoption Act 1976 the child's welfare merely had to be considered 'first', in contrast to the paramountcy of the child's welfare under the Children Act 1989. The Human Rights Act 1998 has led to a new focus on the ways in which the state should respect the birth family's rights and when it is legitimate and proportionate to disregard those rights.

Perhaps more important than the changes in the legal landscape is the transformation of family life and of understandings of what can constitute a family during the last twenty-five years. Unmarried partnerships and same-sex relationships are increasingly recognized as valid alternatives to traditional marriage. Single parents bring children up successfully. Further, there is a growing body of evidence that children are able to deal with complexity in family relationships. Relationship breakdowns, new partners, new step- and half siblings seem to be accepted and understood by children, as long as they have a stable relationship with a loving adult and feel secure in their own future.

Other attitudes have changed. We are an increasingly open society and recognize the benefits of honesty and openness with children. Adoption is no longer seen as something to be hidden. People who are adopted are increasingly viewed as entitled to information about their adoption. There is also a general understanding that some information is private and, whilst the state may hold it, the person it concerns deserves to have their privacy respected.

The context of adoption itself has changed, mainly as a result of the other transformations in society. Just as adoption is no longer a secret, illegitimacy is not something to be hidden. As a result, babies are less likely to be placed for adoption. This is reflected in the reduction in adoptions from around 20,000 a year in 1970 to 4,100 in 1999. However, older children who are being looked after by the local authority may want the security and permanence of adoption. The number of looked after children adopted has remained relatively stable at around 2,000 per year, but now represents about half of all adoptions. But older children come with established relationships with their birth family and adoption needs to take these relationships into account. Additionally, older children seeking adoption may have physical, mental, and behavioural difficulties and troubled pasts. This increases the challenge of adoption and highlights the need to support the adoption process beyond the adoption order.

Finally, we live in a world transformed by the Internet and mass communications. The speed of travel continues to increase. People thwarted in their desire to adopt a baby in the United Kingdom have looked to other parts of the world, in particular to areas of poverty and war, where families may be desperate to give their children a chance in the prosperous West, or where children are abandoned or sold. The Internet enables them to do this, but it increases the risk of the commodification of children and the possibility that children can in effect be sold to the highest bidder. Yet the Internet can also be a useful resource for adoption, putting people in touch with adoption agencies and support agencies.

BOX 13.1 Modernization of the law—a summary

Reason	Comment
The legislative framework	
• The Children Act 1989	• Increasing legal dissonance between the Adoption Act 1976 and the modern child centred perspective of the Children Act
• The Human Rights Act 1998	• New legal perspectives in particular the right to respect for family life and the right to a fair trial
• Ratification of International Conventions	• International obligations which attempt to ensure respect for the child's rights and resist the commodification of the child
The changing nature and meaning of 'family'	
• Increasing complexity	• Children and society have generally adapted well to more complex family life
• New structures and relationships	• Deviations from the 'norm' of the nuclear family are acceptable and more common
Importance of information	
• Democratic and accountable decision-making	• Increasing structures to support access to and freedom of information
• Relationship between knowledge of our childhood and our identity	• Children and adopted adults have rights to understand decisions made in their childhood
• The state should respect privacy	• The law must hold the balance between information necessary for decision making and respect for individual's privacy
Changing context of adoption	• Few babies available so the legal strategy of denying children's past life less feasible
	• Older children place new demands on adoptive families who will require support post adoption
	• In a multi-cultural diverse society there are new challenges for the adoption process
Need for support	• The state's responsibilities do not end with the adoption order
	• There is a need to encourage more people to be interested in adoption and recognize the support they need
Globalization and the Internet	• New requirements for international regulation to prevent the possibility of abuse
	• The Internet can be a force for harm and for good but needs regulation
	• Challenges posed by migration and movement of people

Implementation of the Adoption and Children Act 2002

The Act is expected to be implemented fully by September 2005. Certain provisions relating to adoption support were implemented in October 2003, the provisions placing restrictions on adoption from overseas were implemented in mid 2003, and the first phase of the Independent Review Mechanism which allows the review of decisions by adoption panels which turn down prospective adopters was implemented at the end of April 2004.

Information on the Act

The Adoption and Children Act 2002 and the Explanatory Notes to the Act are available on the HMSO web site at **www.hmso.gov.uk/acts**. Note that amendments to the Act are not made to the Internet version. The explanatory notes are extremely helpful in understanding the purpose of the statutory provisions. We have quoted from them extensively in our description of the new provisions. The Department of Health provides an excellent web site—**www.doh.gov.uk/adoption**—which provides full and up-to-date information on the Act and its implementation. We will provide a link on our web site and you are advised to consult the Department of Health web site for the latest government information and guidance on adoption. Other useful web sites include the one run by British Agencies for Adoption and Fostering— **www.baaf.org.uk**—which provides resources for would-be adoptive parents, and the latest information on the reforms. You may find their responses to the Act and the consultation on the regulations particularly interesting.

The Adoption and Children Act 2002

The Act affects all adoptions and arrangements for the adoption of children in England and Wales and all adoption applications from people who are resident and settled in England and Wales who seek to adopt children living abroad.

In brief the Adoption and Children Act 2002:

- aligns the principles of adoption law with the principles underpinning the Children Act where relevant to do so;
- improves and extends the regulation of adoption and adoption support services;
- sets out and modernizes the legal basis for the process of adoption;
- provides for both disclosure of and protection of information about adopted people and their birth relatives;
- regulates inter-country adoptions;
- regulates the advertising of children for adoption and payments in connection with adoption;
- provides the legal underpinning for an Adoption and Children Act Register;
- attempts to reduce delay in the adoption process.

The Act is in three Parts. Part 1 sets out the framework of the law on adoption. This chapter concentrates on Part 1 of the Act. Part 2 of the Act makes a series of amendments to the Children Act 1989, such as updating the parental responsibility of unmarried fathers, which we deal with as appropriate elsewhere in this book. However, we do detail within this chapter one particularly important feature of Part 2 which is the provision for a new form of long-term legal provision for children, special guardianship orders. We also explain the additional provisions for step-parent adoption. Part 3 of the Act is a series of miscellaneous provisions designed to regulate and improve adoption some of which we highlight in the chapter.

Human rights and adoption

The Adoption and Children Act 2002 addresses several human rights-based concerns about adoption. In particular it clarifies the role of the unmarried father and sets up a system that allows adopted people access to information about their past. Independent reviews are available for crucial decisions about selection of prospective adopters and where access to information is denied by the state.

However, it is inevitable that the adoption process will raise Human Rights Act considerations for adoption agencies. First, any decision to remove a child from its birth parents must be proportionate and necessary in a democratic society. Second, the views of the birth parents must always be taken into account, and if the matter goes to court they must be able to argue their case properly.

P, C and S v UK (2002) provides an excellent example of the way that precipitate action by the local authority can lead to a breach of the birth parents' and the child's human rights. The facts were as follows: P was convicted in the United States in 1995 of deliberately administering laxatives to her young son and thus endangering his health. She was diagnosed as suffering from Munchausen's syndrome, which led her to induce illness in her child and exaggerate her own medical history. In 1996, P moved to the United Kingdom and married C. Before the birth of their child, S, the local authorities expressed concern about P's conviction in the United States and sought to initiate care proceedings in relation to the unborn child. Upon birth, S was removed from P and C and freed for adoption—a procedure now abolished under the 2002 Act. Despite initial legal representation, P conducted her own legal case. The judge ordered S to be removed from P and C's care. His decision was based upon P's treatment of her previous child. Subsequent appeals were dismissed. P, C, and S applied to the European Court of Human Rights alleging that the adoption process had violated their rights under Article 6(1) (right to a fair trial), Article 8 (right to respect for family life), and Article 12 (right to marry and found a family) of the Convention. The Court held that there had been a violation of Articles 6(1) and 8 both as regards the removal of S at birth and as regards the subsequent care and adoption procedures. It also held that there were no separate issues arising under Article 12. The Court pointed out that the key principle of Article 6 was fairness. In light of the human rights principles of effective access to court and fairness, the complexity of the case, the importance of what was at stake, and the highly emotive nature of the subject matter, the Court concluded that P must receive the assistance of a lawyer. As regards Article 8, the Court made it clear that there must be extraordinarily compelling reasons before a baby can be physically removed from its mother, against her will, immediately after birth as a consequence of a procedure in which neither she nor her partner has been involved. In the particular circumstances of the case, the Court concluded that the draconian step of removing S from her mother shortly after birth was not supported by relevant and sufficient reasons and that it cannot be regarded as having been necessary in a democratic society for the purpose of safeguarding S.

Of course concern for the birth family's rights will often be outweighed by the urgency of the need to protect the child. You may feel that this case is yet another instance where social workers are condemned for taking action, but would also have been condemned for failing to act.

Adoption

The child's welfare

Section 1 is the linch-pin of the Act. It sets out the overarching principles upon which decisions made either by courts or by adoption agencies relating to the adoption of children should be based. The principles dovetail with the principles of the Children Act 1989. The child's welfare is placed at the centre of decision-making:

> 1(2) The paramount consideration of the court or adoption agency must be the child's welfare, throughout his life.

Note, however, that in s. 1(1) of the Children Act, it is court decisions only, and not those of social services or other agencies, which must be guided by the paramount consideration of the welfare of the child. There remains therefore a contrast between the welfare principle in adoption and in other proceedings in respect of children.

The statute then sets out a checklist of matters which a court or an adoption agency must consider. This welfare checklist is very similar to the checklist within the Children Act. It does not provide an exhaustive statement of what needs to be taken into account, nor is it written in order of priority. However, you should notice that decision makers must bear in mind that the decision is one which affects the rest of the child's life—and the long-lasting impact of adoption decisions must be reflected in their decision-making process. We have set the checklist out in Box 13.2.

The importance of s. 1 of the Act cannot be over-emphasized. All decisions relating to adoption are to be based upon it.

Of course we should not give the impression that welfare is not central to adoption even under the Adoption Act 1976. In *Re S and J (Adoption: Non Patrials)* (2004) provides a useful contemporary example. The prospective adopters were of Bangladeshi origin and had settled in Britain. They brought two boys into the country in contravention of the immigration rules and raised them along with their own children. The immigration authorities became aware of the situation in 1999 but did nothing active to deport the

BOX 13.2 The Adoption and Children Act checklist

1(4) The court or adoption agency must have regard to the following matters (among others)—

   (a) The child's ascertainable wishes and feelings regarding the decision (considered in the light of the child's age and understanding),

   (b) The child's particular needs,

   (c) The likely effect on the child (throughout his life) of having ceased to be a member of the original family and become an adopted person,

   (d) The child's age, sex, background and any of the child's characteristics which the court considers relevant,

   (e) Any harm (within the meaning of the Children Act 1989) which the child has suffered or is at risk of suffering,

   (f) The relationship which the child has with relatives, and with any other person in relation to whom the court or agency considers the relationship to be relevant, including—

      (i) the likelihood of any such relationship continuing and the value to the child of its doing so,

      (ii) the ability and willingness of any of the child's relatives, or of any such person, to provide the child with a secure environment in which the child can develop, and otherwise to meet the child's needs,

      (iii) the wishes and feelings of any of the child's relatives, or of any such person, regarding the child.

   References to a relative include the child's mother and father.

1(5) In placing the child for adoption, the adoption agency must give due consideration to the child's religious persuasion, racial origin and cultural and linguistic background.

   This is in line with the duty placed on local authorities under s. 22(5) of the Children Act.

   Note that the requirement is for 'due' consideration. These matters are only one element of the overall decision making process.

boys back to Bangladesh. When the Home Office eventually sought to remove the boys the applicants applied to adopt them. At the time of the hearing the elder boy was almost 18 years old and the younger was 15. The Secretary of State was joined in the proceedings and opposed the adoption application. The orders were granted in respect of both boys. The judge decided that there were sufficient psychological advantages for the younger boy for it to be said that his welfare indicated he should be adopted, with all the short and longer term emotional benefits that this would bring. No case had been made to treat him differently from the elder boy, even though the latter would gain the benefits of adoption primarily after reaching adulthood.

Placement for adoption

There are two stages which must be gone through before a child is adopted. The first of these is placement for adoption. Placement—a new legal process—allows adoption agencies to plan effectively for any subsequent adoption. In most circumstances this will not require court intervention. Placement can either be actual placement with the prospective adopters or it can act as an authority to place with prospective adopters once these have been identified.

Placement of children by adoption agencies for adoption is covered by ss.18–29 of the Act. The placement provisions replace the freeing provisions of the Adoption Act 1976. An adoption agency may place a child for adoption only with the consent of the parent or guardian under s. 19, or under a court placement order under s. 21. The consent of both birth parents is necessary to avoid court proceedings. Babies under six weeks old cannot be placed for adoption.

The purpose of the placement provisions is set out in the explanatory notes to the Act.

> The intention is to ensure key decisions are taken earlier in the adoption process than at present, with court involvement where necessary. This is intended to provide greater certainty and stability for children by dealing with consent to placement for adoption before they have been placed (at present this issue is often not addressed until the final adoption order hearing); to minimize the uncertainty for prospective adopters, who under the current system possibly face a contested court hearing at the adoption order stage; and to reduce the extent to which birth families are faced with a 'fait accompli' at the final adoption hearing (as they may be under the current system, where their child has not been freed for adoption but has been placed with an adoptive family for some time before the application or an adoption order is made).

Section 18(1) provides that an adoption agency (except in the case of a child who is less than six weeks old) may place a child for adoption with prospective adopters or, where it has already placed a child with any persons, leave the child with them as prospective adopters only if it does so with consent under s. 19 or under a placement order. Section 18(2) makes it clear that an adoption agency may place a child for adoption with prospective adopters only if the agency is satisfied that the child ought to be placed for adoption. So there are two placement routes, one with parental consent and the other by court order.

Placement with consent

Section 19 provides the mechanism by which children may be placed for adoption with parental consent and without a court order. Parents or guardians may consent either to the child being placed for adoption with prospective adopters identified in the consent, or being placed for adoption with any prospective adopters who may be chosen by the agency. Consent can be withdrawn at any point before an application for the final adoption order is made. As we explain below, if care proceedings have already been launched under the Children Act, s. 19 consent is not possible. Instead the local authority which is proposing an adoption must apply under s. 22(2) for a placement order—see below. Section 20 provides that parents or guardians may consent at the same time or subsequently to the making of a future adoption order.

Placement by court order

If parents do not consent then a court order is necessary. Section 21 provides that placement orders, court orders authorizing local authorities to place children for adoption with prospective adopters, may be made only if (s. 21(2)):

(a) the child is subject to a care order,

(b) the court is satisfied that the conditions for a care order are met, or

(c) the child has no parent or guardian.

The placement order can be made only if either the parent or guardian has consented to the placement or the court is satisfied that the parent's or guardian's consent should be dispensed with.

In determining whether the conditions are met, a clear link is made with the Children Act 1989. The Adoption and Children Act notes: 'The same threshold for compulsory intervention in family life is to apply where a local authority seeks authority to place a child for adoption without parental consent as applies where an authority seeks to take a child into care under a care order. In placement order cases, where the court is satisfied that the 'significant harm' threshold is met, it will then consider whether a placement order should be made.' That decision will be made using the s. 1 welfare criteria.

Section 22 sets out the circumstances when the local authority must apply for a placement order. We have set these out in Box 13.3.

What happens if the child's future is already being considered by the courts? Sub-section (2) provides that, if an application has been made the outcome of which may be a care order, or the child is subject to a care order, and the parents have not consented to the placement for adoption, the authority must, if satisfied that the child ought to be placed for adoption, apply for a placement order. However, if the child is subject to a care order and the parents are prepared to consent, the authority can choose whether to apply for a placement order or to place with parental consent under s. 19.

Parental consent to placement and adoption

Either the birth parents must consent to the placement or the court must decide that consent can be dispensed with. Consent, and when it can be dispensed with, are obviously critical to the placement and indeed the whole adoption process. The following discussion about consent in relation to placement orders is equally relevant to adoption orders, which we discuss later in this chapter.

Section 52 sets out the necessity for consent, the circumstances in which the court can dispense with consent, and the meaning of consent. We have set out the key subsections for you in full in Box 13.4.

13.3 Section 22(1)

s. 22(1) (a) the child is placed for adoption by them or is being provided with accommodation by them,
(b) no adoption agency is authorised to place the child for adoption,
(c) the child has no parent or guardian or the authority consider that the conditions in s. 31(2) of the 1989 Act are met, and
(d) the authority are satisfied that the child ought to be placed for adoption.

Dispensing with consent

In light of s. 52 it is apparent that consent can be dispensed with only in limited circumstances. When will it be appropriate for the court to dispense with parental consent? The decision of the court will be based upon the criteria in s. 1 of the Act. Each case will be based upon its own facts. Careful judgements will have to be made about the best possible future for the child. In many ways outcomes will be similar to the old law where parental consent to freeing for adoption can be dispensed with where 'the parent or guardian is withholding consent unreasonably'—s. 16(2)(b) of the Adoption Act 1976. However, the court will not be seeking to establish what a reasonable parent may do but will be considering as the 'paramount' consideration the child's welfare throughout his or her life. Under the old law the test was the reasonableness of the parents' refusal and the case law was a logical mess. After all, what reasonable parent, however bad at parenting, agrees to abandon their status as a parent? So, whilst it may be useful for you to read some case law on contested adoption cases, it is not relevant to the new legislation, and what will be most useful is to consider extremely carefully the matters set out in s. 1 of the Act, and ensure that any recommendations to the court that you make address those concerns. However, *S (A Child) (Adoption: Freeing Order)* (2001) provides an example of circumstances where the Court of Appeal was prepared to uphold the refusal of the local authority application for a freeing order. The facts were that S's mother, who was 15 at the time of S's birth, had initially cared for S in a foster home but subsequently abandoned the child. S was made the subject of a care order and had been placed with the prospective adoptive parents. The mother had not initially opposed the local authority's care plan that S be placed for adoption. At the application for the freeing order the mother, then aged 18, gave evidence that she had a new partner, a job, and a

---

 BOX 13.4 Section 52—consent

(1) The court cannot dispense with the consent of any parent or guardian of a child to the child being placed for adoption or to the making of an adoption order in respect of the child unless the court is satisfied that—

    (a) the parent or guardian cannot be found or is incapable of giving consent, or

    (b) the welfare of the child requires the consent to be dispensed with.

(2) . . .

(3) Any consent given by the mother to the making of an adoption order is ineffective if it is given less than six weeks after the child's birth.

(4) The withdrawal of any consent to the placement of a child for adoption, or of any consent given under section 20, is ineffective if it is given after an application for an adoption order is made.

(5) 'Consent' means consent given unconditionally and with full understanding of what is involved; but a person may consent to adoption without knowing the identity of the persons in whose favour the order will be made.

sufficiently stable life to enable her to care for s. The judge held that the mother had not unreasonably withheld her consent to the freeing order. The Court of Appeal dismissed the local authority's appeal. In the Court's opinion the judge had weighed all of the competing factors in the balance and had been impressed by the efforts of the mother and her new partner and the improvement in the mother's circumstances. He was entitled to refuse the application. Under the new law it is not the mother's view, but the court's view, of the child's welfare that matters most. But the decision would probably be the same.

The decision illustrates that a great deal of care must be taken to weigh up all the competing factors. Clearly what was decisive here was the dramatic change in the attitude and behaviour of the mother. It will be rare that there will be such compelling evidence before the court.

Parental responsibility

The impact of placement for adoption on parental responsibility is set out in s. 25. If a child is placed for adoption under s. 19 or an adoption agency is authorized to place a child for adoption under s. 19 or a placement order is in force in respect of a child, then parental responsibility for the child is given to the agency. While the child is placed with prospective adopters, then parental responsibility is given to them. The agency may restrict the exercise of parental responsibility of any parent or guardian, or of prospective adopters, in the same way as they can under a care order (see previous chapter).

Contact while the child is placed

Section 26 empowers the court to make orders for contact with the child placed for adoption or authorized to be placed. Applications for such contact may be made by the child or the agency, a parent, guardian, or relative and any person previously had contact under the Children Act 1989. Applications may also be made by a person who was caring for a baby under six weeks old and had the benefit of a residence order immediately before the adoption agency was authorized to place the child for adoption or placed the child for adoption. Applications may, in the rare cases where this occurs, be made by someone who had the care of a child prior to wardship. Finally, any person may apply who has obtained the court's leave to make the application.

Courts may on their own initiative make contact orders under s. 26. It may for instance become apparent during the court proceedings that the child gains great benefit from contact with a particular person.

Contact orders under s. 26 may be varied or revoked by the court on application by the child, the agency, or a person named in the order. If there are urgent short-term problems with contact, for instance where a child has become extremely upset following a visit and the social worker thinks that a cooling off period is required, then, despite the existence of the contact order, s. 27(2) enables the agency to stop contact for up to seven days in order to safeguard or promote the child's welfare. Clearly where there are longer term concerns then agencies should make proper application to the court for variation or revocation.

Legal implications

Sections 28 and 29 set out the legal relationship between placement, adoption, and other orders. Once a child is placed for adoption or authorized to be placed then the parent or guardian may not apply for residence orders unless an application for an adoption order has been made and the parent or guardian has obtained the court's leave. Likewise, once an application is made for an adoption order, a guardian of the child may not apply for a special guardianship order without the court's leave. We discuss special guardianship below. These provisions operate to restrict the availability of court proceedings and prevent unnecessary disruption to the placement process.

Children placed for adoption, authorized to be placed, or subject to a placement order cannot be given new surnames or removed from the United Kingdom without the leave of the court or the consent of each parent or guardian. Removal for a holiday of less than one month by prospective adopters does not require permission of the court or the parents or guardians.

There are additional legal implications of placement orders. When a placement order is in force it supersedes any care order, any supervision order, and any s. 8 orders. Nor can prohibited steps orders, residence orders, specific issues orders, supervision orders, or child assessment orders be made in respect of the child—s. 29(3). There is an exception in respect of residence orders. These can be applied for where an application for an adoption order has been made in respect of the child and the applying parent or guardian has the court's leave under s. 47 of the Act, or other applicants given leave by the court under s. 29—see above. Similarly, special guardianship orders may be made in respect of a child when an application has been made for an adoption order only when the person applying has the leave of the court. This allows for applications which compete with the adoption but only with the leave of the court.

Modifying the 'looked after' status under the Children Act 1989

The Adoption and Children Act extends the 'looked after' status under s. 22 of the Children Act 1989 (see chapter 10) to children authorised to be placed for adoption, which ensures that the local authority retains clear legal responsibilities for the welfare of the child. However it would be inappropriate if all of the requirements of the 'looked after' status applied to children authorized to be placed for adoption. For instance it may not always be necessary to consult the child's parent before making decisions in respect of that child. Regulations will in due course provide for the appropriate disapplication of sections of the Children Act where necessary—s. 53.

Removal and recovery

Removal means taking a child away from where he or she has been placed. Section 30 sets out extensive general restrictions on the removal of children involved in the placement process. No one can remove children who have been placed for adoption with prospective adopters except the adoption agency; no one, unless they have the leave of the court, may remove children accommodated by the local authority while a placement order is under consideration by the court; and no one can remove a child from accommodation provided by an adoption agency once the agency is authorized to place the child for adoption under s. 19 (this also applies where consent has been given and then withdrawn). In these circumstances only the agency may remove the child. Any person who removes a child in contravention of the section commits an offence.

There are, however, some circumstances where the removal of a child is allowed. First, where the child is arrested and, secondly, in particular circumstances set out in ss. 31 and 32. These sections cover the situation where the child is not subject to a care order. If the child either has been placed for adoption or is being provided with accommodation by an adoption agency prior to being placed, and any parent or guardian withdraws consent to placement and requests that the child is returned to him or her, then the agency must return the child within seven days if the child has not been placed or within fourteen days if the child has been placed. Prospective adopters who do not return the child to the agency commit an offence. If the agency wishes to prevent the removal then it must apply for a placement order. If a placement order is refused and the parent or guardian wishes the child to be returned to him or her then the court which refused the placement order will determine when the child is returned.

Where a placement order is in force or has been revoked but the child remains with the prospective adopters or remains accommodated by the local authority then no one other than the local authority may remove the child except in accordance with any order made by the court. If prospective adopters wish to return a child placed for adoption, or the adoption agency decides that the child should not remain with the prospective adopters then the child should be returned within seven days of the decision and the parents or guardian of the child should be informed by the agency.

Sections 36–40 apply to a child who is the subject of an application for an adoption order and

- where notice of intention to adopt has been given or
- there has been an application for leave to apply for an adoption order
  and
- where the child has not been placed in its current home by an adoption agency.

There is a limit on who can remove children in these circumstances. Generally, only someone who has the leave of the court, someone with parental responsibility, or the local authority may remove the child.

Recovery

Section 41 provides for recovery orders. Where it appears to the court that a child has been or may be removed in contravention of the provisions of the Act, then s. 41(2) permits the court to:

(a) direct any person who is in a position to do so to produce the child on request to any person mentioned in subs. (4);

(b) authorize the removal of the child by any person mentioned in that subs.;

(c) require any person who has information as to the child's whereabouts to disclose that information on request to any constable or officer of the court;

(d) authorize a constable to enter any premises specified in the order and search for the child, using reasonable force if necessary.

Key features of placement

We summarize the key features of placement in Box 13.5.

BOX 13.5 A summary of the key features of placement

Feature	Section	Comment
Parental consent required	s. 19 & s. 20	• consent can be withdrawn at any time • consent may at the same time or subsequently be given for adoption • prospective adopters do not need to have been identified
Placement order necessary if no consent	s. 21	• child must be subject to a care order, or the conditions for care order made out, or the child has no parent or guardian
Parental responsibility	s. 25	• with the adoption agency • with prospective adopters once placed • with birth parents • agency may restrict birth parents', guardians', or prospective adopters' parental responsibility
Contact	s. 26	• contact under CA 1989 ceases to have effect • contact may be ordered by the court with anyone following application from a wide range of persons and anyone with the leave of the court
Lack of consent	s. 52	• either parent cannot be found, or is incapable of giving consent or the welfare of the child requires consent to be dispensed with
Quality of consent	s. 52	• consent must be unconditional and given with full understanding

All decisions are underpinned by s. 1 criteria

Adoption orders

Preliminaries to adoption

Section 42 of the Act requires that the child must live with the adopter(s) before the application to adopt is made. The time periods depend upon the identity of the applicant or applicants and who has placed the child for adoption. We have set the time periods out in Box 13.6.

The section also requires that the court is satisfied that the adoption agency or the local authority has had sufficient opportunities to see the child with the applicant or applicants together in the home environment.

Reporting requirements

Section 43 sets out the reporting requirements imposed on an adoption agency:

> The agency must—
>   (a) submit to the court a report on the suitability of the applicants and on any other matters relevant to the operation of section 1, and
>   (b) assist the court in any manner the court directs.

Notice of intention to adopt

Where proposed adopters wish to adopt a child who is not placed for adoption with them by an adoption agency s. 44 requires them to give notice of intention to adopt to their local authority. They can give this notice as much as two years before applying, or as little as three months. The local authority must then investigate and report to the court on the suitability of the proposed adopters and other matters relevant to s. 1 of the Act.

BOX 13.6 Time periods prior to application

Placed by/applicant	Time period
Placed by adoption agency	Ten weeks preceding application
Placed by High Court	
Applicant a Parent	Ten weeks preceding application
Applicant or one of applicants partner of parent	Six months
Applicant (s) local authority foster parents	One year
Any other applicant	Not less than three years out of the period of five years preceding application
The three year period does not need to have been continuous

Regulations will provide the detail of the matters to be taken into account in the investigation and report. Section 45(2) provides:

> In particular, the regulations may make provision for the purpose of securing that, in determining the suitability of a couple to adopt a child, proper regard is had to the need for stability and permanence in their relationship.

This is designed to ensure that all couples who wish to adopt jointly, whether married or unmarried, demonstrate the strength of their relationship. Individual people can of course adopt. We will discuss the different requirements for individual people and couples who wish to adopt later.

Adoption orders

The adoption order is the court order which gives effect to the adoption. Section 46 of the Act gives parental responsibility for a child to the adopters or adopter. The making of the order extinguishes any other person's parental responsibility and any order under the Children Act 1989, the Children (Northern Ireland) Order 1995, and the Children (Scotland) Act 1995. It also extinguishes any obligation to make payments for the maintenance of the child after the making of the adoption order, whether that obligation arises under an agreement or a court order. Section 46(6) provides that:

> Before making an adoption order, the court must consider whether there should be arrangements for allowing any person contact with the child; and for that purpose the court must consider any existing or proposed arrangements and obtain any views of the parties to the proceedings.

Section 47 is a key section of the Act. It sets out the three conditions, one of which must be met before the court may make an adoption order. The first condition is in s. 47(2) in Box 13.7. The first condition will be appropriate where, for instance, the child is being adopted by a parent and step-parent.

The second condition is set out in Box 13.8. The second condition will be appropriate where the adoption follows a placement by an adoption agency.

Parents or guardians may not oppose the making of adoption orders under either the first or second condition unless they have the leave of the court. The court can only give leave if it is satisfied that there has been a change in circumstances since the consent of the parent or guardian was given or when the placement order was made—s. 47(7).

 BOX 13.7 The first conditions

In the case of each parent or guardian of the child the court must be satisfied that—

(a) the parent or guardian now consents to the making of the adoption order,

(b) the parent or guardian consented at the time of the placement order under section 20 (and has not withdrawn the consent) and does not oppose the making of the adoption order, or

(c) the parent's or guardian's consent should be dispensed with.

 BOX 13.8 The second condition

(a) the child has been placed for adoption by an adoption agency with the prospective adopters in whose favour the order is proposed to be made,

(b) either—
  (i) the child was placed for adoption with the consent of each parent or guardian and the consent of the mother was given when the child was at least six weeks old, or
  (ii) the child was placed for adoption under a placement order, and

(c) no parent or guardian opposes the making of the adoption order.

The third condition is that the child is free for adoption under s. 18 of the Adoption (Scotland) Act 1978 or under Article 17(1) or 18 (1) of the Adoption (Northern Ireland) Order 1987.

Adoption orders may be made even if the child to be adopted is already an adopted child—s. 46(5). However, adoption orders may not be made in relation to someone who is or has been married—s. 47(8), or who is 19 or older—s. 47(9). An application for adoption can be made only if the person to be adopted is at the time of the application under 18—s. 49(4). Applications for adoption may be made by a couple or one person.

Adoption by a couple—s. 50

If the application is made by a couple then at least one of them must be domiciled in a part of the British Islands and both must have been habitually resident for one year prior to the making of the application. Domiciled means that their settled home is in the British Islands. Both should be over 21 unless one is the birth parent of the child to be adopted and is over 18, in which case the other must be over 21. The definition of 'couple' is set out in s. 144(4) of the Act:

A couple means—
(a) a married couple, or
(b) two people (whether of different sexes or the same sex) living as partners in an enduring family relationship . . .

Therefore unmarried heterosexuals and gay and lesbian couples are able to adopt as couples as long as they can demonstrate an enduring family relationship. Allowing couples who are not married to adopt widens the pool of potential adoptive parents and therefore supports the aim of increasing the number of children who are adopted. Of course no couple, however stable their relationship, is automatically entitled to adopt. It will be up to the adoption agencies and ultimately the courts to decide upon individual couple's suitability.

Adoption by a single person—s. 51

Single people who are 21 and over and not married and are domiciled in a part of the British Islands may adopt. One member of a couple who is 21 or over may adopt if the court is satisfied that the person is the partner of a parent of the person to be adopted. This means that a parent is no longer required to make a joint application to adopt his or her own child with his or her partner as was required in step-parent adoptions under the 1976 Act.

Someone who is married may adopt as a single person if the court is satisfied that:

(a) the person's spouse cannot be found,
(b) the spouses have separated and are living apart, and the separation is likely to be permanent, or
(c) the persons spouse is by reason of ill health, whether physical or mental, incapable of making an application for an adoption order.

Parental consent

Parental consent or a court decision that parental consent should be dispensed with is critical to the adoption process. The discussion on the meaning of consent and the circumstances when it can be dispensed with in the context of placement for adoption is equally relevant here.

Key features of the legal process of adoption

We set out the key features of the legal process of adoption in Box 13.9 opposite.

A diagrammatic representation of the process of placement and adoption which is annexed to the explanatory notes is very useful to understanding the process (see p. 426).

The status of adopted children

Section 67 sets out the status of adopted children. We have reproduced this in Box 13.10.

The section has effect from the date of the adoption. You may recall that s. 51(2) is about adoptions by one of a couple where the partner is the birth parent of the child.

Information about a person's adoption

The Act attempts to achieve a balance between information being properly recorded and maintained and available to an adopted person and ensuring that private information is properly controlled. It also sets up a 'gateway' for access to information about adopted persons. The provisions apply only to adoptions which take place after the Act has been implemented.

Adoption registers

The Act provides the statutory basis for three adoption registers. The first two registers provide the infrastructure for the maintenance of key information about adoption. The first is the Adopted Children Register originally set up under the Children Act 1989 which the Registrar General must continue to maintain—s. 77. Entries are made in the Adopted Children Register following adoption orders, or following registrable foreign adoptions (Schedule 1 to the Act—not covered in this chapter). The Registrar General must make traceable the connection between any entry in the registers of live births or other records which has been marked 'Adopted' and any corresponding entry in the Adopted Children Register—s. 79.

The second register which must be kept is the Adoption Contact Register. The register contains information about adopted people who wish to make contact with their birth relatives and birth relatives who wish to make contact with adopted people—see s. 80.

A third adoption register, the Adoption and Children Act Register, is provided for in another part of the Act. This must contain (s. 125(1)):

(a) prescribed information about children who are suitable for adoption and prospective adopters who are suitable to adopt a child,

(b) prescribed information about persons included in the register in pursuance of paragraph (a) in respect of things occurring after their inclusion.

BOX 13.9 The key features of the adoption process

Feature	Section	Comment and Details
The child must live with adopters prior to application	s. 42	• parent of child—10 weeks • placed by agency—10 weeks • placement order—10 weeks • partner of parent—6 months • foster parent—1 year • any one else, total of three out of last five years
Proposed adopters of child not placed by agency must give notice of intention to adopt to local authority	s. 44	• to be given not more than 2 years or less than 3 months before application is made
Local authority to prepare reports for court	s. 44 & s. 45	Regulations to provide detailed requirements but include: • suitability of applicant(s) • stability and permanence of couple's relationship • s. 1 matters
Adoption orders	s. 46, s. 47 & s. 48	• gives parental responsibility to adopters • extinguishes previous parental responsibility • one of three conditions in s. 47 must be complied with, the most important being consent of parents, or court satisfied consent should be dispensed with
Potential applicants	s. 49, s. 50 & s. 51	• couples • single people • domiciled in British Islands • habitually resident for 1 year or more • aged 21 + (unless one of a couple and the birth parent in which case must be 18 +)
Lack of consent	s. 52	• either parent cannot be found, or is incapable of giving consent or the welfare of the child requires consent to be dispensed with
Quality of consent	s. 52	• consent must be unconditional and given with full understanding

Decisions underpinned by s. 1 criteria

Placement for Adoption

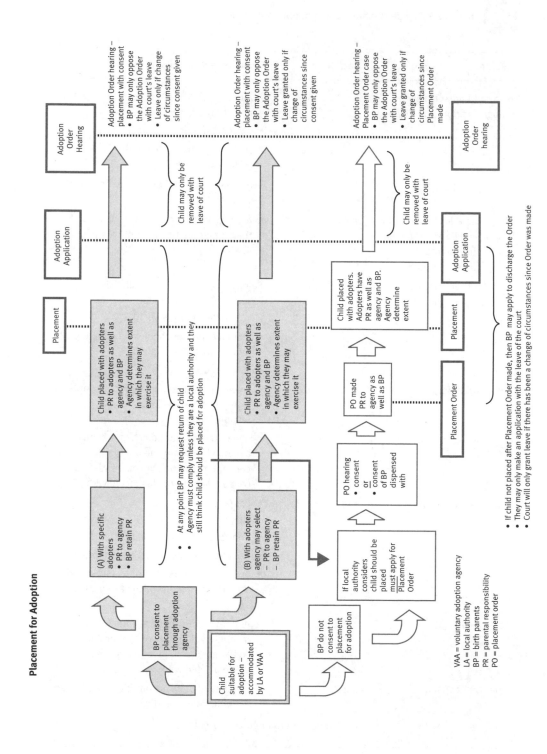

Placement | Adoption Application | Adoption Order Hearing

(A) With specific adopters
- PR to agency and BP
- BP retain PR

Child placed with adopters
- PR to adopters as well as agency and BP
- Agency determines extent in which they may exercise it

Adoption Order hearing – placement with consent
- BP may only oppose the Adoption Order with court's leave
- Leave only if change of circumstances since consent given

Child may only be removed with leave of court

(B) With adopters agency may select
- PR to agency
- BP retain PR

Child placed with adopters
- PR to adopters as well as agency and BP
- Agency determines extent in which they may exercise it

Adoption Order hearing – placement with consent
- BP may only oppose the Adoption Order with court's leave
- Leave granted only if change of circumstances since consent given

BP consent to placement through adoption agency

Child suitable for adoption – accommodated by LA or VAA

BP do not consent to placement for adoption

If local authority considers child should be placed must apply for Placement Order

PO hearing
- consent
  or
- consent of BP dispensed with

PO made PR to agency as well as BP

Child placed with adopters. Adopters have PR as well as agency and BP. Agency determine extent

Adoption Order hearing – Placement Order case
- BP may only oppose the Adoption Order with court's leave
- Leave granted only if change of circumstances since Placement Order made

Child may only be removed with leave of court

Placement Order | Placement | Adoption Application | Adoption Order hearing

At any point BP may request return of child Agency must comply unless they are a local authority and they still think child should be placed for adoption

VAA = voluntary adoption agency
LA = local authority
BP = birth parents
PR = parental responsibility
PO = placement order

- If child not placed after Placement Order made, then BP may apply to discharge the Order
- They may only make an application with the leave of the court
- Court will only grant leave if there has been a change of circumstances since Order was made

BOX 13.10 An adopted person is to be treated in law as if born as the child of the adopters or adopter

(1) An adopted person is the legitimate child of the adopters or adopter and, if adopted by—

(a) a couple, or

(b) one of a couple under section 51(2)

is to be treated as the child of the relationship of the couple in question.

(2) An adopted person—

(a) if adopted by one of a couple under section 51(2), is to be treated in law as not being the child of any person other than the adopted and other one of the couple, and

(b) in any other case, is to be treated in law, subject to subsection (4), as not being the child of any person other than the adopters or adopter;

but this subsection does not affect any reference in this Act to a person's natural parent or to any other natural relationship.

This provision puts onto a statutory basis the Adoption and Children Act Register for England and Wales which was launched in August 2001. The Department of Health adoption web site explains, 'The Register is designed to provide a national infrastructure for adoption services. It will hold information on all children waiting to be adopted and all approved adoptive families from across England and Wales. The Register will tackle delays in finding suitable adoptive families for children from across the country where a local family cannot be found, or the child needs to move away from the area.' The register is therefore designed to support the government aim of increasing the number of children who are adopted and improving the speed of the adoption process. Further information about the operation of the register can be found on the adoption register web site, **www.adoptionregister.net**. This site also lists a range of other useful web sites.

Prescribed information

Section 56 allows for regulations to prescribe the information which an adoption agency must keep in relation to adoption, the form and manner in which it must keep that information, and the circumstances when it may transfer the information to another adoption agency. The explanatory notes tell us that 'The information kept will be about the adopted person, his birth parents and siblings, his adoptive parents and siblings, other relatives, and social workers' reports.'

Protected information

Some prescribed information will be protected information. Protected information is information which allows the adopted person or any other person connected with the adoption to be identified—see s. 57. Any information held by an adoption agency which the agency has obtained from the Registrar General and any other information which would enable the adopted person to obtain a certified copy of the record of his or her birth, or information about an entry relating to the adopted person in the Adoption Contact Register, is identifying information. The explanatory notes set out other examples of identifying information including, 'names, residential, educational and employment addresses, photographic or audio visual material, case records and legal and medical information held by adoption agencies'.

Section 57 restricts the circumstances in which an adoption agency may disclose prescribed information to anyone other than the adopted person except where there has been an agreement to which the adoption agency is a party. Section 58 provides for the disclosure of information which is not protected by an adoption agency where it is necessary for its functions. Such disclosures will be governed by regulations. The explanatory notes suggest, 'This could, for example, be background information about the child's progress to be disclosed to his birth family without disclosing his new identity or his whereabouts.'

Adopted adults' rights to information

Section 60 sets out the rights of an adopted adult (someone over 18) to any information from the adoption agency which enables him or her to obtain his or her birth certificate, (unless the adoption agency successfully applies to the High Court for an order preventing this) and any information disclosed to the adopters by the agency. In this way the adoptive adult is able to access some part of the story of the adoption.

Procedure for disclosure

Not all applications for disclosure of protected information will succeed—see ss. 60–1. An agency is not required to proceed with an application unless it considers it appropriate to do so. In making a decision the agency must consider the welfare of the adopted person, the views of the person to whom the information relates, and all the other circumstances of the case including matters which will be prescribed by regulation. Where the information relates to a child there are additional requirements to consider the views of any parent or guardian of the child and the views of the child, if appropriate to do so having regard to the child's age and understanding and to all the other circumstances of the case. If the child is an adopted child, the child's welfare must be the paramount consideration of the adoption agency in processing the request, and in the case of any other child, the agency must have particular regard to the child's welfare.

Information for pre-commencement adoptions

Section 98(1) allows for the Secretary of State to make regulations for the purpose of helping adults who were adopted prior to the implementation of the Act to obtain information in relation to their adoption, and to facilitate contact between them and their relatives.

The explanatory notes state that

It is intended that this is to be used to provide for a system in which adoption support agencies registered to provide such services may, on application by a person adopted before the Bill is implemented or a birth relative of such a person, act as intermediaries and, with the informed consent of the adopted person, facilitate contact between him and his relatives. It is envisaged that in performing this role adoption support agencies will be obliged, where an adoption agency arranged the adoption, to seek advice and information from that agency. It is also envisaged that the adoption support agency is to be able to obtain information held by the Registrar General where this is necessary in order to perform their intermediary function.

Special guardianship orders

There are some children for whom adoption is not appropriate but who cannot return to their birth parents and could benefit from the permanence provided by a legally secure family placement. The explanatory notes to the Act explain:

> For example some older children (who may, for instance, be being looked after in long term foster placements) do not wish to be adopted and have their legal relationship with their parents severed, but could benefit from greater security and permanence. Adoption may also not be the best option for some children being cared for on a permanent basis by members of their wider family. Some ethnic minority communities have religious or cultural difficulties with adoption in the form provided for in the law of England and Wales.

Section 115 of the Act amends the Children Act 1989 to insert new provisions, s. 14A–G, which create special guardianship. Statutory references in this section of this chapter are therefore references to the Children Act 1989 as amended.

The special guardianship order, as the explanatory notes set out, is intended 'to provide the child with the stability he needs', and therefore 'the special guardian has clear responsibility for all the day to day decisions about caring for the child or young person and for taking decisions about his upbringing'.

Section 14A sets out the basic legal requirements which we reproduce in Box 13.11.

Special guardianship orders may be made following an application from someone who is entitled to make an application or from someone who has the leave of the court to make the application. The people who are entitled to apply for a special guardianship order with respect to a child are set out in s.14A(5): see Box 13.12.

BOX 13.11 Special guardianship

Section 14A(1) A 'special guardianship order' is an order appointing one or more individuals to be a child's 'special guardian' (or 'special guardians')

(2) A special guardian—

    (a) must be aged eighteen or over; and

    (b) must not be a parent of the child in question.

430 RESPONSIBILITIES TOWARDS CHILDREN

BOX 13.12 Those entitled to apply

(a) any guardian of the child;

(b) any individual in whose favour a residence order is in force with respect to the child;

(c) any individual listed in subsection (5) (b) or (c) of section 10 (as read with subsection (10) of that section);

(d) a local authority foster parent with whom the child has lived for a period of at least one year immediately preceding the application.

BOX 13.13 Other circumstances when a court may make a special guardianship order

The court may also make a special guardianship order with respect to a child in any family proceedings in which a question arises with respect to the welfare of the child if—

(a) an application for the order has been made by an individual who falls within subsection (3)(a) or (b); or

(b) the court considers that a special guardianship order should be made even though no such application has been made.

Subsection (6) provides for circumstances where the court may make a special guardianship order. Its provisions are set out in Box 13.13 with respect to a child in any family proceedings in which a question arises with respect to the welfare of the child if—

(a) an application for the order has been made by an individual who falls within subsection (3) (a) or (b); or

(b) the court considers that a special guardianship order should be made even though no such application has been made.

No individual may make an application unless they give written notice of their intention to do so, either to the local authority which is looking after the child in question or otherwise to the local authority in whose area the individual is ordinarily resident.

Subsection (8) provides that on receipt of such a notice, the local authority must investigate the matter and prepare a report for the court dealing with:

(a) the suitability of the applicant to be a special guardian;

(b) such matters (if any) as may be prescribed by the Secretary of State; and

(c) any other matter which the local authority consider to be relevant.

The court may itself ask a local authority to conduct such an investigation and report on the results. The court may only make a special guardianship order if it has received a report from the local authority.

Section 14B sets out other matters to be considered when a special guardianship order is made. We have set this out in Box 13.14 below.

Section 14C(3) (b) prevents the removal of the child from the United Kingdom, without either the written consent of every person who has parental responsibility for the child or the leave of the court. However, the special guardian can remove the child for a period of up to three months.

The effect of a special guardianship order is set out in s. 14C—see Box 13.15.

Special guardianship orders may be varied or discharged following an application by someone listed in s. 14(D)(1) set out in Box 13.16 below

BOX 13.14 Additional matters to be considered

Section 14(B)(1) Before making a special guardianship order, the court must consider whether, if the order were made—

    (a) a contact order should also be made with respect to the child, and

    (b) any section 8 order in force with respect to the child should be varied or discharged.

(2) On making a special guardianship order, the court may also—

    (a) give leave for the child to be known by a new surname;

    (b) grant the leave required by section 14C(3) (b) either generally or for specified purposes.

BOX 13.15 The effect of special guardianship

Whilst the order is in force then—

    (a) a special guardian appointed by the order has parental responsibility for the child in respect of whom it is made; and

    (b) subject to any other order in force with respect to the child under this Act, a special guardian is entitled to exercise parental responsibility to the exclusion of any other person with parental responsibility for the child (apart from another special guardian).

BOX 13.16 Variation and discharge can be applied for by

    (a) the special guardian (or any of them, if there are more than one);

    (b) any parent or guardian of the child concerned;

    (c) any individual in whose favour a residence order is in force with respect to the child;

    (d) any individual not falling within any of paragraphs (a) to (c) who has, or immediately before the making of the special guardianship order had, parental responsibility for the child;

    (e) the child himself; or

    (f) a local authority designated in a care order with respect to the child.

The court may also of its own motion vary or discharge a special guardianship order if it considers that it should be varied or discharged during the course of any family proceedings. Anyone listed in paragraphs (b) to (e) of s. 14D will require leave of the court before they can apply for variation or discharge. In all applications for leave other than that of the child leave will be granted only if there has been a significant change in circumstances since the making of the special guardianship order.

Special guardianship is therefore distinct from adoption. The distinctions lie in the ability to vary or discharge the order and in the continuation of the legal link, although diluted, with the birth parents. As the explanatory notes to the Act put it '. . . unlike adoption, there is the possibility of discharge or variation of the order, and the child's legal relationship with his birth parents is not severed. They remain legally the child's parents, though their ability to exercise their parental responsibility is limited.'

Section 14F sets out the responsibilities of local authorities to make provision for special guardianship support services, which include counselling, advice and information, and financial support. Following a request for support services, the local authority may carry out an assessment of that person's needs for support, and must do so if the regulations prescribe. If the assessment leads to a decision by the local authority that a person has needs for support services then it may decide to provide them, and if it does it must prepare a plan of provision and keep the plan under review. Regulations will provide the detailed requirements of the assessment, planning, and review procedures. Finally, s. 14G provides that local authorities must establish a procedure for considering representations including complaints about the discharge of responsibilities to provide support services.

Key features of special guardianship orders

We summarize the key features of special guardianship orders in Box 13.17 opposite.

Adoptions with a foreign element

Adoptions which do not solely concern children, birth parents, and prospective adopters who are all from the British Islands, whilst still relatively rare, have become more common recently. Concerns about the possible abuse of overseas adoptions led to the Adoption (Inter-country Aspects) Act 1999 (the 1999 Act). Its purpose was explained by Mark Oaten MP, who promoted the Bill:

'Until the Romanian revolution in 1989, inter-country adoption had a low profile in Britain. Although it has risen to about 300 cases a year, we do much less than other countries. In the United States, the annual figure for overseas adoptions is 10,000; in Holland and Sweden, about 2,000. Children come to this country from all over the world. In the past six years, families in the United Kingdom have adopted children from 42 different countries. The most popular are China, India, and Guatemala. . . . There are some problems with the current system. Most inter-country adoptions go through the proper channels. Prospective adopters get approval from local authority social services departments or an approved agency. Although

BOX 13.17 Special guardianship orders

Feature	Section of the Children Act	Comment and details
Special guardians	s. 14A(2)	Must be over 18 Must not be a parent of the child
Applications	s. 14A(3) & (5)	Guardians Individuals with residence orders Local authority foster parents Others with leave Can be appointed on court's own motion
Notice of intention of application	s. 14A(7) & (8)	Must be made Notice initiates investigation and report
Parental responsibility	s. 14C	Special guardian gains parental responsibility Birth parents retain residual parental responsibility
Variation and discharge	s. 14D	Applications may be made as of right or with leave Child can apply with leave Court may make of own motion
Entitlement to support from local authority	s. 14F	Counselling, advice and information, etc.

the process is long and costly, it is legal and operates in the interest of the child. Regrettably it is estimated that in about 100 cases a year, people try to avoid the adoption procedures and bring children into the UK without their suitability as adoptive parents being properly assessed. In such cases, prospective parents may be aware that if they went through the assessment programme, they would not be successful or, worse, they may have gone through it and been considered unsuitable, but believe that taking a foreign child is a back way to adoption' (HC Debs., Vol. 329 col.1140, 23 Apr. 1999).

The need legally to regulate international adoptions, and particularly adoptions organized over the Internet became a political priority following the notorious case of the Kilshaws, the couple who paid an £8,200 fee to adopt twins from the United States. As the *Guardian* put it in an article on 9 April 2001, 'it raised the spectre of a market in children as people became aware that, whatever the facts in this particular case, there is a trade in infants over the net.' The debate provoked by the Kilshaws and other interesting information and articles on adoption can be accessed via the *Guardian*, newspaper web site **www.society.guardian.co.uk/adoption**, a user-friendly and up-to-date site which we recommend.

The 1999 Act was designed to give effect to the Convention on Protection of Children and Cooperation in respect of Inter-country Adoption, concluded at the Hague in 1993, known as the Hague Convention. The Hague Convention sets out minimum standards for the process of inter-country adoption. One of its main aims is to prevent adoption trafficking. The preamble to the Convention sets out its purposes:

> *Recognising* that the child, for the full and harmonious development of his or her personality, should grow up in a family environment, in an atmosphere of happiness, love and understanding,
>
> *Recalling* that each State should take, as a mater of priority, appropriate measures to enable the child to remain in the care of his or her family of origin,
>
> *Recognising* that inter country adoption may offer the advantage of a permanent family to a child for whom a suitable family cannot be found in his or her State of origin,
>
> *Convinced* of the necessity to take measures to ensure that inter-country adoptions are made in the best interest of the child and with respect for his or her fundamental rights, and to prevent the abduction, the sale of, or traffic in children.

The full text of the Convention can be found at **www.webcom/~kmc/adoption/ law/un/un-ica**.

The 1999 Act requires that local authorities provide, or arrange to provide, an inter-country adoption service and provides that children who are the subject of a Convention adoption will receive British nationality automatically. There has been only partial implementation of the Act. The key provisions ban the assessment of adoption by anyone other than approved adoption agencies and local authorities and introducing sanctions against those who bring children in to the UK without following proper procedures were adopted in 2001.

Chapter 6 of the Adoption and Children Act 2002 re-enacts most of the 1999 Act. It aims to improve the legal controls on inter-country adoption by introducing new safeguards and penalties. The 1999 Act will be largely repealed once the Adoption and Children Act is implemented—even before some of it was implemented! However, s. 1 of the 1999 Act (power to make regulations giving effect to the Convention), s. 2 (central authorities and accredited bodies), s. 7 (amendments to the British Nationality Act 1981), and Schedule 1 (which sets out the text of the Convention so far as material) will remain. These provisions, which enable the UK to give effect to the Hague Convention, were implemented in January 2003 and ratified on 1 June 2003.

There are restrictions on children being brought into this country or taken out of it for the purposes of adoption. Section 83 of the Adoption and Children Act 2002 sets out restrictions on people who are habitually resident in the British Islands bringing children into the country either for the purposes of adoption or having been adopted abroad. Unless the child is intended to be adopted under a Convention adoption order by s. 83(4), the person bringing the child into the United Kingdom must apply to an adoption agency for an assessment of his or her suitability to adopt the child and give the agency any information it may require for the purpose of the assessment. Breach of the requirements of the section is a criminal offence.

Convention adoption orders are defined in the Adoption and Children Act as adoptions order made by virtue of regulations made under s. 1 of the 1999 Act. You will recall that s. 1 is the section which implements the provisions of the Convention. The effect, then, is that Convention adoption orders are regulated by the Hague Convention.

Section 84 enables the High Court to make an order giving parental responsibility for a child who is a commonwealth citizen or habitually resident in the United Kingdom to people who the court is satisfied intend to adopt the child under the law of a country outside the British Islands British Islands means the United Kingdom plus the Isle of Man and the Channel Islands (see the Interpretation Act 1978, Schedule 1). The power to make this order is limited to prospective adopters who are not habitually resident in England or Wales. An order can be applied for only by applicants with whom the child has been living during the preceding ten weeks. The child can be taken out of the country for the purposes of adoption only if the prospective adopters have parental responsibility for him or her as a result of s. 84. Removing a child in contravention of the requirements of the section is a criminal offence.

Overseas adoptions

The Act allows for regulations to set out requirements for overseas adoptions. Overseas adoptions do not include Convention adoptions but are adoptions 'of a description specified in an order made by the Secretary of State' which relate to adoptions under other countries' laws. Overseas adoption orders are currently recognised automatically in England and Wales. The explanatory notes state that 'It is intended to review which countries' adoption orders will be recognized in the United Kingdom.' The Secretary of State will be able to specify by regulation clear criteria that must be met for a country to continue to have automatic recognition of its adoption orders.

The High Court is able to intervene in Hague Convention adoptions under s. 88(1) and make a direction that s. 67 (the status of the adopted child) does not apply, or does not apply to any extent specified, where each of the conditions set out in s. 88(2) apply. The conditions are:

(a) that under the law of the country in which the adoption was effected, the adoption is not a full adoption,

(b) that the consents referred to in Article 4(c) and (d) of the Convention have not been given for a full adoption or that the United Kingdom is not the receiving State (within the meaning of Article 2 of the Convention),

(c) that it would be more favourable to the adopted child for a direction to be given under subsection (1).

The reason for this provision is set out in the explanatory notes:

'Adoption law of the United Kingdom recognises only one type of adoption, which is full adoption, and this creates a new and irrevocable legal relationship between the child and adoptive parents which severs all legal ties between the child and his birth parents. A child adopted in England and Wales is to be treated in law as not being the child of any person other than the adopters. In some countries, however, certain forms of adoption do not have the effect of totally severing all ties from the birth parents and these are known as simple adoptions. Article 26 of the Hague Convention provides for the recognition of both full and simple adoptions Article 27 of the Hague Convention allows a receiving State to convert a simple adoption into a full adoption if its law so permits and provided the birth parents and relevant parties under Article 4 of the Hague Convention have given their consent to a full adoption. Where the receiving State is England and Wales, the Central Authority will ensure that in all cases the birth parents are informed of the effects of a simple adoption in England and Wales and seek to obtain their consent to a full adoption prior to a Convention adoption being made in a country outside the British Islands or a Convention adoption order begin made here. Where the receiving State is not England and Wales, it is possible that the child may be brought to this country in circumstances where simple adoption are recognised, both in the State of origin and the receiving State, and so no consent to full adoption has been given. In those cases the adoption will still be treated as a full adoption by operation of law, but if any issue of status arises where it is felt it would be more favourable to the child to treat the adoption otherwise than as a full adoption, an application may be made to the High Court.'

Further, the High Court under s. 89 may annul a Convention adoption or an overseas adoption on the ground that the adoption is contrary to public policy.

The combination of legislative provisions means that adoptions from overseas are now highly regulated. Anyone interested in adopting from abroad will need very good advice. One web site which provides useful information is the overseas adoption helpline at **www.oah.org.uk**.

EXERCISES

Sonia has three children, Anita who is 12, Ben who is 6, and Caitlin who is 2. Sonia suffers from chronic alcoholism. Unfortunately her sober intervals are becoming increasingly rare. She had a serious relapse about eighteen months ago. The children were found on their own in Sonia's flat and it appeared that she had been gone for some days. Care orders were obtained on all three children. Anita is now settled with her grandmother. Ben and Caitlin are living with foster parents. You have been allocated this case and you would like to achieve some permanence for the children. Sonia has recently reluctantly begun to accept that she is unlikely to be able to care for her children again. The three children are very close to each other, and Anita is particularly close to Caitlin as she was her primary carer for large parts of her babyhood. Anita is very happy living with her grandmother. She has made it quite clear that she does not want to end her relationship with her mother. Ben and Caitlin are settled with the foster parents who have expressed a wish to adopt them. Caitlin in particular is very attached to them. The foster parents are white and in their mid-forties. Ben and Caitlin are mixed race.

What suggestions would you make to provide for the children? Why? What further information would you need? Assuming you decide that adoption may be appropriate explain the procedure to Sonia. What contact provisions would you recommend?

COMPANION WEB SITE

 For guidance on how to answer these exercises, visit the companion web site at: www.oup.com/uk/booksites/law

WHERE DO WE GO FROM HERE?

We have now completed our consideration of the public law in relation to children. You have seen that the purpose of the law is to enable the state to protect children. The next chapter has a different focus. It is concerned with the private law of the family and how relationships within families are regulated by the law. There is less of a role for social workers, but family breakdown can lead to a need for public law intervention, and can trigger formal investigation by social services.

ANNOTATED FURTHER READING

The Government's approach to the modernization of the law

The Prime Minister's Review of adoption (2000), A Performance and Innovation Unit Report.

The Performance and Innovation Unit Report.

The White Paper, *Adoption—A New Approach* (December 2000, Cm 5017).

All of these are available on the Department of Health web site: **www.doh.gov.uk/adoption**.

Reform in context

N. Lowe, 'English Adoption Law: Past, Present and Future', in S. Katz, J. Eekelaar, and M. Maclean (eds.), *Cross-Currents: Family Law and Policy in the United States and England* (Oxford University Press, 2000).

Contact

C. Smith and J. Logan, 'Adoptive Parenthood as a "Legal Fiction"—its Consequences for Direct Post-Adoption Contact' (2002) 14(3) C&FLQ 281.

Comparative perspectives

S. Katz, 'Dual Systems of Adoption in the United States', in S. Katz, J. Eekelaar, and M. Maclean (eds), *Cross-Currents: Family Law and Policy in the United States and England* (Oxford University Press, 2000).

C. van Nijnatten and W. de Coraff, 'The Legal Management of (Social) Parenthood: Adoption and Dutch Family Policy' (2002) 24(3) J of SW & FL 263.

Further details on the Adoption and Children Act 2002

C. Bridge and H. Swindells (2003) *Adoption—the Modern Law* (Jordans)—this book is very detailed and informative putting the Act into its historical context and making well informed speculations about the likely response of the courts to particular issues.

N. Allen (2003) *Making Sense of the New Adoption Law—A Guide for Social and Welfare Services* (Wiley).

S. Choudhry, 'The Adoption and Children Act 2002, the Welfare Principle and the Human Rights Act 1998—a missed opportunity' (2003) 15(2) C&FLQ 119—this article seeks to assess the tensions between adoption and human rights.

14 Law of the family

Re H (a child: residence) [2002] 3 FCR 277

The child (H), now aged 8, had been brought up by her grandmother. The mother had agreed on the grandmother having a parental responsibility order. But when the child was 7 the mother contacted social services. She said the grandmother, and the grandmother's husband, had both sexually abused her when she herself was a child. The husband was not named in the residence order, but was now part of H's household. The mother applied under the Children Act 1989 to vary the residence order.

The initial hearing was complicated by the fact that the court had set aside only one day for the hearing, and the grandmother's husband had no representation because he earned too much to get legal aid. The school holidays were coming up and a decision was needed about where H should go. The judge then made a curious decision. He agreed to proceed without investigation of the abuse allegations. But he nevertheless allowed the mother to file a report from a social worker, containing the expert opinion that abuse allegations were credible and likely to be true. The judge then rejected the social worker's evidence because she had taken at face value the mother's allegations without a proper investigation.

The mother's application for a variation in the residence order failed, and the case came to the Court of Appeal. The mother made a number of complaints: the judge had failed to take account of the presumption that a mother was the best person to bring up a child, and had been wrong to ignore the abuse allegations. The judge had suggested new circumstances were required to upset the status quo where there was already a residence order.

The Court of Appeal held that a court starts from only one consideration: the child's welfare is paramount. Past case law, or generalized assumptions, were of little help, since this child's welfare in these circumstances had to be decided. The judge had been wrong to agree to ignore the sex abuse allegations:

> The task which he attempted—the conscientious endeavour to decide the issues on the footing that the events alleged did not take place—would have been a safe enough approach in purely adversarial proceedings in some other realm. But in Children Act proceedings the judge is there in a quasi-inquisitorial role. Child protection is one of his principal responsibilities and allegations of this sort must either be withdrawn or adjudicated upon.

It was also wrong to assume a biological mother was in a better position to care for the child than a psychological mother.

On the facts of the case the Court of Appeal decided the judge had had sufficient evidence of the grandmother's and mother's relative abilities to care for the child, and there was no basis for upsetting the present arrangements. The Court was partly reassured by the fact that the social services authority was aware of the allegations and would be able to investigate any child protection issues.

OVERVIEW AND OBJECTIVES

The case study demonstrates that there is a close overlap between private law disputes about children and the issues that arise in public law cases, including the involvement of social workers to investigate and advise the court. The key linking factor is the welfare of the child, which is not a matter of purely private importance. The child's welfare is paramount where it is the child's future which is being decided.

A social services authority has statutory responsibilities to children (see chapter 1) to support them when in need (chapter 10), and if necessary to protect them if significant harm has occurred or may occur (chapter 12). But, of course, you cannot exercise those responsibilities without taking an interest in the private lives of families, and the Children Act s. 17 and Schedule 2 expects you to help to keep children and their families together. Up to now Part 3 of this book has been about public law and children—i.e. the state's role in protecting them and promoting their interests. This chapter is about those same children when private disputes arise. You will see, we hope, that there is some overlap, since private disputes affect the interests of children and therefore they can trigger the duty of the state to get involved.

The range of problems that may affect families whose children you have responsibilities for is huge. We aim in this chapter to identify the legal aspects of the most pressing or common problems. You will not replace the legal adviser, but you should, after studying this chapter, understand when it is appropriate to make a referral to a specialist lawyer. To do this we hope to provide you with an understanding of what is meant by family, the difference that the status of marriage makes, and how the law deals with the breakdown of family relationships and the disputes this can generate. In particular you will be aware of how the needs, including financial needs, of children are addressed.

The trigger for family tensions to lead to breakdown is often violence; this is separately covered in chapter 18 below.

▮ Preliminary issues

What is family law?

Family law traditionally looked at the fallout from problems resulting from marriage, heterosexual co-habitation or having/bringing up children. Family law, because of commitments and dependency necessary to form intimate relationships and support children, creates enforceable obligations and rights beyond those created by any other relationships. What happens within families creates an interesting tension in law. Families have a right to privacy and autonomy—indeed the European Human Rights Convention enshrines this in Article 8. But the state has always been interested in private morality, though the boundaries of its legitimate interest are at present more relaxed than in previous times. And it has a legitimate interest in the welfare and future of children—indeed the boundaries between private law relating to children and the public law we have looked at so far are blurred because of this. So though the area of law we will look at is private family law, the public interest in families and children mean that standards of behaviour in families, particularly on relationship breakdown, are far more regulated than other areas of private law.

Marriage?

The law carefully defines the ritual necessary to create a valid marriage in England and Wales; it is rare that the validity of a marriage ceremony is in dispute, so for the purposes of this book we will not address issues of the 'void' marriage. As with most areas of family law, whether we cover it in detail or not, a person with a problem including, for example, a potentially void marriage needs to see a specialist lawyer. See below.

It makes no difference whether the parties married abroad. English courts recognize foreign marriages and, so long as one of the parties is now living with some degree of permanence in this country, courts here can make decisions about, and even dissolve, a marriage that took place abroad. Similarly, English or Welsh courts recognize divorces obtained abroad, and other court orders concerning families.

Same sex couples cannot marry. However aspects of same sex relationships, such as a right to inherit a tenancy, are increasingly recognized as creating family rights and obligations (see chapter 2). The Civil Partnership Act 2004 will create recognition of same sex partnerships for purposes of property adjustment on breakdown, intestacy, nearest relative in mental health law, and for example recognition of next of kin for property inheritance. The Act has provisions governing how the partnership is created and how an order can be obtained to end it (similar to divorce, in fact, but without adultery and desertion grounds). We do not have the space to discuss this Act further in this chapter. Additionally the right of people who have undergone gender reassignment to marry in their new gender has been recognised in the Gender Recognition Act 2004 (see chapter 2).

Specialist legal advice

The Legal Services Commission (LSC) contracts with specialist solicitors in family law. To find a specialist solicitor the LSC maintains a directory which can be accessed at **www.justask.org.uk**. If a person with a family problem has no means beyond income support or equivalent, these solicitors can provide free advice. If the case merits it they can then obtain approval to carry out court proceedings. For this the means test is not quite so strict, but there may be a contribution towards the cost. (In any event legal aid in family disputes involving property is not free; the LSC has first claim on any property which a person secures in a family dispute, or if it is the home, will put an extra mortgage onto the home to secure all of its legal costs, not just those which paid for the property dispute to be dealt with.)

A human rights dimension

The Human Rights Act 1998 incorporates the European Convention on Human Rights into English law. The most significant Convention Article in the family context is Article 8, which decrees that, in relation to family affairs:

1 Everyone has the right to respect for his private and family life, his home and his correspondence.
2 There shall be no interference by a public authority with the exercise of this right except such as is in accordance with the law and is necessary . . . for the protection of health or morals. . . .

Article 12 establishes the right to marry and to found a family.

Case law is beginning to develop where there are allegations that existing law does not adequately protect these rights. For example, in *G v UK* (2001), a case decided by the European Court of Human Rights, a father's complaint that the UK authorities had not done enough to facilitate contact with his children was rejected as not being a breach of his Article 8 rights. The authorities had taken all reasonable steps, but could not coerce the mother without breaching her rights. Another example is that of the prisoner denied the right to provide sperm to his wife to start a family. In *R v Secretary of State for the Home Department, ex parte Mellor* (2000), the Queen's Bench Division held that the denial of the Article 12 right was justified, given the lawful imprisonment. By contrast the applicant was successful in *Re H (A child) (Consultation of unmarried fathers)* (2001). He complained that English law did not give an unmarried father a statutory right to be consulted over the adoption arrangements for his child. The ECtHR upheld the father's right to respect under Article 8 for his family life. In each case, whether the case is decided in the English/Welsh courts or in Strasbourg, the right balance between rights of individuals and those of others, or of public policy, has to be decided.

But the real human rights issues arise where the state or a public body is involved. As this chapter focuses on private law, human rights issues will not play such a large part in the discussion as they did in the previous chapters—particularly chapter 12—on public law.

Marriage and legal status

Marriage and immigration status

Being married to someone who has a right of abode in the United Kingdom does not give an automatic right to enter the UK. However, the rules made under the British Nationality Act 1981 state that a spouse in such circumstances will normally be allowed entry, so long as the marriage is deemed to be genuine. Be aware that divorce can occasionally affect immigration status. Competent legal advice should be obtained by anyone whose right to stay in the UK may depend on marital status before starting proceedings. Chapter 21 covers questions of immigration status in a little more detail.

Cohabitation

Cohabitation, however long it has lasted, is usually not recognized in law. There is no such thing as a common law marriage, except—without using the term—when the state takes cohabitees' means into account for state benefits, legal aid, or the council tax, or in exceptional situations, in particular the right to inherit a tenancy on the death of a partner.

Cohabitation does not change legal status in the same way that marriage does. So disputes between cohabitees do not involve matrimonial law. If cohabitees cannot agree on ownership of property, it is resolved according to ordinary property law principles. Who paid what, who contributed what? What was intended? Unlike a spouse, a cohabitee cannot apply for maintenance, unless the right to do so is set out in a contract. However where children are involved the law makes less of a distinction between married and unmarried parents. The state does not with to leave matters involving children solely to the agreement and actions of individuals.

Parental responsibility

A father married to the mother, whether at conception, birth, or later, automatically has parental responsibilities. The unmarried father does not have automatic parental responsibilities. He can acquire them (Children Act 1989, s. 4) by:

- being named on the birth certificate;

- registering an agreement between himself and the mother with the court;

- applying to the magistrates', county, or High Court.

With parental responsibility the father's status is equal to that of the mother, for example, in making decisions about the child's upbringing.

A court presumes it is in a child's interests for the father to exercise parental responsibility. For example the child was in local authority accommodation and the father could do little to exercise his responsibilities, but he still got the order: (*Re G* (1996)). But refusal can happen, as where the father had seen an 11-year-old child only six times in her life and she viewed him as a stranger: (*Re J (Parental Responsibility)* (1998)). Again, the court refused an order where the father was likely to take a sexual interest in the child (*Re P (A Minor) (Parental Responsibility)* (1998)). And a father who, on home leave from prison, conceived a child and committed a robbery which led to another 15 years sentence, was denied a parental responsibility order (*Re P* (1997)). He should have thought about the consequences of his actions. (But if he had married the mother, his irresponsibility would have been of no consequence.)

The court has the power under s. 4 to remove parental responsibility from the unmarried father, which is not possible except following an adoption for the married father. A court can, under s. 8 (see below), limit the way either a mother or a father exercise their parental responsibility, and can (s. 31—see previous chapters) make a care order, which requires the local authority to determine how the parents may exercise parental responsibilities.

Without a parental responsibility order a father can be at a disadvantage. For example, in *Re G (A Child) (Custody Rights: Unmarried Father)* (2002) the father had had a close role in the upbringing of the child, but when his relationship with the mother ended and she took the child to Ireland without his permission and without a court order, he was unable to have this dealt with as child abduction, which a married father or a father with parental responsibility would have been able to do.

Where parental responsibilities are shared, either parent can exercise them independently of the other. If there is a dispute either party can apply to the court for one or more of the Children Act 1989, s. 8, orders which will be considered below.

Parental responsibility and the step-parent

The Children Act, s. 4 provides for a step-parent to assume parental responsibilities, either by court order or agreement of the other parent (unless, being an unmarried father, that other parent does not have parental responsibility). Section 4 does not provide for the divorce of the step-parents to bring this step-parental responsibility to an end, though, as with an unmarried father, a court has the power to terminate it.

Relationship breakdown

Avoidance of breakdown

The Family Law Act 1996 was intended to establish ways of helping families to avoid breakdown. But pilots of the mediation and information processes were unsuccessful and most of the legislation has been shelved. The law will probably always be better at dealing with breakdown than preventing it. Sometimes stress and financial worries lead to the collapse of a family relationship. It is possible that the stress can be reduced by advice in relation to welfare benefits and debt, so a social worker needs to know where to refer a person for advice. We have provided below in Box 14.1 a simplified table of some relevant sources of financial benefits. This is not enough for you to give helpful advice, but to help you to signpost where you recognize a problem. Specialist free help in these areas is available from many local authorities' welfare rights services, or from Legal Services Commission quality marked advisers who can be identified on the LSC **www.justask.org.uk** web site, or via the local Community Legal Service directory. (LSC advice is means tested.) Specialist publications, in particular the Child Poverty Action Group handbooks, are listed at the end of the chapter. For a little more detail of benefits including amounts payable see **www.dwp.gov.uk/lifeevent/benefits/income_support.htm#what**.

Sometimes support is not so much financial but through alleviation of work pressures; Box 14.2 shows one key new provision, leave for a new or adopted child.

Importantly, the work of social services departments to support a child in need (chapter 10) can make a contribution to maintaining some families intact, though you are not required to promote this unless it is in the child's welfare interest.

BOX 14.1 Some sources of financial support for families

Name of benefit and statutory provision	Criteria	Comment
Social services department support for child in need *Children Act s. 17 and Sch 2*	Child must be in need.	Cash payments are possible but there is no statutory right to a payment.
Child Support Agency *Child Support Act 1991*	Non-resident parent must be assessed for ability to pay.	See text below for more detail.
Income Support *Social Security Contributions and Benefits Act 1992 (SSCBA)*	Claimant must be exempt from requirement to be available for work, e.g. sick, carer, or single parent. Must not be working over 16 hours a week.	Means tested, which includes taking into account capital over £3,000 and excluding anyone with over £8,000. Valuable because of 'passported' benefits, e.g. free school meals.
Jobseekers allowance *Jobseekers Act 1995*	Must be available for work.	Means tested after six months, though payable without means test till then following involuntary loss of employment.
Working Tax Credit *Tax Credits Act 2002*	For individual or couple in employment; paid through the employer and administered by Inland Revenue.	Includes element of child care costs; increased for lone parents; increased if disability living allowance payable. Worth applying unless very high income.
Child Tax Credit *Tax Credits Act 2002*	Administered by Inland Revenue, payable as a benefit into bank account. Not necessary to be in work.	Increased for each child and for baby under 12 months; increased where disability living allowance payable. Worth applying unless very high income.
Child Benefit *SSCBA*	Child must be under 16 or under 19 and in secondary education.	No means test. Cannot be split even where child lives in more than one household.
Disability Living Allowance *SSCBA*	Condition must have existed for at least three months. Payable to child or adult under 15. Mobility component at higher and lower rate depending on ability to walk.	No means test. If awarded results in increased Child Tax Credit or Working Tax Credit. Payable for child or adult (must claim before age 65).

	Care component at three rates depending on help needed day and/or night or ability to cook simple meal.	
Social Fund *SSCBA and Social Security Act 1986*	Claimant must already be entitled to means-tested jobseekers allowance or income support. Provides loans for crisis situations, and grants for funeral, maternity, and certain community care needs.	Fund is cash limited unless funeral or maternity application, and therefore even strong case may be refused.
Council tax benefit; Housing benefit	See chapter 20.	

BOX 14.2 Leave for a new or adopted baby; flexible working arrangements for child care

Statute or regulation	Comment
Maternity and Parental Leave etc Regulations 1999; Maternity and Parental Leave etc (Amendment) Regulations 2002	Maternity leave available for 26 weeks; no minimum period of employment necessary. If employed 26 weeks before expected date, statutory maternity pay at 90% normal pay payable via employer for 26 weeks and additional maternity leave without SMP payable for further 26 weeks. (Many employers provide higher levels of payment under employment contract.)
Paternity and Adoption Leave Regulations 2002	Paternity leave two weeks at flat rate £100 pw. Adoption leave (adopter or partner) available for 52 weeks; first 26 weeks flat rate £100 pw payable.
Employment Rights Act 1996 as amended by Flexible Working (Eligibility, Complaints And Remedies) Regulations 2002	Variation of contract to permit flexible working; available for parent, foster parent, spouse, or partner of parent while child under 16 (18 if disabled). Employer can refuse only on cost or efficiency grounds. Disputes resolved by Employment Tribunal.

Ending the relationship

No one is obliged in law to live with their partner, whether married or not. There are practical issues to resolve. It may be that the parties have to live together until property ownership is resolved. A court order may be needed to settle children's future arrangements and division of any property. A court order may be needed to remove a violent or harassing partner (see chapter 18). A person may need to wait for local authority rehousing (see chapter 19).

Where a marriage breaks down neither spouse can be required to leave without a court order, even if one of them is not the tenant or co-owner. (The spouse of the owner can register her rights to live in the property at the Land Registry, to prevent the other spouse from selling or mortgaging the property. Any Family Law solicitor can arrange this.)

Despite being married a person is free at law to form new relationships; the only restriction is on re-marrying before divorce is finalized through decree absolute. A person who is married but not living with her spouse is entitled to assessment for benefits and housing as a single person. So there is no immediate practical difference between terminating a married or an unmarried relationship.

Divorce

There is nothing to compel a person to seek a divorce just because he or she has abandoned the marriage. Often the priority is sorting out housing, income support, child support, and, if necessary, protection from violence or harassment, rather than worrying about marital status. For all divorce does is end the status of being married. Once divorce proceedings are undertaken, all the 'ancillary' matters—children's arrangements, property, maintenance, where to live—will be dealt with (if at all) through the divorce court or by agreement, and that court can make a wider range of orders than a court dealing with the problems of the cohabiting or non-divorcing couple.

Marriage also ends on death; and a court can presume death after a spouse has not been heard of for seven years. Sometimes a marriage can be declared void—for example, where it has never been consummated by sexual intercourse. In that case it never happened, except for sorting out ancillary issues (property, children's arrangements, finance).

But if a party to a marriage wishes to have it dissolved, he or she must issue a petition for divorce in a county court or the Principal Registry of the Family Division. A fee is payable, although those on means-tested benefits are exempted. As an example of moral factors shaping law, spouses cannot petition during the first year of the marriage—even if the marriage is completely failing.

The ground for divorce is, in theory, that the marriage has broken down irretrievably. This never has to be proved. Breakdown is proved instead by evidence of one (or more) of the five statutory criteria, which are set out in the Matrimonial Causes Act 1973, s. 1(2):

(a) Adultery;
(b) Intolerable behaviour;
(c) Desertion lasting two years;
(d) Separation lasting two years, plus agreement on both sides;
(e) Separation lasting five continuous years.

A divorce can be based on desertion, or separation, even where the period of living apart was interrupted by a period of living together for up to six months. If reconciliation fails, the period of desertion or separation can start running again. The divorce can also be based on living apart where the couple lead separate lives under the same roof, which often happens if there is not the money to permit separate homes.

Adultery and behaviour offer the quickest route to divorce, because there is no two-year waiting period, but it means anyone in a hurry has to sling mud—not a good way to encourage a constructive settlement of other issues, particularly if cooperation over children's arrangements is required. Few people defend a divorce petition—there is little to gain apart from scoring points or using this as a negotiation tactic on property or children, and proof of the ground for divorce, if contested, will require a full trial in the High Court. If the petition is not defended, the divorce is dealt with in a county court. Legal aid can pay for a solicitor to draw up the petition, and prepare the rest of the paperwork which triggers the divorce decrees. A statement has to be submitted to the court to say what the arrangements are for the children. Both parents must sign this unless these arrangements are disputed. The court can call in the parties to question them on these arrangements, and the judge has all the powers of a court in family proceedings (see chapter 9), particularly to call for a local authority investigation (see below), but it is highly unusual for the hearing to be more than a formality, and the court usually accepts the arrangements without further question, assuming that the parties will apply to the court where issues remain unresolved.

If everything goes smoothly, as most petitions do, the divorce is dealt with entirely on paper. The decree nisi (provisional approval for the divorce) should be made about eight to twelve weeks after the petition. The marriage is not over until decree absolute. A petitioner can apply for this six weeks after decree nisi, and the respondent can apply three months after that date. Decree absolute ends the marriage, but the courts' involvement is not ended if there are issues of property, finance or children's arrangements still in dispute.

Judicial separation as alternative to divorce

A judicial separation is favoured by those who have moral objections to divorce, or who do not want to let their spouses 'off the hook'. It mirrors the divorce petition in grounds and procedures up to decree nisi. At that point the decree of judicial separation is made, which terminates, for what it is worth, the obligation to live together. More importantly it provides a vehicle for the court to make orders in respect of children, property, and maintenance. A judicial separation does not prevent either party later petitioning for divorce.

▧ Children, property, and maintenance following relationship breakdown

The easiest part of relationship breakdown is ending the relationship. The hard part is untangling the consequences. The Family Law Act 1996 was supposed to usher in a new era of non-confrontational procedures for resolving all of the issues. Most of it has been scrapped. However, s. 29 has survived and can provide legal aid for mediation. The principle is that the mediator does not advise, and the parties have to arrive at their own solution. Such face-to-face discussions can be very demanding for separating couples, and out of the question where violence has entered the relationship. But the naïve hope of making mediation compulsory before getting legal aid has been dropped.

Any negotiation and mediation on ancillary issues takes place in the shadow of the law. What follows is a description of how a court can sort out the issues of children, property, or finance if the parties cannot reach their own agreement.

What happens to the children?

The types of decisions a court can make about where children live, who they have contact with etc., can be made at any time and need not be triggered by relationship breakdown. For in any 'family proceedings' (defined in chapter 9) the court can make orders about the children, whether or not any person has asked it to. For example, in public law proceedings it could refuse a care order application and make a residence order (discussed further below) to the grandmother. Or in private law proceedings concerning violence (chapter 18) it could take a look at the arrangements for the children and make a private law order, such as the same residence order to the grandmother.

If there is a divorce petition underway a petitioner or respondent can apply to the court in the course of the divorce proceedings, or, as we have seen, the court can itself require a hearing if it wants to consider the arrangements for the children. So even where the parties themselves are only concerned about, for example, maintenance or protection from violence (chapter 18), the court can look at whether orders ought to be made in respect of the children.

Who can apply for an order in relation to children? The answer is:

- A parent;

- A guardian;

- A step-parent who treated the child as a member of the family during the marriage;

- A person with whom the child has lived for at least three years (unless it ended more than three months ago);

- The child, if he or she has sufficient understanding;

- Anyone else, with leave, which will be refused if the application will be disruptive to the child.

Before listing a s. 8 case for trial (*Practice Direction (Fam Div: Conciliation)* (2004)), a district judge must hold an informal (that is, all the evidence is off the record) hearing to see if any conciliation is possible. If mediation (see above) has already failed, this hearing is likely to be just a formality.

You may recall from chapter 8 the factors the court takes into account in making any order in respect of the upbringing of the child or the administration of the child's property. The same factors apply if a private law dispute goes to a full hearing. Under the Children Act 1989, s. 1, 'the child's welfare shall be the court's paramount consideration'. So even though it is private law, the needs and desires of the parents, society at large, and others come second—but are not ignored altogether. The court will take into account all the circumstances in deciding what order, if any, to make in relation to a child: the child's own wishes, needs, the likely effect of any change in circumstances (i.e. the status quo is likely to be favoured); age, sex, and background; whether the child has suffered harm or is at risk; and the capability of the parents and other relevant persons to meet his or her needs. Above all the court will consider whether it would be better to make no order; can the parties be left to work things out in the best interests of the child (s. 1(5))? The court must of course hear evidence of any relevant facts. If allegations of abuse or inadequate parenting are made, for example, they must be substantiated by credible evidence. So a video tape of an interview with a child containing allegations of sexual abuse, which had been recorded in breach of the guidelines (see chapter 7), did not persuade the court of the father's unsuitability (*Re M (Sexual Abuse Allegations: Interviewing Techniques) (1999)*).

Before making its decision, the court can also call for a report (oral or in writing) from the Children and Family Court Advisory and Support Service (CAFCASS) or social services department. (See chapter 7 for more on reports.) It may call for the child to be separately represented by CAFCASS. The court should consider such an order in all private law cases, but particularly in cases involving a foreign element, a desire by the child to be separately represented, contact in adoption cases, or any other sensitive issues (*Practice Note (Officers of CAFCASS Legal Services and Special Casework: Appointment in Family Proceedings) (2001)*).

Orders which a court can make in relation to children

The type of order that a court can make about the future of children is dictated by the Children Act 1989, ss. 5 and 8, and Sch. 1.

Section 5 deals with the child who has no parent or guardian. The court can appoint a guardian to take up parental responsibilities for the child. (This section also enables a parent to make a written declaration appointing a guardian for the child after the parent's death, which may avoid the need for someone to apply to the court for a guardian to be appointed where both parents are dead.)

Section 8 does not cover orders about money (dealt with below), the appointment of guardians under s. 5, and care or supervision (see chapter 12); but it covers almost any other dispute about the future arrangements for a child. Orders are known as 'section 8 orders'. They can be made in favour of any person the court thinks appropriate, after hearing all the evidence, not just the applicant and not just a parent; for example, a grandparent, step-parent, an unmarried father, or even a sibling (e.g. *Re W (1996)*, where an older brother applied for contact with his younger brother). Let us look at the range of orders available.

Section 8 contact order
The right to contact is that of the child and the interests of the child are the paramount consideration. An application can be made by anyone, not just a parent—for example, a grandparent. An order can provide that a person who the child is not living with shall have specified contact with the child. The court can lay down the exact nature and

extent of the contact, for example, overnight stays, supervised visits, use of contact centre, telephone contact, or birthday cards.

Each case must be decided on its own facts, and the judge or magistrates, after hearing the evidence, have a wide discretion. Certain predictions can be made based on reported cases. For example, there is a presumption in favour of some form of contact with the natural father; for example, even where the child had no knowledge that the applicant, a man serving a long prison sentence, was the father (*A v L (Contact)* (1998)). The Court of Appeal has ruled that the burden of proof rests with the person who claims a parent should not have contact (*F (A Child) (Contact Order)* (2001)). Even in a case of violence there is no *automatic* presumption against contact (*Re F (A Child) (Contact Order)* (2001)), though each case is to be decided on its own facts. So where contact with the father would cause emotional instability in the mother—not surprisingly in view of the history of violence and rape against her—it was the children who would benefit from the mother not having to cope with him having any form of contact, not even a right to send birthday cards (*Re M and B (Children) (Contact: Domestic Violence)* (2001)). If a child of sufficient understanding, or *Gillick* competent (see chapter 3) does not want contact there is no point imposing it, even if the court would otherwise think it in the child's interest and even if there has been 'parental alienation' against the non-resident parent (*Re S (Contact: Children's Views)* (2002)).

Once a contact order has been made, the courts may take a hard line with parents who obstruct contact. In *Re O* (1995), the Court of Appeal said that non-cooperation was not an option, and ordered the mother not only to allow reasonable contact with the father but also to send progress reports, photographs, etc., to him in between contact visits. In *A v N (Refusal of Contact)* (1997), the Court of Appeal jailed a mother for six weeks for obstructing contact which a court had ordered, even though the father was violent and even though sending her to jail was not in the children's best interests. Again, in *F v F (Contact: Committal)* (1998), the President of the Family Division said that the mother must not sabotage contact by indoctrinating the children against it. However, the pendulum has perhaps sprung back. In *Re M (Minors) (Contact: Violent Parent)* (1998), the Family Division refused contact to a man whose violence to the mother made contact with the children a disturbing experience. The court said it was time to start expecting violent men to change their behaviour. And in *Re M (Contact: Family Assistance: McKenzie Friend)* (1999), the mother's genuine fear was held to be a good enough reason to prevent face-to-face contact, in the interests of the children who were upset by their mother's distress when they returned from seeing their father. Similarly, in *Re K (Contact: Mother's Anxiety)* (1999), where the father had previously kidnapped the child, the mother's anxiety made it in the child's best interest to reduce contact, even though the child was enjoying the contact. However the court may respond with a different solution: in *V v V (Children) (Contact: Implacable Hostility)* (2004) the court found that the mother's implacable hostility to contact, refusal to comply with court orders for contact, and false allegations against the father were themselves contrary to the children's interests. Both could provide a good home, and the children wished to remain with the mother. But the court held that the evidence showed the father was better able to provide emotional support and he should have a residence order.

It is possible for the court to refuse permission even to apply for contact under s. 8, but in *Re B (A Child) (Section 91(14) Order: Duration)* (2003) the Court of Appeal held that such an order was for the most extreme circumstances. Here there was no evidence that the father had abused the court procedures or undermined the mother's care for the child. He was permitted indirect contact, with a view to moving towards direct contact. Reminding us of the presumption in favour of contact, the court considered its primary duty to be that of restoring the child's relationship with her father.

Supported contact may be facilitated by the National Association of Child Contact Centres (**www.naccc.org.uk**; tel. 0115 941 4557), which has 277 centres nationally.

Section 8 residence order

The residence order settles the arrangements as to who the child is to live with. It automatically gives that person parental responsibility for the child while it is in effect. This can, in itself, be sufficient reason to make an order. In *B v B* (1992), for example a grandmother needed a residence order so that she could give consent for school trips, etc. If an unmarried father obtains a residence order, he also gets the parental responsibilities under s. 4, which are not revoked without an explicit court order, even if the residence order itself is cancelled. A residence order can be granted in an emergency without hearing full evidence (*M v C* (1993)). But generally, advance notice is required.

The courts do not presume that one parent is 'better' than another. The UN Declaration of Human Rights states that a child of tender years should only exceptionally be separated from his or her mother, and in *Re W* (1992) the Court of Appeal stated that it would start with that presumption. But more recently, in *Re A (A Minor)* (1997), the Court of Appeal stated that the Declaration was made a long time ago and presumptions about the role of fathers and mothers were out of date. But the courts will always presume that residence with a natural parent is better than with anyone else, unless the evidence against this is strong (*Re D (A Child) (Residence: Natural Parent)* (1999)). This automatic preference was summed up by Lord Templeman in *Re KD (A Minor) (Access: Principles)* (1968): 'The best person to bring up a child is the natural parent. It matters not whether the parent is wise or foolish, rich or poor, educated or illiterate, provided the child's moral and physical health are not endangered.' This is arguably more in keeping with the right to family life approach of the European Convention on Human Rights than the welfare principle of the Children Act 1989.

A residence order can, in exceptional circumstances, be made in favour of more than one person, even specifying how the child's time will be split, if this serves the child's interests. For example, in *G v G* (1993) the father looked after the children when he was not on shift work; the mother covered during the shift work. The court approved a joint residence order because it was working well for the children. The principle was reaffirmed in *Re D (Children) (Shared Residence)* (2001). In *G v F* (1998) a lesbian couple both wanted a residence order in relation to the child, born to one of them by artificial insemination. The biological mother opposed her former partner's application. The judge recognized that both parties loved the child, and the nature of their lesbian relationship should not prevent the court ordering what was best for the child: a shared residence order.

A court can attach conditions to a residence order. In an unusual case, *Re S (A Child) (Residence Order: Condition) (No.2)* (2002), the child, who had Downs syndrome, was emotionally close to her father and paternal grandmother. The mother wanted to move to Cornwall, where her future husband lived and looked after his sick mother. The Court of Appeal, while sympathetic to her wishes, said the child's needs came first and she could have residence only on the condition that she stayed in London, so the child could remain close to her father and paternal grandmother.

Once a residence order has been made, the child's surname cannot be changed unless all those with parental responsibility agree, or the court orders a change (which it will generally be reluctant to do: *Re F* (1994)).

Specific issue order s. 8

The specific issue order is essentially a negative type of order, reducing parental powers. A specific issue is identified which, in normal circumstances, those with parental responsibilities would deal with. The responsibility to decide is instead handed to the court. This order ensures that, where there is disagreement, major decisions, such as where the child is to be educated or whether he or she should have certain treatment, are brought before the court. It can be used in cases such as *Re B* (1991), where the court overruled a mother and permitted her 12-year-old daughter to have an abortion. It was used to resolve a dispute about vaccination, where the mother feared the triple vaccine for MMR and the father wanted the child vaccinated (*Re C (A Child) (Immunization: Parental Rights)* (2003)). The mother's argument was that as primary carer her view, particularly in relation to elective as opposed to emergency treatment, should prevail. She claimed such treatment was in the same category as circumcision or change of name, where by and large courts favour the status quo unless both parents with parental responsibility wish to proceed. The Court of Appeal decided on the basis of expert evidence that it was in the child's best interests to receive the immunization.

A common example of a specific issue order is to obtain a change to a child's surname where one parent objects. The courts, applying s. 1 of the Children Act, generally consider that the interests of the child require there to be no change. They may be more sympathetic where a child has already become used to using a new name before the application comes to court. The court may be sympathetic if other factors are important, for example to help a child to remain connected to the ethnic or cultural heritage of one parent. In *Re S (A Child) (Change of Name: Cultural Factors)* (2001), the father was Sikh and the child had a Sikh name. But the mother, with whom the child lived, was a Bangladeshi Muslim, and the child might suffer some disadvantage in the mother's community unless she was known by a Bangladeshi name. The court ordered that the child should keep her Sikh name as a long-term benefit but be known by her Bangladeshi name at school and at home. By contrast, in *Re M, T, P, K and B (Children) (Care: Change of Name)* (2000), the children had been seriously abused by their father and it would help to prevent him tracking them down and putting them at further risk if they acquired new names which he would not know. In *Re K (Specific Issue Order)* (1999), a mother had told her son that his father was dead. In fact, the father was an alcoholic whom the mother hated intensely. The father wanted his son to be told of his paternity and applied under s. 8 for a specific issue order to require this. The court held that, while in principle it would be in the son's interest to know who his father was, in this instance it would be damaging, though it said the damage arose because of the mother's attitude.

Dawson v Wearmouth (1999) confirms the approach which is probably already apparent to you: each decision must be based upon an assessment of the child's welfare, which prevents any general principles from emerging.

Prohibited steps order s. 8

A reverse image of the specific issue order is the s. 8 prohibited steps order. A court order prevents parental responsibility being exercised in relation to a specified action. This could, for example, prevent a child being taken abroad or living with a certain individual. In *Re J (A Minor) (Prohibited Steps Order: Circumcision)* (1999), the court granted an order prohibiting a boy's circumcision. The father wanted this in accordance with his religious beliefs but the mother, not herself a Muslim, resisted. It was not in the child's interests to proceed unless both parents wanted it.

What else can the court order when considering s. 8 applications?

If an application comes before a court, the court looks at all the circumstances and will make any order under s. 8 that it thinks appropriate on the evidence. So the result may be different from what the applicant was hoping for. A contact application, for example, could lead to a residence order. What is more, the family may exceptionally find the probation service or social services involved, since the court can make a family assistance order (FAO) under s. 16. This FAO requires the probation officer or social services department to advise, assist, and befriend the person named in the order; this may be the child or any parent or person who lives with or has contact with the child and who consents. The FAO lasts for up to six months, but can be revoked earlier on the application of the probation officer or social worker, or any party to the s. 8 proceedings.

Another possible outcome—which emphasizes the blurring of the boundaries between the public and private law quality of family proceedings—is that the court may decide that local authority care or supervision could be appropriate. It cannot make such an order yet, except an interim care order, but it may, under s. 37, require the social services department to investigate, with the task of considering whether it should itself apply for a care or supervision order, provide assistance to the family or take any other action with respect to the child. The authority must inform the court within eight weeks of the results of the investigation and any decision made. An example is *M (Intractable Contact Dispute: Interim Care Order)* (2003); the court had found, in contact proceedings, that the mother had planted a false belief in the children's minds that their father was sexually and physically abusing them. There was expert evidence that it was causing them harm, so the court ordered an investigation under s. 37, and used its powers to order interim care; after the investigation it ordered residence to the father and a two-year supervision order. (Incidentally one of the children applied herself, without success, for a prohibited steps order to prevent contact with the father.)

Any order made in respect of a child's upbringing or any agreement made between the parties without a court order can be altered later by the court.

◼ Discretion to adjust finance and property in divorce cases

Courts have no powers to redistribute assets between cohabitees, except that property may be reallocated to provide a home for children (see below).

The Matrimonial Causes Act 1973 provides broad discretionary powers to the court to redistribute property and income on divorce. (There are no equivalent powers to redistribute assets if the parties are not married.) The system is not like that in Scotland, where there is a starting presumption of a 50:50 split of property and savings acquired during the marriage. It is not like Germany or Sweden, where maintenance for the spouse is extremely rare and the welfare state picks up the additional costs, which it recovers from all taxpayers. It is not even like other areas of English law, where precedent enables lawyers to make good predictions. If an experienced matrimonial lawyer is asked by a client to advise on money and property matters, the following extraordinarily unhelpful remarks of Ormrod LJ in *Sharp v Sharp* (1981) indicate how difficult it is to offer it:

> It [is] often said that the Court of Appeal [is] inconsistent when considering family finances. Each family [is] unique and often decisions decided on different facts or even similar facts [are] not helpful. Sometimes a *Mesher* type order [postponing sale of the matrimonial home until the children leave] [is] appropriate, but again on very similar facts such an order might not be appropriate. The judge has to go through the exercise of s. 25 [discussed below] of the Matrimonial Causes Act 1973. There [is] no need to look at the reported cases.

In other words, in trying to settle a marriage breakdown without litigation, a divorcing person is navigating blind. No wonder it can be costly. By the time the case of *Piglowska v Piglowski* (1999) reached the House of Lords, legal costs were £128,000, exactly £1,000 more than the total matriomonial assets. Their Lordships gave lawyers a lecture on costs, stating that a bad settlement may be in fact produce a better result than a good court decision

We will look first at the factors which a divorce court takes into account in making its decisions, before considering property adjustments and then payments out of income.

Factors a court takes into account—needs, resources, length of marriage, and behaviour

For most couples there simply are not enough assets to allow for easy decision making. The needs of the children are the first (but not paramount) consideration. Once these needs are catered for, is there any presumption in favour of equality? The answer from the House of Lords, after 30 years of decisions giving the lion's share to the richer spouse, is, tentatively, yes to equality if there are any assets left once children's needs are met (*White v White* (2000)). In *Lambert v Lambert* (2002), the Court of Appeal urged courts to avoid the sex discrimination which used to favour the male earner over the female homemaker. Only exceptionally—where for example a person has unusual entrepreneurial skills—should one spouse get more than half the available assets, once issues which we consider below such as length of marriage, needs of children, or extreme behaviour had been taken into account.

A person starting a property dispute with the benefit of legal aid should be reminded of the right of the Legal Services Commission to deduct legal costs from the value of disputed matrimonial assets. The home may end up subject to a massive extra charge. The same applies to those paying their own costs. In *White v White*, above, legal costs exceeded £1 million, in relation to joint assets of £4 million (Law Society Gazette (2001) 24 Oct., 5).

The other factors the court will consider, after looking at the needs of the children, are the needs and resources of the parties, and their relative capacities to earn (including potential, where, for example, a wife could return to work). The length of the marriage will be relevant; the shorter the marriage, the less the obligation between the parties is likely to be. The court also considers the ages of the parties, what contributions each has made over the years to the welfare of the family, and, lastly, the behaviour of any party if it has been extreme. For example, in *Kyte v Kyte* (1987), the wife had not only had an adulterous and clandestine relationship with another man, but had encouraged the husband to attempt suicide. Her lump sum award was reduced. In *Re B (Financial Provision: Welfare of Child and Conduct)* (2002), the husband had been jailed for abducting the child, had failed to cooperate over the sale of the home, and had failed to disclose to the court that he had taken money from an account. In these circumstances the Court of Appeal was willing to award the wife all of the equity (value after paying off the mortgage) in the home. Note that behaviour is not allowed to take precedence over the needs of the children, which are the court's first consideration (but unlike proceedings *about* children, their needs are not paramount).

Powers to redistribute property—divorcing couples

At the same time as dealing with a divorce petition, the court can adjust all the interests in ownership of the property to suit the current position of the parties and the children (Matrimonial Causes Act 1973, s. 24). As well as property which is owned, a tenancy of the matrimonial home is subject to adjustment in divorce proceedings: it can be transferred from one spouse to the other, or from joint names to one only. The landlord cannot veto such a court order. Even furniture, cars, etc. can be considered, though they will rarely be worth as much as the legal costs involved.

Powers to redistribute property—unmarried couples

If there are no children, unmarried parties who own or have a joint interest in property together have to apply to the Chancery Division for an order that the property be sold and divided up. Joint ownership is—though most owners do not realize this—a matter of trust law. When the relationship ends, so does the trust, and a sale must be ordered if requested. It may be possible to avoid this by the party who wants to remain raising a loan and buying the other person's share.

However, if there are children, the trust normally continues until the need to house the children in the trust property has also ended. So an order for sale may be postponed, permitting the parent and the children a limited time in the property, until the children do not need it. In determining shares in the sale proceeds the court can only look at the financial or cash equivalent input to the property (such as improvements), together with attempting a fair interpretation of what the parties intended when the property was acquired. Unless she can prove that an explicit promise was made to give her a share of the property, or it can be inferred from the circumstances, a woman who has stayed at home to bring up the children is unlikely to gain any credit for this in the final balance sheet; but if she built an extension, or paid money into the common kitty for household and mortgage expenses, then she may build up a financial interest in the property accordingly.

Also, where parties are unmarried and there is a child of the relationship, the court has certain additional powers. It can order amongst other things a transfer of property between the parents for the benefit of that child. An order of this type is designed to benefit only the child, and the transfer may be only for the duration of the child's dependence, leaving the parent who looked after them with nothing once the child leaves home (*T v S* (1994)).

Using the court's powers to adjust property and order maintenance on divorce

The first possibility is that the parties agree on who will live where, how the ownership will be adjusted, and who will pay what maintenance (if any). This is the simplest option, but not necessarily the best. For example, the wife may think she is entitled only to a half share of any property, not realizing a court is likely to award more. She may forgo maintenance only to realize later that her earning capacity is far less than her former husband's. So specialist legal advice is recommended before agreeing any property division.

The first issue is deciding who will live where. Only when the arrangements for the children are known—if necessary the court has to make a s. 8 residence order—can other parts of the jigsaw fall into place. The parent with care of the children will, if possible, usually keep the matrimonial home or, if it is owned, sell it and use any proceeds of sale to buy another. The parent without care of the children (let's call him the father for now, as is most often the case) may have been the biggest financial contributor to the family, but still may be entitled to well under half the value of the home, in recognition of his greater earning capacity, the mother's needs, and the children's need for a home; the wife can often increase her share by forgoing maintenance for herself in the future, possibly leading to an outright transfer to herself or the possibility of raising enough cash to buy out the husband's share.

If there are not enough resources for the parent with care to obtain a full transfer of the ownership it will be necessary either to order the property sold or to make a deferred order (sale delayed until the children grow up or until she remarries/cohabits—either way, a delayed headache). (Usually both parties remain liable for the mortgage, as the lender will refuse consent to a transfer of ownership to a low earner.)

Maintenance payments to a spouse after divorce

Maintenance for children is now normally dictated by a formula under the Child Support Act 1991 (see below). So we will not consider them here. We also have to ignore cohabitees, as courts have no powers to order maintenance.

Spouses can ask a court to order maintenance. But is it worth it? It frequently happens that, however much maintenance is paid, the recipient will still have to rely on income support or income-related jobseekers allowance, and the maintenance received is offset by reduced benefit. There are still reasons why an application for maintenance should be considered: first, if the wife later becomes employed, maintenance will be a real addition to her resources; second, former spouses are obliged in law to maintain each other. Where benefits are paid, the Department for Work and Pensions can itself take proceedings against a former spouse for the maintenance. If the wife fears that her ex-partner's maintenance payments will not be reliable, she can sign the maintenance over to the DWP while she receives full income support.

Notwithstanding the obligation to support a former spouse, the courts are encouraged, under the Matrimonial Causes Act 1973, ss. 25(1) and 25A, to try to obtain a clean break between the parties, by adjusting property once and for all, and, if a maintenance order is made between spouses, limiting its duration. But even after a clean break, carefully considered by a court, the DWP can insist on a spouse paying towards the cost of the ex-spouse's means-tested benefits.

Fleming v Fleming (2003) demonstrates the courts' commitment to the clean break. An ex-wife applied for maintenance to be renewed, particularly in light of her disability. The former husband argued that she could take steps to reduce the effect of her disability, and in any event he had new responsibilities by way of a cohabitation equivalent to marriage. The Court of Appeal accepted his argument and confirmed that there should now be a clean break, noting also that the ex-wife and her partner could earn more than they claimed.

The court can order pension fund trustees to make pension payments directly to a former spouse. Therefore a divorce court can treat present or future pension expectations as part of the matrimonial assets. There is a power to order the payments to continue even after the death of the pension holder. This is called pension splitting. This will reduce the amount of pension benefits available, because the pension fund is now required to pay out on two lives, not one.

Where a court has a divorce case before it, it can make the final, considered maintenance and property adjustment orders only when a divorce order has been made. However, the court may make an interim maintenance order as soon as divorce proceedings start.

Enforcement and variation of orders

Unlike child support (below), court maintenance orders for a spouse have no automatic enforcement mechanisms. If a maintenance order falls into arrears, the unfortunate payee has to go back to court to get it enforced. There are various possibilities for enforcement. Commonly, a court will order an employer to make regular deductions from wages and pay them direct to the court. Or a court can order the non-payer to be committed to prison—usually a threat of last resort. But on any application for enforcement, the court may also remit, i.e. cancel, some or all of the arrears, or may vary any maintenance order. It can also do this on the application of a person—payer or recipient—whether or not there are arrears. Many men, in our experience of legal practice, are quick to assume new financial burdens after a relationship breakdown, and then to ask the court to reduce their payments and remit the arrears. Since their alleged ability to pay has to be taken into account, it may be better for the recipient of maintenance to try to obtain the best possible property and lump sum order initially, and trade that off against uncertain maintenance in the future. (As we see below, the maintenance of the children cannot be traded in this way.)

If a maintenance order is in force, either party can go back to court to apply for a variation based on new circumstances. To preserve the option of an upwards variation, a wife is usually advised to agree nominal maintenance—say 5p a year—which can be varied if her needs change, rather than to agree to no maintenance order at all.

■ Maintenance for children

Non-resident parents are expected in law to pay towards the maintenance of their children, whether or not the children need the payments (e.g. the parent with care may actually be very rich), and even where the payments will not actually benefit the children (because means-tested benefits will then be cut).

Maintenance can be paid by agreement. Otherwise the non-resident parent can be made to pay maintenance in one of two ways: exceptionally, by a court order; or, usually, by the Child Support Agency.

The Child Support Agency (CSA)

The Child Support Act 1991 stripped the courts of most of their powers to decide on child maintenance and handed them to the CSA. How much the absent parent pays is calculated by the CSA according to formulae. These formulae are not as complex as they once were, and the starting point is that the non-resident parent must pay 15 per cent of net income for the first child, 20 per cent for two children, and 25 per cent for three or more. If the non-resident parent supports a second family, when calculating his or her net income the CSA reduces it in the same way—15 per cent for the first additional child, etc.)

If the parent with care is receiving means-tested benefits (income support, means-tested jobseekers allowance, tax credits) then any CSA payment reduces the benefit. There would be a temptation not to apply for CSA maintenance in this situation, but the CSA can require the parent with care who receives these benefits to make an application. (It cannot do so where a parent with care receives no such benefits.) The CSA also has the right to enquire into the identity and whereabouts of the non-resident parent. A parent can have their benefits reduced for up to eighteen months for not cooperating, unless she or he can convince the CSA that there is a good reason for not divulging the information. Privacy is not considered a good reason, but fear of harm or 'undue' distress is a good reason under s. 6 of the Act. Sometimes it is better for the parent and the children for a violent parent to have no involvement in the life of the children—not even through making payments. But CSA administration is not family proceedings and the welfare of the children is not only not paramount, it is not mentioned. So what is 'undue'? Guidelines suggest that only physical violence, or fear of it, counts. They also say the claimant should be believed, and should not be required to prove any past violence.

Who is a non-resident parent?
Where paternity is disputed, the courts must settle that issue before the Agency can decide on the correct level of maintenance. The court will rely on scientific evidence. However, no proof is necessary if the man has previously adopted the child, or in other proceedings (such as Children Act 1989 contact proceedings) he was already found to be the father. But a court will not necessarily order a blood or DNA test, because doing so may exceptionally not be in the child's interests.

The child support agency as a cause of disputes
A non-resident parent gets to pay less in maintenance the more the child stays with him or her (unless it is fewer than fifty-three nights in the year). This may be an incentive for disputing staying contact arrangements for the wrong reasons.

Enforcing an agency order
Once a payment has been calculated, the Agency is responsible for enforcement. Payments can be made by standing order or direct debit. Enforcement can be via deductions from earnings (s. 31) or direct from benefits (s. 43). Property of a non-payer can be seized by order of the magistrates' court (ss. 33 and 35), and ultimately he can be committed to prison. The non-payer can even be banned, on application to the magistrates court, from driving (s. 39A). Agency inspectors carrying out an assessment of the non-resident parent's means have powers to interview him, to search property, and to inspect documents. They can obtain information from the tax office, housing benefit department, and the Benefits Agency or Department of Employment (ss. 14 and 15).

More details of the Agency can be obtained free from **www.dss.gov.uk/csa.** There is a free advice phone line on 08457 133 133. A CAB, law centre, or solicitor can also help. An application to obtain an assessment is made on a form available from any DWP office. (A child cannot apply, only the absent parent or the person caring for the child.)

Appeals against agency decisions
Agency decisions, including reductions of benefit for non-cooperation, but also relating to assessments of maintenance payments, can be appealed to the Appeals Service tribunal. The right to appeal must usually be exercised within twenty-eight days of the decision. There is also a right to a review of the decision, which is carried out by the Agency itself.

The role of the courts in provision for children

The court has the power under s. 8 of the Act to decide questions of provision for a child in the following circumstances:

(a) the child is disabled;

(b) the application relates to school fees;

(c) the application is for a top-up over and above the Agency assessment (relevant to the rich only);

(d) there is a court endorsed agreement in effect between the parties (but if the parent with care gets means-tested benefits, the Agency takes over; and the parent with care can still apply to the Agency one year after the agreement was endorsed by the court).

Where a non-residential parent enjoys extreme wealth, applications to the court can result in considerable payments: *Re P (A Child)* (2003)—here, £1 million for the home, £100,000 to furnish it, £70,000 a year for maintenance. (However, had the parties been married the wife could have made far greater claims in her own right.)

Courts also have powers to make lump sum orders in favour of children, whether or not the parents were married, and whether or not the CSA has been involved in support for a child. The considerations taken into account are set out in Schedule 1 to the Children Act 1989 or s. 25 Matrimonial Causes Act 1973.) Lump sum payments can cover expenses incurred before the application, for example in connection with or anticipation of the birth. It is not just the other parent who can be ordered to make a payment: it could also be a step-parent who accepted the child as a child of the marriage. (In contrast, the Agency has no powers to make a step-parent pay.)

Orders for children, whether lump sum or maintenance, are rarely made in isolation. If the parents are splitting up, their needs and resources have to be taken into account too. Indeed, the court may at the same time be hearing applications for property adjustment and maintenance between spouses. The court will also have to be aware of how much the CSA payments will be. When considering financial orders in favour of a child, the court does not have to make the welfare of the child its paramount consideration, as it does when considering where the child shall live and who he or she shall have contact with. What the court must consider are the needs of the child, the child's resources, physical and mental attributes, and educational expectations, and also the needs and resources of both the paying party and the party who the child is living with. It may decide, in the end, to balance these requirements instead of putting a child's needs above all other needs (and there may be other children whose needs have to be met, such as new step- or half siblings).

Any financial order that relates to children, or agreement between the parties—even an agreement expressed to be unalterable and final—can be varied by the court on application, and a child of 16 or over can him- or herself apply to vary an order. Court orders for child maintenance generally last until the child is 17, or ceases full-time training or education.

How does the CSA measure up to the Human Rights Act? In *R (on the application of*

Kehoe) v Secretary of State for Work and Pensions (2004) the parent with care claimed that the CSA regime denied her a fair hearing in relation to her civil rights, and was therefore in breach of Article 6 of the Human Rights Convention. The Court of Appeal held that having an administrative mechanism rather than a judicial process was a proportionate response to the problem of collecting payments from absent parents, even though in this case the CSA had been very ineffective in obtaining any maintenance payments from the father and the mother could do nothing about it.

Child abduction

A parent may decide to take questions of residence and contact with a child into his or her own hands. If the child is removed within England and Wales, the court can make a residence, contact, or specific issue order (see above) to ensure the child's return. The bigger problem arises if there is a risk of the child being taken abroad. If that risk is foreseen, urgent action is necessary, and it is wise to instruct a specialist lawyer. Assuming, for the sake of simplicity, the child is living with the mother, and it is feared that the father may remove the child abroad, steps can include:

(a) an agreement, or court order under Children Act s. 8, for the father to surrender his passport (not always effective if the father has a foreign passport, as a replacement may be provided by an embassy);

(b) a ports warning, carried out by the police. Again this is not guaranteed to succeed, especially with the reduction of passport controls in the European Union.

Where the child has already been removed, legal action becomes necessary in the country to which the child was taken. This is horrifically distressing and difficult. In some countries, laws give custody to fathers automatically, so a court order will be impossible. However, any country which has signed the Hague Convention on Civil Aspects of Child Abduction is bound to assist with returning a child to the country where he or she is 'habitually resident', unless this is quite clearly contrary to the best interests of the child (for example where the children are violently opposed to returning and evidence suggests this will cause psychological harm: *Re M (Abduction: Psychological Harm)* (1997)—an application to return abducted children to Greece). The Department for Constitutional Affairs in the United Kingdom contacts the authorities in the country concerned, and those authorities must take steps to obtain the child's return.

Child abduction (removal of a child from the United Kingdom without the consent of the other parent) is a criminal offence. (For this purpose, consent of a father without parental responsibility is not required.)

An organization providing support to parents whose children have been abducted is: International Child Abduction Centre, PO Box 4, London WC1X 3DX; tel 0207 357 3440; **www.reunite.org**.

EXERCISES

You have been involved with the Patel family. Consider the following situations.

- The eldest child Sandy, age 14, is blind. The parents disagree about her education, Mr Patel wanting to send her to a private boarding school and Mrs Patel wanting her to be educated at a local authority school with special facilities. How can this disagreement be resolved?

- Mr and Mrs Patel have been married for fifteen years. Mrs Patel says that Mr Patel has lost interest in the relationship, stays out late, and has threatened violence against her. She wants a divorce. Consider whether she has grounds.

- The Patels own their home, subject to a small mortgage. Mrs Patel has severe arthritis and the home has been adapted for wheelchair use. Mr Patel says that as he worked all hours to pay for the home he should be free to sell the property and keep the equity for himself. How might a court go about allocating the property?

- Mrs Patel approaches the Child Support Agency but does not feel the formula provides enough support for Mandy's needs. Can she obtain additional money from either Mr Patel or from any other source?

COMPANION WEB SITE

 For guidance on how to answer these exercises, visit the companion web site at: **www.oup.com/uk/booksites/law**

WHERE DO WE GO FROM HERE?

Family breakdown is associated with social exclusion. While we have included the law on family breakdown within the part of the book dealing with children—because private and public law have such a large overlap and are often triggered by common problems within the family—there are other areas of law relevant to other problems such families will face. Violence and housing deprivation are key indicators of social exclusion affecting families and children, and you will benefit from seeing Part 5 of the book within a context of supporting families and children, as well as vulnerable adults.

The final chapter of Part 2, however, is concerned with the question of children who are in trouble with the criminal law. A child suspected of crime or before the criminal courts is a child in need, and a range of social service duties are triggered.

ANNOTATED FURTHER READING

S. Cretney, J. Masson, and R. Bailey-Harris, *Principles of Family Law* (7th edn., Sweet & Maxwell, 2002)—an up-to-date, authoritative, and well-written account of all relevant areas of family law.

B. Hoggett, D. Pearl, E. Cooke, and P. Bates, *The Family, Law and Society, Cases and Materials* (5th edn., Butterworths, 2002)—probably the most stimulating collection of materials available, providing excellent insight into law and policy issues.

G. Douglas, *An Introduction to Family Law* (Clarendon Press, 2001)—well reviewed, easy to read, and shows how one part of family law affects other aspects of family law and family life.

The Rt. Hon. N. Wall (ed.), *Rayden and Jackson on Divorce and Family Matters* (Butterworths)—an encylopaedia kept up to date by looseleaf supplements contains all the legislation and regulations, together with commentary.

Child Poverty Action Group, *Welfare Benefits and Tax Credits Handbook* (7th edn., Child Poverty Action Group 2005), Child Support Handbook (12th edn., 2005), and *Debt Advice Handbook* (6th edn., Child Poverty Action Group, 2004)—these annual CPAG handbooks contain up-to-date core information which can assist you in identifying possible alleviation of financial problems.

Solicitors Family Law Association web site, **www.sfla.org.uk** gives a flavour of the standards and approach adopted by a good family lawyer; the web site has a range of leaflets such as 'Divorce Procedure' designed for non-lawyers.

15 Children in the criminal justice system

CASE STUDY

Case 0002488/94, V v United Kingdom, European Court of Human Rights (1999)

Two boys, aged 10 and 11 at the time, in a highly publicized case, were alleged to have abducted and killed a 2-year-old boy, James Bulger. They were tried in the adult Crown Court, and vilified in the press before and during the trial. Following conviction V appealed, eventually, to the European Court of Human Rights. He did not appeal against conviction; his complaint was a breach of Article 5 (right not to suffer inhuman and degrading treatment), Article 6 (right to a fair trial) and Article 14 (that as a 10 year old he was discriminated against in comparison with a 9 year old who would not have been tried). He also complained that detention 'according to Her Majesty's pleasure' was a breach of his right to liberty (Article 5) and that the decision to increase the 'tariff' (the length of time he would actually spend in custody) was made by a politician and not an independent body (breach of Article 6).

The case illustrates a range of difficulties concerning how to deal with young suspects and, if they are convicted, how to sentence them. The ECtHR ruled in a lengthy but readable judgment that the welfare of the child defendant must be a guiding factor in all decisions; that the right to understand and participate in the trial was the right of the child, not of his lawyers. He should have been personally able to follow and understand. Finally, his sentence should be determined by a court, not by a politician. The claim that V had been subjected to inhuman or degrading treatment was rejected, as was the claim that he was discriminated against. The Court ruled that the age of criminal responsibility in each state had to start at some arbitrary age.

OVERVIEW AND OBJECTIVES

The case study illustrates that the fact that a person is a child affects almost every aspect of the way the courts (and police) should conduct the proceedings, and the fact that human rights considerations underpin every stage of the proceedings. Though you will learn mainly about children in the criminal justice process, where appropriate we will also refer you to considerations which apply if the vulnerable person is an adult.

Although there is an ever-changing rhetoric about crime and young people, what endures is the need for those who work with vulnerable suspects and offenders to help them at a time when they are at their most vulnerable, and to steer them away from involvement in criminal processes in their own best interests. We hope this chapter can make a contribution to the tools you will need for this work, as social workers are involved at many stages of the youth justice process.

You will need an understanding of police station procedures, and the role of the appropriate adult in ensuring that the questioning and gathering of evidence is fair; you could well be involved in helping to decide whether a child should be prosecuted, and you need to know what is the range of alternatives. How could it happen that a 10 year old was brought to trial in the glare of publicity in a Crown Court? We introduce you to the various courts that deal with young offenders, including adult courts, so you should gain an overview of their different roles, and the roles you may play within them. You need to know where children are accommodated if remanded during investigations, or while waiting for trial or sentence. Finally, we look at the sentencing options available to courts, with the intention that you can support the young person and also, when required, both advise the court on an appropriate sentence and be equipped to play a role in administering restorative or community punishments.

◼ Social work responsibilities

The situations where you may have a statutory responsibility are set out in Box 14.1. (Note that social workers or social service departments may be mentioned in statutes in this chapter which are not mentioned as duties in LASSA—but there is no doubt that the duty exists, since the target group of children and vulnerable adults does come within LASSA duties.)

◼ Children's age in the justice system

A child who has not reached the age of 10 cannot, as a matter of English law, commit a crime, and so cannot be subjected to criminal proceedings (Children and Young Persons Act 1933, s. 50). Behaviour which in an older child could lead to arrest, charge, and trial in the youth court will, if the alleged wrongdoer is under 10, have to be dealt with either informally, by the police and/or social services (a telling-off and a word with the parents), or formally, by application for a Child Safety Order (see chapter 18), the institution of care/supervision proceedings or, in an urgent case, by an application for an Emergency Protection Order (see chapter 12). The criminal or deviant behaviour could be evidence of significant harm under the Children Act 1989, s. 31.

After his or her 10th birthday, an age younger than in almost every European country, a child can be charged with, tried and convicted of a criminal offence, and this can happen in an adult Crown Court. However, under the age of 18 the law does treat them in a number of different ways, some of which are inconsistent and confusing:

• They are called juveniles in the criminal courts, but juvenile courts have been renamed youth courts.

• Children of 17 are treated as adults when being questioned in the police station as suspects.

BOX 15.1 Statutory duties involving social workers in the justice system

Duties of an overarching nature	Legislation
Social services department must produce an annual youth justice plan	Crime and Disorder Act 1998, s. 40
Children in trouble trigger the social services duty to investigate and if necessary act to protect the child	Children Act 1989, s. 47
Children in need to be provided with support and in particular to be kept out of criminal justice system	Children Act 1989 s. 17 and Schedule 2
Local authority must provide support for child awaiting trial or sentence	Crime and Disorder Act 1998, s. 38
Vulnerable adults to be provided with support services	National Assistance Act 1948, s. 29
Social workers may be involved when a court sentences a person with a mental disorder	Mental Health Act 1983, s. 37
Every local authority must carry out all of its work in a way designed to reduce crime and disorder	Crime and Disorder Act 1998, s. 17

Services listed in Crime and Disorder Act 1998 s. 39 which social services authorities must ensure Youth Offending Teams can carry out; and additional statutory material relating to such services

(a) appropriate adults to be available when the police interview juveniles	Police and Criminal Evidence Act 1984 Code of Practice
(b) rehabilitation following a police warning	Children Act s. 17; Crime and Disorder Act 1998 s. 65
(c) support for children awaiting trial or sentence	Children and Young Persons Act 1933, ss. 34 and 34A; CYPA 1969 s. 5(8)
(d) accommodation for children who are denied bail	Children and Young Persons Act 1969, s. 23; Children Act 1989, s. 20
(e) making reports to the court	Children and Young Persons Act 1969, s. 9
(f) persons to act as responsible officers where a court has made a parenting order	Crime and Disorder Act 1998, s. 8
(g) supervision of community sentences	Powers of Criminal Courts (Sentencing) Act 2000, ss. 63–7
(h) supervision of detention and training orders or supervision orders	Powers of Criminal Courts (Sentencing) Act 2000, ss. 102–7
(i) supervision of children who are released from custody	Powers of Criminal Courts (Sentencing) Act 2000, ss. 102–7
(j) arranging for convicted juveniles to go into secure accommodation if sentenced to a detention and training order	Powers of Criminal Courts (Sentencing) Act 2000, ss. 102–7

- Where the police or the courts refuse bail to a 17 year old, he or she is not accommodated by the local authority as a child, but is detained at the police station or remanded to a remand centre like an adult.

- Under 18s in most of the legislation are divided into children (aged 10 to 13) and young persons (aged 14 to 17), which is why two of the statutes you will come across are called the Children and Young Persons Acts (1933 and 1969). (The differences add nothing to our understanding so we use the term children or juveniles in this chapter.)

- Once suspects or offenders reach the age of 18, the criminal courts treat them as adults, though if incarcerated they go to young offender institutions until the age of 21.

Youth justice philosophy and politics

Two statutory duties virtually contradict each other. The new, 'tough on crime' Labour Government made it clear under s. 37 of the Crime and Disorder Act 1998 (CDA) that 'It shall be the principal aim of the youth justice system to *prevent offending* by children and young persons'. But s. 44 of the Children and Young Persons Act 1933 (CYPA) still governs most of the procedures for trying young people; it was not amended in 1998 and it continues to make the *welfare of the juvenile* the number one priority. This latter requirement is in accordance with the UN Convention on the Rights of the Child.

The tension between these two concepts was revealed in *R (on the application of Ellis) v Chief Constable of Wales* (2003). The police had displayed a picture of a convicted juvenile. This was encouraged under the national Offender Naming Scheme, as a deterrent to other would-be criminals. The police conceded that doing this necessarily interfered with the juvenile's right to respect for private life under Article 8 of the Human Rights Convention. Balancing up the government's legitimate role in deterrence of crime and the individual's right to respect for private life, as the court must do, it held the public policy outweighed the human rights argument. However, it also held that the police must carefully evaluate for each person whose picture they wish to display whether the use of the scheme is justified in her or his case—taking into account for example the effect on schooling, or on family life.

Giving consideration to the welfare of the child, s. 39 of the 1933 Act permits a court to ban or restrict press reports, particularly detail by which the child may be identified. The press can challenge such an order in the Divisional Court, which must balance safeguarding the child's welfare against the public interest in open justice. In *R v Manchester Crown Court, ex parte H* (2000), for example, the Divisional Court permitted identification of two 15 year olds convicted of murder.

For the social worker involved in youth justice, we suggest that your starting point should be the Children Act 1989, s. 17 and Sch. 2: promoting the welfare of children and keeping them out of the criminal courts (see further chapter 10). This continues to be a duty of a social services department under the Local Authority Social Services

Act 1970. But you carry out this duty towards children in need in the new context of getting tough on crime, and the duty of every local authority under the 1998 Act to 'exercise its various functions with due regard to the likely effect of the exercise of those functions on, and the need to do all that it reasonably can to prevent, crime and disorder in its area'.

To provide direction to the drive to cut down youth crime, the Government has established a Youth Justice Board which sets standards and gives advice to the Government on policy. The Board can make grants to local authorities who have good ideas. See 'further reading' below for their web address.

Youth offending teams: liaison with police and other agencies

Police

To simplify the discussion, we have assumed that it is the police who instigate action in criminal proceedings. In fact an arrest may be carried out by a store detective, or a charge could be made by the transport police, for example where fare dodging is alleged. But by the time a social worker is involved the investigation will be in the hands of the police. The overriding reason you liaise with the police on questions of youth crime is because it is your duty under the Children Act 1989 to keep children out of the criminal justice system. Three ways exist to achieve this ambitious goal: to cause children not to commit crimes (a very long-term aim involving self-esteem, protection, education, housing, etc.); to persuade the police, as a member of a YOT, where appropriate not to charge them (a short-term goal); and, later in the process, to advise a court on the sentence most likely to cut future offending.

Even if they do not consult you, if the case is clear cut, the police must notify the local authority if they decide to prosecute a young person (Children and Young Persons Act 1969, ss. 5 and 34).

The Youth Justice Plan

The framework for joint work with other agencies is set out in the CDA. Every local authority (at district, borough, or county level, not just those with social service functions) must now have a youth justice plan (ss. 6 and 40) containing a strategy and targets for reducing crime and disorder.

The Youth Offending Team (YOT)

Who is at the heart of youth justice? Not the police, not the probation services; it is the local authority social services department. Under s. 38, the department must secure all necessary youth justice services—these were listed in Box 14.1 above. It does this, under s. 39, by setting up YOTs for its area, or jointly with another area. The cooperation of police, probation, health, and education authorities in establishing YOTs is required by the statute. The functions of the YOT in Box 14.1 must be secured by the social services department, but need not necessarily be provided directly by it. Curiously, none of these appears in LASSA as a statutory duty (see chapter 1).

The social worker in the police station

A suspect may have been arrested and brought immediately to the police station, or, under a power introduced into the Police and Criminal Evidence Act 1984 (PACE) in 2004, bailed by the arresting officer with a requirement to attend at a future date. In the following section we assume the suspect is now at the police station.

What goes on when a suspect is held in the police station is governed by PACE, and codes made by the Home Office using PACE powers. The particular code of interest here is Code C on Detention Treatment and Questioning (Code C), as updated in August 2004. Code C is available for consultation by detainees and members of the public in every police station and also at **www.homeoffice.gov.uk/docs3/pacecode_c.pdf**.

Being at the police station for interview is stressful. Code C recognizes that some groups of vulnerable people should not have to undergo the experience alone. An 'appropriate adult' should be called to assist the suspect, and no police questioning should normally take place until that person is available. A social worker will frequently be asked to be that appropriate adult.

The code recognizes two groups as being vulnerable. The first is 'juveniles', which covers children up to but not including the age of 17. (But see the case of *R (on the application of the Director of Public Prosecutions) v Stratford Youth Court* (2001) below for a challenge to this lack of protection for the 17-year-old child suspect.) The other is a suspect who is mentally vulnerable (Code C, s. 11). (There are additional duties on the police if a person may be blind or deaf or for some other reason unable to communicate without assistance—but this will not trigger the calling of an appropriate adult and therefore we will not consider this.) How can the police be expected to know whether a person falls into this category? Under Code C, s. 1, if they have any suspicion, or are told in good faith, that a person is a juvenile or mentally vulnerable, they must act accordingly unless they have clear and reliable evidence to the contrary.

The appropriate adult

Code C contains several references to the appropriate adult: see Box 15.2.

The police need an appropriate adult. It is not in their interests to have doubt cast on the evidence they get during questioning. Evidence of confession can be rejected by a court if the appropriate adult was not there. For example, the defendant was certified fit for interview by a police doctor, but was known to suffer from schizophrenia. He should not be interviewed in the absence of an appropriate adult (*R v Aspinall* (1999)) and what he said in the interview should not have been used in evidence. (Even with an appropriate adult to safeguard the detainee's interests, a confession obtained from a detainee who is suffering at the time of interview from a mental disorder is unlikely to be admissible at trial, and the appropriate adult is likely to be called to give evidence as to the circumstances surrounding the confession: *R v Heslop* (1996).)

Where a juvenile or other person at risk is detained, s. 3.9 of Code C requires the police to inform the appropriate adult—which means the person they have identified

BOX 15.2 Extract from Code C s. 1.7, defining who is an appropriate adult, with emphasis added to show where social workers can be involved.

(a) in the case of a juvenile:
    (i)   the parent or guardian (or, if the juvenile is in care, the *care authority* or voluntary organisation. The term 'in care' covers all cases in which a juvenile is 'looked after' by a local authority under the Children Act 1989);
    (ii)   a *social worker* or a *member of a local youth offending team*;
    (iii) failing either of the above, another responsible adult aged 18 or over who is not a police officer or employed by the police.

(b) in the case of a person who is mentally disordered or otherwise mentally vulnerable:
    (i)   a relative, *guardian*, or other person responsible for their care or custody;
    (ii)   *someone who has experience of dealing with mentally disordered or mentally vulnerable* people but who is not a police officer or employed by the police (such as an *approved social worker* as defined by the Mental Health Act 1983, a specialist social worker, or a community psychiatric nurse); or
    (iii) failing either of the above, some other responsible adult aged 18 or over who is not a police officer or employed by the police.

as such—as soon as practicable of the reason for detention, where the person is being detained, and to request the appropriate adult to come to the police station.

Entirely independently of the need to enlist an appropriate adult before interviewing, the police must attempt to inform the person responsible for the child's welfare (usually a parent or guardian) of the arrest and detention of any juvenile (Children and Young Persons Act 1933, s. 34(2)), and, if the juvenile is under supervision, the supervisor. They must also inform the local authority where the child is in local authority care or accommodation, even if they call another appropriate adult (Code C, 3.7).

We have seen that the department must ensure the availability of appropriate adults, but there is no statutory duty to send someone in any given case to the police station. So should you agree to be the appropriate adult simply because the police have requested a social worker? Clearly where a juvenile is in your care, there is no doubt that a social worker from that authority is the appropriate adult. But in the other situations listed, someone else, a parent or carer, may be better, and the police should be advised to contact that person. Home Office Study No. 174 of 1997 found that for juveniles the appropriate adult is a social worker in 23 per cent of cases.

Sometimes a social worker is more appropriate than a parent. For example, in *DPP v Blake* (1989), Norfolk social services, at the time, had a blanket policy of not sending a social worker to be the appropriate adult if a parent was available. In this case the father of a 16 year old had been contacted. The detained juvenile did not want him, as she had no real relationship with him. She wanted her social worker. During the police station interview the father played no part; in fact his daughter ignored him. She eventually confessed to the charge and was convicted. The Court of Appeal held that this confession should not have been put before the court as evidence, because of the circumstances in which it was obtained, notably the fact that the appropriate adult had not assisted the juvenile in any way. In *R v Jefferson* (1994), the appropriate adult was the father, who intervened on the side of the police, often contradicting the boy's account. As we will see below, this is not what is expected of the appropriate adult—but the boy's eventual confession to riot and violent disorder was allowed to stand by the Court of Appeal.

The Home Office research confirms this impression that frequently the social worker does a far better job than parents, relatives, or other adults. The social worker is calmer, more supportive, and, of course (having read this chapter), understands the task. In deciding whether a social worker should attend, the duty social worker will need to ask the police if there is any known reason why the parent is not appropriate. But a social worker to whom the juvenile has previously admitted the offence is not the appropriate adult—another social worker will be required (Code C, Notes for Guidance 1D). If you refuse to attend, do not, of course, give this as the reason to the police (see chapter 4 for guidance on confidentiality).

There may be a temptation to use a family member as both appropriate adult and interpreter, where the detainee does not speak fluent English. This flouts two important principles: first, that the appropriate adult must have only one task, that of assisting the detainee; second, that an interpreter must be wholly independent (*R v West London Youth Court, ex parte J* (2000)).

In exceptional cases, Code C, s. 11.18, entitled 'Urgent Interviews', allows the police to interview a juvenile or mentally ill/handicapped person in the absence of an appropriate adult if an officer of at least superintendent rank believes that delay will lead to immediate risk of harm to anyone, tip-offs to other suspects, or interference with evidence, and that proceeding without the appropriate adult will not harm the suspect mentally or physically. But the Code warns that the evidence obtained may be unreliable (and, consequently, as we see below, unusable):

> 11C It is important to bear in mind that, although juveniles or people who are mentally disordered or otherwise mentally vulnerable are often capable of providing reliable evidence, they may, without knowing or wishing to do so, be particularly prone in certain circumstances to provide information which is unreliable, misleading or self-incriminating. Special care should therefore always be exercised in questioning such a person, and the appropriate adult should be involved, if there is any doubt about a person's age, mental state or capacity. Because of the risk of unreliable evidence it is also important to obtain corroboration of any facts admitted whenever possible.

Despite this clear warning the Home Office research found that in 9 per cent of juvenile interviews an appropriate adult was not present.

Where the detainee is mentally vulnerable, Code C (Notes for Guidance 1E) recommends that someone with experience and training may often be better as appropriate adult than a relative, though the detainee's wishes are, if possible, to be respected in choosing or rejecting someone. The Home Office study mentioned earlier found that the appropriate adult is a social worker in 60 per cent of cases.

If you decide that you are the appropriate person to attend, it is important to go as soon as possible, to minimize the period of detention. Once you arrive, you should first talk to the custody officer to obtain basic details—suspected offence, time of arrest, what the police are intending to do. Beware of ever being asked at this stage to abandon your own professional judgement ('Between you and me, if you could persuade him to tell us what happened, he'll be out of here much quicker . . .'). Your role is described below; do not allow the police to define it for you.

The detainee is entitled to consult you privately at any time (Code C, s. 3.12). You should delay talking until this privacy is arranged, for conversations overheard by the police could be used in evidence at trial (*R v Ali* (1991)). Many solicitors refuse to talk to clients through partitions, which require microphones and are vulnerable to eavesdropping (*Law Society's Gazette*, 14 Sept. 1994, p. 7). The police, some time ago, admitted that interview rooms routinely have eavesdropping facilities (*Law Society's Gazette*, 25 May 1991) and solicitors have reported that it takes place ('Anger at police station bugging', *Law Society's Gazette*, 23 Oct. 1996). This is a breach of the suspect's human rights: *Brennan v UK* (2001), and you have no choice but to assume the police will not do this.

If a solicitor has been called, he or she will probably wish to hold the first interview with the juvenile without you being present. This is because the solicitor's duty of confidentiality is virtually absolute, whereas something said in front of a social worker could, exceptionally, be ordered to be revealed in court. Law Society guidance (*Law Society's Gazette*, 19 May 1993, p. 41) states:

> [T]he appropriate adult may then disclose what was said during the consultation to the police as their Code of Conduct allows them to breach confidentiality in this way if they believe that the safety of the public may be at risk from the suspect.

And a recent case confirms that the Law Society is right to fear that social workers and probation officers cannot guarantee confidences: *R v Elleray* (2003). In interview for the purpose of preparing a pre-sentence report following a guilty plea, the defendant told the probation officer that he had also committed two offences of rape on the victim. The probation officer mentioned this confession in his report, and consequently the defendant was charged with the additional offences. The defendant asked the court to declare that the revelation had been in confidence and it would be an abuse to use it. The court refused and he was convicted of the additional offences.

Police powers of detention

PACE empowers the police to detain a suspect before charge for up to 36 hours after arrival at the police station (s. 41) to obtain evidence; the principal evidence will come from questioning the person who is detained. This period of detention can be extended up to a maximum of ninety-six hours if a magistrates' court gives authorization (s. 43). (The procedures are different where terrorism is suspected, but you are unlikely to be involved in such a case.)

Extensions beyond 36 hours are allowed only for questioning on a 'serious arrestable offence'; s. 116 lists, for example, murder, rape, and possession of firearms with intent to injure, but in fact any arrestable offence can be serious if the consequences are serious, such as causing death or serious injury, or substantial financial gain or loss. Home Office Circular 60/2003 states that a child should not be detained for more than 24 hours unless the offence is a serious arrestable offence and bail has been considered inappropriate. Code C says that detention of a juvenile or mentally disordered suspect beyond 24 hours will involve consideration of:

(a) special vulnerability;

(b) the legal obligation to provide an opportunity for representations to be made prior to a decision about extending detention;

(c) the need to consult and consider the views of any appropriate adult; and

(d) any alternatives to police custody.

Whatever the length of the detention, its only lawful purpose is for the police to obtain enough evidence to make a decision whether to charge or not. They should take that decision to charge or release as soon as possible, which means as soon as they have obtained evidence on which to base such a decision (s. 37 and Code C, s. 16); most detention ends therefore before the time limits expire.

Decisions concerning detention and charge are made by an officer called the 'custody officer' (ss. 37 and 38), who is not involved in the investigation into the offence. Complaints or problems should be addressed to the custody officer.

One of the first things to ask the custody officer is whether the suspect is detained or not. If the suspect is not detained they are a 'volunteer' and free to leave. Of course, once they say they wish to leave this may trigger an arrest; but at least at that point the time clock for maximum periods of detention before charge has started to run.

Right to legal advice

PACE, s. 58, and Code C give all detainees and volunteers the right to legal advice. Suspects are entitled to receive such advice, in person or on the telephone, and in private, before they are questioned. They are then entitled to have the legal adviser (either a solicitor or an accredited solicitor's representative) present during a police interview. This service is paid for by the Legal Services Commission and is not means-tested; if the detainee cannot nominate a solicitor, a duty solicitor on a twenty-four-hour rota is contacted. A detainee must sign the custody record to confirm, with reasons, if he or she does not want a solicitor. However, our own experience in criminal work indicates that many sign the custody record not knowing they are signing away this right, and Home Office research in 1997 (Study 155, *PACE ten years on*) shows that only 41 per cent of juveniles requested legal advice, an alarmingly low figure. Even this is higher than the adult rate and is attributed to the policy of social workers routinely insisting on a lawyer.

If an appropriate adult finds legal advice has been refused, he or she may exercise the right to call a solicitor on behalf of the detainee, or advise the suspect to do so (s. 58 right to see a solicitor continues to apply even after declining the opportunity, so a change of mind is available at any time). But it is the decision of the suspect whether to actually see the solicitor or not (Code C, para 6.5).

If a solicitor is called, the advice on law can usually be left to him or her, unless exceptionally you have reason to fear he or she is not doing so adequately.

Right to have someone informed of the detention

A detainee is entitled on request to have the police notify one person who is likely to have an interest in their welfare (s. 56 of the Act, s. 5 of the Code). If the police cannot contact the person chosen, they must try at least two further people chosen by the suspect. Code C requires the police in most cases to allow the detainee to speak to one person by telephone, and to have writing materials to send letters (Code C, s. 5).

Right to written notice of rights

All suspects are entitled to written notice of their rights under the Code, which must to be available in a range of languages. This includes an entitlement to an audio version (see Note for Guidance 3B) for anyone who may be unable to read.

Denial of PACE rights

Both the right to legal advice and the right to have someone notified depend on a request being made by the suspect; Code C provides in s. 3 that, on arrival, the suspect must be told of these rights, together with the right to consult the code. When the appropriate adult arrives, the suspect should be told this again, in the adult's presence.

Refusal or delay in the right to legal advice and to have someone notified requires the authority of a superintendent or higher-ranking officer, and can only occur where the offence is a serious arrestable offence (discussed above). The delay cannot continue beyond thirty-six hours from the start of the detention. The officer must be satisfied that the exercise of the right *will* (not may) lead to harm to others, interference with evidence, or a tip-off of other suspects, or hinder the recovery of property (PACE, s. 58, and Annex B to Code C). Refusal of the right to a solicitor additionally requires the police to have grounds for suspecting the solicitor would be committing what amounts to a criminal offence. So this will rarely, if ever, cause you difficulty.

Once a solicitor has been requested, there must be no further questioning until he or she arrives, unless the superintendent believes that delay will lead to immediate risk of harm to persons or serious damage to property, or will unreasonable delay to the investigation, or unless the suspect consents. In this latter case the appropriate adult can override the juvenile's consent and insist on a solicitor being called.

We have seen that the police can detain a person only for the purpose of deciding whether or not to charge. That decision is taken by the custody officer. This officer must also review the detention after six hours, and then every nine hours, to see whether detention is still required or the decision could be made now. If a person is charged, he or she should then be released on bail, unless the custody officer refuses (see bail from the police station, below). If a decision is made not to charge, the suspect must be released; but if the police need to make further enquiries the suspect may be bailed and required to report to the police station on a later occasion, by which time the police will have been able to decide whether to charge.

Drug testing of children in the police station

The Criminal Justice Act 2003 has amended PACE s. 63B so that from August 2004 a police inspector, in approved police authorities, is empowered to authorize a sample to test for Class A drugs for detainees aged over 14 in police custody.

> Trigger offences include: from the Theft Act 1968—theft, robbery, burglary, aggravated burglary, taking a motor vehicle (or other conveyance) without authority, aggravated vehicle-taking, obtaining property by deception, going equipped for stealing etc.; and from the Misuse of Drugs Act 1971 (but only if committed in respect of a specified Class A drug)—producing and supplying a controlled drug, possessing a controlled drug, and possessing a controlled drug with intent to supply. (Code C s. 17E)

Code C gives the detainee the right to seek legal advice before the sample is taken. The sample must be taken in the presence of the appropriate adult. Refusal to give a sample is a criminal offence.

The Home Office has so far approved arrangements in Cleveland, Greater Manchester, Merseyside, London metropolitan police district, Nottinghamshire and West Yorkshire—the power cannot yet be exercised by police in other areas.

(A court can also order a sample to be taken before deciding on a sentence to determine if the offender has any illegal drugs in his or her body. Refusal to provide the sample can lead to a fine. The sample will be taken in the presence of an appropriate adult. No regulations are yet available to explain how and where samples will be taken.)

The role of the appropriate adult at the police station

> Where the appropriate adult is present at an interview, they shall be informed that they are not expected to act simply as an *observer*, and that the purposes of their presence are, first, to *advise* the person being questioned and to observe whether or not the interview is being conducted properly and fairly, and secondly, to *facilitate communication* with the person being interviewed [emphasis added]. (Code C, s.11.17)

Let us take these in turn together with issues connected to these roles which you will need to understand.

Observer

Your presence should be a guarantee that correct procedures will be followed. You have the opportunity to object if they are not, and to have your objections recorded in the custody record: this could lead to evidence being excluded, which the police do not want. We set out the framework for admissibility in chapter 6, but now need to explain in particular rules for admitting and excluding evidence obtained by the police.

The starting rule, as explained in chapter 6, is that relevant evidence is admissible. However, that simple rule is modified by ss. 76 and 78 of PACE and by Article 6 of the European Convention. These deal with admissibility of confessions, exclusion of unfair evidence, and the right to a fair hearing. They all overlap where confessions are concerned, for a fair trial is impossible if a confession has been obtained unfairly. It is up to the prosecution to prove, if they wish to use a confession at trial, that it meets the fair trial requirements: if they cannot do so beyond reasonable doubt, it is not used (under PACE s. 76). They must prove to the court that there was no oppression and there were no other circumstances in play at the time it was obtained which might cause it to be unreliable.

As a social worker, you will not have to argue these points at trial. But if you were present when, or before, the confession was obtained, or they interviewed notwithstanding that you had told them you were on your way, you could be an important witness during a mini-trial which the court must hold to decide if the confession is to be admitted. To anticipate being a witness yourself means to recall what happened. Therefore, bearing in mind the principle (see chapter 5) that you can refresh your memory in the witness box from notes made at or near the time of the facts you are talking about, you should always go to the police station with paper, pens, and an accurate watch. You should record the time, to the minute, of every stage of the procedure—arrival, talking to the custody officer, waiting to see the detainee, length of interview, etc.—and the names, rank, and numbers of the people you deal with. Ask them for this. If the police see you noting these details, they will respect your professional approach, and may resist the temptation to do anything in breach of the code. So keeping a careful note means you will probably not have to use it!

Section 78 PACE allows the court to exclude any evidence which is unfair in the circumstances. Courts typically look at confessions in light of s. 78 as well as s. 76. They can use this power where, for example there is no reason to think a confession may be unreliable, but it was unfairly obtained nevertheless. Examples have included tricking the suspect by saying that the solicitor was not available, when he was; or lying about having fingerprint evidence against the detainee.

There is a close connection between s. 78 and the Article 6 right to a fair trial. For example in *Allan v UK* (2002), the ECtHR ruled against the UK. The police had disguised a policeman as a prisoner to try to get a prisoner to talk about, and if possible admit to, a murder; the suspect did not know he was suspected of this murder and this amounted to questioning of a suspect without the usual safeguards (caution, tape, etc.). It was, ruled the court, a breach of the right to a fair trial under Article 6, and anything said by the suspect should not have been used at trial.

Taking Code C, PACE ss. 58, 76 and 78, and Article 6 into account, courts tend to exclude evidence of interviews in a non-urgent case without the presence of an appropriate adult (*R v Delaney* (1989)).

The police may talk to the suspect about the offence 'informally' before you or the lawyer are allowed to see him or her, and obtain damaging evidence. You obviously cannot prevent this, as you were not present. But if at the same time you have a record that you were waiting in the foyer and available, it is possible that any evidence obtained will be ruled inadmissible (*R v Franklin* (1994)). If you are kept waiting unnecessarily, make a complaint to the custody officer, so that it is registered in the custody record and the defence solicitor will become aware of it. Code C (para. 11.1) in fact forbids this type of informal questioning, except where there is a risk to property or people, or the likelihood of evidence being tampered with, unless questions are asked.

Adviser

On arrival at the police station, you need to find out, in as much detail as possible, what has already been said and what evidence the police have, so that you can discuss it with the detainee. You need then to find out from the detainee what he or she says has been happening. If there has already been an informal interview, it will help to advise the detainee to answer the questions in the formal interview afresh, or remain silent, and to avoid any reference back to earlier conversations and understandings reached with the police. As we just saw the contents of the earlier interview are not likely to be admissible at trial; what may have been happening is that the police have been preparing the detainee to give the 'correct' answers at the formal interview stage. If before the interview the suspect has made any statement that may be important if the case goes to court, or alternatively failed to answer any significant question which a court could take into account, the police must put it to him or her at the start of the formal interview (Code C, 11.4).

Where a lawyer is available, legal advice is usually best left to the lawyer. However, some solicitors, or their representatives, fail in their duty. A really bad case was *R v Miller, Paris and Abdullah* (1993), where the Lord Chief Justice had this to say about the police: 'Short of physical violence, it is hard to conceive of a more hostile and intimidating approach by officers to a suspect.' Yet the solicitor had been present and done nothing to protect his client. At least the old practice of sending untrained staff to advise at the police station has been eliminated—to get public funding for attending, the firm must send a solicitor or someone who has had special training.

Assuming you have confidence in the solicitor, your task is to help the suspect communicate with the lawyer, and ensure that he or she genuinely understands what the advice is. What follows should help you to understand the context in which that advice is given.

As we saw earlier, the reason the police detain before charge is to obtain evidence, principally by questioning, to enable them to decide whether or not to charge. Gathering evidence for the trial is technically only a by-product, although the police will obviously see that as a high priority. They have a natural desire to get that evidence; the detainee has a desire to get out of this unpleasant environment. The detainee quickly realizes—and may be encouraged to think—that there is a connection between confessing and getting out quicker. Confessing may indeed bring about an earlier release, because the police now have enough information to decide to charge. So the confession leads to charge, and court proceedings, and a likelihood of conviction.

The right to silence

This is such a big issue that it deserves a fresh heading, but essentially the reason you need to know about this is that the suspect is going to need advice from the solicitor, or exceptionally from you, about whether to answer questions. So we are still looking at your role as appropriate adult.

Although this right is an ancient feature of the common law, a good way of understanding it is to start with the European Convention on Human Rights, Article 6, which includes the following:

> Everyone charged with a criminal offence shall be presumed innocent until proved guilty in accordance with the law.

It is not up to the suspect to prove anything or to provide evidence by answering questions to help the prosecution case. But if the suspect refuses can the court then draw adverse conclusions? The European Court of Human Rights has consistently ruled that to draw inferences from silence is not, on its own, a breach of Article 6 (e.g. *Murray v UK* (1996)).

The Criminal Justice and Public Order Act 1994 (ss. 31–8) first permitted a court, and in particular a jury, to draw adverse conclusions from silence. Previously it was impossible in law to place any reliance on failing to answer questions.

The risk of failing to answer questions must be explained to the suspect in a caution before police questioning starts. There are two available cautions (Code C, s. 10). The first is used where the police believe that silence could be referred to in court. This runs as follows:

> You do not have to say anything. But it may harm your defence if you do not mention when questioned something which you later rely on in court. Anything you do say may be given in evidence.

This caution is unsatisfactory. At this stage there is no reason to assume there will be a prosecution; in fact if the police have already decided to charge they have no right to detain for questioning. It is also very complex, and you or the solicitor will probably have to explain what it means.

If the police interview a suspect who has requested a solicitor but before one is available, no inferences can be drawn from silence, so a simpler caution can be used:

> You do not have to say anything, but anything you do say may be given in evidence.

An adverse inference can be drawn, if the case comes to trial, only if the accused then suggests a version of events that he or she could reasonably have put forward during questioning. This does not automatically mean all questions should be answered, however. Police questioning is, even with the safeguards in Code C, a frightening affair. It takes great strength of mind to give simple, consistent answers, and to avoid being tripped up by skilled police interviewers. A vulnerable person, who may have particular difficulties in dealing with others in positions of power, may be tempted to confess to please the questioner or escape the continuing questioning. Inferences are less damaging at trial than a confession.

Good legal advice can be vital. Solicitors do advise suspects to remain silent where appropriate, and often make sure that the reason for the silence ('My client will refuse to answer questions, in accordance with my advice') is recorded on tape and known to the court. Adverse inferences can still be drawn, even if he or she stayed silent on the advice of a solicitor (*R v Daniel* (1998)) and even where the detainee was of low intelligence

(*R v Friend* (1997): a 14 year old with an IQ of 63). One ground for a lawyer to advise a detainee not to answer questions is that the police have failed to outline the allegations which have to be answered. The normal right of disclosure of all relevant evidence in support of the allegations is invoked only later between charge and trial, but one of the suspect's rights at the police station is to know and understand, before questioning, the allegations themselves. In fact, failure to provide this information would be a breach of the European Convention on Human Rights, Article 6(1) (right to a fair trial), and the case of *Edwards v UK* (1992) establishes that this right to disclosure applies at all stages of a criminal case.

Case law since the Human Rights Act has made it more difficult for the prosecution to ask the court to make inferences. In *R v Betts and Hall* (2001) the court stated that an adverse inference should only be drawn if the only viable reason for not answering the questions was that the suspect was unable to answer the allegations. Many solicitors use the practice of handing in a written statement setting out the suspect's version of events at the beginning or end of an interview, and this has been upheld as a way of avoiding the adverse inference (so long as the story does not change at trial): *R v Knight* (2003), *R v Turner* (2003).

Even if an inference is drawn, the silence on its own is not enough for a conviction. This was established in *R v Condron* (1997), where the appellants were advised by their solicitor to say nothing. The trial judge gave the jury the option of drawing an adverse inference from this silence and convicting the defendant. The Court of Appeal made it clear that the prosecution must still have good independent evidence of guilt—the inference was not enough on its own for a conviction. The Court of Appeal then upheld the conviction, having noted there was indeed plenty of other evidence of the appellant dealing in drugs. But in a final twist which makes this ruling very important the ECtHR ruled the trial was flawed, Article 6 was breached, and the conviction was wrong for this reason alone, regardless of the other evidence (*Condron v UK (No. 2)* (2000)).

If the right is to be exercised, the whole of the formal interview should generally be 'no reply': partial silence leads to the suspicion that the accused was hiding something when the questions came too near to the target, even though in *R v Welch* (1992) the Court of Appeal said that questions to which no reply was given should be removed from the evidence put to court. We still believe, however, that consistently either answering no questions, or all questions, is the best advice. The police are skilful at persuading a person who has said a little then to say more. The Home Office research indicates that only 6 per cent of interviewees make no comment. By contrast, 58 per cent confess.

Normally, the legal adviser will help the detainee come to the best decisions on how to approach the questioning, and your job will be to help the detainee to understand that advice and reach the best decision.

Communicating and advocating on behalf of the detainee

The facilitating of communication means ensuring that the suspect understands what is going on, and anything he or she wishes to communicate is properly understood by the police and lawyer. But it also includes an advocacy role. If, for example, a senior officer wishes to delay the right to see a solicitor, to continue to detain for questioning, or to refuse bail after charge, he or she does not require the consent of anyone else (subject to time limits being observed). However, police will listen to the views of the solicitor and the appropriate adult and, in relation to bail in particular, your views will be important.

Advocating on behalf of the detainee means noting when there is any breach of the proper procedures, ensuring that it is noted on the custody record, and exercising, if appropriate, any rights the detainee has, for example, to legal advice or to medical assistance (see below). It means interrupting during questioning if the questioning is oppressive (e.g. repetition of questions already dealt with) or incomprehensible. It means communicating the needs and wishes of the detainee, for example, for a break, for refreshment, or to have someone informed of the detention. If the interview is extremely oppressive you will need to consider whether to state your concerns and then leave.

Conditions of detention

As soon as someone is detained (but not helping as a 'volunteer') at the police station, a custody record must be opened, to record all events, decisions, and reviews, as well as listing the property of the detainee. Code C gives the detainee and the appropriate adult a right to inspect the record. You will particularly be looking to see reasons for any refusal of the right to legal advice, either by the detainee or by the police. If any complaints are made they must be noted in the record—this includes complaints by the appropriate adult. The detainee must sign the custody record if a solicitor is not wanted. If an interview proceeds after a request for legal advice, but before that advice has been obtained, the reasons must be recorded.

Code C sets out how detainees must be treated. Requirements include adequate heating and lighting, temperature, toilet facilities, and sufficient meals, taking account of special dietary requirements. These could be summarized as an application of humane common sense. A juvenile should not be kept in a cell unless the custody officer considers that no other suitable accommodation or supervision is available; the reason must be entered in the custody record. If you suspect treatment may be improper, check s. 8 of Code C (you must be allowed to see a copy) and if appropriate make your complaint, which has to be recorded.

Section 9 of Code C deals with medical treatment. A police surgeon must be called (or, if unavailable, another GP, or the detainee must be taken to hospital) if there is any indication of physical illness or mental disorder, injury, or other apparent need, or upon request by the detainee. It is therefore vital that if you are aware of any medical problem or needs of the detainee—for example, a supply of medication, such as insulin—the custody officer be told without delay.

Under s. 5 the police should allow the detainee to receive visits (but may refuse if short-staffed). A social worker can assist in this by contacting family or friends of a detainee. (Be careful of course not to inadvertently pass on messages that may help to dispose of evidence or enable another suspect to avoid arrest.)

The interview

The interview should not proceed while the suspect is unfit through drink or drugs—if you think this applies, you need to insist on a delay. If necessary, insist on delay and ask for a doctor.

The first thing that happens is that a tape recorder, with two tapes, is switched on and the parties present identify themselves. One tape is used as a working copy, and one is kept sealed in case of allegations of tampering. The suspect will later be provided, via the solicitor, with a transcript, and can ask for the tape as well. A suspect must be cautioned or re-cautioned before any questioning starts.

No interview should proceed for more than two hours without a break, and breaks should be taken at usual mealtimes. There must normally be a break from questioning of eight continuous hours every twenty-four hours, usually at night-time. Inducements to confess should not be offered, although if a suspect asks what course the police will take if he or she divulges certain information ('If I tell you, will I be out of here quicker?') the police are allowed to answer.

The informal interview which may have taken place in the police car or at the scene of arrest lacks these safeguards, though a caution is required. As a result, there is more likelihood of a confession. Generally, the courts take a robust attitude to such confessions, particularly where juveniles are concerned. For example, in *R v Weekes* (1993), a 16 year old seen in the area of a robbery was questioned in the police car. The confession was ruled inadmissible at trial.

But you should not get the impression from what we have said that questioning someone outside the police station is wrong. Police need to invoke the formal procedures only once they have formed a suspicion that the person has committed a crime. But evidence obtained from such earlier questioning will not normally be admissible in court (*R v Nelson* (1998)).

When talking to the detainee before the formal interview starts, therefore, it is wise to explain to the detainee the difference between what has happened up to now, informally, and the formal interview, which is more likely to be accepted as evidence by a court. It is not necessary to tell the police something just because that is what the person told them earlier. It may be appropriate on the formal occasion to exercise the right to remain silent; or to tell the story as it should have been told. (But a social worker, like a lawyer, must not in any way assist in fabricating a story.)

Identification, intimate samples, fingerprinting

There are special rules governing these procedures and much case law on identification evidence which we will not consider. The *Code of Practice for the Identification of Persons by Police Officers*, Annex A, like the other codes, is available at the police station for consultation. The most important advice here is that the detainee, or you on his or her behalf, can and should exercise the right to legal advice before he or she agrees to any of them. The appropriate adult cannot as such give consent to fingerprints etc., on behalf of a juvenile; only a parent or guardian can. If the police insist on proceeding before the solicitor arrives, ensure that the reasons are given and recorded, and stay with the detainee to observe what happens and also to reduce the risk of an informal interview taking place.

If an identification parade is offered, the opportunity should be given for a solicitor to be present. The detainee has the right to refuse a parade. But the alternative methods of identification—direct confrontation or identification by photographs—are more likely to lead to a positive identification.

The time limit before release or charge

The custody officer must decide within the twenty-four or thirty-six-hour time limits (or longer if extended by a court) whether the detainee is to be charged, released without charge, or released pending further investigation. The release may be on bail or unconditional. If released without charge, the detainee may be required to return at a later date once the police have made further enquiries or, in the case of a juvenile, had discussions with social services about whether they should charge, caution, or do nothing. What follows assumes that the police have charged the detainee.

▉ Charges, reprimands, warnings, or no action

The alternatives open to the police with a juvenile suspect are to charge and prosecute, to reprimand/warn, or to take no further action. With a juvenile, for reasons we are about to explore, the decision may take time, in which case police bail is appropriate.

The decision on alternatives must take place before charge, because a charge starts court proceedings, and these can be discontinued only with leave of the court. The police, since amendments to PACE in 2004, refer the decision whether to charge to the CPS unless it is a clear case in terms of seriousness. The CPS now provide twenty-four hour cover to assist in this process.

But as well as consulting the CPS, if the suspect is a juvenile, the police should consult with the YOT. They can only avoid this if it is obvious that there should be a charge because of the seriousness of the offence. (They must still notify the social services department. This is independent of any requirement to obtain the presence of an appropriate adult for pre-charge procedures.) If the case is so trivial that no charge is appropriate, the police do not need to consult.

In between these clear-cut cases, liaison with appropriate agencies is normal before a decision is made; but the decision is still that of the police. Home Office Circulars 59/1990 and 18/1994, *Cautioning of Offenders*, described the old cautioning system, and encouraged such liaison. The guiding principle was the desirability of keeping juveniles out of the criminal justice system, recognizing that if their formal entry into the process could be delayed for long enough, it might never happen at all. The 1990 circular also emphasized the needs of victims of crime to feel that something has been done; but did not outweigh the public interest in keeping juveniles out of courts. However, since 1990 the political climate in relation to juvenile offending has moved, in the words of a former Prime Minister, away from understanding and towards condemning. The 1994 circular already discouraged repeat cautions and any use of cautions at all in serious offences. The new system of reprimands and warnings is guided by the belief that 'many young people can be successfully diverted from crime without recourse to court proceedings, provided the response is clear, firm and constructive' (Home Office Consultation Paper on Tackling Youth Crime, 1997).

As a social worker your involvement in all this comes from the statutory requirement for the authority to coordinate a Youth Offending Team (see above), but your statutory responsibility, in our view, still revolves around the Children Act, s. 17, the welfare of the juvenile, and avoiding criminal proceedings.

The system of reprimands and warnings is governed by the Crime and Disorder Act 1998, s. 65. The scheme is best viewed as a first step into the formal criminal justice system. It is not, therefore, available for anyone with previous convictions; such a person has reached the second step.

Guidance has been published which helps the police decide whether to prosecute, warn, or reprimand. Essentially a reprimand is issued for a first offence if it is not too serious (however this is defined—the Act does not say what 'serious' means), and a warning is the next step for a person who has previously been reprimanded, or for a first more serious offence. Following a warning, the police cannot warn the offender again within two years, so a subsequent allegation of criminal behaviour would have to be dealt with (if at all) through the courts. This has meant more cases coming to court than previously. For example, a child who has been warned already will end up in court over the theft of a sandwich, unless the police take no action at all.

Warnings and reprimands for children under 17 years of age have to be given in the presence of an appropriate adult. Additionally the police can administer a reprimand or warning only if the juvenile admits the offence and their parent or guardian consents. That admission must be genuine and not in any way be obtained by inducement or pressure (*R v Commissioner of Police of the Metropolis, ex parte Thompson* (1997)). The guidance makes clear that a warning or reprimand should not be administered where the evidence against the juvenile is weak. If the police do not consider on the evidence they have that a conviction is more likely than an acquittal, if the case went to trial, it is appropriate to drop the case. This guidance has been reinforced by the case of *DPP v Ara* (2001). The police wanted to caution A (it was before cautions were replaced with reprimands and warnings), but his solicitor could not yet advise whether to accept the caution because the police would not say what evidence they had. So the police went ahead and charged A instead. The magistrates dismissed the charge as an abuse of process, and the High Court agreed. What this means in practice is that the police must reveal their evidence before a suspect has to decide whether to accept the reprimand or warning, so that the suspect can be advised whether to accept guilt and a warning/ reprimand.

Detailed guidance was published by the Home Office in 2002—*The Final Warning Scheme: Guidance to Youth Offending Teams*. See **www.homeoffice.gov.uk/docs/final_ warning_scheme.pdf**. One part of the guidance to note is that child prostitutes should not be subject to warnings or reprimands. They are victims, not criminals.

A warning or reprimand is not a criminal conviction, for example for job applications. However, should a person later be found guilty of an offence, the earlier reprimand or warning can be mentioned when it comes to sentencing. A reprimand or warning, therefore, should not be treated as getting off lightly. The child also, in a sense, uses up a chance. This is because, if convicted of an offence within the next two years, the court will not consider a discharge but will move to a more serious sentence (see below for discharge after conviction). A warning in relation to a sexual offence will result in the offender being placed on the register of sex offenders. Failure to explain fully such consequences of a warning or reprimand will make it invalid: *R (on the application of U and another) v Commissioner of Police for the Metropolis and another* (2002).

A warning triggers action from the YOT, who must try to get the offender involved in a rehabilitation programme (s. 66). There is no sanction for refusing to participate in these activities, except that failure to take part can be mentioned in court at sentencing stage if the offender is convicted of a further offence.

Sending the charge in the post

By focusing up to now on the police station we may have given you the impression that all criminal proceedings start with arrest, detention, and interrogation. In fact in most cases a charge (what used to be called a summons) is sent in the post or served by the police on the defendant. The procedure is appropriate in less urgent, less serious cases, and where there is no doubt about the correct identity and address of the person concerned. This process is more likely to be used for less serious offences involving adults than juveniles, since it may be inappropriate to charge the juvenile at all in less serious cases.

■ Legal advice and representation in criminal cases

Help from a solicitor out of public funds is governed by the Access to Justice Act 1999, Part 2.

In the police station, as we have seen under PACE, s. 58, any suspect can insist on seeing a solicitor. The scheme is known as the police station duty solicitor scheme. A similar scheme, again without charge or contribution, operates at court for a person who is brought to court following arrest and detention at the police station or a first appearance following release on police bail. The court duty solicitor can deal with bail applications, ask for an adjournment, and make a plea in mitigation if there is a guilty plea and no adjournments for reports.

For representation and advice beyond this a specialist solicitor has to be identified. This will normally be a solicitor working in a private firm, but in some areas there are pilots of government-employed solicitors called public defenders. (Where public defenders are available there is no requirement to choose them—free choice of solicitor is an important principle underpinning the criminal justice system.) If you do not know who to recommend, a list of specialists contracted to provide advice on behalf of the Legal Services Commission (LSC) can be obtained for your area by phoning the Commission on 0845 608 1122. You can download the LSC leaflet on criminal advice and representation from **www.legalservices.gov.uk/leaflets/lsc/prac-guide-cds(apr)03.htm**. It is common, and often desirable for the sake of continuity, for the police duty solicitor or the court duty solicitor to apply to the court for an order to continue with the representation; but there is no obligation and the client must be free to choose her or his own solicitor at this point (though, unless paying privately, will have to chose from those who have a contract with the LSC).

There is no means test and no charge for using a duty solicitor. To obtain advice from a solicitor in any other circumstance there is a means test, which in the case of a juvenile under 17 means those of the parent or guardian. But if a person needs representation—which is likely if they have been charged—the first task of the solicitor is to apply to the court for a representation order. The application form is signed by the parent or guardian of a juvenile.

The court will decide to grant representation if it considers the accused person needs representation in the interests of justice, which is more likely to be the case for a juvenile than for an adult. No financial contribution is payable if there is an eventual acquittal (or the charge is dropped), but in the event of a conviction in the Crown Court the accused person may be ordered to pay a contribution depending on her or his means (which in the case of a juvenile means their own, not those of the parent or guardian). (The Government is planning to bring back means assessments and contributions towards the cost of criminal representation, which is likely to mean a return to an assessment of parental means.)

Refusal of police bail after charge

If a juvenile is charged, he or she should normally then be released on bail. The police can refuse bail only on grounds set out in PACE, s. 38. The first three grounds also apply to adults:

(a) the custody officer is not satisfied of the identity or address of the person charged;

(b) the custody officer believes that the person will not answer to bail, will interfere with evidence or witnesses, cause injury to themselves or others, or damage to property;

(c) the custody officer believes that it is necessary for the person's own protection; or

(d) granting bail would not be in the juvenile's own interests.

Section 38 does not, unfortunately, offer any guidance on what the interests of the juvenile are in this situation; but, as we shall see, on refusal of bail, the juvenile must be transferred to local authority accommodation, and it will be this that the police will probably see as being in the juvenile's interests.

Police, like courts, can make bail conditional—for example, requiring as a condition of bail that the charged person live at a certain address or keep away from the scene of the alleged crime. Another person can be asked to stand surety, which means that person becomes liable to pay a penalty if the person absconds. A court can also impose bail conditions which have nothing to do with preventing offending or securing attendance at court, and under the Bail Act 1976 as amended s. 3(6)(ca) can impose conditions 'for his own protection or, if he is a child or young person, for his own welfare or in his own interests'.

A social worker present at the time these decisions are made will be able to offer relevant information and advice on some, if not all, of these points, and particularly on what is in the interests of the juvenile.

A breach of police bail or of the conditions of police bail is a criminal offence. It also makes it less likely that the court will grant bail when an application is made.

Detention after refusal of police bail

If a suspect is charged and bail is refused, he or she must be brought before a court at the earliest practicable time.

Until that point, PACE, s. 38(6) requires the custody officer to make arrangements for the juvenile to be taken into accommodation provided by the local authority and detained by it. The subsection goes on to say that it shall be lawful for the local authority to detain the juvenile (but no mention is made of any obligation to do so). Therefore, the local authority is entitled to keep the juvenile in secure accommodation until the court appearance. It will be up to the authority to transport the juvenile to court.

Under s. 38(6), following a refusal of bail, the custody officer can refuse to transfer the detained juvenile to local authority accommodation on either of two grounds:

(a) If the juvenile is 15 or older, the custody officer considers that the juvenile is a danger to the public *and* that the local authority lacks adequate secure accommodation.

(b) It is not practical to make the arrangements for a transfer. This should be exceptional, e.g. social services are on strike, or the roads are blocked by snow.

The custody officer must give a certificate to this effect and may then detain the juvenile in the same way as an adult until the first court appearance, i.e. in the police station (but not in a cell if this can be avoided).

Remand by the court

Remand is what happens every time a criminal court adjourns without unconditional release of the defendant. But if (see **chapter 5** for procedure) the magistrates send the accused for trial or sentencing in the Crown Court, the word remand is replaced by the word **committal**. The effect is the same. Remand or committal will be on bail or in custody.

The grounds for a court to refuse bail, although set out in different legislation (Bail Act 1976 s. 4), are almost identical to those which the police must use under PACE (see above). Breach of court bail or bail conditions is a criminal offence and will make further bail applications more difficult.

If the remand or committal is to be in custody, and the child is below 17 years of age, it will normally be in local authority accommodation (Children and Young Persons Act 1969, s. 23). Why 'normally' and not always? Legislation was passed by Parliament in 1991 which would have prevented prison being used for any child on remand, because it was widely held to be an unsuitable environment. This legislation has never been implemented. The present position is that for a child of 17 years of age there is no restriction on using prison. But girls under 17 years of age and boys under 15 years of age cannot be sent to prison or to a remand home while on remand. So a boy of 15 or 16 years of age can be remanded to prison or a remand home, or as with younger boys or girls of this age, to the local authority. The grounds for remanding a boy to prison or a remand home are that it is necessary in order to protect the public from serious harm and, in addition, *either*:

- the alleged offence is a violent or sexual offence, or
- it is serious enough to attract (for an adult) fourteen years in prison, or
- the boy has a history of absconding from local authority remands.

We predicted in earlier editions that this discrimination against boys would not survive a Human Rights Act challenge. But it did in *R (on the application of SR) v Nottingham Magistrates Court* (2001). The High Court held that the state could legitimately discriminate between boys and girls. Why? The small number of female offenders meant that, if sent to prison on remand, most would be accommodated far from home (unlike boys, where provision is found in most areas of the country). It was noted in this case that it was also legitimate to give first priority in allocating secure remand places in local authority accommodation to girls. We think this decision was fundamentally flawed.

Remand to the local authority

The authority will be the one either where the defendant resides, or where the offence was committed. The remand will be either with or without a security requirement.

Remand without a security requirement

Once the juvenile has been remanded to local authority accommodation, the authority decides how to accommodate the juvenile, and the considerations are the same as for any child it is looking after (see Chapter 10) except that, under the Children and Young Persons Act 1969, s. 23, the authority can lawfully detain the child without a further court order. (Detention in secure accommodation would otherwise require a court order under s. 25 of the Children Act 1989—see chapter 10.)

The court has no power to tell the authority where to accommodate the juvenile, though it may exclude accommodation with certain named people (e.g. with a parent; with an adult accomplice). The Children and Young Persons Act 1969, s. 23, allows the court to impose a range of other conditions. These conditions are the same as a court can impose when granting conditional bail to an adult, and are designed to prevent the juvenile from absconding, offending while in local authority accommodation, or tampering with evidence. Typical conditions include: to report to a police station daily or, say, twice a week; not to approach a witness; to refrain from certain activities (perhaps not going to a particular part of a town where the offending has been taking place). The juvenile who breaches these conditions may be arrested and brought before the court, when further conditions may be imposed. As it will be for the local authority to enforce compliance with bail conditions, the court must consult the authority before imposing them.

Remand with a security requirement

In the absence of a security requirement, we saw that a court cannot tell the authority where to accommodate the juvenile.

In certain circumstances, the court can require the authority to detain the juvenile in secure accommodation, or require it to use electronic tagging. The local authority must be consulted before such a security requirement is imposed. The circumstances are set out in Box 15.3. Our comments on the unjustified discrimination between boys and girls again apply.

Remand to hospital

A court can remand any person accused of a criminal offence to a hospital if it is necessary for the purpose of obtaining a medical report on a person who may be mentally disordered, or for their treatment: Mental Health Acts ss. 35 and 36.

▨ Going to court following charge/summons

Box 15.4 indicates some of the ways in which the juvenile's vulnerability is recognized by the courts.

BOX 15.3 Children and Young Persons Act 1969 s. 23—grounds for courts to remand with a security requirement

Boy must be under 15 or 'vulnerable' (emotionally immature or at risk of self harm); *girl* must be under 17

Ground 1. Security requirement is *essential for public protection from serious harm*
AND

either	*or*
the alleged crime is violent or a sexual offence or could attract 14 years prison if committed by an adult	the child has a recent history of absconding while on remand and the present offence if proved was committed while on remand

Ground 2. The alleged crime(s) are part of a *recent history of committing imprisonable offences* while on bail or remanded to local authority accommodation and *only* a security requirement would

either	*or*
protect the public from serious harm	prevent further imprisonable offences

BOX 15.4 Statutes or rules recognizing children as accused are vulnerable

Court shall have regard to welfare of child	Children and Young Persons Act 1933 (CYPA 1933) s. 44
Local authority to be notified of proceedings	Children and Young Persons Act 1969 (CYPA 1969) s. 5
Explain the charge and proceedings in language child will understand	Magistrates Courts (Children and Young Persons) Rules 1992 ('Rules') ss. 6 and 17
Child may be required to withdraw if hearing evidence would be damaging	Rules, s. 19
Parent or guardian (local authority if in care) may be present (normally *must* if juvenile under 16)	CYPA 1933 s. 34
Local authority must provide support for child awaiting trial or sentence	Crime and Disorder Act 1998, s. 38
No one not involved in case or press to be present in the youth court	CYPA 1933 s. 47
Press reports not to identify child unless court permits	CYPA 1933 ss. 39 and 49
No child to be tried in adult court unless murder or other very serious ('grave') crime alleged or adult is co-accused	CYPA 1933 s. 46; Magistrates Courts Act 1980 s. 24

Allocation to youth, magistrates' or Crown Court

Most cases involving a juvenile will be dealt with, from start to finish, in the youth court. But an adult cannot be tried in the youth court, so if an adult and a juvenile are to be tried together, the adult court will have to be used. This is one of the three exceptions to trial in the youth court for a juvenile, which are shown in Box 15.5.

What happens if the juvenile turns 18 years of age during the course of the proceedings? Before the Crime and Disorder Act 1998, a juvenile who turned 18 after the plea was taken stayed in the youth court. Now he or she can be sent to the adult court at any time before trial, or, after conviction in a youth court, at any time before sentence (s. 47). But it is not compulsory to move the trial or the sentencing to the adult court, and if the youth court decides not to do so it has the power to sentence him or her as if still under 18 (CYPA 1969 s. 29, *A v Director of Public Prosecutions* (2002), where an 18 year old was sentenced to a detention and training order, even though such a sentence is not available for adult offenders). In fact in *R v Ghafoor* (2002) the Court of Appeal has reminded the courts that it is a breach of human rights to impose a harsher penalty on an offender than applied at the date the offence was committed. In this case an 18 year old convicted of riot had been sentenced to four and a half years in a young offenders institution; but he was only 17 at the time of the offence and the maximum for a 17 year old is a twenty-four months' detention and training order.

BOX 15.5 Use of adult courts for juvenile accused

Case factually connected to an adult Children and Young Persons Act 1933 s. 16; 1969 s. 18; Magistrates Courts Act 1980 s. 24	Decision to link juvenile to adult trial or not is made by magistrates before summary trial or committal to Crown Court (see Chapter 5) • Summary (magistrates) trial for adult: magistrates *must* try juvenile with adult if joint charge; *may* send juvenile to youth court if adult pleading guilty and juvenile not guilty or charges are connected not joint. • Crown Court committal for adult: magistrates *must* separate juvenile from adult if in interest of justice—e.g. wide difference in ages; evidential issues not closely connected.
Very serious offence (grave crime) *charged and Crown Court sentencing powers required* Powers of Criminal Courts (Sentencing) Act 2000 (PCCSA), s. 91	Very serious means: • could attract 14-year prison sentence if committed by adult; • indecent assault; • death by dangerous driving, careless driving while under the influence of alcohol or drugs, or firearms offence and accused at least 14; Magistrates must commit case to Crown Court for trial if maximum powers of punishment of youth court (two years' custody) would be clearly insufficient. The decision must be made before conviction of the juvenile, which also means before a guilty plea. Should not use these powers if no real prospect of custody of more than two years: *R (on the application of W) v Thetford Youth Court* (2002), even if the offence is very nasty (*R (on the application of D) v Manchester City Youth Court* (2001)—a 13 year old made an 8 year old masturbate him at knife point).
Murder charge Powers of Criminal Courts (Sentencing) Act 2000, s. 90	Magistrates *must* commit case to Crown Court for trial.

▨ Supporting a child defendant in the criminal court

We do not have space to describe the trial process. Some of this was discussed in chapter 5. Your role will be supporting the child through this process rather than participating. The guidance in Box 15.6 is an extract from *Youth Court Cases—Defence Good Practice*, which was prepared by the Law Society for lawyers using the youth courts, but equally useful for social workers, and aspects are relevant to all cases where children are on trial. (see **www.lawsoc.org.uk/dcs/pdf/youth_court.pdf**).

BOX 15.6 Extract from Law Society Guidance for Lawyers, *Youth Court Cases—Defence Good Practice*

When dealing with a client who is at court for the first time, explain the lay out of the court and the roles of all those present. This need not take long as few are allowed to be present and if this is a pre-trial hearing should usually consist of:

- the client, who in most courts, wherever possible, sits next to his or her legal representative— if not, the client sits in the 'front row' before the bench;
- the parent, guardian or appropriate adult who sits behind;
- the YOT court officer who sits usually behind a table at right angles to the bench, to the right of the prosecutor;
- the bench of three lay magistrates, or single district judge who sits at the 'top' of the room opposite all other seating places;
- the court clerk who sits next to or sometimes in front of the bench; and
- the prosecutor who sits to the left of the defence.

The Youth Court 2001—The Changing Culture of the Youth Court—Good Practice Guide (March 2001) 19 suggests that parents should be seated next to their dependant children, and that justices should be moved from a raised bench to sit at or near the same level as defendants. However, the *Guide* recognizes that existing architecture in courts around the country may restrict what can be achieved, though all courts should aim for a more approachable court layout.

The layout of courts vary and you should not be embarrassed to ask the usher where the personnel all sit. Some courts have a picture of the layout of the court in the waiting area outside the court. If there is any other person in court and you don't know their identity, then ask the usher.

You should explain the procedure you expect at the hearing to the client but mental health problems or communication problems, you should prepare the client for this possibility. All magistrates sitting in the Youth Court are receiving 'engagement' training and you may find that your clients are increasingly expected to engage with the court. If questions are put to the client and parents you should be invited to make representations on what has been said. Before considering sentence, if the defendant has pleaded guilty or been found guilty, the chairman is likely to try to talk to the defendant and parents/guardians, focusing on the offending behaviour and how to change it. Adverse inferences should not be drawn by the failure or the inability of the defendant to reply. Also see *The Youth Court 2001—The Changing Culture of the Youth Court—Good Practice Guide* (March 2001) referred to earlier.

Youth Courts are encouraged to have an open local protocol covering matters including attendance of advocates, involvement and engagement of defendants and their parents, attendance of victims and witnesses, attendance of the public and the media, and reporting restrictions. Find out from the court whether such a protocol is in existence and ask for a copy.

The informality of the Youth Court is generally observed but within limits. You should also advise the client about the impact of their body language and physical attitude—it won't help your client if he or she is slouching, chewing, or apparently ignoring the proceedings, even if

> their attitude is clearly a result of fear or bravado. In the atmosphere of the court a youth may behave in a disruptive manner, including in the public area, to impress other youths in the vicinity. You should advise such a client that excessive disruptive behaviour may lead to exclusion from the court building and will not make a good impression with the court.

Where the trial takes place in the Crown Court the Lord Chief Justice has published guidelines for measures to reduce formality and stress, such as regular breaks, removal of wigs, access to social workers and guardians, etc.: see *Practice Direction* (2002). These guidelines are the result of the criticism voiced by the European Court of Human Rights in relation to the trial arrangements in the Jamie Bulger murder trial, where the young boys on trial had been intimidated by the formality (see case study at beginning of chapter). The steps do not extend to permitting the child defendant to give his or her evidence with the protection of the special measures which are available to the vulnerable witness (see chapter 7): *R (on the application of S) v Waltham Forest Youth Court* (2004).

Sentencing of juveniles

The sentencing powers of courts are largely found in one Act, the Powers of Criminal Courts (Sentencing) Act 2000 (PCCSA). However, significant changes to the approach to sentencing are contained in Part 12 of the Criminal Justice Act 2003 (CJA), which is being brought into force in stages. In what follows we have anticipated that the Act is fully in force.

The CJA results from a sentencing tussle between government and judges, in which the press has sided with the judges in criticizing perceptions of leniency. The sentencing provisions in the Act are designed to increase government and parliamentary control and consistency over the sentencing decisions of courts. Central to the approach is the creation of a Sentencing Guidelines Council, which will, at the Government's request, provide advice to the courts which they must take into account. However, the Government may still be unhappy: 'The home secretary, David Blunkett, yesterday set himself on a collision course with Lord Woolf, the lord chief justice, over new sentencing guidelines that could allow murderers up to a third off their prison terms in return for pleading guilty' (*Guardian*, 9 November 2004).

Sentencing courts must refer to the guidelines and justify in particular any departure. The Council has not published any guidelines yet, but they will be available on **www.sentencing-guidelines.gov.uk/sgchome.html**. Your pre-sentence reports must, of course, refer to these guidelines.

The 2003 Act states the purpose of sentencing of adults to be:

- the punishment of offenders,
- the reduction of crime (including its reduction by deterrence),
- the reform and rehabilitation of offenders,

- the protection of the public, and

- the making of reparation by offenders to persons affected by their offences.

But the CJA does not change the dual philosophy of the youth justice system which we discussed above: children's welfare of the child under the CYPA 1933 Act, and preventing offending under the CDA1998.

Which courts have which sentencing powers?

You are likely to be involved in the sentencing process because you will be required to prepare a pre-sentence report for the court before a juvenile is sentenced. Your report must be prepared in the knowledge of which court is dealing with sentencing and what its powers are. (When we talk about sentencing powers, there is a theoretical maximum sentence for each offence and a theoretical maximum for each court. The actual sentencing power in a given case is whichever of these is lower in the circumstances.)

(Adult) magistrates' court

This court is involved in sentencing only where it has dealt with a connected adult (see Box 15.5 above). It cannot impose custody on a juvenile: it can only fine, discharge, or order parents to enter a recognizance. If it wishes to impose any other type of order, it must remit the case to the youth court, which has greater powers (PCCSA, s. 8).

Youth court

This court has the power to impose any of the orders discussed below. Its most severe sentence is custody under a detention and training order, which cannot exceed two years in total.

Crown Court

A Crown Court dealing with a juvenile offender because of a linked adult should not normally sentence a juvenile but should remit the case to the youth court, unless the judge is satisfied that it would be undesirable to do so (PCCSA, s. 8). In practice, where the Crown Court is dealing with the juvenile because an adult is also charged, it will usually sentence a convicted juvenile itself, rather than send the case to a youth court, in order to avoid delay and inconsistency of approach.

If the youth court magistrates send the case to the Crown Court for trial because it is a very serious crime (see Box 15.5 above) this will be because it considers its maximum sentencing power of a two-year detention and training order is insufficient, or because it is a case of murder. Under ss. 90–92, the Crown Court then has the power to order detention of the juvenile for a period up to the maximum that could have been imposed on an adult. So a juvenile can be detained 'during Her Majesty's pleasure' for crimes which carry a life sentence. (However, the court must set a target date for eligibility for release. Failure to do so leaves this decision in the hands of the Home Secretary rather than an independent body, and was a breach of the human rights of the juveniles who murdered James Bulger: see *T v UK* (2000); *Practice Statement (Juveniles: Murder Tariff)* (2000); *Re Thompson and Venables (Tariff Recommendation)* (2000).)

Procedure

The court must order a pre-sentence report before sentencing a juvenile. How to approach writing such a report was discussed in chapter 5. (Local authorities can by agreement leave this to probation officers where the child is aged 13 or over.)

Frequently, you will be asked by the court to prepare one before the finding of guilt, where it is known that the juvenile will admit the offence. The Children and Young Persons Act 1969, s. 9, requires you to start making the necessary investigations and preparing the information for the court as soon as the young person is charged, and not to wait until conviction. But there is no reason why the juvenile should be required to cooperate with the preparation of the report if he or she intends to deny the charge. The preparation of the report is likely to make the juvenile think that his or her guilt has been pre-judged. So if you have not been able to prepare the report at the time of conviction, the case will need to be adjourned; as with all adjournments, the juvenile may be released on bail, remanded to the accommodation of the local authority, or remanded in custody.

The court should not sentence without a report. It cannot lawfully impose custody if there is no rerpot (CJA Part 12). Magistrates' Courts (Children and Young Persons) Rules 1992 require the court to have evidence on the child's circumstances before sentencing, so a report will usually be needed, though apart from custody, lack of a report does not invalidate the sentence.

Your report will be in writing. You do not have to be in court to give it, but a representative of your department must be there. The court, or the defence, may wish you to be present to explain and justify what has been put in the report. You are performing this reporting role as an officer of the court. The juvenile is not your client; it is not your job to get a lenient outcome. Your role derives from your department's duties under the Children Act 1989, Schedule 2—advancing the child's welfare. Your task is to advise on the individual needs and circumstances of the juvenile, something which cannot be done by the court without your help. As a result, the court is more likely to adopt an individualized, rather than a punitive, approach.

Sentencing where courts have no discretion

Sometimes the courts may not have a choice of sentence. The penalty for murder is fixed, even for a juvenile (see above). The CJA creates the concept of the *dangerous offender*, who also must be sentenced to custody for life. This applies if the offender:

- is under 18,
- has committed a violent or sexual offence,
- will pose a significant danger to the public,
- the offence is a grave offence (see above Box 14.4).

In the absence of exceptional circumstances the minimum penalty for a number of other offences is fixed if the offender has a previous record of such offending. See the PCCSA, ss. 109–15, where, for example, domestic burglary committed for a third time attracts at least three years' imprisonment. These minimum sentences do not apply to offenders aged under 18. However, their juvenile offending record goes through with them into adulthood, and may trigger very harsh adult sentences where the offending is repeated.

Referral order

For a social worker, the new referral order is the fixed outcome of perhaps the most relevance; that is our starting point and in many circumstances the court's starting point.

These orders are made under the PCCSA, ss. 16–32. The essence of the approach is that in suitable cases the court passes·the decision to a special panel instead of deciding on a sentence in court. The panel's task is then to reach an agreement with the offender, failing which it gives the task back to the court to decide on a sentence. You need to understand and apply the concept of restorative justice to work with referral orders—this is beyond the scope of our book but the Home Office maintains a Restorative Justice web site (**www.homeoffice.gov.uk** then search for 'restorative justice').

Here, in brief, is how referral orders work:

A court *must* make a referral to the youth offender panel following conviction for any offence (since 2003 not just one which can carry a custodial sentence) if the following conditions apply:

- the offender is under 18, pleads guilty to all the offences, and has no previous convictions (a reprimand or warning is not a conviction)
- the court decides that custody is not appropriate but something greater than an absolute discharge should be imposed.

A court *may* make a referral where such an offender has pleaded guilty to at least one offence and following a trial has been found guilty on others.

Referral means that the young offender goes before a panel, and together with that panel works out a contract of behaviour which is to last between three and twelve months (the period is pre-determined by the court). The consequence of not agreeing (or of the panel deciding that this approach is not going to work) is that the offender will be sent back to court for sentencing.

The panel is nominated by the local YOT and must have a member of that team on it. A new panel is constituted for each offender who is referred.

As a result of the CJA, a parenting order can be made at the same time as a referral order. These are discussed in chapter 18.

Seriousness and sentencing

In all other cases courts exercise discretion in determining, within statutory upper limits and taking into account previous court guidance, what the appropriate sentence will be.

Parliament lays down maximum penalties; the courts (guided by the Court of Appeal) then decide. In 1991, Parliament (in the Criminal Justice Act 1991) brought in an element of control, in that courts were told to sentence only for the present offence or offences, and not to give an offender a greater sentence because of their bad record. The backlash was immediate and in 1993 something close to the old status quo was restored. Courts now look at the present offence(s) *and* any previous record *and* any mitigating factors before deciding how the present offence is to be sentenced.

The court should first look at how serious this offence is, and the level of punishment appropriate to that seriousness. It is worth looking at the Magistrates' Association's guidelines on offence seriousness, to see where the court will be starting from. Unfortunately, the Association charges £25 for a copy rather than putting them on the web, though you can locate them in a sentencing encyclopaedia such as David Thomas (ed.), *Current Sentencing Practice* (Sweet & Maxwell, looseleaf).

The Association sets an 'entry point' for each offence, then looks at aspects of the offence that are 'aggravating' or 'mitigating'. For example, the defendant has been convicted of taking a vehicle without the owner's consent (TWOC) under the Theft Act 1968, s. 12, and the statutory maximum punishment is six months' custody (unless it is 'aggravated vehicle taking'—a different offence). The guidelines suggest that a community penalty is a starting point. Factors pushing the seriousness upwards could be, for example, driving while disqualified, offending while on bail, driving badly, or the taking was premeditated. Mitigating factors could be, for example, that no damage was caused, the owner left the keys in the car, or the driving was not itself bad. The sentencing court then looks at any case law guidance, which may be in relation to the offence itself or general. For example, in *Attorney General's Reference (Nos. 54, 55, and 56 of 2004)* (2004), three juveniles had approached the 14-year-old victim at night, took his bicycle; knocked him to the ground; punched and kicked him about the face and head; threatened to kill him; broke his arm and threw him into a canal. The Court of Appeal agreed with the Attorney General that community punishment and rehabilitation orders were too lenient, even thought each defendant had personal mitigation in their background, and three years custody should be imposed. Another example of guidance from the Court of Appeal is *R v Howells* (1998) 836, which was on the question: seriousness in whose eyes? The old 'what would right-thinking people regard as serious?' test was dismissed as useless—the judges admitted they simply had no evidence on this, only their own opinions. Instead the Lord Chief Justice, Lord Bingham, told sentencing courts to look at the following issues: was the offence spontaneous or premeditated? Was the victim physically or mentally injured? Was there an admission of guilt? Does the offender have a previous record?

The PCCSA gives further guidance on aspects of what makes an offence serious for sentencing puposes. Under s. 153, racial aggravation explicitly increases seriousness. Pleading guilty—the sooner the better—reduces seriousness under s. 152. (This means that the maximum sentence is often avoided for even the most brutal of crimes to allow some discount for the early plea: *R v Hussain* (2002).) The CJA additionally requires seriousness to be calculated with reference to culpability, harm caused which was intended or foreseeable; it says that seriousness is aggravated by each previous offence on the offender's record, particularly recent offences. It is also aggravated if an offence was committed while the offender was already on bail and if it involves racial or religious aggravation, or hostility towards gay or disabled persons.

Each penalty that a court is thinking of imposing—whether custody, a community penalty, or a particular level of fine—should be imposed only if the court considers the offence to be so serious that only that level of sentencing is appropriate. But under s. 166 CJA the court must take into account any mitigating factors, and not decide the sentence just on seriousness. Mitigating factors may include for example remorse, or the effect that the punishment will have on the offender and/or other people.

There is, therefore, much for the probation officer or social worker to say in a pre-sentence report. A good record, or a bad record with redeeming features, can be used to mitigate the sentence—to reduce it below the sentence the court would think of imposing if seriousness alone were taken into account. Put another way, what is known about the offender can reduce the penalty but not increase it.

Box 15.7 shows a simplified step-by-step approach to deciding on sentence which mirrors the court's decision making process.

When sentencing juveniles, the courts should also be aware of s. 44 of the Children and Young Persons Act 1933:

> Every court in dealing with a child or young person who is brought before it, either as an offender or otherwise, shall have regard to the welfare of the child or young person, and shall in a proper case take steps for removing him from undesirable surroundings, and for securing that proper provision is made for his education and training.

This does not mean the child's welfare is paramount, for the court has a statutory duty—as do social workers as parts of the youth justice system—'to prevent offending by children and young persons' (Crime and Disorder Act 1998, s. 37). But welfare must be a factor in deciding on the appropriateness of a sentence, and gives you some leverage if you wish to suggest outcomes which will benefit the child as well as punish. The Court of Appeal frequently notes that juveniles should receive shorter custodial sentences than adults, and that reform of the young offender is the best way of protecting society. When we look at community sentences, you will see that the criteria

---

 BOX 15.7 Choosing the right sentence

(a) Does the court have a choice, or is the sentence fixed by law?

(b) How serious is the offence? (Consider issues such as violence; effect on the victim; amount of gain or loss; planning; breach of trust; racial aggravation.)

(c) Is it so serious that only custody is appropriate?

(d) If not, is it so serious that only a community sentence involving restrictions on liberty is appropriate? Is such a sentence appropriate for this offender?

(e) If not, is another community sentence appropriate, or a fine?

(f) If not, a discharge should be ordered, unless a warning or a reprimand was given within the last two years.

tie s. 37 CDA in with s. 44 CYPA, in that a community sentence must be appropriate to the seriousness of the offence, and also to reforming the offender.

Sentencing options

It could be, as we indicated above, that the court must make a referral order or, in the case of a murder sentence, to custody during Her Majesty's pleasure. But if the court has to decide, it will do so from the options set out below. The court cannot exceed the maximum penalty for a particular offence and its own maximum powers—for example for theft the sentence must not exceed ten years, in the youth court twelve months, or if a juvenile is dealt with in the magistrates court a fine.

Custody

We have to continually be reminded that the UK is signatory to the UN Convention on the Rights of the Child, and that custody has to be an absolutely last resort for the tiniest minority. What history does show us without a doubt is that the types of young people going [into custody] are going to be high- and multiple-risk. Everything has gone wrong for them, and they are among the most vulnerable people we will meet. We can change the name and culture of the intervention, but persistent young offenders are perennial. Whatever we do, they need very careful and—inevitably—very expensive interventions if we are actually going to reduce crime [Ann Hazel, *Criminal Justice Matters* No. 41, Autumn 2000, p. 30].

In the spirit of treating young offenders as children with important welfare needs, it is heartening to see that children in custody are recognized as children in need under the Children Act, s. 17: *R (on behalf of the Howard League) v Secretary of State for the Home Department* (2002). The trigger for this case was a guidance note from the Home Office to young offenders institutions and secure training centres telling them that the Children Act does not apply. The court agreed it imposed no duties on the prison service, but that imprisonment made no difference to local authority duties. The authority must continue to assess and meet the needs of children whom the courts have locked up in the prison system, in so far as a prison sentence allows. (For more about this case, see the case study in chapter 8.)

It may help you if you are called on to prepare a pre-sentence report where custody is likely to recall that the statutory purpose the criminal justice system (see above) is the prevention of offending. It follows logically that sentences that reduce offending fulfill this purpose better than those which do not do so. The Youth Justice Board has published research showing that work to address offending behaviour not only starts quicker but also achieves a greater investment of time when the young person receives intensive supervision and surveillance community orders, rather than short detention and training orders—see *Key Elements of Effective Practice—Intensive Supervision and Surveillance Programmes* which can be downloaded at **www.youth-justice-board.gov.uk/Publications/Scripts/prodList.asp?idcategory=12&curPage= 2&sortField=description&eP=YJB.**

Nevertheless, despite its manifest problems in dealing with young offenders' problems, custody is in certain circumstances an option for the sentencing court. There are two regimes for locking up children:

(a) *Custody for murder or grave crimes* (PCCSA, ss. 90–2, see above). The Crown Court sentences the juvenile to be detained for a defined term or 'during Her Majesty's pleasure', and the place of detention is left to the Home Secretary to determine. It can include detention in local authority accommodation (Children and Young Persons Act 1969, s. 30). While the offender is under 21 prison is not used; he or she is held in a young offenders institution.

(b) *A detention and training order*. The custodial part of the detention and training order is served either in a young offenders institution or a secure training centre (but as yet there are only three of these).

In either case, the statutory criteria must be met, which are:

- *the juvenile* must be represented (or has refused to apply for publicly funded representation, or it was withdrawn as a result of his or her behaviour); and

- *the offence* meets one of the following tests:

    (i)   it was so serious, on its own or taking into account one or more associated offences, that neither a fine alone nor a community sentence can be justified for the offence; or

    (ii) it is a violent or sexual offence and *only* custody will adequately protect the public from *serious* harm (injury or death); or

    (iii) the juvenile refuses to accept the requirements of a proposed community order; or

    (iv) the offender fails to comply with an order under s. 161(2) CJA to undergo pre-sentence drug testing.

- *the court* has obtained a pre-sentence report (s. 156 CJA).

Even if the court decides that custody is justified, it is still entitled to consider whether what is known about the offender mitigates the sentence in favour of something non-custodial. Under CJA s. 166 it must always take into account any mental disorder before considering a custodial sentence, even if the offence is sufficiently serious for custody. A pre-sentence report can contain very important information about the likely effect of custody versus community or other sentences; the offender's past record and attitude, and prospects for avoiding further offending. The minimum period for custody for a juvenile is four months and it cannot be suspended. (There is no corresponding minimum for an adult of 21 or over. Is this unfair on the juvenile? The idea is that courts are deterred from the idea of a short, sharp shock; custody is wrong unless the offence is serious enough to merit lots of it!)

The actual imposed custodial sentence should be no longer than is necessary to reflect the seriousness of the offence or to the need to protect the public from violence: s. 153 CJA. However, we referred above to sentencing 'dangerous offenders' to custody for life for 'grave' crimes where the juvenile has committed a sexual or violent offence and there is significant danger to the public. Grave crimes were defined in Box 15.5. If the conditions are otherwise met, but it is not a grave crime as defined, the court has the power not only to impose the appropriate custodial sentence, but to add a period on licence of up to five years (for a violent offender) and eight years (for a sexual offender). This means he or she can be recalled to custody for breach of licence conditions, or continue to be detained if the Parole Board consider that he or she remains a danger.

If a young offender is still serving a period of detention at the age of 21 he or she is transferred to a prison sentence for the remainder of the custodial term (PCCSA, s. 99, as inserted by the CJA 2003).

Detention and training orders

Detention and training orders are now governed by the PCCSA, ss. 102–7. The provisions were implemented for 12 to 17 year olds in 1999. The Act provides a power to make orders for 10 and 11 year olds; according to the Government, these will be implemented only if it should prove necessary or desirable to include them. (If these powers are brought into effect, the court must be satisfied that, in addition to the normal custody criteria, custody is the *only* way of protecting the public. Until these powers are brought in, custody is a possibility for 10 and 11 year olds only for the most serious of crimes, as described above.)

For all offenders, the general custody criteria that we saw above apply: in particular, is this offence so serious that custody is the only answer? For offenders below the age of 15, the courts additionally have to find that the child is a 'persistent' offender. The Home Office Circular, *Tackling Delays in the Youth Justice System*, defines this as someone sentenced 'on three or more separate occasions' for a recordable offence. However, this is not a statutory definition, and courts will, it seems, define 'persistent' for themselves. See *R v C (A Juvenile) (Persistent Offender)* (2000), where C was convicted of burglary and aggravated vehicle taking, committed while on bail for an earlier burglary. This was enough to make his offending persistent, even though he had never been convicted of anything before.

The maximum term of the detention and training order is two years, or less if the maximum prison term for an adult would be less. The actual term has to be one of the following: four months; six months; eight months; ten months; twelve months; eighteen months; or twenty-four months. Half of the term will be served in custody undergoing training. For orders of eight, ten, or twelve months, an extra month can be taken off the custodial half of the sentence for good behaviour; for orders of eighteen or twenty-four months, two months can be lopped off the custodial half for good behaviour. The period of detention is to be served in an a secure training centre (at the time of writing only three exist), a young offenders institution, or in local authority secure accommodation.

After release, the offender is supervised for the remaining period by a social worker, probation officer, or other member of the youth offending team. The offender must comply with the requirements of the supervisor. Unfortunately, as with the definition of 'persistent' offending, the nature of 'requirements' has not been specified in the legislation, but according to the Home Office guidance is similar to powers exercised where an offender is subject to a community rehabilitation order or supervision: see below. Breach of any requirements can be reported to the court, which then has the power to fine or to order detention for up to three further months. Commission of an imprisonable offence during the period can put the offender back into custody for some or all of the remaining supervision period, with punishment for the new offence being added to the total term, so long as this does not exceed twenty-four months in total.

Community sentences

The Criminal Justice Act 1991 attempted to create a range of sentencing options called community sentences which are not custodial but are nevertheless tough. The range and importance of community sentences for juvenile offenders were significantly increased in 2000, when action plan orders and reparation orders came into effect, and again under the CJA 2003, particularly when the sections listed below in relation to offenders age 16 and 17 come into force.

A principal feature of the community sentence is that it is a punishment (before 1991 things like supervision orders were considered an alternative to punishment and were part of a comprehensive scheme, child protection legislation which, when designed, did not distinguish between children in trouble because of criminality and because of misfortune).

To count as punishment, the offence must be serious enough to warrant the particular type of community order chosen. Seriousness has already been discussed, but the s. 148 CJA repeats the guidance on what seriousness means specifically for deciding if a community sentence is appropriate.

(1) A court must not pass a community sentence on an offender unless it is of the opinion that the offence, or the combination of the offence and one or more offences associated with it, was serious enough to warrant such a sentence.

(2) Where a court passes a community sentence which consists of or includes a community order—

   (a) the particular requirement or requirements forming part of the community order must be such as, in the opinion of the court, is, or taken together are, the most suitable for the offender, and

   (b) the restrictions on liberty imposed by the order must be such as in the opinion of the court are commensurate with the seriousness of the offence, or the combination of the offence and one or more offences associated with it.

(3) Where a court passes a community sentence which consists of or includes one or more youth community orders—

   (a) the particular order or orders forming part of the sentence must be such as, in the opinion of the court, is, or taken together are, the most suitable for the offender, and

   (b) the restrictions on liberty imposed by the order or orders must be such as in the opinion of the court are commensurate with the seriousness of the offence, or the combination of the offence and one or more offences associated with it.

Under CJA s. 151 a juvenile offender of 16 or over who has not committed a serious enough offence for a community sentence, but who has been previously fined at least three times, can be given a community sentence anyway.

An offender must consent to a community sentence. But refusal is not advisable, as this is itself a ground for triggering custody and enables the court to bypass the seriousness requirement.

The specific community sentences available depend on the age of the offender. We look at each in turn. None can last more than three years, though if a community sentence contains different elements they do not all have to run for an identical period—for example residence requirements can expire after, say, three months while educational requirements could run for three years, within the same supervision order.

Supervision order

Age range: 10–17. You may recall that supervision is a possible outcome in child protection proceedings (see chapter 11). Unless the juvenile is found guilty of murder, where an indefinite period of custody ('during Her Majesty's pleasure') is the only available outcome, a supervision order is also available after a finding of guilt in any criminal proceedings. Although there are many similarities, particularly the supervisor's duty to advise, assist, and befriend, the criminal supervision order is a different one from a civil supervision order, and governed by different legislation: PCCSA, ss. 34, 63–7, and Schedules 6 and 7. The court can designate as supervisor either the local authority, a probation officer, or a member of the Youth Offending Team. An order can be made for up to three years, which means that it can continue after the supervisee reaches 18. (The supervisor is a probation officer in such a case.)

The key difference between civil and criminal supervision orders is the restrictions that can be attached to the latter, which will give a bench a chance, if that is what they need, to feel that they are imposing a punishment. The fact that conditions can be attached to an order is attractive to magistrates seeking to restrict the liberty, or correct the conduct, of a juvenile they feel needs control. We set out below the three types of condition that can (but need not) be imposed with a supervision order under s. 12.

1. Supervision with condition of residence in local authority accommodation

This is a surprising condition, given that the Children Act 1989 abolished care orders in criminal cases. It seems to bring about a similar result by the back door. Until the amendments brought in by the Crime and Disorder Act 1998, it was available only for serious offending. Now the criteria are no more than breach of a supervision order and a belief that such residence will sort out the bad behaviour.

This residence requirement can be imposed if the following conditions are *all* satisfied:

(a) the relevant local authority has been consulted (but it has not necessarily agreed);

(b) the juvenile is already subject to a supervision order with requirements;

(c) the juvenile has either breached a requirement or committed an offence;

(d) the court is satisfied that the offending or the non-compliance results from the circumstances in which the juvenile is living and that a residence requirement will help towards rehabilitation;

(e) the juvenile is represented, or has refused the offer of representation; and

(f) there is a pre-sentence report.

Your report must therefore address the issue of circumstances of the offence or breach of supervision and its seriousness, and of course give the view of the local authority as to whether a residence requirement is recommended, and why, and how it would be applied.

The maximum length of a residence requirement is six months, though the supervision itself continues after that. It is not a custodial sentence, and (in contrast to a remand after refusal of bail) does not give the authority a power to lock up the juvenile (though, as with all children looked after by local authorities, a court's permission can be sought to detain in secure accommodation—see chapter 9). Where does the juvenile actually live while subject to this order? This is up to the local authority; he or she could live at home, with relatives, friends, in a foster home, or a community home. But the court can order that he or she must not live with a particular individual while the order is in force.

2. Supervision with condition—other requirements which the court may impose

Subject to trying to avoid conflicts with the offender's religious beliefs or education, the court can impose any of the following requirements:

(a) to live with a named individual;

(b) to take part in certain supervised activities;

(c) to present him- or herself at stated times to the supervisor (e.g. Saturday afternoons if the offence is connected to soccer violence);

(d) to make reparations to the victim or to the community at large (this is similar to the freestanding reparation order—see below);

(e) to observe a curfew in one or more designated places for up to ten hours between 6.00 p.m. and 6.00 a.m. (to a maximum of thirty nights, which do not have to be consecutive);

(f) to comply with arrangements made for his or her education; or

(g) to submit to medical treatment (before this condition is imposed there must be medical evidence in relation to the juvenile's mental condition).

The first four requirements can be imposed only for the ninety days following the making of the order (unless the juvenile is in breach of the requirements, in which case the clock stops running until the breach ends). After that the supervision order can continue, of course.

3. Supervision subject to requirements made by the supervisor

If none of the above requirements is imposed, the court can instead make an order requiring the supervised person to comply with the directions of the supervisor.

These directions are then given at the discretion of the supervisor, but can cover only:

(a) living at a specified address for a given period or periods;

(b) presenting himself or herself to the supervisor at required times; and

(c) participating in specified activities at stated times.

The court decides how long this power shall last, up to a maximum of ninety days. You will see that it is this third option that gives a supervisor the real control over the offender, particularly the third one. If you wish to work with the offender, you should specify in your report what activities you—or you together with other agencies—have in mind for the initial up to ninety-day period of the supervision order. (See further chapter 6.)

Supervision orders were previously an alternative to custody. That meant that an offence meriting custody because of its seriousness could be disposed of by supervision, if the defence solicitor was persuasive and the pre-sentencing report encouraging. As the current statute does not make supervision a way of avoiding custody, the term 'intermediate treatment' (IT), used to describe the regime of a supervision order, is arguably no longer correct. But before making a supervision order, as before, the court will want to know, in the report prepared for sentencing, what regime is proposed for the supervisee, and to be satisfied that it is appropriate. Once the court makes the supervision order, it has no control over the form of the regime of activities and, strictly speaking, the supervisor can depart entirely from the proposals made. In the long term, that supervisor and that authority begin to lose credence with the court, however, if word gets around that the regime is not as 'tough' as the court was promised.

We consider below what happens if the conditions of a supervision order are breached.

Action plan order

Age range: 10–17. Any juvenile offender can, under the PCCSA, ss. 69–72, be placed under a three-month action plan order. The order will set out an immediate plan of action and whereabouts for the juvenile during this period. Activities can include doing good things, not doing bad things, education, and even reparation. Supervision is the same as for reparation orders (below). The court will, again, need a report setting out the proposed arrangements.

A court can order offenders of 14 or over to submit to drug testing and treatment during the course of both an action plan order or supervision order (s. 70 PCCSA, as amended by CJA).

Reparation order

Age range: 10–17. Under a reparation order a juvenile convicted of an offence can, under the PCCSA, ss. 73–5, be ordered to make reparation either to specified persons (victims of crime or, at least, those affected by the crime) or to the community at large. A report will be needed from the social worker, probation officer or YOT member to indicate that appropriate work is available and, if the victims have been specified, that the victims are genuinely willing. The total work carried out must not exceed twenty-four hours, and the order should not be combined with a community service order or combination order (below). The order must be completed within three months and is supervised by a social worker, probation officer, or member of the YOT.

Community rehabilitation order (formerly probation)

Age range: 16 plus. The court has to be satisfied that the offence is serious enough to warrant a rehabilitation order, and that such an order will either:

(a) secure the rehabilitation of the offender; or

(b) protect the public.

The offender is placed under the supervision of a probation officer for a period, fixed by the court, of between six months and three years. (For a shorter period, supervision is available.)

The offender must keep in touch with the probation officer, and may have to comply with additional requirements under the PCCSA, ss. 41 and 42. These requirements are imposed by the court at the time of sentencing if the court thinks them necessary for securing rehabilitation or protecting the public (the same factors for imposing the order in the first place).

Possible requirements are:

(a) residence at a particular address, such as a bail hostel;

(b) participation in certain reforming activities, or keeping away from certain activities thought to be associated with offending. Participation or keeping away cannot exceed sixty days in total, unless the offence was sexual, in which case activities and—less importantly—prohibitions can continue throughout the probation. This enables longer-term therapeutic work to be undertaken;

(c) treatment for mental disorder. The court requires medical evidence before making this a requirement; or

(d) treatment for drug or alcohol problems, if such problems were connected with the offending. Treatment can be residential. (This power has hardly been used, and is effectively replaced with the new drug treatment and testing order—see below.)

Community punishment order

Age range: 16 plus. The community punishment order used to be called community service, and is governed by the PCCSA, ss. 46–50. It must be shown to be available in the pre-sentence report. The offence must be one for which an adult could have been sent to prison. The number of hours which must be carried out is between forty and 240. Breach of the order, by committing a further offence or failure to comply with the requirements, can lead to the court revoking the order and sentencing the person afresh.

Combination orders

Age range: 16 plus (PCCSA, s. 51). Only community rehabilitation and community punishment can be combined in this order. The seriousness and suitability criteria must again be met, and the court must believe the order is desirable to rehabilitate the offender or protect the public.

The court can attach requirements to the rehabilitation side of the order. The number of hours of the community punishment element is between forty and one hundred.

Attendance centre order

Age range: 10 plus. The attendance centre order is governed by the PCCSA, ss. 60–2. The offence must be one for which imprisonment could have been imposed on an adult. The order will require the offender to attend for between twelve and thirty-six hours in total, usually on a Saturday for perhaps two hours. (If the offender is under 14, up to twelve hours can be ordered. For an offender under 16, the maximum is twenty-four hours.) Attendance centres are usually run by police officers in places such as youth clubs and schools. The court can make an attendance centre order only if it has been informed, through the pre-sentence report, that a suitable centre is available locally. Suitable, according to the Home Office, means within one-and-a-half hours' travel and not more than fifteen miles; or one hour and ten miles for an offender under 14.

Curfew orders

Age range: 10 plus. The curfew order is a form of community sentence which allows the court to impose a curfew of from two to twelve hours a day for up to three months, or, for a juvenile of 16 or 17, up to six months (PCCSA, ss. 37–40), and the order must not interfere with the juvenile's education or religious practices. Powers to enforce the order by electronic tagging (s. 13) are available if the monitoring facilities exist in the juvenile's home area.

Drug treatment and testing order

Age range: 16 to adult. If the offender is a drug abuser, the drug treatment and testing order provides for treatment over a period of between six months and three years (PCCSA, s. 52). The treatment may include residential treatment. It is supervised by an expert named in the order. The court must, of course, be informed that appropriate facilities are available, and, as with all community punishments, the offender has to agree. During the period of the order the offender must provide samples for testing and keep in touch with a 'responsible officer', normally a probation officer. The success or otherwise of this order is kept under review by the court which made the order—a unique provision which does not apply to other community orders unless there has been a breach.

New *à la carte* requirements within community orders for offenders over 16

New provisions in CJA ss. 177 to 218 have recast the sentencing framework for community punishments for offenders aged 16 upwards. The framework provides what is effectively an *à la carte* menu for any court imposing a community sentence, comprising the following:

(a) an unpaid work requirement (s. 199);

(b) an activity requirement, which means to present her or himself for participation in activities at certain times (s. 201);

(c) a requirement to take part in an approved programme (s. 202);

(d) a prohibited activity requirement (s. 203);

(e) a curfew requirement for between two and twelve hours a day, monitored with electonic tagging (s. 204);

(f) an exclusion requirement to stay away from specified places, monitored with electonic tagging (s. 205);

(g) a residence requirement (s. 206);

(h) a mental health treatment requirement (s. 207);

(i) a drug rehabilitation requirement (s. 209);

(j) an alcohol treatment requirement (s. 212);

(k) a supervision requirement (s. 213); and

(l) an attendance centre requirement (s. 214).

Breach of community sentences

The person who supervises a community sentence can report to the youth court a breach of any of the conditions in the order such as residence, activities, attendance, and the court (PCCSA, Schedules 3, 5, 7–9) can then:

(a) fine the juvenile up to £250 if he or she is under 14, £1,000 otherwise;

(b) order up to sixty hours' community punishment (240 if the offender is already doing community punishment);

(c) make an attendance centre order for a breach of probation;

(d) order a curfew for a breach of supervision or reparation;

(e) start again, i.e. sentence the offender afresh. The court may then decide on custody on the ground that the offender's behaviour under the community sentence is effectively a refusal of a community sentence.

Other powers on sentencing

Fines

A court can fine for any offence. It cannot impose a fine greater than the maximum that an adult could be made to pay, and the youth court has a top limit of £250 for an offender under 14, and £1,000 for one of 14 to 17 (PCCSA, s. 135). There is no top limit in the Crown Court.

If the offender is under 16, the parent or guardian pays, unless it would be unreasonable to make them pay in the circumstances (PCCSA, s. 137). It is unreasonable if the court thinks the offending is not in any way a result of parental influence or neglect. For an offender of 16 or 17, the assumption is reversed: the offender pays, unless the court thinks the parent or guardian should pay in the circumstances. The court must, before ordering the parent or guardian to pay, allow them to address the court and argue that they should not have to.

What if the offender is in local authority care? The local authority must normally pay the fine if it has acquired parental responsibility through a care order. The authority can, however, convince the court that it has done all that it reasonably could to keep a child in its care from offending (*D v DPP* (1995)). A remand (or provision of accommodation without a court order) is not the same as care, which arises only from a care order (see chapter 11). In *North Yorkshire County Council v Selby Youth Court Justices* (1994), the court had tried to make the council pay where the offenders had been remanded to local authority accommodation. It was held on appeal that the authority should not have to pay the fine.

All courts must fine on the same broad principles—taking both the seriousness of the offence and ability to pay into account. The court must enquire into ability to pay (which means the parent's or guardian's ability—see above and PCCSA, s. 138). But the court is not told how to apply its discretion. The court fixes a fine that feels right, subject to any maximum levels set by statute for the offence.

The court can order the fine to be paid by instalments. If it remains unpaid the court must hold a means inquiry. After such inquiry, the court can enforce the fine against the parents or guardian. It can make a money supervision order by appointing a suitable person to oversee the payments, or instead make an attendance centre order (see above) or, where the juvenile is employed, an attachment of earnings order (i.e. deduction by the employer). It can also remit, that is cancel, all or part of the remaining balance. Fines are deductible from income support.

Binding parents over

When a court convicts a juvenile of under 16, it must normally also bind over the parents (but it cannot bind over the local authority where the child is in care). If the juvenile is over 16 it can still choose to do this. This means the parent or guardian promises to take care of and exercise proper control over the child to prevent reoffending (PCCSA, s. 150). A sum is fixed by the court, and the parent or guardian is liable on breach to forfeit some or all of this sum. Forfeiture is unlikely to be triggered unless a further offence is committed. The maximum sum is £1,000, and the period during which this sword of Damocles hangs over the parent must not exceed three years, and it stops on the offender's eighteenth birthday. The court should take into account the relationship of the juvenile to the parents and whether the parents could have had any influence over the juvenile's behaviour, in deciding whether to use its power not to bind over. For more guidance see LAC (92) 5, para. 41.

A parent can refuse to be bound over, but it is risky. If the court thinks a refusal is unreasonable, it can fine the parents up to £1,000. This is on top of any fine they may already have to pay for the juvenile's offence.

Deferred sentence

Under the PCCSA, s. 1, a court has the power to defer (i.e. postpone) the decision on sentence for up to six months. It should do so only if some change in the offender's life is imminent—e.g. leaving school and taking up employment—which the court ought to take into account. The offender must consent to deferment, and the court can impose conditions which the offender must comply with pending the return to court. The compliance will usually be monitored by a probation officer, though the court can appoint another person. Breach of any conditions can lead to arrest and return to the court. All going well, however, a day is fixed for the return to court and sentence to be imposed. There will probably need to be a fresh pre-sentence report. The court will sentence in the light of the new circumstances. It will not normally be appropriate to order custody after deferment if the offender's circumstances are now looking more stable. The court can only order what the court could have ordered at the time of deferment—so if the offender is now 18 the court cannot treat him or her as an adult.

Discharge

This is an option where in all the circumstances (the offence and the offender's past history) no punishment is appropriate. It is governed by the PCCSA, ss. 12–15. If the offender had been prepared to admit the offence before charge, it might with hindsight have been more appropriate to reprimand or warn the offender. If the court orders an absolute discharge then, apart from showing on the offender's record if ever he or she is sentenced again, it does not count as a conviction. But the court can order a conditional discharge; the discharge is then conditional for a period of up to three years. If the offender commits an offence within that period, the court dealing with that further offence can sentence for the original offence as well. The later court will only have the powers of the original sentencing court, save that if the offender has now reached 18 they will be treated as an adult (unlike in the deferred sentence described above). A conditional discharge is available only in exceptional circumstances if an offender has already had a warning in the last two years (Crime and Disorder Act 1998, s. 66).

Compensation orders

Any person found guilty of an offence can be ordered to pay compensation to the victim. (This is one reason why a caution is sometimes inappropriate—there must be a conviction for a compensation order.) Indeed, a court should make such an order if appropriate, or give its reasons for not doing so (PCCSA, s. 130). This order can stand alone, without the court making any other order against the offender, or it can accompany any other order made by the court. As with a fine, the juvenile's means are taken into account; and the parents can be ordered to pay the compensation (but not where they were not in control of the juvenile at the time of the offence—e.g. the child was in local authority accommodation—*A v DPP* (1996)). Where the offender has limited means, a compensation order should be made before a fine.

Parenting order

If the appropriate conditions apply, a court can, at the time of sentencing, order the parents of a child who has been convicted of an offence to receive counselling and support via a parenting order—this is discussed in more detail in chapter 18, which relates to anti-social behaviour.

Sex offender orders: Crime and Disorder Act 1998, s. 2

These enable the police to apply to a court to restrict the activities of convicted sex offenders. The police can apply at any point after conviction. In that sense it is not a sentencing power.

These orders could be confused with the sex offenders register, which we mentioned in chapter 3. The difference is that all convicted sex offenders must register with the police, who can then use the information to monitor their activities and keep relevant agencies informed. By contrast, the sex offender order is not about monitoring—it concerns obtaining an order to address an identified risk. The idea is to keep an individual sex offender away from an area where they may commit offences. So a convicted sex offender who represents a danger to schoolchildren may be ordered to stay away from school gates when he has been seen hanging about. As a social worker you may be involved in asking the police to seek such an order. You may also be in a situation where you have a statutory responsibility to work with a child or adult who is subject to an order.

There are two grounds both of which the police must establish before the court when applying for an order:

(a) The person is a convicted sex offender under the Sex Offenders Act 1997, which can mean anyone over ten years old. (Without a conviction there can be no order, whatever the perceived risk.)

(b) There is a risk of serious harm to the public, which in this context can mean one individual.

As these are civil proceedings the court—a magistrates' court—will apply the civil standard of the balance of probabilities. The Queen's Bench Division has confirmed that to require a civil standard of proof is not a breach of the Human Rights Act 1998, since an offender had already been convicted in a criminal court using a criminal standard of proof (*B v Chief Constable of Avon and Somerset* (2001)). What the police need to establish, on balance, is that they have reasonable cause to believe that an order is necessary to protect the public from serious harm from this offender. (This is not the same as showing on balance that the order is actually necessary. No one needs to give evidence except the officer who believes the order to be necessary.)

The sex offender order lasts for a minimum of five years and there is no upper time limit. The effect of the order is to forbid named activities. For example, the sex offender must stay away from school gates or from a defined area. It is in everybody's interest that the area involved is clearly defined. This means that the person knows where he may and may not go. It also enables the breach of such an order to be clear. The order can only be prohibitive: it cannot require the person to do anything, such as obtain treatment (though that result might be obtained through an appropriate sentence in the earlier criminal proceedings).

Breach of the order is a criminal offence and can lead to a fine or imprisonment.

EXERCISES

Consider the statutory responsibilities of a social worker and appropriate actions you might take in each of the following situations:

- Jennifer, who is 14, is currently in local authority accommodation because her mother cannot cope. You feel you have established quite a good relationship with her, and having begun to gain her trust you have been able to talk to her about her life, which has included recent shoplifting and drug use. The police inform you that they have arrested her for supplying cannabis and wish to question her.

- You have arrived at Sunderfield police station following a request to be present as appropriate adult for the questioning of Abdul, who is 16 and is suspected of arson at a local school. The police sergeant tells you Abdul has refused legal advice and therefore they are ready to interview him. He has been in the police station for twenty hours, and when you see him you can see he is tired. The police have not told you what evidence they have to connect Abdul with the offence, but Abdul tells you that he was with a group of friends and someone, perhaps himself, did accidentally drop a lighted match onto some paper. Abdul tells you the police have told him he will not be allowed to leave until he admits it.

- Assume Abdul has been charged. You know he has no past history of offending and comes from what you believe to be a stable family. Consider his right to bail and what will happen if bail is refused.

  We have not provided detail on sentences for different offences. Using one of the research tools indicated in the reading list, find out what the penalty for arson is.

- If Abdul is found guilty what opportunity would a social worker have to influence the court, and what approach might a court or courts take when deciding the appropriate sentence?

COMPANION WEB SITE

For guidance on how to answer these exercises, visit the companion web site at: **www.oup.com/uk/booksites/law**

WHERE DO WE GO FROM HERE?

Most of the contents of this chapter were, at root, triggered by statutory duties involving social workers promoting the welfare of children in need under the Children Act, s. 17. We have touched on vulnerable adults, particularly those with mental health problems and particularly in the police station. We have not considered the sentencing of adults with mental health problems, and this will be dealt with in chapter 16.

This chapter concludes the Part relating to children. But the division of the book, and the law, into different topics is to some extent artificial. Your work with children will be informed by an understanding of family law and the housing of families, all of which are covered in Part 5; and there is a range of quasi-criminal orders which could have been covered in this chapter, such as the anti-social behaviour order or child curfew order, which affect children and which are dealt with in chapter 17, or the child safety order which we have covered as an issue relating to anti-social behaviour, also in chapter 17.

Part 4, which is next, will look at duties to vulnerable adults, which are in some respects similar to those a social worker owes to children. You will find that compulsory powers—to detain those with a mental disorder or to remove people compulsorily into residential accommodation—are not given to social services departments, so in that respect they differ from those relating to children. You will find that in mental health there is one set of legislation, and that most of the work is carried out within the NHS, not by social services. But in community care, which includes residential care, the primary responsibility is with social services, and the legislation is the most complex of all. That follows next.

ANNOTATED FURTHER READING

H. Brayne and G. Broadbent, *Legal Materials for Social Workers* (Oxford University Press, 2002), chapter 6, provides access to most of the relevant primary legislation and official guidance.

If you are really interested in the up-to-date and full details of a particular aspect of how the criminal process works, one of the standard reference works can provide the answer, if you use the contents or index carefully. The following are published annually: *Stone's Justices' Manual* (Butterworths) deals with the work of the youth courts; *Blackstone's Criminal Practice* (Oxford University Press) deals with all aspects of criminal law and practice, as does *Archbold's Criminal Pleadings Evidence and Practice* (Sweet & Maxwell). *Current Sentencing Practice* (Sweet & Maxwell), a looseleaf encyclopaedia edited by D.Thomas, is very useful for the detail on sentencing, including how the courts approach particular offences.

C. Ball, K. McCormac, and N. Stone, *Young Offenders: Law, Policy and Practice* (2nd edn., Sweet & Maxwell, 2003) provides a thorough and up-to-date overview of the area.

N. Stone, *A Companion Guide to Sentencing: General Issues and Provisions, Part 2* (Shaw & Sons, 2001) is particularly aimed at social workers and probation officers, and works through the types of sentence available.

A. Edwards, *Advising a Suspect in the Police Station* (5th edn., Sweet & Maxwell, 2003). The author, Anthony Edwards, is a leading writer and practitioner, and this book is of value to anyone working as an appropriate adult, though it covers all suspects who are being questioned.

C. Taylor and D. Postgate, *Advising Mentally Disordered Offenders* (2nd edn., Law Society Publications, 2003). Notwithstanding the date of publication this volume is useful for those attending the police station in particular.

R. Ward, *Young Offenders Law, Practice and Procedure* (Jordans, 2001) provides a good general overview.

A. Bottoms, L. Gelsthorpe, and S. Rex (eds.), *Community Penalties Change and Challenges* (Willan Publishing, 2002). A series of essays giving a variety of critical perspectives on concepts such as restorative justice.

R. Matthews and J. Young (eds.), *The New Politics of Crime and Punishment* (Willan Publishing, 2003). An up-to-date analysis by a number of contributors to the political dimensions of the justice system.

A. Crawford and T. Newburn, *Youth Offending and Restorative Justice Implementing Reform in Youth Justice* (Willan Publishing, 2003). This book critically explores youth offender panels and referral orders.

The Youth Justice Board is an agency with a statutory responsibility to prevent offending by children. Its web site is usefully and accessibly organized, for example to take you through custodial and community sentences one at a time **www.youth-justice-board.gov.uk/ Youth+Justice+Board**.

NACRO (National Association for the Care and Resettlement of Offenders) has an excellent list of publications, too long for inclusion but worth visiting: **www.nacro.org.uk/about/ index.htm**.

PART IV

Responsibilities towards adults

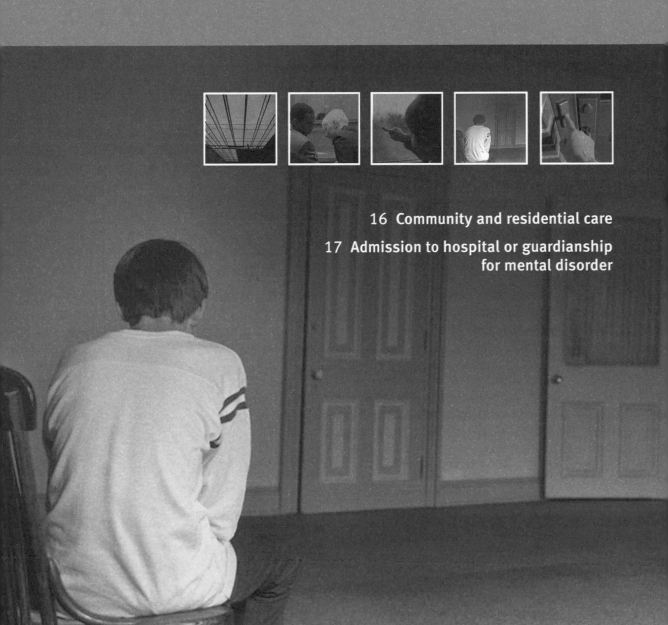

16 Community and residential care
17 Admission to hospital or guardianship for mental disorder

PART IV Responsibilities towards adults

Part 3 has dealt with a range of services for children, including for child protection purposes compulsory measures. Part 4 deals with services provided for adults and compulsory interventions where adults have mental health problems.

Despite the theoretical unification of social services under the 1970 legislation, the legislation for children which we have looked at is largely freestanding and separate from the mass of community care legislation. There is an overlap, and the Mental Health Act in particular covers all ages; some of the community care legislation is addressed to the needs of families with young children. And, of course, where adults have problems requiring community care services, children often become carers, or for other reasons themselves become children in need. Departments have increasingly been organized with separate children and adult sections, and when the Children Act 2004 comes into force children's services will be managed together with education. The separation will then be complete.

This fragmentation into adult and children's services is compounded by the fact that the welfare state, which was designed largely after the Second World War, apportions responsibility for social care, housing, and education to elected local authorities (but under separate legislation and to separate departments) and health and economic support to national government. (This legislative history can be explored further in Brayne and Broadbent, chapter 1.) The fragmentation is made worse—to the point where the best description of community care law is simply that it is a collection of historical legislative remnants with thirty-five years of piecemeal adjustments. There is no blueprint, there is no map; and there is no reason to think it is your fault if you get confused.

Our division of topics into community care and mental health is itself a little artificial. Many community care service users have mental health problems. Our community care chapter covers all users, including those with mental health problems. **Chapter 17**, which deals with mental health, is essentially about admission to hospital or guardianship. These form part of the overall framework for providing services within the community or, where required, in hospital, but because liberties and rights are concerned, there is a separate set of procedures and safeguards. There is also a different, defined, role for certain social workers who have been approved to deal with mental health admissions.

Chapter 16 explains community care services for adults—one of the most unsatisfactory areas of law you will encounter. **Chapter 17** then goes on to explain the powers under the Mental Health Act for treating mental disorder, both in hospital and in the community.

R (on the application of L) v Mayor and Burgesses of the London Borough of Barking and Dagenham (2001)

Schiemann LJ described the circumstances as follows:

> The applicant is a severely disabled woman aged 43. She has for many years suffered from cerebral palsy as well as having learning difficulties, limited oral communication and other problems. She requires care to be available on a 24-hour basis and is dependent on a wheelchair for personal mobility. At the date when these proceedings started in 1997 she had lived for some 24 years at Sweetland Court, a residential care home owned and managed by the respondent authority in performance of its duties under Part 3 of the National Assistance Act 1948. That home in October 1997 had 12 people living there, all of them disabled.

The Council decided this home needed redeveloping; the applicant, Ms Lloyd, would, on completion of the redevelopment, be provided with her own tenancy within the new development. They thought she would benefit from greater independence. She—or more accurately her mother as her litigation friend and the solicitors her mother consulted—believed she had not been properly assessed or consulted in relation to this move, and started judicial review proceedings claiming the council was acting unlawfully. The council reacted by agreeing to carry out an assessment, and indeed made a legally binding undertaking to the court to carry out a proper assessment which took into account Ms Lynne's special needs. The terms of this agreement included:

> (1) The respondent will now carry out a lawful multi-disciplinary assessment of Marie Lloyd's needs for community care services in accordance with its statutory obligations and Governmental guidance, and thereafter reach a lawful service provision decision in the form of a Care Plan. The assessment of need shall include an assessment of her capacity, including her capacity to sign a tenancy agreement, as well as a risk assessment, and all the elements of a lawful assessment necessary to comply with the respondent's obligations.
> (2) The respondent will ensure that appropriate health professionals are involved in and contribute to the assessment, including an occupational therapist, physiotherapist, appropriate consultant, and Ms Lloyd's general practitioner and any other relevant professionals.
> (3) The first Care Plan shall identify which, if any, needs are being met at Ms Lloyd's current accommodation at Sweetland Court. Following the identification of suitable 'temporary' accommodation, the respondent will produce a second Care Plan identifying which services are required at that accommodation to meet the assessed needs, as well as a third plan identifying those services required to meet the assessed needs at the re-modelled Sweetland Court site.

The undertaking allowed Ms Lloyd to veto any exchange of contracts until she was satisfied with the assessment. But she was not. Her case was that the promised assessment had not been properly carried out under s. 47 of the National Health Service and Community Care Act 1990. Her main concern was that the new home was to have independent kitchens for each tenant; the lack of communal dining would deprive her of social contacts. So the case ended up before a High Court judge and from there the Court of Appeal. There her case was rejected and the agreement which prevented the Council from proceeding until Ms Lloyd consented was torn up.

The Court of Appeal made three important decisions:

1 It is important not to confuse a need with the way or ways in which that need could be met. It is for the care plan to cover the latter. . . . [Ms Lloyd's barrister argues that] the latest assessment still has a number of deficiencies. That does not make it unlawful. There may be more than one view which can properly be held among social workers as to the adequacy of a particular assessment of needs. Such disagreements do not render it unlawful.

2 The Council must have a discretion in how to meet needs and cannot be dictated to by a court over the precise arrangements. 'It seems to us . . . that the court is not the appropriate organ to be prescriptive as to the degree of detail which should go into a care plan or as to the amount of consultation to be carried out with Ms Lloyd's advisers. In practice these are matters for the Council, and if necessary its complaints procedure. If the council has failed to follow the Secretary of State's guidance and is arguably in breach of its statutory duties in relation to the way it carries out its assessment and what it puts into its care plans then aggrieved persons should in an appropriate case turn first to the Secretary of State. Where there is room for differences of judgment the Secretary of State and his advisers may have a useful input. The court is here as a last resort where there is illegality. Here there is not.

3 The undertaking to the court to carry out a lawful and proper assessment under s. 47 was no more than the law already required them to do, so there was no need to have such an undertaking.

But the Court was strongly critical of the Council for its failure to consult adequately with Ms Lloyd. It had failed to reveal the nature of the discussions with the housing association, and even whether the new home would be registered as a care home. How could they hope to avoid challenge if they kept their service users in the dark? 'As a result, it is only in this court that the real issue has been isolated and the argument narrowed to something quite manageable.'

OVERVIEW AND OBJECTIVES

The court is, the Court of Appeal has indicated in our case study, not the place to challenge local authority decisions. Yet this chapter and the law reports are riddled with challenges, many of which are successful. Indeed government is so concerned with social exclusion in relation to welfare services that the Legal Services Commission is encouraging solicitors to obtain specialist contracts in community care law in order to use the law to ensure that in a given case care is provided in accordance with legal requirements. The Court of Appeal, even in this case, acknowledged that it had taken a court challenge to get the council to explain to the service user what was going on.

It is not surprising there are mistakes and challenges. The statutory requirements date back to 1948. Parliament has never attempted to review and consolidate the legislation into one coherent set of principles and practice, as it did with the Children Act in 1989. The legislation, instead, is allowed to grow like an untended garden shrub which gets hacked back by the occasional legislative pruning, only to sprout elsewhere with renewed vigour. It was the clearly stated intention of Parliament when creating unified social services departments under the Local Authority Social Services Act in 1970 that the next step would be for the legislation defining the duties of these departments to be rationalised (see Brayne and Broadbent, chapter 1, for a flavour of the parliamentary debates).

Legislative inertia creates avoidable problems. But even if they were, one day, sorted, the nature of community care creates unavoidable problems: one service user can have physical health problems, mental health problems, housing problems, care needs, perhaps residential needs (with or without medical care), and more. The needs may well be compounded by financial needs. Their carers and families will also have a range of needs. These needs are going to have to be met by a range of agencies. You may consider, for example, that the service user has housing needs but find that your colleagues in the housing department are unable or unwilling to provide the housing required. Where does the buck stop? Any services to meet these needs must be delivered in a manner which respects fundamental human rights, but within a cash-limited budget; and they are delivered in the shadow of potential legal challenge to your decisions.

Must you meet every need? Can your department change provision without being dragged to court? Who will pay if you cannot agree whether the need is for NHS services or social care?

Additionally people requiring services may lack the ability to make all their own decisions, so who is the statutory service user? Where you are dealing with a service user whom many people claim to speak on behalf of, who do you listen to? In the opening case study, the judge made a passing reference to the fact that it was not the applicant but her advisers who were unhappy with the arrangements.

In light of these rather pessimistic words we acknowledge that understanding community care law is not going to be easy. You will see in Box 15.1 that there is more legislation in this field than in the other areas you have worked in—which is why we need a box just to introduce it. There is a great deal of case law in which the meaning of many of these legislative provisions have been explained, or obscured—we will introduce you to some of this, and hope that you feel it was explained, not obscured, by our attempt. Our overall aim is to provide you with an overview of who the social services department owes duties to, and to enable you to work through the statutory steps in assessing and meeting needs, whether in the community or residential care. We will outline the ways in which the service user can be required to pay for services, including the use of direct payments for the purchase by the service user of services. The chapter ends with a discussion on decision making for service users who lack the capacity to decide for themselves.

■ Community care: the concept

Community care means the provision of services, where possible in the community, for those who need them. What does 'in the community' mean? For our purposes it means not as an in-patient in a hospital, and in practice it means care provided or coordinated by the social services department. It can include residential care. After we have looked at assessment, we deal with non-residential and residential care in turn.

BOX 16.1 Community care legislation

Name of statute (and initials if used frequently in this chapter)	Comment
National Assistance Act 1948 (NAA)	Originally this Act provided for social security too; it still specifies the core local authority duties to provide community and residential care services to those who need them because disabled or otherwise unable to cope.
Disabled Persons (Employment) Act 1958	Provision of work facilities for people with serious disabilities.
Mental Health Act 1959 (MHA)	Duty to prosecute those who sexually abuse mental patients.
Health Services and Public Health Act 1968 (HSPHA)	Requires local authorities to promote the welfare of older people (even if not disabled under NAA).
Chronically Sick and Disabled Persons Act 1970 (CSDPA)	Requires social services departments to provide assistance in the home for service users who are disabled under NAA.
Local Authority (Social Services) Act 1970 (LASSA)	Specifies in Schedule 1 the duties of social services departments under other legislation; provides for complaints procedure. See chapter 3.
National Health Service Act 1977 (NHSA)	Extends social services to expectant mothers and mothers of young children; after-care following hospital treatment; services for those received into mental health guardianship; home help facilities as needed.
Mental Health Act 1983 (MHA)	Regulates compulsory admission and treatment; appointment of approved social workers and after-care of discharged patients are responsibility of social services. See chapter 17.
Health and Social Services and Social Security Adjudications Act 1983 (HASSASSA)	Requires local authorities to charge for services according to ability to pay and penalizes those who dispose of capital in order to avoid payment for residential care. Enables district councils to provide meals on wheels and recreational facilities for older people (which may involve social services departments in metropolitan districts).
Disabled Persons (Services, Consultation and Representation) Act 1986 (DPSCRA)	Enables a disabled person (or their representative) to insist on an assessment of need and reasons for a decision; ability of any carer to be assessed.
National Health Service and Community Care Act 1990 (NHSCCA)	Provides framework within which assessment of needs in authority area and assessment of individual needs are carried out.

Carers (Recognition and Services) Act 1995 (CRSA)	Carers can insist on having their ability to care assessed.
Community Care (Direct Payments) Act 1996 (CCDPA)	Power to provide cash to person following assessment of need, or to the carer, to purchase services.
Health Act 1999 (HA)	Establishes framework for cooperation between social services and health authorities and planning for health and community care provision; enables payments to be made for services provided on behalf of NHS (and vice versa).
Carers and Disabled Children Act 2000 (CDCA)	Extends right of carer to assessment and creates direct right to services for carer.
Care Standards Act 2000 (CSA)	Establishes framework for quality assurance of care and residential services.
Health and Social Care Act 2001 (HSCA)	Delineates boundaries between social care and medical care, prevents local authorities from providing nursing care as part of residential care; extends scope for direct payments to service users.
Community Care (Delayed Discharges Act) 2003 (CCDDA)	Requires assessment of those facing discharge from hospital into community care and penalizes local authority if they cannot make arrangements in time for the discharge.

■ The NHS and Community Care Act 1990

The NHSCCA 1990 was the first Act to use the words 'community care'. But it did not invent the term. Social services department already had a wide range of powers and duties, and were able to make direct provision of services, or arrange with voluntary or commercial providers to meet the needs of the vulnerable. But several things shifted with, or since, the 1990 Act.

The first was the emphasis on managing services for the vulnerable, rather than providing these directly: 'It will be [social services'] responsibility to make maximum possible use of private and voluntary providers and to increase the available range of options and widen consumer choice' (DoH Circular, *Community Care: Review of Residential Homes Provision and Transfers* (LAC (91) 12, para. 3)).

The second was the requirement for social services to plan services, and assess the need of individuals for those services, in partnership with health authorities and other agencies.

A third, more recent, shift is the idea that users and their carers can be given money rather than provided with a direct service. We deal with direct payments later.

A fourth, aspirational, shift is one which does not specify particular responsibilities for social services departments. This is the Government's ambition to reduce the need for acute health or care services by getting all local authorities to try to improve preventive welfare services. The Audit Commission identified the problem in its report, *Home Alone: The Role of Housing in Community Care* (May 1998):

> A picture emerges of significant resources invested by housing, social services and health authorities in crisis-based services—homelessness, high-intensity support in specialised schemes, hospitalisation in short-stay psychiatric beds, etc.—in large part because funding is available for these services, but is lacking for more basic, and often less costly, support . . . for all vulnerable groups . . .

This problem is to be addressed through the provision by central government of special funds for welfare services under Part V of the Local Government Act 2000. All local authorities—not just those with social services functions—should apply for grants for developing welfare services for local people. Welfare, it is believed, should not be confined to the acute personal care services for which statute already provides, such as homelessness provision and the community care powers and duties we cover shortly.

To assist in achieving this shift in approach the powers of all authorities are broadened by s. 2 of the Act (see Box 16.1 above) to enable any service to be provided which will enhance well-being at an individual or community level. (Identical provisions in s. 93(2) apply in relation to the Welsh Assembly.) It is worth bearing in mind that this s. 2 power provides a means of delivering any welfare service the authority wishes. It can be used as an argument—which has been accepted by the courts—when a local authority would otherwise say 'we do not have the power': see *R (on the application of J) v Enfield London Borough Council* (2002), which is also discussed in chapter 21. The only restriction on this power is that you cannot use it to overcome a clear statutory prohibition, in particular the prohibition on using community care powers to relieve the destitution of asylum seekers (see chapter 21). The social worker's powers and duties in relation to community care provision are not changed by this legislation, even though the context in which you carry out your work is changed, with more agencies and authorities working on the same patch. The intention is laudable, as we said, but it remains to be seen whether the funding might have been better targeted to improved social work resources.

The key elements of community care which have evolved since 1993, are:

(a) Encouragement through financial incentives and government guidance to use the private and voluntary sector. All provisions described below may well be bought in rather than provided in-house.

(b) Planning of community care services with all other service providers.

(c) Social workers as assessors of need and coordinators or funders of service provision, more than as care providers.

(d) (Reading between the lines.) Careful scrutiny of budgets before assessing any vulnerable person as requiring services.

(e) Providing service users with cash where appropriate, so that they can directly purchase the required service.

Guidance and direction from Government

Social services are provided by *local* authorities, each subject to different financial and political priorities. Provision varies, and this variation is accepted by government: LAC (2002/13), *Fair Access To Care Services Guidance On Eligibility Criteria For Adult Social Care.* However, as we explained in chapter 1 under LASSA 1970, s. 7A, social service functions must be exercised under the 'general guidance of the Secretary of State' (meaning the Health Secretary). This includes the exercise of discretionary powers, which play a prominent part in community care. We will refer to the appropriate government circulars, since, as a matter of law, you are obliged to pay attention to their guidance. (However, the guidance may, exceptionally, be wrong in law, in which case the statute— as interpreted by a court—prevails. See *R v Wandsworth BC ex parte Beckwith* (1996), discussed below.)

Understanding the statutory powers and duties

Warning: you are about to enter difficult territory. Why?

- There are many different types of vulnerable people needing support within the community or residential care.

- You may owe different types of duty depending on the service user's needs.

- You will find descriptions of the types of service users, the range of needs, and the powers and duties you must exercise in different pieces of legislation, regulations, and circulars.

- Courts interpret your powers and duties in ways that may be hard to comprehend.

Let us take an example of the last problem. The question was whether a social services department could reduce care to a service user, Mr Barry, on the ground that the authority could not afford to maintain the high level of care previously provided. Mr Barry's challenge to the decision was finally decided in the House of Lords in *R v Gloucestershire County Council ex parte Barry* (1997). Here is an extract from the judgment of Lord Nicholson:

> [N]either the fact that the section imposes the duty towards the individual, with the corresponding right in the individual to the enforcement of the duty, nor the fact that consideration of resources is not relevant to the question of whether the duty is to be performed or not, means that a consideration of resources may not be relevant to the earlier stages of the implementation of the section which lead up to the stage when satisfaction is achieved.

This is actually an important part of the judgment. But what does it mean? We think that Lord Nicholson is saying that:

(a) statute requires the council to make provision for Mr Barry;

(b) Mr Barry is entitled to ask the court to force the council to carry out its duty;

(c) the council cannot plead poverty as a way out of the duty; but

(d) the council's resources can be relevant in assessing what it can actually be required to do for Mr Barry.

If this excerpt from a leading case is anything to go by, it is not going to be easy to find a pathway through the legal maze in this field. A good entry point for a local authority social worker is to ask: 'What statutory duties and powers do I have?'. Refer to Box 15.1 for the full list, but, according to NHSCCA 1990, s. 46(3), the powers and responsibilities can be summarized as providing, paying for, or arranging:

(a) residential accommodation for the old, infirm, disabled, or destitute;

(b) care services and employment facilities for the disabled;

(c) care services following discharge from mental hospital;

(d) welfare services for the old; and

(e) services for mothers of young children.

Assessment of need

Assessment of need at community level

There are two levels at which a social services department must assess need: for the whole community, and for the individual. We will start with the former.

NHSCCA, s. 46, requires every social services department, in consultation with the District Health Authority (i.e. hospital services), Family Health Services Authority, voluntary groups, housing departments, housing associations, and any other appropriate organizations, every year to publish its plan for community care in its area.

The Government's intention, according to government statements when the Bill was debated in Parliament, was that authorities must devise services that meet the needs of the population, rather than develop services and see who wants them. Even if only a small number of people in the area have a particular need for a particular service it should be in the plan. Flexibility in meeting the various needs can then be obtained by using a range of service providers, with the department in the coordinating seat.

Assessing the need of the individual service user—statutory framework and guidance

NHSCCA, s. 47 sets out the statutory duties governing assessments and plans for the individual. This is worth quoting in full (with added emphasis):

(1) Subject to subsections (5) and (6) below [not quoted—they allow you to meet needs without an assessment in order to deal with an emergency], where it appears to a local authority that any person for whom they may provide or arrange for the provision of community care services may be in need of any such services, the authority—

(a) *shall* carry out an assessment of his needs for those services; and

(b) having regard to the results of that assessment, *shall* then *decide* whether his needs call for the provision by them of any such services.

The social services department—with assistance from other bodies—must in fact, under NHSCCA s. 46, assess the needs of all vulnerable people in the area. And it is clear from the wording of s. 47 that an individual does not have to ask for help; the local authority has to carry out an assessment of anyone who might be eligible for community care services. The community care plan should already have identified, in broad terms, the numbers and needs of people who might need the services. Section 47(3) requires you, when assessing an individual, to notify the health authority or housing authority if you think that that agency may need to provide services. And s. 47(6) requires you, in urgent cases, to provide services first and to complete the assessment second—common sense to any social worker.

Section 47 goes on to make special provision for an automatic assessment of needs of any persons who are disabled (as defined in the NAA—see below):

(2) If at any time during the assessment of the needs of any person under subsection (1)(a) above it appears to a local authority that he is a disabled person, the authority—

(a) shall proceed to make such a decision as to the services he requires as is mentioned in section 4 of the Disabled Persons (Services, Consultation and Representation) Act 1986 without his requesting them to do so under that section; and

(b) shall inform him that they will be doing so and of his rights under that section.

The reference in s. 47(2) to s. 4 of the DPSCRA is the beginning of a legislative paper chase and illustrates some of the complexities of community care legislation. If you turn to s.4 of the DPSCRA that section refers you on to CSDPA, s. 2; that in turn asks you to refer to National Assistance Act 1948 (NAA), s. 29. These three sections of the three Acts mean, in outline, that certain individuals who are defined as disabled are *entitled* to have certain needs met, once the assessment shows those needs to exist. (The particular services a disabled person is entitled to receive, if he or she is assessed as needing these, are set out in CSDPA, s. 2(1), and LAC (93) 10 (see below).) But only the disabled are entitled to be informed of this right before their needs are assessed. Is that clear? If not, rather than blame us, please blame the legislators who missed the opportunity to clarify the statutes.

The assessment should be carried out by specialist staff, not by the service providers. And the approach should be needs driven, not defined by what is actually available. Government guidance on assessment is contained in circular LAC (2002)13, *Fair Access to Care Services*. The assessor is charged, under this guidance, with one overarching task:

councils should operate just one eligibility decision for all adults seeking social care support—namely, should people be helped or not?

The Department of Health's *Policy Guidance*, at paragraph 3.24, refines this guidance by stating that 'service provision should, as far as possible, preserve or restore normal living'. The order of priorities in helping any individual will be:

(a) support so that the client can live at home;

(b) a move to more suitable accommodation;

(c) a move to another household;

(d) a move to residential care;

(e) a move to a nursing home; and

(f) long-stay hospital care.

Circular LAC (92)12, *Housing and Community Care* (still current) requires the assessment to focus on the difficulties an individual is facing, and to take into account the following:

(a) capacity/incapacity;

(b) preferences and aspirations;

(c) the living situation;

(d) support from relatives and friends; and

(e) other sources of help.

   Each council should establish its eligibility criteria; the circular accepts that these will vary from one council to another, and that the council's resources have to be taken into account in setting them. The assessment should look in particular at the autonomy of the service user, issues of health and safety, the ability to manage daily routines, their family life and ability to engage with their community. The individual's need for services should be categorized as being in one of four bands: critical, substantial, moderate, or low. (But it is for the council then to determine whether the service must be provided—some councils will provide some services when the need is substantial, others only when it is critical. The circular permits this approach.)

National Service Frameworks and assessment

The Department of Health has published frameworks in a number of areas. These cover both assessment and delivery. Those of particular interest cover services for older persons (LAC (2001)12) and services relating to mental health problems (HSC99/223). The older people framework, for example, requires the assessment to be from the user's perspective, taking into account the clinical background, disease prevention, personal care and physical well-being, senses, mental health, relationships, safety, and environment. The web page for accessing all NSF's is **www.nhsia.nhs.uk/nsf/pages/default.asp**.

Case law on assessment of need

A department is obliged to *assess* the needs and the court can order you to carry out an assessment if you have not complied (*R v Sutton LBC ex parte Tucker* (1996)). It must assess those needs even if it already knows that it cannot afford to meet them (*R v Bristol City Council ex parte Penfold* (1998)). An inadequate assessment can be struck down by a court on judicial review. In *R v Birmingham City Council ex parte Killigrew* (2000), the council had reassessed the service user as needing only six hours' daily care for her physical needs, where previously she required twelve. There was, it was held, no basis at all for this reduction. The reassessment was carried out without even looking at medical reports or consulting the service user's GP. An assessment must be carried out in full: in *R (on the application of HP) v Islington LBC* (2004) the Council had lawfully decided on the basis of psychiatric evidence that HP did not qualify for specialist community mental health services, but it was not entitled to refuse an assessment of his other needs. Failure to assess cannot, of course, be used as an excuse not to make appropriate provision: *R (on the application of AA) v Lambeth LBC* (2001) 741.

R (on the application of Goldsmith) v Wandsworth London Borough (2004) illuminates the interesting boundary between NHS care and community care, discussed below, but for our purposes it is an excellent illustration of the principle that an assessment must be properly carried out, which means according to statute and guidance, involving the service user and any carers. See Box 16.2 for the detail.

 BOX 16.2 *R (on the application of Goldsmith) v Wandsworth London Borough* **(2004)**

An elderly widow broke her hip and was admitted to hospital. The local authority, who were providing residential accommodation, decided that she now needed nursing care. They wanted therefore to move her out of the care home into an NHS nursing home. They had tried to close the home previously, but this woman's legal challenge had already thwarted that. The claimant asked for clarification: what needs did she have which could no longer be met in the care home? So the local authority commissioned a consultant geriatrician to provide a report, and this supported their view that she needed nursing care which could not be provided in a residential home. So the claimant went for judicial review of the decision to transfer her. (Actually they could not force her to move into a nursing home against her will, but she needed a court declaration to benefit from the local authority funded accommodation.)

The Health and Social Care Act 2001, as we see when we discuss the relationship between the NHS and the local authority, provides that a local authority cannot itself provide nursing care; the NHS must make this provision for those in residential care. But this does not mean that any requirement for nursing care means a person cannot remain in a residential home. Even the healthiest person needs medical attention from time to time. But what grounds did she have for a challenge? First, statutory guidance requires the provision of nursing care to be seen as a last resort (see above). Second, assessment requires consultation with carers—but the claimant's daughter had been barred from the meeting where the needs were discussed, and not been permitted any involvement in the assessment by the geriatrician. Third, it turned out that the information on which the geriatrician had been instructed was factually inaccurate—for example he was wrongly told that the claimant could not manage her own toilet needs and was incontinent. Fourth, the local authority had not kept proper minutes of the relevant meetings. Fifth, the consultant geriatrician appeared biased, since he was instructed merely to *confirm* that—not assess whether—the residential home was no longer able to meet the claimant's needs.

The issues are not just technical points. As Wall LJ noted at para. 91: 'These are not academic considerations. It is not in dispute that a change to a strange environment for a person of the Appellant's frailty could have serious if not fatal consequences. The proportionality of the response is, therefore, of the utmost importance. In my judgment it is not good enough for Wandsworth, after the institution of proceedings, to produce evidence that this was a factor in its mind when it made the decision (whenever that was). In my judgment, the court has to look at the decision at the time it was made and at the manner in which it was communicated to the person or persons affected by it. And in that process, I find a complete absence of any suggestion that Wandsworth had addressed the Appellant's Article 8 [respect for private life] rights.'

The case is an object lesson in how assessments and decisions should not be made. The decision was quashed, and the local authority have to make the decision again. It is still possible that they can lawfully reach the same conclusion as before, but they must comply with the statutory guidelines and demonstrate that the relevant issues have been considered by the relevant people.

R (on the application of J) v Newham LBC (2001) confirms assessments must not be delayed. Here the court suggested thirty-five days would be too much delay.

Assessment of the carer

A press release from Help the Aged dated 24 October 2001 states: 'more than a million older carers are having to look after the sick without adequate support from health, social services or homecare agencies'. In attempting to tackle this issue the CRSA was strengthened by the CDCA in 2000. The authority must not only assess the needs of the person who is being cared for; it must assess the ability of any persons aged over 16 caring for that person. This assessment must be realistic and not turn a blind eye to the burden carers take on. The intention of the two Acts taken together is to ensure that the silent army of voluntary carers—including young children looking after sick parents—is monitored by the authority, and their efforts supplemented by care services to both service users; that is, the carer and the person being cared for. The right of the carer to their own life, particularly education and leisure opportunities, must also be considered in the assessment. Where this was good practice before, it is now a statutory requirement—when in force—as a result of the Carers (Equal Opportunities) Act 2004. It is a statutory requirement to ask: what would the carer do if they did not have these caring responsibilities? What services will free up the carer to continue to have a reasonable caring/personal life balance?

The approach to working with the carer is summed up in government guidance in a 2004 circular—see Box 16.3.

Assessment of the service user's means

Government guidance makes it clear that the individual service user's needs are to be assessed, and decisions made on how to address those needs, before looking at whether that service user can be called on to pay for or contribute towards any services. If the need is established it should be met. So far this is reasonably clear, but read in the context of LAC (92)12, a Department of Health Circular, it is a little less clear: 'An authority may take into account the resources available when deciding how to respond

BOX 16.3 *The Community Care Assessment Directions* 2004 LAC (2004) 24

2.1 The Community Care Assessment Directions do not change the requirements of best practice or the guidance available at www.carers.gov.uk/carersdisabledchildact2000.htm or **www.dh.gov.uk/PolicyAndGuidance/HealthAndSocialCareTopics/SocialCare/Single AssessmentProcess/fs/en.** The Directions, however, ensure that this existing practice and guidance on conducting care assessments and care planning is placed within a legal framework. For example when assessing older people the requirements of the Single Assessment Process and the National Service Framework should be observed and where necessary joint assessments involving health partners should be completed. Assessments for all adults with complex needs should take account of physical, cognitive, behavioural and social participation needs.

2.2 Full involvement of individuals and their carers in both assessment and care planning has long been recognized as good practice and the importance of doing so has been highlighted in previous guidance. Carers are entitled, under the Carers and Disabled Children Act 2000, to request an assessment of their needs in supporting the person they care for. It is, in any case, good practice that an assessment is offered to a carer who is going to be involved in providing part of the care package. The involvement of the carer in the assessment and care planning process ensures there is a realistic account taken of the care a carer is able to provide and that the caring relationship is sustainable. A carer's refusal of the offer of an assessment should not be used as a reason to exclude the carer from assisting with care planning.

2.3 There will be cases where the person whose care is being planned lacks the capacity to consent to the involvement of carers, or to the care plan itself. In these situations best practice suggests that the carers should be involved as much as possible, currently local authorities have a responsibility to make decisions in the best interests of the person being cared for.

2.4 If disagreements occur between the person and their carer these should be handled sensitively, safeguarding the best interests of the individual and the carer. In many cases it may be appropriate for a resolution to be sought through independent or statutory advocacy.

2.5 If it is felt to be inappropriate to involve the carer local authorities should retain a written account of why it was felt inappropriate. This should show that the carer's involvement has been actively considered and, if excluded from care planning, the reasons why. It is not enough to state that the reasons were considered, without recording those reasons.

2.6 Local authorities should continue to ensure that up to date and appropriate information on the range of support, entitlements and assistance available for carers is accessible in a variety of formats. This information should be offered to all carers, irrespective of whether the carer receives an assessment.

to an individual's assessment.' This potentially allows the assessor to say that a need does not exist because the service user can pay to eliminate it.

Meeting the needs once assessed

Carrying out an assessment cannot be avoided as it is required under NHSCCA, s. 47. However, the extent to which the needs must be met will depend on whether the authority has a *power* or a *duty* to meet that need. If there is a power, then the authority has a discretion. If the discretion is exercised reasonably (taking into account relevant factors, ignoring irrelevant factors) the decision should be beyond challenge, unless human rights are breached, government direction is ignored, or the proposed provision does address the assessed need. But where there is a statutory obligation to meet assessed needs, there is no discretion and the need must be met (at least until the need can be reassessed): see *R v Kensington and Chelsea Royal London Borough, ex parte Kujtim* (1999), a case relating to residential accommodation.

So the next topic is to identify the services that can, and those that must, be provided to the service user following the assessment.

We will be looking in some detail at the legislation and guidance. Before you get bogged down in that detail, however, we offer an overview of the main service user groups covered by community care, and the legislation (in brackets) which governs what is or can be provided.

- Support services for those who have a *physical or mental handicap* (NAA).
- Support services for *old people* (HSPHA).
- Support services for *expectant and nursing mothers* (NHSA).
- Services for prevention of illness and after-care of *those who have been suffering from illness* (particularly relevant for mental illness and drug or alcohol dependency) (NHSA and MHA).
- *Home help and laundry services for those who need them* (NHSA).
- *Accommodation* for people who need it because of *age, illness, disability, or other circumstances* (NAA).
- Although not specified in s. 46, it may be convenient to add to the list the needs of *any carer aged 16 or more* (CDCA).

You can see that community care is defined both by the type of person who may need a service, and by the type of service provided. Looking at the user not the service makes sense, and it is perhaps a shame the legislation is not framed clearly in this manner. This approach is reinforced by the development of National Service Frameworks, which we have already referred to, and which look at the user as the focus for assessment and delivery of services (so far, frameworks exist for the elderly and those with mental health needs).

Not every vulnerable person is covered by this list. In particular, the needs of children as a group—except indirectly by providing services for the mothers of the under-fives and directly for carers over 16—are not to be met under community care legislation, but under the Children Act (see Part 3 of the book). However, there is an overlap for carers under 16, as they are automatically classed as children in need under s. 17 of the Children Act 1989 and entitled to support from social services in that capacity.

Health and safety issues involved in meeting need

If there is a statutory duty to provide a certain level of assessed need, difficulties with health and safety are just like difficulties with finance: they cannot provide an excuse for the authority not to meet that assessed need, though they may affect what it is reasonable to provide. In *R (on the application of A and B, X and Y) v East Sussex County Council* (2003) the Council, rightly concerned for the health of its employees, imposed a blanket ban on manual lifting of service users. Unfortunately this resulted in the applicants not receiving the community care to which they claimed they were entitled. There are detailed guidelines on manual lifting set out in the *Manual Handling Operations* of 1992, but the court held that these did not prohibit manual handling of people, nor operate a cut off above which they would be too heavy to lift manually. The problem of lifting an overweight person must be solved not ignored. Failure to provide lifting services was in fact a potential breach of the right not to be subject to inhuman or degrading treatment (Article 2); it could leave a service user stuck in a bath or on a lavatory, or suffering from bedsores—and though the carers' rights to a safe working environment must be respected, that requires safe work practices to be devised, not blanket bans which restrict required levels of service.

Responsibilities of other agencies in meeting need

In reaching an assessment the local authority can expect other public authorities (eg housing or health authorities) to meet reasonable requests to provide appropriate services. Where this was previously an implicit obligation, it is now statutory: Carers (Equal Opportunities) Act 2004. But we will examine in a bit more detail the issues arising with the two principal partners, the NHS and the housing authorities.

Overlap with NHS in meeting need

The National Service Framework talks in slightly fuzzy terms about 'the social care community'. Who is this nebulous and benign group of people? Essentially those with the statutory duties are the social services department and the NHS, supported of course by statutory agencies (e.g. housing departments) and non-statutory agencies (providers of residential facilities and charitable organisations). The government department responsible for social service provision is the Department of Health. The NHS is a direct government responsibility, whereas community care is provided by an elected authority which raises much of its funding and allocates according to local as well as national priorities.

The care needs of an individual do not necessarily fall neatly into the category of social care or health care. Who provides? Who pays?

The NHS is charged, under the NHSA, s. 1(1), with providing a 'comprehensive health service designed to secure improvement . . . in the physical and mental health of the people . . . and in the prevention, diagnosis, and treatment of illness'. Specific duties include medical, dental, nursing, and ambulance services, care for mothers and children, and preventive care, and after-care services for ill people and, of course, provision of hospitals. Health and local authorities are also under a statutory duty to cooperate to advance health and welfare (NHSA, s. 22) and to provide after-care for released mental patients (MHA, s. 117).

As you will see below, NHSA, Schedule 8, gives local authorities a wide range of powers in relation to mothers and young children, prevention of illness, care, and after-care. These are services where the health service also has statutory duties. Then there are issues around the discharge of the old or infirm from hospital into residential care: who is responsible? Circular 99 (30) is designed to ensure that the NHS does not abdicate responsibility for long-term health-care need. No patient must be allowed to fall into the gap between social services and NHS services.

The Community Care (Delayed Discharges) Act 2003 was introduced to force local authorities to make as quickly as possible the necessary arrangements for community care so that a person can be discharged from hospital. Circular LAC 2003(21), also entitled *The Community Care (Delayed Discharges) Act 2003*, points out that 'Delayed discharges are people, often frail older people whose future care is uncertain. Hospital is not the ideal place to be while waiting for arrangements for care to be put into place.' During the parliamentary debates on the bill, the government estimated that over 5,000 NHS beds were being blocked because of these avoidable delays (Hansard vol 39 col 501). The Act—adopting methods used in Scandinavia—requires health authorities to notify social services of anyone likely to need community care in order to be safely discharged from hospital, and for the NHS and the local authority jointly to assess the need, together with any carer. Failure to put any services in place which results in the patient's discharge being delayed can result in the NHS passing the bill to social services—an incentive to cooperate, but of course an incentive to give priority to discharged patients at the expense of other service users.

There is not space here to set out the detailed provisions governing financial arrangements between health and social services authorities. Three circulars—LAC (95)5, *NHS Responsibilities for Meeting Continuing Health Care Needs*, HSG(95)45, *Arrangements between Health Authorities and NHS Trusts*, and LAC 99(30) (see below)— are useful, if for no other purpose than to ensure that there is no 'buck passing'. Additionally you should note that under the HSCA the NHS must provide any element of care to service users, whether they are in NHS care or community care, if it involves nursing services—that is not a social services responsibility. This is a helpful dividing line.

The main problems seem to arise when a service user falls into the gap between the NHS and the local authority, and a disagreement occurs over who pays. And there has indeed been litigation on this. *R v North and East Devon Health Authority ex parte Coughlan* (2001) involved a case where the NHS had been providing long-term care— indeed it had promised life-time care—to the victim of a road accident. But the

Department of Health required NHS authorities to review their eligibility criteria, and to distinguish between care which required specialist care and that which required generalist care. As a result the applicant, and other residents of the home, were told the home would be sold and they would have to go into community care. We will see that this is not only disruptive: NHS care is free and National Assistance Act residential care is means-tested. She brought proceedings for judicial review to prevent closure of the home she was in and reneging on the promise. The Divisional Court and the Court of Appeal held that the Secretary of State was wrong in drawing up clear distinctions between specialist and general care, and that the real question was whether a person's needs were primarily for health care or primarily for social services. This patient's needs were essentially health needs. In this case therefore the NHS ended up having to pay, though the Court of Appeal accepted that there could be 'no precise legal line drawn between those nursing services which are and those which are not capable of being treated as included in a [social services] package of care'.

Not surprisingly, given the difficulty in drawing boundaries, in *R (on the application of Collins) v Lincolnshire Health Authority* (2001) the result was the opposite. The applicant was 35 year of age and had severe learning difficulties. The Health Authority thought she would benefit from greater independence and that she should be discharged from hospital, even though she had been accommodated since 1986 in an NHS specialist unit. The judge accepted that the kind of care she needed was better provided within a community setting and that the NHS was not liable to continue to accommodate her, since her needs were not of a medical nature.

Such challenges are inevitable because of the difficulty in drawing the dividing line between health and social care needs. But the more important issue is, perhaps, joint planning. The HA, ss. 28–31, requires local authorities (not explicitly their social services departments) to cooperate with local health authorities to set up local Health Improvement Programmes. The Act permits—indeed encourages—a pooling of resources to achieve common aims, so the care services can be either jointly funded or jointly provided or provided by one service and funded by the other. Statutory duties are not changed. For example, if the NHS pays for and provides after-care services for the patient discharged from a mental hospital, it still remains a social services duty under MHA, s. 117, to ensure that such services are provided. Further guidance on these partnership arrangements may be found in *Implementation of Health Act Partnership Arrangements*, LAC (2000) 9.

Non-residential community care

Community care covers services which can be provided to a person living at home and also residential accommodation. In carrying out assessments of the needs of individuals, you have to be able to consider all possible outcomes together—if remaining in the community with support is not possible, is residential accommodation appropriate? However, the statutory criteria for offering a person accommodation are different from those that dictate who is eligible to receive services at home or in non-residential centres. For convenience we will take each in turn, starting with non-residential care services.

Identifying the service users for non-residential care

The next task is to define who is entitled to receive particular services. Most groups to whom a social services department owes a responsibility are easily identified—the elderly, children, mothers of young children, for example. But one group is defined in statute as 'disabled', and you will need to know the definition. The NAA, s. 29, which we have broken down into a list, refers to persons aged 18 or over who as a result of disability are one of the following:

- blind;
- deaf;
- dumb;
- suffering from a mental disorder;
- substantially and permanently handicapped by illness, injury, or congenital deformity.

Therefore, under the heading of 'the disabled', the statute is aiming to identify people who have some kind of mental or physical disability. Circular DoH (93)10, *Approvals and Directions for Arrangements from 1 April 1993 made under Schedule 8 to The National Health Service Act 1977 and ss. 21 and 29 of The National Assistance Act 1948*, gives guidance on what exactly is meant by words like 'handicapped' and 'deaf'. You will need a copy of this circular if you work with disabled clients. Old age is not, on its own, a sufficient criterion mentioned in s. 29: you have duties to any adult who falls within s. 29, whatever their age, but you do have special duties to the old (but under a different statute, as we shall see) just because of their age.

It will perhaps be clearest if we to approach the statutory definition of services which can, or must, be made available from two perspectives: first, a strategic approach, not aimed at any single service user, is the setting up of schemes for provision (broadly a managerial decision); and second, the provision of services after an assessment of an individual service user (more an individual social worker's or team decision).

Schemes for non-residential care

The schemes that can be set up are not described in detail in the legislation or the circulars, so each authority can arrange them to the extent that their will matches their resources. The schemes that all authorities either must have in place, or may choose to put in place, are identified in Box 16.4.

Non-residential care services to individuals

Limitations on money, staff, and expertise mean that not every possible welfare need of vulnerable individuals can be met—even if the individual falls within one of the statutory criteria and a scheme has been set up to provide the relevant service. As we

BOX 16.4 Schemes for providing non-residential care

Compulsory schemes

Disabled persons under NAA, s. 29

general social work support and advice, in the home or elsewhere (DHSS Circular
   LAC (93)10)
facilities for rehabilitation and adjustment (DHSS Circular LAC (93)10)
facilities for occupational, cultural and recreational activities (DoH Circular LAC (93) 10)
keep a register of such service users (DoH Circular LAC (93) 10)

*The elderly, the ill, expectant mothers, those handicapped by illness or congenital deformity,
   persons suffering from or at risk of suffering from mental disorder*

home help on an adequate scale (NHSA, Sch. 8)
centres for training or occupation (DoH Circular LAC (93) 10)
social work support (DoH Circular LAC (93) 10)
appointment of approved social workers (DoH Circular LAC (93) 10)
Appointment of suitable staff to deal with assessment and mental health guardianship
   (DoH Circular LAC (93) 10)

Drug or alcohol abusers

(Only if the Department receives a government grant) payments to voluntary organizations to
   provide residential and non-residential facilities (Local Authority Social Services Act 1970,
   s. 7E(b) and Payments to Voluntary Organizations (Alcohol or Drug Misusers) Directions
   1990)

Discretionary schemes

Disabled persons under NAA s. 29

providing information about services available (NAA, s. 29)
giving instructions on overcoming problems (NAA, s. 29)
recreational facilities (NAA, s. 29)
holiday homes (DoH Circular LAC (93) 10)
travel subsidies (DoH Circular LAC (93) 10)
help with finding accommodation (DoH Circular (93) 10)
contributing to the cost of wardens in assisted housing schemes (DoH Circular (93) 10)

The handicapped or disabled

sheltered employment or training facilities and hostel accommodation for those whose
   handicap or disability makes them unlikely to obtain work (DPEA, s. 3(1) and NAA, s. 29)

The elderly

wardens (or part of the cost of wardens) (HSPHA, s. 45)
meals on wheels and recreational schemes (HSPHA, s. 45 DHSS Circular 19/71)
laundry facilities (NHSA, Sch. 8)

For parents and children

schemes for the care of expectant mothers and the under fives who are not at state school
   (NHSA, Sch. 8)

The physically ill or mentally disordered (including those at risk)

training, recreational, and occupation facilities, including day centre, meals, social work
   support, respite care, and night-sitting, for prevention, care, and after-care of the ill (NHSA,
   Sch. 8 and DoH Circular LAC (93) 10)
laundry facilities (NHSA, Sch. 8)
residential accommodation for expectant and nursing mothers (DoH Circular LAC (93) 10)

shall see, even where you have not just a discretion but a duty to provide the service to
an individual, you have to do so only if the department first decides as a result of the
assessment that the individual needs that service and (although there are conflicting
court decisions on this) that it is reasonable to meet it from within the department's
available resources.

   If you are deciding what services to offer, you must take into account the ability of any
person who is currently caring for the person to make the necessary provision (C(RS)A).
This should mean more than saying 'Oh good, I see your daughter-in-law can look after
you, so we don't need to bother'. It means assessing how to meet the needs in partnership, without exploitation. (See more on assessment above, and on working with the
carer below.)

   Box 16.5 sets out the services that must be provided to individuals and then the
services which may be offered in the department's discretion. (In both cases we are
talking about responsibilities to service users who normally live within your local
authority's boundaries; if there is a dispute as to where the person is ordinarily
resident, the decision of the Secretary of State is final—NAA, s. 32(3). Guidance is
available in Circular LAC (93)7.) All services which are set out in Box 16.5 can be
bought in rather than provided by the authority, or purchased by the service user out of
funds provided. (We discuss direct payments later.) In the authority's community care
plan there must be a statement of its plans to purchase services from the independent
sector.

Challenges to local authority decisions on non-residential care

We look at the power of courts to review local authority decisions at this point in
relation to non-residential services. The principles will be the same for the provision of
accommodation, but perhaps looking at some case law on both occasions will provide a
small amount of human interest as you plough through this chapter.

   Let us start, by way of a break, with a trip to the picture house. You may recall from
chapter 5 that there is a process called judicial review. This is where the High Court is
asked to rectify decisions of public authorities when such authorities are behaving
irrationally. In the landmark case of *Associated Provincial Picture Houses v Wednesbury
Corporation* (1948), Lord Greene stated:

> The court is entitled to investigate the action of the local authority with a view to seeing
> whether they have taken into account matters which they ought not to take into account; or
> conversely, have refused to take into account matters which they ought to take into account

BOX 16.5 Services to individual service users following assessment of need

These services *must* be provided if the service user is assessed as needing them

Disabled service users (CSDPA, s. 2)

practical assistance in the home (no further guidance is given on this, so you are left with a discretion to weigh up what should be provided; it will cover home visits)

providing or helping to obtain radio, television, library, or similar recreational facilities

providing, or assisting the person to take advantage of, lectures, games, outings, or other recreational facilities outside the home

providing travel or assisting with travel arrangements for the purpose of obtaining the services you provide

providing or helping with adaptations or special facilities in the home, for the purpose of greater comfort or safety. (DHSS Circular LASSL 20/73 gives guidance on such aids for the disabled, such as telephones, page turners, special locks, the costs of which can be recovered from the DSS)

providing or helping a person to obtain a holiday

providing meals, whether at home or elsewhere

providing a telephone, and if necessary any special equipment to enable a person to use it (such as voice amplification for the deaf)

Disabled clients, the mentally disordered, and physically ill

home help and laundry facilities if the person needs them because of the illness or handicap (NHSA, Sch. 8)

The elderly

home help and laundry if needed because of age (NHSA, Sch. 8)

Any person in hospital or local authority residential care

protection of property and possessions while away from home (NAA, ss. 43–45). (This requires liaison with the hospital and the managers of the residential homes)

These services may be provided if the service user is assessed as needing them

Service users who are registered disabled

the person must be registered as disabled with the Department of Employment, and be unlikely to obtain employment for a considerable time because of the disability or handicap; you can then offer sheltered employment, training, and assistance in finding work (DPEA, s. 3(1))

The elderly

meals and recreation, in the home or elsewhere (HSPHA, s. 45 and DHSS Circular 19/71). (District councils can also provide this service in county areas, HASSASSA, Sch. 9)

practical assistance in the home to improve safety, comfort, or convenience (HSPHA, s. 45 and DHSS Circular 19/71)

helping find suitable accommodation (HSPHA, s. 45 and DHSS Circular 19/71)

. . . once that question is answered in favour of the local authority, it may still be possible to say that, although the local authority have kept within the four corners of the matters they ought to consider, they have nevertheless come to a conclusion so unreasonable that no reasonable authority could ever have come to it. In such a case . . . I think the court can interfere.

Unfortunately, but inevitably, the law is imprecise, and great discretion rests with the individual social worker or the department. The exercise of that discretion can only be successfully challenged in a court if one of the following can be shown:

- that you acted so irrationally in making your decision, for example by failing even to consider a request, that no reasonable person/department would have acted in that way;

- that in the exercise of your discretion you abused the human rights of the service user.

The courts prefer an aggrieved individual to use the complaints procedure established under LASSA, s. 7, and not to use the courts. Lord Denning, for example, went so far as to say that it was better to rely on the Secretary of State to use default powers to take over local authority services than for courts to order the local authority what to do. So he refused judicial review for the woman who thought she should have more home help because of her incapacity (*Wyatt v London Borough of Hillingdon* (1978)). This is an old decision, and it has clearly not blocked courts from considering requests for judicial review. But it is difficult to show that the opportunity to make an internal complaint was inadequate redress. A further hurdle is that the applicant must prove an authority's decision is not just wrong but, effectively, bizarre. Notwithstanding these difficulties in challenging the way in which decisions are made, there is a lot of litigation in this area, of which we will give you a flavour only. (Extracts from some cases can also be read in Brayne and Broadbent, chapter 1.)

An example of a successful challenge was *R v Ealing London Borough Council ex parte Leaman* (1984). A service that must be provided, if the service user is assessed as needing it, is to make holiday arrangements for a disabled client (see Box 15.3 above). The local authority refused the request outright because the service user had already made the arrangements privately. The court ruled that it acted unlawfully: had it decided, following an assessment, that she did not need a holiday at all, or arguably that she could afford the arrangements herself, the result would probably have been different.

The normal principle, however, is that courts are reluctant to intervene. The male client who was upset about having his carer withdrawn and replaced with a younger, female carer failed in his challenge (*R v Essex County Council ex parte Bucke* (1996)). The court held that the local authority must be able to decide without judicial interference how to provide the care the service user needs. Similarly, the disabled service user who had initially been promised a stairlift could not show that the council behaved unreasonably when it took the cheaper option of transferring the applicant to a ground-floor flat (*R v Kirklees MBC ex parte Daykin* (1997)).

Another avenue for the dissatisfied service user could be to sue the social service department for compensation for its failure to provide a proper service. Although set in a different context, the case of *Phelps v Hillingdon LBC* (1997) suggests that local authorities do owe duties in the law of tort to their clients which can be pursued in a court. (The most important part of tort law is negligence, which enables a person to sue another person or organization whose negligence has caused them harm.) The claimant in this case was dyslexic and had had a poor education. She succeeded in persuading the court that an education authority which failed to diagnose her dyslexia had been negligent. Could this principle work in the field of mental health? *Clunis v Camden and Islington Health Authority* (1997) suggests that professionals may be protected from liability, although the case was decided on its particular facts and before the advent of the Human Rights Act. Mr Clunis had a mental disorder which needed treatment which the health authority should have provided. In his untreated state he attacked and killed a stranger. His case for compensation was eventually struck out by the Court of Appeal, but solely on the ground that it was against public policy; Mr Clunis should not get compensation for committing a criminal act, even though he wanted to use the money to pay the victim's widow. But could the widow herself have sued? Although the Court did not have to decide this issue, it did state its opinion that s. 117 of the MHA (duty to provide after-care for patients released from mental hospitals) did not, in its view, create a right to sue for breach of statutory duty.

The law is still developing in this area and, in relation to children suffering from abuse which the local authority should have prevented, *Z and others v United Kingdom* (2001) (discussed in chapter 2) human rights principles mean that a victim of social work negligence does have the right to sue. And a health authority has been found liable to a patient whose suicide attempt left her disabled. The authority had not properly assessed and treated the patient for her suicidal tendency: *Drake v Pontefract Health Authority* (1998).

Under NHSCCA, a local authority must have a well-publicized complaints procedure. Also, in theory, the Secretary of State can order the authority to carry out a particular duty, which might have solved the problem of Mrs Wyatt and her home help. This power is relatively recent, and we not discovered any occasions when it has been exercised.

Working with the family to provide non-residential care

How does the local authority assess what contribution to non-residential services a carer—friend or relative, it does not matter—can make? A carer is someone who 'provides or intends to provide a substantial amount of care on a regular basis' (CRSA, s. 1) and can be anyone aged 16 upwards (CDCA, s. 1).

When making an assessment of a client's needs under NHSCCA, s. 47, you must listen to the carer's views and consider the role that he or she can play. You must assess the carer's needs for services as well as those of the vulnerable person (CDCA, s. 1). You can then plan, for example, to supplement the carer's support, or to take over while he or she has a break. Your authority can make direct payments to the carer, or provide vouchers for a short-term break (CDCA, ss. 2 and 3).

Direct payments to service users to purchase services

The CCDPA 1996, together with the HSCA 2001, s.57, and Community Care, Services for Carers and Children's Services (Direct Payments) (England) Regulations 2003, enables local authorities to pay all (or, subject to means, part) of the cost of buying community care services direct to a disabled individual or his or her spouse, cohabitee, or a relative living with the individual. This ability to provide cash does not cover residential accommodation unless for a period of less than four weeks—for example for respite care.

The philosophy is set out in the government guidance:

> Day-to-day control of the money and care package passes to the person who has the strongest incentive to ensure that it is spent properly on the necessary services, and who is best placed to judge how to match available resources to needs. When setting up a direct payments scheme, local authorities should consider how to include people with different kinds of impairment, people from different ethnic backgrounds and people of different ages. They should think imaginatively about the provision of direct payments for both intensive packages and lower level services, about long and short term provision and about how direct payments can be assimilated into preventive and rehabilitative strategies. The Government wants to see more extensive use made of direct payments (*Community Care (Direct Payments) Act 1996 Policy and Practice Guidance*, Introduction, paragraph 2).

A user-friendly guide to the scheme is available at **www.doh.gov.uk/directp.htm** and an audio-tape version can be obtained from the DoH at the address provided.

The Act does not compel an individual to accept money instead of services, nor does it compel the authority to make direct payments on every request. In fact direct payments cannot be used where the service user is in guardianship under the MHA (see chapter 17) or where the provision of the service is under a criminal court order such as a community rehabilitation order. Each service user's needs must be considered on his or her merits, but under the HSCA, s. 57, and regulations the authority must make a direct payment if the service user is assessed as needing a community care or carer service, consents to a direct payment, and is able to manage the direct payment either alone or with the assistance of another person (which can include an independent user trust set up specifically to handle the payments: *R (on the application of A and B, X and Y) v East Sussex County Council* (2003).

The guidance suggests there can be a mix of direct provision and direct payment. The local authority can also provide direct payments through vouchers rather than cash: *Carers and Disabled Children (Vouchers) (England) Regulations 2003*.

Residential care for the vulnerable

Part III and other accommodation

We are going to talk mainly about NAA Part III accommodation, which means it is provided under that part of the NAA (s. 21 of the NAA in fact, which is within Part III of the Act). To satisfy s. 21 it must be shown that the service user cannot cope if the accommodation is not supplied.

But, first, there are two statutory powers to provide residential accommodation which fall outside s. 21 where the requirement that the service user cannot cope does not arise, and which we list briefly.

1. Disabled service users under NAA, s. 29

In addition to all the non-residential support work you can offer, social services can provide hostel accommodation to enable people to take up, or train for, employment; and residential holiday facilities (NAA, s. 29 and DPEA, s. 3(1)).

2. Mentally disordered or physically ill service users

The department can provide residential accommodation for the prevention of illness, and the care and after-care of the ill (NHSA, Sch. 8; DoH Circular LAC (93)10). (This is particularly useful for those discharged from mental hospital or admitted to guardianship.) The person does not have to have a 'mental illness' as defined in the MHA (see chapter 16). Any person with any mental disorder, or recovering from one, or at risk of one, can be offered accommodation.

We will now turn to the duties to provide residential accommodation under Part III. The NAA, s. 21, states that:

> a local authority may with the approval of the Secretary of State, and to such extent as he may direct shall, make arrangements for providing—
>   (a) residential accommodation for persons aged eighteen or over who by reason of age, illness, disability or any other circumstances are in need of care and attention which is not otherwise available to them; and
>   (aa) residential accommodation for expectant and nursing mothers who are in need of care and attention which is not otherwise available to them.

The following subsection was inserted by the 1999 Immigration and Asylum Act; we will touch on it below, and it will explored in greater depth in chapter 21.

> (1A) A person to whom section 115 of the Immigration and Asylum Act 1999 (exclusion from benefits) applies may not be provided with residential accommodation under subsection (1)(a) if his need for care and attention has arisen solely—
>   (a) because he is destitute; or
>   (b) because of the physical effects, or anticipated physical effects, of his being destitute.

Government guidance has indicated that the assessment of need for s. 21 services must take into account drug and alcohol abusers, and must cover those whose needs arise because of HIV or AIDS. Part III accommodation is particularly relevant for those discharged from hospital, who are not yet ready to live in the community but whose needs are no longer primarily medical.

Section 21 covers people who for some reason, normally because of age or some mental or physical incapacity, cannot cope at home. We are talking of people who cannot cope even with help. If, from family, friends, social services, or voluntary organizations, they are receiving sufficient help to manage, then the definition does not apply, for they do have care and attention available to them. As we saw above, residential care is to be used only where support in the home or in another household cannot be achieved. So Part III accommodation cannot be provided where there are alternative ways of keeping the person within the community. (This does not mean that the family must support an impossible relative at all costs; the Act merely states that the person is not receiving care and attention. If the would-be carers refuse to provide it, they cannot be forced. But see 'Liability of the Family to Maintain', below.)

What would happen if the service user could avoid the need for s.21 accommodation by spending their own money? The answer is straightforward. Circular (98)19, *Community Care (Residential Accommodation) Act 1998*, issued as a result of the 1998 Act of the same title, states in relation to a person who has resources: 'However, that does not exempt the Social Services Department from its duty to make arrangements for those people who are themselves unable to make care arrangements and have no-one to make arrangements for them.' A local authority cannot expect a person to spend their own capital to buy their way out of needing residential care. However, we will see later that available capital will be taken into account in assessing their ability to pay a contribution or indeed the entire cost of such care and attention.

Litigation and legislation around residential care and asylum seekers

Can s. 21 assist people whose only reason for not coping is destitution? The welfare benefits system (originally one of the pillars of the welfare state set up under the 1948 NAA) is the normal way of addressing purely economic welfare problems. But in the final phases of the last Conservative Government, legislation was introduced to forbid asylum seekers from obtaining means-tested benefits. (The Government had attempted at first to do this by delegated legislation, but the Court of Appeal said—even before we had a Human Rights Act—that it was inconceivable that Parliament would have given the government the power to leave people destitute and therefore the regulations had been illegal. Undeterred the Government then achieved the same end through judge-proof primary legislation. See also chapter 21 below.)

Some asylum seekers, as an alternative to destitution, then approached a local authority and asked to be assessed for residential accommodation under s. 21 of the NAA. The authority refused, stating that s. 21 was not aimed at economic destitution but social care. In *R v Hammersmith and Fulham LBC, ex parte M* (1998) the Court of Appeal declared that financial destitution could, and indeed should, be included in the phrase 'any other circumstances' (see the exact wording of the legislation above) and therefore entitled destitute asylum seekers to Part III accommodation. But, as discussed in chapter 21 and plainly set out in the amended s. 21 above, the present Government has legislated explicitly to exclude provision of Part III accommodation to asylum seekers on grounds of destitution (but not on any of the other grounds).

What accommodation must be provided?

DoH Circular LAC (93)10, which has the snappy title *Approvals and directions for arrangements from 1 April 1993 made under schedule 8 to the National Health Service Act 1977 and ss. 21 and 29 of the National Assistance Act 1948*, directs that if the s. 21 criteria are met social services *must* arrange the accommodation if the person in need lives in the authority's boundaries; and, if the need is urgent, they must do so even if the person normally lives elsewhere. (If the need is not urgent, your department still has a discretion to accommodate someone from another area.) When accommodation is arranged under Part III, the circular requires it to be backed up with necessary welfare services (i.e. social work support), proper supervision of hygiene, and medical attention, nursing attention during illnesses which would normally be nursed at home, and 'such other services, amenities and requisites' as the authority considers necessary: catering, cleaning, recreation, and so on—whatever it is decided is needed must be provided.

A local authority may provide the accommodation itself, or use commercial or voluntary organizations for some or all accommodation. Although Circular (93)10 states that a local authority must retain some direct provision, the House of Lords was happy to declare this Circular to be wrong on this point (*R v Wandsworth BC ex parte Beckwith* (1996)). (This is also a reminder that Government guidance is not law. Only statute, regulations and case law are law.)

Choice of residential provision

DoH Circular LAC (92)27, *National Assistance Act 1948 (Choice of Accommodation) Directions 1992* (as amended) encourages choice for the resident within England and Wales. A local authority can restrict choice only on the grounds that the chosen accommodation is not suitable for the resident's needs, is more expensive than usually paid to meet those needs, is outside England and Wales, or does not meet the authority's standards, for example for access, monitoring anti-discriminatory practice, or insurance. (It may still be registered without meeting the standards of the paying authority, as it could be in a different local authority area with different requirements.)

If the resident or family wishes to obtain higher standard accommodation than the department provides as a standard, it must provide top-up payments to the local authority.

Does it have to be a care home?

Part III accommodation must meet the assessed needs of the client. If those needs are best met in a residential care home, a place must be found. If they are best met in other accommodation, such other accommodation must be found. The case of *Bernard v London Borough of Enfield* (2002), which is used as a case study in chapter 18, shows this can include a normal house, if that is what is needed. Mrs Bernard was virtually imprisoned in an inadequate house in which she could not use her electric wheelchair and in which she often could not even make it to the toilet without soiling herself. She and her husband were awarded damages for a breach of their human rights under Article 8 (right to respect for family life), since the council had taken far too long to find them a suitable home. Such damages are payable by the social services authority, even if the failure to provide the accommodation could be blamed on the housing department, since that is where the statutory duty lies).

However, if there has been a proper assessment, the applicant cannot sue if she does not get the accommodation she wants. The authority, as we also saw in the opening case study, must have some flexibility in meeting need. In *R (on the application of Khana) v London Borough of Southwark* (2001) the applicant was an elderly Kurd, whose family claimed they could provide extensive support if the applicant did not go into a home, and that their ability to support her would be seriously restricted if she did go into a home. What she needed, they argued, was moving from an upper-floor flat to a ground-floor flat, and that was what social services must provide. They also argued that the council had acted unlawfully in ignoring Government policy guidance (outlined above) which says that normal living should be preserved for clients. As it happens, the court rejected the applicants' argument, preferring to accept on the facts that the council was correct in assessing Mrs Khana as needing twenty-four-hour care and not just family support. But if the facts had been otherwise and the assessment had been that her needs were best met by providing a ground floor flat, such accommodation in the community would indeed have had to be found.

Registration and inspection of residential accommodation

Any establishment which provides residential care for illness, mental disorder, disability, or dependency on alcohol or drugs must be registered. This applies to the local authority's care homes as much as it does to private homes. Registration is with the Commission for Social Care Inspection (in Wales, with the National Assembly). Failure to register a care home is a criminal offence. Registration must be granted if the applicant meets the standards set out in CSA, s. 22, and regulations made under that section. The standards cover management, staffing, facilities, record-keeping, training, accounts, etc. The Commission can cancel registration where the manager has been convicted of an offence relating to registration, or if the home has failed to comply with the requirements. The legislation permits the local magistrates' court to order immediate cancellation of registration in urgent cases (s. 20). The Commission has the power to inspect both premises and records (s. 31).

Balancing the individual's needs and the department's resources

What is the relationship between the needs of the individual—which once assessed as existing must be met if the service is one of the obligatory services set out in Box 15.3 above—and the resources of the authority? Mr Barry was 79 and severely disabled. He was assessed as requiring cleaning and laundry services, and these were provided according to a schedule which seemed to work fine. But the authority, under financial pressure, decided to reassess him. Not surprisingly, given the reason for the reassessment, it 'discovered' that what he really needed was reduced laundry services and no cleaning at all. But Mr Barry's circumstances had not themselves changed. His health had not improved and his needs remained the same, so how could the authority say he no longer needed the same services? The Court of Appeal decided that under CSDPA, s. 2, he should have the services he was assessed as needing; resource problems did not change those needs. The House of Lords—in a majority decision with some powerful dissenting judgments—in *R v Gloucestershire County Council, ex parte Barry* (1997) ruled that the authority has a duty to provide only what it can reasonably afford, and can assess, or reassess, the service user's needs in the light of financial constraints. But—prepare for mental gymnastics here—once the need is found to exist, the authority must meet that need, even if it lacks resources. So it is not wise to make an assessment without, in advance, taking carefully into account what can be afforded. If you fall into the trap of saying a service user needs a service, and it falls into the list of those that must be provided, identifying the lack of resources at this late stage is irrelevant: *R v Sefton MBC ex parte Help the Aged* (1997), where the authority was ordered to provide residential accommodation to an elderly client because she had been assessed as needing it.

Much will turn on the language used in the assessment. 'We can't meet your needs because we can't afford it' won't work. 'We can meet your needs but only in this limited way because of our limited resources' may work. The *Barry* case was decided before the Human Rights Act was in force. And it clashes, in our opinion, with a House of Lords decision on providing home education to a girl with ME. In *R v East Sussex County Council ex parte Tandy* (1998), Lord Browne-Wilkinson stated:

> Parliament has chosen to impose a statutory duty, as opposed to a power, requiring the local authority to do certain things. In my judgment the court should be slow to downgrade such duties into what are, in effect, mere discretions. . . . If Parliament wishes to reduce public expenditure on meeting the needs of sick children then it is up to Parliament so to provide.

Tandy related to a different statutory duty and can technically be distinguished from *Barry*. In spirit, however, *Barry* must be questionable if *Tandy* is correct.

Following *Barry*, the Department of Health issued a Guidance Note (LASSA (97)13) telling local authorities not to use the judgment as an excuse to take decisions on resource grounds only. Decisions must always be based on a needs assessment.

Care entitlement and human rights

Anufrijeva v London Borough of Southwark (2003) shows the limitations of the Human Rights Act in relation to the provision of community care services. The appellants were accommodated under s. 21 NAA. It was an application for damages resulting from what was alleged to be maladministration. An elderly mother was disabled and effectively trapped upstairs. In the course of the two years before she died, the authority had made efforts but had failed to provide 'less inappropriate' accommodation. In other words she was trapped because her needs for appropriate housing as a disabled person were not met. After her death the family applied for damages under the Human Right Act. The Court of Appeal held that this was not a breach of either Article 3 (inhuman or degrading treatment) or Article 8 (respect for family life). There was no positive obligation to provide welfare support under the Convention Rights. The Court stated that Article 8 is about the right to live one's personal life without unjustified interference; the right to one's integrity. Economic provision only comes into this where members of a family are prevented from sharing family life together or where the family has no accommodation at all. However, welfare provision under the Convention is more likely to be triggered, if at all, under Article 3, but degrading and inhuman treatment is a high threshold to substantiate. Inappropriate accommodation did not, in this case, cross that threshold.

[Two factors should be noted in trying to understand this decision. First, although the family concerned here were asylum seekers, this was not a relevant factor in the decision. Second, this was an application for damages. A judicial review application for an order to make appropriate provision in accordance with the service user's assessed needs—during the lifetime of the disabled mother—might, though the court did not comment on this point, have been more successful. We have cited examples above where courts have required authorities to comply with statutory duties.]

Litigation around provision of residential care

Local authorities must think very carefully about closing a home if the residents have been promised care for the rest of their lives: we examined the case above of *R v North and East Devon Health Authority, ex parte Coughlan* (2001), where the health authority was criticized for seeking to evict a long-term resident in such circumstances. The same criticism would apply to social services who seek to close a home. In *Cowl v Plymouth City Council* (2001) the Court of Appeal, in a much-criticized decision, had said that instead of going to court when the home was closed, the resident should have tried mediation; but the Court endorsed a settlement whereby the authority agreed to an independent investigation, and that investigation then produced a scathing indictment of the decision to close the home, in particular of the authority's breaches of Articles 2, 3, 6, and 8 of the European Convention.

Judicial support for the view that a closure brings up human rights issues was restated by Richards J in *R (on the application of Madden) v Bury Metropolitan Borough Council* (2002). He held that the decision will be unlawful if the balance between the residents' rights and grounds for interference with these rights are not carefully considered and articulated to those affected by the decision.

Where a private or a voluntary organization closes a home, it is not subject to the Human Rights Act because, even though relying on local authority funding, it is not a public authority: *R v Leonard Cheshire Foundation* (2002). So the private foundation could close the home, even where residents who had lived there for seventeen years would be uprooted. But the local authority's statutory duty under Part III is not affected; therefore before any change in accommodation, even if resulting from the decision of a private organization, the service user must be reassessed (*R v North and East Devon Health Authority ex parte Coughlan* (2001)), and they must be accommodated under s. 21 if the need still exists.

We have referred above to the case of *R v Gloucestershire County Council ex parte Barry* (1997). To remind you of the reasoning, the majority of the House of Lords permitted Mr Barry to be reassessed in light of the local authority's financial problems. But we noted that assessed needs still have to be met, whatever the available resources. The same tension applies in relation to residential care, for example in the case of *R (on the application of Batantu) v Islington London Borough Council* (2001), where Henriques J said:

I should point out that once a local authority conclude in a particular case that the need which triggers their duty under s. 21(a) exists, they must provide Part III accommodation of a kind which will meet the need for care and attention which arises in that case. They cannot at that stage parade their own lack of resources as an excuse for failing to make the necessary provision, though of course they are entitled to take that factor into account in deciding how they meet the need by provision of Part III accommodation, provided it meets that need.

Nor, he went on to add, can the social services department simply blame the housing department, for the duty falls on social services under s. 21 by virtue of being designated in LASSA, Schedule 1 (see chapters 1 and 3).

Charging for community care

Services provided by the NHS are always free of charge. However, a social services department may, with two exceptions, charge for any or all of the services which have been discussed above (HASSASSA, s. 17). The exceptions are:

(a) after-care of mental patients who have been discharged following detention (MHA, s. 117—see chapter 17); and

(b) advice on community care and assessment of need.

There are no national rates for charges. They must be reasonable, and it is good practice to inform the service user what the charges will be before providing the service and to publish full information on charging policy, including means testing.

Minor adaptations (costing up to £1000) to the service user's home, and the provision of equipment, must be provided free of charge under the 2003 Community Care (Delayed Discharges etc.) Act (Qualifying Services) (England) Regulations 2003, and identical regulations applying in Wales.

Services must not be withdrawn on the ground of non-payment; instead the debt should be pursued in court as an entirely separate matter. (The charity 'Scope' has found that almost one in five people liable to charges for services turn down the help because they cannot afford it.) Where services are provided by voluntary or commercial agencies, the agency can receive payment from the individual up to the amount they are assessed as able to afford, and the local authority tops the payments up. Further guidance on charging may be found in DoH Circular 2001(32), *Fairer charging policies for home care and other non-residential social services—guidance for councils with social services responsibilities*.

Residential care charges

Provision of accommodation is mandatory if the need is accepted. A person's right to it is independent, therefore, of any decision by the local authority to collect contributions. As with other care services, non-payment is a debt-collection problem.

In principle, the system is simple. It is governed by NAA, s. 22, as amended. If a person is not assessed as needing residential care, any provision must be paid for privately.

(A private payer is entitled to a re-assessment, which could result in entitlement to funded care, however.) If the social services department assesses the individual as needing residential care, the authority pays initially, either by directly providing the service or by paying a private or voluntary registered home. But it must under s. 22 recover from the service user the amount it has assessed that person as liable to pay, which can range from nothing up to the entire cost. It is for the authority to set out its charges, and there has been no national charging structure since 2001.

Any element of the care which relates to medical or nursing care must be provided free of charge by the NHS and therefore cannot be included in the cost. (The arrangements for funding NHS nursing care where the accommodation is provided under NAA Part III is explained in circular LAC 2003(7) *Guidance on NHS funded nursing care*). Additionally, under the Community Care (Delayed Discharges etc.) Act (Qualifying Services) (England) Regulations 2003, residential care for up to six weeks, provided in order to assist the service user to return home, must be free of charge.

The actual calculation is not simple, and we will not address it in detail. The assessment of ability to pay is carried out on a national scale updated each year. The applicable version at the time of preparing this edition is issued with Circular 2004(9) entitled *Charging for Residential Accommodation Guide*. A brief summary of how the income is assessed is that all income of the resident (but not the spouse) is relevant. Whether the resident's income derives entirely from social security benefits or from private means, he or she must under the NAA be left with a residual sum for personal expenditure (this is regularly revised, and was set in April 2005 at £18.80; it is not to be spent on basics such as food or essential clothing, which should be provided as part of the care). This amount can be increased if the resident has dependants. A resident must pay a contribution out of capital if this exceeds £12,500 (revised April 2005), and must pay the entire cost if capital exceeds £20,500 (revised April 2005). For this purpose, capital given away to avoid liability counts as available; though any decision on whether the service user is guilty of a disposal with this intention must be fairly and independently handled in accordance with the Article 6 human right to fair and independent decision making (*Secretary of State for Health v Personal Representative of Christopher Beeson* (2002)). The value of the resident's home is disregarded if it is on the market, if a return home is likely, or if a spouse/relative or estranged single parent lives there (National Assistance (Assessment of Resources) Regulations 1992). If the value of the home is taken into account it need not be sold, but is charged by way of a mortgage payable at the latest on the death of the resident.

Special rates of income support were available to pay fees for private residential accommodation before April 1993. For existing residents, these arrangements continue until they die or leave residential accommodation.

People approaching old age and their families naturally worry about the cost of (and the possible forced sale of the old person's home to pay for) care. Family pressure on the old person to give the property away to reduce the risk of a forced sale may be contrary to the interests of that person. The beneficiaries of such a gift (usually the children) cannot be guaranteed to keep it available for the former owner, whose state of dependency is increased to no advantage. This is a complex area of law, but a disposition under duress can in principle be treated as void (and the property recoverable) if the other party knew or had reason to suspect the old person was acting under this kind of duress. Support for the older person before it happens by social services, plus vigilance on behalf of lawyers who should not take instructions unless freely given by a client with proper decision-making capacity, would reduce but never eliminate this kind of problem.

Payment for residential care after mental health act detention

Section 117 of the MHA requires after-care services to be provided to patients released from detention in a mental hospital. See chapter 17 for details. If the services include residential accommodation, it cannot be charged for, a rule recently confirmed by the House of Lords in *R v Manchester City Council ex parte Stennett* (2002). This is a quirk of the community care legislation and its piecemeal origins.

Liability of the spouse to maintain

What happens if a person has to be taken into Part III accommodation because their family does not maintain them? Or if, having been taken into Part III accommodation, their family does not contribute to their costs? The relevant principle is set out in the NAA, s. 42. A person is liable to maintain his or her spouse; failure to do so, in fact, is a criminal offence. If this failure to maintain results in reception into Part III accommodation, this results in a further offence being committed under s. 51. Social services are then, assuming you have nothing better to do at the time, entitled to prosecute the alleged offender.

If Part III accommodation becomes necessary—perhaps despite your efforts with supportive social work—you can ask the spouse who would be liable to maintain the resident to *agree* a contribution towards the actual cost of accommodation. If agreement cannot be reached, the department may ask a magistrates' court under s. 43 to assess the amount that the spouse must pay and to order payment. If you take this course, do not forget that the spouse should be advised of their right to obtain independent advice.

■ Cooperation with housing agencies in providing care—*Supporting People*

Where, having assessed the needs of the individual, the local authority believes that the health or housing authorities could help, it should pass on the information (NHSCCA, s. 47). An important example of this cooperation arises with the housing of vulnerable people. The Housing Act 1996 introduced new powers to evict anti-social tenants. One of these measures allows local authorities and Housing Action Trusts to grant new tenants a year's trial tenancy (an introductory tenancy) before they gain proper security against repossession. The landlord has the legal power to evict them without any ground having to be proved during this period. Given the prevalence of prejudice against people with mental disorders, housing authorities may listen to neighbours' concerns (as they should, of course) and decide to repossess. Where the tenant is known to social services and is owed a duty under the statutory duties listed in Box 16.1, your job is likely to be to assist him or her to retain the tenancy. This requires helping the tenant as necessary, and liaising with the landlord and, perhaps, the neighbours. (If the vulnerability amounts to a disability, to fail to take this into account could in fact be an act of discrimination—see chapter 2, in particular the case of *North Devon Homes Ltd v Brazier* (2003). For more detail on liaison with housing departments see chapter 19.)

Supporting people within the community requires a wide range of services, such as assistance with life skills, budgeting, managing a tenancy and/or dealing with a neighbour dispute. These services can make the difference between remaining in the community and requiring residential care; they are essential for rehabilitation back into the community from prison or other long-term institutionalization. But whose job is it to pay? While social service departments have statutory responsibility, there are many other branches of local and national government who clearly have a role to play. Health has already been considered. But for much of the post war period the state's responsibility for organization and funding of support services has been unclear. This is particularly the case in relation to accommodation of vulnerable people. The cost of support, whether delivered in specialist settings such as hostels or delivered in people's own homes and described as floating support, was met in a variety of ways, principally through Housing Benefit, through grants from local authorities and through grants paid by the Housing Corporation. This lack of clarity led to a series of funding crises as government tried to cut back on Housing Benefit expenditure and social services budgets were under strain. It was impossible for individual projects to work effectively with the high level of uncertainty imposed upon them. The lack of clarity also meant that the government was uncertain how much money was spent on support services and led to uncoordinated and patchy provision of support.

In December 1998 the incoming government set out its proposals to deal with the problem in *Supporting People: A New Policy and Funding Framework for Support Services*. This proposed transferring the financing of supported housing from Housing Benefit and other funding streams to a new fixed budget, the *Supporting People* fund, which would be created by pooling the existing funding streams for support services into a single budget. This was designed to create a framework within which local authorities and other statutory agencies would work with voluntary organizations, housing and other service providers, and individuals to plan, commission and fund joined-up accommodation support services for vulnerable people.

Supporting People was launched April 2003. At that date all supported housing services in operation had the support element of their funding switched to *Supporting People*. The *Supporting People* programme is huge; it provides housing related support services to over 1.2 million vulnerable people. The programme is delivered locally by 150 Administering Authorities, over 6,000 providers of housing related support, and an estimated 37,000 individual contracts. The budget is administered by local authorities in partnership with health bodies, the voluntary sector and probation services (now part of the National Offender Management Service), users, providers and other representative groups It has not been cheap. In 2003–4 the cost of the programme was £1.8 billion. In 2000 there were estimated to be 100,000 'units of housing' support, but by 2004 this had risen to an estimated 250,000. Inevitably this has led to a government review of expenditure and cuts are to be implemented with the aim of reducing expenditure to £1.7 billion by 2006/7

Box 16.6 provides an explanation of the funding of housing support.

However *Supporting People* is not simply about funding. It is targeted at vulnerable people including the homeless, people with mental health problems and/or substance misuse problems, people with learning difficulties, older people, young people, rough sleepers, women fleeing domestic violence, ex-offenders and a number of other needy groups. It aims to provide vulnerable people with the necessary housing related support to enable them to live independently in the community.

BOX 16.6 Funding arrangements for housing support

Expenditure and Income Headings	Who Pays?
Care, Specialist Support or Counselling % Staffing % Overheads	Social Services, Health, Probation, Charity, etc.
Housing Related Support % Staffing % Overheads	Supporting People Grant*
Service Costs (not eligible for housing benefit) Personal light and heat Water Rates Food TV Rental Personal cleaning (unless resident incapable)	Resident/Tenant
Service Costs (eligible for housing benefit) Communal light and heat Communal cleaning/gardening Furnishing and Equipment Entry Phones Servicing and maintaining cookers, fridges, etc. % overheads and staff costs Used to include general support and counselling	Resident/Tenant (Housing Benefit)
Basic Rent Basic housing management = % staff costs % overheads	Transitional Housing Benefit (THB) Resident/Tenant (Housing Benefit)

It involves local strategic planning of support services, and includes commissioning of services, monitoring of service provision, and a focus on user perspectives. All support provision is to be reviewed by administering authorities, that is local authorities, before 2007. There are five criteria on which services will be assessed during a service review. The service must demonstrate that it:

- is strategically relevant,
- meets identified current and future demands for the service,
- provides a quality service which effectively meets the needs/preferences of service users and potential users,
- performs efficiently and effectively, and
- is cost effective.

The implementation of strategic review should result in more coherent and effective local provision of services. So, for instance, new floating support should be developed where there is local demand. On the other hand it may prove difficult to develop new services in a climate of cuts, however necessary it is to open for instance a local hostel for women fleeing domestic violence.

Social workers are likely to encounter *Supporting People* in a variety of contexts. They may be involved in the assessment of needs for support services, they may be involved in locating appropriate support services for a service user, or they may be contacted by support providers for extra help in providing for a particular resident's needs. Social workers are also likely to be involved in the monitoring and strategic review of provision.

Overview of welfare benefits which can assist service users

A community care assessment must cover a benefits assessment. If benefits are maximized then some problems can be reduced without further services being required, for example housing, heating, and social support. Many social services departments run dedicated welfare advice units, and, given the complexity of the law in this area, an outline understanding will have to suffice for non-specialists. Welfare benefits and debt are both specific categories for specialist Legal Services Commission-funded legal help, and any advisor recognized by the LSC will display the LSC quality mark. You can identify local agencies via the **www.justask.org.uk** web site, or via the Community Legal Service Directory available in all LSC-recognized signposting agencies (e.g. libraries). Advice is also available from the following:

Benefits Enquiry Line: 0800 882200 (Mon.–Fri. 8.30–18.30, Sat. 9.00–13.00); Textphone: 0800 243355.

Disability Benefits Helpline: 0845 7123456.

DIAL (Disability Information Advice Line) In local phone book, or DIAL-UK 01302 310123.

The Disability Alliance Helpline: (020) 7247 8763 (Mon. & Wed. 14.00–16.00); web site: **www.disabilityalliance.org.**

Box 16.7 sets out some of the relevant sources of support for adults with community care needs. (Needs of families are not included—but see the equivalent tables in chapter 13, Box 13.1.) For detailed guidance see the *Child Poverty Action Guides* (see further reading below) and for a quick overview with more detail than we can provide see **www.community-care.co.uk/Reference/default.asp?lisectionID=18&liParentID=17**.

BOX 16.7 Some sources of financial support for families

Name of benefit and statutory provision	Criteria	Comment
Income Support *Social Security Contributions and Benefits Act 1992 (SSCBA)*	Claimant must be exempt from requirement to be available for work, e.g. sick, carer, over 60, or single parent. Must not be working over 16 hours a week.	Means-tested, which includes taking into account capital over £3,000 and excluding anyone with over £8,000. Valuable because of 'passported' benefits, e.g. free school meals.
Working Tax Credit *Tax Credits Act 2002*	For individual or couple in employment; paid through the employer and administered by Inland Revenue.	Includes element of child-care costs; increased for lone parents; increased if disability living allowance payable. Worth applying unless very high income.
Disability Living Allowance *SSCBA*	Condition must have existed for at least three months. Payable to child or adult under 65. Mobility component at higher and lower rate depending on ability to walk. Care component at three rates depending on extent of assistance or supervision required.	No means test. If awarded results in increased Child Tax Credit or Working Tax Credit, highest rate care triggers eligibility for ILF (below).
Attendance Allowance *SSCBA*	Payable at two rates. No mobility component.	Similar to care component of DLA above—but must be at least 65.
Carers' Allowance *SSCBA*	Available for the carer of person receiving DLA or AA care component day or night time rate.	Carer must be providing 35 hours per week care.

Social Fund *SSCBA and Social Security Act 1986*	Claimant must already be entitled to means-tested jobseekers allowance or income support. Provides loans for crisis situations, and grants for funeral, maternity, and certain community care needs.	Fund is cash-limited unless funeral or maternity application, and therefore even strong case may be refused.
Incapacity Benefit *SSCBA*	Person under 60 (65 men) and incapable of work.	Not available if insufficient national insurance contributions.
Bereavement Payment *SSCBA*	Payable to spouse aged under 60 (65 men) at death of spouse.	Not available if insufficient national insurance contributions; must have been living together.
Retirement pension *SSCBA*	Payable when 60 (65 men).	Not available if insufficient national insurance contributions. May need topping up with income support.
Winter fuel payments	Payable to anyone over 60.	No need to claim unless not in receipt of retirement pension or means tested benefits.
Council tax benefit; Housing benefit	See chapter 19.	
The Independent Living (1993) Fund (ILF) (see www.ilf.org.uk/)	Must be over 16 and under 66 when first payment is made; must be receiving highest rate care component of DLA (see above).	Discretionary fund which gives cash to help pay for personal and domestic care which enables severely disabled people to live at home. 1993 refers to date fund set up.

Incapacity and protection

[handwritten in margin: Wsc for Protection of children]

In Part 3 of this book a core issue was the power of the state to take over the responsibilities of parents in decision making about children, even removing them from home. This is not because there is anything wrong with the children but because there is something wrong in the arrangements for looking after them—abuse or neglect or inadequate arrangements. The powers seem self-evidently necessary—what else can the state do to fulfil its responsibilities to protect children and enable them to fulfil their physical and emotional potential in accordance with their fundamental human rights?

Why, with vulnerable adults, is the law different? The obvious answer is that adults choose how to spend their lives and are free to leave abusive relationships or themselves to initiate legal proceedings. The adult can use the Family Law Act, Part IV, to obtain court orders (which covers more than conventional families—see chapter 17) for protection against violence or threats. If abusive behaviour is sufficiently bad, it becomes a matter for the criminal law. But there is overlap with the approach to children in need of protection if the adult suffers from a mental health problem as defined in the Mental Health Act, when the state can assume compulsory powers to detain and treat. These are dealt with in the next chapter.

But is there a gap? There will be situations where the adult lacks effective control over their circumstances, not through a mental disorder sufficient to warrant use of those powers, but through confusion or perhaps through abuse. In this final part of the chapter we will provide an overview of the legal powers currently available to assist an adult in such a situation. The powers that exist are not necessarily available to a social worker, but given your responsibilities to provide services to vulnerable adults (because they are old, disabled, or have mental health problems) you are inevitably going to be involved in trying to ensure that powers are used appropriately to protect the interests of the service user.

A good starting point for the social worker is to ascertain, in the statutory context, who is the service user for whom you have a responsibility. Where a person is living with family members much of the discussion will be with those carers (or, in the worst situation, so-called 'carers'), but you must not overlook the fact that your responsibilities are to provide services to the statutory service user and, where issues of consent apply, to be sure that the consent to receive a service is provided by that person and not by someone else. Be aware of the guidance provided in the *National Service Framework for Older People*, which is issued with a circular under LASSA, s. 7, and therefore has the force of law (see chapter 3). This circular states that:

> The need for an NSF for older people was triggered by concerns about widespread infringement of dignity and unfair discrimination in older people's access to care.

Core standard number 2 in the Framework states:

> NHS and social care services treat older people as individuals and enable them to make choices about their own care.

Where you are in doubt about whether consent (choice) is possible you will need both medical and legal advice that any consent apparently given or choice apparently exercised is genuine and is that of the service user, not an expression of the wishes of others.

Situations can arise, though, particularly with elderly people, where the service user cannot give consent or wishes to make choices which are fundamentally at odds with their own interests. The word 'fundamental' is ours, not taken from legislation or case law, but we think it appropriate in light of the Human Rights Act and Articles 5 (liberty) and 8 (respect for private life). Any interference with these rights has to be arrived at through a balanced and independent process (Article 6), and must be proportionate and specified by law. The state (whether social workers or other manifestations of the state such as doctors) owes to the individual a respect for these rights, and the state also owes a duty to ensure that a vulnerable individual is protected against interference from other individuals in the enjoyment of these rights. Translating these principles to your work with, say, the older service user who is confused, you have a responsibility to address abuse by a family member which infringes these rights and you have a responsibility in the exercise of your own powers to respect these rights.

If a person needs assessment or treatment for a mental disorder, compulsory powers are available under the MHA, and these are discussed in chapter 17. Where a person does not have a mental disorder or has a mental disorder which does not require intervention under the Mental Health Act, powers of compulsory intervention by the state—that is overriding the absence of consent—are limited to three areas:

(a) removal from home;

(b) managing financial and property affairs;

(c) medical treatment for the person's benefit.

No other compulsory intervention is acceptable or lawful. It makes no difference if the relatives are well motivated or persuasive, or the action you would like to take is considered by you to be clearly in the individual's best interests,

Compulsory removal from home

The powers we are about to explore are rarely used. The only statistic we are aware of is very old, but indicates around 200 orders a year. These powers are not even mentioned in the *National Service Framework for Older People*. We are not sure they would withstand a Human Rights Act challenge, so it is possible their use will decline further. Most people enter hospital or Part III accommodation voluntarily. What can be done if they refuse to go, but are a danger to themselves or others if they stay where they are living? For example, the person constantly leaves the gas on, or his or her living conditions attract rats. You have done all you can to organize help, including cleaning, change of gas appliances, visits, support for carers, etc. but the danger persists. Perhaps the person does not want your help or that of others. We are in a difficult area, where the rights of the individual are set against what, in the opinion of someone representing state authority, is their own best interests or the interests of society.

The social worker, in this case, is not that part of the state which has the power to remove a person against his or her will. But you cannot avoid some responsibility in this area. First, you are in the front line of the support work which would obviate any need for compulsory removal; secondly, in exercising your powers and duties to provide support to vulnerable people, you, sooner than anyone else, are the person likely to recognize when the need for residential accommodation has arisen. The person who actually exercises the power to apply for compulsory removal is a person appointed by the district or borough council and is called the 'proper officer'. The person appointed will not be part of a social services team unless the authority is a unitary authority. Where a county council runs social services, the 'proper officer' will be an officer from the district or borough council, i.e. not a member of social services staff. Usually the proper officer will be the medical officer of health.

The process is formally triggered by a certificate from the medical officer of health that 'he is satisfied after thorough inquiry and consideration that in the interests of any such person as aforesaid residing in the area of the authority, or for preventing injury to the health of, or serious nuisance to, other persons, it is necessary to remove any such person as aforesaid from the premises in which he is residing'. The proper officer (probably the same medical officer of health) must then seek an order from the magistrates' court. The order can be obtained in an emergency without any notice being given even to the person concerned (see below), so you will appreciate that it is a draconian power. It is essential to follow the correct procedure and be sure that the statutory criteria are met. Even if they are met, you should be aware that what is proposed is to remove basic liberties; could your goal—assisting the person to manage his or her life—be met without compulsory removal, by further support? Or could you justify allowing that person the dignity of living the way he or she wishes?

The power of compulsory removal under NAA, s. 47 applies to persons who:

(a) are suffering from grave chronic disease or, being aged, infirm, or physically incapacitated, are living in insanitary conditions; *and*

(b) are unable to devote to themselves, and are not receiving from other persons, proper care and attention.

We have emphasized the 'and', because it is not enough merely to be infirm and living in squalor—it must be shown that the person is also unable to look after himself or herself, and is not just choosing to live in that way.

The proper officer must supply to the court a certificate that he or she has made thorough enquiries, and considers that it is necessary to remove the person from the premises where he or she is, either because:

(a) it is in the interest of that person; or

(b) removal will prevent injury to someone else's health, or prevent a serious nuisance being caused to someone else.

The proper officer must also give oral evidence of these facts at the hearing before the magistrates.

The person who is at the centre of these proceedings—or the person known to be caring for him or her—must be given notice of the magistrates' court hearing at least seven days in advance. Also the manager of the proposed accommodation must be notified at least seven days before the hearing, unless the manager comes to court to give oral evidence that suitable accommodation is available. In the case of Part III accommodation provided by the local authority, the manager means a person representing social services.

But in an emergency, the procedural safeguards drop away; an application can be made without informing the subject of the application in advance. Nevertheless, the proper officer plus another doctor must certify that it is in the person's interest to remove him or her without delay (National Assistance (Amendment) Act 1951, s. 1). An order allowing removal in an emergency gives the applicant a power to detain the person for up to three weeks, during which period a further application can be made with the seven days' notice. A non-emergency order lasts for three months, and can be renewed by the magistrates as many times as necessary. If the compulsory detention lapses, the person can leave, or remain voluntarily.

The person can be detained against his or her will only in the place mentioned in the court order; any variation requires a magistrates' court order. This is a sweeping power, made more so by the fact that there is often no funding for legal representation before the magistrates for the 'victim'. The Access to Justice Act 1999, shamefully, explicitly excludes this from the scope of Community Legal Service funding, though since liberty is at stake we would argue that this is incompatible with the right to a fair trial under Article 6. There is not even any requirement that the person be represented or receive legal advice before an order is made, which is surprising by the standards of 1948, let alone the standards of the Human Rights Act, given that the person whose future is being considered may lack the ability in many cases to be able to argue the case against removal in person.

The magistrates themselves can be asked to revoke the order, but such an application cannot be made until six weeks after the order was made—over half way through the period of detention and probably another breach of Article 3 (right to liberty) and Article 6 (right to have individual rights determined fairly). There is no right of appeal, unless the magistrates have exceeded their powers or made an irrational decision (another possible incompatibility with Article 6, though the availability of judicial review in the High Court is probably sufficient, even though a huge obstacle for a vulnerable person who has had no legal advice).

There is no statutory requirement to do so, but our advice is to ensure that a person in this situation is advised by a solicitor, if possible one with a Community Legal Service contract to provide legal help in relation to community care (see your local CLS directory or consult the **www.justask.org.uk** web site.)

Managing the affairs of the mentally disordered, confused, or elderly person

Community care legislation is not of much use. It is not itself concerned with property or affairs—except that under the NAA, s. 48, social services must protect the personal property of people admitted to hospital or Part III accommodation, if they believe such steps are required. Apart from s. 47 applications, which we have just considered, all services are provided with the consent of the service user or not at all. So we need to look at a different legal framework in relation to actions to which the service user is unable to provide consent.

What follows should be read in the light of the discussion in chapter 3 on capacity issues in general. The starting point is always that a person is capable of managing their own affairs, but if not, decisions are to be made in line with their known wishes and preferences, and of course, their welfare interests.

A person who is incapable of forming normal legal relationships—buying goods, opening a bank account etc.—lacks legal competence. Any dealings they have with people when in that state cannot be enforced—so no bank manager or business will be able to have normal dealings with them. In addition a person who is becoming confused or demented may lack the ability to manage their financial affairs wisely and will be at risk of exploitation or neglect. You may find yourself advising a relative (not necessarily the nearest relative—a term used in the Mental Health Act and discussed in the next chapter) or friend of a service user or patient about, for example, how to free some of the service user's money to buy items for him or her or for a family member or to pay for residential care. You may exceptionally yourself have to take steps on the service user's behalf if the friend or relative proposes steps contrary to the interests of the service user, or there is no friend or relative.

There is a range of solutions available. Many people anticipate that they may later become incapacitated and can give advance instructions about medical treatment or powers to act in relation to property and money. The Court of Protection can intervene. But, from day to day, ordinary people—friends, families and professionals—are empowered to act in the interest of the person, subject to safeguards.

Proposed powers to take action under the Mental Capacity Bill

A person may be coping at home, or within a residential home, but lacking capacity to spend money, consent to medical treatment, buy a present for a relative, or sign up for an outing. They may also need a little physical handling—to prevent danger, to assist to the toilet. Part 1 of the Bill clarifies what used to be informal practice, by giving clear legal indemnity for those who take action on behalf of such people for the overall purpose of their care or treatment. Section 5 states:

(1) If a person ('D') does an act in connection with the care or treatment of another person ('P'), the act is one to which this section applies if—
  (a) before doing the act, D takes reasonable steps to establish whether P lacks capacity in relation to the matter in question, and
  (b) when doing the act, D reasonably believes—
    (i) that P lacks capacity in relation to the matter, and
    (ii) that it will be in P's best interests for the act to be done.

(2) D does not incur any liability in relation to the act that he would not have incurred if P—
  (a) had had capacity to consent in relation to the matter, and
  (b) had consented to D's doing the act.
(3) Nothing in this section excludes a person's civil liability for loss or damage, or his criminal liability, resulting from his negligence in doing the act.

Section 7 provides a similar power to spend the person's money.

Note the final part of section 5—there can still be legal liability, and squabbles will continue to arise within families over whether a person's affairs were handled for the patient's best interests of for other motives. The Bill includes a power to physically restrain the service user. It does not create a power either to override express instructions set out in a power of attorney, an advance directive, or the decisions of an attorney.

If the NHS or a local authority wish to use the powers available under the Bill to place a service user into NHS or Part 3 accommodation, they must consult with an appropriate carer or, if not available, a member of an independent panel appointed for the purpose.

Instructing a lawyer

In a situation where there could be conflicts of wishes, the early involvement of a specialist solicitor is advisable. But the first issue will be: who gives the instructions? And who is the client? If the advice sought purports to be on behalf of the service user, then the solicitor will take steps to make that person his or her client. If the service user needs legal advice or action, a solicitor can be instructed directly, if the person has sufficient understanding (the solicitor will assess this, if necessary after taking medical advice). Otherwise the solicitor can be instructed on behalf of the service user, either by a carer using powers under the Mental Capacity Bill, by the donee of a power of attorney, or the Court of Protection. The solicitor treats the service user as his or her client, and can only act in the interests of their client, not, where there is a conflict, in the interests of the carer or family. If proceedings are started, the court will have to appoint a Litigation Friend—that is, a person who conducts the litigation on behalf of the person. The solicitor will check that there is no conflict of interest and must certify this to the court.

Powers of attorney and advance directives

A person with the necessary understanding can, by executing a deed, confer their own powers to carry out transactions onto another person. The power can be limited to specified transactions, or all matters on their behalf. Until the Enduring Powers of Attorney Act 1985, such a power was legally useless (though widely used), for it lapsed when a person became incapable of handling their own affairs—the very moment when it was most needed. So it was only of use to people, for example, going abroad who might have to sign a contract while unavailable. The enduring power (under the Mental Capacity Bill renamed a lasting power) lasts beyond the loss of capacity. But it has to be set up at a time when the donor of the power—the person making arrangements for someone else to handle their affairs—is in sufficient control of his or her faculties to understand broadly what powers he or she is giving away; the power must be registered with a new creation, the Public Guardian (previously it was the Court of Protection) once it needs to be used. It is a useful mechanism for a person approaching old age, presently of reasonably sound mind, but fearing dementia. A person wishing to draw up such a power or have one created for a friend or relative should take legal advice both when the donor has capacity and at the stage when the power needs to be registered. The solicitor will need to check that the person has the capacity to draw up a power of attorney and will, if necessary, seek a medical opinion. The new lasting power of attorney covers finance and property decisions, but is mirrored by legal recognition for advance directives, which enable the person to give instructions on consent or refusal of medical treatment. This has been criticized by some commentators as risking old people signing away their right to medical treatment once they are perceived to be a nuisance to their family or to the hospital.

Application to the Court of Protection

If the person cannot execute a power of attorney in a lucid moment, the second way to intervene is more cumbersome. This is an application to the Court of Protection, under, when in force, the Mental Capacity Bill Part 1. The rules have not been drawn up, but probably will at least to some extent mirror the procedures under the previous legislation, the Mental Health Act 1983. We therefore describe what is at the time of writing the present position. The application is supported by a medical opinion that the patient is unable to act, but there is no attempt to define what 'to act' means, and no scrutiny by the court's own medical experts of the medical opinion sent with the application. An application can be made by any interested person on behalf of the patient. If the application succeeds the Court can make decisions for the benefit of the patient in relation to his or her affairs, which can include present affairs (such as paying for residential care) or future affairs (such as drafting a will for the patient or giving away assets to family or charity). The Court will assume that, but for the disability, the patient would have applied 'normal decent' standards in deciding how to dispose of his or her property (*Re C* (1991)).

The Court appoints a receiver, generally the person who cares for or is otherwise involved in the life of, the patient. The receiver must send the Court accounts to show how the money has been spent. Legal advice is generally desirable but unlikely to be available at public expense; and public funding for representation before the court is not available.

Other ways of intervening

Where a person is in receipt of welfare benefits from the Department for Work and Pensions (DWP), arrangements can be made for payment to another person on their behalf if they are unable to act. That person is appointed by the DWP. It can be any-one—a social worker, even a DWP employee. No medical evidence is required. If the person is in residential care, the DWP will notify social services of any appointment. No other legal safeguards exist and no monitoring of the appointee's use of the money takes place, save for a requirement to keep a record of expenditure. If you take on this role you may become liable if the person then alleges that you mismanaged or appropriated the money. The procedure may even turn out to be a breach of the client's rights, under the Human Rights Act 1998 and the Protocol to the Convention, not to be deprived of his or her property without a proper legal process. However, this procedure is quick and easy, compared to the Court of Protection.

Apart from these specific powers to engage in the affairs of people unable to understand for themselves what they are doing, there is no legal mechanism for running someone else's affairs without their genuine consent, and any such action could lead, for example, to the person who does so being sued after recovery of capacity or by the executors following the death of the person concerned.

People having difficulty managing their affairs are at risk of exploitation from friends and relatives. People may think they know better than the elderly person what is good for that person. Relatives may have become impatient at the perceived burden of care, and begin to look at the elderly person's money as their own to use. But social workers, and lawyers, must remind themselves that the service user or client is the elderly person, whose wishes are to be respected unless the evidence is clear that intervention against their wishes is appropriate. Medical and legal advice will give some protection from exploitation and/or well-meaning but unnecessary interference. If you think you know best, check with your lawyer whether the action you propose to take is legal. Never allow yourself to be dictated to by the relatives as to what is best for the elderly person. The relatives are not your statutory responsibility except when they are carers.

EXERCISES

1 Mrs Bennet and three other residents live in Wellesley Road Centre, which is a home for older people provided under the NAA by Camminster Borough Council. When they were admitted they understood that this would be a home for life for her. Their circumstances are as follows:

Doris Bodimeade, age 80, has problems with mobility. Deaf, suffers from dementia with behavioural problems. In residential care for nine years.

Winnie Bennet, 102, has limited mobility. Frail. Swollen ankles. Does not wish to move and is anxious about the consequences if forced. In residential care for three years.

Adelaide Turner, 93, Wheel chair user. Deaf. Local resident with supportive locally based family. Visits local market. Opposed to move.

William Hanton, 88, local resident. Learning disabilities. Walks with aid of frame. Attends local day centre. Exhibits behavioural problems when faced by change. Took months to settle in to Wellesley Road Centre.

On 20 December the residents receive the following letter:

The Borough's Social Services Committee agreed that Wellesley Road would close to allow major works to take place to develop a new facility for frail older people on the site. This means that we will be seeking to move current residents at Wellesley Road to alternative appropriate accommodation in the New Year. The assessment of the individual needs of all residents has been completed and we will now begin to identify alternative accommodation with residents, their relatives and carers.

We will be contacting individual residents, their relatives and carers early in the New Year to discuss the accommodation available, and will be arranging visits. We aim to be arranging the moves to be completed by the end of February.

The intention is to redevelop the site in order to provide a state of the art facility for 'frail older people'. Mrs Bennett's solicitor discovers that the Committee made its decision (he has obtained the minutes) before any assessment was carried out. She suggests to the Council that they are acting illegally. What do you think?

2 Ms Potter, who is white, is a 52-year-old single mother with a dependent teenage daughter, Ellen, who is mixed race Afro-Caribbean. She suffers from anxiety, depression and claustrophobia, and receives help and care from her daughter. She lives in a small high-rise flat and applies to the council for rehousing as a homeless person because of her claustrophobia (see chapter 18 for local authority obligations to the homeless). She is offered accommodation in a neighbourhood where there are virtually no ethnic minority children, and she rejects it. She applies to social services for an assessment of her needs and those of Ellen. The Council say they are not obliged to carry out any assessment because all she is asking for is housing, and that is not a social services department problem but a housing department responsibility. What do you think are the authority's obligations here?

COMPANION WEB SITE

 For guidance on how to answer these exercises, visit the companion web site at: www.oup.com/uk/booksites/law

WHERE DO WE GO FROM HERE?

We have looked in this chapter at a wide range of powers and duties which enable, or require, social services departments to provide services to identified adult service users, either within the community or through provision of appropriate residential facilities. The need may have arisen because of a physical problem such as mobility, sensory impairment, or other disability; it may have arisen from a generalized duty to provide services for a particular type of service user, such as an older person or a pregnant mother. We have also noted that it may be required because the service user is suffering from a mental disorder: this can include after-care on release from detention in hospital, residential support, and support within the community. Sometimes these powers to provide services within the community are not sufficient to meet the needs of the mentally disordered person or to protect the public, and the person needs to be admitted to hospital for treatment or to guardianship within the community. Such a person will not cease to require community care services once a hospital or guardianship admission has taken place, for in most cases long-term admissions are not required and a return to the community is possible. So care of the mentally disordered can involve a period of detention or informal admission, or admission to guardianship. The criteria and procedures are explained in the next chapter.

ANNOTATED FURTHER READING

A. Goodenough, *An Introductory Guide to Community Care* (Age Concern, 2002). A relatively straightforward account, placing particular emphasis on working with older people.

P. Thompson, *Money at Home* (Age Concern, 2004). Covers handling other people's money and belongings.

G. Ashton, *Elderly People and the Law* (2nd edn., Butterworths, 2002). The author is a leading lawyer in this field and also a judge. An authoritative textbook covering all important issues. (New edition due Dec. 2005).

G. Ashton (ed.), *Butterworths Older Client Legal Service* (Butterworth, looseleaf). This contains primary source material as well as explanations, and is updated periodically. A valuable reference tool.

L. Clements, *Community Care and the Law* (3rd edn., Legal Action Group, 2000). The author is widely acknowledged as a leading authority in the field, and the book provides an accurate (though now slightly out of date) and critical account of the practical aspects of the law.

M. Mandelstam, *Community Care Practice and the Law* (3rd edn., Jessica Kingsley Publishers, 2005). As well as providing a good overview the book is useful for its case reports from the courts and, importantly, the ombudsman.

M. Richards, *Long Term Care for Older People: Law and Financial Planning* (2nd edn., Jordans, 2001). Particularly relevant for those concerned with charging for residential care and protecting the assets of the service user.

Department of Health, *A Practical Guide for Disabled People or Carers*, published at **www.doh.gov.uk/disabledguide/index.htm**—a very good entry point providing a comprehensive overview of provision and criteria, plus links to other organizations.

Communitycare.co.uk www.community-care.co.uk/articles/article.asp?liarticleid= 37458&liSectionID=18&liParentID=17—this web site provides a range of articles, news briefings, and updates. Of interest may also be the guide to relevant benefits.

DoH Circulars on the Internet (COIN)—**www.info.doh.gov.uk/doh/coin4.nsf/ Circulars?ReadForm**—we have referred to a large number of circulars, and these can be accessed (together with those we have not listed and new ones) at this invaluable site. Find the list of publications and then go for LAC (which is on the second alphabetical page) for a date-ordered list of local authority circulars.

Age Concern, **www.ageconcern.org.uk/**—see in particular their information and fact sheets page for useful and wide-ranging advice.

Action on elder abuse, **www.elderabuse.org.uk/**—not a lot of material on law but a campaigning web site worth visiting.

Help the Aged, **www.helptheaged.org.uk/default.htm**—good fact sheets, for example on paying for residential care.

www.twylife.com/ A web site comprising links to other web sites relating to the needs of older people.

www.disabilityalliance.org/index.shtml has a particular focus and expertise on issues of benefits.

Admission to hospital or guardianship for mental disorder

Re F (adult: court's jurisdiction) (2001)

Although the case name is *F*, the Court of Appeal judges refer to the patient in this case as *T*. This is how Butler-Sloss P described the family background of T, an 18 year old with a behavioural age of around 5:

> The father was 75 at the date of his death in 1999. The mother is 49 or 50. They married in 1984. The case for the local authority disclosed a picture of chronic neglect, a lack of minimum standards of hygiene and cleanliness in the home, a serious lack of adequate parenting and worrying exposure to those engaged in sexual exploitation and possible sexual abuse of one or more of the children including T. The eight children were said to be suffering significant harm and at risk of so doing, based upon these numerous allegations.

T had been looked after by the local authority with the parents' consent. When T was 17 the parents withdrew their consent, and the local authority tried to obtain mental health guardianship. To do this it had to get an order from the court that the mother should be replaced by it as the 'nearest relative' (only a nearest relative can apply for guardianship). But that application failed, for the 1983 Mental Health Act provides for guardianship in the case of a mental impairment only where that is associated with seriously irresponsible behaviour. Wanting to live with her family might be against F's interests, but it did not meet that test. So it was held in the Court of Appeal that there were no grounds for guardianship. That decision was reported as *Re F (Mental Health Act guardianship)* (2000). The Court of Appeal advised wardship, but by that time there were six weeks until T turned 18, when neither wardship nor Children Act powers would be available.

The local authority still could not use the Mental Health Act and applied to the court for a declaration that it would be legal for it to direct the living arrangements of T, thereby preventing her living at home and coming to harm. Complex legal arguments around ancient legal doctrines giving the Crown parental powers over its subjects and the doctrine of necessity took place in the absence of clear statutory powers to intervene in F's living arrangements. The Official Solicitor was brought in to join in the arguments on T's behalf, since T was unable because of her mental impairment to instruct a solicitor.

So here, in the words of her ladyship, was the problem:

> There is an obvious gap in the framework of care for mentally incapacitated adults. If the court cannot act and the local authority case is correct, this vulnerable young woman would be

left at serious risk with no recourse to protection, other than the future possibility of the criminal law.

As stated by Sedley J:

T is so unable to judge what is in her own best interests that no humane society could leave her adrift and at risk simply because she has reached the age of 18.

According to Butler-Sloss P.:

The assumption of jurisdiction by the High Court on a case-by-case basis does not, however, detract from the obvious need expressed by the Law Commission and by the Government for a well-structured and clearly defined framework of protection of vulnerable, mentally incapacitated adults, particularly since the whole essence of declarations under the inherent jurisdiction is to meet a recognised individual problem and not to provide general guidance for mentally incapacitated adults. Until Parliament puts in place that defined framework, the High Court will still be required to help out where there is no other practicable alternative.

The local authority therefore got the declaration it sought in the Court of Appeal, enabling it to accommodate this young adult away from her family. Sedley J said that no human rights were infringed:

The purpose [of Article 8, respect for private life and family life], in my view, is to assure within proper limits the entitlement of individuals to the benefit of what is benign and positive in family life. It is not to allow other individuals, however closely related and well-intentioned, to create or perpetuate situations which jeopardise their welfare.

OVERVIEW AND OBJECTIVES

The case study throws up a number of questions to bear in mind while reading this chapter:

- Whose job is it to make decisions about the welfare of adults when they themselves cannot make those decisions?
- Why are there so many perceived gaps in the mental health legislation? Is it time for reform?
- Why is there so much litigation involving mental health decision making?
- How do service users' human rights relate to the need to protect society's interests?
- When are social workers involved in mental health decision making?

In relation to the final question, we will shortly see that each social services department is required to appoint specialist mental health social workers to deal with hospital and guardianship admissions. So can the intricate details of the legislation be left to them? We doubt it. What are you going to do about a person who is showing clear signs of disturbance and threatening to jump off a window ledge or to attack you? Or, even if there is no immediate danger, a person with whom you come into professional contact needs medical help because of what you see to be their mental disturbance? Or maybe you are supporting a service user who appears incapable of managing because of dementia? You cannot avoid taking decisions in such a crisis; you cannot hide behind the fact that this is not your field. At the very least you need to contact the right person, sometimes urgently, and that involves knowing enough about the procedures to know who that person is.

The chapter will provide you with a broad view of the powers available to admit to hospital and detain people with mental disorder; you will understand the difference between informal admissions, admissions for assessment, and admissions for treatment and admissions following a criminal conviction; you will also gain an overview of the ways in which detention can be renewed or challenged, and how someone who is detained is to be treated, including treatment without consent. You will see how guardianship provides a complementary range of powers which avoid compulsory admissions. We will explain the responsibility you and health professionals have to provide after-care following hospital detentions.

We intend to show how human rights principles apply at every stage. A new Mental Health Bill is promised, to deal with human rights inadequacies of the present legislation. It will also attempt to address the controversial gap in the present legislation, which is the lack of a power to compulsorily detain or treat dangerous people even if they have committed no offence and any treatment offers them no benefit. We will introduce you briefly to these proposed reforms at the end of the chapter.

◼ Statutory functions of social workers under the Mental Health Act. The National Service Framework

What is the relationship between mental health and community care legislation? In the previous chapter we identified a number of circumstances in which a mental health problem triggers a power, or a duty, to provide community care services. These arise under the community care legislation, most notably the National Health Service and Community Care Act 1990 and the National Assistance Act 1948. The present chapter has a more specialist focus, the mental health framework for hospital and guardianship admissions and discharges.

The main statutory responsibilities for admission and discharge rest with health professionals, though approved social workers (ASW's) are involved in both, and social workers of all types need to know about admission and discharge procedures, because these patients, before admission and after discharge, are likely to be the same service users we discussed in the previous chapter. Additionally to avoid hospital but create some powers of control, patients may be admitted, on the evidence of the health-care professionals, not to hospital, but to guardianship in the community. And community care can itself help to avoid admission to hospital or guardianship.

The MHA in its historical context

The 1983 Act is an old and a long piece of legislation. It is in fact even older than it appears, for all that happened in 1983 was that old legislation dating back to 1959 was helpfully consolidated. In 1959 the Act was, according to the Lawlord Baroness Hale, writing under her academic name, Brenda Hoggett, in *Mental Health Law* (Sweet & Maxwell, 1996) it was 'revolutionary'. Modern treatment would enable rights to replace straitjackets. Patients would obtain hospital treatment with as little fuss as any other medical treatment, leaving compulsory powers for exceptional circumstances.

Criminals as well as others deserved good medical care. Patients who could not benefit from hospital treatment would be treated in the community.

An issue Hoggett identifies is that the Act precedes a modern understanding of rights, and places compulsory powers of admission in the hands of the doctors and (to some extent) social workers rather than law and independent tribunals. The Act also envisages that mental health treatment is for the benefit of the patient. If there is no benefit, no treatment possible, then by and large there should be no compulsion.

Statutory duties

We will examine most parts of the Act, starting with the role of the social services department. Unless we indicate otherwise, in this chapter section numbers refer to the Mental Health Act 1983. Further detail is contained in the Mental Health (Hospital, Guardianship and Consent to Treatment) Regulations 1983. Where we refer to regulations, we mean these regulations unless we indicate otherwise.

Social work functions under the Act are almost entirely carried out by approved mental health specialists. It is the social worker's employing authority who gives this approval to social workers, after training (s. 114), and every social services department must have enough such ASWs to deal with admissions of mental patients and their treatment (DoH Circular LAC (93) 10). ASW cover must be available on a twenty-four-hour basis (Mental Health Act 1983 Code of Practice, para. 2.37).

The social services authority itself can be appointed as a guardian of a mental patient. It must approve a guardianship application if someone else is to be appointed guardian. The authority also has duties to provide after-care following discharge, already touched on in the previous chapter.

We cover all these issues below.

Beyond MHA statutory duties

Perhaps the metaphor of 'tip of the iceberg' can be used to explain the relationship between MHA duties and community care duties. Much of this chapter is at the visible tip, where mental health problems are sufficiently acute or chronic to require compulsory powers and/or hospital admission. But many people suffer a mental disorder—one in six at any given time, according to the Secretary of State in his introduction to the *National Service Framework for Mental Health* (see below)—and the vast majority of problems will not trigger the use of MHA powers. Below the waterline that part of the iceberg where the mental health problem makes the person vulnerable is partly governed by community care laws, and if not sufficiently acute to be picked up for community care assessment, just another health-care need.

The National Service Framework

We noted at the beginning of the community care chapter that the service user may have many problems, and each may be the statutory responsibility of a different agency. The same can arise where a person has a mental health problem. In order to provide a service which is not fragmented, the Department of Health has published a framework setting out core standards for all agencies involved in providing services. You will possibly recall from reading chapter 1 that the guidance published by the Department of Health to social service departments has legal effect under the Local Authority Social Services Act 1970, s. 7. Therefore the *National Service Framework for Mental Health*, published under circular HSC 1999/223 LAC (99)34, has legal effect—any services you provide under any community care or mental health legislation must comply with these guidelines. The circular itself states:

> Chief executives of health authorities, local authorities and NHS Trusts and Directors of Social Services should establish local implementation teams to translate national standards and service models into local delivery plans. The strategies for the implementation of these plans should be reflected in health improvement programmes, joint investment plans, service and financial frameworks, long term service agreements and clinical governance arrangments from April 2000.

Extracts from the framework standards are set out in Box 17.1.

In carrying out any duties, whether triggered under community care or mental health legislation, these standards provide a unifying approach to the duties of the various agencies involved. The framework should be studied in depth—a lot of it is preventative, and therefore relevant to support work with children as well as adults, and relevant to people not assessed as being in need of services.

◼ Accountability for mental health work

Those working in social care generally are accountable through their organizational complaints procedures (see chapter 5), through the courts (we will see examples relating to mental health during this chapter) and through the normal channels of political and public scrutiny. Additionally in mental health work there is a Mental Health Act Commission, which includes laypeople, lawyers, doctors, nurses, social workers, psychologists, and other specialists, and is set up under the Act to monitor aspects of the work which is carried out under the Act's compulsory powers:

- To review MHA powers of detention.
- To visit patients detained under the Act.
- To investigate complaints.
- To review decisions to withhold the mail of patients detained in the High Security Hospitals.
- To appoint medical practitioners and others to give second opinions.
- To monitor the implementation of the Code of Practice (see below).

◼ Mental health work—helping but also controlling people

The problem with mental disorder, from the legal point of view, is that sufferers may not be able to make the best decisions about their own welfare. Society then expects experts

BOX 17.1 National Service Framework for Mental Health standards

Standard one—health and social services should:
— promote mental health for all, working with individuals and communities
— combat discrimination against individuals and groups with mental health problems, and promote their social inclusion

Standard three—any individual with a common mental health problem should:
— be able to make contact round the clock with the local services necessary to meet their needs and receive adequate care

Standard four—all mental health service users of CPA should:
— receive care which optimizes engagement, anticipates or prevents a crisis, and reduces risk
— have a copy of a written care plan which: includes the action to be taken in a crisis by the service user, their carer, and their care coordinator; advises their GP how they should respond if the service user needs additional help; is regularly reviewed by their care coordinator
— be able to access services 24 hours a day, 365 days a year

Standard five—each service user who is assessed as requiring a period of care away from their home should have:
— timely access to an appropriate hospital bed or alternative bed or place, which is: in the least restrictive environment consistent with the need to protect them and the public; as close to home as possible
— a copy of a written after care plan agreed on discharge which sets out the care to be provided, identifies the care co-ordinator, and specifies the action to be taken in a crisis

Standard six—all individuals who provide regular and substantial care for a person on CPA should have:
— an assessment of their caring, physical and mental health needs, repeated on at least an annual basis
— their own written care plan which is given to them and implemented in discussion with them

Standard seven—ensure that staff are competent to assess the risk of suicide among individuals at greatest risk
— develop local systems for suicide audit to learn lessons and take any necessary action

to judge what is in the patient's best interests. But the power of these professionals to override the wishes of the patient, or sometimes the patient's family, is sometimes a power to deprive a person of basic liberties. You should keep in mind the words of McCullough J in the case of *R v Hallstrom* (1986):

> Unless clear statutory authority to the contrary exists, no one is to be detained in hospital or to undergo medical treatment or even to submit himself to a medical examination without his consent. That is as true of a mentally disordered person as of anyone else.

This approach is now underpinned by Article 5 of the European Convention on Human Rights, which provides a right to liberty. An example of the interpretation of this Article can be seen in *Kay v United Kingdom* (1998). Mr Kay was subject to a hospital restriction order for a killing in 1971. He had been conditionally discharged in 1985 and subsequently committed two further violent offences for which he went to prison. While in prison he obtained evidence that he was not suffering from mental disorder and tried to get the 1971 restriction order discharged. The Mental Health Review Tribunal agreed that he had no mental disorder but refused the discharge. The hospital then recalled him, so that on release from prison he was detained again under the 1971 order. A fair result for a dangerous man? Perhaps. But it was all done without considering up-to-date medical evidence. Mr Kay's right to liberty had been breached, because the evidence needed by the state which would justify the continued detention had not been demonstrated and had not been open to challenge, according to the European Court of Human Rights.

The legislation has to provide procedures which ensure that abuse of powers by mental health professionals does not occur, while necessary treatment and containment can still be provided. The 1983 Act was a consolidation of even older legislation, so it is not surprising, particularly in light of the acute awareness of human rights principles resulting from the Human Rights Act 1989, that it is frequently challenged.

The Mental Health Act 1983 Code of Practice (Department of Health and Welsh Office 1999) is essential reading for all professionals working in the mental health field. Some key extracts from the Code are set out in Box 17.2.

 BOX 17.2 Extracts from paragraph 1 of the 1999 Code of Practice

1.1 The detailed guidance provided in the Code needs to be read in the light of the following broad principles, that people to whom the Act applies (including those being assessed for possible admission) should:

— receive recognition of their basic human rights under the European Convention on Human Rights (ECHR);

— be given respect for their qualities, abilities and diverse backgrounds as individuals and be assured that account will be taken of their age, gender, sexual orientation, social, ethnic, cultural and religious background, but that general assumptions will not be made on the basis of any one of these characteristics;

— have their needs taken fully into account, though it is recognised that, within available resources, it may not always be practicable to meet them;

— be given any necessary treatment or care in the least controlled and segregated facilities compatible with ensuring their own health and safety or the safety of other people;

— be treated or cared for in such a way as to promote to the greatest practicable degree their self determination and personal responsibility, consistent with their own needs and wishes;

— be discharged from detention or other powers provided by the Act as soon as it is clear that their application is no longer justified.

Communicating with patients

1.2 As a general principle, it is the responsibility of staff to ensure that effective communication takes place between themselves and patients. All those involved in the assessment, treatment and care of patients should ensure that everything possible is done to overcome any barriers to communication that may exist.

1.3 Local and Health Authorities and Trusts should ensure that ASWs, doctors, nurses and others receive sufficient guidance in the use of interpreters and should make arrangements for there to be an easily accessible pool of trained interpreters. Authorities and Trusts should consider cooperating in making this provision.

1.4 Barriers to communication may be caused by any one of a number of reasons, e.g. the patient's first language is not English or he or she may have difficulty understanding technical terms and jargon; he or she may have a hearing or visual impairment or have difficulty reading. There may also be barriers to communication associated with the person's mental disorder, for example, the patient may lack mental capacity.

1.5 Staff need to be aware of how communication difficulties affect each patient individually so that they can address the needs of patients in ways that best suit them. This will require patience and sensitivity. Specialist help should always be made available to staff as required, either from within the hospital itself, or from the local social services authority or a voluntary organization. The patient's relatives or friends should not normally be used as an intermediary or interpreter. When the need arises, staff should make every attempt to identify interpreters who match the patient in gender, religion, dialect, and as closely as possible in age.

1.6 It will at times be necessary to convey the same information on a number of different occasions and frequently check that the patient has fully understood it. Information given to a patient who is unwell may need to be repeated when they have improved.

Confidentiality

1.7 Managers and staff in all Trusts, Authorities, Mental Nursing Homes, Social Service Departments and other organisations which provide services for patients should be familiar with the DoH Guidance on confidentiality (The Protection and Use of Patient Information, Department of Health 1996, HSG(96)24). Ordinarily, information about a patient should not be disclosed without the patient's consent. Occasionally, it may be necessary to pass on particular information to professionals or others.

■ MHA definitions

We use the word 'patient' frequently. The legislation uses it as a shorthand for any person suffering from mental disorder. It is not necessary to be a patient in hospital to be called a patient under the Act.

Definitions of mental disorder are given in Box 17.3. It is for mental health professionals not lawyers to assess who has and who does not have a mental disorder, though

BOX 17.3 Mental disorders as defined in MHA, s. 1

Mental disorder: 'Mental illness, arrested or incomplete development of mind, psychopathic disorder and any other disorder or disability of mind' (s. 1(2)). It is sufficient for a compulsory admission for assessment.

Mental illness is not defined.

Mental impairment: 'a state of arrested or incomplete development of mind which includes significant impairment of intelligence and social functioning and is associated with abnormally aggressive or seriously irresponsible conduct'.*

Severe mental impairment: as for mental impairment, but the impairment must be severe, not just significant.

Psychopathic disorder: 'a persistent disorder or disability of mind (whether or not including significant impairment of intelligence) which results in abnormally aggressive or seriously irresponsible conduct'.

(* Note that the aggressive or irresponsible conduct does not actually have to be caused by the impairment, so for example a patient whose violence is caused by emotional disturbance, and not mental handicap, could come within this definition.)

that decision can be challenged in court or tribunal. This assessment should be formed by each professional independently of the others: the Code (paragraph 2.31) makes clear that there is nothing wrong with disagreement, so long as the needs of the patient are not ignored while the disagreement is resolved. An approved social worker is an expert in this matter and should not automatically concur with medical opinion.

A diagnosis of mental disorder must not be founded solely on evidence of promiscuity, immoral conduct, sexual deviancy, or drug abuse (MHA, s. 1(3)). Neither can it be founded on bizarre and irrational behaviour. A woman refusing to undergo a caesarian, despite advice that she was putting herself and her baby at grave risk by insisting on a natural birth, is not, without other evidence, suffering from a mental disorder. This Court of Appeal ruling, in *St George's NHS Trust v S* (1998), came too late to stop the caesarian being carried out against her will, but has made it clear that the Act should be used to deal with mental health issues and not social control. Nevertheless, life-threatening anorexia nervosa can be a mental illness (*Re KB (Adult) (Mental Patient: Medical Treatment)* (1994)). (In chapter 3 we noted a more recent case where the refusal of a caesarian was addressed by the courts not through mental health law but by assuming the mother was incapable of making an informed decision on her own welfare.)

The professional assessment is reviewable by the courts, particularly where words like 'seriously irresponsible conduct' have to be interpreted. For example in *Re F (Mental Health Act: Guardianship)* (2000), the Court of Appeal disagreed with the assessment of the doctors that the wishes of a 17-year-old girl to return to an unhappy, abusive home amounted to such conduct; on the other hand in *R (on the application of P) v Mental Health Review Tribunal* (2002), the court agreed with the doctors that disorder (in this case psychopathic disorder) can exist under the Act even if it is currently dormant, if there is a risk of recurrence.

The other definition required for an understanding of the workings of the Act is the 'nearest relative'. This is a person who the ASW often has to work with. Only one person can fill this role at any given moment for a particular patient. Section 26 defines who this is, and this is summarized in Box 17.4.

The final point to mention when defining the patient is that there is no age requirement. The MHA applies to children, except that for admission to guardianship the child must be at least 16 years old.

Discharge or replacement of nearest relative

A patient may be without a nearest relative in this country who is both willing to and capable of acting. Or the professionals may disagree with how the nearest relative

---

 BOX 17.4 The nearest relative, in order of priority

- Spouse (but excluding any spouse who has deserted the patient, or been separated by court order or formal agreement; when the Civil Partnership Act comes into force, this will include a registered same sex partner)
- Cohabitee of six months' standing
- Son or daughter
- Parent
- Brother or sister
- Grandparent
- Grandchild
- Uncle or aunt
- Niece or nephew
- Any other person who has lived with the patient for at least five years (but only if there is no spouse)

If a person on the list actually lives with and cares for the patient, he or she takes precedence, even if lower down the list. Anyone who lives abroad is ignored altogether. And, conversely, if the patient reasonably objects to the nearest relative (in the case of *R (on the application of M) v Secretary of State for Health* (2003) where she had no relationship of trust with her adoptive father) that person must not take on the role. The reference above to a cohabitee now includes a same-sex partner: *R (on the application of SG) v Liverpool City Council* (2002).

Illegitimacy is irrelevant. Where there is more than one person competing for the position on the same level in the list (e.g. a brother and a sister; two parents) then the oldest takes precedence. Relationships of the whole blood take precedence over those of half blood (e.g. a sister comes before a half sister).

If a child is in care under the Children Act 1989 the nearest relative is the authority named in the care order, even if the child is accommodated at home (s. 27, MHA).

wishes to exercise his or her powers. In such a situation, any relative, any person with whom the patient normally resides, or an ASW can apply to the county court to be appointed or to have someone else appointed—for example, the ASW might apply to have a relative further down the list appointed (s. 29) or a suitable friend of the person. The doctors, incidentally, cannot make this application and are reliant on the ASW. Alternatively, the nearest relative can give written authorization to allow another person to discharge their role (reg. 14).

A decision to make such an application raises human rights issues. Because it involves determination of the nearest relative's responsibilities under Article 6 of the Convention, which have to be determined in a fair manner, even the decision to apply to have her replaced triggers amongst other things the right of the nearest relative to access to relevant documents: *R (on the application of S) v Plymouth City Council* (2002), a case also discussed in chapter 4.

The court can make the s. 29 order only if one of the following grounds is established:

(a) no nearest relative can be found; or

(b) the present nearest relative is incapable of acting because of mental disorder or other illness; or

(c) the nearest relative unreasonably refuses to consent to an application for admission to hospital or guardianship under the MHA; or

(d) the nearest relative has unreasonably exercised his or her power to discharge the patient without taking into account the public interest or the welfare of the patient (s. 26(3)).

(e) (implicit in the judgment in *R (on the application of M) v Secretary of State for Health*, above) the patient reasonably objects to that relative acting.

As soon as a s. 29 application is submitted to the court the current nearest relative loses the power (see below) to discharge the patient. This means an ASW can use a s. 29 application to prevent the discharge of a patient by a nearest relative. The hospital authorities, as we will see, also have ways of preventing discharge.

The nearest relative has the right, at any time, to appoint an independent doctor to visit the patient in hospital, and look at all relevant records. This is important, for the nearest relative has rights to apply to the Mental Health Review Tribunal, and to discharge a detained patient, and should be told of this right to obtain medical advice before taking that kind of decision.

■ Admissions to mental hospital

Informal admission to hospital

Before we talk about compulsory powers, it is useful to bear in mind that most admissions to hospital are not compulsory. The MHA (s. 131) and the Code of Practice (paragraph 2.7) explicitly encourage informal admissions. These patients should not strictly be called voluntary, since it is the fact that they do not object to admission, or to remaining in hospital, rather than any positive agreement, that enables the hospital to admit or keep them there.

The lawfulness of admitting patients on this informal rather than voluntary basis was reaffirmed by the House of Lords in *R v Bournewood Community and Mental Health NHS Trust ex parte L* (1998). L had a thirty-year history of in-patient treatment, but had recently been looked after in the community. His carers brought him in to the hospital one day because he was getting agitated, only to find that they could not get him out again. L himself, being severely autistic, could not insist on leaving, but was not objecting to his stay. His carers claimed in judicial review that this amounted to compulsory detention and that he should either have been released, or the compulsory detention procedure, with its safeguards, time limits and discharge mechanisms, should have been used. They were successful in the Court of Appeal, but the *status quo* was restored in the Lords. The Code of Practice now explicitly endorses this outcome: if a patient does not object, informal admission is lawful (paragraph 2.8). But the Department of Health also issued guidance (HSC 1998/122), stating that the wishes of the patient and his or her carers must be taken into account before informal admission, and the fact that a patient does not object should not be taken as evidence of compliance with an informal admission.

Even if the informal patient is capable of exercising his or her right to leave, no one is required to inform them of this right. Patients detained under MHA powers have greater rights: they must be informed that they can refuse treatment and apply for discharge (s. 132). Additionally there are powers to detain the informal patient at the stroke of a doctor's or nurse's pen (see below). So informal patients should not be seen as entirely free to leave, a fact which may influence the decision to become an informal patient in the first place.

Any person of 16 or over can become an informal patient regardless of the wishes of his or her parent or guardian. Below that age an informal admission decision can only be made by the patient's parent or guardian (s. 131(2)). But the question of *Gillick* competence must be addressed in such a case. (*Gillick* is the case discussed in chapter 3, concerning consent by children to medical treatment). In *R v Kirklees MBC ex parte C (A Minor)* (1993), the court, on a challenge by the parents, held that where a child is in care, the local authority, exercising parental responsibility, can admit the child to a hospital against that child's will, even if there are no grounds for a compulsory MHA admission, and even if the result is to deprive the child of his or her liberty without a court order. (By contrast, the local authority must have a court order to lock up children in care for more than seventy-two hours.) The Court of Appeal ruled that if the child had been '*Gillick* competent' she would have been entitled to refuse admission. Despite the involvement of a court, this was still an 'informal admission', in that no powers under the MHA were exercised. The admission took place under the parental responsibility of the local authority.

Application for compulsory admission to hospital

We will discuss in turn the grounds for compulsory admission for assessment, emergency assessment, and admission for treatment. These all have, in common, the requirement that there must be an application, so we look at that first. After that we will consider the powers of the criminal court to make a hospital order following a conviction or a decision that an accused person is unfit to plead, and the power of a police officer to detain a presumed mental patient at a place of safety.

But is the word 'application' actually appropriate? Compulsory admission does not require an order of any court or tribunal (apart from admission for treatment following a criminal conviction (see below)). The liberty of the patient is removed on the completion of a purely administrative procedure: the ASW or the nearest relative makes an application, supported by two (or, in an emergency, one) doctors' statements. Neither the managers nor the hospital doctors actually consider the application's merits. They only consider whether they have space. Indeed, once the application for admission has been completed, before the ink is dry, let alone delivered to the hospital, it gives rise to compulsory MHA powers: the applicant or his or her authorized agent is now empowered to take the patient to the named hospital. However, the detention ceases to be lawful if the hospital managers realize that the facts stated in the forms are untrue (*R v Central London County Court ex parte London* (1999)).

Applicants should remind themselves that 'Compulsory admission should only be exercised in the last resort' (Code, para. 2.7).

Who is the applicant? An ASW is usually a better person to make the application than the nearest relative, 'bearing in mind professional training, knowledge of the legislation and of local resources, together with the potential adverse effects that an application by the nearest relative might have on the latter's relationship with the patient' (Code, para. 2.35). The ASW must consult the nearest relative, however (MHA, s. 11(4)). Consulting the wrong relative in fact makes the ensuing admission and detention unlawful (*Re S-C (Mental Patient) (Habeas Corpus)* (1996)).

The nearest relative's or ASW's application is addressed to the managers of the proposed hospital (s. 11); this means the health authority or, if it is a private mental nursing home, the person registered with the Commission for Healthcare Audit and Inspection to run it, or, if the hospital is secure (e.g. Broadmoor), the Secretary of State for Health.

An ASW *must* make an application where in his or her professional opinion that is the appropriate course (s. 13(1)). This is a matter for the social worker; it is not a departmental decision. And he or she must reach the decision independently, even if it is a different decision from that of the doctors (*St George's Healthcare NHS Trust v S* (1998), where the ASW should have realized that a woman refusing a caesarian was not suffering from a mental disorder). Before making the application, the ASW must interview the patient 'in a suitable manner', and be satisfied that compulsory admission is the most appropriate way of providing the care and medical treatment which the patient needs (s. 13(2)). A suitable manner means taking into account any language barriers, hearing difficulties, and other obstacles such as cultural differences which could interfere with communication with the patient. Guidance is given in the Code, para. 2.11. As soon as the ASW has made a decision—to apply or not to apply for compulsory admission—he or she must explain the decision to the patient, the doctors, the nearest relative (if possible), the patient's key worker and GP (Code, para. 2.17).

Certain pre-application requirements must be satisfied. The applicant for a compulsory admission must have seen the patient within the last fourteen days. The application must be supported by the signed medical recommendations of two doctors, one from a Department of Health-approved mental health specialist, the other, if possible, from a doctor who knows the patient. Both doctors must have examined the patient within five days of each other. They must sign the recommendations before the applicant signs the application, otherwise the application is invalid.

The five-day and fourteen-day time periods are shortened in the case of an emergency admission (which is discussed below): the applicant must have seen the patient not more than twenty-four hours before making the application, and the admission must be carried out within twenty-four hours of the medical examination (s. 6(2)(b)).

A completed application gives the applicant power to take the patient to hospital. This power lapses fourteen days after the last of the two medical examinations (s. 6(1)), which means that the medical information must be reasonably up to date at the time of the admission.

Once a patient is compulsorily detained, the managers must inform the patient of the grounds for detention, and their rights to a discharge and to apply to the Mental Health Review Tribunal. If the application was by an ASW, the nearest relative must be similarly informed unless the patient objects to this (s. 132).

Where the application was by a nearest relative, the managers of the hospital must notify the patient's local social services department; a social worker (who does not have to be an ASW) must then interview the patient and provide the hospital with a social circumstances report (s. 14). The report should set out not only the history of the patient and the disorder, but also state whether alternative methods of dealing with the patient are available and appropriate. Alternative methods means community care— can anything be organised under the powers described in chapter 16?

Grounds for compulsory admission to hospital for twenty-eight-day assessment

The medical grounds will vary according to whether the application is to be for admission for assessment under s. 2, admission for treatment under s. 3, or emergency assessment under s. 4. For assessment, the doctors must certify on the application that they are satisfied that the patient:

(a) is suffering from mental disorder of a nature or degree which warrants the detention of the patient in a hospital for assessment (or for assessment followed by medical treatment) for at least a limited period; *and*

(b) he ought to be so detained in the interests of his own health or safety or with a view to the protection of other persons (s. 2(2)).

The words 'is suffering' still apply even if the condition is currently under control through medication (*Devon County Council v Hawkins* (1967)).

We have seen that a correctly completed application gives the applicant immediate powers to convey the patient to hospital. The hospital may then detain the patient for up to twenty-eight days (s. 2(4)). After that, the patient must be discharged unless he or she remains as an informal patient, or detention is authorized for treatment using the s. 3 powers discussed below.

Grounds for seventy-two-hour admission for assessment in an emergency

The s. 2 procedure above requires two doctors' recommendations. But in an emergency under s. 4, an application can be founded on only one, if the applicant certifies that the need for admission is urgent and that obtaining two recommendations would involve undesirable delay (s. 4(2)). The single medical recommendation should, if possible, come from a doctor who knows the patient; the grounds are the same as under a s. 2 admission for assessment. The doctor must also state that the need for admission for assessment is a matter of urgency.

The Code (para. 6.3) advises that urgency is more than a matter of administrative convenience. There must be evidence of:

- an immediate and significant risk of mental or physical harm to the patient or others, and/or
- the danger of serious harm to property, and/or
- the need for physical restraint of the patient.

The completion of the application gives the applicant a power to convey the patient to the hospital, where he or she can be detained for up to seventy-two hours. During these seventy-two hours, if the second doctor's recommendation is received by the managers, containing the required recommendation under s. 2, the detention is converted into a twenty-eight-day admission, starting from the day of the admission. Otherwise, at the end of the seventy-two-hour period the patient is free to leave, or remain informally.

Grounds for admission to hospital for treatment

One difference between admission for assessment, and for treatment, which is governed by s. 3, is that the ASW cannot usually proceed with admission for treatment against the wishes of the nearest relative. This is because the ASW must consult the person who appears to be the nearest relative before making an application for admission for treatment (s. 11(1)), unless it is 'not reasonably practicable or would involve unreasonable delay'. The nearest relative can then prevent the application going ahead by simply informing the ASW or his or her department that he or she objects (s. 11(4)). If, therefore, an ASW still wishes to make an application for treatment, an application to displace the nearest relative must first be made to the county court (see above).

The medical grounds for admission for treatment are more rigorous than for assessment, which is not surprising given that the doctors are now, by definition, satisfied that treatment is appropriate. Suffering from a mental disorder on its own is not enough. Both doctors making the recommendations must agree on which of the four defined categories of mental disorder the patient is suffering from—mental illness, severe mental impairment, mental impairment, or psychopathic disorder (s. 1: see above Box 17.1). (We saw in relation to s. 2 admissions that 'suffering from' applies even where the condition is currently controlled by medication or is dormant.)

The doctors must also be satisfied that the patient's 'mental disorder is of a nature or degree which makes it appropriate for him to receive medical treatment *in a hospital*'. Having just one of the mental disorders is not ground enough, therefore, if it can be treated in the community. 'Treatment' itself is a broad concept. A patient refusing to eat was capable of treatment consisting of force-feeding (*B v Croydon Health Authority (No. 2)* (1996)); group therapy is treatment, even if the patient does not want to participate: *B v Croydon Health Authority (No. 2)* (1996).

If the patient is diagnosed as suffering from one of the 'minor' disorders—mental impairment or pyschopathic disorder—the doctors must be satisfied that 'such treatment is likely to alleviate or prevent a deterioration of his condition' (the 'treatability test'). In other words, since the disorders are minor, no one should compulsorily be sent to hospital for treatment unless he or she will benefit from it. A psychopathic patient who is dangerous and yet untreatable cannot (until the legislation is reformed—see a summary of the proposals below) be detained under s. 3. But where there was treatment available which the patient refused, she still counted as treatable (*R v Canons Park MHRT ex parte A* (1994)). (Note that the treatability test does not apply on admission for assessment, for assessment by definition has to precede a decision on treatment.)

On top of the required diagnosis of a disorder, the doctors must be satisfied that treatment is necessary 'for the health or safety of the patient or for the protection of other persons'—i.e. the patient is a risk to himself or others—and that 'it cannot be provided unless he is admitted *under this section*'. So if the patient could be treated in the community, or be admitted voluntarily, the s. 3 grounds would not be established.

There is no emergency admission for treatment. If the need is already known, it should be a s. 3 admission for treatment; if it has only just arisen, by definition, assessment is needed first, and if necessary an emergency admission for assessment can be sought.

Detention for treatment then lasts up to six months unless it is renewed (see below).

New grounds for admissions?

The Government has drafted legislation which gives powers to detain 'dangerous people with severe personality disorder', even where the detainee does not meet the treatability test for detention under the MHA and has committed no offence. Any new legislation will have to comply with the Human Rights Act 1998 and Article 5 of the European Convention, which allows for detention of persons of unsound mind but, according to case law, only if the deprivation of liberty is outweighed by the public interest in protection. See the final section of this chapter.

Conveying a patient to hospital following admission

The completion of the admission procedures gives the applicant (usually, as we have seen, the ASW) the power to convey the patient to hospital or to delegate that power. Chapter 10 of the Code should be read before embarking on this, and you should be aware of any local agreements between social service departments, the ambulance service, and the police. Taking a patient in your car without an escort is strongly discouraged. If the task is delegated to police or ambulance staff, the ASW is still in charge (Code, para. 11.4).

Admission to hospital for treatment from a criminal court

Home Office Circular 66/90 provides a useful background to work in this area. As with juveniles, it makes clear that police and Crown Prosecutors should avoid prosecution of a mentally disordered suspect unless this would be in the public interest. And if a prosecution is necessary, and a conviction results, courts should if possible impose sentences which are therapeutic rather than punitive.

If a criminal court is dealing with an offence for which it could have imposed a custodial sentence, it can instead make a hospital order under the Mental Health Act 1983, s. 37 It can make this order even where the offender is a child of ten or more (children under 10 cannot offend—see chapter 15).

The court must be satisfied that the offender is suffering from mental illness, psychopathic disorder, mental impairment, or severe mental impairment, and that detention in a hospital for treatment would be appropriate. As with admission for treatment under s. 3, if the mental condition consists of mental impairment or psychopathic disorder, the court must also be satisfied that a hospital order would alleviate the condition or prevent deterioration. Medical evidence on these requirements will be required by the court from at least two doctors, together with evidence from the proposed hospital that a place is available. The court, in reaching its decision, must take into account the likely effect of any sentence on the offender's mental disorder (Criminal Justice Act 1991, s. 4). There is, strangely, no need for proof of a connection between the mental disorder and the criminal offence.

As an alternative we saw in chapter 15 that a court can impose a community rehabilitation order with a requirement to obtain treatment for a mental disorder. But this is not appropriate if the grounds for detaining the offender in hospital are established: Powers of Criminal Courts Act 1973, Schedule 1A.

The court can name the hospital that the offender is to be sent to (a power introduced by the Crime (Sentences) Act 1997) in order to achieve a particular level of security, rather than leaving it to the NHS to decide this.

Powers of detention and restriction following a hospital order

The hospital order empowers the hospital to detain the offender for up to six months. Once the offender is in the hospital he or she is now a patient, and will be treated the same as any other patient. The Crown Court can, however, add to a hospital order a restriction order designed to protect the public from serious harm (MHA, s. 41). A youth court or magistrates' court cannot do this, but if it considers that such an order would be appropriate it should commit the offender, if he or she is over 14, to the Crown Court (even if the offence itself was not triable in the Crown Court). But the Crown Court is then free to dispose of the case in any way which the sentencing court could have done. It can choose not to make a hospital order or, if it does, to attach a restriction order.

The restriction period can be for a stated period or it can be indefinite. The essence of a restriction order is that the detainee cannot be released, even for leave of absence, during the period of such order without an order of the Home Secretary or the Mental Health Review Tribunal. This is in contrast to other detained patients, who can and indeed should be released by the hospital, if the doctors think this appropriate. We will consider restriction orders again when looking at discharge from hospital.

Transfers from prison to hospital (and back)

Section 47 allows the Home Secretary to make a transfer order to move any prisoner to hospital, on receiving reports from two doctors that certain conditions apply. These conditions are almost identical to the conditions which a court would look for before making a hospital order (see above), and are not repeated here. Once made, the transfer order is identical to a hospital order with restrictions, which was described above. The patient remains in hospital until the mental condition which precipitated the transfer no longer requires treatment, or is not susceptible to treatment. He or she then reverts to being a prisoner for the remainder of the term or, if it has expired, is released.

Where the offender has been diagnosed as a psychopath, the Crown Court now has the power to sentence to hospital followed by transfer to prison (ss. 45A and 45B of the MHA (inserted by the Crime (Sentences) Act 1997)). So the sentence starts out with detention in hospital with restrictions (limitations is just another word for restrictions). The detained psychopath stays in hospital until the condition cannot be treated, or no longer requires treatment, and then he or she is taken back to prison for the rest of the sentence.

Unfitness to plead

A person accused of a crime before the Crown Court may be declared unfit to plead. This is a matter for the jury, not for medical experts. If unfitness to plead is found, the Crown Court must still have a trial on the facts. If the facts of the crime are proven, the court may order detention without time limit in a mental hospital (with or without a restriction order), a guardianship order, a supervision and treatment order, or an absolute discharge. Details are set out in the Criminal Procedure (Insanity and Unfitness to Plead) Act 1991 and Circular 93/1991.

Admission for assessment or treatment from a police station

There is no special procedure for admission from a police station. We saw in chapter 15 that a doctor should be called to assess a detainee in the police station when mental disorder is suspected. From there, informal admission, or formal admission under the MHA, ss. 2–4, can take place. The decision whether to continue with any criminal proceedings will be taken by the police, who will take into account the guidance referred to above that they should only charge a mentally disordered suspect if it is in the public interest.

■ Police powers of temporary detention of mental patients

At the beginning of the chapter, we talked about someone threatening suicide or violence. Your instinct may be to call the police. That is correct. The police can arrest someone committing any kind of offence that is likely to be threatening, and in particular a person committing a breach of the peace. But the police also have powers to detain a mentally disordered person. Section 136 enables a police officer to detain in a place of safety any person found in a public place who appears to be mentally disordered. Every police authority must have a policy on using this power, agreed between the police, social services, and the health authority (Code, para. 10.1). A public place is defined in case law as somewhere to which the public have access (e.g. the landings in a block of flats—*Knox v Anderton* (1983)). The officer must consider that detention is necessary, either in the interests of the mentally disordered person or to protect any other person. The place of safety can be a police station, a hospital, Part III accommodation provided by the local authority (see chapter 16), a mental nursing home, or any other suitable place. 'The purpose of removing a person to a place of safety . . . is to enable him or her to be examined by a doctor and interviewed by an ASW and for any necessary arrangements for his care and treatment to be made' (Code, para. 10.2). The Code suggests that the best place of safety is the hospital (para. 10.5). Any person detained in a police station has the right to a lawyer under s. 58 of PACE 1984 and to the presence of an appropriate adult under PACE Code C (see chapter 14). This power of detention lasts only seventy-two hours, and any longer detention requires an admission for assessment or treatment.

The power to detain in a place of safety is not given to a social worker, even an ASW. You must call the police if you cannot yourself deal safely with the situation.

Searching out and protecting the mentally disordered

Section 135 enables a magistrates' court to issue a warrant for the police to enter premises, by force if necessary, and remove a mentally disordered person to a place of safety for up to seventy-two hours. Anyone, including a social worker, can apply. You will have to satisfy the magistrates that there is evidence that either:

(a) a person suffering from a mental disorder has been or is being ill-treated, neglected, or kept otherwise than under proper control, or is living alone and unable to look after himself or herself; or

(b) you are being denied access to a patient who has absconded from hospital or the place the patient is required to live by the guardian; or in respect of whom the proper admission procedures have been completed.

Admission to guardianship

We saw when looking at the criteria for admission for treatment that patients should not go to hospital if they can be treated in the community. But some power to direct the patient's life may be necessary, and this is where the concept of guardianship may fill the gap. The Mental Health Act Code in para. 13.3 advises that 'ASWs and doctors should consider guardianship as a possible alternative to admission to, or continuing care in, hospital'. And in para. 13.4: 'An application for guardianship should be accompanied by a comprehensive care plan established on the basis of multi-disciplinary discussions.' A guardian can be either an individual or a social services department.

We have seen that there is no minimum age for admitting a person to hospital, either informally or formally. However, age does matter in guardianship. If the patient is under 16, guardianship under the Act is not available: the parents (or other person with parental responsibility) are already the guardians. If the local authority wishes to intervene, mental disorder which the parents are unable to cope with could be grounds for care or supervision proceedings, as outlined in chapter 11, or compulsory admission to hospital under ss. 2–4. Wardship, where the court is unfettered by statutory requirements, may well be better suited to meeting the needs of a child of 16 or 17 (*Re F (Mental Health Act: Guardianship)* (2000)).

Application procedures for admission to guardianship

The application procedures for admission to guardianship are very similar to those for admission to hospital for treatment. In this case, however, the application is made not to a hospital but to a social services department (s. 11; 1983 Regulations, reg. 5). As with the application for a hospital admission the application must be made by the ASW or nearest relative. But the mere completion of the application is not enough, unlike with applications for admission to hospital (see above). The application must also be accepted by the social services authority for the area where the proposed guardian lives or by the authority which it is proposed will be the guardian.

Procedures for an application for guardianship are otherwise the same as those for admission for treatment. The applicant must have seen the patient within the past fourteen days, the nearest relative must be consulted and has the same power of veto, and there must be the two medical recommendations. There is no equivalent to the emergency procedure.

The grounds on which the doctors must be satisfied are slightly different from the grounds for admission to hospital (s. 7). The patient must still be suffering from one of the four mental disorders, to a degree that warrants reception into guardianship. This can be reviewed by a court, and if the grounds are not made out the guardianship order will be quashed. See *Re F* (mentioned above, in relation to wardship, and discussed again below). The doctors must confirm that guardianship will benefit the welfare of the patient or, if not, will protect other persons. Welfare is not such a stringent requirement as the health or safety of the patient, which we have seen is the basis of admission for treatment; if the doctors think that guardianship would improve the quality of the patient's life, that is enough for reception into guardianship.

There is no requirement that the disorder be treatable, since guardianship is not, essentially, about treatment.

Guardianship orders following criminal conviction

As an alternative to the hospital order, s. 37 empowers any criminal court to make a guardianship order on the offender. The guardian will be nominated by social services and may well be the ASW. The local authority will have to provide the court with details of how the guardian will exercise his or her powers. The guardianship order, once made, is identical in effect to such an order made outside criminal proceedings—see below.

Powers and duties of the guardian (s. 8 and 1983 Regulations, reg. 12)

If the local authority accepts the application, the person named as guardian in the application assumes certain powers over the patient's life: to specify where the patient shall live, to require the patient to go for medical treatment, to become involved in occupation, education, or training, and to require whoever the patient lives with to give access to a doctor, ASW, or other named person. The particular place the patient might be required to live could well be Part III of the National Assistance Act accommodation (chapter 16).

There is no sanction against a patient who breaches these requirements, except the power to fetch back an absconding patient. If the patient cannot comply with the requirements then guardianship is not appropriate and the order should be discharged (Code, para. 13.8).

Regulation 12 requires that the guardian visit the patient at least every three months, keep the social services authority informed of any changes in the patient's address, comply with any directions given by social services, and nominate a doctor to attend on the patient. Social services must arrange for the patient to be seen every three months, and by a doctor every twelve months (reg. 13).

Guardianship lasts initially for six months. The doctor in charge must review the guardianship during the last two months of any period of guardianship. If the doctor reports to the social services authority that he or she is satisfied that the conditions for continuation of guardianship are fulfilled, the guardianship is automatically renewed for six months on the first occasion, and after that for twelve months (s. 20).

Transfer from guardianship to hospital or vice versa

What happens if a patient presently under guardianship needs to be admitted to hospital, for assessment or treatment, and refuses? An application can be made by the ASW or the nearest relative to the managers of the hospital. The procedure is similar to the original admission procedures, and in particular the same medical recommendations are required (s. 79).

The converse is a transfer from hospital detention into guardianship, either to an individual or to a social services authority. Here the full guardianship procedure is not necessary—if the proposed guardian and the relevant social services department agree, the hospital managers can simply authorise the transfer (s. 19; reg. 7). Re-admission to hospital after such a transfer would require consent or the usual application under the MHA, s. 2, 3, or 4.

◼ Continuing powers of detention in the hospital

The informal patient

If there is time to do so before the informal patient leaves, the applicant can simply invoke the normal admission procedures. There will normally be no need for assessment, so admission is under the s. 3 treatment procedure.

But if time is short—the patient is packing his or her bags, the taxi is waiting—the informal patient can be temporarily detained using s. 5 powers. First, the doctor in charge of treatment (or his or her delegate) can, without having to get any kind of second opinion, detain any hospital patient by writing a report to the managers of the hospital stating that detention is necessary. As soon as the report is delivered to the managers, a seventy-two-hour power of detention commences. This then gives the authorities time to consider compulsory admission for treatment.

Second, if the doctor in charge is unavailable, a six-hour detention can be made by a nurse (so long as she or he is registered for mental disorder work under the Nurses, Midwives and Health Visitors Act 1979). In this case the power of detention begins as soon as the report is written, even before it is delivered to the managers. Again, there is no requirement for the nurse to consult anyone else.

The doctor can use this procedure to detain a patient who is in hospital for a totally unrelated matter, in which case the doctor is unlikely even to be a mental health specialist. The nurse, on the other hand, can only detain a patient admitted originally for mental disorder.

The detained patient

When the time limit expires, detention is unlawful and the patient can leave unless compulsory powers are used. These are:

* The six-hour nurse's detention can become a seventy-two-hour detention on receipt of the report of the doctor in charge.

* The seventy-two-hour doctor's detention can become an admission for treatment or assessment by following the normal procedures.

* The seventy-two-hour detention for assessment in an emergency can be converted to a twenty-eight-day detention by obtaining the second medical recommendation.

* The twenty-eight-day detention for assessment can become a six-month detention for treatment under the normal procedure for admission for treatment.

(In all of these cases, any time already spent detained counts towards the new detention period.)

But these all hit the metaphorical buffers at six months, which is the time limit for detention for treatment (except under a hospital order with an accompanying restriction order).

Section 20 provides the procedure for review and, if appropriate, renewal of detention for treatment beyond six months. This must be invoked in the last two of the six months of a s. 3 detention, or if the patient came to hospital under a s. 37 hospital order following a conviction, and is subject to a restriction order under s. 41, the last two months of the restriction period. The doctor in charge must do two things: first, examine the patient, and, secondly, consult at least one other person who has been professionally concerned with the patient's medical treatment—such as a social worker in the hospital. The doctor must then report to the managers if he or she is satisfied that the conditions for continued detention apply.

The conditions for renewed detention mirror, with slight differences, the original conditions for admission for treatment:

(a) one of the four disorders applies (it must be treatable if it is only a 'minor' disorder; if it is a major disorder, if discharged the patient would be at risk of exploitation, or unlikely to be able to care for himself or herself); *and*

(b) detention is necessary for the health or safety of the patient or the protection of others; *and*

(c) detention in the hospital is necessary for the treatment.

When the managers receive this report, they can detain the patient for treatment for a further six months on the first occasion, and on future occasions for a further twelve months. This review is then repeated during the last two months of each new period of detention.

Leave of absence and patients who abscond

A doctor in charge of a patient's treatment can give leave of absence under s. 17, and can recall a patient from that leave. The power to renew the period of detention (see above) can be used if the patient is still receiving some in-patient treatment (*Barker v Barking Havering and Brentwood Community NHS Trust* (1998)). But if the patient is on leave without treatment, compulsory recall is impossible and, if grounds arise, a fresh application for admission will be needed.

However, powers exist to detain a patient who is absent from hospital without leave, or who fails to live at the place where their guardian requires. A detained hospital patient absent without leave can be detained and returned by an ASW, a member of the hospital staff, a police constable, or any person authorized by the managers of the hospital. A guardianship patient absent from the place where the guardian requires him or her to live can also be detained and returned by any of this list of people, except a delegate of the hospital managers (s. 18).

The power to return the patient lapses when:

(a) six months have elapsed since the 'escape'; or, if later,

(b) the period of compulsory detention has expired.

A patient can therefore be brought back to hospital even though the compulsory detention has elapsed. There is then a one-week power of detention (MHA, s. 21, as amended in 1995) during which the hospital can consider extending detention under s. 20(3) (renewal of detention for treatment) or s. 20(6) (renewal of guardianship).

■ Discharge

Discharge of a detained patient

Where patients are detained for assessment or treatment the courts have declared that they must be discharged as soon as they are found not to be suffering from a mental disorder (*Kynaston v Secretary of State for Home Affairs* (1981)). So the twenty-eight-day or six-month period is not to be seen as time to serve, but a maximum period.

Who can exercise this power of discharge? Section 23 gives the power to the managers, the doctor in charge, or the nearest relative. But the nearest relative has less power to discharge than the doctor or managers: first, he or she has no power of discharge during the period of a hospital order made by a criminal court (s. 23 and Schedule 1); second, the nearest relative must always give seventy-two hours' notice before exercising the power of discharge. During that period the discharge can be vetoed (see below).

The criteria for discharge are not stated in s. 23, but the case of *Kynaston* implies that those in charge should constantly be checking to ascertain whether the initial admission criteria are still met; they should not wait until the s. 20 review which takes place in the last two months of a detention for treatment.

If the patient is subject to a restriction order imposed by the Crown Court the release has to be approved by the Secretary of State.

Discharge subject to supervision

If the doctor in charge believes that the patient, on discharge, is a risk to himself or herself or to others, or open to serious exploitation, there are powers under the Mental Health (Patients in the Community) Act 1995 to obtain a supervision requirement, known as 'after-care under supervision' (MHA, s. 25, as amended). As the supervision of after-care gives a measure of control over the patient, there is an application and consultation procedure to attempt to ensure that powers to direct the patient's life are not obtained where it is unnecessary to do so. Further details are set out below. After-care with supervision is not available for patients detained under a criminal court hospital order.

Discharge by Parole Board

Section 74 now permits mental patients held under a restriction order as a result of a criminal conviction to apply to the Parole Board like any other prisoner. If the Parole Board orders release the power to detain under the hospital order ceases, notwithstanding the restriction order.

Discharge from guardianship

Guardianship can be terminated before the end of the six- or twelve-month period by the nearest relative, the social services authority, or the doctor in charge (s. 23)—but not by the individual guardian unless he or she is also the nearest relative.

But where the guardianship order was made by a criminal court, discharge under s. 23 can be made only by the social services department, not by the doctor in charge or the nearest relative (Sch. 1, Part I, paras. 2 and 8).

Overriding the power of the nearest relative to discharge a detained patient

The doctors may not agree with the nearest relative that the patient should be discharged from hospital. They have seventy-two hours to decide their position. If the doctor in charge wishes to veto the discharge, he or she must submit a report to the managers of the hospital stating that the patient would, if discharged, be a danger to himself or herself or to others. If the managers agree with this view, this blocks the discharge (s. 25). In addition to risking having their decision overridden, nearest relatives have to think hard about even trying to discharge the patient; if the doctor reports against discharge, the nearest relative is barred from discharging the patient for the next six months. (Neither the seventy-two-hour notice period, nor the right of veto, applies to a discharge from guardianship by the nearest relative.)

An ASW can also block discharge, either from hospital or guardianship, by the nearest relative. But unlike a doctor's immediate power to block discharge from hospital, the ASW must go through the more complex route of applying to the county court to displace the nearest relative (see above). Under s. 29, as soon as this application is filed with the court (which could be during the nearest relative's seventy-two-hour notice period) the discharge by the nearest relative is blocked until the court has made a decision. It will probably be too late to use this power to block discharge from guardianship as there is no seventy-two-hour notice requirement.

Discharge by the Mental Health Review Tribunal (MHRT)

The tribunal can order a discharge both from hospital and from guardianship (MHA, Part V). Procedures are governed by the Mental Health Review Tribunal Rules 1983 (SI 1983 No. 942).

Tribunals, as we saw in chapter 5, are in theory simpler, less orientated towards formal legal procedures, than courts. In the case of the MHRT this is a myth, and as a result of previous campaigns waged for the rights of patients, it is now recognized that applicants should have publicly funded specialist legal representation. A solicitor appearing before the MHRT has to be a member of an approved panel of specialists, for there will be a need to marshall evidence of fact and medical opinion, and cross-examine witnesses, including experts in mental health. The ASW will need to consult its own legal department.

Who can apply to the MHRT? The applicant will be either the patient or the nearest relative who has been barred from discharging the patient. The application is submitted to one of the four regional MHRTs and must be in writing; a letter will do (1983 Rules, r. 3), although forms are available. If the patient is detained for treatment beyond the first six months and no one makes an application to the MHRT, the hospital managers must themselves refer the case to the Tribunal. There must be a further reference not more than three years later—so no patient should languish unnoticed for more than that time.

It is important for any applicant to be aware of the time limits which apply to MHRT applications. These are set out in Box 17.5.

At any MHRT hearing there must be an up-to-date social circumstances report, which is usually submitted by the hospital social worker. Where the application relates to a discharge from guardianship, the social services department has three weeks to prepare a statement of information, including the factual background and social circumstances, together with the author's opinion on whether the patient should be discharged (1983 Rules, r. 6).

The task of the MHRT is essentially to consider whether the original criteria for detention or guardianship are still justified. It will take into account not just the evidence heard, but also a medical examination carried out by the medically qualified panel member (1983 Rules, r. 11). If it is satisfied that the criteria are no longer justified, it can order the discharge of the patient—either now or at a specified date (s. 72). (Failure to order discharge where there is no further mental disorder has been declared wrong by the European Court of Human Rights: *Johnson v UK* (1997).) Discharge can be ordered, even if the original admission criteria continue to be satisfied, if under s. 72 the Tribunal is not satisfied that the detention is in the interest of the patient's health or the protection of others.

BOX 17.5 Time Limits for Applications to the MHRT (MHA, ss. 66 and 68)

Application by the nearest relative

Discharge of patient blocked by the doctor in charge	28 days from the date of being informed
Nearest relative displaced by county court order	12 months from that order, and thereafter once every 12 months
Patient detained under a hospital order; patient under a restriction order	not before six months; once during the second six-month period, thereafter once during every 12-month period

Application by the patient

Admission for assessment	14 days
Admission for treatment/reception into guardianship	six months
Patient receiving supervised after-care	no time limit

Where the patient is under a criminal court restriction order, discharge by the Tribunal can be made conditional (s.73). A conditional discharge then gives the Home Secretary a continuing power of recall. Conditions commonly relate to residence, treatment, and supervision, but in one case which withstood a court challenge the condition prevented the patient from going out at all without an escort: *R (on the application of the Secretary of State for the Home Department) v Mental Health Review Tribunal* (2002). A patient who has been conditionally discharged may be re-sectioned under MHA, s. 3, and may be recalled by the Home Secretary (*R v NW London Mental Health Trust, ex parte Stewart* (1996)). Even after such a further detention under s. 3, he or she may be recalled to the hospital chosen by the Home Secretary (*Dlodlo v MHRT for South Thames Region* (1996)). Guidance on recall of discharged patients is set out in Circular HSG(93)20, *Recall of Mentally Disordered Patients*.

There is a difference between a patient under a restriction order imposed by the court, where the MHRT can order a discharge, as above, and a patient transferred from prison to hospital under s. 47, where the MHRT is allowed only to make a recommendation for the release of the patient to the Home Secretary. But this difference has been declared contrary to Article 5 of the European Convention in *Benjamin v United Kingdom* (2003). The patient was serving a life sentence and, having been transferred to hospital under s. 47, could not be released by order of the MHRT but only with the agreement of the Secretary of State. But the Secretary of State refused release. The ECtHR ruled that the patient was entitled to have the lawfulness of his detention decided by an independent tribunal. This represents one of the many occasions in this chapter where human rights scrutiny of the Mental Health Act indicates the need for some reform. We will look at some more in the next section.

Human rights and the MHRT

Article 5 of the European Convention on Human Rights requires there to be a mechanism for challenging the lawfulness of the detention of any person. The existence of the MHRT, save in the case of prisoners transferred to hospital as we have just seen, fulfils the form of such requirement, but does the practice of the Tribunal meet the substance of the right?

First, there are delays. Where liberty is at stake any delay in the Tribunal must be reasonable, otherwise Article 5 is breached: *R (on the application of KB and others) v Mental Health Review Tribunal and Secretary of State for Health* (2002), where the patient was entitled to damages for the resulting detention.

Secondly, the power of the authorities to re-section the newly released patient has not stood up to human rights scrutiny. We have earlier noted that the discharge by the Tribunal does not prevent a compulsory readmission taking place under s. 3—but, if there has been no change in circumstance since the Tribunal discharged the patient, this has been ruled to be an abuse of the patient's right to liberty: *R (on the application of Von Brandenburg) v East London and the City Mental Health NHS Trust* (2003). According to Sedley LJ at the Court of Appeal stage in *Brandenburg*, at paragraph 32, 'In such circumstances I do not see how an approved social worker can properly be satisfied, as required by section 13, that "an application ought to be made" unless aware of circumstances not known to the tribunal which invalidate the decision of the tribunal. In the absence of such circumstances an application by the approved social worker should, on an application for judicial review, be held unlawful on the ground of irrationality'. Lord Bingham made the key point at para. 8 of his judgment: 'the rule of law requires that effect should be loyally given to the decisions of legally constituted tribunals in accordance with what is decided'. If the hospital thinks the tribunal decision is wrong it should, instead, apply for a judicial review. (It was, the Court agreed, wrong to discharge the patient in this case, since the patient was discharged in the absence of suitable after-care facilities.)

Another challenge may arise under the three-year automatic referral to the MHRT discussed above. This period may be too long, given that the patient may lack the capacity to make an application to the MHRT himself or herself. It could be argued that three years without being able to challenge the lawfulness of the detention is effectively a denial of the right itself. This will be significantly shortened if legislation along the lines of the 2002 draft bill is introduced.

A further problem is that there is no requirement for the doctors who state that grounds for continued detention exist to be cross-examined on that evidence: *R (on the application of Wilkinson) v Responsible Medical Officer, Broadmoor Hospital* (2001).

But the main problem is more fundamental. The legislation is not compatible with European Human Rights decisions. The ECtHR case of *Winterwerp v Netherlands* (1979), laid down a number of tests, including a requirement for the state to prove the grounds for detention. Yet the MHRT has no duty to release a patient unless it is satisfied that the person does not suffer from the mental condition. The negatives in the last sentence essentially mean that the tribunal can, in theory, wait until it is proved that the condition no longer exists before ordering release, putting the burden of proving this on to the detained patient. This provision of the MHA has been successfully challenged in the case of *R (on the application of H) v Mental Health Review Tribunal for North East London* (2001). In fact the Court of Appeal declared s. 72 to be incompatible with Article 5, so there is a good prospect of amending legislation. (We said that in the seventh and eighth editions of this book, and still await the reform.)

Further, any recall of a restricted patient by the Secretary of State is open to challenge if there has not been a proper and independent examination of the grounds for renewed detention. Even with consideration of the evidence, recall by a politician on grounds not tested in an independent court or tribunal seems to amount to a denial of Article 5 (right to liberty) and Article 6 (fair and independent determination of rights).

If a discharge is ordered subject to suitable after-care arrangements being made, it will not necessarily be a breach of the patient's human rights (Article 5, right to liberty) if such arrangements cannot be made. In the case of *R (on the application of W) v Doncaster MBC* (2004), the local authority did not have suitable trained staff to supervise the applicant in the hostel to which he would be discharged, resulting in a seven month continuation of detention. The Court of Appeal held that this was a rational and lawful reason for refusing the discharge. Additionally the local authority was not responsible for detaining the patient, only for dealing with after-care, so the Court could not make any order against them in relation to the detention itself. *R (on the application of B) v Mental Health Review Tribunal and others* (2003) further confirms that a discharge from detention can be delayed to enable the local authority to arrange the necessary after-care, where this will remove the danger of the patient acting in a dangerous manner towards other people or him/herself. In this case the application to the MHRT was by a nearest relative, whose discharge of the patient had been blocked under s. 25.

Treatment while in hospital

Treatment for the mental disorder

Detention for the purposes of treatment under s. 3, or following a criminal conviction (s. 37), enables treatment to be given for the disorder that led to the admission. 'Treatment' was been quite broadly defined, and was held to include a power to search patients and their property, to control and to discipline them, and even to override the objection of a doctor to such discipline (*R v Broadmoor Special Hospital Authority, ex parte S* (1998)).

Restrictions on civil rights

But the starting point is that a detained patient loses none of his or her human rights or civil rights, except those that are necessarily lost by the fact of the detention or by clear legal limitation. For example the Representation of the People Act 2000 allows all mental patients except those detained by a criminal court to vote in elections. But how are actual decisions reached on what restrictions are necessary and, in the language of the Human Rights Act, proportionate? *R (on the application of Munjaz) v Mersey Care NHS Trust* (2003) provides an example. Two patients sought judicial review of the hospital's practice of secluding patients. This practice was recognized, in this particular case, to be a diminution of their rights under the European Human Rights Convention Art.3 (inhuman or degrading treatment) and Article 8 (respect for private life). The Court held that seclusion must be viewed as part of the medical treatment, and must be continually reviewed in accordance with the Code of Practice. Failure to demonstrate that the seclusion was necessary, proportionate to the medical problem and to the need for protection of others, and failure to monitor in accordance with the Code, rendered it unlawful in this case. But the court refused to accept that seclusion was necessarily an unjustified interference with a patient's liberty under Article 5. Detention was lawful in itself and patients' rights during detention could be protected under Articles 3 and 8.

Another example of a reduction in civil rights is the fact that the hospital can monitor the telephone calls of dangerous patients. This was ruled not to be a breach of the European Convention right (Article 8) to private life: *R (on the application of N) v Ashworth Special Hospital Authority* (2001). The manner of the patient's detention was frequently reviewed by the European Court of Human Rights before the Human Rights Act 1998. An example of this is the case of *A v UK* (1980), where a detainee in Broadmoor

Hospital challenged the conditions imposed on him following his involvement in an arson incident. These included solitary confinement and deprivation of normal clothing and furniture. He alleged breach of Article 3 (i.e. inhuman and degrading treatment). The government conceded the case before final hearing, after the European Commission on Human Rights ruled that the conditions of detention would be reviewable by the full Court.

What is the right of a patient to engage in sexual activity? This was reviewed in *R (on the application of H) v Ashworth Hospital Authority* (2001). H, a detainee, suffered from hepatitis. In order to protect his homosexual partners he demanded the hospital provide him with condoms. But the hospital refused, on two grounds: first, the patient should not be having sex, because it was against hospital rules, and second, it did not believe he was having sex anyway. The patient's complaint that this breached his Article 2 right (right to life) was rejected; the hospital no-sex policy provided a better protection; his claim that his right to respect for private life was infringed was also rejected, as there had to be a balance between this and the need to restrict sexual activity in order to prevent sexual abuse of patients.

Similarly, a hospital did not act disproportionately in restricting a patient's choice of clothing when it refused him women's clothes: *R (on the application of E) v Ashworth Hospital* (2001). The judge Richards J thought the need for this sort of control was 'self-evident'. We are not convinced.

Compulsory treatment

The basis upon which doctors normally treat patients is by consent. Where someone is too young to give consent (which is for the doctors to decide under the *Gillick* principle—see chapter 3), it can be given by a parent or guardian, or by a High Court judge in wardship or under s. 8 of the Children Act 1989. But what is the situation where a mental patient withholds consent from treatment? Or the disorder is such that no such consent is real? Treatment in the absence of lawful authority would be an assault and potentially a crime; so the Act clarifies the circumstances in which consent is needed or can be dispensed with. Further, it contains safeguards to try to ensure that any consent is real.

The Code, para. 15.12, reminds health professionals that mental disorder should not in itself be seen as removing such capacity and gives guidance on circumstances where capacity to consent may not exist.

Under the MHA, s. 57, certain drastic treatments cannot be given without the patient's informed consent; an independent specialist doctor, plus two mental health specialists who are not doctors, must vouch for the fact that the patient did understand the nature and consequences of treatment. This could involve the hospital social worker. Also, a second medical opinion is required, confirming that the treatment is appropriate. Only two treatments at present fall into this category: destruction of brain tissue or brain functioning (such as a lobotomy), and surgical implants to reduce male sex drive (reg. 16).

Lower down the scale of drastic treatments comes electro-convulsive therapy and long-term drug treatment (any regime of over three months). This can be administered only if the patient gives informed consent, or if an independent doctor agrees that it is necessary notwithstanding the lack of consent or the lack of capacity to give consent. There is no requirement for an independent specialist to confirm that any consent is informed. If consent is refused the treatment is lawful if the doctors can show—in court if challenged—that it was medically necessary, compared with alternatives. Medical necessity does not require unanimity amongst the profession, since there will always be a need for judgement: *R (on the application of N) v M* (2002). If treatment is to proceed without consent, the doctor providing the second opinion must have consulted two specialists who are not doctors. But the treatment can go ahead after the consultation, whatever they say! The patient is entitled to be given written reasons explaining why his or her consent, for example to a course of anti-psychotic drugs, has been dispensed with: *R (on the application of Wooder) v Fegetter* (2002).

R (on the application of B) v Ashworth Hospital Authority (2003) makes clear that any use of the power of compulsory treatment must relate to the condition for which the patient has been detained, not to any other mental health condition. In this case the patient had both schizophrenia and personality disorder. The personality disorder did not give rise to a power to detain and could therefore not be treated without consent.

The power to treat compulsorily has now been considered in light of the Human Rights Act: *R (on the application of PS) v Dr G and Dr W* (2003). The patient was agreed to have the capacity to refuse consent, but the registered medical officer sought to use the statutory powers to administer anti-psychotic medication in spite of refusal of consent. The patient claimed breach of his right not to suffer inhuman and degrading treatment (Article 5) and right to respect for private life (Article 8). The court held these rights did apply to any decision to use powers of compulsory treatment, but there must be a balancing exercise. Degrading or inhuman treatment does not arise unless the treatment is severe, but even this degrading treatment could be necessary if the patient's disorder is serious, failure to medicate might have serious consequences, and the treatment is likely to be effective. His application for judicial review was unsuccessful.

Treatments which do not relate to the mental disorder

No special rules apply to mental patients. If patients require treatment for physical ailments, their consent must be obtained. If it cannot be obtained because of the lack of capacity of the patient, then there is a common law (i.e. judge-made, rather than statute) power to carry out any treatment necessary for the well-being of the patient. In cases of doubt it is common for a hospital to apply to the court to ensure the proposed treatment is lawful. An example is the case of *F v West Berkshire Health Authority* (1989). The authority sought a declaration that it would be lawful to sterilize a woman with a mental age of 5 who was deemed to be at risk of a pregnancy, with which the doctors felt she could not cope. The House of Lords declared this operation lawful. If the treatment is purely therapeutic (i.e. to treat a condition), the court's permission is not needed. So a mental patient suffering serious menorrhea could be given a hysterectomy even though she could not consent to it herself (*Re GF* (1992)).

The same principles will apply even if the person lacking capacity has not had any mental health problem. In *NHS Hospital Trust v S* (2003) the adult had autism and learning difficulties, and was incapable of consenting to the dialysis treatment needed to keep him alive, a form of treatment which would be painful and invasive, and which he would not understand. The court had to decide what was in his best interests, in a situation where the family and doctors held a variety of views. In fact on these facts the court decided that it would be in the person's own interest to receive the treatment.

A person with a mental disorder, the Code reminds practitioners in para. 15, does not automatically lack the necessary understanding to give or withhold consent. In *Re C (Refusal of Medical treatment)* (1994) the patient refused to allow his gangrenous foot to be amputated and wanted to force the hospital to agree that in future it would not remove the foot without consent. The court held that he knew what he was doing and the right to decide remained his. (According to one newspaper account his foot then recovered.)

Treatment can be for the benefit of the patient in an oblique rather than a direct manner. In *Re Y (Mental Incapacity: Bone Marrow Transplant)* (1996), the High Court ruled that it was in the patient's best interest to donate bone marrow to her sister, whose death would distress the patient.

A person who understands what he or she is doing can give an 'advance directive', so that consent (or withholding of consent) applies even though at the time the need for treatment arises the person lacks capacity. (An advance directive would not limit the power to treat the mental illness itself, however.) See, for example, *Re C* (above); and see *Re AK (Adult Patient) (Medical Treatment: Consent)* (2001), where the court agreed to the patient's request that two weeks after he lost the ability to communicate as a result of his motor neurone disease the ventilator which kept him alive would be switched off. An advance directive is something someone might prepare if they wish to avoid intrusive treatment to keep them alive following the onset of dementia.

If the patient is under 18, the proposed treatment can be authorised by the High Court (*Re M* (1988)). Any person sufficiently interested in the welfare of the young person could make the application, but normally this would be social services, after liaison with the medical staff.

No permission of the court is required, apparently, for an abortion for a mental patient, if doctors consider the criteria of the Abortion Act 1967 to be met (risk to the mother) and the patient is capable of consenting (*Re SG* (1991)).

After-care of the mental patient

Where a patient is discharged from detention in hospital or from guardianship, s. 117 imposes a duty jointly on the health authority and social services to provide after-care services for as long as they are needed. The authorities should cooperate with suitable voluntary agencies. There is no statutory definition of what level of after-care is required. However, DoH Circular of 5 February 1995, *After-care Form for the Discharge of Psychiatric Patients*, sets out a good practice checklist for entering details such as the patient's nominated contact and details of the after-care plan. All discharged patients must have an individual care plan drawn up with an identified keyworker who will ensure that it is implemented.

We have seen in the last chapter that services can, or must, be provided to people who need them by reason of age, mental disorder, or handicap. For example, a number of people in need of Part III accommodation will be old, physically unable to manage, and mentally disordered. Support and accommodation are therefore available under the NAA, ss. 21 and 29 (see above). As we noted in chapter 16 patients released from hospital cannot be charged for their after-care under s. 117.

After-care under supervision

Under provisions inserted into s. 25 of the MHA by the Mental Health (Patients in the Community) Act 1995, there is a regime called after-care under supervision. It does not apply to patients who were admitted under a hospital order following a criminal conviction. The hospital can require a discharged patient to cooperate with a treatment plan under MHA, s. 117. Social services and the health authority will draw up this plan together. The patient who does not cooperate may be readmitted under the MHA powers to admit for assessment or, more probably, treatment.

The power to require cooperation from the patient in the supervision of his or her after-care contrasts with the normal arrangement to work with the discharged patient voluntarily. The power is obtained on the application of the hospital, made to the health authority responsible for the after-care services. The local authority must be consulted, and the application must be supported by both a doctor and an ASW. The application must include an after-care plan which names the doctor and the patient's supervisor after discharge. Social services will be closely involved in preparing this plan. The power lasts six months, and is renewable for six months and then a year at a time. (The health authority responsible for the patient's community care can bring it to an end earlier if the power is no longer needed.) A patient who objects to receiving supervised after-care may apply to the MHRT under MHA, s. 66.

After-care or guardianship?

How does supervised after-care overlap with guardianship? The answer is that the objectives of guardianship and supervised after-care overlap, as do the methods by which control over the patient is exerted—requirement to live at a stated address, to permit the supervisor to visit, etc. The legal regimes are separate though. Indeed, if the patient in after-care is received into guardianship, supervised after-care terminates. Guardianship is essentially a means of providing help independent of compulsory admission to hospital. Supervised after-care aims to keep the former detained patient out of hospital after release. Also the procedure for applying is different, particularly with regard to who is the applicant (ASW for guardianship, hospital for supervised after-care) and who the application is addressed to (local authority for guardianship, health authority for supervised after-care). The other key difference is that supervised after-care gives stronger enforcement powers than guardianship. The social services and health authority, who are jointly responsible for the after-care under MHA, s. 117, can tell the patient where to live, to attend for treatment, occupation, education, or training, and to let any person authorized by the supervisor see the patient. The supervisor can 'take and convey' (i.e. force) the patient to achieve these ends. If the patient still does not co-operate, there are no further powers, and compulsory re-detention may be necessary.

Lastly, whose job is it to supervise? The supervisor must be a named individual, under the amended MHA, s. 117, defined as 'a person professionally concerned with any of the after-care services'. This does not automatically mean a social worker; in theory the doctor in charge could double up as the supervisor (MHA, s. 34 as amended). The responsibility for ensuring that someone is appointed is actually that of the health authority, not the local authority (MHA, s. 117(2)).

Powers to control people not covered by the MHA

You would be forgiven for thinking that the powers of compulsory intervention in the lives of vulnerable people would be clearly set out in the legislation. Two recent cases, taken together, cast doubt on this. They both concern the same mentally incapacitated young woman, and were flagged up in the case study for this chapter. She was 17 years old at the time of the first hearing—too old for a care order. The local authority tried guardianship as its preferred way of removing her from a sexually abusive home environment. There was no doubt that she suffered from a 'state of arrested or incomplete development of mind' under the MHA, s. 1, but her wish to return home, according to the Court of Appeal, could not amount to 'seriously irresponsible conduct'. So guardianship was not available, leaving an obvious gap in the law in terms of affording protection to such persons (*Re F (Mental Health Act: Guardianship)* (2000)).

The local authority then tried another approach, using an old, previously thought defunct, common law doctrine of 'necessity'. The Court of Appeal in *Re F (Adult Patient)* (2000) held that it had the power to make a declaration as to the living arrangements to be made for the mentally incapacitated person, allowing the local authority control. This would be in F's best interests. The result is that the common law provides a power for a court to declare it lawful for the state (the local authority in this case) to control a person's life even where there are no statutory powers. We would hope that any new mental health legislation will lay down clear procedures to replace this *ad hoc* law-making to fill the gaps.

We also looked in chapter 16 at powers of compulsory removal from home under community care legislation. There is no requirement for there to be a mental disorder when those powers are invoked.

Liability of health and social work professionals

We mentioned in the previous chapter the case of *Clunis*, where a mental patient who had killed a stranger wanted to sue the health authority for not controlling his condition, but was refused leave. We mentioned that the whole area of liability law is developing; the rights of children whose needs were not met by social services departments, leaving them exposed to abuse, to sue those departments have been upheld by the European Court of Human Rights. The same principles, we suggest, apply in the mental health field. The most recent case is *Palmer v Tees Health Authority* (1999). The hospital trust had cared for a man for several years, but notwithstanding this the man had sexually assaulted and murdered the 4-year-old daughter of Mrs Palmer. The Court of Appeal rejected her claim for damages on the basis that the hospital, in law, did not owe her a duty of care. Whether this judgment would withstand a Human Rights Act challenge is, in our view, very uncertain, but no case since the Act came into force has been decided to our knowledge. We discussed questions of liability in more detail in chapter 1 above.

New legislation?

For the past three years we have been expecting a Mental Health Act, and have flagged up the various proposals in the eighth and the seventh editions. A new bill has again been published, but was not presented to Parliament in the 2004–2005 parliamentary session. If the bill is brought forward after the 2005 election, we will put the detail on our web site. For now, we are happy to allow the government to describe their intentions, and the following ministerial statements (which we have abbreviated) appeared in their press release in September 2004.

> The revised Bill represents the first major overhaul of the legislation since the 1950s and is an integral part of the Government's wider strategy to improve mental health services for all; reflecting developments in human rights law and providing a legal framework in line with modern services and treatments . . . we believe that we now have a Bill that puts a new focus on the individual, allowing compulsory powers to be used in ways that fit with patients' changing needs.
>
> One of the fundamental aims of the Bill is to help make community care work for the people who need it most. Patients in the community who are ill and vulnerable or at risk will now be able to get the treatment they need.
>
> Safeguards for patients will also be greatly strengthened with choice of representative, access to advocacy and all use of compulsory treatment beyond 28 days having to be authorised by a new independent Mental Health Tribunal.
>
> People will only be subject to treatment under the Bill if they are at risk of harm to themselves or others. The bill means that the small minority of people with mental health problems who need to be treated against their wishes, normally for their protection but occasionally to protect the public, will get the right treatment at the right time. . . .

The provisions that enable dangerous and serious offenders to be detained in hospital for mental health treatment will stay in place. The vast majority of people with mental disorders are not a risk to others, but a minority are—and the law obviously needs to recognise this.

We will not compromise public safety. If we are to protect the public we must ensure that those with a mental disorder who are a risk to others receive the high quality mental health treatment they need. The Bill will help to achieve this.

It also enables non-dangerous offenders who do not pose a risk to others to receive mental health treatment under sanction in the community. This means that the offender will receive the mental health treatment he or she needs to reduce the risk of re-offending.

National Director for Mental Health, Louis Appleby, said:

We are determined to develop an effective Act that best serves the interests of people with mental health problems. It will be for clinical and social care staff to decide whether, in their professional judgement, it is clinically appropriate to treat someone under the act. If they decide that it is not then compulsory powers cannot be used.

The criteria for compulsory treatment under the Bill are carefully drafted—to make sure that only people who need compulsory treatment receive it. Mental health services will have a duty to respond to requests for assessment and patients who are treated under the Bill will have to have an individual care plan focussed on their individual needs.'

The full text can be accessed at **www.dh.gov.uk/assetRoot/04/08/89/14/ 04088914.pdf**. It has over 300 sections and fourteen schedules, and if enacted it will completely replace the existing mental health legislation. It has attracted the hostility of the medical profession and Liberty, and given the track record of previous proposals we do not expect an easy parliamentary passage. Therefore for the time being it is probably wise to stick to the existing law as your guide, while keeping your eye open for developments.

EXERCISE

Steven, aged 20, has a developmental age of around 4 or 5. As a child, he spent a significant amount of time in residential care, provided or paid for by the local authority, though he never required care under a care order. His parents struggled to cope, but managed. Recently his mother, to whom he was very attached, died. Now he is an adult and, though he receives day care, is living at home with his father, Cyril. Since his mother died, Steven has become quite aggressive towards Cyril, who finds it difficult to maintain a safe environment at home for Steven; also Steven tends to wander off, talk with strangers, and stay out for long periods, sometimes having to be brought home by police or others. Recently Cyril hit Steven. A social services assessment of Steven's needs and those of Cyril as his carer, which involved obtaining psychiatric evidence, now recommends that Steven should be accommodated elsewhere as Cyril cannot cope. Cyril is strongly opposed to Steven being removed from his care and, in so far as it can be determined, Steven does not want to live away. In light of community care and mental health law, what options should the various agencies responsible for Steven's welfare consider?

COMPANION WEB SITE

 For guidance on how to answer these exercises, visit the companion web site at: www.oup.com/uk/booksites/law

WHERE DO WE GO FROM HERE?

This chapter concludes the two chapters on work with vulnerable adults. There is one further part to the book. Part 5 collects together issues which could relate to working with both vulnerable children and their families, or vulnerable adults. We look at problems of violence and anti-social behaviour, and attempts by the state to control it or confer rights on its victims; we look at housing rights and in particular rights to be housed if homeless; and, finally, we look at rights to social service provision of those vulnerable people who have restricted immigration status.

ANNOTATED FURTHER READING

Mental Health

H. Brayne and G. Broadbent, *Legal Materials for Social Workers* (Oxford University Press, 2002). Contains much of the important mental health legislation and guidance, with commentary and overview of reform proposals.

R. Jones, *Mental Health Act Manual* (9th edn., Sweet & Maxwell, 2004). This is used as a handbook by many lawyers and is both comprehensive and up to date.

C. Taylor and D. Postgate, *Advising Mentally Disordered Offenders* (Law Society Publications, 2000). The title is misleading, since a lot of this is about suspects, not offenders. But it provides a good insight into an area which we have not had space to focus on: interrogation of mental patients in the police station.

R. Stone, *A Companion Guide to Mentally Disordered Offenders* (2nd edn., Shaw and Sons, 2003). We have the same problem with the title, but otherwise this is an excellent guide to all stages of criminal proceedings involving the mentally disordered, including hospital orders. It also discusses the proposals for reform.

J. Peay, *Decisions and Dilemmas, Working with Mental Health Law* (Hart Publishing, 2003). Examines the interplay between the health and legal disciplines and how decisions are made about patients.

N. Glover-Thomas, *Reconstructing Mental Health Law and Policy* (Butterworths, 2002). This book takes a critical including a historical perspective. How did the law get into its present state? How should it be reformed?

P. Bartlett and R. Sandland, *Mental Health Law Policy and Practice* (Blackstone Press, 2003). Provides a critical perspective on the law and how it works in practice.

R. Brown, and others, *Mental Health Law* (Hodder Arnold, 2005). Written by authors from a range of disciplines, contributions balancing legal with clinical expertise.

Mind, **www.mind.org.uk**—access to a range of helpful materials to help those with mental health problems.

Department of Health, **www.doh.gov.uk/**—not an easy site to navigate, but you will need it to locate press releases and official documents.

National Service Framework for Mental Health, **www.doh.gov.uk/nsf/ mhexecsum.htm#exec**—a guide to the overall standards required, set in conjunction with the NHS.

The Institute of Mental Health Act Practitioners, **www.markwalton.net/**—a very well organized resource bank where, for example, the Code of Practice and circulars can be accessed without having to search the Department of Health.

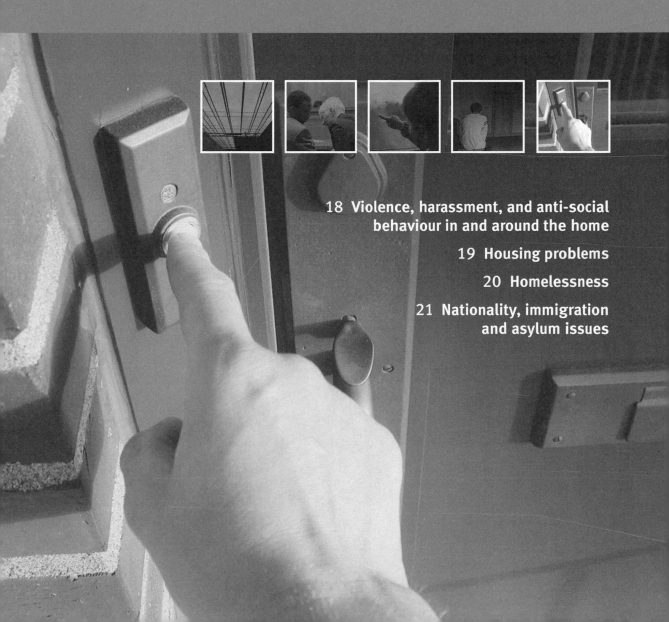

PART V

Social exclusion

PART V Social exclusion

Social exclusion describes the marginalization from employment, income, social networks such as family, neighbourhood and community, decision making and from an adequate quality of life which some people suffer. Policy makers consider that social exclusion increases the likelihood and impact of social harm befalling an individual, so for instance, socially excluded people face a higher risk of family breakdown, a greater likelihood of being the victim of crime and violence, greater fear of crime, poor housing, economic difficulties, debt, unemployment, poor schooling, and uncertain immigration status. Social exclusion has received considerable government attention since 1997 when the incoming Labour Government established the Social Exclusion Unit—see its web site **www.socialexclusionunit.gov.uk**.

Social welfare law provides some, arguably limited, remedies for some of the problems associated with social exclusion. Whilst we cannot address all areas of relevant law within this book, we think that it is important that social workers are aware of the rights and remedies which are available to service users in the particular areas of domestic violence and other anti-social behaviour, housing, homelessness, immigration and asylum support.

In **chapter 18** we will address the ways in which the law provides remedies for problems of violence. Domestic violence impacts particularly seriously on women and families, and we explain the criminal and civil law which may be available to combat it. But there are other forms of violence, harassment and anti-social behaviour, and the chapter explains the powers of local authorities and other agencies to protect victims from unacceptable conduct. We consider racially aggravated offences, anti-social behaviour orders, curfews, and powers available to respond to problems caused by children's behaviour when they are too young to commit a crime. Some of the available orders are punitive, some are preventative and others, for instance parenting orders which enable the court to specify help for parents whose children are in trouble, can be supportive.

Homelessness excludes people from an adequate quality of life. Inadequate or insecure housing impacts particularly on children and vulnerable individuals. Local authorities have a limited duty to provide accommodation to those in priority need if, through no fault of their own, they have no home of their own. Social workers may need to work closely with the housing department to secure accommodation for the benefit of the service user. The law is quite complex and we do our best in **chapter 19** to explain it, and how to make it work for the service user.

Linked to the question of homelessness is the general question of housing. There is lack of decent affordable housing in many parts of England and Wales. Families can lose children because of inadequate housing, housing is central to community care provision and to the successful integration of care leavers into society. We examine in **chapter 20** the ways in which rented housing can be acquired, how it can be afforded and the ways in which landlords can obtain possession from tenants. We also look at other responsibilities that landlords have—for instance their obligations to maintain a property in an adequate state of repair.

Because the duties are modified by a person's immigration status, we set out in **chapter 21** the effect which immigration status will have on your overall duties to children and vulnerable adults. Recent arrivals in the UK, in particular refugees from dangerous situations, or lone children are particularly vulnerable and in need of services. **Chapter 21** also examines the ways in which a person's immigration status is determined, and the ways in which such status can lead to a restriction on eligibility for services from a social services department.

We cannot cover the full range of social welfare law in this part of the book. However you should be familiar with local providers of legal advice in these areas, through personal knowledge eventually, but in any event through using the Community Legal Services Directory, which can be accessed at **www.justask.org.uk**.

CASE STUDY

London Borough of Lambeth v Howard [2001] EWCA Civ 468, (2001) 33 HLR 58

Facts (taken from the judgment of Sedley LJ)

Mr Howard became a secure tenant of a flat in Arden House owned by Lambeth Council in 1976. Ten years later Miss Gabriel moved into the adjoining flat. The flats are built in such a way that Miss Gabriel had to pass Mr Howard's window in order to enter and leave her flat, and so do her child and any visitors. Mr Howard did not have to pass in front of Miss Gabriel's windows. During 1994 when both Miss Gabriel and Mr Howard were living on their own, Mr Howard began to pester Miss Gabriel. On the one hand Mr Howard was seeking her attention and friendship; on the other he was making complaints about her to the local authority housing officers when his approaches were rebuffed. This kind of conduct continued intermittently into 1996 when he began following Miss Gabriel into shops and elsewhere and tried to enter her flat against her will. By the summer of that year, however, he was being remorseful and seeking to build a friendship with her. When that did not work, in the autumn he began to make allegations against Miss Gabriel, which the judge in the county court found were outrageous and unfounded, to the effect that she was involved in drugs and prostitution. He made allegations about the welfare of her daughter to the head teacher and to Social Services, with the predictable result that these complaints were taken seriously if only for fear of the possible consequences if they were not. The effect upon Miss Gabriel and her daughter can be imagined. Then by Christmas of 1996 Mr Howard was again seeking friendship and sending a Christmas card. This on/off conduct continued through 1997. There was a further allegation to the head teacher. Social Services had to become involved. The appellant claimed to be an investigative journalist writing a story for the *News of the World*. He banged on Miss Gabriel's door and verbally abused her and then left apologetic cards with assurances that he would not be any more trouble.

In August of that year the police finally became involved. They spoke to Mr Howard, but it did little good. He tended, when he repeated his conduct and the police were called again, to justify himself by making damaging allegations against Miss Gabriel and her daughter. In October 1997 he pushed open her letterbox, which she had tried to secure against him, and tried to talk to her through it. The following day the police once again came to see him. He again responded with allegations of the most insulting and damaging kind about Miss Gabriel. What is more, in attempting to refute things that the police had put to him, towards Christmas of that year he wrote another letter to the child's head teacher, this time raising fresh and equally spurious grounds for questioning the child's welfare.

In December 1997 Mr Howard was arrested and charged. He was also granted bail pending trial, and in the 11 months that followed, barring one or two incidents which, though unpleasant, were minor by comparison with what had gone before, he left Miss Gabriel and her daughter alone. In November 1998 he was convicted under the Protection from Harassment Act 1997. He was given three months' immediate imprisonment. He had served six weeks when the Crown Court allowed his appeal against sentence. For the sentence of imprisonment the Crown Court substituted a three year probation order. It also imposed a restraint order, first of all prohibiting contact with Miss Gabriel and her daughter, secondly prohibiting any attempt to report anything about them except through his own solicitor and thirdly, forbidding him to go within 50 yards of Arden House. Because it was not clear what was going to be done about the re-housing of either Mr Howard or Miss Gabriel, the Crown Court allowed the geographical restraint order to be the subject of a future application for variation after an interval of six or nine months.

In March 1999 the local authority, knowing of the outcome of the criminal proceedings to date, issued possession proceedings against Mr Howard on the grounds of Mr Howard's persistent and obsessive harassment of Miss Gabriel and her young daughter. It sought outright possession of Mr Howard's flat. The county court judge granted Lambeth council the possession order. Mr Howard appealed. The basis of his appeal was that since his criminal conviction he had ceased to harass Miss Gabriel, that he had been a tenant for 25 years during which time he had been fully involved in the community and in all ways a model tenant, other than his constant abuse of Miss Gabriel, and finally that the granting of an outright possession order was contrary to Article 8 of the ECHR.

The decision

Sedley LJ clearly stated the importance of the right to occupy the home. 'It seems to me that any attempt to evict a person, whether directly or by process of law, from his or her home would on the face of it be a derogation from the respect, that is the integrity to which the home is prima facie entitled.' However, he pointed out that anti-social behaviour has a serious impact on people's lives. He pointed out that, 'not only has the appellant been guilty of the crime of harassment, but Miss Gabriel and her daughter have been denied by him one of the most important freedoms and one of the most important rights in modern urban society, albeit that neither is spelt out in the convention, freedom from fear and the right to live in peace'.

Miss Gabriel and her daughter went through a living nightmare . . .

> The picture . . . is one of real significance to what the judge had to decide and is at least a counterweight (in my judgment more than a counterweight) to the matter relied on by Mr Watkinson [Mr Howard's barrister] of the relatively good conduct in the year in which the appellant was on bail. It illustrates the hard fact that the harassment of neighbours, especially, although not only, those with children, may reach a point where what has been done cannot be undone. So here it may be that the appellant in 1997 to 1998 had demonstrated a capacity to behave himself more or less properly when the stakes were high enough for him. It may even be that he would probably continue to do so if allowed to return to his flat. But although as the judgment points out, the harassment in past years had been intermittent and not continuous, what the appellant cannot do—and it is entirely his own fault that he cannot—is dispel the fear and the tension which his return on the judge's findings will bring to Miss Gabriel. She holds down a job and is often out at work and her daughter, now 13 years old, needs all the concentration that she can get on her schooling and all the protection that she can get from fear and stress.
>
> If from these facts one turns to the Convention questions, just as if one asks whether an outright possession order is reasonable rather than a suspended one, there is only one answer. It is the one that the judge reached: an outright possession order against the appellant was necessary to protect Miss Gabriel and her daughter from the continuing consequences of the

appellant's obsessive harassment of them in the past. It would be necessary even if he were to return next door and commit no acts of harassment in the future. The shadow of the past is too heavy upon the present. Such an order is within the law. It meets a pressing social need. It is proportionate to that need in the straightforward sense that nothing less will do and that it is an acceptable means of achieving a legitimate aim.

OVERVIEW AND OBJECTIVES

This case demonstrates the distress of survivors of persistent harassment and the difficulties that the law has in grappling with it. It illustrates the interface of civil and criminal law. Criminal remedies were not sufficient to enable Miss Gabriel and her daughter to regain a normal life. It required the termination of Mr Howard's tenancy before they felt safe in their home. Yet the case also raises questions about the outcomes for the perpetrator. Mr Howard had been a good tenant for a long time. The courts have to balance a range of factors, and the actions of the state have to be proportionate. This chapter should enable you to understand the range of remedies that the law can provide for people who are suffering violence and harassment in and around their homes. Action can be taken using the criminal and the civil law. Inaction should not be a choice for the state which has the power to protect vulnerable people. However the needs of perpetrators, who are often themselves vulnerable, should be borne in mind.

Community safety

This chapter is concerned with the safety of people within their community. It is broad in scope. We consider the law in relation to violence within the home, often described as domestic violence, racial harassment and violence and anti-social behaviour. The remedies we discuss are appropriate for a wide range of conduct motivated by hate or prejudice. The web site of the Metropolitan Police Community Safety Unit—**www.met.police.uk/csu**—describes the pernicious results of such activities.

> Every crime had a bad effect on the victim but hate crimes are probably the most damaging. They happen when a person hates someone else enough to abuse them, attack them or commit some other offence against them.
>
> Sometimes the crime happens in what should be the peace and safety of your own home and the violence or other abuse comes from someone you know well. Sometimes it happens because someone, a complete stranger to you, doesn't like anyone who is different to them. A different skin colour, a different race, a different religion, a different sexual orientation.

In general, the chapter describes how the law can be used to protect people from violence, but we also recognize that service users may be perpetrators of anti-social behaviour. It is important that you know and can explain to them the possible legal outcomes of their behaviour.

Structure of chapter

The chapter starts with a discussion of the law relating to domestic violence. We then consider the way in which the law can be used to protect people from racial harassment. Finally, we look at the law relating to anti-social behaviour. This area of law is extending rapidly. It can be used to respond to a range of behaviours from homophobia to elder abuse. It can also be used to crack down on young people and children who are causing general nuisance.

> We understand that in talking about such sensitive areas language is important. We have tried not to categorize people as victims, but to consider how the law can help people survive violence and harassment.

Domestic violence

What is domestic violence?

The Lord Chancellor's Department in its guide to remedies for domestic violence (referred to below) quotes the following definition of domestic violence from the inter-government initiative, *Raising the Standard*:

> Domestic violence and abuse is best described as the use of physical and/or emotional abuse or violence, including undermining of self-confidence, sexual violence or the threat of violence, by a person who is or has been in a close relationship.

Domestic violence can go beyond actual physical violence. It can also involve emotional abuse, the destruction of a spouse's or partner's property, their isolation from friends, family, or other potential sources of support, threats to others including children, control over access to money, personal items, food, transportation and the telephone, and stalking.

It includes violence perpetrated by a son, daughter, or any other person who has a close or blood relationship with the survivor. It includes violence inflicted on, or witnessed by, children. It can include violence inflicted upon men by women. Most of the discussion below will be relevant where the survivor is a man.

Scale and extent

> Domestic violence affects and damages whole families across all social classes. The effects are far reaching not only for the families concerned but society in general. We all bear the costs and consequences—not only through the public purse, but more importantly, in terms of the social outcomes for survivors, particularly children. In the twenty first century is shocking to realise that every week, two women die as a result of domestic violence, and that domestic violence accounts for 25% of all violent crime (Rosie Winterton MP, 'Foreword' *LCD guide to domestic violence*, available on the Lord Chancellors Department web site **www.lcd.gov**).

Research on the causes of homelessness indicate that domestic violence is a prime cause of homelessness. More seriously, women fleeing violence appear to become trapped in a vicious cycle of violent relationships and homelessness. Positive intervention and support are required to break that cycle.

Government concern about domestic violence has led to a new Act, the Domestic Violence Crimes and Victims Act 2004. We shall highlight the legal changes it makes where relevant within this chapter.

Social workers and domestic violence

A good place for a social worker to start to understand the implications of violence for his or her statutory duties is Circular (97) 15, *Family Law Act 1996 Part IV, Family Homes and Domestic Violence*. This shows the close link between child protection and dealing with violence, and explains whom you will need to liaise with, particularly health professionals, children's guardians, any local domestic violence forum, child protection team, and the police.

Raising the standard—the inter-government initiative points out that:

> [Domestic violence] ... can also include violence inflicted on or witnessed by, children. The wide adverse effects of living with domestic violence for children must be recognized as a child protection issue. They link to poor education achievement, social exclusion and to juvenile crime, substance abuse, mental health problems and homelessness from running away.

Women's Aid publishes on its web site extensive information about the impact of domestic violence on children. For instance in December 2004 it published a report by Hilary Saunders, *Twenty-nine child homicides: Lessons still to be learnt on domestic violence and child protection* which demonstrates a link between domestic violence and child abuse. The British Crime Survey in 1996 found that 50 per cent of men who have abused their female partners have also been physically abusive to children in the family. It also found that 51 per cent of women subjected to a repeated pattern of abuse had children under the age of 16, and of that group 45 per cent stated that the children had seen or heard the last incident.

Non-legal strategies for responding to domestic violence

Alongside the legal process, or instead of it, other strategies for protecting a woman, and perhaps children, may be necessary.

Immediate safety

If a woman is in danger then the best advice may be to go to a secret address as a refuge from the violence. You will need to be aware of the availability of women's refuges in your vicinity. The Women's Aid National Helpline: tel. 08457 023 468 will provide support, help, and information to women experiencing domestic violence. Local refuges can also be contacted through the police, the Samaritans, the Citizens' Advice Bureau, and social services itself should maintain a list of available refuges. Refuges strive to protect women and children in their care, and are very reluctant to divulge details of who is staying there. They work hard to build trusting relationships with the police, so it is gratifying that a 1998 Court of Appeal decision upheld a refusal by the police to disclose to a father the whereabouts of his child and the child's mother since this would make the refuge less safe (*Chief Constable of West Yorkshire v S* (1998)).

Starting again—housing

If the survivor of violence sees the rift as permanent, and she does not want to apply to get the man out of the home, she can seek re-housing from the housing department as a homeless person. Since no-one can be required to live under threat of violence, she should not be treated as intentionally homeless, which is a ground for refusing accommodation (see chapter 20). There is no need for her to apply to the local housing authority where she is resident. She can apply to an authority where she feels she would be safe. If the woman is a joint tenant of a rented property she can terminate the tenancy by serving notice on the local authority and her partner. Landlords often require women to do this before they will re-house them. Terminating the tenancy will enable the landlord to evict the perpetrator of the violence.

Starting again—income

Problems such as the sudden drop in income will loom large, and an immediate application for income support will be necessary for a woman who has no other source of income. An application to the court for maintenance for herself (if married) and to the Child Support Agency for the children should be urgently considered (see chapter 14). Social Fund applications may be appropriate to provide some assistance in equipping a new home. You should ensure that a woman fleeing violence receives welfare benefits advice as soon as possible.

◼ Domestic violence and the law

The law provides a range of remedies and sanctions for domestic violence. The criminal law can prosecute and imprison the offender; the civil law can make orders, injunctions, forbidding the person from being violent or carrying out other harassing acts; it can send people to prison for contempt of court when they breach these orders (though this is in fact rare). The law is a blunt instrument in protecting a person from domestic violence. It cannot deal with the causes of violence, or resolve the family tension that may be the underlying problem. And it is usually available too late—after the violence has occurred. Decisions about the legal remedies for individual survivors depend on a range of factors.

- The wishes of the survivor about the protection they require from the law;
- The severity and/or nature of the violence or harassment;
- The familial relationship between the abused and the abuser;
- The stricter burden of proof required by the criminal courts compared with the civil courts (see chapter 5 above);
- The actual and perceived protection the law can deliver in practice;
- The availability of support services.

You should always find out what a woman wants from the law before overwhelming her with advice.

Domestic violence and the criminal law

The range of criminal offences

Whilst there is no specific offence of domestic violence within the criminal law, all physical or sexual assault is a criminal offence. The types of criminal offences which may be committed in the context of domestic violence range from murder, rape, grievous bodily harm, and indecent assault to harassment, blackmail, false imprisonment, kidnapping, criminal damage, and malicious communications.

Behaviour which causes psychological injury can also be an assault (*R v Burstow* (1996)), and the Protection from Harassment Act 1997 (which we discuss below) creates the offence of putting a person in fear of violence. These types of offence can lead to lengthy custodial sentences. For example, the accused was sentenced to a total of six years' imprisonment following a concerted campaign of stalking (*R v Haywood* (1998)).

Protection from Harassment Act 1997

The Protection from Harassment Act 1997 provides for two criminal offences: criminal harassment (under s. 2 of the Act) and fear of violence (under s. 4). The sections are set out in Box 18.1.

The police have the power to arrest and charge anyone whom they suspect of committing either of the above offences, and the Crown Prosecution Service can prosecute if the case meets their criteria for deciding whether to proceed (see below). Section 5 of the Protection from Harassment Act 1997 provides a further power enabling the court of protect victims of harassing conduct. The court, when someone has been convicted of an offence under s. 2 or s.4 of the Act may make a restraining order which prohibits further harassing conduct.

The Domestic Violence, Crime and Victims Act extends this power. It provides that a restraining order can be made under the Protection from Harassment Act 1997 following criminal proceedings for any offence, rather than only on conviction for offences under that Act. This will mean that in certain circumstances courts will have the power

---

 BOX 18.1 Criminal offences under the Protection from Harassment Act 1997

Section 2—a person must not pursue a course of conduct which amount to harassment of another

> and which he knows, or ought to know, amounts to the harassment of another, that is, if any 'reasonable person' in possession of the same information would regard the conduct as harassment. A course of conduct must involve conduct on at least two occasions.

Section 4—a person whose course of conduct causes another to fear, on at least two occasions,

> that violence will be used against them is guilty of an offence, if he knows or ought to know that this will cause the other fear.

to make restraining orders even when an alleged perpetrator has been acquitted of a criminal charge.

The role of the police

The police are more willing to get involved in 'domestic disputes' than they were a few years ago. Most forces train recruits to be aware of domestic violence as a serious crime, and have set up specialist units to assist survivors. The Metropolitan Police for instance set out their strategy for responding to domestic violence on their web site, **www.met.police.uk/enoughisenough**. It makes clear the responsibility of the police to take action in response to incidents of domestic violence, stresses the Human Rights Act obligations upon the police to protect survivors of domestic violence, and offers advice on appropriate action to police officers. For example, the web site advises, 'It is the officer's decision to arrest and it is not reliant on the victim's willingness to proceed with a prosecution. This should be stressed to the perpetrator to remove responsibility from the victim. Domestic violence victims have a high risk of repeat victimization due to the proximity of the perpetrator and the violence often escalates in severity. Officers should be aware of the fact that sometimes victims underestimate the future risk.'

One advantage of using the police over any other procedure is their day and night availability in serious cases. (If a solicitor can be contacted, injunctions can also be obtained round the clock—see below.) In addition, the police may decide to arrest a person suspected of violent crime, which provides immediate short-term relief for the survivor while she considers what else to do.

Sometimes the survivor of violence is reluctant to bring in the police; but this is the quickest, and cheapest, process. If the fear is that the perpetrator will be all the more violent when he comes out on bail, there is not a great deal of hope that an order from the civil courts will have much more of a deterrent effect.

Investigation and prosecution of crimes

The police are responsible for investigating criminal offences and deciding whether to charge the suspect. The defendant must be charged within twenty-four hours of the arrest unless the police have been granted an extension. After the police have charged the defendant they refer the file to the Crown Prosecution Service (CPS). The CPS decides whether to proceed with the case. In each regional office of the CPS there is an experienced domestic violence coordinator. Decisions whether to prosecute are based on two tests set out in the Code for Crown Prosecutors. The case must pass the evidential test. This means that there must be sufficient evidence to provide a reasonable prospect of conviction. If the case passes the evidential test, the CPS then consider whether a prosecution is in the public interest. As the Lord Chancellor's Department guide to domestic violence points out:

There are many factors to be taken into account under this test, including the consequences for the survivor of the decision whether or not to prosecute, and the views of the survivor. If the survivor decides to withdraw support for the prosecution, or does not wish to give evidence, the case is not necessarily dropped. For example the CPS may be able to continue on the strength of other evidence gathered at the scene by the police. Alternatively a witness may be compelled to attend court (although in practice the courts rarely use this power). In some domestic violence cases the violence is so serious, or the previous history shows such a real and continuing danger to the survivor or the children or other people, that the public interest in proceeding with the prosecution outweighs the survivor's wishes.

Support for victims and witnesses

A survivor of domestic violence is likely to be the key witness in any subsequent court proceedings. This will put her under a great deal of stress, particularly as she can often be unsure why the case appears to be proceeding slowly. The Youth Justice and Criminal Evidence Act 1999 enables the CPS to give additional support to victims of crimes if they are identified by the police as vulnerable or intimidated. Special measures included separate waiting rooms and facilities for victims and witnesses, giving evidence from behind a screen, or via a TV or video link; or clearing the public gallery. Further detail on special measures is available from the Home Office web site, **www.homeoffice.gov.uk** and in chapter 6. The Domestic Violence, Crime and Victims Act 2004 provide:

- a Code of Practice setting out the services to be provided to victims of criminal conduct;

- an independent Ombudsman to investigate complaint relating to breach of the code;

- the appointment of a Commissioner for Victims and Witnesses who is to represent the interests of victims and witnesses at a national level.

Women's Aid has produced a table of the advantages and disadvantages of using criminal law in the context of domestic violence. We have adapted the table for you and set it out in Box 18.2.

Using the civil courts

When is it appropriate to use the civil courts?

The police may not wish to arrest or charge the violent partner; in any event, he may be released on bail or after conviction, or the survivor may want action that the police cannot provide, particularly an order to remove a person from her home. So she has to take her own case in the civil courts. It is possible to do this without legal representation, particularly in the magistrates' court, but we recommend that you advise a survivor of violence to see a specialist solicitor in any event. There may be other issues which require legal advice, and the solicitor may advise using the county court, or commencing divorce proceedings; or may, after talking it all over, agree with her client that no action should be taken at the moment.

BOX 18.2 Using the Criminal law

Advantages	Disadvantages
• State takes action: not left to women	• Woman is passive witness—the situation is out of her control
• Woman can feel that the violence is taken more seriously	• Proceedings are held in open court
• Abuser can be arrested immediately and easily and he can be held in custody for short periods	• Intended to punish the man, not protect the woman
• Abuser can be punished/removed from circulation for a certain period	• The prosecution process can take a very long time
• There is a clear indication of who is at fault	• Woman may not want the man prosecuted for a number of reasons
• Bail conditions can be more powerful than an injunction (but have limited duration)	• Court personnel attitudes: lack of understanding of nature and dynamics of domestic violence
• Proceedings have a symbolic value—domestic violence is not acceptable	• There is a risk of increasing the threat and danger to the woman and any children
• No problems with costs, or access to legal assistance	• Cannot deal with many 'non-physical' aspects of domestic violence

Funding

Funding of advice may be available under Community Legal Services Funding. To qualify for assistance applicants will have to pass the means test and must show reasonable grounds for pursuing the case. Normally applications for funding will take time, but emergency action can be taken by a solicitor who is contracted with the Legal Services Commission under their devolved powers to grant emergency certificates of Legal Representation.

Part IV of the Family Law Act 1996

The purpose of Part IV of the Family Law Act 1996 is to provide a range of remedies for molestation and violence within family relationships. Part of the protection provided by the law is bound up with the occupation of the family home. Part IV of the Family Law Act 1996 also deals with occupation rights in circumstances of molestation and violence. The Domestic Violence, Crime and Victims Act 2004 will have a dramatic impact upon the operation of the remedies available under the Family Law Act 1996.

Non-molestation orders

A non-molestation order is an order restraining someone from causing or threatening violence to the applicant or to any children or from molesting them. The Domestic Violence, Crime and Victims Bill 2004 makes breach of a non-molestation order a criminal offence.

The Family Law Act 1996 Act does not actually define 'molestation'. Fortunately the old law (the Domestic Violence and Matrimonial Proceedings Act 1976) used the same term, and cases decided under that Act make it clear that the concept is wide, covering physical and sexual violence, or the threat of it; annoying phone calls and letters. In fact the word 'pestering', which is usually the word used in the order which is served on the respondent, sums it up.

Who can apply?

The most common situation is where the survivor of violence or molestation makes the application to court. The applicant applies for an order against her alleged molester, who is called the respondent.

However, three further powers were introduced by the Family Law Act 1996:

(a) The court (s. 62), without an application necessarily being made by anyone, can decide to make an order on behalf of the survivor against the molester. As with similar powers under the Children Act (see chapter 9) to make orders that have not been asked for the court must be already dealing with 'family proceedings'. The order can be made only against a molester who is himself involved as a party in the proceedings. This power can overcome the situation where, under the old law, there was no power in care proceedings to protect a child survivor by getting the abuser out of the home, leaving two equally unsuitable choices to the court—no action, or removal of the child into care.

Allied to this power to make an order in family proceedings is an amendment to the Children Act 1989 which enables the court to make an exclusion order in the course of making an interim care order or an emergency protection order—see below.

(b) A child can apply (s. 43), although if under 16 the court's permission is required. The child will need a children's guardian or next friend for such an application. This is the child's application, and it is likely the courts will not be pleased with adults manipulating children to bring applications to achieve other purposes. Leave will be granted only if the court is satisfied that the child has sufficient understanding to make the necessary application. You may wish to tell a child of this route to an order, and arrange for the child to receive independent legal advice.

(c) If the necessary rules are brought in—Parliament has enacted a power but the Government is still not sure how (and, after so many years, we assume is unwilling) to move forward–a third party (s. 60) such as the police or a social worker may apply directly on behalf of the survivor. You may wish to do so, if and when the rules allow, in order to protect a child where, guided by the 'no order' principle in

Children Act cases (see chapter 9), you would not need to start child protection proceedings if the abuser could be removed. Be aware that intervention on behalf of a woman in this context, without a clear reason under the Children Act aimed at the welfare of a child, may act to disempower a survivor further and would not be within your statutory powers.

The relationship between the survivor and the molester

The purpose of the domestic violence provisions of the Family Law Act 1996 is to provide additional protection, over and beyond the normal provisions of the criminal and civil law, to those people who because of their intimate relationship with the perpetrator of abuse, are particularly vulnerable to that abuse. The law uses the notion of 'associated persons' to define those people who are entitled to this additional protection. The court will not grant a non-molestation order under the Family Law Act 1996 unless the two people concerned are 'associated'. We have set out the list of associated people in Box 18.3. If the two people are not associated as defined under the Act then the proper basis for remedies is the Protection from Harassment Act 1997—we discuss the civil remedies available under that Act later in this chapter. An increasingly broad range of relationships are now recognized to be sufficiently intimate so as to merit the additional protections of the Family Law Act 1996.

You can see from Box 18.4 that the criteria for determining who can apply for an order under the Act is relatively broad but it is made broader by the amendments made in the Domestic Violence, Crime and Victims Act 2004. 'Associated persons' will cover

---

BOX 18.3 Associated persons in s. 62 of the Family Law Act 1996

- a spouse or a 'cohabitant' (this means a heterosexual cohabitant);
- a former spouse or former cohabitant;
- a relative;
- a man and a woman linked by being parents of the same child or having parental responsibility for the same child;
- a person who shares a household (but not as a lodger or tenant);
- they have agreed to marry each other (whether or not that agreement has been terminated).

BOX 18.4 Extending associated persons—the amendments made by the Domestic Violence Crime and Victims Act 2004

- cohabitants are redefined by clause 3 of the Bill to include same sex co-habitants;
- a new category of associated persons is introduced which is defined as people who have or have had an intimate personal relationship with each other which is or was of significant duration.

applications between homosexual couples on the same basis as heterosexual co-habiting couples and long standing intimate relationships regardless of whether they are sexual relationships. Note that parents and adult children are associated so that abuse of elderly parents could be restrained through use of the Act.

From now on we will call the applicant and respondent, for the sake of understanding, the survivor and the perpetrator. But, strictly speaking, the survivor might be a child on whose behalf the applicant is applying; or someone might be applying on the adult survivor's behalf; and of course the term 'perpetrator' assumes that the allegations will be proved.

Applications for non-molestation orders

The Family Law Act 1996 provides that an application can be made to a magistrates' court which is a family proceedings court, to a county court with family jurisdiction, or to the High Court. If funding is available, solicitors will probably continue to prefer the county court. If it is not available the survivor is best advised to make her application to the local family proceedings court. The court staff should help with the paperwork, and the evidence will be given from the witness box. In the other two courts the evidence will be prepared initially in the form of a written statement of evidence, on which the survivor can expect to be cross-examined.

What protection does a non-molestation order provide?

The protections are set out in s. 42(6) and (7) of the Family Law Act reproduced below in Box 18.5.

The actual wording of an order will reflect the particular circumstances. The molester may be ordered not to molest, not to approach, and not to pester the survivor. Together with a property occupation order (see below), an order may require the molester to stay out of the home and not come within, say, 100 metres of it. The courts do not generally like open-ended orders; three months is the normal duration. However, this is not a rule, and orders can be indefinite: *Re BJ (A Child) (Non-molestation Order)* (2000).

Enforcing a non-molestation order

(a) A power of arrest

If the court, when making an order, concludes that the molester has used or threatened violence against the applicant or a child, the order must have a power of arrest attached. A power of arrest means that a police officer can arrest without warrant anyone suspected of breaching the terms of the order, and bring him before the court for

---

 BOX 18.5 Section 42(6) and (7) of the Family Law Act 1996

(6) A non-molestation order may be expressed so as to refer to molestation in general, to particular acts of molestation, or both.

(7) A non-molestation order may be made for a specified period or until further notice.

punishment for contempt of court. (No power of arrest is available under the Protection from Harassment Act 1997, so where survivor and molester are 'associated' we advise use of the Family Law Act 1996.) Without this power of arrest the police would need a warrant, or would have to wait for a further offence to be committed, so enforcement is slower. The power of arrest must be registered at the nearest police station, and the survivor should keep the police telephone number to hand.

(b) The court's powers

Disobeying a court order, for instance by breaching a non-molestation order, is contempt of court. The perpetrator knows that the punishment for contempt of court may be imprisonment because a penal notice is attached to the order warning of the risk of imprisonment. Penal notices are compulsory on non-molestation orders. If, with or without a warrant, the molester is brought back to the court and the court accepts the evidence of breach of the order, it has power to commit to prison for contempt of court, or to remand the molester in custody or on bail so that a medical report can first be obtained. It can send a molester to hospital under the Mental Health Act 1983, s. 37, or make a guardianship order under s. 38 of the Mental Health Act (see chapter 17). However, there is no reason to assume that the courts will abandon the general preference for giving a perpetrator in breach of an order a telling off and 'one last chance' before sending him to prison. Even after eighteen separate breaches of a non-molestation order, thirteen months in prison was considered manifestly excessive in *C v G* (1996). Compare the six weeks' prison sentence for the mother who defied a court and obstructed a violent father's contact with his child. But perhaps the courts are beginning to get tougher. In *N v R* (1998), the Court of Appeal agreed that an immediate custodial order could be necessary to make a violent man obey court orders. (As contempt of court is treated as a criminal matter under the European Convention, it is possible that a committal to prison will be challenged as a human rights abuse under Article 6 (right to fair trial), since the procedure does not at present involve setting out precise allegations in the form of a charge.)

Both these methods of enforcing non-molestation orders are cumbersome. Powers of arrest require that there has been a history of violence or threats of violence and civil courts are reluctant to imprison perpetrators for contempt. The Domestic Violence, Crime and Victims Act is designed to make action to protect survivors more straightforward. First it criminalizes breach of non-molestation orders. A breach is an arrestable offence. Second, common assault becomes an arrestable offence. Anyone reasonably suspected of committing an arrestable offence can be arrested without a warrant. Powers of arrest will therefore become redundant, and proceedings for contempt rare as survivors now have much easier access to police protection.

Applying for a non-molestation order in an emergency

Imagine a situation where there has been a serious and violent incident. The survivor is scared that if the perpetrator hears she is going to court, he will become even more violent. In such a case a solicitor can act under an emergency certificate of Legal

Representation and a judge made available very quickly in court, elsewhere if out of hours, or even over the telephone. The court can make an order without the paperwork being ready, and without the perpetrator having any notice of the case. Such applications are called without notice applications. A person who has an order made against him without notice can apply to have it set aside, and a full hearing with notice and paperwork will generally be held within seven days.

Courts do not like the inherent unfairness of deciding, even for a few days, to grant an order having heard only one side of a case. A court will make an order without notice only if it believes that the applicant or a child will otherwise suffer significant harm, that delay would deter the survivor from making an application at all, or that the molester is trying to avoid being served with the papers for a hearing with notice. Having said that, many judges faced with a desperate and distressed applicant will use humanity and common sense and grant an order without notice even where these requirements are not strictly met. A good lawyer who knows the individual judges is essential.

Occupation orders

Often the most important matter in cases of family violence is getting the perpetrator out of the home. Part IV of the Family Law Act 1996 provides for occupation orders. Occupation orders are orders which regulate the occupation of the family home to protect any party or children from domestic violence.

They may operate to exclude perpetrators of molestation and violence from the home, prevent him from re-entering it, and can order that the applicant regains access to the accommodation.

Although the power of the court to adjust temporarily rights to occupy property is based on different grounds from a non-molestation order, the things you need to be aware of in deciding whether an application can be made are almost the same. The law is set out in ss. 30–41 of the 1996 Act.

Everything we have already said about powers of arrest, applications without notice, punishment by committal to prison, and the need for the survivor and the perpetrator to be associated in some way applies when the court is considering an order to do with occupation rights. Note that there are no proposals to make breach of an occupation order a criminal offence. A child can make an application for an order, as can the court in the course of family proceedings. It is worth bearing in mind, in care proceedings in particular, this power for a court to exclude an abuser, rather than to remove a child survivor into care.

The type of order that can be made, and its duration, depends on the marital or cohabitation status of the parties and their existing property rights in the home. Please note that the order does not adjust property ownership rights. It cannot make the survivor a tenant instead of the molester, and cannot put her name on to the title deeds of freehold property (see chapter 14, by contrast, for property adjustment powers where the parties are divorcing).

Rights of occupation

The Act categorizes the property status of people in two different ways. First, there are people who can be described as entitled people. You are an entitled person if you have some legal right to occupy a property as the freehold owner, the tenant, or the contractual licensee. See chapter 19 for more details on tenants and licensees. People who do not have property rights are non-entitled persons. The type of occupation order an applicant can apply for depends on whether she is entitled or non-entitled. If she is a non-entitled person then the applicant's position depends on whether she was married to the perpetrator. An entitled applicant who applies for an occupation order must be an associated person under the Act. We gave you the list of associated persons and the proposed amendments to that list, earlier in the chapter.

What does the court take into account?

Sections 33–8 describe the circumstances in which a court will adjust occupation rights and the matters it will have to take into account. A court should make an order if to do so would prevent the survivor or a child suffering significant harm. If the court is being asked to interfere with someone's occupation rights to protect a survivor who has no rights as an owner or spouse, the court is required to consider the conduct of the parties before making an order.

The things a court must consider in every case are the financial and other needs of the parties and the children, including issues such as health.

The court can order a person to leave all or part of the home; to keep away (say, not come within 100 metres); and to allow the survivor back in (including, for example, ordering the means to achieve this, such as giving her a key). But remember, it cannot change ownership rights, so it is important to know how long this occupation order can last. Where the survivor has no property ownership rights and is not now married to the molester, the order can last only for six months. What happens, then, after the six months? If the parties are or were previously married, the survivor can go back to court for renewals, if the circumstances justify it, for six months at a time. In any other situation, one six-month renewal is possible, but then the order must lapse. This means that the occupational rights of the molester cannot be interrupted indefinitely and the survivor will have to find some other solution to her accommodation needs. (If there are children, some property ownership adjustment can be applied for; and on divorce, even without children, the court can order property adjustment. See chapter 14. Otherwise the survivor is likely to have to apply to the local authority for accommodation on the basis of her non-intentional homelessness. See chapter 20.)

Will the court be willing to make a person leave?

Occupation orders are to be seen as exceptional orders, and in particular they are hard to obtain without giving notice to the alleged violent person and holding a full hearing of all the evidence. Although the legislation has changed, the leading case is still *Richards v Richards* (1984). Here the House of Lords said that the court has to look not only at the conduct of the parties, which is what the applicant is most concerned with, and the needs of any children, but also at the needs of the parties and their financial resources (so it may be easier for the wealthy to get an order, since the ousted person can find somewhere else to live). But the court has a discretion on the evidence before it, and some judges are more inclined to grant an order than others. Solicitors know this and may time their applications accordingly. You might think that violence is necessary to justify an order—not so. For example, in *Scott v Scott* (1992), an order was made where the husband would not stop pestering his wife for a reconciliation, despite his undertakings to the court. However, an occupation order cannot be granted just because the parties do not get on (*Grant v James* (1993)).

The balance of harm test

Domestic violence tends to evoke images of innocent survivor and guilty perpetrator. Sometimes the law is asked to intervene in less clear-cut circumstances. In *Banks v Banks (Occupation Order: Mental Health)* (1999), the wife suffered from dementia, on top of previous mental illness, but was currently living at home. She was very aggressive towards her husband. He was under great strain, though no physical attack had been made on him (only threatened). The court had to apply (as it does in every case) the 'balance of harm' test. It decided that to evict the wife would be more harmful to her than her staying would be to the husband. Any non-molestation order would be wasted on the wife, given her mental state.

Another case showing the balancing act was *B v B* (1999). The Court of Appeal allowed the violent man to remain because of the needs of his dependent child from a former relationship. His violence, if evicted, made him 'intentionally homeless' (see chapter 20), whereas his wife would be 'unintentionally homeless' and could look to the housing department for housing for herself and their younger child. On balance he could stay and she ended up going, notwithstanding his violence.

Children Act 1989 (amended by Part 4 of the Family Law Act 1996)

When a court makes an order for interim care or emergency protection (see generally chapter 12), it can also, under powers inserted by the Family Law Act 1996, order a suspected abuser to be removed from the home. A power of arrest can be attached if necessary. The court must be satisfied that removal of the person is likely to reduce the significant harm or risk of it. If the child is subsequently removed from home, this order lapses—remember to tell the adult survivor of this.

The Adoption and Children Act 2002

The Adoption and Children Act 2002 amends s. 8 of the Children Act 1989 to make it clear that when a court is considering applications under s. 8 and it is also considering whether a child has suffered, or is likely to suffer, harm, it must consider harm that a child may suffer not just from domestic violence, but from witnessing it.

■ Section 3 of the Protection from Harassment Act 1997

The Protection from Harassment Act 1997 contains criminal remedies which we outlined above, and civil remedies. The Act was originally designed to deal with the problem of 'stalkers' but it is used by people who are unable to apply for an order under Part 4 of the Family Law Act 1996 because they are not associated with the perpetrator.

Applications under the Act

The advantage of the Protection from Harassment Act 1997 is immediately apparent. Anyone can apply for an injunction or damages against anyone else under the Act. Section 3 allows proceedings to be based upon 'an actual or apprehended breach of section 1'. Therefore there is no need for proof of a course of conduct which the criminal proceedings require. As it is a civil application the burden of proof is the balance of probabilities. Applications can be made to the High Court or the county court for injunctions and/or damages. Emergency applications can be made for a temporary injunction.

Enforcement

Breach of an order under s. 3 is a criminal offence. However, there is no provision for attaching a power of arrest as under the Family Law Act 1996. The claimant can apply for a warrant of arrest if the defendant has breached the order. The warrant will be issued if the application is substantiated on oath and the judge has reasonable grounds for believing that the defendant has not complied with the order, or part of the order. Alternatively the claimant can make a committal application, which is an application to commit a defendant to custody or prison. The application is issued by the court staff. At the hearing the defendant must 'show cause', that is provide evidence as to why he should not be committed to prison for disobeying the order.

■ Other civil action

There is a specific ground for possession available to local authority and housing association landlords which enables the landlord to regain possession of a property when one tenant has left it owing to the domestic violence of another tenant. This prevents a perpetrator of violence benefiting from his actions in frightening a woman from her home. See chapter 19 for eviction procedures.

Any action which we describe later under the heading of anti-social behaviour would be available in cases of domestic violence. So, for instance, it may be possible to get an anti-social behaviour order against the perpetrator of violence or the eviction of a violent tenant using powers which allow landlords to regain possession of housing where a tenant is being violent towards another tenant. However ASBOs cannot be used where the victim and the perpetrator are living in the same household and ASBOs do not give the victim access to the same levels of protection and support. See below for more information on ASBOs.

Racial harassment and racially motivated violence

The Government recognizes that racist behaviour does not simply injure the survivor or their property, it affects the whole family and it erodes the standards of decency of the wider community. Trust and understanding built up over many years between communities can be eroded by the climate of fear and anxiety which can surround a racist incident. Service users who are suffering racial harassment and racial violence will require extensive support.

Race crimes

The Association of Chief Police Officers (ACPO) define a racial incident as

> any incident in which it appears to the reporting or investigating officer that the compliant involves an element of racial motivation; or any incident which includes an allegation of racial motivation made by any person.

Someone who harasses or is violent towards someone because of their race is committing a criminal offence. A broad range of criminal offences, from murder to criminal damage, may be relevant. There is a particular offence of incitement to racial hatred which may be committed if a person uses threatening, abusive, or insulting words or behaviour; publishes or distributes threatening, abusive, or insulting written material, or possesses such written material with a view to its publication or distribution.

The Crime and Disorder Act 1998, ss. 29–32 created a number of racially aggravated offences. These are racially aggravated assaults, racially aggravated criminal damage, racially aggravated public order offences, and racially aggravated harassment. The offences are all pre-existing offences which become more serious as a result of the racial motivation for the offence. The meaning of racially aggravated is defined in s. 28 of the Act and set out in Box 18.6.

The role of the police

Racial incidents have been separately recorded by the police since 1988 and figures have risen in almost every year since that date. Most police forces run community safety units with dedicated staff who receive special training in community relations, including local cultural issues to enable them to respond appropriately to racial incidents.

 BOX 18.6 The meaning of 'racially aggravated' in the Crime and Disorder Act

Section 28(1) An offence is racially aggravated for the purposes of sections 29–32 below if—

    (a) at the time of committing the offence, or immediately before or after doing so, the offender demonstrates towards the victim of the offence hostility based on the victim's membership (or presumed membership) of a racial group; or

    (b) the offence is motivated (wholly or partly) by hostility towards member of a racial group based on their membership of that group.

The Crown Prosecution Service

We explained earlier in this chapter the two stages of the decision-making process of the Crown Prosecution Service. First, there must be sufficient evidence to provide a realistic prospect of conviction. Secondly, the public interest must be considered. The code of practice for Crown prosecutors includes as a factor in favour of prosecution; 'the offence was motivated by any form of discrimination against the victim's ethnic or national origin, sex, religious beliefs, political views or sexual preference'.

Local authority responsibilities

It is not only the police who should be concerned with racial harassment. Local authorities have powers and responsibilities to provide useful protection to those who are the target of racist behaviour. See chapter 2 for a discussion of their responsibilities. Where racial incidents occur within housing, the local authority should consider its powers to take possession proceedings against racist tenants, and should consider the possibility of criminal proceedings under the Protection from Eviction Act 1977. The local authority has powers to deal with noise and dangerous dogs, both of which are common weapons of racial harassment, and to prosecute the perpetrators of racist graffiti and posters. The following discussion on anti-social behaviour is relevant to racist behaviour.

▮ Anti-social behaviour

The policy agenda

From the mid-1990s, tackling anti-social behaviour has been a priority for central government. Increasingly, it is a priority of local government. The motivations for tackling anti-social behaviour vary from a concern to eliminate racist behaviour to wider issues of community safety and estate regeneration. There is an extensive range of legal tools available to local authorities (including district councils which do not have a social services function) to tackle anti-social behaviour. Some impact more upon the social worker than others. Your concern is likely to arise either because a service user is a victim of anti-social behaviour or because your service user is or is alleged to be a perpetrator.

What is anti-social behaviour?

The term covers a disparate and broad range of behaviour from tensions between neighbours to violent and intimidatory behaviour. The lack of clarity but a shared intuition about the scope of anti-social behaviour is described in Nixon, *Tackling Anti-social Behaviour in Mixed Tenure Areas* (ODPM Research study, Sheffield Hallam University and Centre for Regional, Economic and Social Research with the Centre for Housing Policy, York 2002):

> . . . the terms 'crime', 'disorder' and 'anti-social behaviour' were frequently used interchange-ably with respondents referring to a whole range of activity from low level nuisance to

criminal behaviour under the umbrella term 'anti-social behaviour'. . . . there was a high level of consensus amongst agencies . . . that the key determinants in decisions whether the behaviour was anti-social or not should be the impact of behaviours on others and the perceptions of local residents. Where such an approach had been adopted agencies were agreed about the activity that need addressing, namely that which 'makes people unhappy living in their homes,' and 'makes people think "I don't want to live around here any more" '.

The focus on where people live has meant that control of anti-social behaviour is seen by many local authorities as a housing management responsibility as well as being behaviour subject to criminal sanctions. Housing authorities have a powerful weapon available to them—the threat of eviction which may be more effective than the penalties imposed by the criminal justice system.

The role of the law

The law controlling anti-social behaviour has to resolve the tension between the need to address the behaviour via speedy and effective remedies and the need to respect due process and the legal rights of the alleged perpetrators of the behaviour. We will discuss three areas of legal controls on anti-social behaviour, housing law, orders under the Crime and Disorder Act 1998, and local strategic responsibilities for disorder.

The role of the social landlord in controlling behaviour

The tenancy agreement between the landlord and tenant sets out the respective rights and responsibilities. Many social landlords in recent years have extended the terms of their tenancy agreements to ban a wide range of unacceptable behaviour from racial harassment to dog fouling and ball games played near residences. The tenant is given responsibility for the behaviour of visitors and children. The presence of such clauses enables the landlord to evict for breach of terms of the tenancy agreement (see chapter 19) and is limited only by the requirements that evictions of secure tenants must be reasonable and the terms in tenancy agreements must be fair. Fairness includes transparency. A vague term prohibiting anti-social behaviour without definition or limits could well fall foul of this requirement.

Extended grounds for possession

The Housing Act 1996 amended the grounds for possession for cases of tenant misconduct. The nuisance grounds (Ground 2 of Schedule 2 to the Housing Act 1985 and Ground 14 of the Housing Act 1988) have been extended. The range of perpetrators is now tenants plus other residents plus visitors; the range of victims extends to persons residing in the properly, visiting, or otherwise engaging in lawful activities; and the potential location of the misconduct is extended to the locality. Therefore tenants can be evicted for the behaviour of a visitor who, for instance, abuses a neighbour even if they do not condone that behaviour.

No notice period

Speed is of the essence in dealing with anti-social behaviour. It is self-defeating if some-one who is behaving in an intimidatory way is able to remain in the property for a substantial period of time pending a court hearing. Section 147 of the 1996 Act recognizes the need for speed by reformulating s. 83 of the Housing Act 1985. This enables possession proceedings against secure tenants on Ground 2 to be commenced immediately upon service of the notice of proceedings rather than giving a minimum of four weeks' notice that all other grounds require.

Reasonableness

The requirement of reasonableness provides a judicial restraint on arbitrary eviction by social landlords. The normal position is that reasonableness is a matter for the trial judge, and in the context of secure tenancies reasonable means having regard to both the interests of the parties and the interest of the public. However, the courts have developed the concept of reasonableness in the context of anti-social behaviour. First, judges must give proper weight to the council's obligations to other tenants on the estate: see *Woking BC v Bistram* (1993). Secondly, in *City of Bristol v Mousah* (1998), the Court of Appeal made it clear that where there are serious breaches of the conditions of the tenancy, it is only in exceptional cases that it is not reasonable to make an order for possession. Decisions of the Court of Appeal from that date indicate that courts of first instance must recognise that the responsibilities of social landlords extend beyond the normal confines of the landlord–tenant relationship and respond appropriately to the seriousness of the behaviour. Despite this judicial activity, social landlords continued to be concerned that there was insufficient predictability in the outcome of possession proceedings for anti-social behaviour. Therefore the Anti-social Behaviour Act 2003 inserted a new s. 85A into the Housing Act 1985 and a new s. 9A into the Housing Act 1988. These sections require that the court consider the past impact of the anti-social conduct on other people, the likely continuing effect of the nuisance and the likely future effect of any repetition of the conduct, when considering whether it is reasonable to make an order for possession.

Introductory tenancies

Part V of the Housing Act 1996 included other statutory initiatives. The best known is the introductory tenancy regime, which operates as an exception to the normal security of tenure of local authority housing for a probationary period of a year. A local housing authority may elect to operate an introductory tenancy regime, and when such an election is in force every new tenancy becomes an introductory tenancy for the first twelve months. During this period the local authority can seek a possession order from the courts subject to certain procedural requirements but without proving grounds. Introductory tenancies have been criticized as a blunt tool. They require election by the local authority, which must then put all new tenants on introductory tenancies and they can be effective only if the tenant behaves in an anti-social manner in the first twelve months of the tenancy.

Reviews

A service user who is an introductory tenant and is threatened with eviction is in a difficult position. He or she can seek a review of the landlord's decision within fourteen days of the service of the notice of proceedings and you should try to persuade them to do so. The procedural requirements for review are set out in the Introductory Tenants (Review) Regulations 1997. The regime has been challenged under the Human Rights Act 1998. The Court of Appeal (in *McLellan v Bracknell Forest Borough Council and the Department of Transport, Local Government and the Regions and Reigate & Banstead Borough Council v Benfield and Forrest* (2001)) held that introductory tenancies were Human Rights Act compliant. The internal review process (coupled with potential judicial scrutiny via judicial review) complies with Article 6 (the right to a fair hearing) and, whilst introductory tenancies do interfere with Article 8 rights, that interference is necessary and responds to pressing social need. The availability of judicial review would ensure that local authorities behaved proportionately.

Demoted tenancies

One particular limitation of introductory tenancies is that they only apply at the start of a tenancy agreement. Anti-social behaviour may arise later during the lifetime of a tenancy. The Anti-social Behaviour Act 2003 introduced demoted tenancies in response to the difficulties caused by anti-social behaviour of secure or assured tenants or their families. From 1 July 2004 local authority and registered social landlords are able to apply to court for a demotion order when the tenant or another resident or visitor to the tenant's home, has behaved in an anti-social manner. This converts secure or assured tenancies to insecure demoted tenancies for a year. The court will only make the order if it is reasonable to do so. During the demotion period the landlord may commence action to evict without proof of reasons if they feel the need to do so. The non-assured demoted tenant will have to be given four weeks notice with reasons for the proceedings and will have the right to a review before the local authority can issue proceedings. The demoted assured tenant has no similar rights. The registered social landlord will be able to evict using the two month notice only ground.

  If no possession proceedings are taken during the demotion period, for example because the tenant's behaviour improves, then the tenancy is automatically promoted up to secure or assured status.

Injunctions

Injunctions, court orders which generally order someone to stop doing something illegal, have always been available to landlords to restrain tenants from breaching their tenancy agreements. The Housing Act 1996 as amended by the Anti-social Behaviour Act 2003 provides strengthened powers (in s. 153A) for social landlords to apply for injunctions to restrain anti-social behaviour. The level of anti-social behaviour needed to trigger an injunction is low. All that is required is conduct which is capable of causing nuisance or annoyance. However there must be a connection between that conduct and the housing management functions (broadly defined) of the landlord. Social landlords can intervene to protect a wide range of victims, not only people who live in the landlord's properties but also people who live in the locality of those properties, people carrying out lawful activities in the locality of the housing accommodation and people who are employed by the landlord in carrying out its housing function. The court will be able to attach an exclusion order and/or a power of arrest to the injunction where the conduct involves violence, threats of violence or a significant risk of harm. Social landlords also have powers under the Housing Act 1996 to obtain injunctions to restrain unlawful use of premises (s. 153B) and breaches of tenancy agreements (s. 153D). Powers of arrest and exclusion orders are available on the same basis as under the antisocial behaviour injunction.

Anti-social behaviour policies

The responsibilities of social landlords to control the behaviour of their tenants for the benefit of the broader community have received statutory recognition in the Anti-social Behaviour Act 2003. Section 12 of the Act imposes a statutory duty upon social landlords to prepare, keep under review and publish their anti-social behaviour policies. The duty is designed to increase social landlords' accountability to local communities. The policies and procedures will feed into performance measurement by central government as well as increasing the capacity of victims to press their case for social landlords to take action. Publication of the policies should act as a deterrent to potential perpetrators who will know the action they will face and additionally should increase the sharing of good practice in managing anti-social behaviour.

The role of the local authority as strategic housing provider

Local authority housing departments have a wider role than simply as landlords of secure tenants. They have a strategic role in the provision of housing, so, for instance, they have responsibilities to allocate social housing and to make decisions on applications by homeless people for housing. The behaviour of potential tenants has always had an impact upon decisions about their housing. These controls are being made more explicit and strengthened. The Homelessness Act 2002 allows a housing authority to decide that an applicant for housing is ineligible for housing on the basis of unacceptable behaviour. The Act requires that housing authorities allocate housing according to need. However, the Act provides that the extent of the priority of a particular applicant may be determined (amongst other factors) by taking into account any behaviour which affects suitability to be a tenant. Finally, local authorities will not be required to give any priority to applicants who are guilty of unacceptable behaviour. Further explanation of homelessness is provided in chapter 20. What you should note here is that anyone who is judged to have behaved unacceptably is going to find it extremely difficult to access social housing.

Other ways of controlling behaviour

Other behaviour management techniques, for instance approved behaviour contracts (ABCs), are promoted by the Home Office to improve community safety. ABCs typically involve local authorities targeting disruptive young people and drawing up explicit behaviour contracts designed to improve their conduct. Social workers may well be involved in ABCs. Such informal controls on behaviour will, if they fail, inevitably feed into decisions about reasonableness if the authority subsequently commences eviction proceedings. These administrative powers are supported by a variety of Home Office initiatives such as funding for CCTV, better lighting, etc., which allow local authorities the resources to provide situational crime prevention in the same way that privately managed blocks do.

The Crime and Disorder Act 1998

The Crime and Disorder Act 1998 introduced a range of quasi-criminal orders, aimed at tackling bad behaviour in order to benefit the community, but not actually taking the form of a criminal prosecution. One of these orders, the Child Safety Order, discussed below, is the responsibility of social services. The district council must apply for the other quasi-criminal orders. However, the orders involve children, who are likely to be not only children in trouble but also children in need, so social services have to be closely involved under their Children Act, s. 17, duties.

The 1998 Act is unusual in that it does not create new duties under the Local Authority Social Services Act 1971 (see chapter 1). This means that although there is a new range of statutory responsibilities for the local authority on a corporate level, they are not specifically the function of the Social Services Committee.

A number of new court orders have been created, which we shall deal with in turn, together with the role that a local authority social worker is likely to play in obtaining or implementing these orders.

Anti-social behaviour orders (ASBO): Crime and Disorder Act 1998, s. 1

It is the anti-social behaviour order (ASBO) contained in s. 1 of the Crime and Disorder Act 1998 which epitomizes this Government's approach to community safety. It provides a local response to a local problem. The law avoids the need for a personal application for the order, as required by the Protection from Harassment Act and therefore reduces the potential fear of intimidation. It requires consultation between the police and the local authority, emphasizing the partnership approach. Its ambit is wide, both in terms of the loose definition of acting anti-socially, meaning in a manner that causes or is likely to cause harassment, alarm, or distress, and in the age range of potential perpetrators, since children as young as 10 can be the subject of the application. A person (child or adult) can be made subject to the ASBO if the court is satisfied on a balance of probabilities that the person has caused the harassment, alarm, or distress as defined in the Act, or might have done so.

Making the application

The application for an ASBO can be made by the responsible authority, which is either:

(a) the local authority; or

(b) the county council;

(c) the police;

(d) registered social landlords;

(e) housing action trusts;

(f) the British Transport Police.

Applicants who are not the police or the local authority will have to consult the police and the local authority before making an application. Registered social landlords' (housing associations') and housing action trusts powers will be limited to where they need to take action against their tenants or to protect their tenants.

ASBOs are also available to the magistrates' court following conviction for a criminal offence (s. 1C). In these circumstances there is no need for an application. The ASBO can be suspended until completion of the sentence.

The county court

ASBOs are available to a county court where the court is already dealing with proceedings relating to anti-social behaviour, such as possession proceedings. If the potential recipient of the ASBO is not a party to the proceedings but his or her behaviour is relevant (for instance it is the adolescent son of the tenant who is being evicted who has terrified the neighbours) then the landlord may apply to have that person made a party. This avoids the cost and inconvenience of issuing separate proceedings for an ASBO when the evidence would be predominantly the same. The standard criteria for making ASBOs apply.

Social workers

There is no requirement for the social worker to be involved in an application. But the guidance, published by the Home Office and available at **www.crimereduction. gov.uk/asbos9.htm**, states that the court hearing the application should satisfy itself that social services have been consulted, and that the person's needs have been assessed, before deciding whether an ASBO is appropriate. For a child, needs must be assessed under the Children Act—see chapter 10; for adults, it will be under the NHS and Community Care Act 1990—see chapter 17.

The grounds for the application

The grounds are set out in Box 18.7.

Interim orders

Interim orders are available under s. 1D to ensure that the community is protected as soon as possible from anti-social activities. Interim orders will be available only if a timetable is set leading to a full hearing.

> **BOX 18.7** Grounds for anti-social behaviour orders—s. 1 of the Crime and Disorder Act
>
> s. 1(1) An application for an order under this section may be made by a relevant authority if it appears to the authority that the following conditions are fulfilled with respect to any person aged 10 or over, namely—
>
> (a) that the person has acted in an anti-social manner, that is to say, in a manner that caused or was likely to cause harassment, alarm or distress to one or more persons not of the same household as himself; and
>
> (b) that such an order is necessary to protect relevant persons from further anti-social acts by him.

Evidence

The evidence for proving these grounds may be presented anonymously, giving the person accused no chance to cross-examine the person making the allegations. The Court of Appeal has held that this is not a breach of the right to a fair trial under Article 6 of the Human Rights Convention (*Clingham v Kensington and Chelsea LBC* (2001)).

Criminal and sub-criminal activities

The guidance states:

> The process is not suitable for private disputes between neighbours (which are usually civil matters), but is intended to deal with criminal or sub-criminal activity which, for one reason or another, cannot be proven to the criminal standard, or where criminal proceedings are not appropriate.

Hybrid nature

Although the ASBO is obtained in civil proceedings, breach of the order is a criminal offence. In *R v Manchester Crown Court ex parte McCann* (2001) the Court of Appeal confirmed that the provisions were to be treated as civil, so there is no requirement to prove the allegations beyond a reasonable doubt, as there would be in a criminal case.

What may be in the order?

Once the magistrates' court accepts that the defendant has behaved in 'a manner that caused or was likely to cause harassment alarm or distress' and that an order is necessary to protect local people from further acts then the court is able to impose those prohibitions which it deems necessary to protect people from further anti-social acts. (Crime and Disorder Act 1998, s. 1(6), set out in Box 18.8 below.) Examples of prohibitions within orders include a ban on riding a bicycle in the city centre, on meeting more than three non-family members in public, on wearing a balaclava in the street, on wearing a single golf glove (a sign of gang membership) and on saying the word 'grass' anywhere in England or Wales until 2010. At first sight such wide-ranging powers appear to have the potential to breach the Human Rights Act 1998. However, judicial concerns about anti-social behaviour expressed in the cases we have discussed earlier

BOX 18.8 The prohibitions

1(6) The prohibitions that may be imposed by an anti-social behaviour order are those necessary for the purpose of protecting persons (whether relevant persons or persons elsewhere in England or Wales) from further anti-social acts by the defendant.

suggest that limits imposed on an individual's freedom would have to be very extreme before they would be found not to be necessary and proportionate.

Parenting orders

When a court makes an ASBO it must make a parenting order at the same time unless it does not consider that the parenting order is desirable in the interests of preventing any repetition of the kind of behaviour which led to the ASBO (s. 9 (1B)). We discuss parenting orders below.

Length of order

Orders must last for not less than two years (s. 1(7)) and can last indefinitely. Although there are provisions to vary the order, the court cannot discharge an order that has not lasted for two years, unless all parties agree.

Breach of order

Doing anything in breach of the order is a criminal offence. On summary conviction the court can sentence to six months in prison or a £1,000 fine. The breach can be dealt with in the Crown Court with a maximum sentence of five years and an unlimited fine. Either court can impose a community penalty—see chapter 15.

Parenting orders: Crime and Disorder Act 1998, s. 8

No one can apply for a parenting order merely because they perceive a risk or a need. One of the decisions provided for in s. 8 of the Act (set out in Box 18.9) must first have been reached about a child (under 18) by the court considering the parenting order.

BOX 18.9 Section 8(1) of the Crime and Disorder Act

8.(1) This section applies where, in any court proceedings—

    (a) a child safety order is made in respect of a child;

    (b) an anti-social behaviour order or sex offender order is made in respect of a child or young person;

    (c) a child or young person is convicted of an offence; or

    (d) a person is convicted of an offence under section 443 (failure to comply with school attendance order) or section 444 (failure to secure regular attendance at school of registered pupil) of the Education Act 1996.

There is no need for anybody to make a separate application to another court: the decision follows, if the court thinks it appropriate, from the order or conviction listed above. But when would it be appropriate? Under s. 8 the court has to believe that a parenting order is desirable in the interests of preventing a repetition of the event (conviction, truanting, etc.) which the court has just been dealing with. Given the range of court orders or convictions which can trigger the parenting order, there is a range of courts with the power to make the order: a family proceedings court; a magistrates' court acting under civil or criminal jurisdiction; or the Crown Court.

What may be in the order?

An order has two elements:

(a) Compulsory attendance at counselling or guidance sessions for up to three months. The programme of counselling or guidance may include a residential element if the court is satisfied that this is likely to be more effective than attendance at a non-residential course and that any interference with family life that would result from the parent attending a residential course is proportionate in all the circumstances. If the parent has already been subject to a parenting order then the court can exercise its discretion as to whether or not it should order further attendance at counseling or guidance

(b) to comply with any requirements specified by the court (see below) for up to twelve months.

Under s. 8(3) a court may make a parenting order only if facilities are available where the parent lives.

Government guidance gives the following suggestions as to what might be included as requirements for the parent:

- ensuring that the child attends specified school or any extra-curricular activities, such as sporting activities or homework clubs;

- ensuring that the child avoids contact with other named children;

- ensuring that the child avoids visiting certain areas, such as shopping centres, unsupervised;

- ensuring that the child is at home during certain hours, probably the evening, and is effectively supervised; or

- attending or ensuring that the child attends a particular course or session to address specific problems.

No requirement should interfere with the child's religious or educational life, unless there is a very good reason.

Who is the parent?

Section 8 talks of a parent being a parent or guardian or the person convicted of the educational offence. So at least the social worker looking after a child in care is not included. But how will the court decide which parent? The family may be dysfunctional because of the father's absence or behaviour, but the court may feel the only hope is via the mother (or vice versa). At first sight this may appear unfair but research indicates that parents believe that they have benefited significantly from the programmes and many parents sign up voluntarily.

> Though some parents had mixed expectations at the outset of what the Programme would be like (and parents on Parenting Orders were especially likely to feel negative), 'exit' ratings at the end of the Programme were very positive. Only 6% were negative or indifferent about whether the Programme had been helpful, and over nine in ten would recommend it to other parents in their situation. Parents were especially positive about the qualities and skills of the project staff. There was no difference in the level of benefit reported by parents who were referred voluntarily as opposed to being referred via a Parenting Order. *Positive Parenting: The National Evaluation of the Youth Justice Board's Parenting Programme* September 2002

The procedure for making a parenting order

Section 9(3) and (4) of the 1998 Act imposes specific requirements on the court which are set out in Box 18.10 below before it can make a parenting order.

The court must name a 'responsible officer' who will ensure that the order is carried out effectively. Guidance on the role can be found at **www.homeoffice.gov.uk/ docs/parent.html**.

Variation, discharge, and breach of the parenting order

While the order is in force, the responsible officer or the parent may apply to discharge or vary it. Any provisions can be taken out or added. The guidance states that it is not possible to extend the length of an existing order, though the legislation does not cover this point. A parent failing to comply with a parenting order commits a criminal offence and can be fined. This could make further work with this family difficult or impossible and is obviously a threat of last resort which has failed if it has to be used.

 BOX 18.10 Court requirements for parenting orders

The court must:

(a) obtain and consider information about the child's family circumstances and the likely effect of the order on those circumstances. This information can be either in oral or written form;

(b) explain to the parent or guardian of the child in ordinary language—
  (i) the effect of the order and of the requirements proposed to be included in it,
  (ii) the consequences which may follow if the parent fails to comply with any of those requirements, and
  (iii) that the court has power to review the order on the application either of the parent or of the responsible officer;

(c) avoid, as far as practicable, imposing requirements which would either conflict with the parent's religious beliefs, or interfere with the times at which the parent normally works or attends an educational establishment.

Parenting orders and human rights

Is a parenting order a breach of the human rights of the parent? After all the parent's private life is being judged and opened to criminal sanctions for the misdeeds of their child—is that an interference with the respect for private life? The High Court ruled that trying to address the causes of youth crime is proportionate and outweighs the effect on the parent's right not to have her private life interfered with: *R (on the applicaton of M) v Inner London Crown Court* (2003).

Free standing parenting orders

The Anti-social Behaviour Act 2003 introduces two new 'free standing' parenting orders. By free standing we mean that there is no requirement for other court proceedings to be taking place before the order can be made, in contrast with the requirements of s. 8 of the Crime and Disorder Act 1998.

Parenting orders and school exclusions

The first of these orders is introduced by s. 20 of the Anti-social Behaviour Act 2003 and applies to school exclusions. The local education authority may apply to the magistrates' court for a parenting order where 'a pupil has been excluded on disciplinary grounds . . . for a fixed period or permanently. The court can may the order 'if it is satisfied that making the order would be desirable in the interests of improving the behaviour of the pupil (s. 20(3)). The Education (Parenting Orders) England Regulations 2004 limit the use of such orders in the case of fixed-term exclusions to situations where a child has been excluded from school for a fixed term on more than one occasion. The definition of these orders and the requirements for them replicate the provisions of s. 8 of the Crime and Disorder Act 1998.

Parenting orders in respect of criminal conduct and anti-social behaviour

The second circumstance is designed to allow the courts to address early patterns of offending behaviour when asked to do so by the youth offending team. Section 26 requires the court to be satisfied that the child or young person has engaged in criminal conduct or anti-social behaviour and that making the order would be desirable in the interests of preventing the child or young person from engaging in further criminal conduct or further anti-social behaviour.

Local child curfew schemes: Crime and Disorder Act 1998, s. 14

These powers of the district council should be noted, but since they have been ignored by councils, despite Government exhortation, it is unlikely that you will come across a curfew scheme.

Curfew schemes

These schemes should not be confused with curfew orders imposed on individual juveniles following their conviction for a criminal offence (see chapter 15). This is not an order made in response to individual children but in response to the behaviour of children in general in the specified area. It is designed to keep all unsupervised children under the age of 16 off the streets in a particular area for a particular period of time, if the police and the local authority think that this is necessary. (Actually the order does not require anything to be proved, in an evidential sense; no evidence is needed of recent bad behaviour by children roaming the streets out of control. All that is required is that the Home Secretary agrees to the request and signs the order.)

Duration

Each order can last up to ninety days, but if the perceived troubles persist a new one can be made once the old one expires. The order empowers the police to take a child home (or elsewhere if they think the child would not be safe at home) if found out, without supervision from a parent or responsible person of at least 18, between the hours specified in the order (the order can be for any time between 9.00 p.m. and 6.00 a.m.). If a child is picked up in this way the social services authority must be notified, and they must start a s. 47 of the Children Act investigation into whether steps need to be taken to protect or assist the child (see chapter 11).

If a child under the age of 10 breaches a curfew order this can trigger an application for a child safety order.

Dispersal powers under the Anti-social Behaviour Act 2003

The unwillingness of local authorities to use curfew powers available to them under the Crime and Disorder Act 1998 appears to have prompted the government into a second attempt. Section 30 of the Anti-social Behaviour Act 2003 includes two powers which bear a close resemblance to the curfew powers. The first of these is the power to disperse groups and the second is the power to remove children and young persons to their place of residence. The use of both these powers is dependent upon the police designating an area as one where the presence of groups or young people has been seen as particularly problematic. The grounds for designation are set out in box 18.11 below

The local authority must consent to the designation which must be publicized and can last up to 6 months.

Once an area has been designated then a police officer can direct a group to disperse if he or she has 'reasonable grounds for believing that the presence or behaviour of a group of two or more persons in any public place in the relevant locality has resulted, or is likely to result, in any member of the public being intimidated, harassed, alarmed or distressed' (s. 30(3)). Once a direction has been given, it is an offence if a person that the direction has been given to knowingly contravenes the direction (s. 32(2)).

 BOX 18.11 Designation of areas under s. 30(1) Anti-social Behaviour Act 2003

(a) that any members of the public have been intimidated, harassed, alarmed or distressed as a result of the presence or behaviour of groups of two or more persons in public places in any locality in his police area (the 'relevant locality') and

(b) that anti-social behaviour is a significant and persistent problem in the relevant locality.

The second power under s. 30, the power to remove a person that a police officer believes to be under 16 to their place of residence, is likely to be of more relevance to the professional practice of a social worker. The power requires that the area has been designated under s. 30, it applies only to children and young person in public places between the hours of 9 p.m. and 6 a.m., and it applies only when the person under the age of 16 is not under the effective control of a parent or adult (s. 30(6)). It is also restricted where the police officer 'has reasonable grounds for believing that the person would, if removed to that place, be likely to suffer significant harm' (s. 30(6)).

Initial evidence suggests that these powers may prove more attractive than the local child curfew schemes. The Home Office anti-social behaviour web site **www.together.gov.uk/news** has news of the police in Bolton designating an area of the town centre under s.30 of ASBA with the intention of targeting anti-social skateboarders, and also indicates several areas of Nottinghamshire have been designated under the Act.

Child safety orders

These are orders brought in by s. 11 of the Crime and Disorder Act 1998. They apply only to children under the age of 10. A child under the age of 10 cannot, in law, commit a criminal offence (see chapter 15). However the child safety order is available to control or protect the child. The grounds for imposing such an order include behaviour that would be criminal but for the child's age. It is the local authority with social services responsibility who has to apply for the order.

The grounds

Box 18.12 sets out the grounds for a child safety order.

'Offence' in s. 11(3)(a) means any criminal offence ranging from murder to dropping litter.

Section 11(3)(c) refers to a breach of a curfew notice imposed by s. 14 of the Crime and Disorder Act 1998.

 BOX 18.12 Section 11(3)—the conditions for imposing a CSO

(a) that the child has committed an act which, if he had been aged 10 or over, would have constituted an offence;

(b) that a child safety order is necessary for the purpose of preventing the commission by the child of such an act as is mentioned in paragraph (a) above;

(c) that the child has contravened a ban imposed by a curfew notice; and

(d) that the child has acted in a manner that caused or was likely to cause harassment, alarm or distress to one or more persons not of the same household as himself.

Section 11(3)(d) is largely self-explanatory. It should be noted that the provision that specifies the person to whom harm, alarm, or distress is caused or likely to be caused should not be of the same household. (Harassed parents cannot apply!)

Applications

The application for a CSO is to the family proceedings court. These are not specified proceedings under s. 41 of the Children Act 1989. This means that there will be no children's guardian appointed. They are, however, family proceedings under the Act. This means the court must apply the s. 1 principles set out in chapter 9, such as the welfare principle, the no-order principle, and so forth. Before making an application the local authority must also consider its duty under s. 17 of the 1989 Act and decide whether the application will safeguard and promote the welfare of the child. In deciding to apply for a CSO, the local authority is not bound by the provisions of s. 37 of the Crime and Disorder Act 1998 (see chapter 15).

What may be in the order?

Section 11(1) of the 1998 Act places the child under the supervision of a responsible officer (who will be either a social worker or a probation officer) for a minimum period of three months, or exceptionally up to twelve months. The court may specify any requirements which the court considers desirable in the interests of:

(a) securing that the child receives appropriate care, protection, and support and is subject to proper control; or

(b) preventing any repetition of the kind of behaviour which led to the CSO being made.

The Act is silent on the actual requirements. The guidance issued by the Home Office gives examples, such as:

• attendance at school or extra-curriculum activities such as sporting activities or homework clubs;

• avoiding contact with disruptive and possibly older children;

• not visiting areas, such as shopping centres, unsupervised;

• being home during certain hours, probably the evenings; or

• attending particular courses/sessions to address specific problems (for example educational support, behavioural management).

The procedure for making a CSO

Section 12 of the Crime and Disorder Act 1998 imposes specific requirements on the court before it can make an order. The court must:

(a) obtain and consider information about the child's family circumstances and the likely effect of the order on those circumstances (this information can be either in oral or written form);

(b) explain to the parent or guardian of the child in ordinary language —
  (i) the effect of the order and of the requirements proposed to be included in it,
  (ii) the consequences which may follow if the child fails to comply with any of those requirements, and

(iii) that the court has power to review the order on the application either of the parent or guardian or of the responsible officer (this normally would be done at court, although the draft guidance does suggest that it could be done in the form of a letter sent by the court); and

(c) avoid, as far as practicable, imposing requirements which would either conflict with the parent's religious beliefs, or interfere with the times at which the child normally attends school.

When making a CSO the court could make a parenting order under s. 9 of the Crime and Disorder Act 1998 (see above).

Variation and discharge of the CSO

While the order is in force, the responsible officer or the parent may apply to discharge or vary the order. Any provisions can be deleted or be added. The guidance states that it is not possible to extend the length of time of an existing order. It is not clear how the guidance comes to this conclusion.

Breach of the CSO

The magistrates' court is given powers under s. 12(6) where it is satisfied that a child has failed to comply with any requirement of a child safety order, following an application by the responsible officer. The court's powers are set out in Box 18.13. The power of the court to make a care order on breach of a child safety order was repealed by the Children Act 2004.

Local strategic duties

This Government has recognised that anti-social behaviour cannot be categorised simply as a matter with housing or criminal consequences for victims. The impact of anti-social behaviour can contribute to social exclusion and local government has a key role in promoting inclusion.

 BOX 18.13 Breach of a CSO—the court's powers—s. 12(6)

The court may vary the original order, either by cancelling any provision in it or by inserting or substituting for an existing provision any provision which could have been included in the child safety order when first made.

Section 222 of the Local Government Act

One particular legal tool, which provides local authorities with the potential for strategic litigation to prevent anti-social behaviour, predates the current debate. A local authority has wide-ranging powers under the Local Government Act 1972, s. 222, to prosecute or defend or appear in legal proceedings and initiate civil proceedings when it considers it expedient for the promotion or protection of the interests of the inhabitants of its area. The use of this power was recently considered by the Court of Appeal in the context of anti-social behaviour in *Nottingham C.C. v Z* (2001). Nottingham County Council was seeking an injunction to restrain a drug dealer from entering a housing estate. The Court of Appeal, overturning the district judge's striking out of the application and held that the authority was entitled to institute proceedings under s. 222 where activities interfered with the interests of local inhabitants, even where such activities were of a criminal nature. The Anti-social Behaviour Act 2003 amends s. 222 to enable a court which grants an injunction under the section to attach a power of arrest where the conduct which is prohibited includes violence, threatened violence or a risk of significant harm.

Strategic duties under the Crime and Disorder Act

A more recent statutory device provides for a broader-based strategic approach. Section 6 of the Crime and Disorder Act 1998 imposes a duty on local authorities, in partnership with the police, probation service, health authorities, and others, to produce and implement a local strategy for the reduction of crime and disorder. The critical importance of the strategies produced by local Crime and Disorder Reduction Partnerships is made explicit by The Social Exclusion Unit in its report, *A New Commitment to Neighbourhood Renewal: National Strategy Action Plan* (Social Exclusion Unit, January 2001). The duty in s. 6 is supplemented by a less well-known duty on local authorities, contained in s. 17 of the Crime and Disorder Act 1998, to consider the crime and disorder implications of their core activities. Taken together these two sections embed the reduction of crime and disorder into the core activities of local authorities.

Victims

The justification for this extensive legal and policy activity is the needs of victims. Local authorities refer to tenant satisfaction surveys urging them to take more action to protect tenants, and ministers talk about the need to protect the majority of social tenants from the impact of the behaviour of the disruptive minority. There is no doubt that the poorest and most vulnerable in society are at the most risk of crime. Despite this the law provides no means whereby tenants of local authorities can force local authorities to take action on anti-social behaviour.

In *Hussain v Lancaster City Council* (2000), confirmed recently by *Mowan v Wandsworth LBC* (2001), the Court of Appeal held that local authorities are liable for nuisance only if they have authorized it or adopted it. This will rarely apply in anti-social behaviour cases. It seems very likely that this limitation on local authority liability will be challenged via the European Convention. If local authority and other social tenants are going to suffer increasing surveillance and diminution of their security of tenure and other rights to control the behaviour of a minority, it must be right that they should be fully contributing to local authority priorities for action.

Legal apparatus and anti-social behaviour—summary

Box 18.14 provides a summary of the range of potential responses to anti-social behaviour by local authorities.

 BOX 18.14 Summary of local authority responsibilities towards controlling anti-social behaviour

Focus	Mechanism	Innovation	Comment
The landlord's role in controlling anti-social behaviour	Tenancy Agreements	Explicit anti-social behaviour clauses added	Tenants should ensure that they are familiar with the terms of their agreement. Terms must be fair
	Grounds for possession	Extended by the Housing Act 1996	Requirement of proportionality
	Reasonableness requirement	Re-interpreted by the Court of Appeal. Structured discretion in cases of anti-social behaviour introduced by the Anti-social Behaviour Act 2003	Needs of landlord and other tenants stressed
	Injunctive powers	Statutory powers introduced by Housing Act 1996 and extended by the Anti-social Behaviour Act 2003	Use not a prerequisite to possession proceedings
	Security of tenure	Introductory tenancies—discretionary probationer tenancies introduced by Housing Act 1996 Demoted tenancies—reduction of security of tenure for anti-social tenants introduced by the Anti-social Behaviour Act 2003	Human Rights Act compliant
Local authority as housing provider	Allocation schemes	Homelessness Act increases the power to exclude potential anti-social tenants from social housing	Anti-social tenants will be forced to rely on the private rented sector

Action against anti-social individuals (including children) Action against anti-social groups in designated areas	Civil controls Criminal penalties for breach	Anti-Social Behaviour Orders—s. 1 Crime and Disorder Act 1998 Parenting orders—s. 14 Child Safety Orders—s. 11 s. 8 of the Crime and Disorder Act 1998 Local Child Curfew Schemes s.30 of the Anti-social Behaviour Act 2003 dispersal of groups and removal of young persons to their place of residence	Status of civil proceedings despite eventual criminal penalties confirmed by Court of Appeal
Local Government	Strategic and planning duties	s. 6 and s. 17 Crime and Disorder Act 1998	Ensures local delivery of central government priorities via Crime and Disorder Reduction Partnerships

EXERCISES

1 You are contacted by Jenny, who is the mother of three young children. She tells you that her husband assaulted her this morning. As you talk to her it emerges that he has beaten her on a number of occasions, and this has sometimes been in front of the children. Jenny is distraught. She does not know what to do, or who to turn to. She is frightened that she will have nowhere to live if she leaves her husband, but she is frightened to stay. The family live in a housing association property. Jenny and her husband are joint tenants.

(a) What are your statutory duties towards Jenny and her children?
(b) What criminal remedies are available to her?
(c) What civil remedies are available to her?

2 Gulzar, 14, has been attacked by a gang of lads on the estate where he lives. The gang were shouting racist slogans. He has not been to the police, but is frightened that the gang will attack again. What advice can you give him?

3 Kylie is a service user. You have had contact with her over the years because of difficulties she has had raising her family of four boys by herself. In general, with support she has managed well. She telephones you to say that the council have told her that they are going to get an ASBO on her eldest boy, aged 15, because of his behaviour. Apparently, he hangs around with other boys on the estate, verbally abusing residents. The council have also told her that if she cannot control him she will be evicted. She is very worried.

(a) Can you explain the council's actions to her?
(b) Is there anything you can do to help?

COMPANION WEB SITE

 For guidance on how to answer these exercises, visit the companion web site at: www.oup.com/uk/booksites/law

WHERE DO WE GO FROM HERE?

This chapter has provided an outline of the law designed to protect individuals from violence, harassment, and anti-social behaviour. Violence and harassment can arise within family relationships, from failed relationships, from neighbours and others living and visiting the local area, and from total strangers. This is an important area of law, and constantly expanding. You should ensure that you are familiar with your own local authority procedures and practices to help people suffering violence. You will have noticed during this chapter how housing is critical to enabling people to feel safe and secure—indeed the case study at the beginning of the chapter involved the eviction of a neighbour who had harassed a woman and her daughter over a long period of time. Suitable housing will be a priority for women fleeing domestic violence and people wanting to escape a racist environment if a landlord is not prepared to evict perpetrators of racial abuse. The next chapter discusses this important and complex area of the law.

ANNOTATED FURTHER READING

Domestic violence

We recommend the straightforward user-friendly guide, *Domestic Violence: a Guide to Civil Remedies and Criminal Sanctions* published in March 2003 and available on the Lord Chancellor's Department web site, **www.lcd.gov.uk**.

A more scholarly article is P. Dobash and R. Dobash, 'Violence against Women in the Family', in S. Katz, J. Eekelaar, and M. Maclean (eds.), *Cross-currents: Family Law and Policy in the United States and England* (Oxford University Press, 2000), this charts responses to domestic violence from isolated reaction to integrated response.

Other guides to the law are available on the Women's Aid web site, **www.womensaid.org**, which additionally provides a great deal of other information to support women suffering violence. There are a number of other web sites which provide useful information on domestic violence. These include:

www.halt.org.uk/ A Leeds based site which provides legal advice to women going through the courts or are thinking about their legal options.

www.rightsofwomen.org.uk/ Rights of Women is a women's voluntary organization committed to informing, educating and empowering women concerning their legal rights. You can buy a DIY guide to injunctions from their site.

www.jfw.org.uk/ Justice For Women is a feminist organization that campaigns and supports women who have fought back against or killed violent male partners.

www.domesticviolencedata.org/ The Domestic Violence Data Source is an information coordinating system on projects relating to domestic violence within England, Wales, Scotland, Northern Ireland and the Republic of Ireland.

Community care published a useful summary of action on domestic violence in 2003 entitled 'The Bigger Picture on domestic violence' which is archived at **www.communitycare.co.uk/ articles/**.

A useful recent article on the Domestic Violence Bill is D.J. Robert Hills, 'The effect of the Domestic Violence Bill on the Family Law Act 1996 June [2004] Fam Law 442.

You may also find *Special Domestic Violence Courts* interesting reading. This report was published by the CPS and the DCA in April 2004.

Racial harassment

The Commission for Racial Equality has a useful web site with links to other organizations involved in combating racism: **www.cre.gov.uk**.

For general information the victim support web site is very helpful: **www.victimsupport.org.uk**—from there you can download their leaflet, *Going to Court*.

Elder abuse

We have not specifically discussed the problem of elder abuse, although the general information on domestic violence and anti-social behaviour should be useful in this context. You may find the following useful: *Elder Abuse No Secrets—Guidance on developing and implementing multi-agency policies and procedures to protect vulnerable adults from abuse*. It is available on the Department of Health web site **www.doh.gov.uk**. The problem received parliamentary attention in *Elder Abuse 2nd Report of The Health Select Committee* published on 20 April 2004 and available on the Parliament web site at **www.parliament.the-stationery-office.co.uk/pa/cm/ cmhealth.htm**.

Anti-social behaviour

A good general guide to the law is C. Hunter, *Tackling Anti-Social Behaviour-Law and Practice in the Management of Social Housing* (Arden's Housing Library, Lemos and Crane, London, 2002).

The Social Exclusion Unit report, Policy Action Team 8, Anti-social Behaviour available on the Social Exclusion Unit web site **www.socialexclusionunit.gov.uk** provides a useful examination of government policy, and Manchester City Council's web site **www.manchester.gov.uk/people/people/issue16/antisocial.htm** provides examples of how one particular local authority is using the powers available to it.

D. Ghate and M. Ramella *Positive Parenting: The National Evaluation of the Youth Justice Board's Parenting Programme*. London: Youth Justice Board for England and Wales (2002) is an interesting evaluation of the impact of parenting orders on families.

Criticism of anti-social behaviour initiatives include the academic, for instance: P. Papps, 'Anti-social Behaviour Strategies—Individualistic or Holistic?', (1998) 13(5) Housing Studies 639, and C. Hunter and J. Nixon, 'Taking the Blame and Losing the Home: Women and Anti-social Behaviour', (2001) 23(4) Journal of Social Welfare and Family Law 1.

There has also been extensive practitioner comment. See for instance:

'Curfew culture is unfair on the silent majority', Municipal Journal, 10 June 2004. Explains why Liberty is challenging child curfews which have been introduced under the Anti-social Behaviour Act.

'What to do about the neighbours', Property People, 15 July 2004. Outlines the powers, duties and responsibilities of landlords when dealing with nuisance neighbours.

'Media campaign catches local "yobs" ', Young People Now, 9–15 June 2004. A newspaper 'shop-a-yob' bingo campaign in South East London and North Kent has resulted in the identification of all 80 young people featured. The campaign used CCTV images of young people, believed to have vandalized buses, as bingo squares and readers who could identify three in a row or four in each corner had a chance of winning a digital camera.

For commentary on the Anti-social Behaviour Act 2003 see H. Carr, M. Waddington, A. Blair, and T. Baldwin, The Anti-social Behaviour Act 2003—a special bulletin, Jordans (2004).

Housing problems

R (on the application of Bernard) v Enfield LBC [2003] HRLR 4

Facts

Mrs Bernard (the second claimant) was a severely disabled woman with very limited mobility. She was dependant on an electronically operated wheelchair. She was doubly incontinent and suffered from diabetes. She was cared for by her husband, the first claimant, who also looked after their six children, aged between 3 and 20 years old.

For about seven years the claimants were owner occupiers of a house in north London. That house had been fully adapted by social services to meet Mrs Bernard's needs. Unfortunately, mortgage arrears built up and the claimants sold the house. The family were housed by Enfield Council at 26 Shrubbery Road in June 2000. In September, Enfield's social services department carried out an assessment of the claimants' needs. The assessment indicated that the property was unsuitable for Mrs Bernard as, amongst other things, she was unable to use her wheelchair in the property and was confined to the lounge room. The social services department recommended that suitable accommodation be provided for her and her family.

Mr Bernard gave powerful evidence of the effect of the unsuitable accommodation on the family.

> Because my wife is doubly incontinent and only gets, frequently, less than one minute warning of the need to use the toilet, she commonly defecates or urinates before we reach the toilet. The result has been that I have had to persistently clean the carpets together with her clothes and bedclothes. This is a problem which arises several times each day. I have to go the laundrette often twice a day, and because of the layout of the house, I have had to buy adult size nappies for my wife together with disposal pants and wipes . . .
>
> We only have benefits to live on and the additional cost of going to the launderette twice a day and having to buy large amounts of floor cleaner and carpet cleaner has left us impoverished. We have not been able to pay the difference between our Housing Benefit and rent because we are so impoverished by these launderette and cleaning costs.
>
> Additionally my wife's role in bringing up the children is greatly limited. She cannot access the upper part of the house at all and it is a real struggle for her to leave her bedroom which is in fact the family's living room.
>
> She has no privacy. We have six children and she is in the living room which is accessed directly from the front street door.
>
> Understandably my wife finds this state of affairs depressing and demeaning . . .

The re-housing recommendation was not acted on by Enfield's housing department. Enfield also failed to act and respond to a series of letters from the claimants' solicitors who also sent the defendant an independent report confirming the defendant's own assessment.

It was only in March 2002, during a hearing of the case, that Enfield accepted that, as a result of the assessments, it had been under a duty to make arrangements for the provision of suitably adapted accommodation for Mrs Bernard under s. 21(1) (a) of the National Assistance Act 1948.

Eventually, the claimants were offered and accepted appropriate accommodation into which they moved on 14 October 2002, more than two years after the September 2000 assessments.

Prior to the offer of appropriate accommodation, the claimants had commenced proceedings for judicial review. The claimants contended, among other things, that the defendant's conduct had been in breach of Articles 3 and 8 of the European Convention on Human Rights.

Held

There was no breach of the claimants' Article 3 rights. Although deplorable, the conditions in 26 Shrubbery Road did not cross the necessary threshold of severity so as to amount to a breach of Article 3. That there was no intention to humiliate or debase the claimants was an important consideration. The claimants' suffering was due to a failure to act, namely the defendant's corporate neglect, and not to a positive decision by the defendant that the claimants should be subjected to such conditions. There was, however, a breach of Article 8. The European Court of Human Rights had recognized that Article 8 may require public authorities to take positive measures to secure respect for private or family life. Not every breach of duty under s. 21 of the National Assistance Act 1948 would result in a breach of Article 8. The state was not required to provide every one of its citizens with a house. Whether Article 8 rights were infringed would depend on all the circumstances of the case.

Following the assessments in September 2000, it was clear the provision of accommodation was necessary not merely to facilitate the normal incidents of family life, but to secure the physical and psychological integrity of the second claimant. The defendant's failure to act on those assessments was incompatible with Article 8 as it condemned the claimants to living conditions which made it virtually impossible for them to have any meaningful private or family life.

Although the breach of Article 8 did not inevitably lead to an award of damages, in this particular case an award was necessary to give just satisfaction to the claimants. The defendant had committed a serious breach of the claimants' rights under Article 8. They and their family had had to live in deplorable conditions wholly inimical to any normal family life, and to the physical and psychological integrity of the second claimant for a considerable period of time. Further, the defendant had repeatedly ignored requests by the claimants' solicitors for it to take action, not acknowledged that it was in error or provided any explanation or apology, and done nothing to indicate that its procedures had been improved so as to avoid the same kind of mistake in the future. £ 8,000 was awarded to Mrs Bernard, and £2,000 to her husband. The level of award was similar to the amount that would have been awarded by the Local Government Ombudsman in a community care case.

OVERVIEW AND OBJECTIVES

This case highlights the critical relationship between decent housing and a satisfactory private and family life. It also demonstrates that it is not sufficient for social services to carry out their duties appropriately. If people are to get the services they need other departments of the local authority must carry out their responsibilities. Housing departments are under a lot of pressure, and, like social services, have limited resources. Yet it is essential that they deliver their responsibilities. The failure here was dramatic and prolonged, such that it interfered with the claimants' Convention rights under Article 8. Yet the problems do not have to be as serious as this to have an impact upon people's lives. Vulnerable people need social services and housing departments to understand each other's priorities. If this chapter helps you understand your service users' housing rights, and the responsibilities of landlords including local authority landlords, then perhaps it will help you communicate properly the urgency and importance of your service users' housing needs. Equally important, if you can assist the people towards whom you have statutory duties to sort out their housing problems, you may avoid the need for more social work intervention.

As you read this chapter, notice how much depends upon people being aware of their rights. Also notice how dependent housing status is upon affordability. If you can afford your rent or your mortgage then you are generally able to sort out your problems. If you cannot, your problems can become intractable. The Bernard family had their own house, fully adapted by social services. It is very unfortunate for everyone, and especially Mrs Bernard, that no support was available to help them continue to afford to live in that property.

This chapter is designed to help you understand the law which underpins housing rights. It works on a very different basis from social services law as it is based on an array of rights which flow from the legal status of the occupier, rather than being based upon statutory duties arising from the needs of the person. We will consider legal status and security, harassment, and illegal eviction and the law relating to disrepair. We will also consider the financial help that is available to help people afford and, in certain limited circumstances, make adaptations to their housing. By the end of the chapter you should be able to identify where people have housing rights. You should be able to recognize the statutory framework of rented housing. You should be able to anticipate when someone will qualify for housing benefit, and give them an outline of the procedure involved in claiming. We do not expect that you will be able to advise on the enforcement of those rights. You should, however, be able to point someone in the direction of more specialist housing advice.

Introduction

Housing law is complex. It is often ignored, both by tenants and other occupiers, who do not know that they have rights, and landlords, who may rely on or share this ignorance. It is an area which occupiers frequently do not recognize as having a legal dimension. For example, there are arrears with the rent, the landlord is threatening to throw the tenant out, and the flat is damp. The tenant may see this as an insoluble problem—the social worker, on the other hand, should recognize rights and obligations; the landlord may have a legal duty to repair; the tenant cannot be thrown out without a court order; the rent may be too high or housing benefit may be available and, once you have told the tenant that there may be something he or she can do, specialist advice should be sought.

The key issues for the non-property owning client are the following:

- obtaining a property;

- keeping the property;

- affording the rent; and

- keeping the property in repair.

The law relating to these matters forms the basis of this chapter. We have 'mapped' the relationship between the relevant law and these issues on our web site.

Owner-occupiers also have problems, particularly relating to affordability and repair, or the need for adaptations to enable them to stay in the home. We provide a brief summary of their legal position at the end of the chapter.

Information on the law

Legislation

There are a multitude of statutes which cover housing law. The most important are the Housing Act 1988, the Housing Act 1985, and the Housing Act 1996. Important statutory provisions on repairing obligations and information requirements are contained in the Landlord and Tenant Act 1985. The Protection from Eviction Act 1977 provides remedies for illegal eviction.

The Office of the Deputy Prime Minster

The Office of the Deputy Prime Minister publishes a very useful series of leaflets on housing topics. The leaflets can be obtained from ODPM Free Literature, PO Box No 236, Wetherby LS23 7NB. Telephone 0870 1226 236 and e-mail odpm@two-ten.press.net. The web site of the Office of the Deputy Prime Minister contains a whole range of useful information about housing. Its address is **www.housing.odpm.gov.uk**. The ODPM leaflets referred to above can be downloaded from the web site.

The Community Legal Service

The Community Legal Service also publishes helpful leaflets on housing and the law. They are available from the Community Legal Service web site at **www.justask.org.uk/legalhelp/leaflets**.

Shelter

Shelter is a national charity which campaigns on behalf of and provides advice to those who are homeless or who have housing problems. They provide three very valuable advice services. First, Shelterline, a twenty-four hour, free, national housing helpline. It provides advice to anyone with a housing problem. The freephone number is 0808 800 4444. Second, Shelternet, a housing advice web site at **www.shelternet.org.uk**. Third, Shelter runs over fifty housing aid centres and projects across Britain. You can find your nearest Housing Advice Centre from the Shelter web site at **www.shelter.org.uk**.

Other sources of advice

Your local Citizens' Advice Bureau will be able to provide housing advice. Law Centres employ lawyers who specialise in housing law. We have a complete list of law centres and their telephone numbers on our web site. Many solicitors also provide housing law advice. Unfortunately, the number that specialise in housing is in decline, due to the low remuneration for legal assistance. However, in most areas of the country there are still many good firms providing an excellent service. The Law Society web site provides a list of firms which specialize in housing.

It is very likely that good housing advice is available within your local authority if it is a unitary authority or within the housing and environmental health departments of your district council. Tenancy relations officers are often employed by local housing authorities to advise both landlords and tenants on the law. We discuss their role later in this chapter. Environmental health officers are able to give advice on standards in housing. Many local authorities have housing advice centres, and some, such as Brent Council, run duty possession schemes which provide help in court on possession days.

◼ Obtaining rented accommodation

You may be asked to help someone who is looking for rented accommodation. The choices open to people are renting from a private sector landlord, a housing association landlord, or a local authority landlord.

Obtaining private sector tenancies

Some people may prefer to rent property in the private sector, or have no choice either because they are not owed housing duties under the Housing Act 1996—we discuss housing authorities' duties to the homeless in chapter 20—or because there is such a high demand for housing locally that there is no real prospect of them being re-housed via the local housing authority waiting list. Renting in the private sector offer tenants fewer legal rights (see later), but it mean greater choice, particularly as to the type of accommodation available and its location. Private accommodation is advertised in local papers and the local authority housing office may have a list of landlords. Accommodation agencies may offer a service to people looking for private sector accommodation, but their services are often expensive and may not be relevant to people on benefits. Their operation is regulated by the Accommodation Agencies Act 1953. Note that private sector landlords can select their tenants in any way they choose, and have no obligations over and above anti-discrimination legislation.

The most important advice for those seeking accommodation in the private rented sector is to check that it is affordable. Most private sector landlords require deposits and rent in advance which are not automatically covered by income support or social fund payments. More importantly, housing benefit, which covers rent payments, is not only means-tested but also has limitations with regard to the level of payments which can be made on any particular property. Several local housing departments run schemes to help people rent in the private rented sector which aim to speed up housing benefit decisions and support tenants in their dealings with their landlord. You should check to see what services are offered in your local area. We provide an outline of housing benefit later in this chapter when we consider affordability in more detail.

Private sector landlords are most likely to offer assured shorthold tenancies under the Housing Act 1988. Private sector landlords have a range of legal responsibilities towards their tenants and we will outline their main legal responsibilities in this chapter. However, private sector landlords are not public bodies for the purposes of the Human Rights Act 1998 and, therefore, obligations under that Act—for instance the Article 8 requirement for respect for the home—are not relevant to them.

Obtaining housing association tenancies

Most housing associations are legally defined as registered social landlords under the Housing Act 1996. Registered social landlords are registered with the Housing Corporation, which regulates their operation. When we talk about housing associations in this chapter we really mean registered social landlords. We use the term housing association because that is how most people recognize this type of landlord. Housing associations are becoming of greater significance as landlords as the role of local housing authorities as landlords is in decline and their stock is transferred to housing associations.

Housing association tenancies are generally obtained either through a waiting list run by the individual housing association or via nominations from the local housing department. Again, you should get to know which housing associations offer accommodation in your area and what their criteria are. Housing association landlords are most likely to offer properties which let on are assured tenancies under the Housing Act 1988.

Housing associations are not automatically public bodies for the purposes of the Human Rights Act 1998. However, this is a developing area of the law, and if an individual's landlord is a housing association which may have taken action which infringes human rights then he or she should get legal advice.

Housing association tenants in England can complain to the Housing Ombudsman Service about maladministration of housing by their landlord. Welsh housing association tenants will be able to complain to the Social Housing Ombudsman for Wales once the relevant provisions of the Housing Act 2004 are implemented. We discuss the role of ombudsmen in chapter 5. The Housing Ombudsman Service web site which contains details on how to make complaints and reports on decisions about housing associations is at **www.ihos.org.uk**.

Obtaining local authority tenancies

Code of Guidance on Allocations

Part 6 of the Housing Act 1996, as amended by the Homelessness Act 2002 together with the Code of Guidance on Allocations published in November 2002, sets out the principles for allocation of local authority housing. The Code of Guidance is on the ODPM web site at **www.housing.odpm.gov.uk/local/allocation/index**.

Eligibility for local authority accommodation

Section 160A of the Housing Act 1996 provides that everyone is eligible to be housed by the local authority except for:

(i) people from abroad who are subject to immigration control with the meaning of the Asylum and Immigration Act 1996 unless they are in a class of people prescribed in the regulations as exempt from being ineligible. Even those people will be ineligible if they are excluded from entitlement to housing benefit by s. 115 of the Immigration and Asylum Act 1999.

(ii) people guilty of unacceptable behaviour as decided by the local housing authority. Unacceptable behaviour is defined as behaviour by the applicant or a member of her/his household which would, if he or she were a secure tenant of the local housing authority, entitle the authority to a possession order under the grounds of possession set out in Schedule 2 to the Housing Act 1985.

Being excluded from eligibility is a very serious matter. Decisions on eligibility can be reviewed under s. 167(4A) of the Housing Act 1996. Whilst there may be little that you can do to support someone subject to immigration control you should be prepared to support a client who is excluded because of unacceptable behaviour. Advise them to seek a review of the decision and be prepared to give evidence on their behalf if you can shed light on the reasons for their behaviour.

Applications to the local housing authority for accommodation

Section 166 of the Housing Act 1996 imposes certain duties on local housing authorities to:

• provide free advice and information about the right to make an application for housing;

• provide free assistance in making an application for housing to anyone who may have difficulty making an application;

• inform every applicant about their rights to a review of decisions about allocations;

• consider every application if it is made in accordance with the procedural requirements of the authority's allocation scheme;

• not divulge to any other member of the public the fact that a person is an applicant without his or her consent.

So, in theory, everyone should be confident that they can make an application for accommodation which will be considered properly. In practice, of course, housing authorities, like social services, are overstretched and people do not necessarily get an appropriate level of service.

Housing authorities must consider all applications for housing and cannot exclude applicants who, for example, are not currently resident in the borough. However, in determining relative priorities for an allocation, authorities are able to have regard to whether or not applicants have a local connection with the district.

Allocation schemes

When local housing authorities decide whom to house, they must give 'reasonable preference' in allocating accommodation to people who are homeless, to people who are owed duties under the homelessness provisions of the Housing Act 1996, to helping people move out of seriously substandard or insecure housing, and to people with medical or other problems, or people who need to move to a particular locality in the district of the authority, where failure to meet that need would cause hardship to themselves or to others (s. 167). Housing authorities may decide to give additional preference to particular categories of people in urgent housing need. Other factors which may be taken into account when housing authorities are devising an allocation scheme include the financial resources available to a person to meet his housing costs, the behaviour of any person or a member of his household which affects suitability to be a tenant, and any local connection which exists between a person and the authority's district. You will notice that anti-social behaviour is again featured in the legal framework of allocations. Local housing authorities can devise schemes which give very low priority to people they consider to be anti-social. We discuss government initiatives on anti-social behaviour in chapter 18.

The authority must publish the criteria it uses to decide how it allocates its accommodation, including how it will apply these statutory priorities. Most local authorities operate a waiting list awarding extra points for particular circumstances such as age, health, number of children, quality of current accommodation, homelessness, etc.

Choice based letting

Recently there has been a move away from bureaucratic allocation systems to choice based lettings. In this system available housing is advertised. The advertisements set out the qualifying conditions, such as household size and the rules for applying along with a reply coupon. Households express interest in a property by sending a reply coupon to the landlord. Household are ranked according to transparent and objective criteria like age, length of residence, waiting time, or combinations of these. The property is offered to the household ranged highest. Feedback is given in the newspaper on the number of applicants for each dwelling advertised and on the qualifying conditions of applicants housed. Unsuccessful applicants can check the qualifying conditions of the successful applicants and can use this feedback information to focus their future applications on properties for which they would have a realistic chance of being ranked highly.

Secure tenancies

Local authority landlords will offer either secure tenancies under the Housing Act 1985 or introductory tenancies under the Housing Act 1996. Because local authorities are public bodies their actions must be compliant with the Human Rights Act 1998 and their decisions are judicially reviewable.

Local authority tenants can complain to the Local Government Ombudsman about local authority maladministration of housing matters. The web site, which includes details on how to complain, is at **www.lgo.org.uk**.

▓ The statutory framework of housing law

The main practical problems which affect occupiers during the course of their occupation are to do with the rent level, the state of repair of the property, and the right to stay in the property. We shall consider each of these in turn, but since the legal rights of tenants and licensees are dependent upon their legal status we must spend some time describing the different legal arrangements that exist within the rented sector.

Identifying status

Legal status depends on a number of things. First, it has to be established whether someone has a tenancy or a licence and then, if a tenancy exists, what kind of tenancy it is. The answer (to the question what type of tenancy) largely depends on the date of commencement of the tenancy and who the landlord is. Finally, you need to check whether the particular tenancy arrangement is one specifically excluded from protection. It is worth pointing out now that the most significant exclusion is of the tenant who has a resident landlord. We will explain this more fully later.

Tenancy or licence?

The requirements of a tenancy

People who pay money—rent—to live in someone else's property are normally called tenants. However, in law, the word tenant describes a particular type of arrangement. To be a tenant, the person or persons renting must be entitled to three things: (i) exclusive possession; (ii) of identifiable premises; (iii) for a known period (such as a weekly period) (*Street v Mountford* (1985)). So they must be able to say that under the contract (that is the verbal or written agreement), while the tenancy continues, they are entitled to live there and to exclude anyone else from being there. A guest, or a cohabitee, or a live-in granny, or grown-up child living with their parents would all fail these tests. Such occupiers are in the premises by permission of the occupier, their right to continue there can be withdrawn, and they are called not tenants but licensees. The problem is that often tenants do not realise that they are tenants. For instance the landlord may tell them that he or she will let themselves in when it is convenient to do so. This may lead the occupier to think that they do not have the right to exclude the landlord. In fact the landlord is behaving illegally—in breach of the covenant of quiet enjoyment which we discuss later. In addition, a landlord may try to describe a letting as a licence, when in fact it is a tenancy. The House of Lords in *Street v Mountford* said it does not matter what the letting is called; what matters is what the person actually gets from the landlord under that agreement.

The safest way to proceed is to assume that the occupier is a tenant unless there are strong indications to the contrary.

The advantages of a tenancy

There are two main advantages to being a tenant. First, it is generally harder for the landlord to recover possession of the premises, because the protection provided by the

Housing Act 1988 extends to tenants only. We shall examine this protection below. Second, the landlord must repair premises let on a tenancy (see below)—this obligation does not apply with a licence, unless the landlord has actually agreed to repair—this would mean that he or she had a contractual obligation to repair. It is important to note that most licensees who have a contract, like most tenants, cannot be evicted without a court order, because of the Protection from Eviction Act 1977, which we discuss below.

Shared accommodation

Difficulties have arisen for the courts in deciding whether an arrangement is a lease or a licence in two particular areas. First, where occupiers share accommodation. These multiple occupancy agreements were discussed by the House of Lords in *Antoniades v Villiers* (1990) and *AG Securities v Vaughan* (1988). In the *Antoniades* case, a young couple were looking for accommodation together. They each signed a separate agreement, described as a licence agreement to share a one-bedroom flat. Each agreement provided that the 'licensor' also had the right to occupy the premises and that he might license others to share occupation with the licensees. The House of Lords held that the arrangement was clearly a lease and that the young couple were joint tenants of the flat even though they had signed separate agreements. The terms allowing occupation by the landlord or others were clearly shams not intended to be used in reality. This contrasts with the other case that the House of Lords heard at the same time, *AG Securities*. Here the premises comprised a flat which had four bedrooms, plus bathroom and kitchen. The flat was occupied by four people who were selected by the owner and who did not previously know one another. Each had arrived at a different time and each paid a different amount for the use of the flat. No exclusive possession of any part of the flat was given. It was a typical student-type house-sharing agreement. The House of Lords was clear that these were genuine licences.

There have been a number of cases since 1988. What we can learn from them is that agreements for flat-sharing should be understood in the light of all the circumstances— the relationship between the sharers, the negotiations which led up to the agreement, the nature and the extent of the accommodation, and the intended and actual way in which the accommodation was used. Do not be swayed by what the landlord or the occupiers think the arrangements are. What matters is the objective reality of the situation.

Hostel accommodation

The second difficulty has arisen around the nature of exclusive possession in the context of hostel accommodation provided by either local authority or housing association landlords—often collectively described as social landlords. Following the decision in *Westminster City Council v Clarke* (1992), it was generally understood that where social landlords provided bedsitters for the vulnerable homeless in hostels and maintained strict controls over the management of the residents and the hostels, licences as opposed to leases were created. This allows a social landlord to optimise short-term provision of accommodation without granting security of tenure. However, in the decision of the House of Lords in *Bruton (AP) v London and Quadrant Housing Trust*

(1999), the judges returned to a very straightforward interpretation of the lease/licence distinction. As Mr Bruton had exclusive possession for an identifiable period (here, for a weekly term) at a rent of a room in the Housing Trust's hostel, he was found to have a tenancy. This was despite the fact that the trust itself only had the premises on licence and that Mr Bruton had understood that he only had a licence. What this means is that in most circumstances, residents who are paying rent for the exclusive use of accommodation will have tenancies, even if this causes difficulties for social landlords attempting to accommodate some very vulnerable people in short-term accommodation. The reason Mr Bruton took his case to court was to get his landlord to carry out repairs. He needed a tenancy so that there would be a legal obligation to repair his accommodation.

Some hostel accommodation provided by local authority landlords and housing association landlords is excluded from the Protection from Eviction Act 1977. This means that the occupier has no security of tenure at all and can be evicted without a court order. We discuss the provisions of the Protection from Eviction Act 1977 later.

■ Legal implications of tenancies

Unfortunately, even when you have solved the initial problem of tenancy or licence, the law governing tenancies is complex, and rights vary depending upon the statutory regime that the tenant falls under. Before we start to unravel those matters, however, we should consider some basic principles which apply to all tenancies.

Written or oral agreement?

Many people renting homes do so without a written tenancy agreement. They may therefore wrongly assume that there is no enforceable contract. This is untrue; only an agreement for a fixed term of over three years has to be in writing. Sometimes the absence of a written agreement is to the tenant's advantage, since most of what is put in written tenancy agreements is worked out by lawyers for landlords, not tenants. This is particularly so when the agreement commenced before 28 February 1997. We will explain this later. For now just remember that a binding agreement comes into effect when its terms are agreed; that agreement can be oral or written, although the best evidence of what has been agreed is what is written. Failing that, the evidence of what has been orally agreed will form the basis of the contract. If the landlord says you can live here for £30 a week, and you pay rent on that basis, a weekly periodic tenancy has been formed. Some terms will, if necessary to the functioning of the contract, be implied by common law. We discuss the meaning of common law in chapter 5. Other terms are implied into the contract by statute. These terms, such as the repair obligations of landlords or the amount of notice which must be given before a tenancy is terminated, are terms which Parliament has decided are necessary to protect the tenant. We will consider these later in the chapter.

Information requirements

There are certain matters which the law requires of a landlord which are important to mention here. First, if the rent is payable weekly, the landlord must supply the tenant with a rent book (Landlord and Tenant Act 1985, ss. 4–7). Failure to do so is a criminal offence. However the requirement only applies where the rent is payable weekly. Most rents are now payable monthly, so it is of limited use. Secondly, there is an obligation (under s. 48 of the Landlord and Tenant Act 1985) on landlords to provide tenants with an address in England and Wales at which notices, including notices relating to legal proceedings, may be served on them by tenants. Failure to comply with this requirement renders any rent or service charge not due until the requirements have been satisfied. What it does not mean is that the tenant will not be required to pay the arrears of rent once the s. 48 notice has been provided. Finally, any tenant who has an assured shorthold tenancy which began after the 27 February 1997 who has not got a written tenancy is entitled to a written statement from the landlord of certain key provisions of the tenancy (s. 20A of the Housing Act 1988). If the landlord fails to provide this he or she commits a criminal offence.

Unfair contract terms

There is one important piece of consumer legislation which protects tenants from exploitative tenancy terms. The Unfair Terms in Consumer Contracts Regulations 1999 (the Regulations) regulate contracts to ensure that terms other than terms which are described as core terms are fair and transparent. Core terms, such as price or statutory terms or individually negotiated terms, are excluded from the Regulations. The Regulations mean that the courts will strike out terms which breach the Regulations, and may provide a useful remedy where, for instance, in a fixed-term tenancy the tenant has had to agree to rent increase provisions which are considerably in excess of the annual inflation rate. In *Camden LBC v McBride* (1999), a county court judge ruled that Camden Council's anti-nuisance clause could not be enforced against one of its tenants because of the 1999 Regulations. It is the Office of Fair Trading which is the main enforcer of the Regulations and its role is probably more important than the courts' in ensuring that tenancy terms are fair. If you are aware that a landlord or a letting agency is using contracts with oppressive terms you can complain to the Office of Fair Trading which may investigate the matter and take action to stop the use of the unfair term. The Office of Fair Trading has published guidance on unfair terms in tenancy agreements. It is available on its web site at **www.oft.gov.uk**.

Other legal characteristics of a tenancy

Tenancies have other characteristics. First, what is called the covenant of quiet enjoyment is implied by law into every tenancy. What this means is that the landlord makes a legally binding promise that the tenant's lawful possession of land will not be substantially interfered with by the landlord. In practical terms, therefore, the landlord cannot go into the tenant's home without permission, he cannot send the tenant threatening letters, neither should he stop the tenant using the premises as he wishes.

The covenant is particularly useful in the context of harassment and illegal eviction. The second characteristic of which it is useful to know is the tenant's obligation to behave in a 'tenant-like' manner. This means that the tenant should look after the property, carry out minor repairs and not let damage occur through carelessness. If they do not do so, then they may be liable to the landlord for damages. It is unfortunate that such significant terms are not self-explanatory. They reflect the medieval origins of landlord and tenant law.

Young people and tenancies

Very few landlords in the private rented sector are going to want to rent accommodation to 16- or 17-year-olds. However local authorities and housing associations should be prepared to do so, particularly in view of the increased priority need that 16- and 17-year-olds receive under the homelessness legislation—see chapter 20. There are two obstacles to young people becoming tenants. First, you have to be 18 or over to acquire a 'legal interest in land', which is what a tenancy is. Second, contracts with young people under 18 are enforceable against the young person only if they are 'contracts for necessities'. This would theoretically make it difficult for the landlord to recover unpaid rent. However, these hurdles can be overcome. In most circumstances a contract to rent accommodation would be considered by the courts to be a 'contract for necessities'. Even if landlords cannot grant legal tenancies to under 18s, they can grant 'equitable leases'. Equitable leases are in very simple terms leases which do not comply with all the legal formalities but the courts consider should be treated as if they do. Such agreements attract the normal provisions of security of tenure. Unfortunately most social landlords do not understand the law, and if they are prepared to rent accommodation at all to young people may try to do so on a variety of arrangements which are less favourable to the young person. If you are trying to help a young person to become established on leaving home or residential care and the landlord will not agree to the young person signing a standard agreement granting them the same rights as their other tenants, we suggest you contact a housing law specialist.

Help for young people

Young people have particular difficulties in accessing accommodation and in retaining it. There are a range of organizations who specialize in supporting the housing of young people for instance, Centrepoint—**www.centrepoint.org.uk**—the Foyer Federation—**www.foyer.net**—and Crisis—**www.crisis.org.uk**.

Recognising the relevant statutory framework—a summary

In order to recognize the relevant statutory regime you need the answers to two key questions:

• Who is the landlord?

• When did the tenancy commence?

The potential landlords are local authorities, housing associations, and private landlords, who can be individuals or companies. The most significant date is 15 January

1989, the date of the commencement of the Housing Act 1988. However, the commencement date of the relevant sections of the Housing Act 1996—28 February 1997—is also important.

In simple terms, all private tenancies created on or after 15 January 1989 are governed by the Housing Act 1988 and must be either assured tenancies or assured shorthold tenancies. All private tenancies created before that time are governed by the Rent Act 1977 and are regulated tenancies. Where the local authority is the landlord then the Housing Act 1985 is the relevant piece of legislation, and local authority tenants generally have secure tenancies regardless of the commencement date. However, there are two exceptions to this. Some local authorities use introductory tenancies for the first year of the tenancy. Introductory tenancies are governed by the provisions of the Housing Act 1996. Local authorities also have the power to apply to court to demote a secure tenancy to a demoted tenancy.

Housing association tenancies are slightly more complex, in that the legislation treated them in different ways depending on whether the Government of the day saw them as part of the private or public sector. Pre-January 1989, the housing association tenant was seen as part of the public sector, with the rent governed by the fair rent provisions of the Rent Act 1977 and the other terms determined by the Housing Act 1985. New tenancies created on or after that date by housing association landlords are governed by the Housing Act 1988 and are generally assured tenancies, although some housing associations are using assured shortholds for probationary periods. Housing Associations can also apply to court to demote assured tenancies. The demotion process creates an assured shorthold tenancy.

The Housing Act 1996 added a final twist from its commencement on 28 February 1997. Prior to that date a private sector landlord had to comply with rigorous technical procedures to create an assured shorthold tenancy. From that date all new tenancies created are assured shorthold tenancies unless the landlord informs the tenant that the agreement is for an assured tenancy. These complex provisions have real significance, particularly in relation to the tenant's right to remain in the property.

Statutory rights

You should now be able to work out which statute covers the tenancy agreement. If so, once we have explained to you the key features of each tenancy type you will be able to identify the rights which are relevant to the tenant and give an indication of the answers to the problems which we discussed at the beginning of the chapter (i.e. what legal protection does the tenant have from rent increases and from eviction from the property).

Exclusions

Note, however, that not all tenancies are covered by statutory regimes, either because the tenancy is one which is specifically excluded from protection by the statute, or because the tenancy agreement itself falls outside the scope of the statute. So, for instance, a tenant of a private landlord started living in the property in July 1990. On the face of it that means that the relevant statute is the Housing Act 1988. However, the tenant also owns a property where she lives five days a week. Section 1 of the Housing

Act 1988 requires that, for the tenant to receive the protection of the statute, she must occupy the property as her only or principal home. Clearly this tenant does not, so she will not be protected by the Act. What protection would such a tenant have? She would be a common law tenant whose tenancy can be ended by a notice to quit. Her only (and limited) protection would be via the Protection from Eviction Act 1977, which we will discuss later.

Our second example relates to those tenancies which are excluded from statutory protection. The same basic facts apply—a tenant moved into the property in July 1990. This time, however, it turns out that she has a resident landlord. Such an agreement is excluded from the Housing Act 1988 on the basis that a landlord should not be obliged by statute to allow a tenant to continue to live in his own house when that relationship has broken down. Again, what the tenant has is a common law tenancy with only the Protection from Eviction Act 1977 for protection. If the tenant shares living accommodation, that is more than a hall or stairway, with the landlord she will receive no protection.

You may begin to agree with us that the law is complicated and that you are happy to have your role limited to signposting! The Law Commission also agrees that the law is complex and proposes to publish a report and draft Bill designed to simplify and modernize the law in 2005. However, for the foreseeable future, you must grapple with the legal complexities. A large number of tenants are covered by the statutory regimes, so we will now consider the rights which these create. We will concentrate on the rights of assured and assured shorthold tenants, and secure and introductory tenants. However, we need to provide a brief outline of the rights of Rent Act 1977 tenants. Rent Act 1977 tenants make up about 8 per cent of the private rented sector. Their numbers are in decline, but you may find that your older service users who live in the private rented sector are Rent Act tenants.

Regulated tenancies under the Rent Act 1977

The Rent Act 1977 created regulated tenancies. Such a tenancy will be either a protected or a statutory tenancy. No new tenancies can be created under the statute and so they are a dying breed. We will limit our discussion here to statutory tenancies because those represent the vast majority of tenancies under the Rent Act 1977.

Strong rights

The Rent Act 1977 created much stronger rights than those in subsequent statutes, so anyone who has the benefit of a statutory tenancy has something of great value and should not give it up without legal advice. The key features of the statutory tenancy are that the tenancy was created before 15 January 1989 and that the tenant resides in the property. The key exclusions from protection are tenancies with payments for board and attendance, holiday tenancies, and student lettings provided by an educational establishment, along with the most important exclusion, that of tenancies with a resident landlord. Once it is established that an occupier has the benefit of a statutory tenancy, however, then he or she becomes entitled to leave the tenancy to a spouse or a member of the family, to the fair rent regime which sets rents at a fair rather than a market level protected by a system of registration, and to strong security of tenure. If anyone other than a spouse or co-habitee succeeds to the tenancy, the tenancy converts to an assured tenancy. The House of Lords in *Ghaidan v Godin-Mendoza* (2004) decided that as a result of the Human Rights Act 1998 the survivor of a same-sex couple succeeds as a spouse.

Dilution of rights

By creating these strong rights the Rent Act 1977 created a regime which gave benefits very similar to those enjoyed by owner occupiers. However, the Housing Act 1988 had an impact upon these rights. Not only did it amend the succession provisions as set out above, it also enabled landlords to argue successfully in the courts that rents of Rent Act tenants should rise to the level of market rents as there was no longer a scarcity of rented accommodation. This led to a great deal of hardship. Tenants who had anticipated that their rents would remain relatively stable found that they doubled and tripled over a period of a few years. The Government intervened to provide additional protection for these tenants. The Rent Acts (Maximum Fair Rent) Order 1999 (SI 1999 No. 6) sets a maximum fair rent limit for regulated tenancies where applications for a fair rent are made after 1 February 1999. An arithmetical formula provides a maximum rent of the existing registered rent plus the difference in the retail price index since the last registration, plus 7.5 per cent for first applications or 5 per cent for subsequent applications. The limit does not apply if there is no existing registered rent or if the increase requested is more than 15 per cent because of improvements carried out by the landlord.

Statutory protection

Statutory tenants under the Rent Act 1977 can be evicted only following notice to quit and a court order. The grounds for eviction are limited and are largely discretionary. In particular eviction for non-payment of rent will only happen at the discretion of the court, which means that the court will only order possession where it is reasonable in all the circumstances to do so.

We do not intend to give you any more detail on the Rent Act 1977. What you need to know is that anyone whose tenancy commenced prior to the 15 January 1989 has potentially a very valuable asset. They should not leave that tenancy without very good specialist advice. Your responsibility should be to try to persuade them to see a good housing lawyer if they are being asked to move by their landlord or experiencing any other housing difficulty.

Assured tenancies under the Housing Act 1988

The Housing Act 1988, as amended by the Housing Act 1996, governs private sector and housing association tenancy agreements commencing from 15 January 1989 to date. It creates two forms of tenancy: the assured tenancy and the assured shorthold tenancy.

Scope

The key feature of the assured tenancy is that the tenant must occupy the property as his or her only or principal home.

Exclusions

The important exclusions from the assured tenancy regime are set out in Box 19.1 below.

Succession

Succession provisions in the 1988 Act are limited. There can be only one succession, and only the spouse or partner of the tenant can succeed.

Rent control

The rent regime is a market system. The tenant is taken to have freely agreed the original rent with the landlord and therefore cannot legally challenge it. If he or she has agreed rent review clauses then he or she is similarly bound. If there are no provisions for rent increases, the landlord may increase the rent annually via a notice procedure. The tenant can challenge the increase, but the Rent Assessment Committee will intervene only if the rent has been raised above the market rent level. As the Committee can raise the rent as well as lower it, the tenant has to be very sure before challenging any increase.

You can see that this means there is very little that the tenant can do to lower the rent, although it is worth pointing out that some housing advisers have successfully negotiated lower rents with landlords where the general market level of rents is falling.

 BOX 19.1 Main exclusions from assured tenancy regime—Housing Act 1988 Schedule 1

Exclusion	Comment
Tenancies made prior to the Act i.e. prior to 15 January 1989	In general such tenancies are covered by the Rent Act 1977
Tenancies with high rateable values/high rents	Statutory protection is to protect the vulnerable within the housing market
Tenancies at low or no rent	Landlords who are acting out of charity should not be burdened with legal regulation and exclusion distinguishes from long leases where a ground rent is paid
Commercial tenancies, tenancies of agricultural holdings; licensed premises	Such tenancies are covered by other statutory codes
Holiday lettings	Statutory protection is designed to protect people in their homes
Lettings to students by educational institutions	Lettings to students by anyone other than an educational institutions are protected by the statute
Lettings by resident landlords	The most significant exclusion. The property must be the landlord's only or principal home
Local authority lettings	Covered by the Housing Act 1985

If the tenant is on housing benefit there will be a limit on what rent the benefit will cover. We discuss this later in the chapter.

Security of tenure—evicting the assured tenant

Security of tenure is the extent to which the tenant has the right to remain in the property after the landlord has decided he or she no longer wants to let to the tenant. In general the assured tenant has a great deal of security of tenure. In order to evict the tenant the landlord must serve a notice called a notice of seeking possession, often referred to as an 'NSP'. The notice must specify the grounds for possession and set out the period of time before which court proceedings cannot be issued. The ground for possession means the reason that the landlord gives for wanting to evict the tenant. The landlord is allowed to use only reasons which the statute allows for. The grounds for possession—the legally acceptable reasons—in the assured tenancy regime are set out in Box 19.2 below.

You will notice that there are two different types of ground. One is described as mandatory. This means that if the facts of that ground are made out then the court has no alternative but to evict the tenant. The other type of ground is discretionary. This means that even if the landlord makes out the facts of the case the court will grant a possession order only if it is reasonable to do so.

Eviction for rent arrears

The biggest difference between the assured tenancy regime and the secure tenancy regime, which is the regime which local authority tenants benefit from, relates to eviction for rent arrears. There is a particular ground for eviction, Ground 8, which is available to the landlords of assured tenants where there are two months' arrears of rent outstanding at the date of the notice of seeking possession and at the date of the eviction. This ground is mandatory. This means that if the facts are made out the court has no option but to grant the possession order. The rent could be in arrears because of housing benefit delays or because of problems within the family. The reasons for the non-payment of rent are irrelevant. The court must order possession. Many housing association landlords choose not to use Ground 8. However, recently there has been an increase in its use by housing associations. Shelter and Citizens' Advice have both produced research on the problem of eviction for non-payment of rent. These reports can be found on the Web at **www.citizensadvice.org.uk/policy** and **www.shelter.org.uk**. They propose that the good practice of some housing associations in supporting tenants with financial problems rather than evicting them should be followed by all housing associations. What you must be aware of is that anyone with an assured tenancy must pay their rent. Failure to do so may well result in eviction.

Eviction for anti-social behaviour

Social landlords are increasingly evicting tenants for anti-social behaviour. This is likely to be of concern to you, either because your service users are threatened with eviction because of anti-social behaviour or because your service users are the victims of anti-social behaviour. We deal with this subject which is of increasing importance in chapter 18.

BOX 19.2 Housing Act 1988 Schedule 2—grounds for possession of dwelling-houses let on assured tenancies

Part I grounds on which court must order possession—the mandatory grounds

	Ground	NSP
Landlord's former/future principal home—notice prior to tenancy or just & equitable to dispense with notice	Grd 1	2 mths
Mortgagee repossessing—notice prior to tenancy or just & equitable to dispense with notice	Grd 2	2 mths
Former holiday let, now fixed term 8 or less months—notice prior to tenancy	Grd 3	2 wks
Former student let, now fixed term 12 or less months—notice prior to tenancy	Grd 4	2 wks
Required for minister of religion—notice prior to tenancy	Grd 5	2 mths
Demolition/reconstruction/substantial works by original landlord, requiring possession	Grd 6	2 mths
Inherited periodic tenancy, 12 or less months after death	Grd 7	2 mths
Rent arrears—8 weeks at NSP & hearing	Grd 8	2 wks

Part II grounds on which court may order possession—the discretionary grounds

Suitable alternative accommodation available	Grd 9	2 mths
Rent arrears (any)—at NSP & issue	Grd 10	2 wks
Rent arrears—persistent delay, even if none now	Grd 11	2 wks
Breach of tenancy agreement	Grd 12	2 wks
Waste/neglect by tenant/resident causing deterioration of dwelling	Grd 13	2 wks
Nuisance or Conviction for immoral/illegal use of arrestable offence in locality	Grd 14	instant
Domestic violence and leaver unlikely to return—RSL landlord only	Grd 14A	2 wks
Ill-treatment of furniture by tenant/resident causing deterioration	Grd 15	2 wks
Ex-employee of landlord	Grd 16	2 mths
False statement to obtain tenancy	Grd 17	2 wks

Assured shorthold tenancies under the Housing Act 1988

Assured shorthold tenancies (ASTs) are a particular type of assured tenancy which gives very limited security of tenure. They provide the normal form of tenure within the private rented sector. The rules set out above which cover the scope of the assured tenancy regime and the exclusions from it apply equally to the assured shorthold tenancy. The distinguishing feature of the assured shorthold tenancy is that tenants can be evicted from the tenancy with two months' notice once the first six months have expired. When the Housing Act 1988 was originally passed there were some procedural requirements which needed to be conformed with before an AST could be validly created. So the tenant had to be given notice that the tenancy was an AST and there had to be a fixed term of a minimum of six months. However, landlords seemed to have difficulty complying with the requirements of the Act, so in the Housing Act 1996 the requirements were abolished. All tenancy agreements created on or after 28 February 1997 are automatically ASTs unless the landlord serves notice otherwise. Housing association landlords usually serve a notice on the tenant saying that the tenancy is to be an assured tenancy. Private landlords do not serve such a notice, therefore all tenancies in the private sector which commenced after 27 February 1997 are likely to be assured shorthold tenancies.

Rent control

The rent control provisions for ASTs are more rigorous than for assured tenancies. However the provisions give very little real benefit to the tenant of an AST. The tenant is allowed to challenge the initial rent during the first six months, but only if the rent is significantly higher than the market rent. It is also extremely unlikely that any tenant with such limited security is going to risk his or her future in the property by commencing such a challenge.

Evicting the assured shorthold tenant

During the initial six months of an AST the landlord can recover possession only by obtaining a possession order from the court based upon a limited range of grounds (which, however, includes all of the rent grounds). After those six months are up a specific procedure for recovering possession is open to the landlord, who can give notice of not less than two months stating that he or she requires possession. The notice may be given before the expiry of the six months, although no order for possession can be applied for before the six months is complete. The court must make an order for possession and has no discretion at all, as long as it is satisfied that the correct notice has been served. No matter how long a tenant has been in the property, the two-month notice period is legally sufficient.

The accelerated possession procedure

Not all possession cases have to go to a full court hearing. If a landlord wishes to evict an assured shorthold tenant, he or she can use a paper-only procedure called the accelerated possession procedure. The landlord has to have given the tenant a written agreement and written notice to benefit from this much cheaper court procedure. If he or she is able to apply to use the accelerated possession procedure, the tenant has only fourteen days within which to respond. If the tenant has any doubt about his or her status then it is critical to get good legal advice. Note that the accelerated possession procedure is also available for some grounds which can be used to evict the assured tenant. The disadvantage to the landlord is that he or she cannot use the accelerated possession procedure to get an order for rent arrears. If the landlord wants to get a court order against the tenant for rent then he or she must use the full court procedure or sue the tenant separately for a rent judgment.

Secure tenancies under the Housing Act 1985

The Housing Act 1985 creates secure tenancies. It covers all local authority tenancy and housing action trust agreements whenever they were commenced, and housing association tenancies created before 15 January 1989. (Do not forget that for pre-1989 housing association tenancies, the relevant rent regime is that of the Rent Act 1977.) Housing action trusts (HATs) are temporary organizations set up in some areas to regenerate particular local authority estates.

Scope
The key requirement of the secure tenancy is that the tenant occupies the property as his or her only or principal home. Subletting the whole of the property removes the tenant from protection.

Exclusions
The principal exclusions to the 1985 Act are set out in Box 19.3 below.

Succession
There can be only one succession under the Housing Act 1985, which can be either by a spouse or a member of the family. There is a statutory list of family members who can succeed and, since the Civil Partnership Act 2004, that list includes civil partners and those that live together as if they are civil partners.

Rent control
There are no rent control provisions in the statute other than the right of landlords to charge reasonable rents for their properties. Tenants must be given notice of rent increases. Reasonableness of rent rises can be challenged via judicial review. However, past challenges have had very little success.

Tenant's charter rights
Secure tenancies come with a bundle of other important rights which are summarized in the Tenant's Charter. These include the right to buy, the right to take in lodgers, the right to consultation, and other significant rights. For a full list of these we suggest you look at the leaflet, *Your Rights as a Council Tenant: The Council Tenant's Charter* available on the ODPM web site at **www.housing.odpm.gov.uk/local/hsg/tenchart/**.

Note that the discounts available to secure tenants exercising their right to buy have recently been reduced. Further restrictions to the right to buy are contained in the Housing Act 2004. Advice on secure tenancies is available from the Tenants Participation Advisory Service: see their web site **www.tpas.org.uk**.

Security of tenure—evicting the secure tenant
Secure tenants have a great deal of security of tenure. Before a secure tenant can be evicted, the landlord must serve a notice, called a notice of seeking possession (NSP). The notice must specify the grounds for possession. The grounds on which a court will grant possession are divided into three categories. These are found in the Housing Act 1985,

BOX 19.3 Main exclusions from the secure tenancy regime—Schedule 1 of the Housing Act 1985

Exclusion	Comment
Introductory tenancies	Covered by the Housing Act 1996
Premises occupied in connection with employment	Therefore school caretakers, park keepers, and others may not be protected by the statute. Local authority employees housed by the local authority should seek advice on their housing status.
Accommodation provided under Part 7 of the Housing Act 1996 (homelessness)	This enables rapid eviction where it is found there are no duties to house, and for re-housing in suitable accommodation where there are duties.
Temporary accommodation during works where the tenant was not previously a secure tenant	This allows housing associations to decant tenants into local authority housing during modernization programmes.
Student lettings	Where the local authority lets the premises specifically for the purpose of the student taking up a course at an educational establishment.
Commercial lettings, agricultural holdings, licensed premises	Covered by other statutory regimes.
Almshouses	Lettings are for charitable purposes so security may be incompatible with charity's objects

Schedule 2. Except for an introductory tenancy, possession is never automatic for a public sector landlord. There is always a discretion; in each case the court must be satisfied that a possession order is reasonable or that there is suitable alternative accommodation for the tenant. Where the property is of a particular type—for example, adapted for a disabled person, or adjacent to special facilities for the elderly—the court has to be satisfied both that there is suitable alternative accommodation and that possession is reasonable. This is set out in Box 19.4 below.

Introductory tenancies under the Housing Act 1996

A local authority or a housing action trust is entitled to grant new tenants a tenancy for a trial period of up to a year as 'introductory tenants' (Housing Act 1996, Part V). If the introductory tenancy is used it must be used for all new tenants, the landlord is not allowed to pick and choose. Not all local authorities use introductory tenancies, although their use has grown recently. The stated purpose of the tenancy is to enable public housing authorities quickly and easily to evict tenants who behave anti-socially

BOX 19.4 Housing Act 1985 Schedule 2—grounds for possession of dwelling-house let under secure tenancies

Reasonableness—Part I grounds

Rent arrears or Breach of tenancy agreement	Ground 1
Nuisance or Conviction for immoral/illegal use or arrestable offence in locality	Ground 2
Domestic violence, and leaver unlikely to return	Ground 2A
Waste/neglect by tenant/resident causing deterioration of dwelling	Ground 3
Ill-treatment of furniture by tenant/resident causing deterioration	Ground 4
False statement to obtain tenancy	Ground 5
Premium paid for s. 92 Mutual Exchange	Ground 6
Abuse of job-related accommodation	Ground 7
Decant given to previously secure tenant	Ground 8

Suitable Alternative Accommodation Available—Part II grounds

Over-crowding (criminal Pt X)	Ground 9
Demolition/reconstruction/works by landlord, requiring possession	Ground 10
Disposal under SoS/HC-approved redevelopment scheme	Ground 10A
Conflict with objects of charity	Ground 11

Reasonableness and Suitable Alternative Accommodation Available—Part III grounds

Ex-employee of job-related accommodation	Ground 12
Specially designed property required for physically disabled person	Ground 13
Specialist HA requires property for person in its client group	Ground 14
Property close to special needs provision, required for person with special needs	Ground 15
Under-occupation by successor 6–12 months after death (particular reasonableness factors—age, time there, support to previous tenant)	Ground 16

in the first year of their tenancy. It is part of a series of measures designed to improve life for the majority of residents on local authority estates. We discuss the legal developments in the area of anti-social behaviour in chapter 18. The provisions also allow tenants with introductory tenancies to be evicted for rent arrears.

The landlord can obtain possession at any time during the year by applying to the court, and the court must order possession if the correct procedure has been followed. There is no need to prove any grounds such as bad behaviour or non-payment of rent; all the tenant can do is to ask (within fourteen days of the notice that the land-lord intends to evict the tenant) for the landlord to review its decision to evict. This power of summary eviction with no consideration of grounds or evidence has been challenged under the Human Rights Act 1998, since the tenant can lose his or her property without any trial, in breach of Article 6 of the European Convention and Article 1 of the First Protocol to the European Convention. The Court of Appeal in *McLellan v Bracknell Forest DC* (2001) decided that introductory tenancies are Human Rights Act 1998compliant. Article 6 was satisfied, as the availability of judicial review combined with the internal review procedure provided sufficient safeguards for tenants. Moreover, the summary eviction procedure was necessary for the protection of the rights and freedoms of others. Guidance provided by the Department of the Environment, now the Office of the Deputy Prime Minister, emphasised that the provisions should not be used against vulnerable tenants when providing support via social services would be more appropriate. For further information see the ODPM web site at **www.odpm.gov.uk**.

Following the introductory year the tenancy becomes secure, and grounds are needed before a court can order eviction.

Demoted tenancies

The Anti-social Behaviour Act 2003 amended both the Housing Act 1985 and the Housing Act 1988 to allow social landlords to apply to the court to reduce the security of tenure of secure and assured tenants. The provisions are very complex but in essence they make the concept of the introductory tenancy available to social landlords during the lifetime of the tenancy. The demoted tenancy lasts one year, during which time it can be terminated without grounds being proved. At the end of one year the tenancy is 'promoted' to its former levels of security.

Summary of statutory protection

The table in Box 19.5 sets out a summary of the main statutory framework.

◼ Termination of a private sector tenancy by the tenant

Although a landlord cannot remove a tenant without a court order, the *tenant* is free to end any tenancy, apart from a fixed-term tenancy, by giving four weeks' notice, or longer if the tenancy agreement requires. With a fixed-term tenancy there is no means to end the tenancy before it expires, except where the landlord has breached the agreement (for example, failing to make repairs) and it would as a result be reasonable for the tenant to leave. If the tenant does leave early, the landlord can recover the rent owing for the remainder of the period, but must try to reduce his or her loss by seeking new tenants.

📄 **BOX 19.5** The main statutory framework—a summary

Rent Act 1977	Regulated tenancies Strong security of tenure 'Fair' rents (including Housing Association tenancies created prior to the commencement of Housing Act 1988) Strong succession rights	Private residential tenancies created prior to 15 January 1989
Housing Act 1985	Secure tenancies Strong security of tenure Including Housing Association tenancies created prior to commencement of Housing Act 1988)	Local authority and Housing Action Trust tenancies whenever created which comply with the landlord and tenant conditions set out in the statute
	Demoted tenancies Very limited security	Created by the Anti-Social Behaviour Act 2003 Last for one year and require a court order
Housing Act 1988	Assured tenancies Strong security of tenure Market rent	Private residential tenancies created on or after 15 January 1989
	Assured shorthold tenancies which comply with statutory criteria Market rents Very limited security of tenure	Housing Associations can demote assured tenancies to assured shorthold for one year following court order
Housing Act 1996	Presumption that a tenancy is assured shorthold unless notice to contrary	Private residential tenancies created on or or after 8 February 1997
	Introductory tenancies	Probationary tenancies for first year of tenancy

---

▣ Protection from eviction

Two questions arise from our consideration of statutory security. First, what security is offered to tenants and other occupiers who do not fall within the scope of the Rent Act 1977, the Housing Act 1985, or the Housing Act 1989? Secondly, what happens if the landlord does not follow the procedures set out in the statutory regimes, that is illegally evicts the tenants? The answers to these questions can be found in the Protection from Eviction Act 1977 (PfEA). This Act provides civil and criminal remedies for illegal eviction and harassment and sets out procedures which provide a minimum of protection for all residential occupiers—except those who are specifically excluded from its provisions.

Criminal offences

Section 1(2) of the Protection from Eviction Act 1977 states:

> If any person unlawfully deprives a residential occupier of any premises of his occupation of the premises or any part thereof, or attempts to do so, he shall be guilty of an offence unless he proves that he believed, and had reasonable cause to believe, that the residential occupier had ceased to reside in the premises.

The key word is 'unlawfully': the landlord cannot change the locks, or throw out the tenant's possessions; he or she must obtain possession, if at all, by way of court order and the court bailiff, as we have already described.

Section 1(3) also makes it an offence to harass the occupier knowing that this is likely to make him or her leave, or to prevent him or her from exercising a right connected with the occupancy. Cutting off services is a prime example of such harassment, and is specifically provided for within s. 1(3). If a landlord's actions appear to be harassment, a tenant should seek urgent legal advice.

A landlord who unlawfully evicts or harasses an occupier in breach of the Act can be prosecuted by the local authority (districts and London boroughs (s. 6)). It is important to note that authorities differ widely in their willingness to take criminal proceedings against offending landlords. You should find out what the practice is in your authority. Illegal eviction or harassment is a criminal offence even if the landlord has cast-iron grounds in law for possession, and even if the tenancy was granted for a fixed period which has now expired. Nor is it necessary that the occupier is a tenant. Note that the statutory provision relates to residential occupiers. You should report cases to the appropriate person from the housing department, who is probably called a tenancy relations officer. Tenancy relations officers are experts in this area of law. They will explain the legal requirements to a landlord and often persuade him or her to stop their illegal behaviour. Where the landlord persists they may take criminal proceedings. If the landlord is found guilty, the court can make a compensation order in favour of the tenant.

Excluded occupiers

But the Act does not protect all residential occupiers. Lettings made on or after 15 January 1989 which are holiday lets, temporary lettings to squatters, where the landlord is a resident landlord who shares living accommodation with the tenant, or is hostel accommodation provided by a social landlord are excluded from the Protection from Eviction Act 1977 by s. 3A of the Act. Therefore, the landlord can recover possession without court proceedings, so long as reasonable notice is given, which will usually be four weeks or contractual notice, which could be as short as a week. The exclusion of hostel accommodation from the requirements of the Protection from Eviction Act 1977 is probably narrower than you would think. The accommodation must not be self-contained and must be provided by the local authority, a registered social landlord, or a charitable housing trust. If someone is evicted from a hostel without a court order you should send them for legal advice.

Civil remedies for illegal eviction

Tenants and licencees may themselves bring a civil case for damages for harassment or unlawful eviction, and should be advised that if they wish to regain possession or prevent further harassment, to apply to the county court for an injunction. Such proceedings can be taken whether or not the local authority has decided to prosecute or even if the landlord was acquitted. Subject to satisfying the means test, the tenant can usually obtain legal assistance, and in an emergency this can be granted very quickly (see further, chapter 14). Tenants can sue for trespass, breach of the covenant of quiet enjoyment, and breach of contract. They can also sue for breach of the statutory duty in s. 3 of the Protection from Eviction Act and under a specific statutory tort under ss. 27 and 28 of the Housing Act 1988. Licensees can sue for breach of contract.

Harassment can lead to very large awards of compensation in the civil courts. In *Tagro v Cafane* (1991), the Court of Appeal upheld an award of £46,538 against a landlord who ransacked the tenant's bedsit. Some £30,000 of this represented the increase in value of the property to the landlord once the tenant had left. Lord Donaldson described the case as 'a cautionary tale for landlords'! Injunctions stopping further harassment or ordering the landlord to let the residential occupier back into the property are probably just as useful to the residential occupier. He or she is unlikely to want to stay in the property for much longer, if the relationship with the landlord has broken down to such an extent, but getting back in can provide a breathing space enabling the residential occupier to look for alternative accommodation.

Procedural requirements

The other important provisions of the Protection from Eviction Act 1977 are procedural protections for licensees and tenants who are not covered by the Rent Act 1977 or the Housing Act 1985 or 1988, but are not excluded from the Protection from Eviction Act 1977—see above. So long as the property is rented as a home, both landlord and tenant have to give at least four weeks' notice before ending the tenancy, whatever the agreement may say to the contrary (s. 5(1)). The notice must contain prescribed information. Section 3 of the Protection from Eviction Act 1977 requires the landlord to obtain a court order to recover possession of the premises.

A summary of the legal protections against harassment and illegal eviction is set out in Box 19.6 below.

Affording a rented property

The third overarching housing problem we identified at the beginning of this chapter concerned affording a property. Running a house involves a lot of outgoings. Tenants will have to find money for deposits and rent in advance, the rent and council tax. Council tax is a part property and part personal tax levied by the local authority. The level of tax relates broadly to the value of the property but is discounted where fewer than 2 residents live in the property.

BOX 19.6 Summary of the legal protections against harassment and illegal eviction for non-excluded residential occupiers

Protection	Legal authority	Comment
Criminal offences of illegal eviction	s. 1 of the Pf EA	Dependent on local authority willingness to prosecute
Criminal offences of harassment	s. 1 of the Pf EA	
Civil actions for statutory torts	s. 3 of the Pf EA ss. 27 & 28 of the Housing Act 1988	Injunctions can be obtained to stop harassment or to enable the occupier to re-enter the premises
		Damages can also be obtained. Damages for breach of s. 27 of the HA 88 calculated by a statutory formula
Civil actions for breach of contract and tort	Common law	Injunctions can be obtained to stop harassment or to enable the occupier to re-enter the premises
		Damages can also be obtained
Procedural protections	Either requirements of notice—grounds—court order under the HA s. 85 or s. 88 Or requirements of notice and court order under s. 5 and s. 3 of the Pf EA '77	

Deposits and rent in advance

People seeking to rent accommodation are often asked for deposits and rent in advance. Housing benefit will not cover such payments, which will also be given a very low priority by the social fund. The social services department has the power to pay deposits and rent in advance for families where children are in need under s. 17 of the Children Act 1989.

One real difficulty that many people have with deposits is getting them back at the end of the tenancy. Citizens Advice published a report (*Unsafe Deposits*, Citizens' Advice Bureau, 1998) on the problem. If a landlord refuses to return a deposit or wishes to retain a larger proportion of it than seems justifiable, then the former tenant can sue in the small claims court for its return. It is good practice to insist on a comprehensive inventory which records the state of repair in the property as well as the actual contents of the property at the commencement of the lease. The government is to implement a tenancy deposit protection scheme in the Housing Act 2004. The full details of the scheme will be included on our web site when the regulations are available.

Housing benefit

The principal way that unemployed tenants or tenants on low or irregular wages afford rent is through housing benefit.

Housing benefit is a notoriously complex benefit. What we intend to do is to provide you with a basic outline of the workings of the benefit. If a service user requires further advice you should refer him or her to an agency such as Citizens' Advice. For further information on referring to specialist advice centres see chapter 10.

What is housing benefit?

Housing benefit is an income-related benefit designed to assist people on income support and low income to pay their rent.

Who is entitled to claim housing benefit?

Someone may be entitled to housing benefit if:

- they are liable to pay rent;
- their capital (i.e. savings and investments) is less than £16,000;
- they receive income support or income-based jobseekers allowance or are on a low income as prescribed by the Housing Benefit Regulations 1987.

Certain people are generally excluded from housing benefit. These include:

- people who live in residential care homes;
- people subject to immigration control or defined as persons from abroad;
- full-time students (there are exceptions here, and further advice will be necessary);
- people who live with their landlord or are a close relative;
- people whose landlord is a former partner of the claimant;
- people whose landlord is a parent of the claimant's child;
- people whose tenancy is not made on a commercial basis.

Anyone excluded from housing benefit should seek further advice.

How much rent is payable by housing benefit?

Not all of the money which is payable to the landlord will be covered by housing benefit. Payments for charges such as water charges, fuel costs, meals, and other services provided by the landlord are excluded.

There are other restrictions that may affect the amount of housing benefit which will be paid. These restrictions are most relevant where the claimant is renting in the private rented sector. No housing benefit will be paid above the maximum rent level. The maximum rent may be based on the reasonable market rent for the property. It may be based on the local reference rent which is based on the rent officer's valuation of the average of all rents in the particular area which are in a reasonable state of repair and the same size as the claimant's. It may be based on a smaller home that the one the claimant is renting if the rent officer considers that the house is too large for the claimant's needs. In most cases if the claimant is under 25 years of age, the rent officer will assess a single room rent which is based on the average costs for one-room homes with shared use of toilet and kitchen. This is the case even if the claimant is living in a bigger property.

Certain groups of claimants are protected from rent restrictions. If your service user's rent is restricted it is important to get further advice. It is possible to appeal against a decision if the rent has been wrongly restricted. The best way to understand the rent restriction regime within housing benefit is to see it as a way that the state controls its expenditure on housing costs for the poor. The regulations ensure that people on benefit do not rent a quality of property that is inappropriate for benefit recipients, nor are they able to rent a property which is too large for benefit recipients.

The amount of rent that housing benefit will cover for a particular claimant renting a particular property is called the eligible rent.

How to claim housing benefit

If the claimant is on income support or income-based jobseekers allowance then he or she obtains the claim form from job centre plus. The claimant should complete the form promptly—within four weeks of the claim for income support or income-based jobseekers allowance.

If the claimant is not on income support or income-based jobseekers allowance then he or she obtains the form from the housing benefit department of the local authority. Certain documents need to be provided with the claim. These include evidence of the rent, such as a rent book or tenancy agreement, evidence of income and possibly capital.

Payment of housing benefit

Housing benefit is usually awarded for a fixed period of up to sixty weeks. If the claimant's circumstances change during that period, for instance there is a change in the amount of income or capital that they receive then they must inform the housing benefit department. Failure to do so may mean that the claimant is liable to repay an overpayment of benefit. Housing benefit is paid as a rebate towards the claimant's rent account if the claimant is a local authority tenant. It is paid directly into the claimant's bank account or by giro cheque if the claimant's landlord is a private landlord or a housing association landlord.

Payment direct to the landlord

Housing benefit can be paid directly to the landlord if the claimant's landlord is a housing association or a private landlord. This will happen if the claimant agrees to this, if it is thought to be in the claimant's family's best interests, or if the landlord requests it and can show that the claimant has at least eight weeks of rent arrears. This method of payment of housing benefit direct to the landlord has become the norm in the private sector. Government reforms are attempting to change this practice—see below.

How is housing benefit calculated?

If a claimant is on income support or income-based jobseekers allowance the calculation is quite simple. The claimant's eligible rent is calculated. Then amounts for non-dependents are deducted. A non-dependent is a person who lives with the claimant in his or her home. The definition excludes someone who is financially dependent upon the claimant, is a joint tenant, or someone with whom the claimant shares communal facilities. The most common non-dependent deduction is for an adult child who is living with a parent who is claiming housing benefit.

The weekly housing benefit that will be paid will be the eligible rent minus non-dependent deductions.

The calculation is more complex for a claimant who is not on income support, or income based jobseekers allowance. The weekly eligible rent is calculated. Amounts are deducted for non-dependents. The claimant's weekly income is compared to the amount the claimant would receive if he or she received income support—an amount known as the applicable amount. Certain deductions are made from the weekly income. If the claimant's weekly income is less than the applicable amount then they will receive the same amount of housing benefit as if they were on income support or income-based jobseekers allowance. If the claimant's weekly income is higher the amount of his or her housing benefit will be the weekly eligible rent minus any non-dependent deduction minus 65 per cent of the excess income.

Appeals

Councils must internally review housing benefit decisions, provide written reasons for the decision, or an explanation of the decision, if requested within one month of the decision. If the applicant is not successful on internal review they have a right to an appeal to an independent tribunal.

Information on housing benefit

Information on housing benefit is available on the Department of Work and Pensions web site, **www.dwp.gov.uk/lifeevent/benefits**, and on many local authority web sites, for instance Salford Council provides extensive information and a benefit calculator on **www.salfordgov.uk/benefits**. Application forms for housing benefit are available on the Department of Work and Pensions web site.

Council tax benefit

Council tax benefit is available for people on low incomes who have to pay council tax. Entitlement to council tax benefit is calculated in a similar way to the calculation of housing benefit. Internal reviews and appeals are also similar.

Reform of housing benefit

Housing benefit is a particularly complex benefit. It is not easy to claim, particularly if you are working. It is not easy to anticipate how much you will receive and if it will cover your rent, and local authorities find it extremely difficult to administer. The Department for Work and Pensions is running a 2-year project from October 2003 piloting a different approach to the payment of Housing Benefit in nine local authorities. Claimants in these areas receive a standard allowance based on the area in which they live and the number of occupiers in their property. If they are living in rented property that costs less than average rents in their area, they are entitled to keep the difference. Payment is to be made to the tenant rather than the landlord. The Department for Work and Pensions intends to publish a report on the pilots, known as pathfinder schemes, during the winter of 2005.

Repair problems

The tenant is entitled to a certain level of repair from the landlord.

Contract

The first place that the tenant should look to for repairing obligations is the contract between him or her and the landlord. It is rarely that a landlord commits him- or herself to any level of repair, but there have been cases where local authority landlords have promised that the house provided will be fit for human habitation. If a landlord has made such a commitment, then if he or she or it breaches the commitment they can be sued.

Statutorily implied terms

Sections 11 and 13 of the Landlord and Tenant Act 1985 set out the statutory obligations of the landlord to tenants. These obligations do not apply to licences. A licensee, as opposed to a tenant, can insist only on such repairs as are included in the agreed licence. Landlords must keep in repair the structure and exterior of the residential premises. This includes drains, gutters, and pipes. The landlord is also responsible for keeping in working order the supply of gas, electricity, and water, and any appliances for heating and water heating. Additionally, the landlord must ensure the sanitation facilities are in working order—lavatories, sinks, baths, and showers. This leaves the tenant responsible for internal decoration. But if the need to redecorate is the result of the landlord's repairs, the landlord, not the tenant, must carry this out.

The landlord cannot escape these obligations; for they are statutory, and cannot be written out of a tenancy agreement for residential premises (unless it is for a fixed term of at least seven years). The landlord must be allowed reasonable access to the property from time to time, both to inspect and to repair. The landlord should give the tenant notice of his intention to inspect, and should require access only during reasonable hours.

Limits on the obligations

The landlord is not obliged to repair damage caused by the tenant, unless the damage amounts to no more than normal wear and tear. More importantly, a landlord's duty to repair does not arise until he or she knows of the defects. Therefore, the tenant should be encouraged to report disrepair in writing as soon as it arises. There are other restrictions; courts will not order landlords to carry out repairs which are disproportionate to the value of the property or to a standard that is higher than the current standards of the locality. Because the obligations are implied into the contract visitors injured because of disrepair are not able to sue, because they are not parties to the contract.

The definition of disrepair

Sections 11 and 13 of the Landlord and Tenant Act do not require the landlord to *improve* property but to repair it. Frequently, a landlord can defend a repairs case by showing, for example, that serious damp is a design fault and not a disrepair matter.

Suing the landlord

These repairing obligations are implied into the contractual relationship between land-lord and tenant. Therefore, a failure to carry out the repair is a breach of contract for which the tenant can sue. Damages may include not only the cost of putting the premises right, if the tenant has had to do this, but may also include resulting losses, such as damage to clothing and furniture, additional heating costs, and compensation for health effects and inconvenience. If it is suspected that disrepair has caused medical symptoms, the sufferer should see a doctor at a very early stage, so that if the matter ever comes to court, the evidence is documented in health records from the start. If it can be shown that the disrepair has caused problems for other persons living with the tenant—particularly spouse and children—the effect on them, and damages for such effect, can be included in the claim, for example children suffering from respiratory disease caused by damp (if the damp is due to disrepair).

   The tenant can therefore claim damages from a landlord in breach of the repair obligations. The tenant can also apply to the court for an order against the landlord, requiring him or her to carry out the repairs or improvement. Legal assistance may well be available for such an application. Of course, the first step is for the tenant to inform the landlord of the defects.

Statutory tort

If the limitations on ss. 11 and 13 cause problems, there is another approach, where the state of the property leads to injury (not just to the tenant, but to anyone) or to damage to the tenant's possessions. In this case, it does not matter whether the damage was caused by disrepair or bad design—the property should be safe (Defective Premises Act 1972, s. 4). The landlord must make the premises safe if he or she knew or ought to have known of the defect. If the landlord has put a term into the contract granting him- or herself permission to inspect the property then he or she will be presumed to have known about the defect, even if the tenant has not informed him or her. This avenue is worth pursuing therefore if there has been injury or damage to the tenant or a visitor as a result of disrepair which has not been formally notified to the landlord.

Tort

The common law of tort of negligence may also provide a remedy to an occupier or a visitor who suffers injury or damage to goods as a result of disrepair. The problem is that tort of negligence applies only where the landlord owes a duty of care to the tenant. The common law does not impose a duty of care on a landlord normally. However, where the landlord has another relationship with the tenant, such as being the builder or designer of the property, then the duty of care will arise. Therefore if the landlord was responsible for conversion or building of the property, which may often be the case with local authority or housing association landlords, then the duty of care may arise. It is not sufficient for there to be a duty of care, the tenant will also have to show that there has been breach of that duty and that the damage suffered was foreseeable. However once the tenant has shown there is a duty of care it is relatively straightforward in most circumstances to overcome the other legal hurdles.

Rent arrears and disrepair

Is there anything a tenant can do without actually commencing proceedings? Withholding rent should never be considered without legal advice because of the high risk of eviction. But if there are arrears and the landlord sues for the rent, the claim by the tenant for damages for disrepair can be either offset against the amount owed or claimed by a process called a counterclaim. If the court agrees that the tenant is entitled to compensation, the amount goes to reduce or cancel altogether any rent arrears—so the landlord may find that the ground for possession disappears.

Public health

There are other ways of making a landlord repair. A local authority or a tenant can prosecute a landlord for statutory nuisance under the Environmental Protection Act 1990, s. 82. A statutory nuisance exists where residential premises are a danger to the health of the occupants. If a landlord is convicted, the court has a power and, unless there is a good reason to the contrary, an obligation to make a compensation order to the tenant. Cases involving unhealthy premises should therefore be referred to the environmental health department, which may be able to obtain improvements by threatening prosecution.

The Housing Health and Safety Rating System

The Housing Act 2004 replaces the housing fitness regime set out in the Housing Act 1985. The criteria in the Housing Act 1985 were first introduced 80 years ago and require modernization. The test of fitness is replaced with an evidence-based risk assessment process, carried out using the Housing Health and Safety Rating System (HHSRS). HHSRS requires local authorities to assess the risks to health and safety in residential premises rather than decide whether a property fails a fitness test. The hazards that can be assessed are set out in Box 19.7. The HHSRS assessment is based on the risk to the potential occupant who is most vulnerable to that hazard. For example, stairs constitute a greater risk to the elderly, so for assessing hazards relating to stairs they are considered the most vulnerable group. Action by authorities will depend upon:

• the hazard rating determined under HHSRS
• whether the authority has a duty or power to act, determined by the presence of a

---

BOX 19.7 The hazards that can be assessed under HHSRS

Damp/mould growth (2)	Radiation	Noise	Fire
Excess heat/cold (2)	Uncombusted fuel gas	Hygiene (2)	Hot surfaces
Asbestos	VOCs	Food safety	Entrapment
Biocides	Crowding & space	Water supply	Explosions
Carbon monoxide etc	Intruders	Falls (4)	Ergonomics
Lead	Lighting	Electrical	Structural

---

hazard above or below a threshold prescribed by regulations (Category 1 and Category 2 hazards); and

- the authority's judgement as to the most appropriate course of action to deal with the hazard.

However, the new system will take some time to implement and is heavily dependent upon unpublished regulations. We will set out details as they become available on our web site.

Right to repair

Where the tenant is a secure (i.e. a local authority) tenant, he or she can notify the landlord of a disrepair; if the landlord then fails to repair, the tenant can, with the landlord's agreement, carry out the work and deduct the cost from the rent (Housing Act 1985, s. 96). The procedure looks simple, but the tenant has to be aware that they become liable to pay the contractors in the first place; and, remote possibility though it is, if the repairs were badly carried out the tenant, and not the landlord, would be liable if anyone were injured.

Statutory regulations

There is a range of regulations imposed upon landlords which cannot be contracted out of. The Gas Safety (Installations and Use) Regulations require landlords to maintain gas fittings and flues provided by the landlord in a safe condition. An annual gas safety check must be carried out on each gas appliance and flue by a CORGI registered installer. All furniture and furnishings provided by a landlord must satisfy the Furniture and Furnishing (Fire) (Safety) Regulations 1988. The regulations cover upholstered furniture, mattresses, cushions, and pillows, but exclude carpets, curtains, and duvets. The regulations are enforced by the Health and Safety Executive. More information is available on their web site—**www.hse.gov.uk**.

Summary of legal remedies

Box 19.8 sets out a summary of the legal remedies for disrepair available to the occupiers of rented housing.

BOX 19.8 Summary of legal remedies for disrepair

Note that any particular instance of disrepair, for instance a leaking toilet or a damaged gas fire, could give rise to several different remedies.

Problem	Example	Legal remedy	Comment
The landlord fails to carry out express repairing obligations set out in the contract	The contract states 'The house will be fit for human habitation' and there is an infestation of cockroaches	Breach of contract	Landlords rarely commit themselves to repairing obligations over and above the legal minimum
Defects in exterior and/or installations	Rain penetration through the window Leaking roof	Breach of contract as a result of statutorily implied contractual terms in s. 11 of the Landlord and Tenant Act 1985	The most effective provision for tenants and landlord cannot contract out of statutory responsibilities but: • landlord must be given notice • there needs to be disrepair • standard of repair that of locality • courts will not order expenditure of a disproportionate amount
Dangerous state of premises	Visitor injures him- or herself falling downstairs as a result of missing stair tread	The Defective Premises Act 1972	Applies where the landlord knew or ought to have known of the defect
Design defect	Design increases amount of condensation in property	Negligence	Only applies where the landlord owes a 'duty of care' to the person who suffers damage as a result of the design defect. No need for notice
Secure tenant with disrepair	Broken front door	s. 96 of Housing Act 1985	Tenant must approach landlord first See the relevant regulations for details
Disrepair with public health implications	Leaking WC Dirty and damaged work surfaces in kitchen	Assessment of hazard under HHSRS	Local authorities have a range of remedies available to them, including powers to act in default and prosecute lack of compliance
The health of the occupant is at risk as a result of conditions in the property	Dampness leading to increased risk of bronchitis	Statutory nuisance under s. 82 of the Environmental Protection Act 1990	Criminal offence prosecuted by Environmental Health Department Local authority tenants can prosecute the local authority under s. 82 EPA
Landlord failure to comply with statutory regulations	Damaged gas appliance	Breach of regulations— enforceable by the Health and Safety Executive	Landlord cannot contract out of responsibilities

▨ Adaptations for disabled occupiers

Occupiers of rented accommodation may need that accommodation to be adapted to their particular needs so that they can continue to live independently. It is not the landlord's responsibility to pay for these adaptations. If the tenant can afford the adaptations then the tenant will have to pay. However, most people who need these adaptations cannot afford them. In such circumstances the tenant may be entitled to a disabled facilities grant from the local authority.

Disabled facilities grants are available under Part I of the Housing Grants, Construction and Regeneration Act 1996. Disabled facilities grants can help towards, for instance, installing an access ramp for wheelchairs, putting in a stair lift, or lowering work tops to make it easier to prepare and cook food. There are two stages in applying for disabled facilities grants. First, the applicant needs to find out the amount and type of work which needs to be done and the likely cost. Occupational therapists should be able to provide advice on this. The proposed works must be necessary and appropriate to meet the disabled person's needs and they must be reasonable and practicable depending on the age and condition of the property. A local authority can refuse a disabled facilities grant if it believes the scheme is not practicable. Secondly, all grant applicants will be subject to a means test which will assess the resources of the applicant and their spouse or partner to see how much, if anything, they must contribute to the cost of the works.

Grants are mandatory for works which provide essential adaptations to the home to give better freedom of movement into and around it and for essential facilities within it. Grants are discretionary for a wide range of other works which make a home suitable for a disabled occupant's accommodation, welfare, or employment needs. Grants will not be payable for work started prior to approval by the local authority.

Application forms for disabled facilities grants can be obtained from the local authority. The council must give the applicant a decision in writing within six months of receipt of a completed valid application together with any additional information it may require. If your service users may benefit from a disabled facilities grant, then you should encourage them to apply as soon as possible. Note that these grants are not limited to tenants; licensees and owner occupiers are equally eligible.

Other grants

Other grants which are available are discretionary. If the local authority has limited resources then it may be more difficult to obtain such a grant. Two particular types of grant are of particular relevance: house renovation grants and home repair assistance.

House renovation grants

House renovation grants may be available if a dwelling falls below the fitness standards set out in the Housing Act 1985 and referred to above, and the council is satisfied that renovation is the best way of dealing with the problem. The grant will be means-tested, and no work commenced prior to the grant will be covered.

Home repair assistance

Home repair assistance is available for help with small repairs to people who are tenants, long-term licensees with a right of exclusive occupation and owner occupiers. The applicant must be claiming an income-related benefit (which includes housing benefit) or be over 60, disabled, or infirm, or a carer of someone who is over 60, disabled, or infirm. The assistance may be available in the form of materials or a grant for carrying out works of repair, improvement, or adaptation to a dwelling. Applications are made to local authorities who have a discretion to decide what works, if any, they will grant aid. Grants are limited to £5,000 per application.

More details on these grants are available from your local council.

Reform of housing law for rental occupiers

You will have noticed from this chapter so far that housing law is complicated and does not necessarily serve the interests of the rental occupier. Recently the Government has commenced a great deal of activity targeted at the reform of many aspects of housing law. We have referred to these reform proposals at various points in this chapter. Box 19.9 provides a summary of this reform activity and the stage it has reached by the time of writing. We will provide updates on progress on our web site.

Owner-occupiers

Most owner-occupiers have the benefit of a substantial capital asset and affordable mortgage repayments. However, an increasingly large number of people struggle to

---

BOX 19.9 Summary of reform proposals

Area	Agency	Stage reached
Housing Benefit	Department of Work and Pensions	Piloting of standard housing allowances in pathfinder authorities
Deposits	Office of the Deputy Prime minister	Housing Act 2004
Fitness standards	Office of the Deputy Prime Minister	Housing Act 2004
Right to Buy	Office of the Deputy Prime Minister	Housing Act 2004
Legal status of rented housing	Law Commission	Final Report and draft Bill 2005
Succession rights	Department of Trade and Industry	Civil Partnership Act 2004

afford to buy their own homes. We have decided to provide a very brief overview of the law as it relates to three key areas of home ownership—possession proceedings by banks and building societies, obtaining income support towards the cost of buying a house, and an overview of grants which may be payable for essential work on the property.

Possession proceedings by a mortgagee

The most common reason for possession proceedings is that the owner-occupier has failed to pay an instalment on the mortgage or another loan secured on the property. Before the lender can succeed in evicting the owner occupier for non-payment a number of procedures must be complied with. The lender must give the owner-occupier an opportunity to put the non-payment right and must be informed that failure to do so will result in legal proceedings. There must be a possession hearing, and at that hearing the owner occupier will get an opportunity to explain his or her position and make an offer to pay off the arrears. Even if a possession order is made an owner-occupier does not have to leave until the lender gets an order to evict. There are many opportunities for preventing the eviction—but the best advice for an owner-occupier in difficulties is to get advice. The sooner the owner-occupier gets advice the better. There will be a greater chance of a satisfactory outcome, and an advisor will be able to negotiate with the mortgagee and represent the owner occupier in court. The organizations we identified at the beginning of this chapter will be able to help.

Help with the cost of mortgages and loans

Service users may be able to get help with housing costs when they are buying their own home if they are entitled to income support or income-based jobseekers allowance. Note that housing benefit is not applicable when someone is buying, as opposed to renting, their home. To see whether someone is entitled to income support you should refer to chapter 14.

Income support will meet payments of mortgage interest and the interest on loans for some repairs to the property. Help is limited to mortgages and loans up to £100,000. Help is available only for mortgage interest so there may be a shortfall between the amount that income support will pay and the total monthly mortgage payment.

Different rules apply depending upon whether the applicant took out their mortgage before 2 October 1995 or after that date.

Mortgages taken out before 2 October 1995

In these circumstances applicants will get no help with the mortgage interest payments for the first eight weeks of the claim. After that 50 per cent of the eligible mortgage interest will be paid for eighteen weeks. After that the claimant will get 100 per cent of the eligible mortgage interest.

Mortgages taken out after 2 October 1995

In these circumstances the claimant will get no help with mortgage interest for the first thirty-nine weeks of the claim. After that 100 per cent of the eligible mortgage interest will be paid.

Some claimants will be treated as if they took out their mortgage before 2 October

1995. This includes some carers and someone with a mortgage protection policy which did not pay out because the claimant was ill when they took out the policy, or because they are HIV positive.

Grants

Owner-occupiers are eligible for the grants which we have outlined above. Owner-occupiers who need adaptations should contact their local authority housing department.

EXERCISES

1 Jane and Jim started renting a property from a private landlord in January 2002. They have no written contract. The landlord does not live in the property. The landlord told them that they could stay for six months but he would want the property back sometime around the end of November 2002. In October he told them that he was quite happy for them to stay for a few more months. Last week he sent Jane and Jim a letter telling them they had to be out of the property at the end of the month.

- What is Jane and Jim's status?
- Do they have to leave at the end of the month?
- What difference would it make if the landlord was a resident landlord?
- Where would you send Jane and Jim for further advice?

2 Tanya is a single mother who lives with her three children, Lewis (14), Claire (10), and Kate (3) in a three-bedroom flat which she has rented from Camlington Council since 1999. The property suffers from disrepair, the windows will not close properly, the toilet leaks, and there is severe condensation which has led to mould growth in two of the bedrooms. Lewis and Claire suffer from asthma.

- What is Tanya's status?
- What legal action may Tanya take about the disrepair?
- What difference would it make if Tanya's landlord was Happytown Housing Association?
- Where would you send Tanya for further advice?

3 Fred has been a tenant of Happytown Housing Association since 1992. Recently he lost his job and he has begun to fall into rent arrears. He has received a notice of intention to seek possession from his landlord. It is based upon ground 8 of the Housing Act 1988.

- What is Fred's status?
- What is ground 8 of the Housing Act 1988 and does Fred have a defence to the possession proceedings?
- What benefits may Fred be entitled to?
- Where would you send Fred for further advice?

COMPANION WEB SITE

For guidance on how to answer these exercises, visit the companion web site at: www.oup.com/uk/booksites/law

WHERE DO WE GO FROM HERE?

This chapter is long and covers a number of difficult legal areas. We believe that it is important for you to understand these areas in outline because, as the case study at the beginning of this chapter demonstrates, decent housing is essential to an individual's human dignity. Unfortunately, a great deal of housing in Britain is either expensive or not in good condition or is insecure. Many service users are likely to be living in inadequate housing. You should ensure that you are familiar with local sources of housing advice and refer service users appropriately. It is inevitable that many of your service users will not be able to retain their current accommodation. They may have to turn to the local housing authority because they are homeless. The next chapter of our book explains the law on homelessness.

ANNOTATED FURTHER READING

General housing law

For a full and authoritative account of housing law you should refer to A. Arden and C. Hunter, *Manual of Housing Law* (7th edn., Sweet & Maxwell, 2003).

We would also recommend D. Hughes, M. Davis, V. Matthews, and A. Jones (OUP) 2004 for a full explanation of the law. For a more theoretical but thoroughly enjoyable approach to housing law, read D. Cowan, *Housing Law and Policy* (Macmillan, 1999).

Both the Legal Action Group and the Citizens' Advice Bureau publish well-informed and practical accounts of particular areas of housing law in their monthly magazines, *Legal Action* and *The Adviser*. In addition *Legal Action* publishes a range of housing law books aimed at the practitioner but accessible and informative for the general reader. These include:

J. Luba, N. Madge, and D. McConnell, *Defending Possession Proceedings* (5th edn., Legal Action, 2002).

A. Arden, D. Carter, and A. Dymond, *Quiet Enjoyment* (6th edn., Legal Action, 2002).

J. Luba and S. Knafler, *Repairs—Tenants' Rights* (3rd edn., Legal Action, 1999).

The Law Commission's consultation papers No 162, *Renting Homes (1) Status and Security*, and No. 168, *Renting Homes (2) Co-occupation etc.* and the interim report *Renting Homes* No 284 provide clear explanations of the current law as well as proposals to reform the law. They are available from TSO and from the Law Commission web site, **www.lawcom.gov.uk**.

For a general commentary on the important provisions of the Housing Act 2004 see H. Carr, T. Baldwin, S. Castle, and M. King, The Housing Act 2004, Jordans.

Human rights and housing

Christopher Baker, David Carter, and Caroline Hunter, *Housing and Human Rights Law* (Legal Action Camp, 2001).

20 | Homelessness

CASE STUDY

Osmani v Camden London Borough Council [2004] EWCA CIV 1706

Mr Osmani, who came from Kosovo, applied to Camden local housing authority for accommodation as a homeless person with a priority need, on the basis of his vulnerability arising from his suffering from depression and post-traumatic stress. Camden applied the well established test of vulnerability in homelessness cases. It had to decide whether Mr Osmani would be less able to fend for himself than an ordinary homeless person so that injury or detriment to him would result when a less vulnerable person would be able to cope without harmful effects. The local authority found that Mr Osmani was not vulnerable in that sense, and refused to secure for him and his wife interim accommodation. Mr Osmani requested a review of that decision, and submitted medical evidence concerning his vulnerable psychiatric state. Whilst the local authority was undertaking the review, Mr and Mrs Osmani were evicted from their privately rented accommodation, and the local authority subsequently provided them with temporary accommodation pending completion of the review. In due course, Camden confirmed its earlier determination. Mr Osmani appealed against that decision under s. 204 of the 1996 Act. The judge dismissed his appeal, having found that the defendant's decision was not unreasonable or otherwise unlawful. Mr Osmani appealed to the Court of Appeal.

His argument was that in making its determination, the local authority had applied the wrong test in that it had not considered, or considered adequately, the effect on his frail psychiatric condition of his becoming homeless as distinct from his current state when not homeless and in temporary accommodation provided by Camden.

The Court of Appeal dismissed his appeal.

It was pointed out that the homelessness provisions of the Housing Act 1996 involved first a system for determining 'priority' between homeless persons, and second, a scheme of social welfare conferring benefits at public expense on grounds of public policy on those who were identified as entitled to such priority. The scheme defined a number of circumstances, one of which was vulnerability, by which a person might qualify as having a priority need for housing assistance. According to settled authority, a person was vulnerable if he had such a lesser ability than that of a hypothetically 'ordinary homeless person' to fend for himself that he would suffer greater harm from homelessness than would such a person. That test did not impose as the sole, or even an integral, requirement of the notice of fending for oneself that an applicant should also be less able than normal to fend for himself in finding accommodation. For the purpose of applying the vulnerability test, a local housing authority should take care to assess and apply it on the assumption that an applicant had become or would become street homeless, not on his ability to fend for himself while still housed. In that respect, it should have regard to the debilitating effects of depressive disorders and the fragility of those suffering from them if suddenly deprived of the support provided by their own home. Nevertheless, although authorities should look for and pay close regard to medical evidence submitted in supports of applicants' claims of vulnerability on account of mental illness or handicap, it would be for an authority, not medical experts, to determine this statutory issue of vulnerability.

In this case Camden had met all those requirements when assessing the risk as to the future vulnerability of Mr Osmani. Whilst there was no doubt that he suffered from a depressive illness, it was not such, when he was still being housed by the defendant, as to prevent him from fending for himself and his wife in maintaining all their normal support systems and in his daily activities. The defendant's conclusion that the claimant was not vulnerable to that extent had been one which was reasonably open to it and which was not perverse.

OVERVIEW AND OBJECTIVES

Mr Osmani is clearly a very vulnerable individual suffering from mental illness. However, his need for housing was not sufficient for him to be in priority need for housing under the Housing Act 1996. This demonstrates the limited legal responsibilities upon housing authorities to provide housing for the homeless.

Whilst this case is primarily about the extent of social services responsibilities to children in need, it is very closely linked to the limited legal responsibilities upon housing authorities to provide housing for the homeless. Local authorities are not obliged to house people who are found to be intentionally homeless, who are from abroad, or who are housed in unsuitable accommodation, even where they have children, It illustrates some of the difficulties faced by vulnerable people in trying to get access to accommodation. It also highlights the difficulties faced by housing authorities which are having to ration their accommodation so that it is available to the most vulnerable applicants who are also deserving, in the sense that they have not lost or given up accommodation without very good reason. As you read this chapter, consider the limits on the legal duties towards homeless people. Think about the people who are given priority by the legislation, and, if you were devising a system to ration housing, whether you would go about it in the same way. You will notice how complex the provisions are. Why do you think the law is so complicated? Think also about the people who fall through the homelessness safety net. What is social services' role in providing for those people, particularly where there are children involved? By the end of the chapter you should understand the basic provisions of the homelessness legislation and understand what housing officers are trying to do when they interview applicants under the legislation. You should also understand that as a social worker you have duties to help those who fall through the net, but you will also see that those duties are very limited.

▇ Introduction

It is not easy for people with limited resources to obtain and keep accommodation. The law does not provide accommodation for every homeless person via homelessness legislation. Only those people who are homeless through no fault of their own and are in priority need as defined by the law are entitled to housing. The law is complex and subject to frequent challenge. We can provide you with only an outline and anyone considering applying to their local housing authority will require good legal advice. We remind you of our signposting advice in chapter 9. We will refer you to further reading at the end of the chapter if you need to know more.

Information on the law

This area of law is governed by Part 7 of the Housing Act 1996, and references to sections within the chapter are to this Act unless otherwise stated. Important amendments to the Housing Act 1996 have been made by the Homelessness Act 2002 which also introduces strategic responsibilities for homelessness on local housing authorities. The Homelessness (Priority Need for Accommodation) (England) Order 2002, SI 2051 and the Welsh equivalent, the Homeless Persons (Priority Need) (Wales) Order 2001 No. 607 (W.30) make important additions to the classes of people who should be considered to be in priority need of accommodation. The Acts, the statutory instrument, and the explanatory notes are available on the web site, **www.hmso.gov.uk**. Shelter, the homelessness charity, runs an excellent web site on the Homelessness Act 2002— **www.HomelessnessAct.org.uk**—which provides links to key government materials, together with useful information on the law, on good practice, and hosts discussion groups on the practical workings of the legislation.

Case law on homelessness is extensive. Many cases decided under the old legislation remain valid, as the basic principles were retained in the 1996 Act.

District and borough councils must also take into account the Homelessness Code of Guidance for Local Authorities, published by the Office of the Deputy Prime Minister in July 2002; this provides a thorough and wide-ranging explanation of the council's obligations, and is worth having and quoting on behalf of a homeless applicant. A revised Code is due to be published in 2005. Note, however, that where the statute and the Code are not in agreement then the statute prevails—*R (on the application of Tower Hamlets) v Secretary of State for the Environment* (1993). The Code contains extensive references to the duties of social workers dealing with clients who are vulnerable and at risk of homelessness. As it refers to clients as opposed to service users, that is the term we have used in this chapter. The Code also makes clear the extent of the duty of social services departments to cooperate with local housing authorities. It is available free of charge from the ODPM web site, **www.odpm.gov.uk**. The ODPM web site contains a great deal of other useful information about homelessness and government projects to respond to the problem. The structure of our chapter follows the structure of the Code since it provides the most straightforward way of explaining the legislation.

The law talks about local housing authorities. If you work within a unitary authority then the local housing authority will be the same authority as the social services authority. In non-unitary authorities social services and housing are in different authorities. Unitary authorities are in London and in the metropolitan areas. Otherwise, your authority is a non-unitary authority.

Summary of the duties in Part 7 of the Housing Act 1996

The basic objective of Part 7 of the Housing Act 1996 is to place a duty upon local housing authorities to provide advice and assistance and, in certain limited circumstances, accommodation for the homeless. You will realize from this that local authorities do not have to house everyone who is homeless. In many parts of the country there is a shortage of decent affordable housing and the law serves to ration that accommodation to those who are both in need and, according to the criteria set out in the Act, deserve it. The statutory obligation placed upon local authorities is to make available suitable accommodation for a person who meets the four criteria of the Act. The person must be eligible for assistance, homeless, in priority need of accommodation, and not intentionally homeless. The duty is also subject to the local connection provisions of the Act. Your clients may seek your advice and support directly about their homelessness, but may also need advice in the context of relationship breakdown, mortgage possession proceedings, eviction, immigration, or dissatisfaction with their housing conditions.

The key definitions of 'eligibility for assistance', 'homelessness', 'priority need', and 'intentionality' need to be understood before advising on anyone's rights under the legislation. It is also important to be aware of the relevant local authority's policies and practice and the local authority's allocation scheme, and to understand what accommodation can be described as suitable. We will examine these questions later in this chapter. First of all, however, we should consider the context of homelessness and the need for strategic responses.

Who are the homeless?

The homelessness statistics published quarterly by the Office of the Deputy Prime Minister and available on its web site provide a great deal of information about the characteristics, trends, and numbers of households found to be homeless through no fault of their own and to have a priority need for help. Between October and December 2003, 32,100 households were accepted for re-housing by local authorities. This represents a decrease of 11 per cent from the last quarter but is 3 per cent higher than a year ago. Of these over 22 per cent were from black and ethnic minority communities which are massively overrepresented amongst the homeless. Around 50 per cent all homeless households were families with children and a further 11 per cent were households containing a pregnant woman. At the end of December 2003 there were 95,060 households living in temporary accommodation, an increase of 13 per cent on the previous year. The number of families with children in bed and breakfast hotels was around 1,680—a decline of more than two thirds since the government set a target for the end of the use of bed and breakfast hotels for homeless families except in emergencies and for no more than six weeks. The biggest reason for homelessness was parents, family, or friends no longer being able or willing to provide accommodation. This reason accounted for 37 per cent of all homelessness acceptances. Relationship breakdown was the second biggest cause of homelessness, with 20 per cent of acceptances.

These statistics are the official statistics compiled by local authorities in England and Wales. They do not take into account people who may not have anywhere to live that we would consider satisfactory but who do not make applications to the local housing authority. Nor do they take into account people who are turned away because they are not in priority need or are homeless intentionally. It is difficult to work out the true facts about homelessness in this country. There is no doubt that it is a greater problem than the official statistics suggest.

The statistics indicate that homelessness is caused by a wide range of personal and social problems. The Government and many voluntary sector organizations working within housing believe that a more coherent approach to homelessness by housing authorities would reduce the extent of homelessness, reduce the numbers accommodated within temporary housing, particularly bed and breakfast, and improve the chances of homeless people being successfully settled into permanent accommodation. One of the major drivers behind the Homelessness Act 2002 is the need to ensure that local housing authorities take a more strategic response to this important social problem.

Homelessness reviews and strategies

The Homelessness Act 2002 imposes strategic responsibilities for homelessness on local housing authorities. Section 1 of the Act provides that local authorities should review their homelessness provisions and publish a strategy based upon that review. Section 1(3) imposes a duty on local housing authorities to publish the first homelessness strategy for their district within twelve months of s. 1 coming into force (in July 2002) and subsequent homelessness strategies must be published every five years. Social service departments in unitary authorities will need to co-operate with the housing department in producing the strategy. In non-unitary authorities social services authorities have a duty under s. 1(2) of the Act to provide assistance in the production of the strategy.

Section 2(1) sets out what a review must consider. We have set it out in Box 20.1 below.

The type of assistance that social services authorities may be expected to provide to housing authorities is set out in para. 1.58 of the Code of Guidance. The suggestions include:

- providing information about current and likely future numbers of social services client groups who are likely to be homeless or at risk of homelessness, e.g. young people in need and those with community care needs;

- details of social services' current programme of activity and the resources available to them for meeting the accommodation needs of these groups;

- details of social services' current programme of activity and the resources available to them for providing support for vulnerable people who are homeless or likely to become homeless.

BOX 20.1 Reviews of homelessness

This includes:

(a) the levels and likely future levels of homelessness

(b) activities for
   (i)   preventing homelessness,
   (ii) securing that accommodation is available for homeless people, and
   (iii) providing support for people who
        — are homeless,
        — may become homeless, or
        — have been homeless and need support to prevent them becoming homeless again.

The Code reminds readers of the duty upon local housing authorities under s. 27 of the Children Act 1989 to cooperate with social services.

Finally, once the review has been carried out and the strategy published, local housing authorities and social services authorities are required to take the homelessness strategy into account when exercising their functions.

We suggest you read your local authority homelessness strategy, which will be available on the web, and notice what commitments it makes to tackling homelessness and what the role of social services will be.

The provision of advisory services

Advice and information about homelessness and how it can be prevented form an essential part of a strategic response to homelessness. Section 179(1) of the Housing Act 1996 sets out the duty of local housing authorities to provide advice and information free of charge to anyone in their district. The Code of Guidance suggests that advice could be made available on, for instance, housing opportunities within the district, including the private rented sector; and on the housing authority's allocation scheme and details of housing associations in the district that accept direct applications. Other examples of useful advice include rights to benefits, rent guarantee and deposit schemes, and running duty representation schemes to help people in court who are facing possession proceedings. You should find out what advice services are available in your area and ensure that you refer people to them.

The procedural requirements of homelessness legislation— applications, inquiries, decisions, and notifications

The procedure

Whenever a person applies to a housing authority for accommodation or help in obtaining accommodation, and the housing authority has reason to believe that he or she may be homeless or threatened with homelessness, the housing authority must make inquiries under s. 184 of the Housing Act 1996 to satisfy itself whether the applicant is eligible for assistance and, if so, whether a duty is owed to that person under Part 7 of the 1996 Act.

Applications

The key word that triggers the homelessness investigation process is that a person must *apply*. Applications need not be in writing, or in any particular form. An application can be made by any member of a household. There is no reference to an age limit in the 1996 Act, so in theory a minor can apply, but courts have excluded applications from dependent children, as we shall explain later in this chapter. The Code of Guidance at para. 3.4 recommends that housing authorities have arrangements in place to ensure that, where they receive applications from young people aged 16 or 17, including those who are single parents, they can undertake a joint assessment with social services of the applicant's housing, care, and support needs. An authority owes a duty only to someone who has the mental capacity to understand and respond to an offer of accommodation and, if accepted, to understand the responsibilities involved. Whether a person has sufficient mental capacity to make an application is to be decided by the authority, and its decision can be challenged only on the basis that no reasonable authority could make such a decision. Although joint applications can be made, for instance by husband and wife, each individual is entitled to separate consideration of his or her case.

Applicants can apply to more than one housing authority simultaneously. The housing authorities can agree amongst themselves which will take the lead on the inquires. Housing authorities are also entitled to consider decisions made on previous applications to be treated as homeless made by the applicant. However, they cannot rely on previous decisions but must make their own, independent, inquiries in response to all applications in order to reach a fresh and independent decision.

The Code of Guidance at paras. 3.7–3.9 sets out the level of service that applicants should expect. For instance applications should be able to be made at all times, with twenty-four-hour emergency cover. Applicants should receive clear written explanations of the procedures and be kept informed of the progress of their applications, and the time scales involved and be given a realistic expectation of the housing assistance to which they may be entitled. At para. 3.18 the Code suggests that housing authorities should aim to complete inquiries within thirty-three days from the date of application.

Inquiries

Once an application is made the authority is under a duty under s. 184 to inquire into:

(a) whether the applicant is eligible for assistance;

(b) homelessness or threatened homelessness;

(c) priority need; and

(d) intentionality.

There is a power, not a duty, to make inquiries into local connection. The meaning of these key legislative phrases will be considered later in the chapter.

Inquiries by the housing department should be made in a caring and sympathetic way directed towards the relevant issues. They should not be carried out in the manner of a CID inquiry but can be, and indeed should be, rigorously and fairly pursued. The applicant must be given an opportunity to explain matters which the authority is minded to regard as weighing substantially against him or her. The housing authority is under a duty to inquire; it is not for the applicant to prove their case. Therefore if inquiries lead to doubt or uncertainty, the issue should be resolved in the applicant's favour. A ten-minute conversation was not sufficient exploration of the reasons why the applicant was homeless in *R v Dacorum Borough Council ex parte Brown* (1989). If medical evidence is relevant, where the council's decision was based on the report of a doctor who had not even seen the applicant, the investigation was ruled inadequate by the court: *R v Lambeth London Borough Council ex parte Carroll* (1988). The greater the applicant's problem, the more thorough the assessment required. In *R v Ealing LBC ex parte C (A Minor)* (2000), C was a 9 year old suffering from dyspraxia, asthma, incontinence, dyslexia, and partial blindness. He was having to share a bed with his mother in a small flat. The council's failure to assess his practical difficulties before turning down his application as homeless was unlawful because it was unreasonable. If the person is homeless because he or she failed to pay rent, the department must find out if it was deliberate or accidental (*R v Westminster City Council ex parte Ali and Bibi* (1992)).

Inquiries into applications where there are allegations of violence will have to be handled particularly carefully by the housing authority. As the Code of Guidance points out at para. 3.14, 'it is not advisable for the housing authority to approach the alleged perpetrator, since this could generate further violence, and may delay the assessment. Housing authorities may, however, wish to seek information from friends and relatives of the applicant, social services and the police as appropriate. In cases involving domestic violence, the applicant may be in considerable distress and for inquiries to be effective an officer of the same sex as the applicant, trained in dealing with circumstances of this kind, should conduct the interview.'

Social services departments may be required to assist in inquiries where the applicant has care, health, or other support needs. This may well be necessary to answer queries about priority need and to determine what non-housing support needs the applicant has.

Interim duty to accommodate

There is an interim duty to accommodate the applicant where the housing authority believes that he or she is homeless, eligible for assistance, and in priority need while inquiries are ongoing (s. 188). The accommodation should be suitable for the needs of the applicant. The Code of Guidance suggests that 'whilst bed and breakfast accommodation may need to be used in an emergency, where other, more suitable forms of accommodation are not available, housing authorities should avoid using this wherever possible'. We will discuss the meaning of suitable accommodation later. Just note at this point that an applicant has no right to any review of the suitability of interim accommodation.

Notification

As soon as possible after completing its inquiries, the authority must notify the applicant in writing of its decision and, so far as any issue is decided against his or her interest, inform him or her of the reasons for the decision. Any notice of any decision by the authority must inform the applicant of his or her right to request a review of the decision and of the time limit for doing so (s. 184). The Code of Guidance also recommends that housing authorities advise applicants about their procedures on conducting reviews and about the applicant's right to appeal to the county court against a review decision.

The interim duty to accommodate ceases when the authority's decision is notified to the applicant, even if the applicant requests a review of the decision, although the authority may continue to secure that the accommodation remains available. The applicant should be given reasonable notice to quit the accommodation.

Box 20.2 sets out a summary of the procedural requirements.

 BOX 20.2 Summary of the procedural requirements

Procedure	Section	Requirements	Comment
Applications	s. 183	No requirements stipulated, therefore no particular form of application required	An application triggers the inquiry process
Inquiries	s. 184	Into the key factors of eligibility, homelessness, priority need, and intentionality	Even those not eligible for assistance under the Act are entitled to advice and assistance in finding housing It is the duty of the housing authority to inquire, not the applicant to prove their case
Interim duty to accommodate	s. 188	Applies where the applicant is homeless, eligible for assistance, and has a priority need	No review available on suitability of accommodation provided on the interim basis
Notification	s. 184	Notify applicant of decision in writing giving reasons for the decision Must also notify applicants of local connection referral, and the right to request a review and the time limit of the review procedure.	Notification should also inform applicants of review procedure and of the right of appeal to the county court

Eligibility for assistance—the first key inquiry

People from abroad

No duty is owed by the housing department to anyone, however dire their situation, if the legislation and the regulations taken together make them ineligible for assistance (s. 185). The philosophy behind this is to remove the right to emergency housing assistance for anyone whose immigration status is restricted (see chapter 21). There is one exception: a duty is owed to a person seeking asylum but whose status as asylum seeker has not yet been determined by the Home Office. However, no duty will be owed if that person has any accommodation of any sort, including hostel accommodation but excluding totally unsuitable accommodation (s. 186). The Homelessness (England) Regulations 2000 (SI 2000 No. 701) have been made under s. 185. A similar statutory instrument has been implemented for Wales. The provisions that deny eligibility to certain groups of people from abroad are complex. The Code of Guidance provides a great deal of further information, much of it in the annexes to the Code. It does point out that housing officers will require training not only in the complexities of the legislation but also in the authority's duties and responsibilities under race relations legislation and how to deal with applicants in a sensitive manner.

Homelessness—the second key inquiry

What is meant by homelessness?

If a person's immigration status is not restricted and therefore the applicant is eligible, the authority moves on to investigate his or her homelessness. It is not necessary to have, literally, no roof over a person's head. A person is homeless if he or she, together with any person he or she can reasonably be expected to live with, has no accommodation which they are entitled to occupy and which it would be reasonable for them to continue to occupy (s. 175). Accommodation includes accommodation overseas. A person does not have to be actually homeless to qualify under the Act, if he or she is likely to become homeless within the next twenty-eight days.

The Code at para. 6.2 states that housing authorities must not wait until homelessness is imminent before providing assistance. However, in *R v Newham LBC ex parte Sacupima and others* (2000), it was made clear that Newham Council was able to decide that tenants did not become homeless until actual execution of a bailiff's order, despite the fact that there was no defence to the proceedings. It is worth pointing out to the housing department that in such circumstances the applicants are threatened with homelessness and therefore they are owed duties under the Act. If they still will not listen you should refer the applicants to a good housing lawyer.

What is meant by accommodation which the applicant is entitled to occupy?

A person is entitled to occupy a place he or she owns, or has a tenancy or licence of, or has a right to occupy by marriage (under the Family Law Act 1996, see chapter 19). A cohabitee living in his or her partner's premises has an entitlement to occupy as a licensee, unless that right is withdrawn on relationship breakdown.

The applicant may have rights which he or she cannot exercise. The landlord has changed the locks—the tenant has the theoretical right to occupy, and may eventually be able to enforce it. Or the applicant has a caravan, but nowhere where he or she is entitled to place it. People in these circumstances are usually treated as homeless.

Guests

An informal licence which a person has by virtue of living with relatives or friends could be terminated at any moment; it nevertheless constitutes a right to occupy, so a person is homeless 'intentionally', with all the disastrous consequences that follow from this label, if he or she gives this up for no valid reason. But if the hosts genuinely want that person to leave, and are not colluding to get him or her a home with the local authority, that person is threatened with unintentional homelessness.

16 and 17 year olds

16 and 17 year olds have informal licences with their parents. The Code (at paragraph 6.9) states, 'The government considers that, generally, it will be in the best interests of 16- and 17-year-old children to live in the family home, unless it would be unsafe or unsuitable for them to do so because they would be at risk of violence or abuse. It is not unusual for 16 and 17 year olds to have a turbulent relationship with their family and this can occasionally led to temporary disagreements and even temporary estrangement. However such temporary breakdowns in the family relationship will not always amount to actual homelessness. Housing authorities will need to give careful consideration to whether applicants who are 16 and 17 are actually homeless. Where the housing authority are satisfied there is genuine homelessness, the first response should be to consider the possibility of reconciliation with the applicant's immediate family, or the possibility of him or her residing with another member of the wider family.' Several local authorities run mediation schemes particularly focussed on enabling teenagers to remain in their family homes.

When is it reasonable to continue to occupy accommodation?

Domestic violence and other violence

The Act gives some indication of when it would *not* be reasonable. For example, under s. 177(1), it will not be reasonable:

... if it is probable that this will lead to domestic violence or other violence against [the applicant] or against—

(a) a person who normally resides with him as a member of his family, or
(b) any other person who might reasonably be expected to reside with him.

Section 177(1A) provides that violence means violence from another person or threats of violence from another person which are likely to be carried out. So it includes threats as well as actual violence.

Domestic violence is defined as violence or threats of violence from an 'associated person' with whom the applicant was living, such as a relative, a cohabitee, or a member of the same household. Domestic violence is not confined to violence within the home, but includes violence outside the home from an associated person.

Remedies

Victims of domestic violence can go to court to obtain an injunction to enable them to return to a property. Victims of other violence can obtain similar remedies. We set out the legal position in chapter 18. Quite often a victim does not want to go to court as he or she is frightened to do so. Will your client be obliged by the local authority to obtain an injunction to allow him or her to return to the property? The Code of Guidance (at para. 6.20) says: 'Housing authorities should recognise that injunctions ordering persons not to molest, or enter the home of, the applicant will not always be effective in deterring perpetrators from carrying out further violence or incursions. Applicants should not automatically be expected to return home on the strength of an injunction.' Some local authorities try to insist that an applicant obtains an injunction. There is useful support for approach of the Code in a Court of Appeal decision *Bond v Leicester City Council* (2001). In the High Court the judge had accepted Leicester City Council's view that it was entitled to take into account, in assessing the reasonableness of her action in leaving her accommodation, the applicant's failure to seek protection through the pursuit of civil or criminal action against her former partner. The Court pointed out that in situations involving domestic violence, the sole test in determining whether an individual was intentionally homeless was the probability of the occurrence of violence given continued occupation of the property. The issue was one of fact and did not allow for value judgements on an individual's approach to taking civil or criminal action.

Perpetrators

What of the person who commits the violence? Such a person is not homeless within the Act; he (and we have decided to refer to perpetrators of violence as male) is able to exercise his rights of occupation. (If an injunction is obtained requiring him to leave the property, or if his local authority or housing association landlord evicts him under a ground specifically designed to remove the perpetrators of domestic violence from family homes, he is then homeless; but, as we shall see below, it is treated as intentional homelessness, because he is the cause of his own misfortune.) However, while it is not necessarily your job to worry about such a person, you should bear in mind the provisions of the Children Act 1989, para. 5 of Sch. 2 (see chapter 10); a suspected abuser of children can be assisted by social services in finding accommodation, including cash assistance such as paying a deposit or even an advance of rent. (No statutory obligation is placed on the local authority housing department by this provision, but the social worker should liaise with it when helping the abuser find somewhere to live.)

Other factors

These could include the physical conditions in the property, overcrowding, type of accommodation (so that, for instance, crisis accommodation such as women's refuges or direct access hostels should not be regarded as suitable for occupation in the longer term). It is important to note, however, that in deciding whether it is reasonable for a person to continue to occupy accommodation, a local authority may have regard to the general circumstances prevailing in relation to housing within its area. So, if the prevailing housing conditions are overcrowded or in serious disrepair, then the local authority is unlikely to find that it is unreasonable to continue to occupy the accommodation. You saw the impact of this requirement on the case study at the beginning of the chapter. If your service user is not accepted as homeless on these grounds, you can advise him or her to use the review proceedings which we explain later.

One factor that should always be considered in the inquiry into whether it is reasonable to give up accommodation is affordability. The Homelessness (Suitability of Accommodation) Order 1996 (SI 1996 No. 3204) states that a housing authority must take into account whether the accommodation is affordable for the applicant and must in particular, take account of:

(a) the financial resources available to him or her;

(b) the costs in respect of the accommodation;

(c) the maintenance payments (in respect of ex-family members); and

(d) his or her reasonable living expenses.

Who may live with the applicant?

The right to respect for family life (Article 8 of the European Convention: see chapter 2) is a fundamental human right and suggests that families should be able to live together. The 1996 Act recognises this. The definition of homelessness covers not only the applicant, but people he or she could reasonably be expected to live with (s. 176)—a spouse, a cohabitee, dependent children, or relatives. It also includes other people who are established members of the household or who could reasonably be expected to live with the applicant as part of his or her household. The Code suggests in paragraph 6.3 that this 'might include a housekeeper or a companion or an elderly or disabled person or children who are being fostered by the applicant or a member of his or her family'. A pregnant woman should be considered as herself plus the baby (the baby being a person she could reasonably expect to live with): *R v Newham London Borough Council ex parte Dada* [1995] 1 FLR 842. In *R v London Borough of Ealing ex parte Sidhu* (1983) 2 HLR 41, the court said the Borough housing department was wrong to require that the applicant, a single parent, obtain a custody order (now known as a residence order) before it would be reasonable for the children to live with him. We have summarized the legislative meaning of homelessness in Box 20.3.

BOX 20.3 Summary of the meaning of homelessness

Element of homelessness	Subsection of s. 175	Comment
No accommodation available for his occupation *or*	(1)	This means no accommodation anywhere in the world Accommodation needs to be available for anyone who resides with him or may be expected to reside with him (s. 176)
Unable to secure entry to accommodation *or*	(2a)	For instance landlord changing the locks
Nowhere to place a moveable home	(2b)	Applies to caravans and house boats
Applicant has no accommodation if it is not reasonable to continue to occupy accommodation	(3)	s. 177—it is not reasonable to occupy accommodation where there is probability of domestic violence, or other violence other factors such as affordability can affect reasonableness general housing conditions can be taken into in assessing reasonableness
Someone threatened with homelessness within 28 days is homeless	(4)	

Priority need—the third key inquiry

The categories in outline

In order to decide whether the applicant is entitled to the benefit of the main duties of the Act which we discuss later the authority has to decide whether the applicant, or someone who can be expected to live with the applicant, is in *priority need*. Section 189(1) sets out that the following are in priority need:

(a) a pregnant woman or someone with whom she resides or may reasonably be expected to reside;

(b) a person with whom dependent children reside or may be expected to reside (including a child who could reasonably be expected to if the applicant had a home);

(c) a person who is vulnerable as a result of old age, mental illness or handicap, or physical disability, or who has some other special reason for being vulnerable or with whom such a person resides or may reasonably be expected to reside;

(d) a person whose homelessness, or threatened homelessness, results from flood, fire, or similar emergency or disaster.

The Homelessness (Priority Need for Accommodation) England) Order (SI 2002 No. 2051) sets out six further categories of applicants with priority need. We will list them and then explain any aspects that are not self evident:

(a) a person aged 16 or 17 who is not a relevant child or a child in need to whom a local authority owes a duty under s. 20 of the Children Act 1989;

(b) a person under 21 who was (but is no longer) looked after, accommodated, or fostered between the ages of 16 and 18 (except a person who is a 'relevant student');

(c) a person aged 21 or more who is vulnerable as a result of having been looked after, accommodated, or fostered (except a person who is a 'relevant student');

(d) a person who is vulnerable as a result of having been a member of Her Majesty's regular naval, military, or air forces;

(e) a person who is vulnerable as a result of:
    (i) having served a custodial sentence,
    (ii) having been committed for contempt of court or any other kindred offence, or
    (iii) having been remanded in custody;

(f) a person who is vulnerable as a result of ceasing to occupy accommodation because of violence from another person or threats of violence from another person which are likely to be carried out.

In categories (b) and (c) the words 'looked after, accommodated or fostered' have the same meaning as in s. 24(2) of the Children Act 1989 (as amended by the Children Leaving Care Act 2000). The term 'relevant student' means a care leaver to whom s. 24B(3) of the Children Act 1989 applies, who is in full-time further or higher education and whose term time accommodation is not available during a vacation. See chapter 10. These additional categories reflect the vulnerability of these particular groups to homelessness. The term 'relevant child' is a child aged 16 or 17 who has been looked after by a local authority for at least thirteen weeks since the age of 14 and has been looked after at some time while 16 or 17 and who is not currently being looked after. In addition, a child may be a relevant child if he or she would have qualified but for the fact that on his or her sixteenth birthday he or she was detained through the criminal justice system or in hospital, or if he or she has returned home on family placement and that has broken down. See the Children Act 1989, s. 23A, and the Children (Leaving Care) Regulations 2001, discussed in chapter 10.

The Welsh Assembly similarly extended the categories of priority need. However, unlike the regulations in England, there is no requirement for an applicant to establish that they are vulnerable as a result of fleeing violence, leaving the armed forces or being released from custody. However those leaving custody will only be in priority need if they have a local connection with the local housing authority they have approached. The Welsh categories are set out in the Homeless Persons (Priority Need) (Wales) Order 2001 No. 607 (W. 30).

■ The categories in detail

Pregnant women

A pregnant woman and anyone with whom she lives or may reasonably be expected to live has a priority need for accommodation regardless of the length of time that the woman has been pregnant. The housing authority should accept evidence from a midwife or a doctor that she is pregnant.

Dependent children

Applicants have a priority need if they have a dependent child who lives with them or who may reasonably be expected to live with them. Problems can arise where a child shares his or her time with two parents living apart. It is not a requirement in law, but is nevertheless helpful to the homeless applicant, to have a s. 8 of the Children Act residence order. The Code of Guidance states (at para. 8.6) that 'there must be actual residence (or a reasonable expectation of residence) with some degree of permanence or regularity, rather than a temporary arrangement whereby the children are merely staying with the applicant for a limited period'. The Code also points out at para. 8.10 that it will be only in exceptional cases that the child may be considered to reside with both parents. If the child normally lives with the applicant, or would do so but for the lack of a home, the applicant is in priority need (*R v Lewisham Borough Council ex parte C* (1992)). Social workers, in liaising with the housing department, should bear in mind that their duty under the Children Act includes keeping families together, if this is in the child's interests. The housing department does not have this duty. The Code also raises the problem of children who are being looked after by social services and are not currently living with the applicant. In these circumstances it states (para. 8.11) that 'liaison with the social services authority will be essential. Joint consideration with social services will ensure that the best interests of the applicant and the children are served'.

Dependent children are not defined in the Act, but the Code suggests (at paragraph 8.7) that housing authorities 'may wish to treat as dependent all children under 16, and all children aged 16–18 who are in, or are about to begin, full time education or training or who for other reasons are unable to support themselves and who live at home'.

Dependent children can never be treated as vulnerable applicants in their own right, even if they suffer from one of the specified conditions, as Parliament has provided for them by giving a priority right to accommodation to their parents or carers (*R v MBC of Oldham ex parte G; R v LB Bexley ex parte B* (1993)).

Vulnerability

The legal meaning of vulnerability in the context of homelessness is restrictive. In *R (on the application of Pereira) v Camden* (1998) it was decided that a drug addict was vulnerable only if his condition made him less able to obtain and keep a home than other homeless people. The fact that, like an applicant with children, being housed is a good thing for a drug addict does not seem to have convinced the Divisional Court. On the other hand, an alleged paedophile who had been driven from his home and who received death threats in temporary accommodation was vulnerable and entitled to accommodation (*R v Tower Hamlets LBC ex parte G* (2000)).

The Code of Guidance published in July 2002 set out a more generous test of vulnerability. It stated at para. 8.13 that vulnerability meant that, 'the applicant would be less able to fend for himself than an ordinary homeless person so that he would be likely to suffer injury or detriment, in circumstances where a less vulnerable person would be able to cope without harmful effects'. This differed from the test set out in *Pereira* as it added the words 'would be likely to' to the test. In *Griffin v Westminster CC* (2004) the question for the court was whether the Review Officer had applied the correct test, as he did not use the Code of Guidance test but the less generous interpretation of the statute set out in *Pereira*. The judge held that the Review Officer was correct. The question which had to be answered was, 'Would the claimant, when homeless, because of his reactive depression, be less well able to fend for himself than an ordinary homeless person so that he **would** suffer injury or detriment?'

Old age

Old age puts the applicant into priority need only if it makes the applicant less able to fend for him- or herself. The Code (at para. 8.14) states that 'All applications from people aged over 60 need to be considered carefully, particularly where the applicant is leaving tied accommodation. However, housing authorities should not use 60 (or any other age) as a fixed age beyond which vulnerability occurs automatically (or below which it can be ruled out); each case will need to be considered in the light of the individual circumstances.'

Mental illness, learning, or physical disability

Advice from social services and medical advice will be important in helping housing authorities decide the vulnerability of applicants with these particular problems. However, the final decision rests with the housing authority. This principle is endorsed by the Court of Appeal in the case study at the start of this chapter. The Code of Guidance points out that 'Health authorities have an express duty to implement a specifically tailored care programme for all patients considered for discharge from psychiatric hospitals and all new patients accepted by the specialist psychiatric services' (see Department of Health circulars HC (90)223, LASSA (90)11, HSG (94) 27 and LASSA (94) 4). People discharged from psychiatric hospitals and local authority hostels for people with mental health problems are likely to be vulnerable. Effective liaison between housing, social services and health authorities will be essential in such cases but authorities will also need to be sensitive to direct approaches form former patients who have been discharged and may be homeless.

Homelessness as a result of an emergency

Applicants have a priority need for accommodation if they are homeless or threatened with homelessness as a result of an emergency such as fire, flood, or other disaster. The

Code points out (at paragraph 8.42) that 'the disaster must be in the nature of a flood or fire, and involve some form of physical damage or threat of damage'. The volcanic activity on the island of Montserrat was treated by various London housing authorities as an example of 'other disaster' when the inhabitants fled Montserrat. There is no need for applicants who are in priority need by reason of such an emergency to be vulnerable for any other reason or to have dependent children.

Other special reasons

The list of categories of priority need can never be exhaustive. The legislation allows for some people who do not fall within the specific categories to be considered vulnerable by housing authorities. Housing authorities must not make blanket decisions always to include or exclude certain groups of people from priority need. Each application should be considered carefully, taking into account the specific facts and circumstances arising. The Code makes some suggestions as to people who may be considered in priority need because of their particular circumstances. For instance, it suggests chronically sick people including people with AIDS and HIV-related illnesses may be in priority need even before their illness has progressed to the point where they would be in priority need under one of the other categories. Young people who fall outside the categories set out in the 2002 Order may be vulnerable because they suffered sexual or physical abuse at home and therefore lack the support that other young people may take for granted. Young people living on the streets may be at risk because of drugs, abuse, or prostitution and therefore in priority need. People fleeing harassment and former asylum seekers are other people whose needs should be considered carefully by housing officers.

The extended categories

The Homeless Persons (Priority Need for Accommodation) England Order 2002 came into force on 31 July 2002. The equivalent order for Wales is the Homeless Persons (Priority Need) (Wales) Order (SI 2001 No. 607). As yet it does not appear to have had a noticeable impact upon the statistics of homelessness acceptances. The extension of categories was made in response to the numbers of young people, people fleeing violence, and people leaving institutional settings amongst the street homeless.

16 and 17 year olds

All 16- and 17-year-old homeless applicants are in priority need unless they are a 'relevant' child or a child in need who is owed a duty under s. 20 of the Children Act 1989. There is no need for the applicant to have any additional vulnerability.

We discussed the meaning of 'relevant' child earlier in the chapter. As you will know, certain 16 and 17 year olds are owed a duty under s. 20 of the Children Act which places a duty on social services authorities to provide accommodation for a child in need aged 16 or over whose welfare is otherwise likely to be seriously prejudiced if they do not provide accommodation. The section also places a duty on local authorities to provide accommodation for other children in need in particular circumstances. Responsibility for providing suitable accommodation for a relevant child or a child in need to whom the local authority owes a duty rests with social service.

If there is uncertainty as to the status of a 16- or 17-year-old applicant then the housing authority should contact social services. The Code of Guidance at para. 8.37 recommends 'a framework for joint assessment of 16 and 17 year olds is established by housing and social services to facilitate the seamless discharge of duties and appropriate services to this client group'.

Many local authorities, either in a bid to reduce the number of young people they are required to house, or because they believe that 16–17 year olds are better housed with their families, have set up mediation schemes designed to reconcile young people and their parents. A homeless 17 year old loses their automatic priority need status on their eighteenth birthday.

Care leavers under 21

Applicants who are under 21 who were (but are no longer) looked after, accommodated, or fostered between the ages of 16 and 18 have a priority need for accommodation—except those who are 'relevant' students. We set out the meaning of relevant student earlier in the chapter. There is no need for care leavers under 21 to demonstrate any further vulnerability.

Having been looked after, accommodated, or fostered

A person aged 21 or over who is vulnerable because they have been looked after, accommodated, or fostered is in priority need. The terms are defined in s. 24 of the Children Act and discussed in chapter 10. Housing officers will have to inquire into an applicant's childhood to establish their history. The factors which may be considered in making decisions about vulnerability are suggested within the Code as including:

(i) the length of time that the applicant was looked after, accommodated, or fostered;

(ii) the length of time since the applicant was looked after, accommodated, or fostered, and whether the applicant had been able to obtain and or maintain accommodation during any of the period;

(iii) whether the applicant has any existing support networks, particularly by way of family, friends, or mentor.

Having been a member of the armed forces

People who are vulnerable following discharge from the armed forces have a priority need for accommodation. Housing authorities should consider the length of time someone has been in the forces, whether they were on active service, stays in military hospitals, and any other matter which may suggest vulnerability.

Having been in custody

Applicants discharged from custodial sentences who are also vulnerable as a result of having served a period in prison are in priority need. The Code points out in paragraph 8.24 that 'Those who have served a sentence of more than one year will have probation supervision on release, and the probation service have primary responsibility for ensuring that their accommodation needs are met'. The Code suggests the following factors may be relevant to housing officers decisions on vulnerability:

(i) the length of time the applicant served in prison;

(ii) whether the applicant is receiving probation service supervision;

(iii) the length of time since the applicant was released from prison or custody, and whether the applicant has been able to obtain and/or maintain accommodation during that time;

(iv) whether the applicant has any existing support networks, particularly by way of family or friends.

Many applicants who may be in priority need as a result of these provisions are likely to find themselves deemed to be intentionally homeless. We will discuss this later.

Having fled accommodation because of violence

A person has a priority need if he or she is vulnerable as a result of having to leave accommodation because of violence from another person or threats of violence from another person that are likely to be carried out. The Code points out at paragraph 8.26 that 'In cases involving violence, the safety of the applicant, and ensuring confidentiality, must be of paramount concern. It is not only domestic violence that is relevant but all forms of violence, including racially motivated violence or threats of violence likely to be carried out.' The factors likely to be relevant are:

(i) the nature of the violence or threats of violence (there may have been a single but significant incident or a number of incidents over an extended period of time which have had a cumulative effect);

(ii) the impact and likely effects of the violence or threats of violence on the applicant's physical and mental health and well being;

(iii) whether the applicant has any existing support networks, particularly by way of family or friends.

We have summarized the priority need categories in Box 20.4.

Intentionality—the fourth key inquiry

The housing authority has to decide whether the applicant became homeless *intentionally* (s. 184), which means that the applicant has to have had accommodation which it would be reasonable to continue to occupy, and by some deliberate act loses it (s. 191). The same criteria apply to threatened homelessness (s. 196).

Deliberate

The key to this is 'deliberate'. A person who suffers domestic violence leaves in consequence of an act of someone else—this is not deliberate. This interpretation is upheld in several cases. For example, in *R v Northampton Borough Council ex parte Clarkson*

BOX 20.4 Summary of priority need categories

Priority needs categories	Act/Priority Need SI	Comment
Pregnant woman	s. 189 (1) (a)	Includes anyone who might reasonably be expected to live with the applicant—for instance a partner Any stage of pregnancy relevant
Person with dependent children	s. 189 (1) (b)	Includes anyone who might reasonably be expected to live with the applicant—a partner Generally only the main carer is in priority need
Vulnerable as a result of old age, mental illness or handicap, or physical disability, or some other special reason	s. 189 (1) (c)	Includes anyone who might reasonably be expected to live with the applicant—a partner, a carer, a child for instance Vulnerability must relate to housing
Applicant homeless as a result of an emergency, flood fire or other disaster	s. 189 (1) (d)	Includes anyone who might reasonably be expected to live with the applicant No need to qualify under any other priority need category
16- and 17-year-olds	Homelessness (Priority Need for Accommodation) England) Order 2002	Includes anyone who might reasonably be expected to live with the applicant—for instance a parent Applicants are in priority need only whilst they are under 18 Excludes relevant children Automatically vulnerable
Over 21 having been looked after, accommodated or fostered by social services and vulnerable as a result	Homelessness (Priority Need for Accommodation) England) Order 2002	Includes anyone who might reasonably be expected to live with the applicant There will be inquiries into vulnerability
Care leavers under 21	Homelessness (Priority Need for Accommodation) England) Order 2002	Automatically vulnerable
Applicant having been a member of the armed forces and vulnerable as a result	Homelessness (Priority Need for Accommodation) England) Order 2002	There will be inquiries into vulnerability
Applicant having been in custody and vulnerable as a result	Homelessness (Priority Need for Accommodation) England) Order 2002	Applicants run the risk of failing the intentionality test (below) There will be inquiries into vulnerability
Applicant fleeing violence or threats of violence and vulnerable as a result	Homelessness (Priority Need for Accommodation) England) Order 2002	There will be inquiries into vulnerability

(1992), a woman suffering sexual advances from her half-brother applied to another authority as a homeless person. Without investigating her allegations of harassment, they said she could have carried on living near the half-brother. The court said that the council must investigate the circumstances. Exactly the same happened to a wife who left the area because of her husband's violence: *R v Tynedale District Council ex parte McCabe* (1992).

According to the Code, at para. 7.13, a person in rent or mortgage arrears through careless financial management whose property is repossessed is homeless intentionally, whereas the person whose arrears arose from genuine difficulties will be unintentionally homeless. It is the housing department, subject to review and appeals procedures, which makes the decisions. It should give applicants an opportunity to explain their behaviour. The applicant can try to blame his or her partner for the failure to pay the mortgage (and therefore prove that he or she had no intention of default). This argument failed in *R v Barnet LBC ex parte O'Connor* (1990), but in this case the applicant was partly to blame for re-mortgaging the house beyond the family's means. It should succeed if she was genuinely blameless—see para. 15.2 of the Code. In *R v Exeter City Council ex parte Trankle* (1993), the applicants had lost their home by securing a loan to run a hopeless pub. They had acted unwisely, but in good faith, so their homelessness was not intentional.

The applicant's act or omission

The decision about intentionality is about the intentionality of the applicant. Since every applicant is entitled to individual consideration of his or her application, if one person is found to be intentionally homeless, there is nothing to stop another member of the family who was not implicated in the act or omission which led to the loss of accommodation from applying as homeless. As the Code points out in para. 7.7, 'A person may have deliberately failed to pay the rent or defaulted on the mortgage payments which resulted in homelessness or threatened homelessness, against the wishes or without the knowledge of his or her partner. However, where applicants were not directly responsible for the act or omission which led to their family or household becoming homeless, they may be treated as having become homeless intentionally themselves, if they acquiesced in that behaviour.' A partner may be put into the position of having to prove that they did not agree to the act or omission which led to the homelessness despite the fact that it is not for the applicant to prove his or her case.

A vulnerable person who does not know how to manage his or her affairs, thereby becoming homeless, cannot be said to have acted intentionally (Code, para. 7.12); but with proper support from social services that person would not have been allowed to drift into that position in the first place.

Examples

There is much litigation on intentional homelessness. For example, the court upheld the local authority which considered a person intentionally homeless who left a home because of poltergeists (*R v Nottingham County Council ex parte Costello* (1989)); tenants who had a reasonable counterclaim for disrepair but consented to the landlord's possession application were held to be deliberately homeless (*R v London Borough of Wandsworth ex parte Henderson and Hayes* (1986)); where the tenant's children caused the nuisance which led to the possession claim the tenant herself was held to be deliberately homeless (*R v East Herts District Council ex parte Bannon* (1986)). But when children damaged property in *R v Rochester City Council ex parte Williams* (1994), and the landlord locked the applicant out, she was held to be unintentionally homeless.

The tenant who lost his home through being sent to prison for child abuse was intentionally homeless (*R v Hounslow LBC* (1997)). Indeed losing accommodation as a result of imprisonment will generally justify a finding of intentionality. The recent Court of Appeal case *Stewart v Lambeth LBC* (2002) is a good illustration of this. S had a secure tenancy which started in 1983. In 1997 a possession order was made, suspended on terms that he pay the rent and a sum towards arrears of rent each week. In 1998 he was remanded in custody for supplying heroin and subsequently sentenced to five years in prison. He arranged for his sister to pay the rent on the property while he was in prison. No payments were actually made. On 7 February 1999, a warrant for possession was executed. In December 2000, S was released from prison and he applied to the council for accommodation as a homeless person. He was found intentionally homeless. The council took the view that the loss of the accommodation was caused by his deliberate act in knowingly committing a criminal offence. S appealed to the county court but his appeal was dismissed. He subsequently appealed to the county court. The Court of Appeal made it clear that the loss of accommodation was directly caused by S's deliberate act in supplying heroin. The arrangement for his sister to pay the rent was ineffectual and did not break the chain of causation. The additional priority offered as a result of the Homelessness (Priority Need for Accommodation) England) Order 2002 is unlikely therefore to make a difference to the number of homeless ex-offenders since ex-offenders whose imprisonment itself led to the loss of their home are likely to be found to be intentionally homeless. If they are homeless for some other reason, then they are also likely to be in priority need.

Collusion

Under s. 191(3), collusion between the landlord and the applicant ('You kick me out so that I can get a local authority tenancy') is intentional conduct. Collusion may also happen between friends and families. As the Code points out, however, 'for collusion to amount to intentional homelessness, s. 191(3) specified that there should be no other good reason for the applicant's homelessness'.

Families with children under 18

Section 213A of the 1996 Act requires housing authorities to have arrangements in place to ensure that social services are alerted as quickly as possible to cases where the applicant has children under 18 and the housing authority considers the applicant may be intentionally homeless. We will consider social services responsibilities in these circumstances later in this chapter.

Summary of intentionality

Each element of s. 191 (or s. 196 if threatened with homelessness intentionally) needs to be present before a finding of intentionality is made. It is always worth returning to the words of the statute to challenge any decision on intentionality. Do not forget it requires a deliberate act or omission, that act or omission must cause the loss of accommodation, that accommodation must have been available for the applicant's occupation, and it must have been reasonable for the applicant to continue to occupy it. The key words in the section are set out in Box 20.5.

Applicants who are found to be intentionally homeless must obtain accommodation for themselves for a settled period in order to break the chain of causation between an act causing homelessness and the current homelessness. Whether accommodation is settled is a question of fact. The relevant factors will be security of tenure and length of residence. An assured shorthold tenancy is capable of constituting settled accommodation (*Knight v Vale Royal BC* (2003)). If people become homeless from settled accommodation unintentionally, they can then apply to the local authority and their application will not be tainted by their former intentionality.

Local connection

Once an applicant has been accepted as in priority need and not intentionally homeless, there can occasionally be a problem identifying which local authority housing department has the duty of providing accommodation.

Under s. 198, local connection means being normally resident in the area, or employed there, or having family ties. The House of Lords (in *Osmani v Harrow LBC; Al-Ameri v Kensington & Chelsea RLBC* (2004)) decided that accommodation provided to asylum seekers following their compulsory dispersal did not create a local connection since it was not a residence of choice. However the government has indicated its intention to reverse the impact of the decision through amendments to the Asylum and Immigration Bill.

 BOX 20.5 The key words of s. 191

Deliberately

Does or fails to do

Anything

In consequence of which

He ceases to occupy accommodation

Which is available for occupation

And which it would have been reasonable for him to continue to occupy

---

Local connection should not be misunderstood: the applicant is *not* required to have a local connection to obtain housing under these provisions. It is more subtle; if neither the applicant nor a person who would reasonably be expected to live with them has a local connection, but does have a local connection with another local authority's area, the buck can be passed by notifying that other authority. It is therefore unlawful for a housing authority to refer all cases elsewhere just because the applicant has a connection elsewhere (*R v Harrow London Borough Council ex parte Carter* (1992)). It is also unlawful to pass the buck where the applicant has a good reason to leave the area where she had a connection (*R v East Devon DC ex parte Robb* (1998), where Aberdeen was too cold for the applicant's skin condition). While the buck is in the process of being passed, the first authority approached must provide temporary accommodation until accommodation is available in the area where the local connection applies. The local connection proviso does not apply to an applicant who has a local connection, if to return there would be to return to the probability of violence including domestic violence.

◼ The duties owed by housing authorities to applicants once inquiries are complete

The duties in respect of homeless people are the duties of housing authorities. We will discuss the duties of social services to people who are not owed duties by housing authorities later in the chapter.

Here, then, is a summary of what the housing department must do in the different circumstances after its investigations are complete. It is based on chapter 9 of the Code of Guidance which sets the duties out clearly:

Notification and review

Under s. 184 the housing authority must tell the applicant, in writing and with reasons, the result of its inquiries and what help, if any, it will give. It must give the applicant details of the right to seek, within twenty-one days of notification, a review of the decision (s. 202). The housing authority will make one of the following decisions.

No duty is owed

This may be because the applicant is ineligible (wrong immigration status), or not deemed homeless/threatened with homelessness. Actually a duty is still owed, in the sense that under s. 179 the department must give free advice on homelessness to anyone in its district. The department has a power, not a duty, to assist such a person to obtain housing.

The applicant is homeless/threatened with homelessness but not in priority need

The duty is confined to giving advice and assistance to help the applicant to get or keep housing (s. 192). (A social worker is unlikely to be involved, since your statutory clients are likely to be in priority need.)

The applicant is homeless, is in priority need, but the situation is intentional

The duty is to provide interim accommodation or to secure it from elsewhere for the applicant, but only for such a period as will enable the applicant to find accommodation with the department's assistance (s. 190). Case law under similar legislation before the Housing Act 1996 indicates that an interim period is short, even a few days, and that use of bed and breakfast accommodation is frequent. The Code of Guidance (paragraph 9.30) suggests a period of twenty-eight days, although an authority that did not consider each case individually would be acting unreasonably. The interim accommodation does not, under the legislation, have to be 'suitable', unlike the accommodation provided under the next heading but one. It must be capable of being called accommodation, of course. And it is not good enough if it splits up the family unit (*R v Ealing LBC ex parte Surdonja* (1998), where the local authority split the family between hostels in Ealing and Southall).

The applicant is threatened with homelessness, is in priority need, but the situation is intentional

The duty is to give such advice and assistance as will avert the homelessness (s. 195), failing which the need for interim accommodation (see above) arises.

The applicant is homeless, in priority need, and it is unintentional

A refusal by the applicant to act on the advice offered or to accept the assistance turns the homelessness from unintentional to intentional, with the disastrous consequence that the department can wash its hands of the problem after a period of interim accommodation is secured. (Leaving the problem, almost inevitably, with social services, since priority need plus homelessness probably means a child in need or a vulnerable adult.)

The applicant is unintentionally threatened with homelessness, and in priority need

The department must help prevent the homelessness occurring (s. 195). If it fails, the situation is dealt with under the previous heading. In trying to avert the homelessness it may be that social services can help; for example, a vulnerable person is at risk of eviction from an introductory local authority tenancy because of behaviour that upsets neighbours. Talking to all parties and support to the vulnerable person could make a difference. Box 20.6 sets out the housing duties and powers of the housing authority.

■ Securing accommodation

Local housing authorities may discharge their duty to secure that accommodation is provided for the applicant only by providing accommodation themselves for the applicant, by ensuring that some other person provides it, or by giving such advice and

BOX 20.6 Summary of housing duties and powers

Decision of housing authority	Housing Act 1996	→ Duties → *Powers*
Unintentionally homeless and have a priority need	s. 193	→ Duty to secure accommodation
Unintentionally homeless and no priority need	s. 192	→ Duty to provide advice and assistance → *Power to secure accommodation*
Unintentionally threatened with homelessness and have priority need	s. 195(2)	→ Duty to take reasonable steps to ensure that accommodation does not cease to be available
Unintentionally threatened with homelessness and do not have a priority need	s. 195(5)	→Duty to provide advice and assistance → *Power to take reasonable steps to ensure that accommodation does not cease to be available*
Intentionally homeless and have a priority need	s. 190 (2)	→ Duty to provide advice and assistance and secure accommodation for such period as will give applicant a reasonable period to secure accommodation for him/herself
Intentionally homeless and no priority need	s. 190(3)	→ Duty to provide advice and assistance
Threatened with homelessness intentionally and have a priority need	s. 195(5)	→ Duty to provide advice and assistance
Threatened with homelessness intentionally and no priority need	s. 195(5)	→ Duty to provide advice and assistance

assistance as will enable the applicant to secure accommodation. The housing authority can discharge its duty by offering an allocation of permanent accommodation under Part 6 of the Act (see chapter 18) if the applicant meets its own waiting list criteria. Otherwise, permanent accommodation may be provided by a housing association or a private sector landlord.

The accommodation offered must be suitable for the applicant and his or her household. Refusal of an offer of suitable accommodation will discharge the duty of the housing authority. An applicant must be very clear of the consequences of refusal. Refusing a suitable offer would mean that any future applications would run the risk of failure because of intentionality.

The Act does not specify within what time limit accommodation must be secured for those in priority need who are unintentionally homeless, and it is well known that many people have to wait indefinitely in unsuitable temporary accommodation. The Code (paragraph 20.16) suggests that temporary arrangements should be as short as possible. An applicant in priority need (or a member of their household) who is homeless intentionally can expect no more than temporary accommodation in any event.

Suitability

The accommodation that the local housing authority makes available to eligible applicants under Part 7 of the Housing Act 1996 must be suitable—s. 206. The Code of Guidance makes it clear that 'this applies in respect of all powers and duties . . . including interim duties such as those under s. 188 and s. 200' (para. 12.1). The Code sets out what 'suitable' means in paragraph 12.4: 'The accommodation must be suitable in relation to the applicant and to all members of his or her household who normally reside with him or her, or who might reasonable be expected to reside with him or her . . . Housing authorities should therefore have regard to all the relevant circumstances of the applicant and his or her household. Account will need to be taken of any medical and/or physical needs, and any social considerations relating to the applicant and his or her household that might affect the suitability of accommodation. Any risk of violence or racial harassment must also be taken into account.' Accommodation which is not affordable (see para. 12.7 of the Code of Guidance) or is located at a distance from essential facilities may be found to be unsuitable. An offer of an assured shorthold tenancy may be suitable accommodation in certain circumstances (*R (Bibi) v Newham LBC*).

Social workers liaising with the housing authorities should note the needs of children. Bed and breakfast accommodation is particularly inappropriate for young families and can damage the physical and emotional development of children. Since the 1 April 2004, bed and breakfast accommodation in the private sector is not in most circumstances to be treated as suitable accommodation for longer than 6 weeks where an applicant has 'family commitments'—see SI 2003 No. 3326 and statutory guidance issued by ODPM available on the ODPM web site.

Case examples

To put a homeless Bangladeshi man into housing where there were intolerable levels of racial harassment was not considered an offer of suitable accommodation in *R v Tower Hamlets London Borough ex parte Subhan* (1992). Likewise, to place a woman on the twenty-seventh floor of a tower block when she produced psychiatric evidence that she and her daughter suffered from vertigo was unacceptable (*R v Kensington and Chelsea RLBC ex parte Campbell* (1996)). Sending a family to accommodation a long way from the children's school also was unacceptable (*R v Newham LBC ex parte Ojuri* (1998)) but, in the absence of special needs, a mere change of school was acceptable (*R v South Holland DC ex parte Baxter* (1998)). Sending a homeless family to live in seaside accommodation, applying a policy that took no account of children's schooling needs, was, however, declared unlawful (*R v Newham LBC ex parte Sacupima* (2000)). Expecting a

Nigerian family to live in a house daubed with racist slogans was hard for the housing department to justify (*R v Islington LBC ex parte Okocha* (1997)).

Right to request review of suitability

Applicants may ask for a review of the suitability of the accommodation that is offered to them—s. 202(1) (f)—although the right does not apply to duties to accommodate on an interim basis. An applicant may request a review of the suitability of the accommodation regardless of whether or not she or he accepts the accommodation. This means that suitability may be challenged without the applicant putting at risk his or her right to be accommodated, since a refusal of an offer of suitable accommodation terminates the housing authority's duty. For details of the review process see the next section of this chapter.

■ Challenging the local authority's decision

Internal review

Section 202 of the Housing Act 1996 creates a right to a review by the housing department of certain decisions on homelessness, followed by a right to appeal to the county court. The procedure of the review is prescribed in *The Allocation of Housing and Homelessness (Review Procedures) Regulations 1999* (SI 1999 No. 71). The review must be requested within twenty-one days of the authority's decision. Decisions which may be reviewed are:

- any decision about eligibility for assistance;
- any decision as to what duty if any is owed under ss. 190, 191, 192, 193, and 195;
- local connection decisions;
- suitability.

An applicant should use the review procedure to explain why they are challenging the housing authority's decision and to set out any new information which would be relevant to the decision. The applicant can provide written representations or oral representations. He or she can be represented. We would certainly advise representation by an experienced housing lawyer if at all possible. Housing authorities have the power to accommodate the applicant pending a review. Decisions whether to provide accommodation in these circumstances should be made reasonably.

Appeals to the county court

Section 204 of the Housing Act 1996 provides a right of appeal on a point of law to the county court where the applicant is dissatisfied with the decision on review or the applicant is not notified of the decision on the review within a prescribed time period. Legal advice should be obtained urgently if the decision of the internal review is unfavourable. The appeal must be brought within twenty-one days of the decision. The court may give permission for an appeal to be brought after twenty-one days, but only where it is satisfied that there is good reason for the applicant's delay. The county court can confirm, quash, or vary the decision of the housing authority. The county court can also hear appeals from decisions of housing authorities not to accommodate the applicant pending the appeal.

Human Rights Act compliance

The case of *Runa Begum v Tower Hamlets LBC* (2003) raised interesting points about whether the statutory right of appeal on a point of law was compatible with Article 6 of the European Convention. The facts were that Runa Begum applied to Tower Hamlets for accommodation under Part 7 of the Housing Act 1996. Tower Hamlets accepted a full housing duty and offered her a secure tenancy of a two-bedroom flat on the third floor of a tower block. Runa Begum believed that the accommodation was unsuitable for four reasons. First, the area was drug addicted; secondly, it was racist; thirdly, she had been robbed by two youths near the property; fourthly, her husband, from whom she was estranged, frequently visited the block to see friends. At the internal review, where the facts were examined, Tower Hamlets upheld its own decision. Runa Begum appealed to the county court, where the issue of whether the internal review complied with Article 6 was raised. The House of Lords decided that whilst the internal review was not independent as required by Article 6, the county court appeal was sufficient to ensure that Runa Begum's civil rights were properly determined.

Local government ombudsman

An applicant has the right to complain to the local government ombudsman if she or believes that there has been maladministration (see chapter 5).

Social services responsibilities

This chapter has been primarily concerned with housing authorities' responsibilities towards the homeless, although we have endeavoured to make it clear that housing and social services must cooperate if the problems of homelessness are to be minimised. However, as the case study at the beginning of the chapter indicated social services also have some limited responsibilities and the remainder of this chapter is concerned with the duties of social services departments to people who are ineligible for housing department help or who are found to be intentionally homeless.

Ineligibility

Your duties to the vulnerable and to children are not affected in any way by their immigration status (unless the only reason for there being a need for a service is destitution) and a child in need of protection or services under the Children Act, or an adult under the National Assistance Act, must be catered for whatever their background. The Court of Appeal ruled in the case of *R v Hammersmith and Fulham LBC ex parte M* (1998), in a landmark judgment, that social services must accommodate a person who is financially destitute (in this case an asylum seeker whose entitlement to benefit the Government had just abolished) because that person meets the criterion of being 'by reason of age, illness, disability or any other circumstance ... in need of care and attention which is not otherwise available to them' (National Assistance Act 1948, s. 21). The duty may even be owed to a person who has entered, or remained in, the country illegally. In *R v Brent LBC ex parte D* (1998), the applicant was too ill to leave the country, and the court had to decide between two competing principles: compassion and not benefiting from his own wrongdoing. Compassion won in this case, and social services were ordered to accommodate the applicant, but only until he was fit to return home. This duty, incidentally, cannot be discharged by giving the homeless destitute person cash instead of accommodation (*R v Secretary of State for Health ex parte Hammersmith and Fulham LBC* (1998)).

Intentionally homeless applicants with children

Social services departments also provide a final safety net for homeless applicants with children where it is found that the applicant became homeless intentionally and therefore the housing department does not owe them any duties. The scope of s. 17 of the Children Act 1989 has been provided by s. 116 of the Adoption and Children Act 2002, which amends s. 17 of the Children Act to make it explicit that accommodation can be provided for children in need and their families. Guidance is available from the Department of Health in LAC (2003) 13. However, the House of Lords decision discussed in chapter 10, *R (on the application of G) v Barnet London Borough Council; R (on the application of W) v Lambeth London Borough Council; R (on the application of A) v Lambeth London Borough Council* (2003) makes it clear that s. 17 imposes a general duty upon local authorities and not a specific duty towards particular individuals. This means that a homeless family may be accommodated by social services departments, but they do not have to provide accommodation for the whole family. It is perfectly legitimate for social services, in appropriate circumstances, to take the children of a homeless family into care and leave the parents or carers to fend for themselves.

Duty to cooperate

How do social workers find out that there are homeless children who are not going to be helped by the housing department? They have to rely on the housing department to tell them. Section 213A of the Housing Act 1996 applies where the housing department of a local authority are dealing with a homelessness application from a person whose household includes a child under 18 years of age, and they have reason to believe that the applicant may be either intentionally homeless or not eligible for assistance under Part 7 of the Housing Act 1996. The section requires that housing departments have arrangements in place to ensure that all such applicants are invited to agree to the housing department notifying the social services of the essential facts of their case. The arrangements must also provide that, where the applicant consents, the social services authority is made aware of the essential facts and in due course made aware of the subsequent decision on the homelessness case. If the applicant refuses permission for the housing department to disclose the information to social services then, if the housing department considers that a child is or may be at risk of significant harm then it can disclose information to social services.

Once the social services department is aware that applicants with children may be found intentionally homeless then they may request that the local housing authority provide them with advice and assistance under s. 27 of the Children Act 1989. By s. 213A(5) of the Housing Act 1996 the housing authority must comply with such a request. The Code of Guidance suggests that 'Advice and assistance as is reasonable in the circumstances might include, for example, help with locating suitable accommodation and making an inspection of the property to ensure that it meets adequate standards of fitness and safety.' The duty does not extend to a requirement on the housing authority to provide accommodation for the family. Social services themselves could use their powers under s. 17 of the Children Act to pay for a deposit to secure private rented accommodation or to pay for temporary accommodation whilst the family makes more permanent arrangements.

EXERCISES

1 Katy is 17. She has run away from home because of violence from her step-father. What responsibilities does the housing department have towards her under Part 7 of the Housing Act 1996?

2 Joe is 19. He is sleeping rough. What questions would you need to ask him to find out if he is owed any duties under Part 7 of the Housing Act 1996?

3 Mandy is a single parent with two children under 10. Her landlord, Camlington Council, is seeking a possession order because of rent arrears. She cannot afford the property because she has extensive debts. What advice can you give her? If the local housing authority finds her to be intentionally homeless is there anything you can do to help house the family?

4 Nadim has left his previous accommodation because of racial harassment. Whilst living there he received letters threatening violence towards him. He is 30 and single and has returned home to live with his elderly mother in her one-bedroom flat. He has become very withdrawn and is receiving treatment for depression. Does the local housing authority owe him any duties?

5 George(30) is an alcoholic and suffers from depression. He left his mother's accommodation after disputes with his stepfather. He applied to Camlington Council as homeless. Camlington has decided that his medical condition is not sufficiently serious for him to be considered vulnerable. Can George challenge the local housing authority decision?

COMPANION WEB SITE

 For guidance on how to answer these exercises, visit the companion web site at: www.oup.com/uk/booksites/law

WHERE DO WE GO FROM HERE?

This chapter has endeavoured to provide a description of the legal safety net that is available to some people who are homeless. We hope that we have made clear that it is not everyone who is homeless who will be housed, that the rules are technical and are designed to ration accommodation which is in short supply. Only those who are eligible for housing assistance, are homeless, in priority need, and not intentionally homeless are owed substantial housing duties by housing authorities. We think it is important that social workers understand the law on homelessness to enable them to advise their service users appropriately and also to be able to look after their accommodation needs. We think it is also clear that very many of those who are homeless are likely to be the concern of social services. The closer the cooperation between social services and housing departments the better. Cooperation is going to be critical to the success of local authority homelessness strategies. Each department needs to understand the concerns and priorities of the other. At the moment there is some evidence of mutual misunderstandings. The Shelter web site suggests that secondments, job shadowing, and regular meetings between front-line social workers and housing officers would help both departments better to achieve their goals. What needs to be avoided is both departments 'passing the buck' when it comes to housing the most vulnerable in society.

You will have noted the limited legal responsibilities you have to asylum seekers both in this chapter and throughout the book. The next chapter outlines the law relating to immigration, and asylum. You will see that it is a very complex area of law.

ANNOTED FURTHER READING

For an overview of the government's policy on homelessness see 'More than a Roof', a report into tackling homelessness (ODPM, March 2002).

For an authoritative book which includes the Homelessness Act 2002 see A. Arden and C. Hunter, *Homelessness and Allocations* (Legal Action Group, 2002).

For a more critical approach read D. Cowan, *Homelessness: The (In-)appropriate Applicant* (Ashgate, 1997).

An interesting article is I. Loveland, 'Cathy Sod Off! The End of Homelessness Legislation', [1994] Journal of Social Welfare Law 367.

For an overview of the House of Lords decision on the limits on the duty on social services authorities to accommodate homeless families see:

S. Rai, 'Accommodating Families with Children—The Final Chapter', Journal of Housing Law (Sweet & Maxwell 2004) p. 21.

21 Nationality, immigration, and asylum issues

CASE STUDY

R (on the application of J) v Enfield London Borough Council (2002)

H was a citizen of Ghana. She had overstayed her visa. She also had HIV. She had no means of supporting herself and her daughter. Her local authority said they had no power to provide her with accommodation or to support her, so she applied for judicial review, claiming a breach of Article 8 of the European Convention (right to family life). The council conceded the breach but said that it still had no power, because the National Assistance Act 1948 and the Children Act 1989 explicitly prohibits providing support to an asylum seeker if the sole purpose is to alleviate destitution.

The court agreed with the local authority that the Acts were clear and gave no power to provide services merely to relieve financial destitution, even if this breached the Convention. However, the court found a loophole. Section 2 of the Local Government Act 2000 provided not only a way round this but—to avoid breach of Article 8—a duty. Section 2 reads as follows:

(1) Every local authority are to have a power to do anything which they consider is likely to achieve any one or more of the following objects—

   . . .

   (b) the promotion or improvement of the social well-being of their area . . .

(2) The power under subsection (1) may be exercised in relation to or for the benefit of . . .

   (b) all or any persons resident or present in the local authority's area.

This was held to apply even though s. 3 of the 2000 Act goes on to prohibit s. 1 being used wherever another statute prohibits the proposed action.

OVERVIEW AND OBJECTIVES

A social worker has statutory duties, underpinned by professional codes and personal values, to support the most vulnerable members of society. The welfare state, with its strengths and imperfections, is society's collective response to poverty and vulnerability. Refugees and immigrants are likely to be vulnerable. These three propositions ought, logically, to lead to social workers having significant roles to play in helping refugees and other immigrants, particularly in light of the increasing numbers of vulnerable people coming to the UK because of disasters and wars elsewhere.

Unfortunately, questions of immigration in general, and asylum in particular, have been allowed by the media and even encouraged by many politicians to become politically charged and, since 9/11, even confused with issues of terrorism. One response from government has been to gradually restrict the services it allows the welfare state, including social services departments, to provide. The case study above reveals the type of conflict that can arise as a result. Although the party to the case was the unfortunate asylum seeker, the real dispute was between an agency of national government, the National Asylum Support Service (NASS), and an agency of local government (Birmingham social services).

This area of law is confusing and complex. As a social worker you may encounter adults or children who do not have an unrestricted right to stay in the UK. To what extent will the lack of this right limit the services you or other state agencies can provide?

Our main objective in this chapter is to explain the extent to which your statutory duties to provide community care services and services to children in need can still be carried out. The main restriction on helping vulnerable people whose immigration status is restricted is that you cannot provide economic support if its only purpose is to relieve destitution. The other main restriction is that no service can be provided to an adult former asylum seeker once they have been directed to leave the UK.

In order to achieve this main objective, we aim to provide a broad understanding of immigration and nationality law, so that you can have a shared understanding of the issues some of the service users you work with will face. You may be in a position to point them to services where they can obtain advice on their immigration status and rights to further services.

The chapter provides an overview of the following three topics:

- Who is subject to immigration control for entering in or remaining in the UK;

- Who can claim, and the procedure for claiming, asylum;

- Welfare services and social service obligations in relation to these categories.

You should not try yourself to provide immigration advice, for immigration advisers have to meet standards laid down by the Office of the Immigration Services Commissioner. Anyone giving immigration advice must be accredited, either by the Commission directly or through recognized professional bodies (in particular the Law Society and the Bar). In fact apart from educational institutions, who can advise prospective students, anyone giving immigration advice for reward commits a criminal offence (Immigration and Asylum Act 1999, s. 91). The Legal Services Commission has attempted to ensure nationwide availability of publicly funded advice, and the best way to access this is through their Just Ask web site, **www.justask.org.uk/** (which has advice in several languages). Advice and support services on immigration are also available through The Refugee Council, **www.refugeecouncil.org.uk/**, the Joint Council for the Welfare of Immigrants, **www.jcwi.org.uk/** or the UK Immigration Advisory Service, **www.iasuk.org/**.

We use the term UK law in this chapter, because there is no separation of English, Scottish, Welsh, or Northern Irish nationality. We will refer on occasion to the Immigration Rules, made by the Home Office. These are not made by statutory instrument, and do not have a date. They are frequently amended.

▓ Who is subject to immigration control?

The following do not require leave to remain:

• a British Citizen;

• a Citizen of the European Economic Area;

• a person with right of abode.

Everyone else is subject to immigration control, and this status affects the right to work and the right to receive many welfare services.

British Citizens can enter and remain in the UK without control

The law determining who is a British Citizen is complex, and our summary does not claim to be complete. The complexity is caused in particular by the UK's history of empire and by changing political attitude to citizens of former colonies. Until 1983, British Citizens were called Citizens of the United Kingdom and Colonies. This was an outdated term, for such citizenship gave some of its citizens restricted or even no rights actually to live in the UK. This was replaced in 1983 with British Citizenship; it permits British Citizens to live in the UK, and it excludes all others (aliens and citizens of Commonwealth countries alike) unless they have received leave to enter or possess the right to enter under European Community Law (Treaty of Rome 1957, Articles 17 and 18).

British Citizenship confers civic rights, in particular the right to vote (Representation of the People Act 2000, ss. 1 and 2). Interestingly citizens of Commonwealth nations and Irish nationals who are settled here can also vote. But aliens (anyone else) cannot vote, even if settled in the UK with a right of abode, or as European Economic Area citizens, they enjoy the freedom to come and go.

Box 21.1 summarizes the ways to become a British citizen, which is set out in the British Nationality Act 1981 (BNA) ss. 1–9.

Citizens of the European Economic Area

European Community law gives the right to free movement, residence, and work to its Member States' citizens, and to many other European states' citizens.

Leave to enter and remain

Anyone else is subject to immigration control. Leave to enter will be granted at the point of entry by an immigration officer, or in advance by an overseas embassy or High Commission. Leave to remain once in the UK will be granted by the Home Office. Any leave given may be time limited or open ended, and conditions may be imposed (for example a requirement to register with the police under s. 1 of the 1971 Immigration Act). Some overseas citizens are known as 'visa nationals'. They come from a list of countries selected because their citizens are perceived as potential economic migrants. A visa national must present a valid visa on arrival in the UK.

BOX 21.1 How to acquire British Citizenship

By birth or adoption in the UK if at the time:

- mother or father a British Citizen; or
- mother or father settled in the UK ('settled' is defined below).

By birth or adoption in the UK if stateless and settled in UK for five years.

By descent if born before 21 May 2002 and:

- mother or father is/was a British Citizen by birth (or by descent if in the government service); or
- grandparent is/was a British Citizen by birth and citizenship was registered within twelve months of birth.

By descent if mother, father, or grandparent is/was British Citizen by birth and citizenship registered before age 18 or after living in UK for three years.

By right of abode if already acquired before 1 January 1983 and:

- citizen of UK and Colonies and right of abode was acquired (or acquired by a parent) through birth, adoption, naturalization, or registration in the UK (some restrictions if acquired by a woman through marriage);
- citizen of UK and Colonies settled in UK for five years as at 1 January 1983;
- Commonwealth Citizen born to/ adopted by parent born/adopted in UK.

By naturalization if:

- settled in UK for five years (three for a spouse); requirements include knowledge of English/ Welsh/Gaelic and oath of allegiance.

The Immigration Act 1971, Immigration and Asylum Act 1999, and Immigration Rules spell out the requirements for leave to enter or remain. Some of the criteria for entry and leave to remain are summarized in Box 21.2 below. In addition to those we have listed, there are some additional general requirements. These include satisfying the Home Office that the person will not rely on public funds for economic support (which does not prevent use of community care services, child care services, state education, or health care). Decisions are discretionary, so meeting the criteria is not guaranteed to result in admission/leave to remain.

Appeal against a refusal is to an Immigration Adjudicator, and then to an Immigration Appeal Tribunal (shortly to be merged into a single process).

The Home Secretary can exclude or, if here, deport a person and their dependants if he deems this to be conducive to the public good. He has additional powers to remove acquired British Citizenship from suspected terrorists, which would then enable them to be expelled. (He cannot do this for citizens born here or entitled to it by descent.) Any leave given to enter can be rescinded or restricted if a person has not complied with a condition of leave, such as the condition not to have recourse to public funds.

BOX 21.2 Leave to enter or remain under Immigration Act 1971

No sponsor required:

1. *Visitor not intending to work*: must be self supporting and able to return after six months (though may be permitted to stay on to study, to work (Commonwealth Citizen and parent or grandparent born in UK); or following marriage or cohabitation with person with right of abode);

2. *Student*: must demonstrate means of support and intention to leave after course;

3. *Worker with work permit*, or exempted from having one (e.g. journalist);

4. *Entrepreneur* who can invest at least £200,000 in the business.

Sponsor (settled in UK with leave to remain) required:

1. *Fiancé(e)*: must have met and intend to live together; marriage must take place within six months. May bring in own child(ren) if compelling family reasons, and no one outside UK could provide care;

2. *Dependent spouse*: leave initially for twelve months, which will not be renewed if marriage breaks down* (unless court order or social services letter evidences domestic violence†);

3. *Dependent parent, grandparent*: if no other support available outside UK;

4. *Other dependent relative*: if exceptional compassionate reasons exist;

5. *Parent wishing to exercise access (sic) to child in UK*: must produce evidence of right to access, normally UK court order.

Child under 18‡:

1. Prospective adopted child where natural parents genuinely unable to bring up child and adoptive parents settled in UK;

2. Both parents (or one, if one dead) settled in UK, or other compelling family reason to admit child;

3. Child born in UK on or after 1 January 1983 and British Citizen (allowed to have recourse to public funds);

4. Child previously settled in UK returns after not more than two years: may enter to remain with parents or where local authority has full parental responsibility;

5. Child previously settled in UK returns after more than two years abroad: may re-enter for no more than three months and only if no-one outside UK can care for child.

* Evidence of the circumstances of the breakdown will not normally make any difference. In *Secretary of State for the Home Department v Patel (Veena)* (1992) the husband informed the immigration authorities he no longer wished to be married. She was refused leave to re-enter the UK after a holiday in India, even though pregnant with the husband's child.

† Even where a court accepts that domestic violence has caused the breakdown, there are strict requirements before the victim is allowed to remain: *R (on the application of McKenzie) v Secretary of State for the Home Department* (2001).

‡ Home Office policy is currently not to remove a child under 16 unless satisfied that adequate arrangements are in place to care for child.

Applications for a work permit are decided by the Home Office and refusals are not subject to appeal (though judicial review of alleged procedural irregularities may be available, as with all administrative decisions—see chapter 5). Leave to remain may be extended; normally this is granted to a person who has worked in the UK for at least four years, and to their dependant spouse and children. We do not address either of these issues in further detail, and specialist immigration advice should be obtained by any person needing to determine their status.

Removal from the UK

A British Citizen cannot be removed, though a person who acquired citizenship through a false statement can have it removed. Anyone who is not a British Citizen can be removed if the Home Secretary deems it to be in the public interest (though, if the decision is an irrational one, an application for judicial review can be made to the High Court). Criminal courts which convict a person who is not a British Citizen can make a deportation recommendation.

A person who enters without leave is deemed an illegal immigrant and can be removed summarily (Immigration Act 1971, s. 3(5)). However a person claiming asylum is not an illegal immigrant, even though she or he has entered without leave. All those who claim asylum are entitled to a fair determination of their claim. The law does not recognise the word 'bogus'. As we see below, the claim for asylum has to be determined before removal is permitted (though the 2002 Immigration Nationality and Asylum Act, s. 93 provides authority for an asylum seeker to be removed to a third country before having a right of appeal against a refusal. This section is not yet in force).

If a person is given unlimited leave to remain in the UK they have a 'right of abode' (and under the Immigration Nationality and Asylum Act 2002 may be required to obtain a certificate to confirm this right). Such a person is not subject to the restrictions on the provision of welfare services set out in Box 21.3 below.

Immigration control, human rights, and race discrimination

Inevitably a decision to exclude a person from the UK will impact on that person's human rights, for example the right to family life, which is a right recognized in English law through the Human Rights Act (see chapter 2). Inevitably immigration decisions adversely affect greater numbers of people of non-British origin than those of British origin. White people are more likely to have been born in the UK, descended from those with British Citizenship, or to be citizens of the European Economic Area (see above) and are therefore subject to immigration control in smaller numbers than those of, say, African or Asian origin. How do the grand principles of the Human Rights Act and the Race Relations Act apply? The answer is that there is little impact.

Let us first illustrate this with a pre-HRA case. In 1996, the then Government withdrew social security entitlement from asylum seekers. They did this by way of regulations, using powers to make regulations granted to the government under the Social Security Contributions and Benefits Act 1992. In *R v Secretary of State for Social Security ex parte Joint Council for the Welfare of Immigrants* the Joint Council for the Welfare of

Immigrants challenged the legality of the regulations, on the basis that they were *ultra vires*, meaning the content went beyond the power granted to the government. In the Court of Appeal Simon Brown LJ and the majority of the Court agreed with JWCI that the regulations should be declared illegal, saying:

> [T]hese regulations, for some genuine asylum seekers at least, must now be regarded as rendering [the rights to claim asylum under the Geneva Convention]nugatory. Either that, or the 1996 regulations necessarily contemplate for some a life so destitute that, to my mind, no civilised nation can tolerate it. So basic are the human rights here at issue, that it cannot be necessary to resort to the Convention for the Protection of Human Rights and Fundamental Freedoms . . . to take note of their violation. Nearly 200 years ago Lord Ellenborough CJ in *R v Eastbourne (Inhabitants)* (1803) said:
>
> > As to there being no obligation for maintaining poor foreigners before the statutes ascertaining the different methods of acquiring settlements, the law of humanity, which is anterior to all positive laws, obliges us to afford them relief, to save them from starving . . .
>
> True, no obligation arises under art 24 of the 1951 convention until asylum seekers are recognised as refugees. But that is not to say that up to that point their fundamental needs can properly be ignored. I do not accept they can. Rather, I would hold it unlawful to alter the benefit regime so drastically as must inevitably not merely prejudice, but on occasion defeat, the statutory right of asylum seekers to claim refugee status.
>
> If and when that status is recognised, refugees become entitled under art 24 to benefit rights equivalent to nationals. Not for one moment would I suggest that prior to that time their rights are remotely the same; only that some basic provision should be made, sufficient for genuine claimants to survive and pursue their claims.

The Court of Appeal ruled that in making regulations certain basic principles—common humanity requiring asylum seekers to have the means of support, the absence of which would make the right to asylum ineffective—are automatically a part of the law, a lens through which the regulations could be viewed. This was a case decided before the Human Rights Act, but you will note the statement that English law assumes such fundamental rights to exist without a reference to the European Convention on Human Rights even being required. But, as you may recall from Part 1, there is a doctrine of parliamentary supremacy which even the Human Rights Act and the European Convention on Human Rights cannot override. Through clear primary legislation—which means Acts of Parliament—any law can be enacted. And that is what happened in response to this case: the Government used Parliament to bring in a new Act to achieve the desired effect of removing welfare benefit entitlement from asylum seekers. Where wording is clear—as it was in the new legislation—courts must follow it and not conscience or international conventions. But that is not the end of the struggle between courts and Parliament over what the Lord Justice had called the duty of a 'civilized nation'.

Let us complete this history of welfare support entitlement for asylum seekers, before returning to look at the impact of the right to family life and the race discrimination legislation on immigration law. The Government overruled the *JWCI* decision on entitlement to benefits through primary legislation, the Asylum and Immigration Act 1996, again leaving destitute asylum seekers with no welfare benefit entitlement. But, as you have seen in chapter 16, the National Assistance Act 1948, Part III, requires a local authority to provide accommodation to those who are unable to fend for themselves, whether for reasons of disability 'or otherwise'. Although the Government—and indeed several local authorities—were not keen on this being used as a way round the withdrawal of benefits, the courts ruled that in the absence of clearly worded statutory prohibitions, existing legislation could and must be used to support asylum seekers if the alternative is destitution. In *R v Westminster City Council ex parte A* (1998), the Court of Appeal echoed its own sentiments in the earlier *JWCI* case. Westminster and other social services authorities were refusing to provide Part III accommodation. This is how Lord Woolf described the operation of the 1948 Act, in light of the withdrawal of benefits in 1996:

> What they are entitled to claim (and this is the result of the 1996 Act) is that they can as a result of their predicament after they arrive in this country reach a state where they qualify under the subsection because of the effect upon them of the problems under which they are labouring. In addition to the lack of food and accommodation is to be added their inability to speak the language, their ignorance of this country and the fact they have been subject to the stress of coming to this country in circumstances which at least involve their contending to be refugees. Inevitably the combined effect of these factors with the passage of time will produce one or more of the conditions specifically referred to in section 21(1)(a) [of the 1948 Act]. It is for the authority to decide whether they qualify.

Destitute asylum seekers—alongside anyone destitute and without alternative means of support for any other reason—continued to be provided with the means of survival under the NAA until the implementation of the National Asylum Support Service (NASS), which we deal with below. NASS is now the only permitted government-funded mechanism for addressing the economic needs—but not other welfare needs such as health education and community care—of asylum seekers.

What these two cases show is that courts can apply human rights and humanitarian principles to difficult cases. However it is governments, using their control of Parliament, not courts, which seem determined to have the last word; and the last word—surprisingly for a government which brought in human rights legislation—is that asylum seekers who fail to apply for asylum at the first opportunity can be left destitute. We will discuss later the inevitable and so far successful challenges to this new attempt to leave some refugees without publicly funded support.

How has the HRA itself impacted on the way in which immigration decisions are made? Let us illustrate the problem with reference to the right to family life under Article 8. In the case of *R (on the application of Samaroo) v Secretary of State for the Home Department* (2001) Mr Samaroo, a native of Guyana, had lived lawfully in the UK for twelve years; his close family members, his children and step-children, and his wife's family were in the UK. But he had been convicted of a serious drugs offence, and on release was due to be deported on the recommendation of the trial court. There are two conflicting policy objectives here: the right to family life, which would be disrupted even if his family followed him to Guyana, for in that country they would be strangers; and the desire of the Home Secretary to deal firmly with serious drugs offences. Dyson LJ refused to overrule the deportation order, and expressed the Court of Appeal's reasoning as follows:

> Fair balance involves comparing the weight to be given to the wider interests of the community with the weight to be given to an individual's Convention rights. Some rights are regarded as of especial importance and should for that reason be accorded particular weight. Broadly speaking, the more serious the interference with a fundamental right and the graver its effects, the greater the justification that will be required for the interference.

In relation to human rights, in summary, the legitimate objectives of Government in maintaining its governmental role, such as a firm and fair immigration regime and an effective criminal justice system, will—if reviewed by the courts—be balanced against individual rights under the Human Rights Act.

How does race relations law apply to immigration? (For more detail than we have given you may wish to turn to the Immigration Law Practitioners Association, **www.ilpa.org.uk/publications/rractintro.htm**, whose guidance on the 'race exemption' for immigration law provides a readable overview.) You may perhaps recall from chapter 2 that the Race Relations Act 1976 (RRA) does not prevent all forms of discrimination on racial grounds. Under s. 71, discrimination authorised by statute is not unlawful. The whole immigration regime is statutory, including any discrimination resulting from restrictions on rights of entry and abode. Therefore, if the statute is clear any resulting discrimination cannot be unlawful.

However, statute purports to limit, without preventing, discrimination in immigration decisions on racial grounds. How does this work? Is it just rhetoric? We saw in chapter 2 that public bodies must not discriminate on grounds of colour, race, nationality, ethnic or national origins (RRA, s. 19B). But for immigration decisions this prohibition is reduced by s. 19D to not discriminating on grounds of colour, race, and ethnic origin. Discrimination on nationality and national origins remains lawful. According to Lord Lester, protesting against this diluted form of wording in the Parliamentary debates in 1999, when the RRA was amended:

> Unlike discrimination on grounds of nationality or place or residence, discrimination based on ethnic or national origins is as much racial discrimination as is discrimination based on colour or race, as the definition of racial discrimination in Article 1 of the United Nations Convention on the Elimination of All Forms of Discrimination 1966 makes crystal clear. Such discrimination involves treating one individual less favourably than another for what is not chosen by them but for what is innate in them at birth—their genetic inheritance—whether as ethnic Jews, Roma gypsies or Hong Kong Indians. It is as invidious and unfair as is discrimination based on the colour of a person's skin. That is why the Race Relations Act 1976 forbids direct discrimination on any of those racial grounds, apart from a range of clearly defined exceptions.

There is little case law on the effect of s.19D and its attempt to stop immigration officers discriminating on grounds of race. The case of *European Roma Rights Centre and others v Immigration Officer at Prague Airport and another* (2004) was discussed in chapter 2. Far more Roma than non-Roma were detained for long interviews at Prague airport and ultimately refused entry. While the Court of Appeal, ignoring the principles of indirect discrimination (see chapter 2) said that this was not discrimination, the House of Lords recognized that the selective screening was unlawful, as Roma people were almost always the victims.

It seems to us inevitable that if there are to be immigration criteria, however phrased, discrimination on racial or ethnic grounds will occur. When you look through the criteria in Box 21.1 or Box 21.2 for granting rights of entry or for grant-ing British Citizenship, you will notice that in certain situations it is helpful that a parent or grandparent lived in the UK or had British Citizenship. This is direct dis-crimination based on national origins (which, as we have just seen, is lawful in immi-gration); but it is hard to avoid the conclusion that it is also indirect discrimination based on racial or ethnic origins (since it affects some racial or ethnic groups more than it affects others). If this were employment or service discrimination the victims would have the right to be treated in the same way as the majority ethnic, national, or racial group. But immigration statute permits, indeed requires, such discrimination.

Asylum

We start with a look at who is entitled to asylum. Welfare support for those subject to immigration control, which includes asylum seekers, is dealt with below.

The UK has accepted through international treaty—the 1951 (Geneva) Convention Relating to the Status of Refugees—particular obligations to any person who has a well founded fear of persecution on grounds of race, religion, nationality, membership of a particular social group, or political opinion. Such a person should be granted asylum if removal would require him or her to go to a country where his or her life or freedom would be threatened. (A country in the European Union or one of those listed under the 2002 Nationality Immigration and Asylum Act, s. 94, is automatically considered a safe country, and a person with the right to live there cannot apply for asylum, whatever the circumstances in that country. We noted in chapter 2 the comments of the Parlia-mentary Human Rights Committee, that this legislation is likely to breach the Conven-tion rights (Article 3) not to suffer inhuman treatment and (Article 6) to have a fair hearing.) Once a person has made a claim to asylum under the Geneva Convention there is, with limited exception, no power to remove the person or her/his dependent spouse or child until the claim has been determined (Immigration and Asylum Act 1999, s. 15). The exceptions are:

- the Geneva Convention allows expulsion if he or she is a danger to the security of the state;
- the 1999 Act allows a person to be removed to another EU country which accepts it has the responsibility under the Convention, or to a non-EU country if the Home Secretary can show that that country will comply with the Convention.

Decisions on asylum claims are made by the Home Office, with a right of appeal under the Immigration and Asylum Act 1999, s. 69, to an immigration adjudicator (unless asylum is refused on grounds of national security). Under the 2002 Act, the Home Secretary may require the asylum seeker to return to any third country through which he or she passed and to appeal from there.

The claim to asylum can be made on arrival or later. (There are powers in the Nationality Asylum and Immigration Act 2002 to establish overseas centres where asylum can be claimed before arrival in the UK.) It can be made by a child as well as by an adult, in which case the Refugee Council must immediately be notified by the Home Office for the purpose of safeguarding the child's welfare (but welfare is not paramount when reaching a decision on the child's asylum application as it would be under Part 1 of the Children Act 1989). Those claiming asylum can be required to report to the police under powers brought in in the Nationality Asylum and Immigration Act 2002, and for the first fourteen days, to live at a specified address in order to receive an induction programme (s. 70). Unless they have independent means, an asylum seeker can be required to live at an accommodation centre as a condition of obtaining support (see below).

▨ Welfare support for those subject to immigration control

Some people are explicitly excluded from some of the services of the welfare state because of their immigration status. The legislation makes this explicit, as we are about to see. (A person who has leave to remain subject to a condition not to rely on public funds risks expulsion of themselves and their dependants by applying for welfare benefits—though this does not cover non-economic benefits such as community care, health, education, and support for children under the Children Act.)

Economic support for asylum seekers

Once accepted for asylum the person has indefinite leave to remain and there can be no restriction on availability of welfare services. But before achieving refugee status, the right of an asylum seeker to use the welfare state for their economic support alongside other members of society has been progressively eroded through legislation over the past ten years. Such state-provided economic support for asylum seekers as exists is now set out in the Immigration and Asylum Act 1999.

The essence of the economic support regime for those without other means of support has the following characteristics:

(a) compulsory dispersal;

(b) maintenance at below income support levels;

(c) prohibiting social services providing services to relieve destitution;

(d) withdrawal of support for asylum seekers who fail to make their claim at the first opportunity (this does not apply where the asylum seeker has a dependent child or has special needs); and

(e) power to insist that an asylum seeker live in an accommodation centre to obtain support.

Dispersal to where the Home Office directs (based on agreements with local authorities and availability of housing in those areas) is a precondition of asylum support. There is no statutory right to be dispersed to where the asylum seeker has personal or family ties, and facilities in the South East are stretched. But completely to ignore the person's circumstances could be a breach of the Human Rights Act. Thus in *R (on the application of Blackwood) v Secretary of State for the Home Department* (2003) the asylum seeker had, unusually, been brought up, educated, worked, and had a child in London, and to send her out of London where she had family support was a breach of her right to family life under Article 8. Although the regime assumes cooperation between Home Office and local authorities, the Act allows the Government to direct a local authority to receive and accommodate asylum seekers. We assume that, by the time the social worker encounters asylum seeker support, dispersal has already taken place and that we do not need to discuss it further.

The NASS system

Part IV of the Act establishes a support regime separate both from the welfare benefit system and from the safety net for those who are otherwise destitute provided by the Children Act or the National Assistance Act. (This does not mean, as we shall see, that social welfare legislation has no relevance to asylum seekers in need of services such as community care, services for children, health, or education; it means that social welfare provision cannot be used to take asylum seekers out of destitution, for the asylum support system has the sole statutory responsibility for doing this.) Asylum seekers under 18 who are not accompanied are the exception: they are not provided for by the asylum support system and social services must deal with economic as well as other needs of such children under the Children Act s. 17 as children in need.

The scheme for asylum support is the National Asylum Support Scheme (NASS) established under Part VI of the 1999 Act. Asylum seekers are entitled to NASS support if they—taken together with any dependent children or disabled adults—are likely to be destitute. Destitution means they do not have adequate accommodation, including shared and temporary accommodation, and/or they are not able to meet essential living needs. 'Adequate' and 'essential' are defined in restrictive terms: for example, toys are non-essentials, as are travel and entertainment. For accommodation to be adequate the standard is no higher than is to be expected of temporary accommodation; and the preference of the asylum seeker is not to be taken into account in deciding its adequacy. (However, the Human Rights Act still applies—asylum seekers' right to family life, for example, is no different from that of any other group of people, so family separation could be challenged.)

The support which the Home Office provides, under s. 96, amounts to providing accommodation and meeting other needs to a level which the Secretary of State considers adequate. (What is adequate may, exceptionally, be open to challenge in a court. For example, in *R (on the application of T and another) v Secretary of State for the Home Department* (2002) NASS was ordered to provide milk where a breast-feeding mother would otherwise risk passing HIV to her baby.) Payment of support by way of money is allowed (following a three-year experiment with vouchers instead of cash). Support is capped at around 70 per cent of the income support equivalent level. Section 99 allows the Secretary of State to pay local authorities to provide the support to the asylum seekers. Support includes accommodation; this is provided by the local authority, which must provide information on request so that the Home Office can decide on dispersals. The Secretary of State is forbidden to take into account the preference of the asylum seeker in determining where the person will live.

If support is refused or it is provided only upon conditions, the applicant can appeal to the Asylum Support Adjudicator. Assistance for asylum seekers in establishing support and bringing appeals if necessary is available—though stretched—through a national network of refugee support services (details on **www.refugee.org.uk/links**).

Changes to asylum support under the Immigration Asylum and Nationality Act 2002

The Act introduces accommodation centres, initially on a trial basis, to accommodate and provide services for asylum-seekers and their dependants on one site. Once the scheme is introduced, asylum-seekers who are eligible for support may be offered places in accommodation centres. Those who refuse, leave, or breach their conditions of residence will then lose the right to asylum support. (It does not affect those asylum seekers who do not need support.) Unless sufficient accommodation centres exist for all asylum seekers to be offered this support, the NASS support regime will continue alongside accommodation centres.

The Act gives the Home Office the power to use the new centres as the sole vehicle for providing welfare services to asylum seekers and their dependants, in place of either NASS (see above), the local authority (see below), or other welfare agencies (such as the NHS, not considered in this chapter). These will include food and other essential items, money, assistance with transport and expenses, healthcare, and education and training. This means, on implementation of s. 36, if the refugee centre has educational facilities the deplorable implementation of a regime of segregation of children of asylum seekers from normal state education—though in special circumstances the accommodation centre will be able to request the education authority to provide educational facilities.

Perhaps the most striking aspect of the legislation and regulations made under it is the withdrawal of all support from an asylum seeker who does not claim asylum at the first reasonable opportunity. As we see below, this has been repeatedly and successfully challenged in court. This is despite the statistics which show that those who claim later than the port of entry are in fact more likely to succeed (and that their claim to asylum is therefore more likely to be genuine).

Availability of economic and other welfare services for asylum seekers subject to immigration control

A person who is subject to immigration control is a person who is not a British Citizen and who does not have indefinite leave to remain. This includes an asylum seeker.

The restrictions on welfare services available to a person subject to immigration control are summarized in Box 20.3. It is important to be aware that except for 'failed' adult
asylum seekers the restrictions do not in fact mean that the provisions of legislation
such as the Children Act or the National Assistance Act are altogether irrelevant to
a person subject to immigration control. (A person ceases to be an asylum seeker if
their claim is refused. They are often called failed asylum seekers. Eventually a removal
direction will be issued, and at that point the rights to support of any kind virtually
cease. This category of people, for whom the welfare state is a closed book, are worse off
than anyone else, and are considered at the end of the chapter.)

Social services departments continue to have duties to children in need or adults
assessed as being in need. Where such duties are restricted is in the fact that the services
are not allowed to be used just to provide economic support. This is not a straightforward issue—we have trouble making sense of it, as lawyers, and even more trouble
in terms of the ethics; so partly to demonstrate that you are not alone if you find it
difficult, and partly to throw some light onto the area, so that you are not deterred from

---

 **BOX 21.3 Restrictions on local authority and other welfare services to people subject
to immigration control with no right of abode (under the 1999 Immigration and Asylum
Act or amendments to other Acts)**

The following cannot be provided:

- Non-contributory welfare benefits such as child support;
- Any of the following where the need for the service is *solely* brought about by destitution:
- residential care, prevention of illness, care of the ill, and after-care services under the
  National Assistance Act;
- services for old people under Health and Public Services Act 1968;
- general housing assistance or tenancies under Housing Act 1996 (though asylum seekers
  who are homeless can apply to the local authority under a recent relaxation of the Housing Act
  1996).
- Assistance to accompanied children under the Children Act, s. 17, so long as the Home Office
  is providing support for the children under NASS (but, if withdrawn or inadequate, social
  services departments' powers and duties are not reduced). Unaccompanied children in need
  must be supported under s. 17, and this explicitly includes providing accommodation.
- All Children Act or NASS services to overstayers and illegal immigrants.

Under the 2002 Act, s. 54, social services departments must additionally report to the Home
Office claims for services under National Assistance Act 1948 to community care, Children Act
1989 services to children, Health Service and Public Health Act 1968 services to elderly people
if brought by the following:

- Failed asylum seekers who are not cooperating with removal directions;
- Non-asylum seekers unlawfully in UK;
- Refugees granted asylum in another country;
- Dependants of any of these people.

providing services that are available and which your department may have a legal obligation to provide, we will at the end of the chapter consider examples of problems from the case law that these restrictions on services have thrown up.

Destitution—how the courts view the role of social service departments

The Government's 1998 White Paper, which led to the 1999 Act, stated at paragraph 8.23:

> The 1948 Act will be amended to make clear that social services departments should not carry the burden of looking after healthy and able-bodied asylum-seekers. This role will fall to the new national support machinery.

But is the result as clear-cut as the government intended? We have set out below a summary of recent cases where social services work overlaps with immigration law. (The case law has mainly arisen in relation to asylum seekers, but potentially the same issues could arise from any other persons subject to immigration control needing a combination of economic support and community care or child services.) If one principle emerges, it is that, whatever a person's immigration status, there is no restriction on the social services department's obligation to assess the need for services for a child in need (Children Act, s. 17), child protection (Children Act, Parts 3 and 4), or community care (National Health Service and Community Care Act 1990, s. 47). This was clearly stated in *R v Wandsworth LBC ex parte. O* (2000): immigration status is irrelevant except for the purpose of explaining any destitution (which it is then not the social service's task to address). And it is worth being aware that, while NASS and not social services have responsibility for relief of problems arising from destitution, destitution cannot be ignored in a full assessment of need for community care: *Murua v Crodydon LBC* (2002).

The first of our cases is *R (on the application of Westminster City Council) v National Asylum Support Service* (2002). A Kuwaiti asylum seeker needed treatment for spinal cancer. The local authority assessed her needs for accommodation—as it must—under the National Assistance Act 1948, s. 21, and as a result provided her with accommodation close to the hospital, with wheelchair access and room for a carer. But should NASS or the local authority pay? The local authority argued that NASS should pay under its obligation to support 'destitute' asylum seekers, which we have examined already. NASS argued that this was the responsibility of the local authority under s. 21(1)(a) of the National Assistance Act 1948, which requires that the local authority must provide residential accommodation to those in need of care and attention not otherwise available to them. NASS further argued that section 21(1A), which provides that such accommodation may not be provided to a person whose need for care and attention has arisen 'solely' because he or she was destitute, does not prevent the local authority from carrying out its statutory duty to assess and provide residential accommodation.

The ruling of the House of Lords made clear that the local authority's obligation to provide and fund community care services is not diminished by the status of the asylum seeker. Her need for this care had not arisen solely because she was destitute (which

NASS and NASS alone would have had to meet), but also because she was ill. Only able-bodied destitute asylum seekers were actually excluded from the provision of services by local authorities under s. 21(1)(a).

R (on the application of Mani) v Lambeth LBC (2003) shows that the law is becoming quite settled. M was an asylum seeker. He had a disability limiting his mobility, and claimed a need for care and attention under the National Assistance Act 1948 s. 21. The Court of Appeal held that he was entitled to s. 21 support to meet the needs resulting from this disability. The House of Lords has refused leave to appeal, so this case is now settled law.

One problem that can arise is the passing of the buck between NASS and social services. *O v Haringey LBC* (2004) illustrates this horribly. Ms O was an asylum seeker with HIV. She had two children. The Court of Appeal said the local authority had a duty to her as a disabled person under s. 21, and must support and accommodate her. But the children had no disability and the authority was barred from supporting them, as their only problem was destitution. They should not be left destitute, and their support was the responsibility of NASS. The Court insisted that NASS and the authority should work together to agree the best support arrangements for the family as a whole—the authority to house the family and NASS to meet the costs as far as the children were concerned. So social workers need good working relations with NASS.

The next case example reiterates the need for the social services department to meet the needs of a child in need. It is *R (on the application of Ouji) v Secretary of State for the Home Department* (2002). An asylum seeker's 13-year-old daughter suffered from a range of disabilities including incontinence, requiring additional bedding. The Children Act 1989, s. 17, provides that social services have a duty to provide support, since such a child is a 'child in need' (see chapter 10). The standard support available through NASS did not meet these types of need. The Divisional Court held that the cost fell not on NASS but Birmingham social services.

The following case is more complex, and illustrates the problems the Government faces through its emphasis on human rights, on the one hand, and ever tougher immigration laws on the other. It is *R (on the application of Q and others) v Secretary of State for the Home Department* (2003). Section 55 of the Nationality Immigration and Asylum Act 2002 denies asylum support to any adult where 'the Secretary of State is not satisfied that the claim was made as soon as reasonably practicable after the person's arrival in the United Kingdom'. But s. 55 goes on to say—in what Philips LJ describes as a 'conundrum'—that 'This section shall not prevent . . . the exercise of a power by the Secretary of State to the extent necessary for the purpose of avoiding a breach of a person's Convention rights (within the meaning of the Human Rights Act 1998).'

Six asylum seekers were left destitute under s. 55 and applied for a judicial review under the Human Rights Act, which incorporates the ECHR, Article 3 (inhuman and degrading treatment) and Article 8 (respect for private and family life). Phillips LJ noted that (paragraph 57): 'The imposition by the legislature of a regime which prohibits asylum seekers from working and further prohibits the grant to them, when they are destitute, of support amounts to positive action directed against asylum seekers and not to mere inaction.' It therefore counts as 'treatment'. The Home Secretary must take each case on its merits and consider the reasonableness of reasons for not claiming asylum at a particular stage. The judge then quoted with approval a previous statement from the Strasbourg Court: 'Where treatment humiliates or debases an individual showing lack of respect for, or diminishing, his or her human dignity or arouses feelings of fear, anguish or inferiority capable of breaking an individual's moral and physical resistance, it may be characterised as degrading.' The Court of Appeal therefore ruled that to comply with the asylum seekers' Convention rights, which s. 55 expressly requires him to do, the Secretary of State must provide support in these circumstances.

The final case, *R (on the application of Limbuela) v Secretary of State for the Home Department* (2004) provides strong and probably unpopular judicial guidance to the Home Office on its priorities. Mr Limbuela, an asylum seeker from Angola, was excluded by s. 55 from NASS support. The Home Office knew he had no means of support, no accommodation, no source of food, no access to sanitary facilities and no choice but to sleep on the street. This was sufficient to establish inhuman and degrading treatment under Article 3 of the Convention, particularly. While it would normally be necessary to show, to satisfy article 3, that there was a risk to health, in winter it would be common sense to expect a real threat to arise to health. The Court then gave a useful lecture to the Home Office: if it would only take a slightly more flexible approach to problems faced by asylum seekers, huge sums of public money spent on judicial review could be saved.

'Failed' asylum seekers

The Nationality, Immigration and Asylum Act 2002, Schedule 3, starkly removes the right to the following services for all those whose asylum claim has failed and who have not complied with a Home Office direction to leave the UK. (Letters (d)(f) and (h) refer to Northern Ireland and Scotland and are omitted.)

(a) section 21 or 29 of the National Assistance Act 1948 (local authority: accommodation and welfare);

(b) section 45 of the Health Services and Public Health Act 1968 (local authority: welfare of elderly);

(c) section 12 or 13A of the Social Work (Scotland) Act 1968 (social welfare services);

(e) section 21 of and Schedule 8 to the National Health Service Act 1977 (social services);

(g) section 17, 23C, 24A or 24B of the Children Act 1989 (welfare and other powers which can be exercised in relation to adults);

(j) section 188(3) or 204(4) of the Housing Act 1996 (accommodation pending review or appeal);

(k) section 2 of the Local Government Act 2000 (c 22) (promotion of well-being).

However it does not remove the powers and duties to promote the welfare of children under the Children Act 1989—the reference here to the Children Act is only to services under that Act provided to adults. But, as amended in 2004, it does remove the right of a parent to support as part of the support provided to a child. The result, inevitably, is that parents or guardians have no other means of support, care or accommodation and a care order may have to be sought by the local authority to fulfil its duties to the child. Is this a breach of the Human Rights Act, article 8? If it is, the 2002 legislation, as amended in 2004, tries to have it both ways, by stating that withdrawal of these services must not be in breach of the Human Rights Act. This echoes similar provisions in relation to NASS support, which we discussed above, and on which there has been extensive litigation, largely resulting in human rights winning out over Home Office intentions when it comes to withdrawal of NASS support as a penalty for not claiming asylum promptly.

Similarly 'failed' asylum seekers who remain in the UK, unless they have been in the UK for at least twelve months, lose entitlement to free NHS care, except in an emergency or for continuing treatment, and are liable to charges under the NHS (Charges to Overseas Visitors) Regulations 2004.

EXERCISES

What difference does the immigration or asylum status of the individuals in the following examples make to their entitlement to services or to any issues you should be aware of when talking with them? (You may find these problems easier to address by also referring to parts 3 and 4 of this book.)

Mr and Mrs A have arrived in the UK with their 5-year-old daughter and Mrs A's 60-year-old mother. They have fled war and persecution in their country of origin.

- The family has nowhere to live.
- Mrs A's mother suffers serious mental health problems as a result of recent traumas. She needs to see a doctor and you think the doctor will probably want her to be admitted to hospital for assessment.
- The daughter seems to be undernourished because Mrs A finds it difficult to prepare nutritious food in the circumstances she is living in.
- Mr and Mrs A would like more spacious accommodation; the house they have been sent to in a northern English city also suffers from damp.

Mr B was born and brought up in the UK. His parents came originally from another country and Mr B recently went to that country in order to marry Ms C. Following the marriage, Ms C has come to live in the UK.

- Ms C, who is now pregnant, is unhappy in the marriage. She wishes to remain in the UK and to commence divorce proceedings against Mr B. She tells you that as a divorced single parent, she would be severely mistreated if she returned to her country of origin. She does not know where to turn for legal advice.

COMPANION WEB SITE

For guidance on how to answer these exercises, visit the companion web site at:
www.oup.com/uk/booksites/law

WHERE DO WE GO FROM HERE?

This chapter is the last within Part 5, which has examined a range of areas of law which impact on social exclusion. Unstable immigration status can lead to economic problems, loss of control over living arrangements, and a fear of being removed from the UK and separated from family members. A person of whatever immigration status can still be a service user of social services, and your duties—unless the only problem is economic—are not affected. Even if the problem is economic you cannot ignore the needs of a child.

Other issues of social exclusion could have been covered. We have not dealt in particular with employment law, debt advice, or welfare benefit advice (except in summary form in relation to families in chapter 14, community care in chapter 16, and housing in chapter 18). These are issues where advice from a specialist agency can be obtained, subject to a means test, free of charge—see the Community Legal Service Directory for your area or **www.justask.org.uk**.

You have come to the end of *Law for Social Workers*, but not to the end, we hope, of an active interest in developments in law and a realization of law's importance for those who you are helping to achieve better lives. We wish you well and hope our contribution has been helpful.

ANNOTATED FURTHER READING

If your department cannot provide a service for an asylum seeker, you may need to contact NASS, which has a twenty-four-hour telephone line 0870 606 7766: see **www.workpermits.gov.uk/default.asp?pageid=2762**.

UK Immigration Advisory Service, **www.iasuk.org/**—contains easily readable guides to aspects of immigration law and through local branches can provide direct advice.

The Legal Services Commission web site contains directories of advisers and some guidance on law: **www.justask.org.uk/**.

Advice and support services on immigration are available through The Refugee Council, **www.refugeecouncil.org.uk/**, the Joint Council for the Welfare of Immigrants, **www.jcwi.org.uk/**, or the UK Immigration Advisory Service, **www.iasuk.org/**. The Immigration Rules can be found on the Home Office web site at **www.194.203.40.90/default.asp?PageId=3185**.

S. Willman, s. Knafler, and s. Pierce, *Support For Asylum-Seekers, a Guide to Legal and Welfare Rights* (Legal Action Group, 2001). Provides comprehensive practical guidance for those helping asylum seekers, and contains examples of forms and sample letters.

K. Browne and J. Pothecary, *Welfare Benefits and Immigration Law* (Jordans, 2004). This book is written for trainee solicitors but is kept up to date and contains a clear overview of all aspects of the law.